Cressman Library
Cedar Crest College
Allentown, Pa. 18104

DEMCO

The Green Guide

D. Thierry/DIAF

Alsace
Lorraine
Champagne

Travel Publications

38 Clarendon Road - Watford Herts WD1 1SX - U.K.
☎ (01923) 415 000
www.ViaMichelin.com
TheGreenGuide-uk@uk.michelin.com

Manufacture française des pneumatiques Michelin

Société en commandite par actions au capital de 2 000 000 000 de francs
Place des Carmes-Déchaux – 63 Clermont-Ferrand (France)
R.C.S. Clermont-Fd B 855 200 507

No part of this publication may be reproduced in any form
without the prior permission of the publisher.

© *Michelin et Cie, propriétaires-éditeurs, 2001*
Dépôt légal Juillet 2001 – ISBN 2-06-000089-0 – ISSN 0763-1383

Printed in France 07-2001/2.1

Typesetting: A.P.S./Chromostyle, Tours
Printing and binding : MAME, Tours
Cover design : Agence Carré Noir à Paris 17e

THE GREEN GUIDE:
The Spirit of Discovery

The exhilaration of new horizons, the fun of seeing the world, the excitement of discovery: this is what we seek to share with you. To help you make the most of your travel experience, we offer first-hand knowledge and turn a discerning eye on places to visit.

This wealth of information gives you the expertise to plan your own enriching adventure. With THE GREEN GUIDE showing you the way, you can explore new destinations with confidence or rediscover old ones.

Leisure time spent with The Green Guide is also a time for refreshing your spirit, enjoying yourself, and taking advantage of our selection of fine restaurants, hotels and other places for relaxing.

So turn the page and open a window on the world. Join THE GREEN GUIDE in the spirit of discovery.

Contents

D. Fouss/DIAF

Old-fashioned shop sign
in Mulhouse

R. Mattes/MICHELIN

The fruit of the vine,
luscious and ripe

Maps and plans

Thematic maps

Monuments

Local maps for touring

Routes du Champ p. 100

Town plans

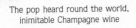

The pop heard round the world,
inimitable Champagne wine

Cephas/TOP

Ready for a healthful pause
in Contrexéville?

Ch. Boisvieux/HOA QUI

Michelin maps

Michelin products are complementary: for each of the sites listed in The Green Guide, map references are indicated which help you find your location on our range of maps. The image below shows the maps to use for each geographic area covered in this guide. To travel the roads in this region, you may use any of the following:

● the **regional maps** at a scale of 1:200 000 nos 237, 241, 242 and 243 which cover the main roads and secondary roads, and include useful indications for finding tourist attractions. These are good maps to choose for travelling in a wide area. In addition to identifying the nature of the road ways, the maps show castles, churches and other religious edifices, scenic view points, megalithic monuments, swimming beaches on lakes and rivers, swimming pools, golf courses, race tracks, air fields, and more.

● the **detailed maps** are based on the regional map data, but with a reduced format (about half a region), which makes them easier to consult and fold. For the region covered in this guide, use maps 53, 56, 57, 61, 62, 65, 66 and 87.

● the **departmental maps** at a scale of 1:150 000 (an enlargement of the 1:200 000 maps) are very easy to read, and facilitate travelling on all of the roads in the following departments: Ardennes (4008), Marne (4051), Haute-Marne (4052), Meurthe-et-Moselle (4054), Meuse (4055), Moselle (4057), Haut-Rhin (4068) and Vosges (4088). They come with a complete index of place names and include a plan of the towns which serve as administrative seats (*préfectures*).

And remember to travel with the latest edition of the **map of France no 989** (1:1 000 000), which gives an overall view of the regions of Alsace, Lorraine and Champagne-Ardenne, and the main access roads which connect it to the rest of France. Also available in atlas format: spiral bound, hard back, and the new mini-atlas – perfect for your glove box.

Michelin is pleased to offer a route-planning service on the Internet: **www.ViaMichelin.com.** Choose the shortest route, a route without tolls, or the Michelin recommended route to your destination; you can also access information about hotels and restaurants from The Red Guide, and tourists sites from The Green Guide. *Bon voyage!*

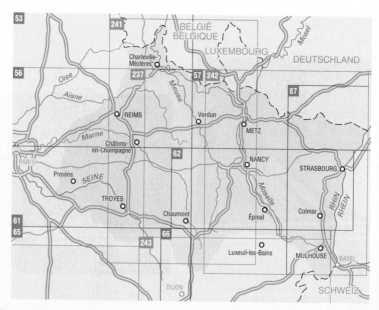

Using this guide

● The **summary maps** on the following pages are designed to assist you in planning your trip: the **Map of principal sights** identifies major sights and attractions, the **Map of driving tours** defines selected itineraries.

● We recommend that you read the **Introduction** before setting out on your trip. The background information it contains on history, the arts and traditional culture will prove most instructive and make your visit more meaningful.

● The main towns and attractions are presented in alphabetical order in the **Sights** section. In order to ensure quick, easy identification, original place names have been used throughout the guide. The clock symbol ⊙, placed after monuments or other sights, refers to the **Admission times and charges** section at the end of the guide.

● The **Practical information** section offers useful addresses for planning your trip, seeking accommodation, enjoying outdoor activities and more. Consult this section for the opening hours and admission prices for monuments, museums and other tourist attractions; festival and carnival dates; suggestions for thematic tours on scenic railways and through nature reserves etc.

● We have selected **hotels and restaurants**, and other places for **entertainment** in many of the towns in this guide. Turn to the pages bordered in blue.

● The **Index** lists attractions, famous people and events, and other subjects covered in the guide.

Let us hear from you. We are interested in your reaction to our guide, in any ideas you have to offer or good addresses you would like to share. Send your comments to Michelin Travel Publications, 38 Clarendon Road, Watford, Herts WD1 1SX, UK or by e-mail to thegreenguide-uk@uk.michelin.com.

F. Zuardon/PLURIEL

Key

Selected monuments and sights

	Tour - Departure point
	Catholic church
	Protestant church, other temple
	Synagogue - Mosque
	Building
	Statue, small building
	Calvary, wayside cross
	Fountain
	Rampart - Tower - Gate
	Château, castle, historic house
	Ruins
	Dam
	Factory, power plant
	Fort
	Cave
	Prehistoric site
	Viewing table
	Viewpoint
	Other place of interest

Sports and recreation

	Racecourse
	Skating rink
	Outdoor, indoor swimming pool
	Marina, sailing centre
	Trail refuge hut
	Cable cars, gondolas
	Funicular, rack railway
	Tourist train
	Recreation area, park
	Theme, amusement park
	Wildlife park, zoo
	Gardens, park, arboretum
	Bird sanctuary, aviary
	Walking tour, footpath
	Of special interest to children

Abbreviations

A	Agricultural office (Chambre d'agriculture)
C	Chamber of Commerce (Chambre de commerce)
H	Town hall (Hôtel de ville)
J	Law courts (Palais de justice)
M	Museum (Musée)
P	Local authority offices (Préfecture, sous-préfecture)
POL.	Police station (Police)
	Police station (Gendarmerie)
T	Theatre (Théatre)
U	University (Université)

	Sight	Seaside resort	Winter sports resort	Spa
Highly recommended	★★★	�☺☺	✳✳✳	♇♇♇
Recommended	★★	☺☺	✳✳	♇♇
Interesting	★	☺	✳	♇

Additional symbols

🛈		Tourist information
═══	═══	Motorway or other primary route
➊	➊	Junction: complete, limited
⊏═══⊐	═══	Pedestrian street
I═══I		Unsuitable for traffic, street subject to restrictions
⊥⊥⊥⊥	----	Steps - Footpath
🚆	🚉	Train station - Auto-train station
🚌	S.N.C.F.	Coach (bus) station
•——•——		Tram
Ⓜ		Metro, underground
P+R		Park-and-Ride
♿		Access for the disabled
✉		Post office
☏		Telephone
⊠		Covered market
◦×◦×◦		Barracks
△		Drawbridge
℧		Quarry
✗		Mine
B	F	Car ferry (river or lake)
⛴		Ferry service: cars and passengers
⛵		Foot passengers only
③		Access route number common to Michelin maps and town plans
Bert (R.)...		Main shopping street
AZ **B**		Map co-ordinates

hotels and restaurants

20 rooms: Number of rooms:
250/375F price for one person/ double room

half-board or Price per person, based
full board: 280F on double occupancy

⊐ *45F* Price of breakfast; when not given, it is included in the price of the room (i.e., for bed-and-breakfasts)

up to 5 pers: Maximum capacity of lodging
week 2400F Price per week

3 "gîtes" : Number of lodgings
2/7 pers Capacity smallest/largest unit
week Weekly rate for
2300/6000F smallest/largest unit

100 apt: Number of apartments (residential hotel or holiday
2/7 pers: camp) mini/maxi capacity
week of apartments, mini/maxi
2000/5000 rate per week

100 beds: Number of beds and price
50F per person (hostel)

120 sites: Number of camp sites and cost
80F for 2 people with a car

110/250 Restaurant mini/maxi price fixed menu (lunch and dinner) or à la carte

rest. Lodging where meals are served
110/250F mini/maxi price fixed menu or à la carte

food service Light meals and snacks available

meal 85F "Family style" meal

reserv Reservation recommended

⊄ No credit cards accepted

P Reserved parking for hotel patrons

The prices correspond to the higher rates of the tourist season

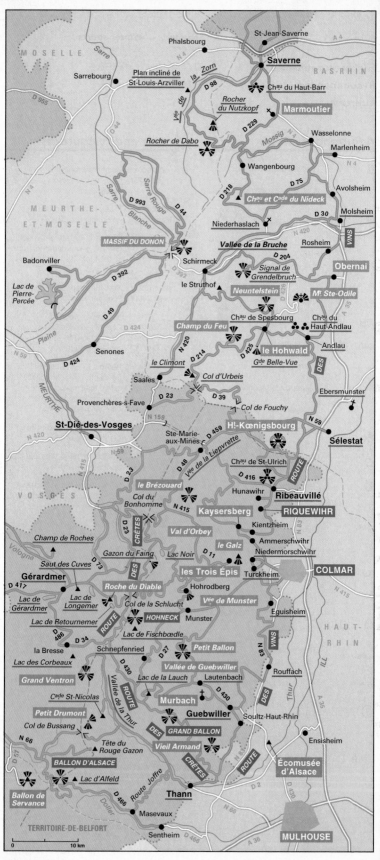

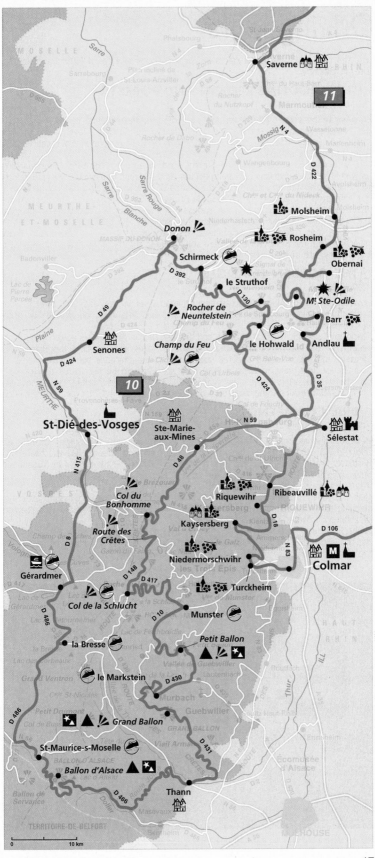

11

10

Saverne

Molsheim

Rosheim

Obernai

Donon

Schirmeck

le Struthof

Mt Ste-Odile

Rocher de
Neuntelstein

Barr

Champ du Feu

le Hohwald

Andlau

Senones

St-Dié-des-Vosges

Ste-Marie-
aux-Mines

Sélestat

Col du
Bonhomme

Riquewihr

Ribeauvillé

Kaysersberg

Route des
Crêtes

Niedermorschwihr

Colmar

Gérardmer

Turckheim

Col de la Schlucht

Munster

la Bresse

Petit Ballon

le Markstein

Grand Ballon

St-Maurice-s-Moselle

Ballon d'Alsace

Thann

0   10 km

17

Driving tours

You can read more about the places on these tours by looking up individual towns and sites in the index.

① THE ARGONNE REGION AND FOREST
200km/120mi

Located at the border of Champagne and Lorraine, the Argonne region has its own distinctive geographic characteristics. The hilly, wooded land is a lovely place for long walks or cycling trips; horseback riding and off-road biking are also great ways to enjoy the natural setting.

Ste-Menehould is a good starting point for such adventures. The terrain is rewarding, as it changes and provides new perspectives to the attentive traveller who crosses the ridges and plateaux or who follows the course of a river deep in a narrow gorge.

You may stop and admire the Château de Braux-Ste-Cohière, home to the Champagne-Argonne cultural association, which sponsors many events and festivities to promote the region, and also the site of an interesting regional museum.

The wars that ravaged the Argonne at different times have left their scars. Some trenches from the First World War are still visible in the forest outside of Varennes, at the historic site of Haute-Chevauchée.

② THE GOLDEN TRIANGLE
120km/72mi

Between Reims, Châlons, Épernay and Château-Thierry, the vineyards stretch along the sunny hillsides. Villages seem to float and bob like ships on the sea of green in summer months.

The "gold" in this tour is bottled and bubbly. Many fine cellars await you in the regions of the Montagne de Reims, the Marne Valley and the Côte des Blancs. The vintners will welcome you and tell you all about the methods behind the magic. Of course, you will want to taste a little, and are likely to be persuaded to pick up a few bottles to bring home — sunshine with a cork on it! Certain places have set up interesting exhibits and museums devoted to the fine art of Champagne-making.

③ BRIE CHAMPENOISE
165km/100mi

Between the regions of Île-de-France and Champagne, the landscapes of Brie are adorned with historic old towns set along the rivers and streams like the beads of a necklace. You may want to stop and take in the sights or have a meal in Nogent-sur-Seine, Villenauxe-la-Grande, Montmirail or Verdelot.

The finest jewel in this setting is certainly Provins, a medieval city standing on a hilltop that has been occupied since Roman times. You can spend a pleasant afternoon strolling along the high ramparts and in summer you may enjoy a jousting tournament or a falconry demonstration.

While Provins is famed for its red roses, the gardens at Viels-Maisons are famous for the thousands of varieties of fragrant flowers, herbs, bushes etc that grow there. The big park is divided into gardens both formal and "English-style", a feast for the senses.

Ph. Cajic/MICHELIN

St-Loup-de-Naud — Columns on the church doorway

[4] THE LAKES OF THE DER REGION
170km/102mi

If your idea of a holiday includes relaxing and enjoying outdoor activities in a beautiful natural environment, this is the route for you! Swimming, boating and fishing are on the agenda on the big lake at Der-Chantecoq.
Birdwatchers will want to bring along their binoculars to study the many species of migratory waterfowl, including the *grue cendrée*, a grey crane. The *Maison de l'oiseau et du poisson*, with exhibits on the local ecosystem, is a good place to stop before setting out to observe the natural inhabitants of the lake and its shores. As you drive around the region, you will notice the local half-timber architecture, which has also been used for churches.
Further north, the Forêt de l'Orient is a lovely forest that also has many lakes where visitors may relax and play. If you are patient and quiet, you may go to the *parc de vision animalier* in the eastern part of the Regional Nature Park, which has been set up to enable visitors to observe animals in semi-captivity.
The Lac d'Orient is a bird sanctuary, and also offers opportunities for scuba diving, sailing and swimming; the road that runs around it is a pretty drive. Anglers and canoeists prefer the Lac du Temple, whereas the smaller Lac Amance is reserved for motorised craft. Fresh air for all, and you may choose the peace and quiet of secluded natural sites for observing wildlife or fishing, or lively sports and games at the beaches and recreation areas.

[5] CHAMPAGNE: FROM BAR TO BAR
225km/135mi

The title is not meant to encourage you to drink and drive ... it is a reference to the region know as the Côte des Bars. The towns of Bar-sur-Aube and Bar-sur-Seine derive their names from the old Celtic word *barr*, signifying summit. This route passes through a lovely variety of landscapes: vineyards, forest and fields. The town of Riceys is unique in that it is the only commune in France to produce three wines labelled *appellation d'origine contrôlée*, including the delightful rosé for which it is best known. If you are travelling with children, treat them to an afternoon at the Nigloland amusement park (there are plenty of shaded areas to sit and rest).

[6] ARTS AND CRAFTS IN HAUTE-MARNE
200km/120mi

Begin your journey in the old town of Langres, and enjoy the view from the ramparts. Langres was once the centre of the knife-making trade in France; the town's most famous native son, Denis Diderot (author of the first Encyclopaedia) was the son of a cutler.
Carry on to Fayl-Billot, where there is a national school of wickerwork, and look for a basket to put the rest of your souvenirs in. There are a number of artisans who give demonstrations in their shops.
In Bourbonne-les-Bains, you may be tempted to ease your aches and pains in a warm mineral water bath or go up for a massage. In Nogent, the *Musée de la coutellerie* is devoted to the cutlery trade, and includes an old-fashioned workshop with a large wheel dating from the 18C.

[7] REMEMBERING TWO WORLD WARS
272km/163mi

Begin this drive in Verdun. Although the First and Second World Wars are an ever more distant memory for older travellers, and may seem like ancient history to youth, this tour brings the events that rent Europe asunder into sharp focus and remind one and all of the absurd tragedy of combat.
Verdun is famous for its fortifications and as the site of numerous battles, but the peaceful old town is well worth a visit, too. In the national cemetery, there is a memorial to seven unknown soldiers, and the Douaumont ossuary is the resting place of soldiers who once fought under different colours. The fort and the "bayonet trench" are startling reminders of the violence of the First World War – which was thought at the time to be the last war that Europe would ever experience.
The once-vaunted, later taunted Maginot Line is still marked by several forts and defensive works: Fermont Fort and its military museum, the Immerhof defensive works, the Zeiterholz shelter and Fort Guentrange. In Longwy, you may admire the works of enamel artisans, and in Thionville the Château de la Grange. Continue the tour of military installations at Hackenberg, impressive in its size. In the busy city of Metz, visit the cathedral and the old town.
Complete the tour by way of Briey, where the visionary architect Le Corbusier built one of his *cités radieuses*, and Étain, entirely rebuilt after 1918.

8 BETWEEN MEUSE AND MOSELLE
261km/157mi

This drive leads you along one river and another, and through different periods of French history. Begin in Metz, where the past is associated with wars and religion, but also with culture and fine architecture (especially lovely at night under the many lights installed to accent the features and proportions of buildings).

In Pont-à-Mousson, the old abbey dates from the 18C; the town greeted American troops in 1944. Nancy is the former capital of the dukes of Lorraine. The beautiful monuments and public squares are evidence of its rich cultural and artistic heritage.

Vaucouleurs and nearby Domrémy-la-Pucelle are forever linked to the most famous of all French heroines, Joan of Arc. Born in Domrémy, the simple peasant girl first took her quest to the governor of Vaucouleurs, whose condescension did nothing to dissuade her fervour.

Commercy is reputed to be the best source of the soft cakes favoured by Marcel Proust, *madeleines*. On your way back to Metz, visit the Château de Stanislas, the old town of Bar-le-Duc and the 17C church in St-Mihiel.

9 SPA RESORTS IN THE VOSGES
219km/131mi

The French are very fond of their *cures*, or spa treatments, which are prescribed for a variety of chronic ailments. In addition to the therapeutic virtues of the waters at each place, the spa experience enhances overall health and well-being in other ways, such as enabling patients to take a break from medication, reducing stress, improving sleeping and eating habits and encouraging outdoor exercise. The course of treatment generally runs for three weeks, but some spas offer short stays for a quick program of revitalisation. Most of these resorts are well equipped to entertain *curistes* and their families, often with casinos, racetracks, facilities for tennis and golf, and they are usually located in a pleasant and accessible natural settings.

This tour takes you through Vittel (kidney and liver problems, rheumatism), Contrexé-ville (obesity, kidney and urinary problems), Bourbonne (rheumatism, respiratory ailments), Luxeuil (phlebology, gynaecology), Plombières (digestive and nutritional problems, rheumatism, bone and joint ailments or surgical recovery) and Bains-les-Bains (heart and artery problems, rheumatism). For information on spa treatments, contact the local tourist office *(see Practical information)* or log on to www.tourisme.fr (click on "Special Breacks – Relaxation and fitness holidays") and choose the spa that interests you from the list for a direct link to individual web sites.

Vologne Valley from the Roche du Diable

10 THE VOSGES FOREST
377km/226mi

Put on your walking shoes as you leave St-Dié and head out to the hills and dales of the Vosges. You will be enchanted and exhilarated, and all the family will enjoy this beautiful forest.

After visiting the cathedral and cloisters in St-Dié, this itinerary leads to the old town of Senones. The Donon range begins here, defining the border of Alsace and Lorraine and providing wonderful views of the Vosges mountains. There are several nice walks to take starting from Schirmeck. The former concentration camp of Struthof is open to visitors interested in this tragic chapter of the history of the Second World War.

For more outdoor excursions, you may climb the Neuntelstein rock, discover the Hohwald or (in season), ski on the slopes at Champ du Feu. Ste-Marie-aux-Mines is the ancestral home of the Pennsylvania Dutch, and you will find fabric displays in the textile museum which echo Amish designs. Travel the high passes on the Route des Crêtes: Col du Bonhomme, Col de la Schlucht. Stop at Munster for the eponymous cheese, then on to the Petit Ballon and the Markstein ski resort. From the Grand Ballon, the view is panoramic.

Thann is at a lower altitude, and you can admire the church there before climbing to the highest point in the range, the Ballon d'Alsace.

Around St-Maurice-sur-Moselle and La Bresse there are many ski areas. In Gérardmer, you can ski in winter, or take a pedal boat out on the lake in fine weather. A tour for active folks who like to stay on the move!

11 THE ALSATIAN WINE ROAD
277km/166mi

Begin your wine tour in the European capital of Strasbourg. The city has long been an economic, cultural and intellectual magnet for the region. It is well worth a visit.

Likewise, Haguenau has historic importance, and traces of its old fortifications remain. Bouxwiller, once the home of princes and princesses, seems to huddle for warmth at the base of mount Batsburg, legendary repair of sorcerers and witches. Then it is on to Saverne to visit the marina and château. The wine begins flowing in earnest in Molsheim; the nearby hillsides are covered in Riesling grapes. Obernai is a lovely wine-growing town infused with a golden glow and surrounded by vineyards. Climb to the top of Mont Ste-Odile for a visit to the old convent – this is one of the most popular tourist attractions in Alsace. Some come for the view (all the way to the Black Forest on a clear day), others for sacred inspiration, and still others are drawn by the mystery of the so-called "pagan wall".

The city of Barr is awash in excitement during the Wine Fair; at any time of year you can enjoy local Sylvaner and Gewürztraminer wines. Following along the wine road, you will pass by the ruins of Andlau Abbey, guarded by a stone bear. The fortifications of Sélestat, storks nests and a castle at Ribeauvillé mark your route as you continue to the famous village of Riquewihr, the capital of Riesling.

Kaysersberg is another picturesque hamlet; it seems to have sprung straight off the pages of a book of fairy tales with its ruined medieval castle, half-timbered houses, pots of bright geraniums and fortified bridge. Continuing the route, you will appreciate the charms of Niedermorschwihr and the towers of Turckheim on the way to the city of Colmar. This is the capital city of the wine-growing region; the old town and the area known as *la Petite Venise* are unforgettable. Return to Strasbourg by way of the Rhine Valley.

Strasbourg – La Petite France

Hunawihr

Introduction

Landscapes

ADMINISTRATION

This guide covers three of France's 22 *Régions* (the largest type of administrative district): Alsace, Lorraine, and Champagne-Ardenne. Each Region is made up of *départements* (numbered 01 to 96 alphabetically – their numbers are used as identification on automobile number plates and in postal codes). Thus, Alsace includes Bas-Rhin (67) and Haut-Rhin (68); Lorraine is made up of Meurthe-et-Moselle (54), Meuse (55), Moselle (67) and Vosges (88); Champagne-Ardenne includes the Ardennes (08), Aube (10), Marne (51) and Haute-Marne (52). The French *départements* were created in 1790 and generally given the name of the main river within their territory. The country is further divided into *arrondissements*, which are split into *cantons* and finally *communes* which are managed by an elected mayor. There are 36 556 mayoralties in France.

REGIONS

The easternmost portion of the area covered in this guide is the **Alsatian plain**. Barely 30km/19mi in width, it stretches, north to south, over 170km/106mi. The border with Germany is traced by the Rhine, which forms an alluvial basin with the Ill; a porous, friable blanket of marl and loam deposits, consisting predominantly of silt (known as *loess*). At the southern end, the pebbly soil of the **Sundgau** region links it to the Jura range.

Like a wall at the other edge of the narrow plain, the **Vosges** mountains rise abruptly, running parallel to the Rhine for the whole length of Alsace. This ancient range formed by folding movements of the earth 300 million years ago is made of crystalline rock (granites, porphyries) and ancient sedimentary rock, mostly sandstone. At the southern end, the mountain tops have distinctive, rounded shapes locally known as *ballons*. The glaciers of the Quaternary period left behind high mountain lakes. To the north, the lower altitude has resulted in a thicker sedimentary crust, and a forest cover.

The western slope of the range is more gradual than the Alsatian side. The geological history of the **Ardennes** uplands is a complex one, the result of intense folding, faulting, uplifts and denudations, with some of the older strata of rock thrust above the younger. The highest point of the plateau in France is the Croix de Scalle (502m/1 647ft), on the border with Belgium. The Meuse flows through deeply entrenched meanders between the tip of the French Ardennes, Givet, and Charleville-Mézières. The rugged **Argonne** Forest is drained by the River Aisne.

The region of **Champagne** is part of the Paris Basin, a vast bowl-like formation contained by the Ardennes and the Vosges (north and east) and the Morvan and Massif Armoricain (south and west). The landscape has been shaped by a series of concentric layers, one on top of the other in diminishing size, like a stack of saucers, with the oldest and smallest on top. The **Lorraine** plateau marks the eastern rim of the basin.

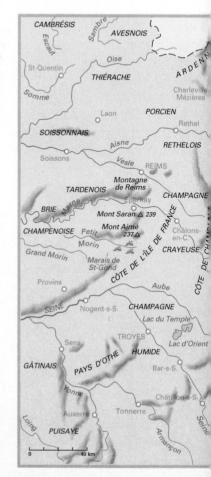

HOW THE LAND WAS FORMED

The Vosges and Alsace

Primary (Paleozoic) Era – About 560 million years ago, France was covered in water. The earth's crust underwent a great upheaval and the so-called "Hercynian folds" pushed up the bedrock of the Vosges and what is now the Black Forest, constituting a crystalline massif dominated by granite.

Secondary (Mesozoic) Era – This era began about 200 million years ago. The Vosges, planed down by erosion, were surrounded by the sea which filled the Paris Basin at different periods. At the end of the Secondary Era, the range was covered in water; sedimentary soils (sandstone, limestone, marl, clay, chalk) piled up on top of the primitive bedrock.

Tertiary Era – About 65 million years ago, a tremendous folding of the crust of the earth brought out the Alps. In reaction to this movement, the old Hercynian hills slowly lifted up. In the first phase, the Vosges and the Black Forest reached an altitude of nearly 3 000m/9 843ft. In the second phase, the central zone, unbalanced by the upheaval, collapsed inward. This sunken area was to become the Alsatian plain, separating the Vosges from the Black Forest, and explaining the symmetry of the structure and relief found between the two areas.

Quaternary (Glacial) Era – The earth underwent a global cooling period some two million years ago. Glaciers covered the southern Vosges. Descending slowly, they widened the valleys and steepened the slopes, gouged the rock and left hollows which were later filled with water (Lac Noir, Lac Blanc). When the climate warmed, the accumulated earth and stones carried by the glaciers were finally deposited in formations known as *moraines*, some of which created natural dams and lakes (Lac de Gérardmer). Since the glaciers retreated, rainwater, rivers and streams have further eroded the Vosges. The old stone peaks have been laid bare in the south, whereas the northern end of the range, preserved from the harshest glacier aggression, has retained a thick sandstone mantle.

Ardennes: Hercynian history

At the end of the Paleozoic Era, the European continent was subject to a period of mountain-building resulting from the collision between the African and the North American-North European continent. The Hercynian belt extends in western Europe for more than 3 000km/1 860mi from Portugal, Ireland and England in the west through Spain, France (Brittany, Massif Central, Vosges and Corsica), and Germany (Black Forest, Harz) to the Czech Republic in the Bohemian Massif. Analyses of the

rocks and geological structures found in these zones indicate that they are the result of the seabed spreading, subduction of the oceanic crust and plate collision. The lateral compression of the upper layers of the earth pushed accumulated sediment upward, bringing ridges of hard, old rocks together like the jaws of a clamp.

Thus, the Ardennes uplands emerged around 550 to 220 million years BC. Spreading over the countries of France, Germany and Belgium, the region has been eroded over time until it now appears as a mostly flat plain. The River Meuse has marked a course through the very hard stone, revealed in the dramatic canyon-like walls of dark rock through which it winds *(see Meanders of the MEUSE)*. Near Givet, the river valleys widen as the water passes over bands of shale and limestone.

Lorraine and Champagne

These two regions form the eastern part of the **Paris Basin**. At the end of the Primary Era, and into the early Tertiary Era, this vast depression was a sea. A great variety of sedimentary deposits – sandstone, limestone, marl, clay, chalk – piled up 2 000m/6 562ft deep. By the middle of the Tertiary Era, the water began to drain from this wide "saucer", whereas the rim, in particular to the east and south-east, rose under the effects of Alpine folding. Erosion worked to flatten out the land, creating the **Lorraine plateau**, where geology served to create a homogeneous landscape; greater diversity of soil composition created the more diversified landscapes of the **Pays des Côtes**.

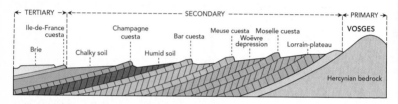

The illustration of the eastern part of the Paris Basin shows the formation of cuestas *(côtes)*. The characteristic of this type of escarpment is a steep cliff on one side and a gentler dip or back slope on the other. This landform occurs in areas of inclined strata and is caused by the manner in which different types of soil and rock react to weathering and erosion. Here, the resistant layers (limestone) surmount softer layers (clay, marl). Running water works a channel in the hard layer until it reaches the more porous zones below. The softer areas are washed away and leave a depression, which is hemmed in by the abrupt rise of the hard rock (the *front de côte* or steep face); the softer surface slopes back at a gentle angle. This back slope, protected from wind, is characterised by loose, fertile soil whose chalky layers below the surface help the soil warm up quickly in the spring. These areas are ideal for cultivating vineyards.

The Champagne region is made up of many small *pays*, areas with distinct climates and soils. **Champagne crayeuse** refers to the chalky soil which gave the region its name (etymological descendent of "calcareous plain"). This zone forms a circle with a circumference of about 80km/50mi, with Paris near the centre. The **Brie and Tardenois plateau** is crossed by a few rivers (the Marne, the two Morins and the Seine); impenetrable marl holds in humidity, whereas siliceous limestone forms the upper layer. The **Barrois** is another plateau, crossed by the valleys of the Saulx and the Ornain, home to the towns of Bar-le-Duc and Ligny-en-Barrois. It extends into the **Côte de Bars**, where the vineyards of the Aube *département* grow.

Between the Champagne and Bars cuestas lies the region known as **Champagne humide**, a verdant and well-watered area of woodlands, pastures, and orchards. The creation of the lake-reservoirs in the **Der-Chantecoq** and **Orient** forests have further transformed the lay of the land, where the heavy, clay rich soil is more suited to grazing than growing.

FORESTS AND WILDLIFE
Alsace and the Vosges

The Vosges mountains are particularly lovely for the forest cover, which changes subtly according to altitude, orientation and the composition of the soil. The southern part of the range is known as *Vosges cristallines*, in reference to the granite content of the high mountains. The *ballons* and other summits are rounded, with moderate slopes on the western side. Facing the Alsatian plain, however, the rocky faces appear sharper and steeper. The River Bruche marks the separation with the *Vosges gréseuses* – the "sandy" northern end. The range diminishes in altitude and the red sandstone so prevalent in the construction of castles and churches has also sculpted the landscape. The forest blanketing the whole hilly area is sometimes a harmonious mixture of species, and sometimes dominated by a single species, creating a variety of colours and distinctive woodland environments.

Facing the region of **Lorraine**, the lower hills of the north are exposed to the wet western winds, and dominated by beech trees. Firs grow at an altitude of 400m/1 312ft altitude. In the higher southern peaks, Scotch pine grow above

700m/2 297ft. Beyond 1 000m/3 280ft, conifers yield to deciduous varieties, including beech, maple and mountain ash. On the highest ridge tops, there are no trees at all, just low brush and bilberry bushes. On the warmer slope facing the **Alsatian plain**, firs begin to grow at 600m/1 968ft. Just above the vineyards, groves of chestnut trees can be found; in the past their wood was used to stake out the grape vines. The warm, dry climate is congenial to spruce. A large population of oak flourishes in the Harth Forest, east of Mulhouse.

Storks – No discussion of the wildlife in Alsace would be complete without the mention of storks. These stately, long-necked creatures from the Ciconiidae family are symbolic of the region, where they are believed to bring good luck. Each spring, their return is awaited anxiously. After years of decline (due to hunting in their winter habitat in Africa, and accidents involving high-voltage electric lines), the population seems to be stabilising and the gracious birds are once again a common sight. It is

THE VOSGES FOREST

Deciduous trees
- Beech
- Other species

Conifers
- Fir
- Fir and spruce
- Pine

- High meadows

Wissembourg
Haguenau
STRASBOURG
Meurthe
St-Dié-des-Vosges
Épinal
Moselle
Gérardmer
Hohneck
Colmar
Grand Ballon
Ballon d'Alsace
MULHOUSE
Belfort
RHIN / RHEIN
DEUTSCHLAND
0   20 km

estimated that about 200 couples now live in Alsace, some year-round. The migrating storks come to roost, typically atop chimneys, in the month of March. Storks are voiceless, or nearly so, but announce their presence by clattering their bills loudly. The male arrives first, and begins work on a large platform of twigs and vines. The circular nest is refurbished yearly, and may weigh up to 500kg/1 100lb for 2m/6.5ft in diameter. Most nests are under 1m/3ft high, but exceptionally they may reach double that height.

When the chosen mate has arrived, the couple produce three to six eggs in a season, which hatch after 36 days of incubation by both parents. Generously nourished with insects, larva, lizards, newts, mice, moles and snakes, baby storks grow quickly; they begin testing their wings at about four weeks and are flying one month later.

Vosges lakes – On each side of the crest of the Vosges, many lakes add to the pleasure of an excursion to the mountains. The largest is Gérardmer (115ha/284 acres), on the Lorraine side; one of the region's most popular winter resorts is located along its banks. The deepest lake is Lac Blanc (71m/233ft), on the Alsatian side.

B.Kaufmann/MICHELIN

Lac Blanc

27

The lakes were created by the glaciers which once covered the range, hundreds of centuries ago. Most are found at high altitudes, in bowl-like formations with steep waterfront terrain (Lac des Corbeaux, Lac Noir, Lac Blanc etc). Many of them are now used as reservoirs, particularly useful for meeting the needs of textile plants when water is in short supply.

Other lakes, in the valleys, were formed by glacier deposits, moraines, which retain or deviate waters. Gérardmer and Longemer are such lakes.

Ardenne

The French Region of Ardenne is the south-west margin of the larger Ardennes highlands and the adjacent lowlands in the Meuse and Aisne valleys. The thick, apparently impenetrable forest has been the scene of battles since the French Revolution. In addition to the sandstone, limestone and quartzite found in neighbouring regions, the Ardenne is famous for the blue slate quarried there. The oldest sections of the forest are majestic with hardwoods such as oak, beech and yellow birch; younger growth includes European white birch and willows. The variety of soil quality has a strong influence on the height of trees: on the plateau a mature oak may yield only a dozen logs for the fire; an ash further south in the Signy-l'Abbaye area may climb more than 30m/110ft.

S. Sauvignier/MICHELIN

Sanglier des Ardennes

Game is abundant in the Ardennes forest, where hunting is popular. The region's emblematic animal is the wild boar, *sanglier*. The wild population has returned from the brink of extinction thanks to better management. There is also a limited hunting season (two to six weeks, depending on the district) on the plains, for pheasant, partridge and hare. Each hunting permit is delivered with tags which the hunter must affix to the animals captured. Deer are now found only in animal parks; few escaped the devastation of the Second World War, however, the population has been restored thanks to the Belval animal reserve. Things have changed considerably since the days of Charlemagne: on 8 December 799, the Emperor and his party bagged two bison, two aurochs, 46 boar, 28 stags and a wolf, using spears, bows and arrows.

Argonne

The southernmost part of the French Ardenne is wooded and hilly, more temperate in every way than the highlands. The massif is a natural barrier between Champagne and Lorraine, about 65km/40mi long and 15km/10mi wide, rarely exceeding 200m/650ft in altitude. The Aire and Aisne river systems cut deep valleys through this region which has been of great strategic importance. Beech groves are common on the slopes, and it is not unusual to see regal chestnuts atop the crests. Shrubs, berry bushes and reeds provide shelter for birds and other creatures; bluebells, lungwort and daffodils grow wild on the forest floor. Some species have migrated to the area from other regions of France, including heather from Brittany; specialists may look out for a non-indigenous blue lily from England, a souvenir from soldiers of the First World War.

Recognise common species by looking for distinctive features of bark, leaves, and shape:

Beech trees can be recognised by their limbs which divide into flexible twigs; the long, pointed buds grow alternately. The leaves are well-shaped ovals, fringed with cilia when young; light green in spring and summer, they turn a familiar copper colour in autumn. The bark is smooth, light grey, and often marked by white patches of lichen.

Spruce have twisted needles which grow two-by-two and are blue-green. The pale bark comes off in thin strips from young shoots; as the tree ages, the bark turns grey-brown, thickens and develops deep cracks.

Fir bear horizontal branches with light green needles; these are flat and disposed in a regular pattern

Beech

like the teeth of a comb. The underside is clearly marked with two silvery lines. The crown of older trees is rounded. The grey bark is dotted with resin bubbles. The cones sit upright on the branches and fall apart when they reach maturity – this is why cones of the fir tree are not found scattered on the ground.

Scotch pine trees have pointed crowns and the branches dip downwards, hanging in a thick fringe said to resemble the tail of a spaniel. The dark green needles are sharp, growing in a circle around the branch. The cones hang down from the ends of twigs. At maturity, the seeds fall out and the cone remains on the tree intact for several months. The reddish bark forms scales which are more distinct in older trees.

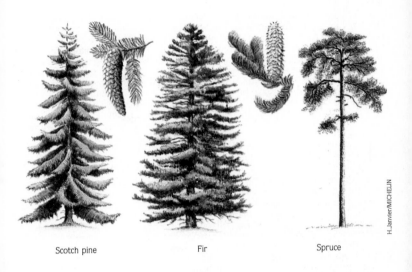

H. Janvier/MICHELIN

| Scotch pine | Fir | Spruce |

Oak trees are a genus of the beech family, and there are about 450 known species. Recognise oak by the alternate simple leaves, usually lobed or toothed. The most familiar feature of oaks is the acorn, which varies slightly in appearance (arrangement of scales on the cup, fused scales, hairy lined shells) from one subgenus to another.

Chestnuts are tall trees with furrowed bark and lance-shaped leaves. In spring, the male flowers stand upright like candles on the end of branches; the female flowers are arranged at the base of these catkins. The spiky fruit contains two or three edible nuts (used as feed for livestock or milled into flour); the table variety, *marrons*, come from choice trees bred to produce one large nut in the bur.

Bird sanctuaries and other animal reserves are found around many of the region's lakes and nature parks. There are numerous "discovery trails" and nature centres where visitors can learn more about the environment, the flora and fauna of the region. For more detailed information turn to *Practical information* at the end of this guide.

Big Bad Wolf

The Ardennes Forest extends over the present-day borders of Belgium and Luxembourg; for many local inhabitants, being an *Ardennais* is more significant than being French or Belgian. At the end of the 19C, the thick forest was the perfect environment for smuggling cheap coffee and tobacco into France. Dogs were trained to make runs at night, and "Little Red Riding Hoods" carried innocent baskets for "Grandmother" while they stuffed their underclothes with contraband. Notorious customs officers, known as *noirs* because of their black uniforms, developed the habit of thoroughly searching any young lady found alone in the forest, and were generally despised as predators by the native country folk.

Economy

Alsace – This region has become a symbol of the transnational European economy. For the past 30 years, regional development has centred around this theme. Strasbourg, seat of the Council of Europe, was one of the first "Eurocities" on the continent. Mulhouse has expanded its commercial activities through close ties with the cities of Basel and Fribourg across the Rhine. Because of its history, language and traditions, Alsace is able to develop privileged trading partnerships with the bordering nations of Germany and Switzerland. The valley of the River Rhine, long a significant communications corridor, has contributed to regional prosperity. As early as the 8C-9C, boats left Strasbourg for the North Sea, where they sold wine to the English, Danish and Swedish. Steam ships made their appearance in 1826. But it was the construction of the Canal d'Alsace, begun in 1920, which modernised navigation on the Rhine, at the same time harnessing the considerable energy resources provided by the river between Basel and Strasbourg. A strong local policy for encouraging investment has made Alsace the second most dynamic region in France for capital growth. Of 160 regions in the European Union, Alsace is ranked 13th for prosperity.

The fertile plain of Alsace could be used for growing many different crops, but the long strip at the foot of the Vosges is used almost exclusively for the cultivation of grapes: 14 566ha/36 212 acres. All of the wines are bottled in the region of production (almost 150 million bottles), and represent more than 18% of total French still white wine production. This activity involves 7 000 wine-growers. Grapes make up more than half of overall crop production in the region (40% of total agricultural output). On the domestic market, one-third of still white AOC wines consumed in France are from Alsace. The export market takes up 25% of the yearly production (about 40 million bottles).

Lorraine – Its reputation as an industrial leader has been tarnished since its most brilliant period in the late 19C. First the textile crisis, then the decline of the steel industry and the closure of coal mines pushed the area into a deep economic slump. Local policy makers have had to work overtime to find innovative solutions for recovery. These include the creation of "technopoles" in Metz and Nancy, districts zoned for the development of high-tech industries. Subsidies have been allotted to areas around the Meuse Valley, Longwy and Thionville for similar development projects.

Diversification is slowly making inroads where heavy industry once dominated: manufacture of synthetic fabrics for tyre manufacture, paper products, service industries and tourism are expanding. Lorraine is also involved in joint development projects with its neighbours in Germany and Luxembourg.

Recently, 2 000 new jobs were created in Hambach for the manufacture of the innovative Smart Car. A collaborative effort, the mixed diesel/electric or petrol automobile has design by Swatch and quality by Mercedes.

Farms in Lorraine are France's leading producers of rape seed, used for making cooking and salad oil; the flowering plants make bright yellow fields. The region actively promotes "quality labelling" of agricultural products, including beef, cheese and eggs. Wood and wood-processing operations (parquet flooring, panelling, furniture etc) also account for a significant share of French production.

Champagne – Clearly the most important export (20% of total) for this region is its namesake sparkling wine. But it should be noted that in recent years, an accumulation of stock and subsequent lowering of prices have pushed leading traders to rethink their marketing philosophy. Related economic activities include bottling and processing plants and farm machine manufacture. The "Packaging Valley" association brings together 250 businesses specialising in packaging products and processes.

Agriculture, shored up by government subsidies, has also made steps towards increased profitability through diversification. Milk products have taken on an impor-

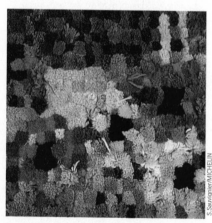

Textile colour chart

tant role; the region produces 25% of all the ice cream in France (mostly in Haute-Marne). Research is underway on the chemical components of natural substances, used in non-food products: biological fuels from rape seed, alcohol and ethanol from sugar beets, paper products and adhesives from wheat starch. Research is carried out in a European institute, the *Agropôle*, in Reims.

The textile industry offers employment to a significant number of people in Champagne-Ardenne, especially in Troyes and the Aube *département*. Among the world famous manufactures of knitted goods: Absorba, Petit Bateau, Lacoste (the alligator shirts were created in Saint-Dizier and Troyes), Dior, Benetton. 35% of all French socks and 58% of infant layettes are made here.

Ardenne – Foundry and metalworks are leading sources of employment, and many automobile and appliance makers place orders with local plants (Citroën, Ford, Électro-lux, General Motors, BMW, Porsche). Various industries related to automobile equipment have also set up shop (automotive textiles, safety parts, machine tools), as well as plants producing parts for high-tech projects such as Ariane rockets, TGV trains, Airbus, Rafale fighter jets and the Channel Tunnel. More recently plastics have taken off, in some instances replacing metal parts and devices, and also in the packaging field.

Most of the businesses in Ardenne are small and medium-sized firms engaged in subcontracting. The network of companies is supported by the CRITT (Regional Centre for Technology Transfer) in Charleville-Mézières, which works in research and development of new and rare materials, microanalysis, non-destructive controls, thermic and thermionic treatments and other highly specialised testing. In an immense effort to revitalise the region after the damage of the Second World War and the decline of heavy industry, the government offers significant fiscal advantages to companies choosing to locate in Ardenne. Their employees benefit from the exceptionally clean and quiet natural environment and the transport network which puts them no more than a few hours away from major European capitals.

Tourism has become an important economic factor in all of the regions covered in this guide. Local authorities have sought to enhance and promote the value of the many historic towns and sites, natural resources and the recreational opportunities they provide. Improvements in the **transportation network** have helped this effort. International airports in Strasbourg and Basel-Mulhouse provide connections to European capitals. A high-speed train (TGV) is scheduled to begin serving eastern France in the near future. The network of *autoroutes* is dense and practical, making it easy to reach the area by car, from the north or south. The waterways have adapted to tourism as well, and there are many possibilities for short trips and longer cruises through the countryside. Major investments around the region have stimulated the development of golf courses, marinas and water sports recreation areas, trails for walking, riding and cycling, and various mountain sports resorts. Many tourists also enjoy a stay at one of the spas – especially after enjoying the fine wines and hearty cuisine of the region *(see Practical information for more details on spas)*!

Arriving at the spa...

...Leaving the spa

Historical table and notes

Prehistoric inhabitants

Human settlements in Champagne and the Ardenne had developed into small villages by the Neolithic Era (4500-2000 BC). By the Bronze Age (1800-750 BC), the region had already established what would become a long tradition of metal working. Different tribes gave their names to future cities: *Lingones* (Langres), *Remi* (Reims), *Catalauni* (Châlons), *Tricasses* (Troyes). In Alsace and Lorraine, Celtic and Germanic tribes occupied the land at the time of the Roman invasion.

BC

58-52	Roman conquest. In Champagne and Ardenne, the people lent their support to Ceasar's troops. In Alsace, the Germanic tribes were forced to retreat to the east of the Rhine.
27	Under Emperor Augustus (27BC-14AD), Champagne was part of the province of Belgium. A sophisticated civilisation developed under the *Pax Romana*; villas were built, trading centres grew and roads improved communication. The area's thermal springs were appreciated for their curative powers.

Christianity and monarchy take root

AD

69-70	Following the death of Nero, the Roman Empire weakened. Assembly held in Reims.
3-5C	Missionaries travelled the region; Germanic invasions: Alemanni, Vandals and Huns successively carried out raids.
486	The regions of the Meuse and Moselle came under the control of the Merovingian king Clovis, establishing a Frankish kingdom. While the Franks were not numerous, they became the ruling class of the territories conquered.
498	St Remi persuaded Clovis to convert on Christmas day.
511	Death of Clovis. Champagne was divided into incoherent parcels, constituting several small kingdoms.
683	The duke of Étichon, father of St Odile, ruled Alsace. After his reign, the land was divided into Nordgau and Sundgau, each ruled by a count.
774	Charles Martel seized some church property for the secular state. At the same time, the region was organised into parishes, and the power and authority of the church grew stronger; a balance of powers developed.
800	The title of emperor was revived and conferred upon Charlemagne. The Holy Roman Empire was a complex of lands in Western and Central Europe ruled by Frankish then German kings for 10 centuries (until renunciation of the imperial title in 1806). The empire and the papacy were the two most important institutions of Western Europe through the Middle Ages.
816	Louis I, (known as The Pious and also The Debonair), son of Charlemagne and Hildegarde the Swabian, was crowned emperor in Reims by Pope Stephen IV; a forceful French monarchy began to take shape.
817	Louis I, in accordance with his father's will, divided Charlemagne's realm among three sons from his first marriage: Bavaria to Louis the German, Aquitaine to Pepin, and Lothair he named co-emperor and heir.
829	Louis' second marriage to Judith of Bavaria had produced a son (Charles the Bald), to whom he granted the realm then known as Alemannia. From this time on, the sons formed and dissolved alliances, overthrew their father twice, and territories were passed back and forth or seized outright by the brothers who continued fighting for decades after their father's death.
839	Pepin dead, another attempt at partition divided the empire between Lothair and Charles, with Bavaria left in the hands of Louis the German. The following year, Louis I died.
843	Under the Treaty of Verdun, Lothair received *Francia Media* (today, parts of Belgium, the Netherlands, western Germany, eastern France, Switzerland and much of Italy); Louis the German received *Francia Orientalis* (land east of the Rhine); Charles received *Francia Occidentalis* (the remainder of present-day France). This treaty marked the dissolution of Charlemagne's empire, and foreshadowed the formation of the modern countries of Western Europe.

| 870 | Lothair left the land of Lotharingia (Greater Lorraine) to a son (Lothair II) who died without a legitimate heir. By the Treaty of Meersen, Charles received western Lorraine and Louis the German an extremely large expansion of his territories west of the Rhine. The region today known as Alsace remained separate from the rest of the French kingdom for the next seven centuries. |

Crowning of Lothair II
Vincent de Beauvais, *Le Miroir historial*, Musée Condé de Chantilly

911	Louis IV died, the last of the east Frankish Carolingians. The many dukes controlling the feudal states in the region elected Conrad, duke of Franconia, as successor; he was followed by Henry (918) and thus began more than a century of Saxon rule in the region.
959	Lotharingia was divided into two parts: Upper Lorraine (Ardennes, Moselle Valley, Upper Meuse Valley) and Lower Lorraine (northern part of the realm, including parts of modern Belgium and the Netherlands).
late 9C and 10C	Raids by Northmen destabilised Charles' reign; power struggles continued as rival dynasties emerged and the feudal system took hold of the people. In France, the Carolingian dynasty waned.

The Middle Ages

987	Hugues Capet crowned, the first of 13 French kings in the Capetian dynasty, which lasted until 1328.
11C	The domains of Tardenois, Château-Thierry, Provins, Reims, Châlons and Troyes, through marriage agreements, came under the authority of the counts of Blois (the king's immediate vassals, but also his most dangerous rivals).
1098	Robert de Molesmes founded the abbey at Cîteaux.
25 June 1115	Clairvaux Abbey founded by St Bernard.
1125-52	Thibaud II, count of Blois, strengthened the economy by creating sound currency and cashing in on trade between Italy and the Netherlands. Communication routes improved, many trade fairs (Lagny, Provins, Sézanne, Troyes, Bar-sur-Aube) were the meeting place for Nordic and Mediterranean merchants.
1015	On the site of a temple to Hercules, a Romanesque cathedral was begun in Strasbourg. St Bernard said Mass there in 1145, before it was destroyed by fire.
1152	French King Louis VII repudiated Eleanor of Aquitaine, who later married Henry Plantagenet, bringing western France under the English crown. For three centuries, the French and English remained "hereditary enemies".
1176	The new cathedral at Strasbourg was begun, inspired by the Gothic style.
1179-1223	Philippe Auguste reigned as the "king of France" rather than the "king of the Franks".
1210	Construction started on the cathedral at Reims.
1284	The brilliant court and unified counties of Champagne joined the French crown with the marriage of Jeanne, Countess of Champagne and Navarre, to Philippe le Bel.
1337	Beginning of the Hundred Years War.
14C	In Alsace, 10 cities formed the Decapole, to resist the excesses of the feudal system; gradually these cities (Strasbourg, Colmar, Haguenau, and others) freed themselves from their overlords.
1429	Joan of Arc, aged 17, led the French armies to victory over the English at Orléans, thus opening the way for the coronation of Charles VII at Reims.

| 1434 | Gutenberg settled in Strasbourg and formed a partnership with three local men for the development of a secret invention. Their association ended acrimoniously in a court of law; in 1448, in Mainz, his printing press saw the light of day. |
| 1480 | The Upper Duchy of Lorraine (Lower Lorraine was no longer a unified duchy) united with Bar and Vaudémont, and became known simply as Lorraine . |

Héloïse and Abélard

The story of these two lovers is one of the world's best-known tragic tales. **Pierre Abélard** (1079-1142) son of a Breton knight, sacrificed his inheritance to devote himself to the study of philosophy and logic, attracting students from all over Europe. Around 1118, Fulbert, a prominent clergyman at Notre-Dame cathedral in Paris, entrusted the education of his brilliant niece **Héloïse** (1101-64) to the scholar. They fell in love. Héloïse bore a son, Astralabe, and the couple married in secret, to protect the philosopher's career. Her family's outrage caused the young woman to seek refuge in a convent. As for Abélard, the bride's relatives wreaked their vengeance by cutting off "the parts of his body with which he committed the offence". He became a monk at the abbey of St-Denis. Ever a controversial character, he was finally able to obtain authorisation to retreat to a lonely site near Nogent-sur-Seine (in the Aube *département* of Champagne-Ardenne), **Le Paraclet** *(see p 244).* The convent Héloïse had entered at Argenteuil was dispersed in 1129. Abélard received permission to create and endow the Community of the Paraclet for his beloved and her sister nuns. The two met again after 10 years of separation. Moved by the words he had written in his famous *Historium calamitatum* ("History of My Troubles"), Héloïse also wrote of her passionate love for him: *The lovers' tenderness we shared together was so sweet to me, that I could no more condemn it than could I erase its memory without pain.* Yet chaste love was to be their lot for the rest of their days. Abélard was continually criticised for his views, by figures as influential as Bernard de Clairvaux. After a reproof from Pope Innocent II, he retired to the monastery of Cluny in Burgundy. There abbot Peter the Venerable helped him make peace with his faith and his fellows before he died in 1142. His body was first sent to the Paraclet; it now lies alongside Héloïse in one of the most visited tombs in the Père-Lachaise cemetery, in Paris. *(For information on books about Abélard and Héloïse, see Suggested reading, p 430.)*

Riches and power are but gifts of blind fate, whereas goodness is the result of one's own merits.

Letter, Héloïse to Abélard

The Renaissance

Late 15C	After a century of strife in Champagne, trade flourished anew during the reign of Louis XI.
1507	In St-Dié, the *Cosmographiae Introductio*, a work by several scholars, first gave the name America to the continent discovered by Christopher Columbus, in honour of the navigator Amerigo Vespucci.
1515-59	Uprisings against the house of Austria in Mézières, Ste-Menehould, St-Dizier and Vitry.
1525	The revolt of peasants *(Rustauds)* ended with their massacre in the town of Saverne.
1562	The massacre at Wassy signalled the beginning of the Wars of Religion in Champagne, which devastated the region for the following century.

The unification of Lorraine and Alsace with France

1552-53	Henri II occupied Metz, Toul and Verdun, defeating Charles V.
1572	The St Bartholomew's Day massacre undermined the power of Protestants in the regions of Champagne and Ardenne.
1635-37	An outbreak of plague in Lorraine killed half of the population; the Thirty Years War, plague and famine ravaged the entire region.
1648-53	The period was marked by serious unrest caused by the far-reaching peasant revolt known as *la Fronde*, and persistent Spanish offensives in Champagne.
1678	The Nijmegen peace agreement confirmed the unification of Alsace and France.
1681	Louis XIV revoked the independence of Strasbourg.
1738	Stanislas Leszczynski, former king of Poland, father-in-law of Louis XV, named duke of Lorraine.
1766	After the death of Stanislas, Lorraine was definitively annexed by France.

Revolution and the transformation of Europe

1785 | Napoleon Bonaparte became an officer of the French army.

1789 | The French Revolution toppled the king, proclaimed the rights of man and destroyed the Ancien Régime.

1791 | Louis XVI and his family were arrested in Varennes-en-Argonne.

1792 | Rouget de Lisle sang the *Marseillaise*, the future French national anthem, in Strasbourg.

1794 | Near Saverne, Chappe's telegraph began operation.

1798 | Mulhouse, the last independent town in Alsace, united with France.

1799 | Napoleon instituted a military dictatorship and named himself First Consul.

1804-15 | Napoleon had himself crowned emperor after victories in Austria and Russia, and successfully consolidated most of Europe as his empire until about 1810. The revived Allied coalition and his defeat at Waterloo led to his final exile.

1814-15 | The Congress of Vienna reorganised Europe after the Napoleonic Wars. It began in September 1814, 5 months after his first abdication, and completed its "Final Act" just before Waterloo and the end of the Hundred Days of Napoleon's return to power.

1815-71 | France was ruled by a limited monarchy, with the exception of a brief republican period (1848-52).

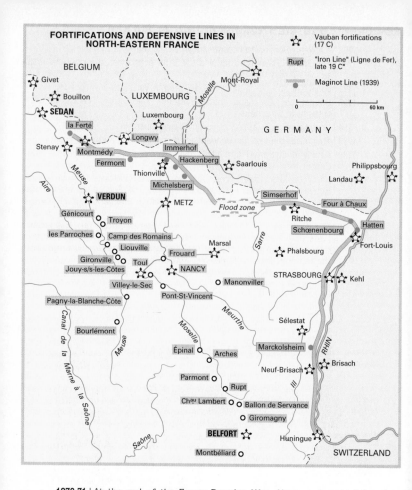

FORTIFICATIONS AND DEFENSIVE LINES IN NORTH-EASTERN FRANCE

☆ Vauban fortifications (17 C)

Rupt ━━ "Iron Line" (Ligne de Fer), late 19 C"

● Maginot Line (1939)

0 ————— 60 km

BELGIUM

Givet
Bouillon
SEDAN
la Ferté
Stenay
Montmédy
Fermont
Thionville
VERDUN
Génicourt
Troyon
les Parroches
Liouville
Camp des Romains
Gironville
Jouy-s/s-les-Côtes
Toul
Villey-le-Sec
Pagny-la-Blanche-Côte
Pont-St-Vincent
Bourlémont
Épinal
Arches
Parmont
Rupt
Chᵘ Lambert
Giromagny
BELFORT
Montbéliard

LUXEMBOURG
Luxembourg
Longwy
Immerhof
Hackenberg
Michelsberg
METZ
Flood zone
Marsal
Frouard
NANCY
Manonviller

Mont-Royal
Moselle

GERMANY

Saarlouis
Philippsbourg
Landau
Simserhof
Four à Chaux
Ritche
Hatten
Schœnenbourg
Fort-Louis
Phalsbourg
STRASBOURG
Kehl
Sélestat
Marckolsheim
RHIN
Neuf-Brisach
Brisach
Ballon de Servance
Huningue
SWITZERLAND

Aire
Meuse
Canal de la Marne à la Saône
Saône
Sarre
Meurthe
Ill

1870-71	At the end of the Franco-Prussian War, Alsace and part of Lorraine were in German hands.
1885	Pasteur administered the first rabies vaccine to a young Alsatian shepherd.
1906	Captain Dreyfus, a native of Mulhouse, was reinstated and decorated with the Legion of Honour, the conclusion of the scandalous "affair" of 1894.

The World at war

1914-18	The violent conflicts of the First World War lasted four years; at the end, Alsace and Lorraine were once again in French territory.
1928	Construction of the Grand Canal of Alsace.
1930-40	Construction of the Maginot Line.
1940-44	Germany invaded France; Alsace and Lorraine occupied.
Late 1944	Lorraine liberated by French and Allied armies.
1945	Final German retreat from Alsace, Armistice signed in Reims.
1949	The Council of Europe established headquarters in Strasbourg.
1952	Dr Albert Schweitzer, of Kaysersberg, awarded the Nobel Peace Prize.
1963	Canalisation of the River Moselle.
1974	Works completed on the Rhine in Alsace, with the inauguration of the hydroelectric plant at Gambsheim.
1976	Paris-Metz-Strasbourg motorway opened.
1977	The Palais de l'Europe (European Economic Community) buildings inaugurated in Strasbourg.
1964-84	Mines and metalworks suffer inexorable decline.
1991	Creation of ARTE (Association Relative à la Télévision Européenne), a joint Franco-German TV station based in Strasbourg.
1993	Strasbourg confirmed as the seat of the European Parliament.
1995-96	Nuclear power plant Chooz B begins operating on the Meuse.
1999	Total solar eclipse observed in Reims. 1 500th anniversary of the baptism of Clovis.

The Franco-Prussian War

From July 1870 to May 1871, the war also known as the Franco-German War came to mark the end of French hegemony on the continent and formed the basis for the Prussian Empire.

Napoleon III's ambitious plans appeared to Prussian chancellor Otto von Bismark as an opportunity to unite northern and southern German states in a confederation against the French. Within four weeks, French troops had been effectively bottled up in the fortress at Metz. The rest of the army, under Marshal Mac-Mahon and accompanied by Napoleon, was surrounded and trapped at Sedan on 31 August. By 2 September, they had surrendered. French resistance fought the desperate odds under a new government of national defence, which had assumed power and deposed the emperor on 4 September 1870, establishing the Third Republic. With Paris under siege, negotiations were stalled while Bismark demanded Alsace and Lorraine. Léon Gambetta, a provisional government leader, organised new armies after escaping from Paris in a balloon. Despite their valiant efforts, and the Paris insurrection which declared the independence of the *Commune de Paris*, capitulation was at hand. The Treaty of Frankfurt was signed on 10 May 1871: Germany annexed all of Alsace and most of Lorraine, with Metz; France had to pay a heavy indemnity. Thus French influence on German states came to a halt and the Prussian domination of Germany was ensured. For the next 40 years, until the First World War, an uneasy peace held sway as further consequences were felt: the papacy lost power and Italian troops entered Rome; the Russian government repudiated the Treaty of Paris and began an aggressive campaign in Eastern Europe.

The First World War (1914-18)

After the Franco-Russian defensive accord of 1892, the Germans responded with the so-called **Schlieffen plan** (named after Marshal von Schlieffen). The plan counted on the slow mobilisation of Russian troops, and called for a six-week campaign to conquer France by way of an invasion of Belgium and a northern attack, bypassing France's solidly defended eastern flank. Once victory in France had been achieved, the plan called for transporting German troops to the Russian front, where the northern giant would be beaten in a few short months.

August-September 1914 – French troops crossed the border on 7 August and entered Mulhouse the following day, but had to withdraw to Belfort under the enemy's counter-attack. On 19 August, after grim combat, Mulhouse was captured anew and the Germans retreated towards the Rhine. Preparing an offensive, the French took control of mountain passes in the Vosges. Meanwhile, on 14 August, the First and Second French Armies had penetrated occupied Lorraine. An assault launched on

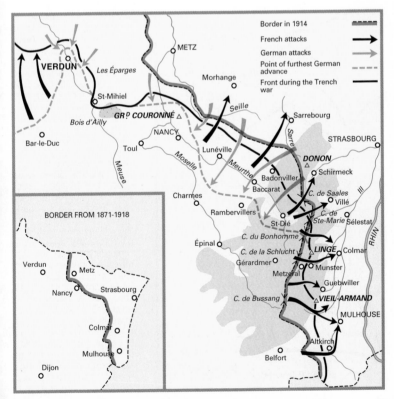

20 August was met with such a violence of firepower that the French troops were decimated, and forced to pull back to the Meurthe. The defensive line between Badonviller and Nancy formed a funnel shape, with the town of Charmes at the small end. The Germans took advantage of this position to attack Charmes, but met with resistance. From 26 August to 9 September they brought their force to bear on the eastern front, the line of the Vosges towards upper Meurthe and on to Nancy.

Yet German commander **Moltke** spread his infantry too thin, and hesitation cost him the **Battle of the Marne** (5-10 September 1914) along with his military command. Marshal **Von Kluck** pushed the German troops towards the Seine. For the French, **Joffre** and **Gallieni** attempted a bold attack on the German's right flank. Four thousand reinforcement troops were carried to the front in the famous **Marne taxis**. British soldiers were able to drive into the opening thus created in the German line, forcing a retreat as far as the Aisne Valley.

A terrible war of attrition settled in along the front from the Jura mountains to the North Sea, through the heart of Alsace and Lorraine.

Trench warfare (1915-18) – After the Battle of the Marne the German position stabilised along the pre-war border in Lorraine, the Vosges and Alsace. Fierce localised combat pitted the armies against each other as they strove to take and hold strategic positions (Les Éparges, Ailly woods, Le Linge, Le Vieil-Armand). In February 1916, the Germans concentrated their efforts on Verdun; the stakes were high as the site became a giant battlefield which was to determine the outcome of the war.

The **Second Battle of the Marne** began with a German incursion in June 1918; Foch led the French forces in powerful resistance. Under pressure from all sides, the Germans fell back to the so-called Hindenburg Line. On 26 September of the same year, Marshal **Foch** launched a general offensive which finally brought about German defeat and the Armistice of 11 November 1918, executed at Rethondes.

The Second World War (1939-45)

Virtually every part of the world was involved in this conflict: the Axis powers (Germany, Italy and Japan) and the Allies (France, Great Britain, the United States, the Soviet Union and, to a lesser extent, China) were, of course the main players. The war was in some ways a continuation of the disputes left unresolved at the end of the First World War. France expected that if another war occurred, it would resemble the last one, and so built up a continuous defensive front, the Maginot Line, which also responded to the very low demographics of the eastern regions of France after the first war. This siege mentality, coupled with the old guard's refusal to modernise offensive and defensive weapons or to develop new strategies, proved poor preparation for the onslaught to come.

The period of 1939-41 is often sardonically referred to as the *Sitzkrieg* or **Phony War** – the French expression is the sheepish *drôle de guerre*. A combination of French procrastination, lack of British military support and German *Blitzkrieg* (lightening war) tactics led to the divided occupation (Nazi and Soviet) of Poland. While a massive Soviet offensive secured Finland, still the other Allies dithered; Norwegian ports were occupied by German naval forces and Denmark taken by Blitzkrieg. Thus the belligerents staked a claim to a vast area of Europe. Perhaps the first significant riposte was the appointment by George VI of Winston Churchill to head the War Cabinet. The great and energetic statesman made the first of many inspirational speeches, prophetically announcing that he had "nothing to offer but blood, toil, tears and sweat".

On 10 May 1940, a German offensive drove the Dutch to surrender within days. Meanwhile, armoured units made their way through the supposedly impenetrable Ardennes Forest – simply bypassing the Maginot Line, France's illusory defence. By 20 May, the Germans had reached the coast. Not until D-Day, 6 June 1944 was the Norman peninsula wrested from German occupation by American, British and Canadian troops. More troops landed in Provence on 15 August. The Allied armies then raced eastward and northward to liberate France. Paris was liberated on 25 August; Verdun at the end of the month. Nancy and Épinal followed in mid September. The fierce German defence did not yield in Metz until 22 November.

Fighting continued in Alsace as German hopes of recovering the region for its own refused to die. But French offensive forces took Belfort and Mulhouse, and encircled German troops in the Battle of Haute-Alsace. To the north, General **Leclerc** launched his Strasbourg campaign from Saverne, taking the city on 23 November. Controlling the two extremities of the Alsatian plain, the Allies then crossed the Vosges and came down into the vineyards, where more brutal fighting awaited them. By 19 December one pocket of resistance remained, around Colmar, protected by the flooded River Ill. On 1 January 1945, the Germans rallied and re-occupied Strasbourg, but the insistence of General de Gaulle (Eisenhower wished to retreat to the mountains) and the hard-fighting local resistance recovered the city for the French. **De Lattre de Tassigny**, meanwhile, was busy squeezing the "Colmar pocket" with French and American divisions. The Wehrmacht was forced over the last bridge still under its control, at Chalampé, on 9 February.

German capitulation was marked by the signature of the Armistice at Reims on 7 May 1945.

European peace and unification

9 May 1950: Robert Schuman proposed the idea of the European Coal and Steel Community (ECSC), later established by the Treaty of Paris (April 1951). Schuman's declaration was inspired by Jean Monnet's idea of "building Europe" step by step. Six States laid the foundations: Belgium, France, Germany, Italy, Luxembourg and The Netherlands. The ECSC was given a "parliamentary assembly", which met for the first time in September 1952 in Strasbourg. By 1979, the European Economic Community, as defined by the Treaty of Rome (1957), saw the European Parliament elected by universal suffrage: 410 Members from nine Member States.

By 1993, the Member States numbered 12, and the Treaty on European Union came into force. In June 1994 the fourth European Parliament elections by direct universal suffrage were held: the number of Members rose to 567 to take account of German unification. In 1995, the accession of Austria, Finland and Sweden increased Membership to 626.

The **European Union**, founded to promote peace and economic stability, freedom of movement, and a unified approach to problems of security, defence, and social welfare, operates through the Parliament, which meets in Strasbourg, but also other bodies: the Commission makes proposals for European legislation and action; the Council of the European Union is made up of one minister for each Member State government and for each subject; the European Council decides broad policy lines for Community policy and for matters of foreign and security policy and justice; the Court of Justice is the supreme court of the European Union (15 judges and nine advocates-general); the Court of Auditors monitors the management of Community finance. Advisory bodies include: the Economic and Social Committee consisting of 222 representatives of various economic and social groups; the Committee of the Regions consisting of 222 representatives of local and regional authorities, who bring a regional and local dimension to the Union.

Among the main aims of the Union, the goal of a single European currency is becoming a reality in many countries. The euro is now the currency used by banking and financial institutions in most EU nations, and will entirely replace French francs, along with the currencies of other participating nations, in the year 2002.

Art

ABC OF ARCHITECTURE

Religious architecture

I. Ground plan of a church

Axial chapel: in churches which are not dedicated to the Virgin this chapel, in the main axis of the building, is often consecrated to the Virgin (Lady Chapel)

Ambulatory: in pilgrimage churches the aisles were extended round the chancel, forming the ambulatory, to allow the faithful to file past the relics

Chancel, nearly always facing east towards Jerusalem

Arm of the transept, often extending outward

Bay: transverse section of the nave between two pillars

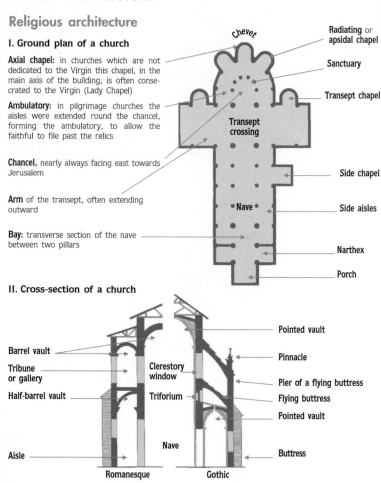

Chevet

Radiating or apsidal chapel

Sanctuary

Transept chapel

Transept crossing

Side chapel

Nave

Side aisles

Narthex

Porch

II. Cross-section of a church

Barrel vault

Tribune or gallery

Half-barrel vault

Aisle

Clerestory window

Triforium

Nave

Romanesque

Pointed vault

Pinnacle

Pier of a flying buttress

Flying buttress

Pointed vault

Buttress

Gothic

III. MÉZIÈRES – Notre-Dame-de-l'Espérance Basilica (15 C)

Keystone pendentive: characteristic of late or Flamboyant Gothic period, embellishments, added in the Renaissance

Lierne: a short, intermediate rib

Tierceron: an intermediate rib between the main ribs

Diagonal rib

Transverse arch: reinforcing arch under a vault

Transverse rib

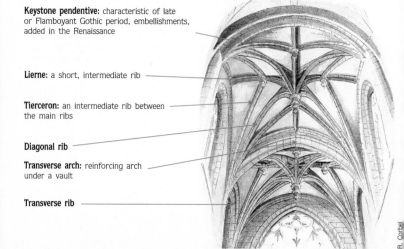

R. Corbel

IV. MARMOUTIER – Romanesque façade of St-Étienne (*c*1140)

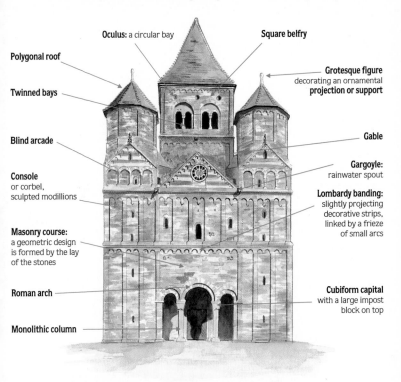

Oculus: a circular bay

Square belfry

Polygonal roof

Twinned bays

Grotesque figure decorating an ornamental **projection or support**

Blind arcade

Gable

Console or corbel, sculpted modillions

Gargoyle: rainwater spout

Lombardy banding: slightly projecting decorative strips, linked by a frieze of small arcs

Masonry course: a geometric design is formed by the lay of the stones

Roman arch

Cubiform capital with a large impost block on top

Monolithic column

V. REIMS – Chevet of the cathedral (1211-1260)

The cathedral in Reims can be compared to Chartres. Both are great works of Gothic architecture, which reached an apogee in Champagne and the Ile-de-France region between the late 12C and mid-13C.

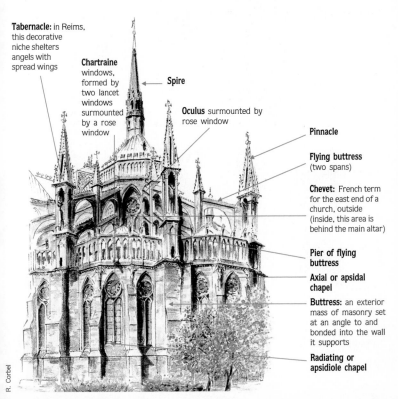

Tabernacle: in Reims, this decorative niche shelters angels with spread wings

Chartraine windows, formed by two lancet windows surmounted by a rose window

Spire

Oculus surmounted by rose window

Pinnacle

Flying buttress (two spans)

Chevet: French term for the east end of a church, outside (inside, this area is behind the main altar)

Pier of flying buttress

Axial or apsidal chapel

Buttress: an exterior mass of masonry set at an angle to and bonded into the wall it supports

Radiating or apsidiole chapel

R. Corbel

VI. Strasbourg – Central façade of Notre-Dame cathedral (12-15C)

The abundant detail of Flamboyant Gothic is evident in the central doorway, richly sculpted and crowned with openwork gables.

Gable: decorative, vertical triangle above certain doorways, here incorporating openwork

Pinnacle

Great rose window, made up of sixteen geminated (split) petals

Sculpted **rose** cornerpieces

Arch: a curved construction which spans an opening; a series of arches forms the **archivolt**

Jamb shaft: vertical member forming part of the jamb of a door

Bronze door leaf

Embrasure embellished with statues

Tympanum made of four historiated bands

Band sculpted ornamental strip

Archivolt: the series of arches

Upright post or bearing shaft of a portal, generally a statue is bonded to it

R. Corbel

42

VII. MOUZON – Interior of the Abbey church (1195-*c*1240)

The elevation of the nave embraces four storeys (arcades, gallery, Triforium, clerestory windows), typical of primitive Gothic art (second half of the 12C).

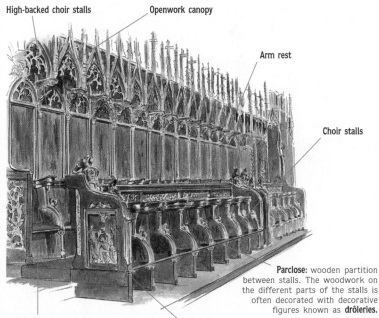

Sexpartite vault, ribbed vault whose lateral triangles are bisected by an intermediate transverse rib producing six triangles within a bay

Clerestory window

Trefoil arch

Blind Triforium: series of simulated openings between the large arcades and the clerestory windows

Corner piece: between the arch and its frame

Engaged column, partly embedded in or bonded to the wall

Crocket capital

Shaft of a column: between the base and the capital

Tribune: upper gallery where small groups can convene

Nave

Keystone

Cell or **Quarter** segment or part of the vault defined by the groins (1) or ribs (2)

Transverse arch

Apse: the eastern end of a church behind the main altar (interior). Compare to chevet

Canopy

Chancel

Main arcade: separates the nave from the aisles

VIII. THANN – Choir stalls in St-Thiébaut (14C-early 16C)

High-backed choir stalls

Openwork canopy

Arm rest

Choir stalls

Parclose: wooden partition between stalls. The woodwork on the different parts of the stalls is often decorated with decorative figures known as **drôleries.**

Misericord (or **Miserere**): a bracket on the underside of a hinged choir stall which can be turned up to support a person standing during long services (from the Latin for "compassion")

Cheek: the vertical uprights at the end of a row of stalls

43

Civil architecture

IX. SAVERNE – Katz House (1605-1668), no 76, Grand'Rue

Half-timbered houses, numerous in Alsace, illustrate the skill of local carpenters, especially between the 17-19C.

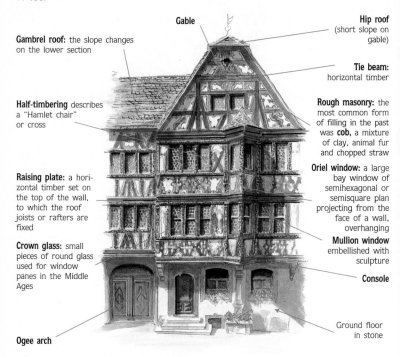

Gable

Hip roof (short slope on gable)

Gambrel roof: the slope changes on the lower section

Tie beam: horizontal timber

Half-timbering describes a "Hamlet chair" or cross

Rough masonry: the most common form of filling in the past was **cob,** a mixture of clay, animal fur and chopped straw

Raising plate: a horizontal timber set on the top of the wall, to which the roof joists or rafters are fixed

Oriel window: a large bay window of semihexagonal or semisquare plan projecting from the face of a wall, overhanging

Mullion window embellished with sculpture

Crown glass: small pieces of round glass used for window panes in the Middle Ages

Console

Ogee arch

Ground floor in stone

X. LUNÉVILLE – Château (18C)

Also known as "Petit-Versailles", this château was designed by the architect Germain Boffrand.

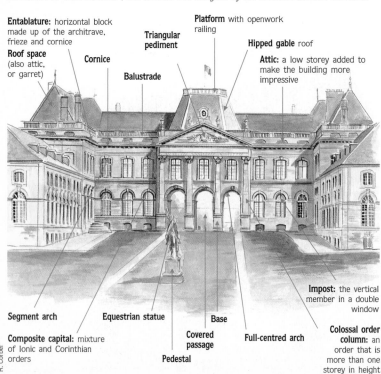

Entablature: horizontal block made up of the architrave, frieze and cornice

Roof space (also attic, or garret)

Cornice

Triangular pediment

Balustrade

Platform with openwork railing

Hipped gable roof

Attic: a low storey added to make the building more impressive

Impost: the vertical member in a double window

Segment arch

Equestrian statue

Base

Colossal order column: an order that is more than one storey in height

Composite capital: mixture of Ionic and Corinthian orders

Covered passage

Full-centred arch

Pedestal

44

XI. CONTREXÉVILLE – Thermal springs gallery and pavilion

The design expresses the architectural eclecticism typical of spa town; neo-Byzantine style predominates.

Drum embellished with decorative brick designs

Cupola: metal frame is pierced to let light in

Doric capitals

Concentric peristyle

Circular pavilion above the spring

Large **bay windows**

Gallery-portico

Fluted columns with mosaic embellishments

Military architecture

XII. HAUT-KOENIGSBOURG – Feudal castle rebuilt in the early 20C

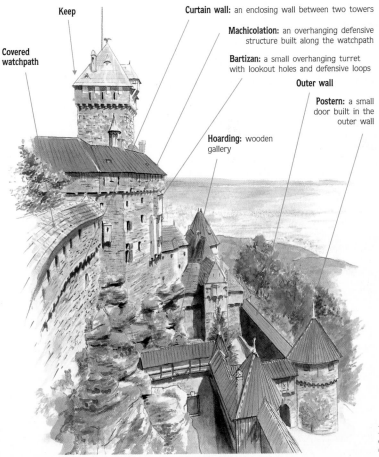

Keep

Curtain wall: an enclosing wall between two towers

Machicolation: an overhanging defensive structure built along the watchpath

Covered watchpath

Bartizan: a small overhanging turret with lookout holes and defensive loops

Outer wall

Postern: a small door built in the outer wall

Hoarding: wooden gallery

R. Corbel

45

XIII. NEUF-BRISACH – Stronghold (1698-1703)

The polygonal stronghold was developed in the early 16C, as firearms became more common in warfare: the cannon mounted on one structure covered the "blind spot" of the neighbouring position. This stronghold was built by Vauban, opposite the formidable Breisach, handed back to the Hapsburgs under the Treaty of Ryswick (1697).

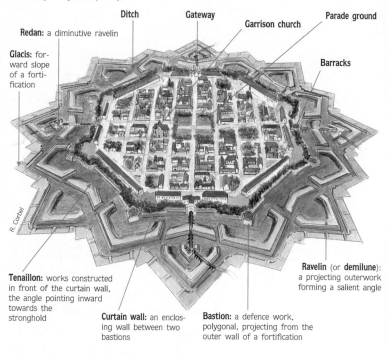

Redan: a diminutive ravelin

Glacis: forward slope of a fortification

Ditch

Gateway

Garrison church

Parade ground

Barracks

R. Corbel

Tenaillon: works constructed in front of the curtain wall, the angle pointing inward towards the stronghold

Curtain wall: an enclosing wall between two bastions

Bastion: a defence work, polygonal, projecting from the outer wall of a fortification

Ravelin (or **demilune**): a projecting outerwork forming a salient angle

Other architectural terms used in this guide

Ashlar	Hewn masonry or squared stones lain in regular courses, as distinguished from rubble work.
Bailey	Space enclosed by the outer walls of a castle (also: *ward*).
Barbican	Outwork of a medieval castle, often with a tower, defending a gate or bridge.
Bartizan	An overhanging battlemented corner turret, corbelled out; sometimes as grandiose as an overhanging gallery (illustration XII).
Battlements	Parapet of medieval fortifications, with a walkway for archers, protected by merlons, with embrasures between them.
Buttress	Vertical mass of masonry built against a wall, so strengthening it and resisting the pressure of a vaulted roof (illustration II).
Clerestory	Upper stage of an elevation, consisting of a range of tall windows (illustration VII).
Crenellation	The low segment of the alternating high and low segments of a battlement.
Donjon	French term for the castle *keep* (illustration XII).
Glacis	A bank sloping down from a castle which acts as a defence against invaders; broad, sloping naked rock or earth on which the attackers are completely exposed (illustration XIII).
Machicolation	In medieval castles, a row of openings below the projecting parapet though which missiles could be rained down upon the enemy.
Merlon	The high segment of the alternating high and low segments of a battlement.
Portcullis	A heavy timber or metal grill that protected the castle entrance and could be raised or lowered from within to block passage or to trap attackers.
Postern Gate	A side or less important gate into a castle; usually for peacetime use by pedestrians (illustration XII).
Rustication	Worked ashlar stone with beveled edges defining conspicuous joints.
Wicket	Person-sized door set into the main gate door.

ARCHITECTURE IN ALSACE
Religious architecture

Romanesque churches – In Alsace, Carolingian influences persisted longer than elsewhere in France; the flowering of Romanesque art took place in the 12C, lagging a century behind the rest of the country.

Yet this lag did produce some happy consequences: Alsace, at the crossroads of France, Germany and Italy, was able to assimilate the most diverse trends and add a regional touch to create a very original style.

Exterior – Most of the churches in Alsace are small or modest, and laid out in the form of a Latin cross with short lateral arms. The 11C church at Ottmarsheim still shows the Carolingian polygonal ground plan, inspired by the Palatine chapel in Aix-la-Chapelle (Aachen).

Among the distinctive local features, **tours lanternes** (lantern towers) are found above the transept crossing (Ste-Foy in Sélestat is a good example). **Belfries**, both square and round, often rise from the angle made by the main body of the church (chancel and nave) and the transept crossing. The western façade, with or without a porch, is flanked by belfries several storeys high.

The east end culminates in a semicircular apse; flattened chevets (Murbach) are the exception. The side walls, gables, apse and façade are embellished with Lombardy banding, slightly projecting decorative strips linked by a frieze of small arcs.

Under the influence of artisans in Basel, arched doorways rest on slender columns; historiated tympana were frequent adornments in the 12C *(doorway of the cathedral at Verdun, p 365)*.

Interior – The architecture is ascetic; arcading and bays without decorative moulding are surmounted by a wall, with one or two windows which flare open wider on the inside. The chancel is not ringed by an ambulatory. Vaulting was not used until late in the 12C.

The main supports are Roman arches which shape the ribbed vault. They rest on thick rectangular pillars flanked on four sides by engaged columns. The side aisles are covered with groined vaulting formed by the intersection of the long vault of the side aisle and the transverse vaults.

Decoration – The spare decoration is mostly found on doorways, in plain geometric patterns; only the church at Andlau has any interesting sculptures.

The **capitals**, the wide upper portion of columns supporting arches, are an important part of the architectural style. Ribs from more than one vault

Flamboyant Gothic doorway, Avioth basilica

can rest on a single pillar. In Alsace, the Romanesque churches usually have very simple, cubic capitals, with little variety of sculpted forms – a few rare figures and some foliage. Some churches have tried to palliate the plain and sober decoration with paintings, such as those in **Ottmarsheim**.

Gothic churches – After some searching, Gothic art in Alsace reached a rare degree of perfection: the cathedral in **Strasbourg** is proof enough. Many Gothic buildings, civil and religious, went up between the 13C and the 14C: in **Colmar**, the Unterlinden cloisters, St-Martin Church, the Koifhus (Customs House); in Wissembourg, St-Pierre-St-Paul; St-George in Sélestat, to name a few.

At the end of the 15C, Flamboyant Gothic appeared on the scene in **Thann** (St-Thiébaut) and Strasbourg (St-Laurent doorway on the cathedral).

During the 16C, while the Renaissance was influencing civil architecture, religious buildings remained true to the Gothic spirit. The churches in **Ammerschwihr** (16C) and **Molsheim** (16C-17C) well reflect this.

Traces of the **Renaissance** are more evident in charming private residences and admirable public buildings.

Classical style – In the 17C, a long period of trials and warfare halted nearly all construction of new civil and religious buildings. Under French authority, Alsace rebuilt and embellished monasteries. Yet there are a few churches dating from this time, including St-Pierre in **Colmar** (Regency style), and Notre-Dame in **Guebwiller**, built by the abbots of Murbach on a strict Classical design.

Baroque influences are apparent in the abbey church at **Ebersmunster**, lavishly decorated with sculptures, mouldings and frescoes.

Civil architecture

Town halls – As early as the Middle Ages, Alsatian towns sought a degree of independence. Town halls were built to serve the municipal authorities, a symbol of power and an illustration of architectural preferences of the times.

The lovely town halls in **Ensisheim, Mulhouse** (the covered porch was inspired by Swiss buildings), **Obernai, Rouffach, Kaysersberg, Molsheim** and **Guebwiller** as well as the old town hall of Strasbourg (today the Chamber of Commerce), testify to the intensity of local politics.

Bourgeois and princely manors – In most of the towns in Alsace, visitors will see neighbourhoods or street corners which recall the prosperity of bygone days.

Picturesque places like **Riquewhir, Kaysersberg**, the Petite France district of **Strasbourg** and Petite Venise in **Colmar** have a rich architectural heritage of traditional 16C-17C private residences. Overhanging elements mark the façade, and the upper storeys culminate in sharp points; both stone and wood are used as building materials.

During the Renaissance, many amusing details were added: fancy gables, wooden galleries around towers, wrought-iron work, sculpted or painted wooden panelling on the façade. The two most distinctive features of Alsatian manors built in the 15C and during the Renaissance are the gables and the oriel windows.

Gables perch ornately atop buildings. In Strasbourg, the Maison de l'Œuvre Notre-Dame is topped with a gable mounting squarely upwards like a set of stairs; in Colmar, curling scrolls adorn the sloping sides of the gable on the Maison des Têtes.

Colmar – Maison des Têtes

Oriel windows – These large bay windows of semihexagonal or semisquare plan project from the façade, creating an overhang, as on the Maison des Têtes *(see photograph)*. The oriel window provides a break in the uniformity of a façade and creates a lively play of light and shadow. For a building located on a narrow street, it can be a precious source of light, and a good vantage point for watching the comings and goings of the town. Prestigious residences built for the powerful lords, prelates and financiers in the 17C – once the devastating Thirty Years War was past and Alsace was in the hands of Louis XIV – and the 18C are distinguished by the increase in French influence on the banks of the Rhine. While 18C residences do not have the imaginative style of Renaissance houses, they are admirable for their graceful balconies, delicate corbels and elegant bay windows, as well as the fine quality of stone.

The luxurious palaces of the Rohan family, in **Strasbourg** and **Saverne**, are splendid examples of Classical architecture.

Wells and fountains – Especially popular during the Renaissance, fountains went up on many town squares, red-sandstone columns supporting a statue of the patron saint, a figure from history or legend or a heraldic emblem.

Military architecture

All along the Vosges hillsides, rising above the plain of Alsace, the vestiges of ancient fortresses and feudal keeps mark the horizon.

More recent vestiges also interest the visitor: magnificent ramparts built and renovated by Vauban; German defences put up between 1870 and 1914; concrete pillboxes and armoured towers from the above and below-ground works that made up the **Maginot Line** *(see p 52)*; numerous forts and blockhouses left from the Second World War.

Defensive castles – Sentinels in times of war, all of these castles have kept their proud allure, even those which are little more than an isolated keep or a lone wall crumbling under moss. The reconstitution of the Haut-Kœnigsbourg Castle, by the order of Kaiser Wilhelm II, was controversial from the outset. Still today, some prefer the romantic reverie of ruins to the academic demonstration of a pristine reconstruction.

Medieval walled cities – In the Middle Ages, towns and cities built fortifications to defend themselves from both feudal lords and enemies from abroad. A city would build a ring of protective walls, with strategically located towers and just a few gateways which could be closed up and protected. These gateways still stand in many towns (Porte Haute); towers (Tour du Diable, Tour des Sorcières) mark the line of the old fortified wall.

ARCHITECTURE IN LORRAINE
Religious architecture

Romanesque churches – In the 10C and early 11C, German prelates held jurisdiction in Metz, Toul and Verdun, bringing the architectural influences of the Rhineland; an example is the western chancel of Verdun Cathedral. But by the end of the 11C, influences from Champagne and Burgundy had grown stronger.
The churches in Lorraine are mostly basilicas, often simplified to the extreme. The smaller churches have only a nave, a chancel and an apse. The doors are crowned with a semicircular tympanum, the façades are sparsely decorated. Ribbed vaulting is common in Romanesque building; it was introduced in Lorraine in the last third of the 12C. Towers are generally square, and placed atop the square shaped by the transept. Among the most characteristic churches of this period, one is in **Mont-Devant-Sassay**; part of **Notre-Dame de Verdun** is also a good illustration of this style.

Gothic churches – Like all regions which were long under German influence, Lorraine was slow moving from Romanesque to Gothic architecture.
In **Toul** and **Metz**, the cathedrals bear the marks of French influence. Indeed, they were designed by masters who had already worked in Champagne and Île-de-France, the cradle of the French Gothic style.
The links between Lorraine and France were numerous at that time, and French predominance was felt in many fields: students from Lorraine travelled to the University of Paris; the famous trade fairs in Lorraine made it an economic centre; the dukes of Lorraine were well aware of the ambitious plans of the Capetian kings next door.
Other Gothic edifices worth citing: **Avioth**, where the great ambulatory of the church was frequented by pilgrims, St-Étienne in **St-Mihiel** and the basilica of **St-Nicolas-de-Port**, whose magnificent façade was completed in the 16C.

Renaissance – The most significant works from this period are the Chapelle des Évêques in the cathedral at **Toul** and the church at **St-Gengoult**.

Civil architecture

Renaissance – The monumental doorway of the old ducal palace at Nancy *(see p 230)*, so finely wrought, dates from the 16C. Few châteaux from the period are still standing, but visitors can admire those at **Louppy-sur-Loison, Cons-la-Grandville** and **Fléville**.

Classical architecture – The 18C was the heyday of this style. Although there was a pronounced taste for French styles, the traditional Italian influence remained present. Robert de Cotte designed the Château de la Grange and the Verdun bishopric in this style.
Germain Boffrand, a student of Jules Hardouin-Mansart, superintendent of buildings for the French king, drew the plans for Lunéville Château, the "Versailles of Lorraine", for the benefit of Duke Leopold. For Marc de Beauvau, *Grand écuyer de Lorraine*, the Duke's Riding Master, he built the lovely Château d'Haroué. But the most impressive examples of Classical architecture are found together in the city of **Nancy**. When he was granted the duchy of Lorraine in 1737, former Polish king Stanislas Leszczynski undertook a plan to beautify his new capital. In particular, he called on Boffrand's disciple, **Emmanuel Héré**, and a metalwork craftsman from Nancy, **Jean Lamour**. Their work still shines on place Stanislas (on the UNESCO World Heritage List), the Arc de Triomphe and place de la Carrière. The ensemble constitutes one of the masterpieces of European urban architecture.

Montmédy

Military architecture

Many defensive castles were erected in the Middle Ages. Today most have been reduced to ruin, or mere vestiges remain: Prény, Sierk, Tour aux Puces (Thionville), Châtel-sur-Moselle.

Few of the former fortified towns have kept all of their walls, exceptions being **Montmédy** and **Neuf-Brisach**. Often, it is the gateways which have remained standing: Porte de France in Longwy, Porte des Allemands in Metz, Porte Chaussée and Porte Châtel in Verdun, Porte de la Craffe in Nancy, Porte de France in Vaucouleurs, Porte de France and Porte d'Allemagne in Phalsbourg.

ARCHITECTURE IN CHAMPAGNE-ARDENNE

Religious architecture

Romanesque churches – As in Lorraine, most of the works dating from the Carolingian period have disappeared. Of the many sanctuaries built in the 9C, only the chancel of the abbey at Isle-Aumont remains.

Architecture in the year 1000 – A period of reconstruction followed the Norman and Hungarian invasions. The East Frankish Ottonian Empire (962-1002) had a strong influence on contemporary artistic style at the time.

Churches from the early 11C often look like big basilicas, with sturdy framework allowing for many openings to provide light; there are towers outside, galleries and sometimes an ambulatory inside. The interior decoration is usually very simple, based on geometric patterns.

Three churches in Champagne illustrate this style: Notre-Dame in **Montier-en-Der** (rebuilt in 1940), St-Étienne in **Vignory** and St-Remi in **Reims**. St-Étienne is one of the most remarkable monuments in the region because it has changed so little over time. St-Remi, on the other hand, has been renovated many times, and yet the Romanesque elements are easily recognisable, in particular the sculpted capitals adorned with foliage and figures.

End of the 11C and 12C – The traditions of the year 1000 continued to grow through the 11C, while at the same time, Gothic influences from the neighbouring Île-de-France were making inroads. Romanesque architecture from this period is mainly represented by a few buildings around Reims and in the Ardenne. Covered porches are common, and because of this are often referred to as *porches champenois*. The Carolingian influence is apparent in the plain decorative effects: capitals and cornices are embellished with rows of geometric designs, palmettos, and notched patterns.

Romanesque traces in vestigial monastic buildings hint at what great beauty must have been there: the cloisters of Notre-Dame-en-Vaux at **Châlons-en-Champagne**, the doorway of St-Ayoul in **Provins**, the chapter-house in St-Remi in **Reims**.

The birth of Gothic – Gothic art originated in the Île-de-France in the 12C and quickly spread to the Champagne region, where manpower and financing made construction possible. The primitive Gothic style has echoes of the Romanesque: the use

Reims Cathedral

of embellished decoration was restrained and structures remained simple. Experimentation was taking place, too, with the edification of the abbey church at **Mouzon**, Notre-Dame-en-Vaux in **Châlons-en-Champagne**, St-Quiriace in **Provins**, the abbey church at **Orbais**, where the architect Jean Orbais designed a remarkable chancel which served as a model for Reims Cathedral. The chancels of Notre-Dame in **Montier-en-Der** and St-Remi in **Reims**, which date from the origins of Gothic art, have a distinctive feature: columns stand in the ambulatory at the entrance to the side chapels, and support ribs of both chapel and ambulatory vaults, forming an elegant and airy colonnade.

The apogee of Gothic art – The golden age of the great cathedrals was the **13C** and **14C**; brilliantly lit by vast bays and vivid rose windows, they are covered in delicately carved sculptures.
When the cathedral at **Reims** was built, architects were already seeking to lighten the walls and interiors with immense bays: St-Amand-sur-Fion, the cathedrals at **Châlons** and **Troyes** and in particular St-Urbain show the accomplished fruits of their labours.

Decline – Gothic architecture then moved into its Flamboyant period (**15C-16C**), just before it began to wane. The over-abundance of decorative elements tended to mask the essential lines of the buildings. In the Champagne region, the basilica of Notre-Dame de l'Épine is the best example.

The Renaissance (16C) – Most of the architectural achievements of the Renaissance concern civil construction, but a few churches which were enlarged or renovated are worth mentioning: St-André-les-Vergers, Pont-Ste-Marie, Les Riceys, Auxon, Bérulle. Many beautiful windows and statues were produced in Troyes during this period.

Civil architecture

Gallo-Roman vestiges – Although not many major monuments are still intact, there are some very interesting vestiges. In **Reims**, remains of the ancient urban settlement include a triumphant arch, the Porte Mars (decorated with farming scenes celebrating the prosperity of the Roman Empire), and a cryptoporticus; in **Langres**, a gateway stands. In **Andilly-en-Bassigny**, archaeological research has uncovered a villa complete with its baths. Museums in Troyes, Reims, Nogent-sur-Seine and Langres have extensive collections including pottery, glass, statuary and domestic objects.
Outside of the cities, the hubs of civilization, the countryside was dotted with estates known as *villae*. At the centre of a farming operation, each villa was a luxurious and well-equipped residence. The main house was not only very comfortable, but also richly decorated with paintings, mosaics, marble floors and wall panels and statues. Nearby, stood buildings for servants and craftsmen, and farther off the farm buildings. These settlements thus were home to a fair number of people, engaged in various activities. The villa-centred organisation of country life went into decline in the 3C as threats of invasion made it necessary to build protective walls.
Indeed, successive waves of invasions destroyed Gallo-Roman civilization in the 5C. Cities locked their gates, monuments were destroyed or abandoned. In the Middle Ages, the final remains were mostly broken apart for other uses.

The Renaissance – Italian influence brought about a major change in style notable for a renewed interest in forms from ancient civilization: columns and superimposed galleries lend grandeur to monuments of the period. Niches, statues and medallions are set into the façades; pilasters frame the bays (**Joinville Château** and Renaissance manors in **Troyes** and **Reims**).

Classical architecture – In the Ardennes region this style is best represented by the masterpiece in the Henri IV-Louis XIII style, place Ducale in **Charleville**. There are many similarities with the famous place des Vosges in Paris.
In the 18C, the construction of large urban squares on the Classical model was popular in France. In Paris, place Louis-XV (now place de la Concorde) inspired similar works in **Reims** (place Royale) and **Châlons-en-Champagne**, where the town hall is further evidence of the Parisian influence.

Military architecture

Located on the French border, the Ardennes still boasts a few fortifications, including the impressive château of Sedan, the largest in Europe, which was built between the 15C and the 18C. There are fortified churches in the Thiérache region of *Champagne humide* dating from the 16C and 17C; a few traditional fortifications erected by Vauban; the **Villy-la-Ferté** fort was part of the Maginot Line.
Most **fortified churches** were built up at the end of the 16C and early 17C to serve as refuges. The region, neighbouring both the Netherlands under Spanish rule and the Prussian Empire was rocked by incessant warfare.

Vauban – **Sébastien le Prestre de Vauban** (1633-1707) took inspiration from his predecessors, and in particular from **Jean Errard** (1554-1610) of Bar-le-Duc, who published a treatise on fortifications in 1600. Able to learn his lessons from the many wars of siege which occurred in his century, Vauban promoted fortifications in the countryside. His opinion was that they should rise up around a stronghold and be organised according to the principle of the fortified camp. The defensive perimeter was stretched as far as possible in order to force the enemy to use more men to hold the siege; thus the number of men available to keep watch was reduced and the enemy became more vulnerable to a surprise attack from rescuers of the besieged. Vauban's system is characterised by bastions which function with advanced ravelins – projecting, arrow-shaped outworks – all surrounded by deep ditches. One of the best examples of his work is in **Rocroi**. Taking advantage of natural obstacles, using materials found nearby, he also sought to bring some beauty to his fortifications, by bestowing monumental stone entrances upon them. On the northern front in the Ardennes Forest, he set up a system known as *Pré carré*. This consisted of two lines of strongholds located near enough to one another to prevent enemy passage, and to offer help in the case of attack. Although most of these fortified places are in today's Flanders and Hainaut regions, the Ardennes was defended by the **Charlemont** fort on the front lines, and by Rocroi, **Mézières** and **Sedan** on the rear lines.

The Maginot Line – Devised by War Minister Paul Painlevé and his successor, **André Maginot** (1877-1932), this line of defensive fortifications was under study by 1925. It includes a series of concrete works placed at the top of a hill or on the hillside all along the north-eastern border from the Ardennes Forest to the Rhine. The fort of **Villy-la-Ferté** is a good example of the defensive architecture of the line. Unfortunately for the French, this stronghold was without troops at the crucial moment, which meant that the resistance of May-June 1940 was pathetically vain.

Besides the famous series of fortifications, the Maginot Line today also has a series of museums and tourist facilities; a tour is both easy to undertake and educational. Turn to page 182 for full details on visiting this historic site.

World Heritage List

In 1972, The United Nations Educational, Scientific and Cultural Organization (UNESCO) adopted a Convention for the preservation of cultural and natural sites. UNESCO World Heritage sites included in this guide are:

Place Stanislas, Place de la Carrière and Place d'Alliance in Nancy

The temporary residence of a king without a kingdom – Stanislas Leszcynski – is an example of an enlightened monarchy responding to the needs of the public. Constructed between 1752 and 1756 by a brilliant team under the direction of the architect Héré, this project illustrates a perfect coherence between the desire for prestige and a concern for functionality.

Strasbourg, Grande île

The historic centre of the Alsatian capital lies between two arms of the River Ill. The district occupied by the Cathedral, four ancient churches and the Palais Rohan recalls the typical medieval city plan, and shows the evolution of the city from the 15C to the 18C.

Cathedral of Notre-Dame, former Abbey of Saint-Remi and Palace of Tau, Reims

The Cathedral, its sculpted decorations embellishing the Gothic architecture, is a masterpiece. The former abbey has conserved its beautiful 9C nave where the holy anointing of the kings of France was first carried out by Saint Remi. The Tau Palace was almost entirely reconstructed in the 17C.

Sculpture and stained glass

ALSACE

The finest examples of **sculpture** in Alsace are found in the embellishment of churches: statues, low-relief sculptures and funerary monuments. The most famous sculptor to come from Alsace was **Auguste Bartholdi**, from Colmar, who made the Belfort Lion (a copy can be found in Paris, place Denfert-Rochereau) and what may be the world's best-known statue, the Statue of Liberty which stands in New York Harbour.

Some of the most remarkable **religious sculptures** in the region are found in **Andlau** on the church porch. In the 13C, Gothic artists had a field day on the cathedral of **Strasbourg** (low-relief sculpture of the Death of the Virgin, the Angels' Pillar); the 14C statuary shows a more fluid style (Virtues and Vices, Wise and Foolish Virgins).

The doorway of St-Thiébaut in **Thann** and St Laurent's doorway on Strasbourg Cathedral illustrate the opulent art of the Flamboyant period (15C). **Hans Hammer** sculpted the pulpit in Strasbourg cathedral, which is often referred to as lace tatted from stone. The best examples of **funerary sculpture** are also found in **Strasbourg**, in St-Thomas Church: the tomb of Bishop Adeloch (12C), in the form of a sarcophagus, and the tomb of Marshal Maurice de Saxe.

The proudest piece of **sculpture in wood** is no doubt the Issenheim altar in the Unterlinden Museum in **Colmar**. The paintings are by Grünewald, but some of the glory must go to **Nicolas de Haguenau**, who carved the gilded statues of saints Anthony, Augustine and Jerôme; Sébastien Beychel crafted the lower section which shows Christ in the midst of his Apostles.

Beautiful carved screens and altars are also on view in **Kaysersberg**, **Dambach** and **Soultzbach-les-Bains**. Elsewhere, there is a profusion of pulpits, organ lofts, and choir stalls **(Marmoutier, Thann)**, which demonstrates the skill and artistry of local artisans.

The windows in **Strasbourg** Cathedral date from the 12C, 13C and 14C, and although they have been damaged over time, they are remarkable in number.

LORRAINE

Romanesque decoration of churches was often rather awkward. The doorway of Mont-Devant-Sassey, dedicated to the Virgin, is in fact an inferior reproduction of statuary in Reims. A better example is Notre-Dame in **Verdun** where the Lion's Door is carved with a Christ in Majesty surrounded by symbols of the Apostles; though some find it lacks elegance, it does have its own original beauty.

In the 16C, **Ligier Richier**, working in **St-Mihiel**, brought new life to the art of sculpture, and his influence is felt throughout Lorraine.

Many mausoleums were embellished with **funerary art** between the 16C and the 18C. Perhaps the most remarkable example of Richer's work is in St-Étienne church (p 86) in Bar-le-Duc; known as the Tormented Soul, the skeletal figure with one arm raised high adorns the tomb of René de Chalon. Richier also sculpted the tomb of Philippa de Gueldre in the Église des Cordeliers in **Nancy**; the tomb of René II in the same church is by Mansuy Gauvain. In Notre-Dame-de-Bon-Secours, the tomb of Stanislas and the mausoleum of his wife Catherine Opalinska are the work of Vassé and the Adam brothers, respectively.

St-Étienne Cathedral in **Metz** was built between the 13C and the 16C. The church has been called God's lantern because of the many stained-glass windows. The oldest date from the 13C, and the most recent are contemporary, including some designed by painter Marc Chagall. Other modern stained-glass windows of interest can be found in the church at **St-Dié**. In **Baccarat**, St-Rémy Church has windows made of crystal.

CHAMPAGNE-ARDENNE

Gothic **sculptures** on buildings are made in fine-grained limestone which is easy to carve, and are both ornamental and figurative. The **Ateliers de Reims** workshops were especially productive in the 13C, and the masterpieces produced there are visible on Reims Cathedral. The famous smiling angel is a good illustration of the delicate mastery of sculptors from the Reims School. During the **14C-15C**, while the Hundred Years War raged, artists favoured funerary art such as *gisants* (recumbent figures) and monumental sepulchres showing scenes from the Passion of Christ.

Angel of Reims Cathedral

The first half of the 16C was an exceptionally creative time for sculptors in **Troyes**, as styles segued from Gothic to Renaissance. The treatment of draped fabric and folds in clothing, of embroideries and jewels shows extraordinary attention to detail. Facial expressions suggest a range of emotion, and in particular give an impression of sweetness, sadness or timidity. The great master of this type of sculpture created the statue of St Martha in Ste-Madeleine Church **(Troyes)**, the *Pietà* in **Bayel** and the Entombment in **Chaource**. The Flamboyant altar screen in Ste-Madeleine is from the same period.

The emergence of the Italian style is also evident in St-Urbain, where a statue of the Virgin holding grapes has graceful posture and a gentle expression, marking a departure from Gothic Realism. As of 1540, such manneristic, refined representations had completely invested the Troyes School of Sculpture, and put an end to its distinctive appearance. Churches installed many works by **Dominique Florentin**, an Italian artist who married a native of Troyes and settled there, training students in his workshops.

Some works in **stained glass** have survived the wars, pollution and the 18C practice of replacing coloured windows with milky white ones (to make it easier to read the liturgy).

The **13C** saw the creation of the windows in the chancel of **Troyes** Cathedral as well as those of Notre-Dame in **Reims** (apse and rose on the façade), a few in St-Étienne in **Châlons-en-Champagne** and finally the great windows of **St-Urbain** in **Troyes**, which are most typical of the era. Very colourful, they portray solitary characters (bishops) in the high panels, whereas the lower panels, more easily studied by visitors, illustrate the lives of the saints or episodes from the life of Christ. The compositions are enlivened by complex backgrounds and the expressive attitudes of the figures; some panels tell us something about the daily life of the time.

Window in Ste-Madeleine Church in Troyes –
The Creation (1500)

In the **16C**, painting on glass became popular and many pieces were ordered for donations to churches (the donor's name or likeness often appearing thereon). Cartoons (basic drawing patterns) made it possible to reproduce the same image over and over, which explains the wealth of windows in the small churches of the Aube region. Some of the artists' names are known to us today: Jehan Soudain, Jean Verrat, Lievin Varin. Early in the 16C, colours exploded on the scene, as seen in the spectacular upper windows in **Troyes Cathedral**, which were installed between 1498 and 1501. In these windows the contours of the drawings are clearly defined and the technical prowess is evident in engraving, pearling, brushed *grisaille* which creates a three-dimensional illusion, and inlays of different coloured glass as used in the stars.

The most common themes are the Passion, the Life of the Virgin, the Tree of Jesse, Genesis, and the Sacrifice of Abraham. Divided into panels, the windows should be read upwards from the bottom. The first rows often represent the donors and their patron saints.

As of 1530, polychrome effects were abandoned by the masters in favour of *grisaille* – tones of a single colour – on white glass with golden yellow and blood red highlights. Italian influence is found in the evolution of the drawings. The architectural backgrounds were inspired by the Fontainebleau School.

In the 17C, the tradition of stained-glass craft continued in Troyes with **Linard Gontier**, who brought back polychrome windows with a new technique of enamelling on white glass, which produced bright hues. He is considered the master of monumental compositions, with works such as the Mystical Press, in Troyes Cathedral. He was also an exceptional miniaturist and portraitist, working in *grisaille*.

Decorative arts and painting

Merovingian treasures

The Merovingian period refers to the first dynasty of Frankish kings founded by Clovis and reigning in France and Germany from about 500 to 751. Recently, art historians have become more interested in works from this often neglected time. In the Champagne-Ardenne region, a trove of funerary objects has been uncovered in the many necropolises that once served local communities. In the archaeological museum in **Troyes**, the tomb of Pouan, a prince, reveals much to us about the artistic temper of the times.

Gold and silver work was highly prized. The decorative items on view in the museums include **fibulae** (clasps resembling safety pins), belt buckles, parts of shields, sword handles, among other things. The eastern influence is obvious in the designs, in particular the fantastic animal turning its head to look back. Styles and techniques were also adapted by Germanic invaders. The rarity of precious metals led to a preference for gold and silver beaten into fine sheets or pulled into threads; other metals were also substituted for a precious effect, including copper, tin and bronze.

Arms made during the Merovingian period are another illustration of the prowess of metalwork masters. Various metals, always high quality, were juxtaposed in the forging process. They were welded together and hammered. The layered structure thus created was both resistant and elastic. The most common arms being long double-edged swords, axes and the *scramasax*, a sort of sabre with one cutting edge. In addition to metalwork, a speciality of Germanic regions, some sculptural works have also survived. In Isle-Aumont, a set of sarcophagi show the evolution of style between the 5C and the 8C.

ALSACE

In the 15C, great **painting** began to appear in Alsace, with the arrival in Colmar of **Gaspard Idenmann**, creator of a Passion inspired by the Flemish style, now on view in the Unterlinden Museum. Another Colmar resident, **Martin Schongauer**, painted the magnificent Virgin in the Rose Bower *(in the Église des Dominicains, see p 121)*. Students under his direction painted a series of Passion works (also in the Unterlin-den), and created other remarkable works, such as the Buhl altar screen. The great German artist **Mathias Grünewald** painted the high altar of the Antonite Church in Issenheim. This screen *(see photograph p 118)* sets a Crucifixion of fearful realism against exquisite figures of the Annunciation and a Heavenly Choir. Some excellent portraitists (Jean-Jacques Henner) were Alsatian, as were a number of draftsmen, engravers and lithographers, including **Gustave Doré**, who was from Strasbourg.

In the realm of **decorative arts**, Alsatian craftsmen excelled in woodwork, ironwork, tinsmithing and working precious metals. They have a reputation as skilled watch and clock makers, as the astronomical clock in Strasbourg Cathedral proves. Ceramics made the **Hannong** family, creators of the "old Strasbourg" style, eminent for generations; their

Traditional pottery, Soufflenheim

R.Mattes/MICHELIN

production is on view in the Strasbourg Museum. In the second half of the 19C, Théodore Deck of Guebwiller brought new ideas to ceramic arts and refined techniques.

LORRAINE

The region, with its wealth and as a cosmopolitan crossroads, produced many painters, miniaturists and engravers over the centuries. Some achieved fame beyond the local area. Arts in the 17C were imprinted with the influence of **Georges Lallemand**, a native of Nancy who established himself in Paris in 1601; **Jacques Bellange**, master of Mannerism; **Claude Deruet**, official court painter par excellence; **Georges de la Tour**, known for his remarkable candlelit and torchlight effects incorporating deep black nights; **Claude Gellée**, a landscape painter; **Jacques Callot**, a great draftsman and engraver (most of his works are together in the museum of the history of Lorraine in Nancy).

In the 19C, **Isabey** was the leading painter of miniature portraits, and one of the favourite painters of Imperial society, alongside **François Dumont**, from Lunéville.

Mention must be made of **Épinal**. In the 18C and 19C, this town specialised in the production of pretty coloured prints, which were sold around France by street vendors. The pictures became so well known that it is common nowadays to use the expression *image d'Épinal* to refer to any simplistic or naive representation of life.

Ceramic production in Lorraine was mostly centred around **Lunéville** and **Sarreguemines**; enamellers settled around **Longwy**.

Crystal — Lorraine has several famous crystal manufacturers, including those in **Baccarat**, **Daum** and **Saint Louis**. This activity was able to develop, especially in the 16C, thanks to the abundance of wood (to stoke the fires), water and sand in the region. Today, in addition to traditional glassware, as appreciated by the royal and imperial courts of Persia, Russia, Germany and Italy, these venerable companies produce objects designed in contemporary styles by Salvador Dali and Philippe Starck, among others.

Art Nouveau and the 20C

At the end of the 19C, a movement to rehabilitate decorative arts and architecture, known as **Art Nouveau**, came to the fore. It is easily recognisable by its use of long, sinuous lines, often expressed in the shapes of vines and tendrils, flower stalks, butterfly wings and other curvaceous natural forms. Some of the artists who made the style famous were Mucha (Czechoslovakian designer immortalised in poster format), Hector Guimard (designed the Art Nouveau entrances to Paris Metro stations), American glassmaker Louis Tiffany (stained-glass lamps), and Spanish architect Antonio Gaudi (works in and around Barcelona), who took the style to the outer limits.

In France, the first works to appear were in Nancy, made by **Émile Gallé**; he produced glassware inspired by the patterns and forms of nature. His work was hailed at the Universal Exhibitions of 1884, 1889 and 1900 in Paris. Soon a group of artists working in various media (glass, wood, ceramic, engraving and sculpture) had gathered around him. Among them were **Daum, Majorelle, Vallin, Prouvé**, and together they formed the **École de Nancy**.

Between 1900 and 1910, the influence of the Nancy School became apparent in local architecture (about 10 years behind decorative arts). Nancy is now, with Brussels, Vienna and Paris, one of the great centres of Art Nouveau architecture in Europe.

The second half of the 20C saw some **architectural achievements** in the larger towns: the Tour de l'Europe in Mulhouse (1966); the Tour Altea in Nancy (1974); the Palais de l'Europe (1977) and the Palais des Droits de l'Homme (1995) in Strasbourg.

Palais des Droits de l'Homme, Strasbourg

The most famous artist of the 20C to come from the region was **Jean (or Hans) Arp** (1887-1966). He was born in Strasbourg when it was spelled Strassburg and part of Germany, and trained there as well as in Weimar and Paris. A leader of the avant-garde, he produced sculptures, paintings and poetry. In Paris, he was acquainted with Modigliani, Picasso and Robert Delaunay as well as writer Max Jacob. He sought refuge in Zurich, Switzerland during the First World War, and while there became one of the founders of the Dada movement along with Tristan Tzara. After 1922, he took the same path to Surrealism as other Dadaists. Their early attitudes of Nihilism and attacks on social and artistic conventions as well as their fascination with the bizarre, the irrational and the fantastic made an indelible mark on the century, and stand at the root of Abstract Expressionism and Conceptual art.

Arp fled to Zurich during the Second World War; his wife, artist Sophie Taeuber died there. After the war he returned to their home in Meudon, just outside Paris. A fine collection of Arp's works and other modern and contemporary art works are assembled in the Musée d'Art Moderne et Contemporain in Strasbourg *(see p 334)*.

Prouvé-Martin:
La Parure leather box

Gallé:
Ceramic dog in costume

Vallin: Masson dining room

Gallé:
Fourcaud
glass vase

École de Nancy

Daum:
"Figuier de
Barbarie"
(prickly pear)
glass lamp

Gruber: water lilies and colocynth, stained glass

Traditions and folklore

ALSACE

Both the mountains and the plain are rich in local colour, and legends abound in Alsace. Of course, visitors today are not likely to see women wearing distinctive, bow-shaped black headdresses, unless there is a local heritage fête in progress. But the preservation of so much architectural patrimony – a miracle considering the strife and wars that long plagued the region – provides a setting which vividly evokes the past.

"How beautiful is our Alsace"

R.Mattes/MICHELIN

Some local traditions do persist, in particular those associated with saints' feast days. Each village celebrates the feast day of its patron saint, **la fête patronale**, also known as *messti* (Bas-Rhin), and *kilwe* or *kilbe* (Haut-Rhin) in local dialect. Folk dancing and traditional costumes enliven the festivities. Ribeauvillé has held its especially popular fair in early September for centuries. Many seasonal traditions would seem very familiar to a visitor from the United Kingdom or North America: brightly lit and sparkling trees, red and green ribbons, gingerbread men, and markets full of "stockingstuffers" in December; carnival celebrated with doughnuts; Easter which brings a rabbit who hides coloured eggs in the garden.

Legends often surround lakes, rivers, and the romantic ruins of castles. There are religious legends as well, often remembered in traditional ceremonies like the one held in Thann every 30 June, when three pines are set afire. While the realm of legend sometimes reflects aspects of reality and history, the advantage here is that good always conquers and evil is inevitably punished. The characters in these legends are knights and ladies, monks and beggars, saints and demons, gnomes and giants.

The most famous legend in Alsace may be the story of **Mont Ste-Odile**. The patron saint of Alsace (Odilia, Ottilia and other variations are found) was the daughter of Duke Adalric; she founded a nunnery on a mountain around the year 700 and was its first abbess. From these historical facts, a legend has grown, which recounts the birth of a blind Odile, rejected by her father, and spirited away to safety by her mother. By this account, Odile, now a beautiful young woman, was baptised by St Erhard, her uncle,

---

The Legend of the Lac du Ballon

Long ago, a green meadow lay like an emerald in the blue velvet folds of the Vosges Forest, below the majestic Grand Ballon. The field belonged to a man who earned his living making charcoal, a *charbonnier*. A covetous bourgeois from the Guebwiller Valley tried to buy the field, and when the collier refused, he bribed a local judge into forcing the forfeit of the land.

The proud new owner arrived with a fancy golden wagon to cut the fragrant hay, and he passed by the collier's simple dwelling with a smug, victorious grin. The wronged man shook his fist, and called on Providence to render the justice which the courts of law had denied him.

Suddenly, a menacing gloom came upon the sky and a violent storm erupted in the high mountains, followed by a downpour so heavy it cut off all sight like a thick dark curtain. When the light returned, a round lake appeared in the place of the field, its deep waters covering the bourgeois, his wagon and horses.

As you gaze on the lake, remember the French proverb: *Charbonnier est maître chez soi* (even a charcoal-burner is master in his own house). Every man's home is his castle.

and miraculously recovered her sight. Her father decided to marry her off, despite the girl's religious vocation, and he pursued her through the forest as she ran from the fate he had devised for her. Suddenly, a rock opened up and enfolded her, protecting Odile from the duke. From that rock, a sacred spring came forth. Adalric got the message and built her a convent instead.

Many pilgrims came to visit the holy woman. It is said that, upon encountering a sick man dying of thirst, Odile struck the ground with her cane and brought forth a spring. He drank and was cured; many people came to pray at the site and wash their eyes with the curative water. Her intercession is still sought after by those with diseases of the eye.

LORRAINE

The traditional emblem of Lorraine is the **Croix de Lorraine**, a cross with two horizontal arms, the shorter one above the longer. It appeared on coins minted by the dukes of Lorraine, was made famous by General de Gaulle who took it for his personal standard, and is found on everything from biscuit tins to postage stamps. Its origins can be traced to the kingdom of Hungary, which used such a cross as its coat of arms. When the Árpád dynasty expired, a series of Angevin kings came to power, beginning with Robert of Anjou (1308-42). Ultimately, René II inherited the title from the dukes of Anjou and brought the emblem to his duchy of Lorraine. In 1477, the cross blazed on banners rallying the people to the Battle of Nancy, and from that time on it has been known as the Lorraine Cross. In an amusing reminder of days long past, when the Metz football club faced Slovakian adversaries, both teams' uniforms bore the emblem!

St Nicholas has also held a special place in the hearts of the people of Lorraine since the days of the Holy Roman Empire. With his bishop's mitre and backpack full of toys, he travels Lorraine on the night of 5-6 December. The patron saint of the region is celebrated in all the towns and villages with festive lights and parades. The beautiful Flamboyant church of St-Nicolas-de-Port was the site of many pilgrimages; the town was once one of the liveliest in Lorraine.

The countryside around Remiremont is reported to be populated by a variety of **fairies**. Some of the local place names give a good indication of this (the French word for fairy is *fée*): Château-des-Fées on the Fays plateau; Pont-des-Fées (Fairies' Bridge) – there is one in Saint-Étienne-lès-Remiremont and another across the Vologne (a tributary of the Moselle which comes down the mountains from Retournemer Lake); Grottes-des-Fées (Fairies' Cave); numerous other names of caves, streams and rocks refer to legends of the diminutive beings with magic powers.

There are fairy bakers and pastry chefs, who make delicious treats in their lairs and send the sweet aroma out to lonely shepherds or field workers. Some have even reported finding lovely cakes laid out on a white cloth, which they enjoyed without any ill effects. Other fairies have a mean streak, such as the laundress fairy, **Fée Herqueuche**, a scaggle-tooth hag, with her bald head under a straw hat and rags on her skinny body. She washes witches' clothes at night, and tramples the clean work of honest washerwomen with her dirty feet.

CHAMPAGNE-ARDENNE

In this region, as elsewhere in France, recent years have seen a renewed interest in ancestral traditions, including religious and pagan festivities and activities related to daily life in the countryside (harvest, crafts, family celebrations etc).

Carnival costume parades are coming back in style in many towns and villages where the custom had nearly died out. Around the textile centre of Sedan, costumes were commonly made from canvas sacks used to hold spools of yarn; five or six people would climb into one and march along broadside. Near Mézières, carnival-goers stick their heads through the rungs of a horizontal ladder draped with white cloth and pop out one or several burlesque faces at a time. Popular games are blindfold races, horseshoe throwing, wheelbarrow races, with the loser buying a round at the nearest café.

At nightfall, the crowd gathers round for the bonfire. A procession through the streets bears a sort of scarecrow who, from village to village, may be named Nicolas, Christophe, Joseph or Pansard, and may be dressed as a ragged beggar or a bridegroom. As the carnival figure burns and sparks fly up, dancing and singing mark the end of the festive day. In some places, the ashes from the fire are believed to have special powers, or bring good luck, especially to young couples.

Although Mardi Gras is associated with the Christian rite, the carnival has well-documented pagan origins and is clearly associated with chasing out winter and preparing for spring.

A funny tradition still observed in villages is the May Day *charivari*. Young rascals band together on the eve of 1 May and spend the dark night going from house to house, where they quietly make off with anything that isn't nailed down or locked up: ladders, barrows, benches, rakes... The whole lot is then piled up on the main square, where everyone gathers the next morning, to laugh or complain according to temper, and to recover the goods.

Life in the countryside

Villages – Most of the people living outside main urban centres live fairly close to their neighbours in villages. This has been the custom since the first settlers arrived. Rather than a response to a perceived need for protection, this pattern is more likely a result of communal farming and forestry techniques.

In **Alsace**, the houses in a village are generally detached from one another, and may even be facing in different directions. Some villages are little more than a group of farmhouses around a belfry. Traces of a more glorious past may remain: a ruined castle rising above the roof line, a lovely church in an otherwise unremarkable place. In any case, one of the most conspicuous features of the Alsatian village is the care the inhabitants take to keep their doorways swept, windows sparkling, and geraniums in bloom.

In **Lorraine**, the houses in the village are generally attached, and stand along both sides of the street in an orderly row. Often, there is an entranceway wide enough to accommodate a tractor or wagon, and a smaller doorway into the building itself. The large entrance opens onto the farmyard, and often the farm extends far back beyond the main house, with the usual collection of buildings and equipment scattered about. Nowadays, most inhabitants reserve the small front yard for a flower garden.

On the dry plain of **Champagne**, sizeable villages grew up around fresh water springs, often quite far from one another. While the streets are narrow and confined, through an open gate you may glimpse a spacious courtyard with neatly kept buildings holding presses and other equipment needed to maintain and harvest grapes. In the southern part of the region, around Bar-sur-Aube, Bar-sur-Seine, Langres and the Blaise Valley, villages can be seen from afar as the buildings are predominately made of bright white limestone. In the Argonne Forest, the linear look of houses lined up along the road is reminiscent of neighbouring Lorraine.

Houses and farms – While houses and farms in rural **Alsace** have many things in common, there are also many subtle differences from one area to another. Gables, the colour, shape and disposition of timbers, the materials, patterns and embellishments used to fill in the frame vary from north to south. In the **vineyard** region, the ground floor, in stone, is used for pressing grapes and storing wine. An outside stair leads to the living areas above. The Écomusée *(see p* 131*)* is a good place to see various building techniques.

In a typical **Lorraine** village, the older buildings have gently sloping roofs covered with a kind of hollow tile. The traditional farmhouse held the living area, barn and stables under one roof. The limestone walls are coated to preserve the mortar joints.

Exhibit in the town museum in Châlons-en-Champagne

M.Roche/Musée de Châlons-en-Champagne

The **Champagne** region is home to many wine-growers. Their houses are typically low, made of millstone, local chalk-stone or brick. In "**dry**" **Champagne**, the farmyards are generally bordered by the living area (facing the street), the barn (facing the fields) and other buildings for animals. In the south-east, half-timbering appears, filled in with blocks of chalk-stone or tuffy-stone covered with plaster. In the greener or "**wet**" **Champagne**, timbers are cut from pine and poplar, held with cross beams and daub, or earthen bricks. Around **Troyes**, brick is commonly used in decorative patterns between the timbers. A traditional dwelling in the **Argonne** Forest has a dark brick façade on the ground floor and a roughcast plaster storey above. The flat tiles of the roof extend out over the sides of the house.

The region of **Ardenne** is rich in schist and quartzite stone, often used for building; the blue slate quarried here is of excellent quality. These materials make the houses rather gloomy looking. To defeat the rigours of winter, all of the farm buildings are close together, making for a single, long building, in contrast to the rectangular courtyard with outbuildings seen in more clement neighbouring areas.

Language and literature

ALSATIAN DIALECT

"His tongue is German, but his sword is French." Thus did Napoleon Bonaparte describe General Jean-François Kléber, a native of Strasbourg who held a prominent position in Bonaparte's Egyptian campaign. In fact, Alsatians do not speak German, but rather an Alemannic dialect which evolved from High German, as did the modern German language spoken in Germany, Austria and parts of Switzerland today. Of course, the influence of the French language has been felt over time, distancing the dialect even further from its origins.

Over time, as the region was controlled by French or German authority, one or the other language was imposed as the official language used in schools and by the administration. As in other corners of the world, distinct regional dialects were not recognised until recently, and years of neglect (and outright repression) have taken their toll. Interest in local history in all of France's regions was renewed as the events of 1968 shook up conventional cultural values. Since that time, the Alsatian dialect has received official recognition and is no longer forbidden in the schoolyard; volumes of poetry and books of popular songs and tales are displayed in bookstores.

ALSATIAN DIALECT

0   30 km
--- Borders of the administrative department
Linguistic border
Border between Alsace and Lorraine

MOSELLE
Haguenau
Sarrebourg
STRASBOURG
BAS-RHIN
Schirmeck
St-Dié-des-Vosges
Sélestat
DEUTSCHLAND
VOSGES
Col de la Schlucht
Colmar
Gérardmer
Munster
Freiburg-im-B.
Col de Bussang
HAUT-RHIN
Thann
TERRITOIRE
Mulhouse
Belfort
DE
BELFORT
BASEL
SCHWEIZ

LITERATURE IN ALSACE-LORRAINE

In this border region, literary tradition has three expressions: French, German and dialect. German works represent the oldest, most prestigious tradition. The **Renaissance**, **Humanism** and the **Reform** marked the golden age of Alsatian literature. Gutenberg worked on developing his printing press in Strasbourg before getting it up and running in Mainz. The wonderful collection of the Humanist library in Sélestat is testimony to the regional attachment to the written word. The German author Goethe lived in Strasbourg in 1770-71, a memorable time because it marked the beginning of the so-called *Sturm und Drang* (storm and stress) movement. This style of literature exalted nature, feelings and human individualism, and was strongly influenced by the ideas of French author Jean-Jacques Rousseau, and by the works of Shakespeare, which had just been translated.

The **20C** was marked by the upheavals of war. German literature was still most prevalent, but by the end of the First World War, numerous works had been published in dialect, certainly in response to the need to express cultural identity in a region caught in the middle of a terrible power struggle. Between the wars, the French language got a foothold and today it is the language most commonly heard and used.

CHAMPAGNE: CRADLE OF FRENCH LITERATURE

In the **12C**, Champagne was home to many authors writing in the emerging French language. Bertrand de Bar-sur-Aube is reputed to have composed *Aimeri de Narbonne*, the best-known chapter of the ballad of William of Orange (later to inspire Victor Hugo). Chrétien de Troyes (c 1135-c 1183) wrote tales of chivalry based on the legends of Brittany, including the characters Lancelot and Perceval. The search for the Holy Grail and the Crusades inspired Geoffroi de Villehardouin (1150-1213), who wrote about his adventures in *History of the Conquest of Constantinople*. Another medieval bard, Jean, Sire de Joinville, described travelling to Egypt with St Louis (1309). The Count of Champagne, Thibaud IV, crowned king of Navarre in 1234, preferred to pen poetry, whereas his countryman Rutebeuf entertained with biting satires of the church, the university and tradesmen.

In the **17C**, **Paul de Gondi, Cardinal de Retz** (1613-79), took time out from politics (as a leader of the rebellion known as the *Fronde*) to note down his favourite maxims. After his retirement, he wrote his *Mémoires*, considered a classic of 17C French literature.

Another major figure from the century was **Jean de la Fontaine**, celebrated for his *Fables*. Born into a bourgeois family in Château-Thierry, he married a local heiress in 1647, but separated from her 11 years later. An outstanding feature of his character was his life-long ability to attract wealthy patrons, thus freeing himself from the pedestrian worries of earning a living so he could devote his time to writing 12 books of fables and other works. The first collection of six books is based on the Aesopic tradition, whereas the second takes its inspiration from East Asian stories. His use of animal characters is a light-hearted ploy for expressing the everyday moral experience of humankind; his poetic technique has been called the exquisite quintessence of the preceding century of French literature. La Fontaine's *Fables* continue to form part of the culture of every French schoolchild, and his reputation has lost none of its glow.

The **18C** brought bold thinkers to the fore. In 1713, the philosopher **Denis Diderot** was born in Langres. His early life was a time of financial and religious crisis. He studied law, aspired to be an actor, wrote sermons for missionaries for a miserable wage and considered an ecclesiastical career. Over time, he progressed from his Roman Catholic faith to deism and finally atheism and philosophical materialism. In 1745 he was engaged to translate the *Cylopaedia*, authored by Ephraim Chambers, but he soon made radical changes in the work. Working with a team of authors including scholars, scientists and priests, he created the *Encyclopédie*, a rational dictionary which covered the basic premises and contemporary applications of all arts and sciences. His unconventional views landed him in prison, but neither incarceration nor censorship prevented him from carrying on with the work, although the later volumes were published in secret. When the *Encyclopédie* was completed in 1772, Diderot was left without an income. The patronage of Catherine the Great of Russia provided for him in his old age. As his friends and contemporaries left this life, he retired into his family circle. His last words were: "The first step towards philosophy is incredulity".

Diderot was well-acquainted with another 18C luminary, **Voltaire** (pseudonym of François-Marie Arouet). Although his classical tragedies for the stage were popularly acclaimed, when Voltaire turned his talents to satire (of the Regency and established religion), he met the same fate as Diderot, imprisonment. After his release, a quarrel with a nobleman resulted in a two-year exile to England, where he mastered the language and enjoyed the company of Alexander Pope, Jonathan Swift, William Congreve and even Queen Caroline. Upon his return to France, Voltaire found refuge in Champagne in the château of Mme du Châtelet in Cirey-sur-Blaise. They lived a life both studious and passionate, translating Newton, conducting experiments in their laboratory, travelling and frequenting high society. She died in childbirth in 1749, ending their complex relationship of 15 years, and leaving her lover bereft.

Voltaire's most famous work is probably *Candide* (1758), a satirical masterpiece on philosophical optimism. His long life spanned the waning of classicism and the dawn of revolution; his ideas and actions had a significant influence on the evolution of European civilization. In particular, his letters stand as a testimony to his defence of clear thinking in a world where complications seek to defeat us at every turn.

The **19C** and **20C** produced two figures whose memory has been perpetuated by modern-day songwriters and film directors: **Paul Verlaine** and **Arthur Rimbaud**.

Musée A. Rimaud

Rimbaud

Fables of La Fontaine

The Cicada and the Ant

The Cobbler and the Financier

The Two Friends

The Heron

*The Frog Who Would be
as Big as an Ox*

*The Bear
and the Lover of Gardening*

Imagerie de Paris, début 19ᵉ s.

Collection Musée Jean de la Fontaine, Château-Thierry

Verlaine was born in Metz in 1844, Rimbaud 10 years later in Charleville. The older poet was from a comfortable background, the well-educated son of an army officer; the younger was raised in poverty by his mother and yet distinguished himself as a gifted student. After graduating with honours from the Lycée Bonaparte, Verlaine became a clerk in an insurance company, then a civil servant. His early work was published in respectable literary reviews; he married and had a son. During the Franco-Prussian War, he was the press officer for the Paris insurgents of the *Commune*. Meanwhile, Rimbaud, a restless and despondent soul, lived on the streets of the capital in squalor, reading everything he could get his hands on – including the poetry of Baudelaire (considered immoral by the cultural establishment at the time) and works on the occult – and shaping his own poetic philosophy.

In 1871 the two met, moved to London and carried on a scandalous affair. While Verlaine vacillated between decadent thrills and anguished repentance, Rimbaud was seen as his friend's evil helmsman on their *Drunken Boat*. In 1873, a violent quarrel in Brussels ended with Rimbaud shot in the wrist and Verlaine in prison for 18 months. Rimbaud, both distraught and exhilarated, feverishly completed *A Season in Hell: ... As for me, I am intact, and I don't care.*

By his 20th birthday, Rimbaud had given up writing and turned to gunrunning in Africa. In 1891, his right leg was amputated, and he died the same year. He has been cited as an inspiration by many, in particular the Beat poets, Jim Morrison, Bob Dylan and Patti Smith.

Verlaine, released from prison, became a devout Catholic and moved to England where he taught French. In 1877, he returned to France and began writing the series of poems to be published as *Sagesse* (*Wisdom* – or perhaps, simply "wising up"). Further heartbreak (the deaths of a favourite student and the poet's mother) and a failure to reconcile with his wife drove Verlaine back to drink, but sympathetic friends encouraged him to continue writing and publishing, and supported him financially. His significant body of work marks a transition between the Romantic poets and the Symbolists.

THE LAST WORD...

Can you identify the quotes below? Half are from the pen of Voltaire, and the other are morals from the Fables of La Fontaine.

In this best of all possible worlds ... all is for the best.

Better to suffer than to die: that is mankind's motto.

The secret of being a bore is to tell everything.

People who make no noise are dangerous.

Love truth, but pardon error.

It is a double pleasure to deceive the deceiver.

History is no more than a portrayal of crimes and misfortunes.

We heed no instincts but our own.

Thought depends on the stomach, but in spite of that, those who have the best stomachs are not the best thinkers.

A hungry stomach cannot hear.

I disapprove of what you say, but I will defend to the death your right to say it.

The opinion of the strongest is always the best.

Answer: The first is Voltaire, the second La Fontaine, the next one is Voltaire, and so on, in alternation.

Regional cuisine

ALSACE–LORRAINE

Charcuteries – Ham and Strasbourg sausages are featured in the classic *assiette alsacienne*, an array of pork meats; but *foies gras* (fattened livers) hold pride of place. This delicacy has been appreciated since the Roman era; in 1778 a young local chef, Jean-Pierre Clause, created the prototype goose liver *pâté en croûte* (wrapped in a crust). Today there are over 40 variations on his theme on sale in local delicatessens. In Lorraine, traditional dishes are loaded with butter, bacon and cream. **Potée** is a pot roast made with salt pork and sausages, white cabbage and other vegetables. Of course, **Quiche Lorraine** is famous fare: a creamy pie made with beaten eggs, thick cream and bacon bits. Pâté from Lorraine is made from veal and pork.

Choucroute – Strasbourg is the capital of this cabbage-based speciality made with white Alsatian wine. The savoury white cabbage is heaped with sausages, pork chops, bacon, ham, and occasionally a bit of partridge, a few crayfish or a truffle find their way in. It is best enjoyed with a big glass of beer or a good regional wine.

Choucroute

Fish and fowl – Chicken dishes are popular in Alsace, and menus often list *coq* and *poularde* (pullet hen), served with mushroom and cream sauce; local *coq au vin* is made with Riesling wine. Fresh trout from mountain streams is a delicious treat, in cream or Riesling sauce. Other local fish recipes are eels stewed in wine sauce *(matelote)*, fried carp, pike and salmon.

Les marcaireries – Dairy farmers and cheesemakers in the Vosges are known as *marcaires*. Traditionally, they take their herds up to the high pasturelands *(chaumes)* on 25 May (the old feast day of St Urbain), and bring them down again on 29 September. Nowadays, farms which serve country fare to travellers may be called by the more usual French name of *ferme-auberge*, but the local traditions remain the same.

Munster and Géromé – The perfect way to polish off an Alsatian meal is with one of these two cheeses which are only made in the Vosges. Munster is an unpasteurised, soft fermented cheese, which many enjoy with a dash of cumin. It was first made in these mountains in the 15C, and is a significant source of income for mountain-dwellers.
On the Lorraine side, Géromé – a word in dialect which means "from Gérardmer" – also has a long-standing reputation. It is made with unheated whole milk to which rennet (for solidifying) is added immediately. The cheese is aged for four months in a cool cellar until the crust turns russet and the interior is creamy. Cumin, aniseed or fennel seeds may be served with a portion.

Pastries – There are as many different tarts in Alsace as there are fruits to make them with. Any chef is proud to pull a perfect **Kugelhopf** out of the oven, a delightful puff of flour, butter, eggs, sweetened milk, raisins and almonds. Other special desserts are *macarons de Boulay* (dainty biscuits of egg whites and almonds), *madeleines de Commercy* (soft, buttery cakes), *bergamotes de Nancy* (hard sweets flavoured with citrus fruit).
Waffles *(gaufres)* were traditionally made at carnival time in irons forged with unique designs, both religious and profane. Hot waffles sprinkled with sugar or dripping with chocolate are still a popular treat, but the old-fashioned irons are now rare collector's items. **Meringues** were first served in France at the table of Duke Stanislas, in Nancy.

Beer – Breweries abound in Alsace (Schiltigheim, Strasbourg, Hochfelden, Obernai, Saverne) – *(for information on tours see Practical information, p 430)*; Stenay is home to the Beer Museum; the Brewery Museum is in St-Nicolas-de-Port. Beer has always been made from the same elements: pure water, barley, hops and yeast. Barley transforms into malt, giving colour and flavour; hops provide the bitterness. Each brewery cultivates its own yeast, which gives each brand its distinctive taste.

Beer has been enjoyed since Antiquity: Egyptians called it liquid bread; Hippocrates defended its use as a therapeutic medicine. Today, beer production starts with the reduction of malt to flour, the addition of water, and heating at a low temperature. While the mixture is stirred, the starch contained in the grain turns to sugar. In another tank, non-malted grain such as corn is prepared in the same way. The two tanks are mixed into a **mash**, which is filtered to become the **stock** or **wort**. The hops are added to the **wort kettle** where the mixture is heated, then filtered again. Fermentation takes place at temperatures between 5-10°C/40-50°F. Pasteurisation makes the final product more stable, and industrial chilling enables year-round production. Beer leaves the brew house and has yeast added to it, which turns the sugar into alcohol over two weeks, in large tanks kept at low temperatures. The yeast is removed after maturation: a final filtration and it's ready for the bottle.

CHAMPAGNE–ARDENNE

Champagne – Savoury sauces, rich meats and fresh produce are the ingredients of fine cuisine in the region. Sauces made with Champagne garnish many recipes for chicken, pullet, thrush, kidneys, stuffed trout, grilled pike, crayfish and snails. Smoked ham and sausage are used in **potée champenoise**, a popular dish at grape harvest time, served with mounds of fresh cabbage, a vegetable which is at its prime in the fall. Brenne-le-Château has its own recipe for *choucroute*, Troyes is celebrated for its *andouillettes* sausage and Ste-Menehould is famous for dishing out pigs feet and mashed potatoes.

In the *pays d'Othe* region, sometimes called little Normandy, apple orchards, though less numerous today than in the past, still produce fruit for making sparkling cider, however it is now more of a hobby than an industry.

Ardenne – The isolation of this region has contributed to the conservation of local traditions. The cuisine is hearty and fortifying, based on natural products found in the wooded hills. Game and fish are prominent on the menu: young boar, venison, rabbit with *sauce chasseur*; woodcock and thrush roasted in sage leaves or served *en terrine* with juniper berries; rich pâtés of marinated veal and pork meats.

Smoked ham cured over juniper or broomwood and *boudin* sausages are on display in local *charcuteries*.

Salads made with fresh wild greens are flavoured with *crétons* or *fritons*, local terms for crunchy bacon bits. A menu offering plain country fare may feature *baïenne*, a satisfying dish of potatoes, onions and garlic.

Cheese from Champagne

Cheese – South of Troyes, the region has specialised in the production of creamy cheeses such as Chaource, which are only slightly aged. This cheese has been served at the best tables since the 12C. It can be enjoyed within five days after it is set out *(frais)* or may be left to firm up for about 20 days *(fait)*. Firmer cheese may be covered with a thin film of white mould. Some other regional cheeses are varieties of **Cendré**, with a powdery dusting of grey ash (Châlons-en-Champagne, Les Riceys and the Marne Valley). **Maroilles** is a fragrant cheese from Thiérache which is usually enjoyed at harvest time. **Mostafait** is a white cream cheese blended with butter and tarragon. **Rocroi** is from the town of the same name; **Igny** shares its name with the Trappist monastery that produces it; **Troyen** is a regional cheese that resembles Camembert.

Pastries – At carnival time, doughnuts are a festive treat, variously known as *frivoles* or *fiverolles* or *crottes d'âne* (donkey turds!). At Easter, little tarts *(dariolles)* are filled with a flan mixture made from milk and eggs. Gingerbread is still made with a reliable recipe from the 13C.

In Reims, many varieties of delicate biscuits are served with Champagne: *massepains, croquignols, bouchons*.

In the Ardennes region, crêpes are called *vautes* or *tantimolles*; hard sugar biscuits are served with coffee; soft cakes served at wedding banquets were sometimes baked with a silver ring inside, for luck. Blueberry pie is delicious in the summer, and at Christmas time there are many sorts of seasonal sweets, including little red candy animals.

Wine and Champagne

VINS D'ALSACE

The vineyards of Alsace stretch from Thann to Wissembourg, over about 100km/60mi, but the main area to explore starts just south of Marlenheim, where travellers join the famous **Route des Vins** *(see the chapter in Sights for touring advice)*. The route meanders through a sea of grape vines and many wine-growing villages; all is devoted to the production of wine. The most exciting time to visit is certainly the autumn, when the harvest is in full swing and the leaves are vivid red. The eastern foothills of the Vosges are well exposed, and the climate is sunny and mild.

Varieties – The wines of Alsace are identified, not by geographical area, but by grape variety. **Riesling** is a bright star in the constellation of white grape varieties. Most of the wine produced in the valley of the River Rhine is made from these grapes, which create a sophisticated, subtle bouquet.
Gewürztraminer is a heady, fragrant wine with an intense bouquet.
The wine to choose if you wish to quench a thirst is **Sylvaner**, dry and light, with a fruity note.
Pinot blanc wines are generally considered well-balanced, with a fresh and supple character.
Pinot gris, called **Tokay Pinot gris**, is a distinguished grape which produces opulent, full-bodied wine.
The flavour of fresh grapes has a strong presence in **Muscat d'Alsace**.
The only red variety is **Pinot noir**. These grapes have grown in popularity in recent years, and go into fruity rosé or red wines marked by a cherry aroma and taste. The red wines are firmer and more complex than the rosés.
Edelzwicker is the name given to the only wine made from a blend of varieties, including the less noble Chasselas.
Vin d'Alsace is an *Appellation d'Origine Contrôlée*, and is always bottled in the region of production. It is generally served in a round glass with a thin green stem. Most Alsace wines are best when fairly young (one to five years after harvest), and should be chilled. Before a meal, a sparkling Crémant or sweet Muscat is a good apéritif; Sylvaner goes well with assorted cold cuts served as a starter. Riesling or Pinot accompany fish, fowl, meats and, of course, *choucroute*. Flavourful cheeses and desserts do well with the rich aroma of Gewürztraminer.

Eaux-de-vie – Cherries, mirabelles and raspberries are used to make sweet liqueurs: kirsche in the Vosges, quetsch and mirabelle in Lorraine. Clear raspberry liqueur is served in a snifter to increase the pleasure of the aroma. The **musée des Eaux-de-vie** in Lapoutroie shows how such liqueurs were traditionally made.

CHAMPAGNE

A long and prestigious past – When Roman soldiers arrived in the Champagne region, grapes were already cultivated on the slopes. The first bishops of Reims encouraged this activity; vineyards flourished around monasteries and the many travellers attending trade fares or coming to the royal court boosted sales. Even the popes favoured Champagne, starting with Urbain II, a native of the region. During the Renaissance, Pope Leo X had his own vineyard to keep him supplied. St Bernard, in Clairvaux, introduced the *arbanne* stock, which created the basis for Côte des Bars vintages.
Champagne has been called the "nectar of the gods" and the "wine of kings". Henri IV, impatient with the Spanish ambassador's recitation of his master's aristocratic titles, interrupted him by saying, "Tell His Majesty the King of Spain, Castille and Aragon that Henri, lord of Ay and Gonesse, is master of the greatest vineyards in the world...".
At that time, Champagne was a still wine with only a hint of sparkle. That sparkle caught the eye of **Dom Pérignon**, who carefully studied the wine's characteristics and developed blending. The popularity of Champagne grew throughout the centuries, admired and imbibed by kings and their courts and figures of romance such as Mme de Pompadour and Casanova.
Political revolutions came and went, but Champagne remained. Napoleon was a faithful client, and Talleyrand plied the participants at the Congress of Vienna with Champagne in hopes of gaining a better settlement. The Prince of Wales, the future Edward VII, speaking of the Most Honourable Order of the Bath, is reputed to have said, "I'd rather have a bath of Champagne".

The vineyards – The vineyards cover about 30 000ha/74 130 acres, in the *départements* of Marne, Aube and Aisne. The most famous areas of production are the Côte des Blancs, the Marne Valley and the Montagne de Reims, where the great vintages originate. The grapes grow half way up the limestone slopes, above the chalky bedrock and in the sandy clay soil of the Côte de l'Île de France. The only varieties allowed are Pinot noir, Pinot Meunier and Chardonnay; the vines are planted close together and pruned low.

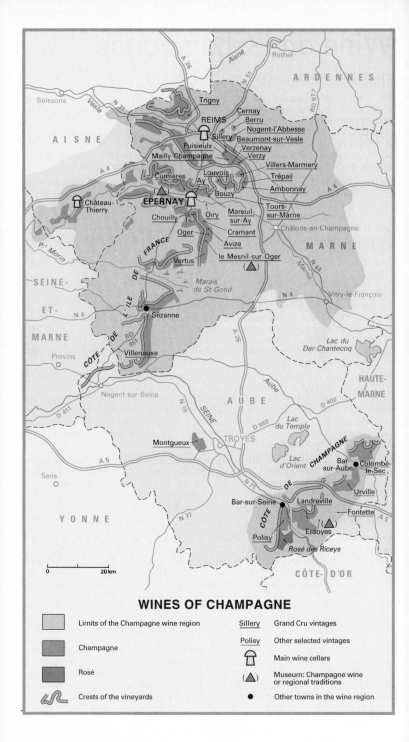

WINES OF CHAMPAGNE

Limits of the Champagne wine region		_Sillery_	Grand Cru vintages
Champagne		_Polisy_	Other selected vintages
Rosé			Main wine cellars
Crests of the vineyards		(△)	Museum: Champagne wine or regional traditions
		●	Other towns in the wine region

A delicate process – Champagne is created through a series of carefully executed steps which take place in the vineyards and in the cellars, where a steady temperature of about 10°C/50°F must be maintained.

Harvest – In October, bunches of grapes are picked and set down in flat trays; they are then sorted and carried to the press.

Pressing – The entire grapes are pressed, which results in a white must, even when dark grapes are used. Only the juice obtained by the first pressing (about 2 550l/660gal from 4 000kg/8 800lb of grapes) is used to make true Champagne wine.

Fermentation – The juice is stored in barrels or vats and fermentation is underway by Christmas.

Vintage and blend – In the spring, the *maître de chais* creates the vintage by blending different still wines, produced by various vineyards in various years. Each Champagne house has its own vintage which respects quality standards. Blendings include wines from the Montagne de Reims (hearty, full-bodied), the Marne Valley (fruity, aromatic wines), the Côte des Blancs (fresh, elegant wines) and the Côte des Bars. Red and white grapes are used in proportions which may vary but are generally about 2/3 to 1/3. Blanc de Blancs sparkling wine is made with only white grapes. Exceptionally, although ever more frequently, Champagne labels bear the vintage year, when the blending includes only wines of the same year.

Second fermentation and foam – The second fermentation is brought about by adding sugar and selected yeasts to the wine. The wine is drawn and put in very thick bottles which withstand pressure. Under the effects of the yeast (in the form of powder collected from the grape skins), the sugar is transformed into alcohol or carbonised into gas which, when the bottle is uncorked, creates foam. The bottles are set on racks in a cellar for 15 months to three years and sometimes more.

Settling and removing sediment – Over time, a deposit forms and must be eliminated. It is forced to settle in the bottle neck by storing the bottles at an angle, upside down. Each day, one person alone gives a slight turn (1/8 rotation) to as many as 40 000 bottles, and adjusts them for gradually increasing verticality. After five or six weeks, the bottle is fully vertical and all of the sediment has settled around the cork. The cork is then removed and the sediment with it. This process is called *dégorgement*. The bottle is topped off with more of the same wine, which may have had sugar added to make the final product sweeter.

Finishing – The corks need to be wired down to contain the pressure of the gas within; then the bottle can be labelled and shipped. Champagne which is already three or four years old will not improve any more in the bottle and should be consumed.

Marketing – Nearly 120 Champagne houses, mostly family-owned, and many dating back to the 18C, produce 70% of all Champagne shipped, with the remaining 30% in the hands of *récoltants-manipulants*, who blend their own wine; there are a few cooperatives as well. Financial backing is necessary for successful operations, because Champagne must be stored – and cared for – for an average of three years before it can be marketed, and thus involves keeping a lot of stock on hand.

A size for every thirst

© MOËT & CHANDON

Every year, more and more Champagne leaves the region for sale elsewhere. In 1995, over 246 million bottles were shipped; sales projections include 110 million bottles for export outside of France. Production of the region's sparkling wine accounts for just four percent of total French wine production, but in 1997, Champagne generated about 33% of France's earnings from wine exports.

A Merry Widow

Veuve Clicquot-Ponsardin is one of France's best-known and best-selling brands of Champagne. The eponymous origin is indeed a *Grande Dame*, Nicole-Barbe Ponsardin. In 1798, she married François Clicquot in a Champagne cellar (the churches had not yet been restored for worship after the Revolution); he left her a widow eight years later. Twenty-seven years old, with a baby daughter and almost no experience in the trade, she took over the family Champagne house, and ran the business until her death in 1866.

She revolutionised the art of blending *(assemblage)* when she developed the technique known as *remuage*. Previously, the wine had to be decanted into new bottles after the second fermentation, an inefficient process which was necessary to remove the sediment, but which reduced precious effervescence. Nowadays, using her technique, the bottles are twisted and tilted so that the dregs settle around the cork, which can then be popped open briefly. A small bit of wine is removed *(dégorgement)*, then the bottle is quickly topped off.

"Champagne," wrote Madame de Pompadour, "is the only wine which leaves a woman beautiful after drinking it. It gives brilliance to the eyes without flushing the face." Good news for merrymakers!

Nancy – Place Stanislas

R. Mathis/MICHELIN

Sights

ALTKIRCH

Population 5 090
Michelin map 87 fold 19 or 242 fold 39

The old town is perched on a hilltop overlooking the Ill Valley. The first settlement was established in the valley, round the old church *(alt kirch)* of St-Christophe, then Altkirch was rebuilt on the hilltop at the end of the 12C. The town, famous for its tiles, lies at the heart of the Sundgau region noted for its characteristic furniture and costumes and it is the ideal base for fishing and horse-riding enthusiasts.

SIGHTS

Église Notre-Dame – The church was built during the 19C in neo-Romanesque style; the north transept contains the remarkable polychrome stone statues of the Mont des Oliviers (Mount of Olives) and a copy of Prud'hon's Christ by Henner. In the south transept, a painting by Oster of Strasbourg depicts St Morand, the patron saint of Sundgau, being welcomed by the count of Ferrette. His sarcophagus is in the nave.

Place de la République – A modern fountain in neo-15C style stands in the centre of the square; its slender pinnacle shelters a statue of the Virgin Mary, which is all that remains of the former church.

Hôtel de ville – The town hall dates from the 18C.
On the right stands the bailiff's former residence, adorned with a wrought-iron balcony, which now houses the Sundgau Museum.

Musée sundgauvien ⊘ – The Sundgau Museum contains collections devoted to the region's history, archaeology and folklore, as well as paintings by local artists (Henner, Lehmann), some fine statues and a model of Altkirch in the past.

Eating out

MODERATE

Wach – *Near the Hôtel de Ville* – *68210 Dannemarie* – *10km/6.2mi W of Altkirch on D 419* – ☎ *03 89 25 00 01* – *closed 16-29 Aug, 23 Dec-9 Jan, evenings and Mon* – *60/180F.* This restaurant is worth visiting for its nice atmosphere and cooking; one can't help noticing that the decor dates from the 1950s, but the place is well run. The simple, mouth-watering dishes are reasonably priced and use regional or more classic recipes.

Where to stay

MODERATE

Camping Municipal Les Lupins – *68580 Seppois-le-Bas* – *13km/8mi SW of Altkirch on D 432, D 17 and D 17*[fl] – ☎ *03 89 25 65 37* – *open Apr-1 Nov* – *booking advisable Jul-Aug* – *158 plots 66F.* A pleasant couple run this camp site, which is on the site of the former station. The plots are well shaded and an amusing detail is the television room, in what was the station hall. Swimming pool and mini golf.

EXCURSIONS

Luemschwiller – *7km/4.3mi NE towards Mulhouse then right along a country road.*
The village **church** ⊘ houses a beautiful **altarpiece**, carved and painted in the 15C: the painted wings depict scenes from the life of the Virgin Mary (believed to be by Hans Baldung Grien) whereas the carved central panel represents the Virgin between St Barbe and St Catherine.

★**Sundgau** – *see SUNDGAU.*

AMNÉVILLE✦✦

Population 8 926
Michelin map 57 fold 3, 241 fold 20 or 242 folds 5 and 9

Access – *Amnéville is situated 5km/3mi from the A4 motorway (exit 35), along D 953.*
Lying at the heart of the Coulange Forest, covering 500ha/1236 acres, this former industrial town has become an important spa town following the discovery of ferruginous water at a temperature of 41°C/105.8°F, as well as a lively resort with a quality environment and good tourist facilities, including a splendid fitness centre, Thermapolis. Moreover, children will no doubt rejoice at the thought that the Walibi-Schtroumpf leisure park is nearby.

★**Parc zoologique du bois de Coulange** ⊘ – About 600 animals representing almost 110 different species from various zoos roam around in pens spread about a forested area covering 8ha/20 acres.

The zoo is committed to international programmes intended to protect endangered species; some of these, such as aurochs, wild oxen from the glacial period, have even been recreated. There are also many magnificent big cats: tigers from Siberia and Sumatra, lions from the Atlas mountains, panthers from Iran (there are only 50 wild specimens left), the snow leopard endangered for its beautiful coat, the strangely graceful serval... as well as free-roaming emus hanging on to visitors who are kind to them.

Located 300m/328yd from the zoo, the **Aquarium Impérator** offers an insight into some aspects of the tropical underwater world: there are species of fish and corals from the Caribbean, other species found only in Australian rivers or in the Amazon Valley, fauna native of Lake Malawi and Lake Tanganika... Several species of sharks share a huge tank.

★**Walibi Schtroumpf** ⊘ – *3km/1.9mi S of Amnéville.*

This 42ha/104-acre leisure park offers visitors of all ages a journey with Walibi, the friendly kangaroo, and the Schtroumpfs, the famous blue characters of Peyo's comic strip.

There is a wide choice of shops, snacks and restaurants, as well as several shows, so that visitors can easily spend a whole day in the park.

Attractions include the Réaktor, a huge wheel with a loop-the-loop track, the **Odisséa**, a buoy tossed about among the rapids, the Waligator which splashes 12m/39ft down a waterfall and the Aquachute, a huge water slide. For the more daring, there is a guaranteed thrill on the **Comet Space** or the **Sismic Panic**... But will you be brave enough to face the **Vengeance de Gargamel**, a fantastic tower which will propel you 55m/60yd upwards in two and a half seconds?

In France, a "Smurf" is a "Schtroumpf"

Eating out

MID-RANGE

La Forêt – *In the Bois de Coulange leisure park – 2.5km/1.5mi S of Amnéville –* ☎ *03 87 70 34 34 – closed 22 Dec-6 Jan, Sun evening and Mon – 120/250F.* This popular restaurant in the Bois de Coulange leisure centre is surrounded by trees, and its dining room and terrace are pleasantly arranged with cane furniture and plants. The cooking is good, too.

Where to stay

MID-RANGE

Hôtel Orion – *In the Bois de Coulange leisure park – 2.5km/1.5mi S of Amnéville –* ☎ *03 87 70 20 20 – closed 25-31 Dec, Fri and Sat Nov-Apr – 44 rooms 260/300F –* ⊡ *45F – restaurant 90F.* This spa resort hotel offers simple, identical rooms with rendered walls and cane furniture. A modern building and a cheap, practical place to stay.

On the town

La Taverne du Brasseur – *R. du Bois-de-Coulange –* ☎ *03 87 70 11 77 – Mon-Thu 10am-midnight, Fri-Sat 10am-2am.* Amnéville beer is traditionally brewed here. Typical local menu.

ANDLAU ★

Population 1 632
Michelin map 87 fold 16 or 242 fold 27 – Local map see Route des VINS

This small flower-decked town, nestling in the green valley of the River Andlau, has retained some old houses and the church of a once-famous monastery. The ridge to the north is crowned with the ruins of the Château du Haut-Andlau *(see p 165)*. Andlau is at the heart of Riesling country, with three famous vintages produced nearby.

Bear legend

The abbey was founded in 880 by Richarde, the wife of Emperor Charles le Gros (the Fat). According to legend, Richarde had a vision telling her to build a convent on the spot where she would meet a female bear building a shelter for her young. She met the animal in the forest and built the convent there; from then on, a live bear was kept at the convent and passing bear-leaders were always given free lodging and food. A hole in the paving of the crypt of St-Pierre-et-St-Paul Church is said to mark the very spot indicated by the bear; it is guarded by the pre-Romanesque stone statue of a bear!

★ÉGLISE ST-PIERRE-ET-ST-PAUL

The church is a fine example of 12C architecture, except for the upper part of the steeple which dates from the 17C. The doorway is surmounted by a massive construction. The west front and north side are decorated with a frieze depicting animals, monsters and a mixture of realistic and allegorical scenes.

The **doorway**★★, which is the most interesting part of the building, is adorned with the most outstanding Romanesque carvings in Alsace. Small characters placed on either side support foliated mouldings entwined around animals; several couples, presumably representing the benefactors of the abbey, are framed by the arcading. The lintel is decorated with scenes from the Creation and the Garden of Eden.

Inside, the **chancel**, situated above the 11C **crypt**★, is decorated with fine 15C stalls; St Richarde's funeral monument, also dating from the 15C, can be seen against the wall.

EXCURSION

Epfig – *6km/3.7mi SE along D 253 and D 335. Drive through the village and follow D 603 towards Kogenheim.*
Situated at the eastern end of the village, above the Rhine Valley, the **Chapelle Ste-Marguerite**, surrounded by the cemetery, was built in the 11C and 12C. According to legend, it was used by a congregation of nuns during the 12C. The ossuary remains a mystery.

The vineyard surrounds Andlau

ARGONNE★

The Argonne region is a geographical entity situated on the border of Champagne and Lorraine. Its rolling landscapes, its forests and beauty spots are attractive tourist areas. The massif which, at its widest point between Clermont and Ste-Menehould, is no more than 12km/7.5mi wide, reaches an altitude of 308m/1 010ft south of Clermont. The eastern side overlooking the plain forms a considerable obstacle which was always highly coveted. The valleys separating the hillocks are the natural passages through which invasions traditionally penetrated the region: the Islettes, Lachalade and Grandpré passes.

In 1792, Prussian troops were held up here after the fall of Verdun, which enabled Dumouriez to get his own troops ready in Valmy and to stop the enemy as it came out of the Argonne passes. During the First World War, the front line ran for four years between Four-de-Paris, Haute-Chevauchée, Vauquois and Avocourt, splitting Argonne into two. Fierce fighting took place near the Vauquois and Beaulieu heights, causing numerous casualties.

> **HOME-STYLE**
>
> **Hostellerie de l'Abbaye** – 7 Grande-Rue – 55250 Beaulieu-en-Argonne – ☎ 03 29 70 72 81 – closed 15 Dec-1 Feb and Sun evening Oct-Mar – 8 rooms 270/320F – ☲ 30F – restaurant 95/180F. In the small village's main street, this property comprises the corner café, a few nicely decorated rooms and a simple restaurant. Family atmosphere, unpretentious.

ROUND TOUR STARTING FROM CLERMONT-EN-ARGONNE

77km/48mi – about 4hr – local map see below

Clermont-en-Argonne – Clermont is picturesquely situated on a wooded hillside above the Aire Valley; the top of the hill reaches 308m/1010ft, the highest point in the Argonne region.

The former capital of the county of Clermontois used to be overlooked by a fortress and surrounded by fortified walls. It belonged in turn to the Holy Roman Empire, to the bishopric of Verdun, to the county of Bar and to the duchy of Lorraine before being joined to the kingdom of France in 1632. Louis XIV later gave it to the Grand Condé after the castle was razed during the Fronde. The **Église St-Didier** ⊙, dating from the 16C, is adorned with two Renaissance doorways. Note the Flamboyant Gothic vaulting of the transept and chancel, the modern stained glass and a 15C Mirror of Death low-relief sculpture. From the terrace behind the

St-Didier church

church, the view extends over the Argonne region and the Hesse Forest.

The **Chapelle Ste-Anne** ⊙ *(access via the path climbing on the right of the church)*, a small edifice erected on the site of the former castle, contains a 16C representation of the Holy Sepulchre comprising six statues. The very beautiful Mary Magdalene, which belongs to a painted group depicting the three Marys, is thought to be the work of Ligier Richier or a sculptor from the same school.

Follow the shaded path leading to the tip of the promontory: the view extends across the Argonne Forest and the plateau carved by the Aire Valley *(viewing table)*.

Leave Clermont-en-Argonne on D 998 towards Neuvilly-en-Argonne. From Neuvilly, follow D 946. In Boureuilles, take D 212 on the right towards Vauquois. As you enter Vauquois, follow the surfaced path on the left, which leads to the hillock. Leave the car and climb along the footpath to the top of the hill.

Butte de Vauquois – Between 1914 and 1918, there was fierce fighting on both sides over this hill. A monument marks the site of the former village destroyed during the war. A narrow path running along the ridge and offering views of the Hesse Forest, the Montfaucon Hill and the Aire Valley, overlooks several mine craters, 30m/98ft deep. The ground all around is completely churned up and it is still possible to see pieces of barbed wire and *chevaux de frise* (defensive spikes).

Return to D 38 which leads to Varennes-en-Argonne.

Varennes-en-Argonne – This small town, built on the banks of the River Aire, is famous as the place where Louis XVI was arrested when he tried to flee from France with his family during the Revolution. The royal coach was stopped by a handful of soldiers at 11pm on 21 June 1791. The king tried to gain time, hoping to be freed by his own troops, but the people of Varennes acted promptly and the royal family was escorted back to Paris by national guards.

The **Musée d'Argonne** ⊙, housed on two levels inside a modern building, features Louis XVI's arrest, arts and crafts of the Argonne region (sigillated ceramics and earthenware from Les Islettes and Waly), as well as mementoes from the First World War (underground fighting and the American intervention).

Between the museum and the church, an itinerary lined with seven explanatory panels commemorates the arrival and the arrest of Louis XVI and his family during the night of 21 to 22 June 1791.

The **Mémorial de Pennsylvanie** is an imposing monument dedicated to American soldiers who died during the fighting which took place in 1918.

There is a lovely view of the River Aire and the surrounding countryside to the north.

Return to D 38 then turn left onto the Haute-Chevauchée road.

Haute-Chevauchée – This is one of the main sites of the First World War; fierce fighting took place here but today the road offers a pleasant walk through the forest to the **Kaisertunnel** and the Forestière military cemetery. Trenches and narrow passageways can still be seen in the undergrowth on either side of the road.

Return to D 38 and continue to Four-de-Paris, then take D 2 to Lachalade.

Lachalade – The village is overlooked by the imposing silhouette of a former Cistercian abbey. Two wings of the 17C monastery buildings *(private property)* are still standing.

The 14C **church** looks oddly proportioned, owing to the fact that it is reduced to two bays, the first three having been destroyed by fire at the beginning of the 17C. Note the Flamboyant Gothic rose on the west front: it originally decorated Ste-Vanne Abbey in Verdun.

Continue towards Les Islettes.

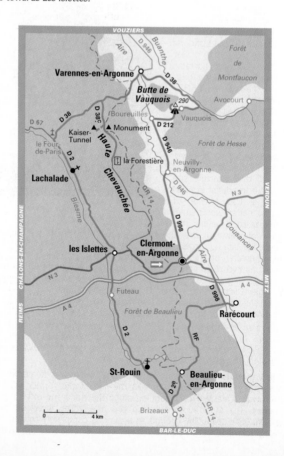

Les Islettes – This once-thriving village was famous for its tileries, glassworks and above all earthenware factories.

Beyond Futeau, D 2 goes through the Beaulieu Forest.

Ermitage de St-Rouin – St Roding (or Rouin), a 7C Irish monk, settled in Argonne and founded a monastery which preceded the Beaulieu Abbey. A greenery cathedral lies in a lovely wooded setting. A solitary building intended for pilgrims, welcomes visitors; further on, under the canopy formed by the trees, stands a modern concrete chapel designed by Father Rayssiguier, a disciple of Le Corbusier. The multicoloured stained-glass windows are the work of a young Japanese artist. A pilgrimage takes place in mid-September.

Continue along D 2 and turn left towards Beaulieu-en-Argonne.

Beaulieu-en-Argonne – This village, brightened up with flowers, occupies a hillock offering fine views of the forested heights. Of the important Benedictine abbey which once stood here, only a few walls remain apart from the huge 13C **winepress★** ⊙, entirely made of oak (except for the hornbeam screw), in which the monks could press 3 000kg/6 615lb of grapes to produce 1 600l/352gal of grape juice.

From Beaulieu-en-Argonne take the forest road running alongside the winepress building (on the left), continue straight on beyond the Trois Pins crossroads then turn left to Rarécourt.

Rarécourt – The **Musée de la Faïence** ⊙ is housed in a 17C fortified building *(on the right of the road beyond the bridge spanning the River Aire)*. More than 800 earthenware and terracotta pieces from the area (Islettes, Lavoye, Waly, Rarécourt...), dating from the 18C and 19C, are exhibited.

From Rarécourt, return to Clermont-en-Argonne along D 998.

Basilique d'AVIOTH★★
Michelin map 57 fold 1 or 241 fold 15

This magnificent church, situated in the centre of a remote village near the Belgian border, offers a striking contrast with it rural setting. Next to it stands a small unusual monument, the Recevresse, intended to receive offerings from pilgrims.

BASILIQUE NOTRE-DAME *about 30min*

The discovery of a statue of the Virgin Mary, believed to perform miracles, led to a pilgrimage during the early 12C and to the construction, in warm-coloured stone, of the basilica from the second half of the 13C to the beginning of the 15C when the Flamboyant Gothic style prevailed.

Exterior – The **west doorway** is well proportioned and its design harmonious: the arching is decorated with 70 figures and Christ's Passion is depicted on the lintel. Above the portal, near the gable, one can see the Last Judgement; note also the statues representing angels sounding trumpets.

The **south doorway** is dedicated to the Virgin and to Christ's childhood. The lower parts are decorated with carved draperies, in typical Champagne style.

Left of the south doorway stands **La Recevresse★**, a small yet elegant edifice in Flamboyant style, adjacent to the door of the old cemetery and decorated with fine tracery work.

Interior – The basilica is very bright inside. There is a walkway (unusual in this region) and an ambulatory; radiating from it are shallow chapels fitted between the buttresses which happen to be inside the church according to a practise used in Champagne. Restoration work has brought to light 14C and 15C paintings and frescoes over the chancel screen and vaulting, in particular near the tabernacle, where a Virgin and Child with St John and St Agnes can be seen.

La Recevresse

R.Mattes/MICHELIN

The basilica has retained several works of popular art. Worth noting in the **chancel** is the 14C high altar decorated with the symbols of the four evangelists. To the left of the altar, one can see the ancient statue of **Notre-Dame d'Avioth**, carved out of lime c 1110 and resting on a 15C stone throne. Note also the 14 polychrome statues placed high against the pillars of the east end, which form a silent court around the Virgin's statue. The Gothic tabernacle on the right of the altar dates from the 15C, its high pinnacle almost touching the top of the arcading forms a frame round it. The elegant pulpit, dating from 1538 carved with Renaissance motifs still shows traces of polychromy; the central panel depicts the Coronation of the Virgin. Next to it, the Ecce Homo is flanked by a Pontius Pilate dressed in the court fashion of the Holy Roman Empire.

BACCARAT

Population 5 015
Michelin map 62 fold 7 or 242 fold 22

This small town lying on both sides of the River Meurthe is famous for its crystal-works founded in 1764.

Crystalworks – *Not open to the public.* In 1764 King Louis XV allowed the bishop of Metz to revive an ancient glass-making tradition; in 1817 the glassworks were turned into crystalworks and since the visit of Charles X in 1828, the works have been supplying kings, presidents and important people throughout the world, including Czar Nicholas II, who commissioned a 3.85m/12.6ft tall candelabrum. There was a time of great prosperity at the beginning of the 19C and again in the 1950s after the sombre period marked by two world wars. The workers' district comprised several long buildings. Glassworkers lived near the crystalworks because they had to run to the factory as soon as the bell rang signalling that the crystal had melted. Today, the high-tech crystalworks use a special furnace which fines down the melted mixture and 38 highly qualified craftsmen have been nominated "best workers in France".

SIGHTS

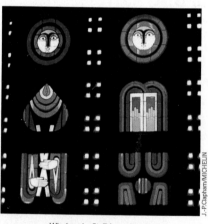

Window in St-Rémy church

Musée du Cristal ⊙ – Located in the directors' house, the museum displays antique and contemporary pieces: 19C opalines, agates, millefiori paperweights, plain, cut or carved glasses, table sets ordered by sovereigns and heads of states. In the last room, the various techniques and tools used are illustrated: work under heat, cutting, carving and gilding process.

Église St-Rémy – Built in 1957, the church has an unusual roof with large awnings. The steeple, a 55m/180ft pyramid, stands beside the church. The interior decoration, which consists in a huge low relief made up of concrete elements and **stained-glass panels ★** in Baccarat crystal (more than 50 different colours), illustrates the creation of the world. The tabernacle and christening font lit by two stained-glass windows depicting the Twelve Apostles, are also noteworthy.

Eating out

MODERATE

Le Wagon du Pré Fleury – *54129 Magnières – 15km/9.3mi W of Baccarat, Bayon direction on D 22 –* ☎ *03 83 72 32 58 – closed Jan, Sun evening and Mon – 87/195F.* An unusual setting for this restaurant, in an old railway carriage and a station! It is run by a former industrial designer and saddler and is pleasantly decorated in a slightly old-fashioned style. Regional cooking. Nearby attractions include fishing, walking and pedal-propelled railcars.

L'Écurie – *54120 Bertrichamps – 5km/3mi E of Baccarat, Raon-l'Étape direction, then minor road –* ☎ *03 83 71 43 14 – closed Feb, 8-15 Jul, Sun evening and Mon – 95/235F. –* This country-style restaurant in a simple rural setting, at the end of a cul-de-sac of houses, serves meals outside in fine weather. Home-made *charcuteries* and regional cooking.

EXCURSIONS

Deneuvre – Excavations, carried out between 1974 and 1986 south of this village adjacent to Baccarat, led to the discovery of a Gallo-Roman sanctuary which has been reconstructed in a museum.

Les Sources d'Hercule – In the entrance hall there are explanations, maps, plans and models dealing with the discovery of the site. Founded in the middle of the 2C AD, the sanctuary was dedicated to Hercules. Three pools were at the disposal of those who wished to perform their ablutions. Those whose wishes came true offered ex-votos, ie stelae or altars which eventually formed a circle round the springs. Hercules is represented on most stelae as he was considered as the protector of the springs.

Fontenoy-la-Joûte – *6km/3.5mi W.* In this typically stretched-out Lorraine village, 18C semi-detached houses have been turned into bookshops and Fontenoy has become a book village with some 15 bookshops, a first-class bookbinder and a printing house. An important market takes place on the last Sunday of the month from April to September.

BALLON D'ALSACE ★★★

Michelin map 66 fold 8 or 242 folds 35 and 39

The Ballon d'Alsace is the highest peak (alt 1 250m/4 101ft) of the **Massif du Ballon d'Alsace** situated at the southern end of the Vosges mountain range. It belongs to the crystalline part of these mountains where granite predominates and owes its name to its rounded shape, although *ballon* could be derived from the name of the Celtic god Bel as there is some evidence that the peak was used as a solar observatory in Celtic times.

The massif is clad with dense forests of spruce and fir trees and the undergrowth is in parts charming; ravines are pleasantly cool and heights are covered with pastures dotted with Alpine flowers.

The Ballon d'Alsace provides one of the most popular excursions in the region in summer as well as in winter (downhill and cross-country skiing).

Where to stay

MODERATE

Grand Hôtel du Sommet – *On the summit of the Ballon d'Alsace – 90200 Lepuix-Gy –* ☎ *03 84 29 30 60 –* 🅿 *– 25 rooms 240F –* 🍴 *30F – restaurant 80/150F.* Imagine waking up on a mountain top, surrounded by nothing but open air and fields of cows, with a view of the Belfort Valley and even, on a clear day, the Swiss Alps. A good night's sleep is guaranteed in the simple but comfortable rooms. Classic cooking.

MID-RANGE

Chambre d'hôte Le Lodge de MonThuy – *70440 Servance – 4.5km/2.8mi N of Servance on D 263 –* ☎ *03 84 20 48 55 – closed 24 Dec-2 Jan – 6 rooms 305/350F – evening meal 125/200F.* Immerse yourself totally in nature in this isolated 18C farm in the forests above the Ognon Valley, facing the Ballon de Servance. Comfortable, simple rooms. The cooking uses local produce. Fishing available in 7ha/17 acres of private lakes.

★★MASSIF DU BALLON D'ALSACE

☐ From St-Maurice-sur-Moselle to Sentheim

38km/23.6mi – allow 2hr – local map see Parc naturel régional des BALLONS DES VOSGES.

The road leading to the Col du Ballon d'Alsace, built in the 18C, is the oldest in the area.

St-Maurice-sur-Moselle – This small industrial town (textiles and sawmills) is close to some remarkable beauty spots as well as the Rouge Gazon and Ballon d'Alsace winter resorts. It is the starting point of excursions to the Ballon de Servance and the Charbonniers Valley *(see p 85).*

On the way up to the Col du Ballon, the road *(D 465)* offers some fine views of the Moselle Valley before going through a splendid forest of firs and beeches.

Plain du Canon – *15min on foot there and back.*

⚑ The path leaves D 465 by an information panel tied to a tree and runs down towards a forest lodge. Go down past the lodge and follow a path on the left which meanders upwards. The place owes its name to a small gun once used by the local gamekeeper to create an echo.

There is a charming view of the wooded Presles Valley over which tower the Ballon d'Alsace and Ballon de Servance, crowned by a fort.

Beyond **La Jumenterie**, whose name (*jument* means mare) is a reminder of a horse-breeding centre founded in 1619 by the dukes of Lorraine, there is a fine view of the Moselle Valley and Ballon de Servance to the right.

The road reaches the high-pasture area.

The **Monument aux Démineurs** by Rivière and Deschler is dedicated to bomb-disposal experts who died while performing their duty.

Col du Ballon – To the right there is a monument celebrating the racing cyclist René Pottier *(at the end of the parking area)*. There is a fine view of the summit of the Ballon d'Alsace, crowned with a statue of the Virgin Mary and, further right, of the Belfort depression dotted with lakes and the northern part of the Jura mountains.

A path leads to Joan of Arc's statue.

★★★ **Ballon d'Alsace** – *30min on foot there and back.*

⚑ The path starts from D 465 in front of the Ferme-Restaurant du Ballon d'Alsace. It runs through pastures towards the statue of the Virgin. Before Alsace became French once more, the statue stood exactly on the border. From the viewing platform, the **panorama★★** extends north to the Donon, east across the plain of Alsace and the Black Forest and south as far as Mont Blanc.

Preserve the environment! Walk along paths, don't cut through pastures or forests, and leave wild flowers and plants as you find them.

The drive down to the Alfeld Lake is very beautiful. Ahead is the Grand Ballon, the highest summit in the Vosges mountains (1 424m/4 672ft); later on there are fine views of the Doller Valley and of the Jura and the Alps.

As the road comes out of the forest, the lake appears inside a glacial cirque.

★ **Lac d'Alfeld** – The Alfeld artificial lake (covering an area of 10ha/25 acres and reaches a depth of 22m/72ft) is one of the most attractive water expanses in the Vosges region. It ensures that the Doller has a regular flow, particularly when the thaw comes. The lake is framed by picturesque wooded heights.

R.Mattes/MICHELIN

La Doller

The dam, built between 1884 and 1887, is 337m/369yd long and leans against a moraine left behind by ancient glaciers.

Lac de Sewen – Close to the Alfeld Lake, this small lake is gradually filling up with peat. Alpine and Nordic plants grow on its shores.

Further downstream, D 466 follows the Doller which flows between high slopes covered with green pastures alternating with woods of fir and beech trees.

The valley is overlooked by the Romanesque church of **Kirchberg** perched on a moraine and, as you enter **Niederbruck**, on the left, by a monumental statue of the Virgin and Child by Antoine Bourdelle.

Masevaux – *See THANN: Excursion.*

Sentheim – The **Maison de la Géologie** ⊙, opposite the church, houses a fine collection of fossils and minerals.

Sentier géologique de Wolfloch – *Drive along D 466 towards Bussang, then turn right 300m/328yd after the church and follow the arrows to the starting point of the geological trail.*

⚑ *The itinerary extends over a distance of 5km/3mi and includes 12 geological sites. Allow 2hr. It is essential to obtain the brochure available at the Maison de la Géologie.*

Start from the presentation panel and walk to the right along the fields, following the markings illustrating a fossil.

The path goes across the great Vosges fault and gives an insight into the geology of the region from the Primary Era until today. The fault separates the primary formations, uplifted when the Alps rose, from more recent sediments, often rich in fossils, which account for the presence of the sea 100 million years ago *(see p 24)*.

Parc naturel régional
des BALLONS DES VOSGES

Population 240 000
Michelin map 62 folds 17 and 18, 66 folds 7, 8 and 9
or 242 folds 27, 31, 34, 35, 38 and 39

The nature park's main attraction is its varied landscapes –
rounded summits *(ballons)* clad with high pastures, peat bogs,
glacial cirques, lakes, rivers and hills covered with conifers – all of
which are responsible for what is called the "blue line of the
Vosges", on the horizon.

The great diversity of ecosystems accounts for the varied fauna:
deer, roe-deer, wild boars, chamois and even lynx. Bird life is also
plentiful in forested and mountainous areas (in particular species
such as the peregrine, capercaillie and blackbirds). Aquatic ecosystems also have a rich fauna (crayfish, common trout, Alpine newt
etc) and specific flora.
Villages, farms and museums illustrate agricultural and industrial
traditions as well as local handicrafts: silver-mine development,
weaving, wood-sledging, Munster-cheese making.
There are numerous walks and hikes and a wide choice of outdoor activities. Mills and
sawmills in the area are open for guided tours and demonstrations. Historic trails,
museums and open-air museums deal with the historic and cultural development of the
region *(information available from the park's headquarters in Munster and from tourist
offices).*

VAL D'ARGENT

④ Round tour from Ste-Marie-aux-Mines

65km/40mi – allow 1hr 30min

The Vosges mountains are particularly rich in mineral resources, silver, copper and
other metals, extracted since the Middle Ages. The mining industry had its heyday
during the 16C and 17C and its decline was completed in the middle of the 19C.
Great efforts have been made to restore the region's mining heritage and develop
its touristic potential. Today, several protected sites, which have been restructured,
are open to the public.

Follow N 59 west out of Ste-Marie-aux-Mines through a green valley. The road
then climbs sharply past a war cemetery on the right.

Col de Ste-Marie – From the pass (alt 772m/2 533ft), one of the highest passes
in the Vosges mountains, look back towards the Cude Valley and ahead to the
Liepvrette Valley, the Plaine d'Alsace and Haut-Kœnigsbourg Castle.

Roc du Haut de Faite – *From the pass, 30min on foot there and back. Walk north along
a path starting on the right of a gravestone.*
🔲 From the top, there is a fine **panorama** of the Vosges summits and the slopes on
the Alsatian and Lorraine side.

*Return to N 59 and drive towards St-Dié. Turn left onto D 23, 2km/1.2mi beyond
Gemaingoutte.*

Circuit minier La Croix-aux-Mines – *5.6km/3.5mi walk – allow 2hr 45min.*
🔲 Start from the Chapelle du Chipal and follow the panels marked with a black
circle against a yellow background and bearing the emblem of the trail (crossed
hammer and pickaxe). Miners extracted galena, a mineral ore of lead sulphide
mixed with silver, from this site at Le Chipal and others in the area.

Continue along D 23 to Fraize and turn left onto N 415.

Col du Bonhomme – *See Val d'ORBEY.*

On reaching the pass, turn left onto D 148.

Le Bonhomme – This pleasant resort was three times caught in heavy fighting
during the two world wars.

★★**Le Brézouard** – *45min on foot there and back.*
🔲 You will be able to get fairly close to the Brézouard by car if you approach it via
the **Col des Bagenelles** *(4km/2.5mi)* which offers a fine view of the Liepvrette Valley.
Leave the car in the parking area, near the Amis de la Nature refuge.

The Brézouard and the surrounding area suffered a complete upheaval during the
First World War.
From the summit, there is a very wide **panorama★★**: the Champ du Feu and
Climont to the north, with the Donon in the background; Strasbourg to the
north-east, the Hohneck and Grand Ballon to the south. When the weather is clear,
Mont Blanc can be seen in the distance.

PARC NATUREL RÉGIONAL DES BALLONS DES VOSGES

🛈	Information centre
M	Museum or exhibit
◗	Historical tour
◰	Environmental learning centre
🚶	Discovery trail

🧗	Climbing centre
🚴	Off-road bike trail
🎿	Downhill ski area
⛷	Cross-country ski area

0   5 km

ST-DIÉ-DES-VOSGES
Bruyères
601 △ Mont-Avison
ÉPINAL ★
D 46
N 420
Champ-le-Duc
D 44
D 60
D 11
Vologne
D 30
Faucompierre
Granges-s-Vologne
Barbey-Serou
★ Champs de Roches
Archette
Chéniménil
Arches
Tête des Cuveaux ★
783
Éloyes
Gr de cascade de Tendon ★
le Tholy
D 11
D 417
GÉRARDME
★ Lac de Gérardmer
St-Amé
D 42
D 417
Vagney
la Bresse
Remiremont
Moselotte
Cornimont
Vée de la Semouse ★
N 57
757 le Beuille
Saulxures-s-Moselotte
Ventre
PLOMBIÈRES-LES-BAINS
★ Cascade du Géhard
D 57
Rupt-s-Moselle
M Ventre
Le Val d'Ajol
620 Col du Mont de Fourche
Ermitage du Frère Joseph
N 66
Moselle
D 486
Fougerolles
M
D 83
D 136
D 6
GR 7
le Thillot
N 66
Bussang
St-Maurice-s-Moselle
St-Bresson
Col des Croix
679
D 16
Raddon
Faucogney-et-la-Mer
Château-Lambert
le Haut-du-Them
2
Plain du Canon
la Jumente
Breuchin
★★ Ballon de Servance
1216
1178 128
Servance
D 486
Col du Ballon
Vée des
Saut de l'Ognon
★★★ BALLON D'ALSACE
D 73
Ognon
D 16
Planche des Belles Filles
1148
Savoureuse
GR 5
Mélisey
Plancher-les-Mines
Lepuix
D 486
Giroma
Auxelles-Haut
D 13
RONCHAMP
RONCHAMP
SERMAMAGNY

Landscape in the Regional nature park

Return to Ste-Marie-aux-Mines along D 48.

The road winds its way through the forest then follows the Liepvrette Valley where orchards take over from high pastures.

Sentier patrimoine de Neuenberg – *In Échery.*

⚐ During the tour of this heritage trail *(short tour: 2hr 30min, long tour: 4hr)*, the mineworkers' tower and the tithe-collector's house, flanked with a turret in characteristic Renaissance style, and a research gallery of the Enigma mine come into view.

Turn right in Échery.

St-Pierre-sur-l'Hâte – There was once a Benedictine priory in this picturesque hamlet framed by wooded slopes, which has retained an ecumenical **church**, known as the miners' church, built in the 15C-16C and restored in 1934.

Ste-Marie-aux-Mines – This small industrial town, located in the Liepvrette Valley, owes its name to its former silver mines. Today, it is the meeting place of collectors of rocks and fossils who gather for the exhibition and exchange market organised every year during the last weekend in June. Ste-Marie has a famous weaving industry specialising in fine woollen cloth, factory or home made by craftsmen who have been passing their skills on from one generation to the next since the 18C. Twice a year, in spring and autumn, a fabrics fair offers buyers from various countries a choice of fabrics woven in Ste-Marie, in particular tartans and a variety of new textiles mostly intended for the Haute-Couture trade.

The **Maison de Pays** ⊙ *(place du Prensureux)* houses a rich collection of rocks on the ground floor. On the first floor, there is the reconstruction of a workshop where visitors can follow the different stages of the manufacturing process of fabrics. The second floor is devoted to the history of mines and the various techniques used: life-size reconstruction of a mine gallery, models, tools, copies of archives.

The birthplace of patchwork

Every year in September, a historic and artistic exhibition on patchwork and the Amish community takes place in Ste-Marie-aux-Mines. Founded in 1693 in Ste-Marie, the Amish movement emigrated to Pennsylvania in 1740. Amish women used to make up blankets with pieces of fabric and thus initiated the art of patchwork. Lessons in patchwork-making are available and there are lectures on the history of the Amish movement and the various techniques of patchwork-making in several venues throughout the valley.

The **Mine St-Barthélemy** ⊙ *(rue St-Louis)* organises tours of the galleries hewn out of the rock by 16C miners and the **Mine d'argent St-Louis-Eisenthur** ⊙ presents the various mining sites and techniques used in the 16C.

A **historic trail** *(1hr 30min, booklet available at the tourist office)* enables visitors to discover miners' houses and mansions which show how flourishing the mining industry was in the 16C and early 17C.

Leave Ste-Marie-aux-Mines by D 459 towards Ste-Croix.

Sentier minier et botanique de Ste-Croix-aux-Mines – *A mining and botanic trail (3.8km/2.4mi, allow 2hr 30min) starts on the left of the road as you leave the town, 100m/110yd before the panel marked "les halles".*

🔼 The trail winds through the Bois de St-Pierremont where several silver mines were located in the 16C. All along the way, panels provide information about the various species of trees.

★**Vallée de la Liepvrette** – North-east of Ste-Marie-aux-Mines, a picturesque stretch of N 59 follows the fresh valley of the River Liepvrette with pastures framed by large forests of firs as far as Sélestat. From Liepvre, it is possible to reach the **Col de Fouchy** *(7km/4.3mi along D 48).* From the pass, there is a fine view of the Champ du Feu and the Hohwald mountains to the north, the Schlossberg and the ruins of Frankenbourg to the east. Look south for Haut-Kœnigsbourg Castle.

★★MASSIF DU BALLON D'ALSACE

① From St-Maurice-sur-Moselle to Sentheim

See BALLON D'ALSACE.

★★BALLON DE SERVANCE

② Itinerary starting from Servance

20km/12.4mi – allow 1hr

Situated a few miles west of the Ballon d'Alsace (crowned by a statue of the Virgin Mary), the Ballon de Servance (crowned by a military fort) reaches the altitude of 1 216m/3 990ft. The River Ognon takes its source there as a modest mountain stream.

Servance – The syenite quarries which produced a fine reddish building stone are no longer worked.

🔼 As you leave the village, a footpath starting on your right *(15min there and back)* leads to the Saut de l'Ognon, a picturesque waterfall gushing forth from a narrow gorge.

Col des Croix – Alt 679m/2 228ft. Overlooked by the Château-Lambert Fort, the pass marks the watershed between the North Sea and the Mediterranean Sea.

Château-Lambert – Situated 1km/0.6mi from the pass, this charming village has an interesting **Musée de la Montagne** ⊙, which includes the house of a farmer-miner, a mill, a smithy, a 17C press, a sawmill, a former classroom...

Return to the Col des Croix and turn left onto D 16; the road rises above the Ognon Valley, offering fine views, before meandering through the forest.

★★**Panorama du Ballon de Servance** – *Leave the car at the beginning of the military road (no entry) for the Fort de Servance and take a marked path on the right which leads (15min on foot there and back) to the summit of the Ballon (alt 1 216m/3 990ft).*

🔼 The panorama is magnificent: the Ognon Valley, the glacial Plateau d'Esmoulières dotted with lakes and the Plateau de Langres to the west; Monts Faucilles to the north-west; the Moselle Valley further to the right; the Vosges mountain range to the north-east and to the east, the nearby rounded summit of the Ballon d'Alsace; the foothills of the Vosges mountains stretching to the south and south-east.

VALLÉE DES CHARBONNIERS

③ Itinerary from St-Maurice-sur-Moselle

12km/7.4mi – allow 30min

St-Maurice-sur-Moselle – *See p 79.*

From St-Maurice-sur-Moselle, drive east along the road which follows the Charbonniers stream.

The inhabitants of this valley are believed to be the descendants of a Swedish and German colony hired by the dukes of Lorraine in the 18C for forestry work and coal mining. In the village of Les Charbonniers, turn left onto the Rouge Gazon road (winter sports): from the **Tête du Rouge Gazon**, there are good views of the Ballon de Servance.

BAR-LE-DUC ★

Population 17 545
Michelin map 62 fold 1 or 241 fold 31

Partly built on top of a promontory, Bar-le-Duc is split into two: the Ville Haute or upper town, where the castle of the dukes of Bar once stood, and the Ville Basse or lower town, lying on both banks of the River Ornain, a tributary of the Marne. In the 10C, Bar was already the capital of a county whose influence rivalled that of the duchy of Lorraine, and in 1354 the counts of Bar became dukes. In 1484 the Barrois region was joined to Lorraine, yet managed to retain its autonomy and in 1766 it was united with France. During the First World War, Bar-le-Duc played an important role in the Battle of Verdun.

Today the city is the administrative centre of the Meuse *département* and a commercial town where regular fairs and markets are held. Redcurrant jam is a famous speciality.

★VILLE HAUTE *30min*

This fine ensemble of 16C, 17C and 18C architecture was Bar's aristocratic district. Behind its façade adorned with statues, columns, trophies and gargoyles, each building comprises a mansion, a courtyard and servants' quarters.

Place St-Pierre – This triangular open area, overlooked by the elegant west front of the Église St-Étienne, is lined with houses dating from different periods.

Three residences standing on the right as you face the church show the evolution of architectural styles from the 15C to the 17C. **No 25**, a timber-framed house with corbelled upper floor, is a good specimen of medieval architecture; whereas **no 21**, formerly the Hôtel de Florainville and today the law courts, has a façade in Alsatian Renaissance style (the graceful wrought-iron balconies were added in the 18C). As for the early-17C façade of **no 29**, now occupied by a magistrates' court, it is decorated in strict Classical style: columns and windows surmounted by scrolled pediments.

Bar-le-Duc

Église St-Étienne ⊘ – This former collegiate church dating from the late 14C has a partly Renaissance west front. It contains several works of art including the famous **Transi**★★ by Ligier Richier (in the south transept), which depicts the Prince of Orange, René de Chalon, killed during the siege of St-Dizier in 1544. This powerful work was commissioned by his widow, Anne de Lorraine. It depicts with gruesome realism the contrast between the miserable state of the decomposed body and his triumphant attitude as he looks up to his heart which he is holding heavenwards at arm's length. A **Calvary** scene, also by Ligier Richier, placed behind the high altar, depicts Christ and the two thieves. In the north transept the **Statue of Notre-Dame-du-Guet** is revered locally. According to legend, it stood by one of the town's gates during the siege of 1440 and warned of a surprise enemy attack. A painting facing the statue illustrates the **Crucifixion** but, in this case, Jerusalem has been replaced by the upper town as it looked in the 17C.

86

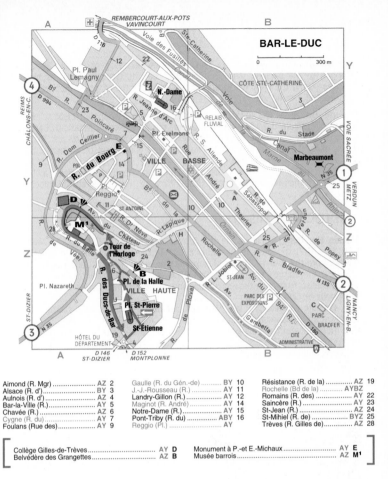

BAR-LE-DUC

0   300 m

Place de la Halle – It is possible to get a glimpse of the arcades of the former covered market through the gateway of no 3, which has a beautiful Baroque façade, unfortunately damaged.

Take rue Chavée and turn right.

Belvédère des Grangettes – This viewpoint offers a pleasant view of the lower town, from the industrial district to the hillside along the River Ornain.

Return to rue Chavée and turn right onto rue de l'Armurier then left onto rue de l'Horloge.

The **clock tower** is all that remains of the former ducal castle. The face, restored in 1994, now looks exactly as it did in the 14C.

Rue de l'Horloge on the left leads to avenue du Château; turn left. From the Esplanade du Château, there is a fine view down to the Romanesque gate and the ruins of the fortifications (on your left before you reach rue Gilles-de-Trèves).

Collège Gilles-de-Trèves – The university college was founded in 1571 by the dean of St-Maxe, Gilles de Trèves, who wished to prevent young aristocrats from going to other universities where the ideas of the Reformation were gaining ground.

The Renaissance façade was remodelled in the 19C but the inner courtyard remained intact. Access is through a long porch with decorated vaulting bearing the inscription in Latin: "Let this house remain standing until ants have drunk the oceans dry and tortoises have gone all the way round the world".

Galleries supported by pillars surround the courtyard. Note the balustrades decorated with complex carvings which could be Flemish.

Continue along rue du Baile.

Rue des Ducs-de-Bar – This former aristocratic high street of the upper town has retained a number of beautiful façades. **No 41**, an interesting example of local 16C architecture, has two friezes decorated with military motifs. **No 47** has retained its gargoyles. At **no 53**, the main door is framed with carved arcading. The façade of **no 73** is adorned with added panels illustrating musical instruments. In a building at the end of the courtyard of **no 75**, there is a 15C **winepress**.

The street is closed at one end by the façade of the Hôtel de Salm.

VILLE BASSE

Château de Marbeaumont – This early-20C extravagant castle, which once belonged to the bankers Varin-Bernier, was used by General Pétain as his headquarters during the First World War. It lies at the centre of a vast park with sports facilities and a camp site.

Rue du Bourg – The lower town was essentially a shopping district, the high street being, from the 16C onwards, one of the most elegant streets of Bar-le-Duc, as some richly decorated façades still testify today (**nos 42, 46, 49** and **51**). **No 26**, dating from 1618, has window frames adorned with busts of women and sirens and a fine carved wooden door.

On the corner of rue du Bourg and rue Maginot, a monument picturing a child and a bicycle commemorates Pierre and Ernest Michaux, who invented the velocipede in 1861.

ADDITIONAL SIGHTS

Musée Barrois ⊘ – Housed in the former tax office (1523) and the new castle built in 1567, the museum contains a rich archaeological collection covering the period from the Bronze Age to Merovingian times with many Gallo-Roman exhibits including the statue of a goddess from Naix-aux-Forges (Nasium), the stela of an eye specialist from Montiers-sur-Saulx and some Merovingian jewellery from the necropolis at Gondrecourt.

The **Chambre du Trésor**, a late-15C hall surmounted by ribbed vaulting, houses medieval and Renaissance sculptures (Pierre de Milan, Gérard Richier).

The museum also contains paintings of the French and Flemish Schools (Heindrick de Clerck, David Teniers Junior and Jan Steen), a collection of 16C and 17C weapons and armours, a collection of ethnography and local-history exhibits.

Église Notre-Dame – This Romanesque church was restored and remodelled in the 17C following a fire; the steeple dates from the 18C.

In the nave there is a Christ on the Cross by Ligier Richier. A late-15C low-relief sculpture in the south-transept chapel depicts the Immaculate Conception: the Virgin, praying beneath God the Father, is surrounded by the symbols of her purity.

EXCURSION

Rembercourt-aux-Pots – *18km/11mi. Drive N out of Bar-le-Duc along D 116 towards Vavincourt.*

The 15C village **church** has a magnificent **west front** in a successful blend of Flamboyant and Renaissance styles. Admire the wealth of decoration, the shell-shaped recesses and the pagan motifs of the Renaissance frieze. The two towers were never completed. The interior conveys an impression of unity.

BAR-SUR-AUBE

Population 6 705
Michelin map 61 fold 19 or 241 fold 38

Situated on the east bank of the River Aube, the town is surrounded by a ring of boulevards, laid on the site of the former ramparts, and has retained many old stone and timber-framed houses.

In medieval times, an important fair took place in Bar-sur-Aube; the region was a lively trading centre at the crossroads of southern and northern Europe.

Today, the town thrives on the Champagne trade.

SIGHTS

Hôtel de ville – The town hall is housed in the former Ursuline convent (1634), where young ladies were educated.

Rue d'Aube – The post office (nos 16 and 18) is housed in a fine 18C mansion with beautiful wrought-iron balconies. No 15 is another 18C house; note the late-18C railing at no 32. No 33 dates from the end of the 16C, whereas no 44 is a Renaissance house with a rounded arch over the door, surmounted by a triangular pediment underlined by a dentil.

Turn left onto rue Jeanne-de-Navarre.

Église St-Maclou – This former chapel of the counts of Bar's castle was built in the 11C and given a Classical front in the 18C. The steeple was the castle's keep. Traces of the portcullis can still be seen.

Walk round the right side of the church.

Eating out

MODERATE

Le Cellier Aux Moines – *R. du Gén.-Vouillemont* – ☎ *03 25 27 08 01* – *closed Sun evening, Mon evening and Tue evening* – *98/175F.* Eating in this vaulted restaurant is a pleasant experience, particularly as the food is good and the prices reasonable. This former storeroom served as headquarters during the 1912 rebellion when the local wine-growers fought to keep the Champagne appellation.

La Toque Baralbine – *18 r. Nationale* – ☎ *03 25 27 20 34* – *closed 15-31 Jan, Sun evening and Mon* – *99/280F.* The slogan outside this town-centre restaurant rightly promises happiness, refinement and pleasure. You will enjoy carefully prepared fresh local products in a classic, understated setting.

Where to stay

MID-RANGE

Moulin du Landion – *R. St-Léger* – *10200 Dolancourt* – *9km/5.6mi NW of Bar-sur-Aube on N 19 towards Troyes* – ☎ *03 25 27 92 17* – *closed 1 Dec-15 Feb* – **P**– *16 rooms 390/460F* – ⌷ *50F* – *restaurant 110/326F.* Peace and quiet reign supreme in this old half-timbered mill. The rooms open onto a landscaped park, while the picture windows of the two-storied restaurant overlook the huge paddle wheel and the millstream. Lovely open-air swimming pool.

A small circular window in the east end made it possible for the Blessed Sacrament to be visible even at night.

Continue along rue Mailly.

Note the elaborate doorway of the *sous-préfecture* building, a former salt store-house.

Walk across rue Nationale, the town's lively shopping street.

At no 14, the deconsecrated Chapelle St-Jean, dating from the 11C and 12C, once belonged to the Order of St John.

Follow rue St-Jean then turn left onto rue du Général-Vouillemont.

Cellier aux Moines ⊘ – Situated near the east end of the church, this former town house of the monks of Clairvaux *(now a restaurant)* has retained a fine 13C cellar, covered with ribbed vaulting; it was used as their headquarters by the local wine-growers during the 1911 rebellion which enabled the Bar area to continue to give its wine-production the name of Champagne.

★**Église St-Pierre** ⊘ – The west front and south side of this 12C church are lined with a covered gallery (making it look like a *halle* or covered market, hence its name Halloy). Ribbed vaulting was later built over the nave and aisles and the chapels were added in the 16C. The high altar was originally in Clairvaux Abbey and the organ in Remiremont Abbey. Some 50 tombstones mark the graves of local lords and wealthy merchants. The 15C polychrome stone statue, known as the *Virgin with the flowers*, is typical of the work produced by the School of Troyes.

Bibliothèque – *13 rue St-Pierre.* The library is housed in the early-17C Hôtel de Brienne.

Walk round the building to admire its Renaissance façade with mullioned windows.

Turn left onto rue Thiers, which has retained some timber-framed houses (note the old carved beam at no 8).

Cross rue Nationale again and follow the narrow rue de la Paume and rue du Poids to return to the town hall.

EXCURSIONS

Chapelle Ste-Germaine – *4km/2.5mi. Leave Bar-sur-Aube by D 4, SW of the town, 3km/1.9mi further on, turn left in a bend onto a steep path and continue on foot.* The path leads to a pilgrimage chapel dedicated to Germaine, a virgin martyred by the Vandals in 407. Walk beyond the chapel and around the house to reach the viewing table which offers glimpses of Bar-sur-Aube, the valley, Colombey-les-Deux-Églises and its cross of Lorraine, as well as the Dhuits and Clairvaux forests.

⚑ Hikers might prefer to walk all the way to the chapel: beyond the bridge on the River Aube, take rue Pierre-Brossolette then continue straight on alongside the *lycée* (secondary school) and follow the path climbing through the woods *(30min)* up to the chapel.

La Rivière Enchantée

Nigloland ⊙ – *9km/5.6mi. Leave Bar-sur-Aube NW by N 19 to Dolancourt.*

◉ This leisure park, in a green setting, offers some 15 attractions including quiet trips in a vintage car dating from 1900, aboard the small train or along the meandering enchanted river. Those who enjoy a thrill will appreciate the Gold Mine Train or the Canadian River. Do not miss the cinema show on the 180° screen or the presentation of the Niglo Company (electronic automata) staged in the theatre of the Canadian Village. A balloon ride enables visitors to get an overall view of the park.

Shops and restaurants make it possible to spend the whole day in the park.

Soulaines-Dhuys – *18km/11.2mi N along D 384.* Follow the white and yellow markings to explore this charming village through which flows the River Laines *(brochure available at the tourist office).* The local tile factory produces tiles decorated with medieval motifs. The village also has a number of fine timber-framed houses (one of them dates from the 13C) and kitchen gardens, a chapel with timber-framed overhang and a 16C church. The Dhuys reappears near the village mill.

Bayel – *7.5km/4.7mi SE along D 396.* Bayel is famous for its prestigious **crystal-works** ⊙ founded in 1666 by the Venitian glass-blower Jean-Baptiste Mazzolay. A mixture of sand, lime, soda and lead heated for 12hr in special ovens to a temperature of 1 450°C/2 642°F produces a kind of paste which is ready to be shaped by blowing or casting; all the items are handmade.

Those who are unable to tour the factory can visit the **Écomusée du centre Mazzolay** ⊙, housed in three small workers' cottages *(entrance through the tourist office).* By means of a series of models, the centre offers an insight into the origins of glass, its various components, the manufacturing process and the different methods used to decorate glass: by guilloche, engraving... A video cassette *(17min)* about the crystalworks, the town and the surrounding area rounds up the visit.

The plain **church** contains a moving 16C polychrome stone **Pietà★**: Mary's simple attitude, the realism of her features and the perfection of the sculpture's outline as well as the harmonious folds of her garment, all point to the work of the Master of Chaource, who also sculpted the famous St Martha housed in the Église Ste-Madeleine in Troyes *(see TROYES)*; a fine 14C Virgin with Child decorates an altar along the north aisle.

Colombé-le-Sec – *About 10km/6mi NE.* The village has retained an interesting wash-house, thought to date back to the 12C. Although remodelled in the 16C, the church still has a Romanesque lintel, decorated with a Greek cross surrounded by an Easter lamb and a wolf.

The nearby **Ferme du Cellier** ⊙ is a farm built in the 16C over 12C Cistercian cellars, which belonged to Clairvaux Abbey *(see Abbaye de CLAIRVAUX)*.

BITCHE

Population 5 517
Michelin map 57 fold 18 or 242 fold 11

Founded in the 17C and lying at the foot of its famous citadel which used to guard one of the main routes through the Vosges, Bitche offers a rather unusual town plan with its main street following the outline of the imposing citadel.

LAKE-SIDE CHALET

Auberge du Lac – *2km/1mi SE of Bitche, at Lake Hasselfurth –* ☎ *03 87 96 27 27 – closed Feb, Tue except lunchtime Jul-Aug, and Wed – 115/295F.* This chalet-like restaurant on the edge of Lake Hasselfurth is not all that easy to find, but once there, you can enjoy simple regional cooking in a peaceful, natural setting. Terrace.

★CITADEL ⊘

1hr 30min

Rebuilt by Vauban c 1680, subsequently dismantled, then rebuilt once more between 1741 and 1754, the citadel successfully repelled Prussian attacks in 1793 and 1870-71. Today, there remain the impressive walls of red sandstone (visible from afar above the dense trees), and the underground structure. The citadel was intended for a garrison of about 1 000 men.

Walk up the ramp and through the vaulted passageway of the northern entrance towards the top mound crowned by a flagpole *(30min on foot there and back)*. There is a panoramic view of Bitche and the wooded heights surrounding the town. It is possible, with a pair of binoculars, to spot some of the armoured domes of the Simserhof structure, which formed part of the Maginot Line. All along the way, as you walk through the maize of galleries and casemates (kitchens, hospital, underground guard-room, officers' quarters), slides, laser sounds and even smells vividly recreate the siege of the 1870-71 War.

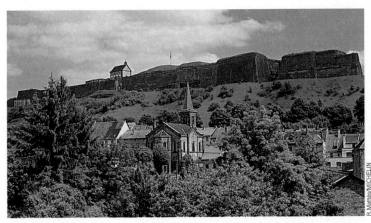

The citadel stands above the town

EXCURSIONS

Reyersviller – *5km/3mi W along N 62.* Just beyond the village on the right stands the impressive **Swedish oak**, said to be more than 400 years old. According to legend, the invading Swedes used it as a gallows during the Thirty Years War.

★Simserhof – *See Ligne MAGINOT.*

Ossuaire de Schorbach – *6km/3.7mi NW along D 962 and D 162[B] to the left.* Near the church there is a small ossuary with Romanesque arcading through which a pile of bones can be seen.

Volmunster – *11km/6.8mi NW along D 35[A] and D 34.* The Église St-Pierre, destroyed during the Second World War, was rebuilt in 1957. The tympanum of the doorway is decorated with a 70m²/84sq yd mosaic depicting Peter as a fisherman.

BOURBONNE-LES-BAINS♨♨

Population 2 764
Michelin map 62 folds 13 and 14 or 242 fold 33

Already known in Roman times, this spa resort overlooking the Apance Valley became very popular between the 16C and 18C. The three hot springs are used in the treatment of rheumatism, arthritis, fractures, osteoporosis and respiratory complaints.

Where to stay and eating out

MODERATE

Hôtel des Sources – *Pl. des Bains* – ☎ *03 25 87 86 00* – *closed Dec-Mar* – *23 rooms 250/300F* – 😋 *35F* – *restaurant 75/200F*. No effort is spared to make you feel comfortable in this hotel near the baths. The bedrooms and dining room are decorated in subtle colours; the latter opens onto a pleasant terrace. Tasty dishes to tempt spa patrons.

Chambre d'hôte Ferme Adrien – *Rte du Val-de-la-Maljoie – 52400 Coiffy-le-Haut – 10km/6.3mi SW of Bourbonne-les-Bains on D 26* – ☎ *03 25 90 06 76* – 🖃 – *5 rooms 180/220F* – *evening meal 75F*. What a treat to stay on this farm, dating from 1845 and surrounded by valleys, meadows and forests! Among its attractions are its massive fireplace in the dining room, its antique furniture and its little rural life museum.

MID-RANGE

Hôtel Jeanne d'Arc – *R. de l'Amiral-Pierre* – ☎ *03 25 90 46 00* – *closed 1 Nov-14 Mar* – 🅿 – *29 rooms 300/350F* – 😋 *45F* – *restaurant 98/190F*. Right next to the baths; enjoy the quiet and the light. Comfortable rooms, really lovely terrace. Open-air swimming pool and solarium to add to your well-being. Classic menu and carefully prepared dishes.

Quartier thermal – The hydrotherapy establishment was entirely renovated in 1978 to the highest standard and the former military hydrotherapy hospital, the first one of its kind to be built in France (1732) has been turned into a hotel and entertainment centre (lectures, shows, various activities...).
The **Parc des Thermes** (Gallo-Roman remains) and **Parc d'Orfeuil** offer peace and quiet, walking facilities and relaxation.

Ville haute – The gatehouse of the former early-16C fortress marks the entrance to the park of the castle. The **museum** ⊙, housed in the outbuildings, contains 19C paintings by René-Xavier Prinet, Georges Freset and Horace Vernet *(the Fall of Constantine)* as well as temporary exhibitions in summer. The **castle**, a fine residence built on the site of the former stronghold and bequeathed to the town as a gesture of gratitude for treatment received, houses the town hall. There is a fine view of the lower part of the town and the valley. The early-13C Église Notre-Dame-de-l'Assomption houses a graceful 14C marble statue of the Virgin Mary.
The **Arboretum de Montmorency** is an English-style park containing 250 species of trees from five continents.

EXCURSIONS

Abbaye de Morimond – *16km/9.9mi NW*. This Cistercian abbey is the fourth house founded by the Abbaye de Cîteaux in 1115. Owing to its favourable geographical position on the border of Champagne and Lorraine, it spearheaded the expansion of the Cistercian order in Germany (in the 13C, 213 abbeys were dependent on Morimond).
In this remote dale, only part of the gatehouse and the Chapelle Ste-Ursule remain; the chapel was remodelled in the 17C, and recently restored. Nearby, the Morimond Forest is the subject of mysterious legends; a path leads to a quiet pond.

Tour of the vineyards

27km/16.8mi – allow 1hr
Drive south-west out of Bourbonne-les-Bains along D 417.

Villars-St-Marcellin – This hillside village is overlooked by its 12C church, restored in the 19C. The Merovingian crypt contains an 8C sarcophagus believed to be that of St Marcellin.

Drive south-west along a narrow road to rejoin D 460 in Genrupt and continue to Montcharvot. Turn right onto D 130 to Coiffy.

Coiffy-le-Haut – The village is famous for the surrounding vineyards which produce quality table wines known as *vins de pays des coteaux de Coiffy*. Destroyed by phylloxera at the end of the 19C, the vineyards reappeared almost a century later and now produce red and white wines. From the village, there are fine overall views of the vineyards and the surrounding deep vales.

Coiffy-le-Bas – Separated from Coiffy-le-Haut by a few rows of vines, this village has retained some old houses including the town hall (16C gate and bartizan).
Follow D 158 then D 26.

Parc animalier de la Bannie ⊘ – *3.5km/2.2mi SW along D 26.*
Deer, does and moufflons roam freely in this 100ha/247-acre park; numerous species of birds can be admired in the park's aviaries.
Return to Bourbonne-les-Bains along D 158.

BRIENNE-LE-CHÂTEAU
Population 3 752
Michelin map 61 folds 8 and 18 or 241 fold 38

Brienne lies across a flat area, close to the River Aube, within the Parc naturel régional de la Forêt d'Orient. The town is now a major supplier of cabbage for sauerkraut; one quarter of the cabbages of France are grown here. A festival celebrating *la choucroute au champagne* (sauerkraut cooked in Champagne) takes place on the third Sunday in September.

Napoleon Bonaparte and Brienne – Napoleon Bonaparte was a student at the local military school from 1779 to 1784. During his stay, he excelled in mathematics and military exercise and was recommended for the military school in Paris. He returned briefly to Brienne in 1814, at the end of the Napoleonic Wars, when he attacked a coalition of Prussian and Russian troops. Later on, during his exile on the island of St Helena, he recalled with emotion his youthful years in Brienne and left the town a considerable sum of money.

SIGHTS *1hr*

Musée Napoléon ⊘ – Housed in the former military school, the museum contains mementoes of Napoleon and relates the various episodes of the French campaign of 1814.
The chapel houses an exhibit of the **Treasuries** of nearby churches in the Parc naturel régional de la Forêt d'Orient: sculptures, paintings, and gold plate.

Hôtel de ville – The sum of money bequeathed by Napoleon was partly used to build a town hall inaugurated in 1859; the pediment of the building bears the effigy of Napoleon surmounted by an eagle.

Church – The nave dates from the 14C and the chancel, surrounded by an ambulatory, from the 16C (lierne and tierceron vaulting); the Renaissance stained-glass windows depict interesting scenes: note the story of Noah on the left and the legend of St Crépin and St Crépinien on the right. The bell-shaped stoup goes back to the 16C whereas the christening fonts and the chancel railing date from the 18C.

Covered market – A market takes place regularly beneath the fine 13C timberwork which supports a large tiled roof.

★**Castle** – *Not open to the public.* The imposing white castle crowns the hill overlooking Brienne; built between 1770 and 1778 in typical Louis XVI style, it now houses a regional centre of psychotherapy and can only be seen through the railings of the main gate.
An alleyway leads past the 18C almshouse to the main entrance of the castle, an elegant building in Louis XVI style.

EXCURSIONS

Brienne-la-Vieille – *1km/0.6mi S of Brienne-le-Château along D 443.*
This port used to be the main timber supplier of the capital by the log-floating method. Rough timber would come by cart from the nearby forests of Orient, Temple and Clairvaux. The logs would then be tied together to form floats which would be guided by mariners down the River Aube, then the Seine until they reached Paris.

Écomusée ⊘ – Administered by the Parc naturel régional de la Forêt d'Orient, this museum devoted to the local environment includes the **Boutique** (former smithy which has been left as it was in 1903 and has retained the tools used at the time) and the **Maison des jours et des champs** (collection of tools and agricultural machinery showing the evolution of techniques between 1850 and 1950).

Rosnay-l'Hôpital – *9km/5.6mi N along D 396.*
The 16C **Église Notre-Dame** ⊘ stands on a once-fortified mound, on the banks of the River Voire. Walk along the left side of the church to reach the stairs leading to the vast **crypt**, erected in the 12C but rebuilt in the 16C at the same time as the church above it.

CHÂLONS-EN-CHAMPAGNE★★

Conurbation 61 452
Michelin map 56 folds 17 and 18 or 241 folds 25 and 26

Formerly known as Châlons-sur-Marne, the town recently resumed its original name of Châlons-en-Champagne.

Two canals, the Mau and the Nau, formed by small arms of the River Marne, meander through the town which is an important crossroads and agricultural market with several food industries (sugar refinery, Champagne wines). To the north-east, an industrial area covering 150ha/371 acres concentrates on agricultural equipment and chemicals.

Châlons is also an administrative and military centre: a number of 17C and 18C mansions confer on the city a certain bourgeois character which contrasts with the charm of its restored timber-framed houses and its old bridges spanning the Mau and the Nau. The banks of the Marne, lined with beautiful trees, form an attractive sight in the western part of the town.

HISTORICAL NOTES

Catalaunum (Châlons-en-Champagne) was an active Gallo-Roman city named after the Catalauni, a Gallic tribe Christianised in the 4C AD. In June 451, the Roman army under the command of General Aetius defeated the Huns led by their powerful chief **Attila**. The exact location of the battle is uncertain, but it was somewhere in the fields around the city of Catalaunum, hence the name of **Champs Catalauniques** which later became a symbol of deliverance from the Barbarian threat.

A site known as the Camp d'Attila, lying 15km/9.3mi north-east of Châlons, is said to be the place where the Huns camped on the eve of the battle.

During the Middle Ages, the town became an important centre administered by bishops who took an active part in the coronation ceremonies in Reims *(see REIMS p 263)*.

During the Wars of Religion, the town remained loyal to the king who declared it to be the "main town of the Champagne region": it became the seat of an annexe of the Paris Parliament and, in 1789, the main administrative town of the Marne *département*.

In 1856, a vast military camp was created near the town and a special pavilion was built for **Napoleon III** who often came to watch manoeuvres and trials of new weapons as well as to perfect the education of the imperial prince.

TOWN WALK

Quartier de la Préfecture

Start from place Foch overlooked by the town hall and the north side of the Église St-Alpin.

Hôtel de ville – The town hall was designed in 1771 by Nicolas Durand; the main hall is Doric and the wedding hall is adorned with Louis XVI pilasters of a colossal order.

Bibliothèque ⊙ – The library is housed in a beautiful 17C residence, once the home of the governors of the city. It was raised by one storey in the 19C. It holds some precious manuscripts and books *(not on display)* such as the **Roman de la Rose**, a famous 13C allegory in medieval French, and Queen Marie-Antoinette's book of prayers bearing her farewell to her children, written on the day of her execution.

Walk through the Henri-Vendel passageway. Note the former doorway of the Église St-Loup at the end of the courtyard and numerous cast-iron plaques along the passageway.

Return to rue d'Orfeuil and continue along rue de Chastillon.

Rue de Chastillon – The street was lined with workshops. Even numbers were occupied by well-off people whereas odd numbers were lived in by manual workers. Note the fine late-16C doorway of no 2, a mansion dating from 1738, the stone-and-brick building at no 10 and the contrasting timber-framed houses at nos 14 and 16.

Turn left onto rue de Jessaint which crosses the Mau.

Couvent Ste-Marie – The back of the 17C convent, overlooking the Mau, is built with a mixture of white limestone and red brick whereas the façade is decorated with fluted pilasters.

Cross rue Carnot and follow rue Vinetz.

A steep passageway leads to **place du Forum-de-l'Europe**; the square is surrounded by old buildings (gallery and timber-framed façade of the Couvent de Vinetz) and by modern ones (county archives), which are fine examples of style blending in an urban environment.

Eating out

MODERATE

Salon de thé Philippe Génin – *27 pl. de la République* – ☎ *03 26 21 46 63 – closed 1-20 Aug and Mon – 85F.* The shop window of this restored local-style house is a real invitation to overindulgence. Enjoy a light lunch of salads, pies and pastries in this tearoom.

Le Chaudron Savoyard – *9 r. des Poissonniers* – ☎ *03 26 68 00 32 – closed 23 Jul-13 Aug, Sat lunchtime and Mon – 98/110F.* Don't be fooled by the Champagne-style façade of the building; here the cooking is devoted to the Savoy region. It can be savoured in two dining rooms: one on the ground floor with exposed beams, and one on the first floor, where the atmosphere is more reminiscent of the mountains.

MID-RANGE

Le Pré St-Alpin – *2 bis r. de l'Abbé-Lambert* – ☎ *03 26 70 20 26 – closed Sun evening – 130/235F.* Good food to be enjoyed in the attractive setting of a 1900 bourgeois town house which has retained all its former charm. Two dining rooms have decorated glass roofs, another is panelled, and on the first floor are two further Edwardian-style dining rooms with pretty blue lace curtains.

Ferme-auberge des Moissons – *8 rte Nationale – 51510 Matougues – 12km/7.5mi W of Châlons on the Épernay road (D 3)* – ☎ *03 26 70 99 17 – www.des-moissons.com – closed Jan, 15-31 Aug, open Sat evening and Sun lunchtime – booking essential – 120F.* Those who enjoy good food will appreciate the home-raised chickens, ducks, rabbits and turkeys. After a hearty meal, don't miss the small farm museum, or a visit to the stables, the garden and the farmyard.

Where to stay

MODERATE

Hôtel Bristol – *77 av. Pierre-Sémard* – ☎ *03 26 68 24 63 – closed during Christmas holidays –* 🅿 *– 24 rooms 240/290F –* ☕ *35F.* If you need a stopover between Troyes and Épernay, this modern, family-run hotel just outside Châlons has spacious, simple rooms.

MID-RANGE

Hôtel Le Pot d'Étain – *18 pl. de la République* – ☎ *03 26 68 09 09 – 27 rooms 300/350F –* ☕ *50F.* Light, freshly decorated rooms and the warmth of a wood fire and leather armchairs will all contribute to the peace and pleasure of your stay. Not to mention the crispy breakfast pastries...

Hôtel d'Angleterre – *19 pl. Mgr-Tissier* – ☎ *03 26 68 21 51 – closed 2-9 Mar, 16 Jul-8 Aug, Christmas holidays, Sat lunchtime and Sun –* 🅿 *– 18 rooms 450/750F –* ☕ *80F – restaurant 180/470F.* Close by the superb Gothic façade of Notre-Dame-en-Vaux, this is a lovely traditional hotel, without being over luxurious. The soundproofed, air-conditioned rooms are attractively furnished. Fine contemporary cooking will delight lovers of good food.

LUXURY

Aux Armes de Champagne – *51460 L'Épine – 8-5km/5.3mi NE of Châlons-en-Champagne on N 3* – ☎ *03 26 69 30 30 – closed 5 Jan-13 Feb, Sun evening and Mon Nov-Mar –* 🅿 *– 37 rooms from 530F –* ☕ *70F – restaurant 240/525F.* Treat yourself to a little peace and pleasure! All the rooms in this opulent, flower-decked inn opposite Notre-Dame-de-l'Épine have a personal touch. The food is carefully prepared by the young chef, who favours Mediterranean-style recipes. Fresh, home-grown produce.

The former **Couvent de Vinetz**, built in the late 17C, now houses the **Hôtel du Département**, the administrative headquarters of the *département*. The façade of the chapel was built to look like a triumphal arch.
Return to rue Carnot.

Préfecture – The Préfecture occupies the former residence of the royal treasurers of the Champagne region, built between 1759 and 1766; the architects Legendre and Durand's design already points to Louis XVI's sober style. **Marie-Antoinette**, who stopped here on her way to marry the heir to the French throne, came back later, during the Revolution, humiliated after she failed to escape with the king and their children and was arrested in Varennes *(see ARGONNE: Varennes-en-Argonne).*

Porte Ste-Croix – This triumphal gateway, erected in 1770 to welcome **Marie-Antoinette**, arriving in France to marry the future Louis XVI, was formerly known as the Porte Dauphine; it was never completed (only one side is decorated with carvings). Beyond the gate, opposite the **Hôtel de Région** (regional administrative headquarters), stands a bronze column by the sculptor Ipoustéguy, dedicated to **Nicolas Appert** (1749-1841), a native of Châlons who invented a method of preserving food.

Le Jard

This former grazing field, which formed part of the bishop's estates, was a convenient meeting place. St Bernard probably preached here in 1147 as no doubt did Pope Eugene III who consecrated the church the same year.
Laid in the 18C, the park is crossed by avenue du Maréchal-Leclerc. It is divided into three sections:

Ph.Gajic/MICHELIN

A turret on the Château du Marché

– the **Petit Jard**, a landscaped garden in the Napoleon III style, with a flower clock, laid on the site of the former ramparts. It extends along the banks of the Nau across which stands the Porte d'Eau of the **Château du Marché**, a fortified construction which has retained a 16C turret;
– the **Grand Jard**, a vast esplanade lined with chestnut trees; from the footbridge linking it to the Jardin Anglais across the canal running along the River Marne, there are pleasant **views** of the cathedral and the Préfecture;
– the **Jardin anglais**, an English-style garden laid along the banks of the Marne in 1817.

SIGHTS

★★ **Cathédrale St-Étienne** ⊘ – Before the Revolution, a cloister, attached to the cathedral, stood on the site of the present square. Two royal marriages took place here during the reign of Louis XIV.

Exterior – The north side is in pure Gothic style: the nave, lined with high buttresses supporting double-course flying buttresses, has tall lancet windows; the transept is adorned with an attractive rose window and flanked by a tower with a Romanesque base which belonged to the previous cathedral destroyed by fire in 1230. The massive west portal dates from the 17C.

Interior – The edifice is nearly 100m/110yd long and looks quite imposing in spite of its relatively short chancel. Daylight pours generously into the 27m/89ft high nave which looks particularly elegant with its graceful triforium surmounted by large windows. The west front and the two bays closest to it were erected in 1628 in strict Gothic style.
The cathedral has retained an interesting number of **stained-glass windows**★, which make it possible to follow the progress of the art of stained-glass making between the 12C and 16C, as well as a few works of art in the transept and the chancel.
– In the chancel stands an imposing baldaquined high altar, dating from the 17C and believed to be the work of Jules Hardouin-Mansart; note the superb Gothic tombstones set all around the chancel. The stained-glass windows above the high altar, dating from the 13C, depict Christ in glory, the Crucifixion and the Holy Mother, accompanied by saints, apostles and prophets.
– Two chapels on the right of the ambulatory contain a 15C painting on wood showing the consecration of the cathedral, Christ restrained by bonds (16C) and Christ in his tomb (17C low-relief sculpture).

Treasury ⊘ – Housed in the lower part of the Romanesque tower adjacent to the north transept, it contains three restored 12C stained-glass panels (representing the Crucifixion and the discovery of St Stephen's relics), a 12C christening font decorated with a carving representing the Resurrection of the Dead and a piece of St Bernard's wicker mat.

★**Église Notre-Dame-en-Vaux** ⊘ – This former collegiate church was built in Romanesque style at the beginning of the 12C, but the vaulting, the chancel and the east end, dating from the late 12C and early 13C, are fine examples of the Early Gothic style. The austere Romanesque west front, flanked by two towers surmounted by lead-covered spires, is reflected in the waters of the Mau Canal; the east end with its ambulatory and radiating chapels is enhanced by two Romanesque towers *(stand on the far side of place Monseigneur-Tissier in order to get a good overall view)*. The 15C south porch precedes a Romanesque doorway; the statue columns were mutilated during the Revolution, but the capitals, which were spared, are interesting. There is a peal of 56 bells.

A garden, situated on the north side of the church *(not open to the public)* marks the site of the former cloister.

Enter the church through the south doorway.

The harmonious proportions and simplicity of the **interior**★★ are quite impressive. In the nave, there is a marked contrast between the pillars topped by Romanesque capitals and supporting vast galleries and the pointed Gothic vaulting. The chancel is characteristic of the region's architectural style.

The nave is lit by a harmonious set of **stained-glass windows**★. The finest, dating from the 16C, are on the north side.

Walk up the north aisle starting from the west doorway:

Second bay: the legend of St James (1525) by the master glass-maker from Picardie, Mathieu Bléville, illustrates the battle which took place in 1212 between Christians and Moors (the pilgrims' route to Santiago de Compostela went through Châlons);

Third bay: the Dormition and Coronation of the Blessed Virgin, red and gold symbolising her glory; dated 1526 under the effigy of the donators;

Ph. Gajic/MICHELIN

Inside Notre-Dame-en-Vaux

Fourth and fifth bays: legends of St Anne and Mary; Christ's childhood;

Sixth bay: The Compassion of the Virgin Mary, against a blue background dotted with silver stars, is illustrated by a Deposition, a *Pietà* and Mary Magdalene (1526).

Walk round the church to rue Nicolas-Durand where the entrance of the Musée du cloître de Notre-Dame-en-Vaux is situated. The late-15C **Maison Clémangis**, opposite the entrance, is used for exhibitions.

★**Musée du cloître de Notre-Dame-en-Vaux** ⊘ – The cloister museum contains some remarkable sculptures from a Romanesque cloister, discovered in 1960. Built in the 12C next to Notre-Dame-en-Vaux, it was demolished in 1759 by the canons who replaced it with their own quarters. Excavations in the immediate surroundings have made it possible to recreate part of this splendid cloister.

A vast room contains sections of the former fortified wall, the reconstruction of four arcades framed by pillars as well as several valuable exhibits such as carved or ringed columns and **55 statue columns**★★: the finest depict prophets, famous biblical characters or saints (Moses, Daniel, Simon and Jesus as a child, St Paul whose face has a wonderful spiritual expression), characters from the Old Testament and from the Middle Ages (kings of Judea, 12C knights in full gear, and the governor of Antioch, Olibrius, torturing St Margaret). The transition from the Romanesque to the Gothic style is emphasized by the expressive features of the characters, and the tendency for some of them to be separate from the column. Note a group of storiated capitals depicting episodes of Christ's life and the saints' legends. The four sides of one capital illustrate in succession the Presentation in the Temple, the Flight to Egypt, Jesus' Christening and the Resurrection of Lazarus. Another capital depicts the Wedding at Cana.

Musée municipal ⊘ – The town museum is organised on two floors.

Ground floor: reconstruction of a typical interior from the Champagne region (mid 19C), collection of Hindu deities (16C-17C), 13C recumbent figure of Blanche de Navarre, Countess of Champagne, 15C Head of Christ from the rood screen of Notre-Dame-en-Vaux, three polychrome wooden altarpieces, including one carved around 1500, representing the Passion, and a Head of St John the Baptist by Rodin.

CHÂLONS-EN-CHAMPAGNE

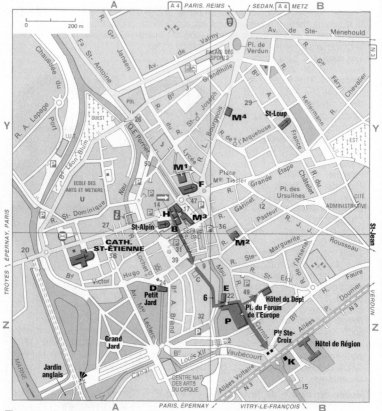

First floor: local archaeological finds from the Paleolithic period to the 17C; the Gallic period is particularly interesting. The fine arts gallery contains paintings from the 14C to the 20C: *Winter Landscape* by Josse de Momper (16C), *Gazotte's Portrait* by Perronneau (18C), *Self-portrait* by Nonotte (18C), *Park of St-Cloud Castle* by Daubigny and several works by the local painter, Antral (20C).
The ornithological collection includes some 3 000 birds mostly from Europe.
The last room contains furniture (16C-20C) and tapestries (15C-17C).

Église St-Alpin ⊙ – Surrounded by houses on its north and east sides, the church, built between the 12C and 16C, is a mixture of Flamboyant Gothic and Renaissance styles. In the chapels of the south aisle, there are **Renaissance windows** with magnificent *grisaille* stained glass representing the Bishop of Châlons, St Alpin, before Attila (first chapel), Emperor Augustus before the Sibyl of Tibur (third chapel), St John the Baptist (sixth chapel) and, in the south transept, the Miracle of the Loaves and Fishes, and the Miracle at Cana. The precious 15C stained-glass windows of the ambulatory have been restored.

The church contains fine works of art: in the north aisle there is a lovely *Christ of Mercy* from the 16C French School; in the nave there are several carved tombstones, including one going back to the 13C, and the gallery houses an organ case dating from 1762.

Musée Garinet ⊘ – This ancient partly Gothic mansion houses a 19C bourgeois interior, enhanced by paintings from the 14C to 19C; particularly remarkable is the *Flagellation* attributed to Preti and *Ruth strolling in Booz's fields* by Cabanel (in the red room). The second floor contains a collection of some 100 models of French churches and cathedrals.

Église St-Loup ⊘ – The church has a neo-Gothic façade dating from 1886. The 15C nave houses a triptych depicting the Adoration of the Magi, attributed to Van Eyck *(second bay on the left)*, a 16C statue of St Christopher in painted wood *(third bay on the right)*, and a 17C painting by Vouet illustrating the Death of Mary Magdalene *(above the sacristy door)*.

Église St-Jean – *Access via rue Jean-Jacques-Rousseau.*
The raised area in front of the church allows access to the west part rebuilt in the 14C. The west front flanked by buttresses, is surmounted by a pointed pediment decorated with 17C vases with flames coming out of them. The crossing is surmounted by a massive quadrangular steeple. In the 15C, a small chapel, known as the Crossbowmen's Chapel, was built off the south aisle: the Romanesque nave, covered with wood-panelled barrel vaulting, ends with a raised chancel and a flat apse. The stained-glass windows date from the 19C.

Musée Schiller-et-Goethe ⊘ – The collections were donated to the museum in 1952 by Baroness von Gleichen-Russwurm, the widow of Schiller's great-grandson. They include Meissen and Wedgwood porcelain, vases, clocks, furniture and clothes having belonged to the German poet, together with a model of Schiller's monument by Thorvaldsen in Stuttgart. There are also a few mementoes of Goethe who was a friend of Schiller. The last room contains a bronze statue by Ernest Dagonet depicting the *Marseillaise*.

EXCURSION

★★**Basilique Notre-Dame de l'Épine** – *8km/5mi E along N 3*. This basilica, which is as large as a cathedral, has been an important place of pilgrimage since the Middle Ages, when shepherds discovered a statue of the Virgin in a burning thorn bush. Built in the early 15C and gradually extended, the edifice has a Flamboyant Gothic west front and radiating chapels dating from the 16C.

Exterior – The richly decorated west front comprises three doorways surmounted by pointed gables (the highest of these bears a crucifix) and topped by openwork spires; the south spire (55m/180ft high) is ringed by a crown made up of fleurs-de-lis; as for the north spire, demolished in 1798 to make room for a telegraph installation, it was rebuilt in 1868.
Stand a short distance from the doorways to admire the successive levels bearing pinnacles, small spires and gargoyles. The kings' gallery is decorated with 28 statues representing Christ's royal descent.
Walk along the south side of the church to observe the numerous realistic **gargoyles**★ at

Curious characters

closer range: they symbolise the vices and evil spirits expelled from the church by the presence of God. They were restored in the 19C and those which were considered too obscene were destroyed. The doorway of the south transept, with deeply splayed sides, is framed by polygonal turrets and adorned with carved draperies similar to those of the main doorway of Reims Cathedral; the lintel is decorated with carved scenes depicting the Life of John the Baptist. Large rings, set in the stone on either side of the doorway, were used to tie horses; note the Gothic inscription for the attention of travellers: "Good people who are passing by, pray to God on behalf of the deceased".

Interior – It expresses without exaggeration the refined perfection of Gothic architecture. The chancel is closed off by an elegant **rood screen** dating from the late 15C (note the 14C statue of the Virgin under the right-hand arcade) and by a stone screen which is Gothic on the right side and Renaissance on the left. Above the rood screen, a monumental 16C rood beam bears a crucifix flanked by the Virgin and St John.

In the north transept, there is a well which is supposed to have been used during the building of the basilica.

Walking round the chancel (starting from the north side) you will see a Gothic **tabernacle-reliquary** with Renaissance ornamentation, and a small oratory where it was possible for pilgrims to touch the relics including a piece of the True Cross. Further on, a chapel houses a fine 16C **Entombment** by members of the Champagne School.

Routes du CHAMPAGNE★★★

Michelin map 56 folds 14-17 or 237 folds 21-23

The Champagne vineyards, known since ancient times, produce a type of wine famous throughout the world.

The reputation of the so-called Devil's Wine grew considerably from the 10C onwards, as a consequence of the fairs which took place during the 12C and 13C and, by the time the Renaissance came, it had spread beyond the borders of France. Yet, up to the 17C, Champagne was a predominantly red wine with a slight tendency to sparkle. According to tradition, modern Champagne was "invented" by Dom Pérignon, a monk from the Benedictine abbey of Hautvillers, who mixed various local wines. Success was almost immediate: kings, princes and European aristocrats elected Champagne as their favourite drink for festive occasions.

The great Champagne firms were set up in Reims and Épernay from the 18C onwards: Ruinart in 1729, Fourneaux (which later became Taittinger) in 1734, Moët in 1743, Clicquot in 1772, Mumm in 1827... Since then, Reims and Épernay have never ceased to prosper as tourists continue to enjoy winding their way through the Champagne vineyards.

★★CHAMPAGNE KINGDOM

1 Round tour starting from Montchenot

See Parc naturel régional de la MONTAGNE DE REIMS.

★★CÔTE DES BLANCS

2 From Épernay to Mont-Aimé

28km/17.4mi – allow 2hr

Stretching between Épernay and Vertus, the Côte des Blancs or Côte Blanche, owes its name to its white-grape vineyards consisting almost exclusively of Chardonnay vines. The refined grapes grown in the area are used to produce vintage and *blanc de blancs* (made solely from white grapes) Champagne.

The majority of the great Champagne firms own vineyards in this area; some of these are even equipped with a heating system to protect the vines from frost.

Like the Montagne de Reims, the Côte des Blancs is a bank sloping down from the edge of the Île-de-France cuesta, facing due east and almost entirely covered with vines. In front of this limestone cuesta stand outliers such as Mont Saran (239m/784ft) and Mont Aimé (240m/787ft).

The twisting lanes of the villages dotted along the slopes are lined with wine-growers' houses with their characteristic high doorways.

The road described below runs half way up the slopes, offering general and close-up views of the vineyards and the vast plain of Châlons.

★**Épernay** – *See ÉPERNAY.*

Leave Épernay S along D 951 and the Sézanne road to Pierry.

Pierry – The town hall now occupies the house where **Jacques Cazotte** lived; the author of *Le Diable amoureux* (the Devil in Love) was guillotined in 1792. A tour of the 18C Château de Pierry reveals reception rooms, small apartments, a wine-press museum and cellars dating from 1750.

In Pierry, turn left onto D 10.

This road offers views of Épernay and the Marne Valley on the left.

Where to stay

MODERATE

Chambre d'hôte Ferme du Grand Clos – *R. Jonquery – 51170 Ville-en-Tardenois – ☎ 03 26 61 83 78 – ⌷ – 4 rooms 220/290F.* In this old farm, built out of local stone, the rooms have been completely refurbished and include their own lounge area. A warm welcome and very reasonable prices make this a good place to stay on the Champagne route.

Chambre d'hôte Les Botterets – *7 r. du Fort – 51190 Oger – ☎ 03 26 57 94 78 – closed 20 Nov-28 Feb – ⌷ – 6 rooms 250/270F.* Recently renovated bed and breakfast rooms in two traditional village houses. The rather charmless decor is compensated by the friendly welcome.

Shopping

Breton et Fils – *12 r. Courte-Pilate – 51270 Congy – ☎ 03 26 59 31 03 – contact@champagne-breton-fils.fr – daily 9am-noon, 2-4.30pm – closed 3rd Sun in May, Christmas Day and 1 Jan.* This vineyard owner and grower will let you visit his cellars, which are typical of the Champagne region and, weather permitting, you may be lucky (or brave!) enough to fly over his vineyards by micro-light, one of the Breton family's hobbies.

Dehu Père & Fils – *3 r. St-Georges – 02650 Fossoy – ☎ 03 23 71 90 47 – varocien@aol.com – Mon-Sat by appointment only.* After visiting the pressing room and museum, which contains a collection of tools associated with the cultivation of vines and winemaking, you will be invited to a Champagne tasting.

F.P. Arnoult Coopérative vinicole – *Rte de Damery – 51480 Fleury-la-Rivière – ☎ 03 26 58 42 53 – Wed-Mon 10.30am-12.30pm, 2-6pm except Sun and public holidays 3-7pm.* The walls of this cooperative cellar are decorated with a superb 550m^2/658sq yd fresco, depicting the region's history. The tasting room, where home-made products are sold, boasts a magnificent view over the vineyard and the Marne Valley.

Henry de Vaugency – *1 r. d'Avize – 51190 Oger – ☎ 03 26 57 50 89 – www.mariage-et-champagne.com – Mon-Sat 9-11am, 2-6pm, Sun 3-6pm. Dec-Feb by appointment only.* This family, which has been making wine since 1732, combines Champagne and celebrations in a display of wedding souvenirs and a collection of wine labels tracing the history of Champagne from 1820 to 1940. The visit ends in the cellar, with the opportunity to taste a selection of the vintages.

Jean Milan – *6 rte d'Avize – 51190 Oger – ☎ 03 26 57 50 09 – Mon-Sat 9.30am-noon, 2-6pm; Jul-Sept: Mon-Sat 9.30am-6pm.* The visit to the cellars and manufacturing premises ends with a tasting of 100% Chardonnay *grands crus* and a demonstration of a spectacular way of opening bottles!

Launois Père & Fils – *2 av. Eugène-Guillaume – 51190 Le Mesnil-sur-Oger – ☎ 03 26 57 50 15 – Maison de Champagne: Mon-Fri 8am-noon, 2-6pm, Sat-Sun 10am-1pm, 3-5pm – museum: by appointment Mon-Fri 10am-3pm, Sat-Sun 10.30am-3pm.* Founded in 1872, this owner-grower's establishment includes a wine museum, and the visit includes a wine tasting. The vineyard can be visited by a little train.

Cuis – The Romanesque church stands on a platform overlooking the village. From D 10, there are interesting vistas of the Montagne de Reims.
Note the huge bottle (over 8m/26ft tall) marking the village of Cramant.

★**Cramant** – This village lies in a pleasant setting, at the heart of an area producing the famous Cramant wine produced from white Chardonnay vines, sometimes called Blanc de Cramant.

Avize – Also famous for its wine, Avize runs a school for future Champagne wine-growers. The 12C church has a 15C chancel and transept. Take a walk above the little town to the west for extended views of the whole area.

Oger – Producing a *premier cru de la Côte Blanche*, one of the area's top quality wines, Oger has a fine church dating from the 12C-13C with a high square tower and flat east end. *Jean Milan*
Musée des Traditions, de l'Amour et du Champagne ⊙ – This museum, devoted to wedding traditions between 1880 and 1920, includes an interesting collection of bouquets made of paper, carton, leather, gilt-metal and shell flowers, with their

La Côte des Blancs, near Cramant

original glass cover. Champagne is of course part of the tradition and there is a display of old labels and a tour of the 18C cellars with their collection of old tools.

Le Mesnil-sur-Oger – This wine-growing village is widely spread out. In the centre of a shaded close stands the Romanesque church with its tower surmounting the crossing and its Renaissance doorway framed by fluted columns. There is an interesting **Musée de la Vigne et du Vin** ⊘ displaying objects, winepresses, tools and machinery which illustrate wine-growing in the past; traditional crafts connected with wine-growing are also dealt with, in particular the production of corks, bottles and barrels.

A small road winds its way across the vineyards to Vertus.

Vertus – This small town surrounded by vineyards was once the property of the counts of Champagne who lived in a castle now demolished except for the Porte Baudet. During the Middle Ages, Vertus, which had several springs, was a busy market town enclosed by a defensive wall. Today, it is a quiet little town dotted with charming squares.
Église St-Martin was built in the late 11C and early 12C. Damaged by fire in 1167, partly destroyed during the Hundred Years War and remodelled several times, it was finally restored after the 1940 fire. The pointed vaulting over the transept and east end dates from the 15C. Note the delicately carved 16C *Pietà* in the south transept and the 16C stone statue of St John the Baptist near the christening fonts. Stairs lead from the north transept to three 11C crypts; note the capitals of the central crypt, beautifully carved with foliage motifs.

On the way down to **Bergères-lès-Vertus** with its small Romanesque country church, the road affords pleasant views of the surrounding area.

South of Bergères-lès-Vertus, turn right onto the road leading to Mont Aimé.

⋆**Mont Aimé** – Once part of the Île-de-France cliff, this isolated hill reaches 237m/778ft. Inhabited since prehistoric times, it was fortified successively by the Gauls, the Romans and the counts of Champagne who built a feudal castle; its ruins are today scattered among the greenery.
On 10 September 1815, a great parade of the Russian army (stationed in the area during the occupation of France by several European countries following the fall of Napoleon) took place at the foot of the hill.
In one of the corners of the old fortifications, a viewpoint *(viewing table)* offers an extended **view** of the Côte des Blancs to the north and of the plain of Châlons to the east.

⋆VALLÉE DE LA MARNE

The round tours starting from Épernay and Château-Thierry offer an opportunity of discovering wine-growing villages climbing the vine-covered hillsides on both banks of the River Marne. During the First World War, the fate of France and of the allies was sealed on these banks during two decisive battles, which took place in 1914 and 1918.

③ Round tour west of Épernay

63km/39mi – allow 4hr

Leave Épernay along N 3, turn right in Mardeuil then cross the Marne to Cumières and follow the north bank of the river.

Cumières – *The pier is by place du Kiosque.* There are boat trips on board the *Champagne Vallée* through vineyard country. Locks are negotiated along the way and it is possible to have lunch or dinner on board *(booking required).*

Damery – Damery offers fine walks along the banks of the River Marne; the 12C-13C **church** once belonged to the Benedictine abbey of St-Médard de Soissons. The Romanesque nave is lit by lancet windows. Note the carved capitals of the pillars supporting the belfry: they represent an interesting bestiary against a background of foliage and intertwined stems. The organ case and the chancel railing date from the 18C.

Turn right towards Fleury-la-Rivière.

Fleury-la-Rivière – The walls of the **Coopérative vinicole** ⊙ (wine-growers' cooperative society) are decorated with a huge fresco by Greg Gawra, which depicts the history of the Champagne region. *Arnouit Co-op*

The road runs through villages and across vineyards and fields.

Châtillon-sur-Marne – Camped on a vine-covered hill overlooking the Marne, this ancient fortified town was the fief of Eudes de Châtillon who became Pope under the name of Urbain II (1088-99) and launched the first crusade.

Leave the car in the parking and follow rue de l'Église then turn right onto rue Berthe-Symonet.

Statue d'Urbain II – The 33m/108ft high statue was erected in 1887 on the mound once crowned by the castle keep. Eighty blocks of granite were brought all the way from Brittany in carts pulled by oxen. Inside, a **staircase** leads up to the arm of the statue. From the nearby viewing table there is a fine **view★** of the valley and the vineyards.

Drive W along D 1 to Vandières.

Vandières – The 18C castle stands in the middle of a park, at the top of the village. The 11C church has a beautiful porch. There are fine views of the valley framed by hills to the south.

Verneuil – The small 12C-13C church, carefully restored, stands beside the Sémoigne, a tributary of the Marne.

Continue to Vincelles then Dormans.

Dormans – The park of this peaceful flower-decked riverside town is the setting of the **castle** (housing the tourist office and temporary exhibitions) and of the **Mémorial des victoires de la Marne** ⊙, a memorial chapel dedicated to the battles of the Marne, consisting of two storeys and a crypt surmounted by a chapel. On the lower level, note the marble sundial to the right of the crypt and the viewing table illustrating the course of events during the second battle of the Marne to the left. The upper level features the chapel and an ossuary.

From the memorial it is possible to reach the mill across the park.

Moulin d'en Haut ⊙ – This former communal mill houses an interesting collection of rural tools for working in the vineyards, in the fields and in the woods.

Church ⊙ – This Gothic church features a square tower above the crossing, with geminated bays on each of the four gables; the north transept is flanked by a turret surmounted by an octagonal pinnacle. The most interesting part of the church is the flat east end dating from the 13C, with High Gothic windows.

Painted wall in the cooperative vineyard at Fleury-la-Rivière

Œuilly – A folk museum has been established in this old fortified hillside village.

Écomusée ⏱ – It includes a typical wine-grower's house, dating from 1642, complete with cellar and attic, the Musée de la Goutte (a famous wine brandy) with the former village still and the village school, dating from the turn of the 20C, with its desks, stove and blackboard.

Follow D 222 to Boursault.

Château de Boursault – Built in 1848 in neo-Renaissance style for the famous Veuve Clicquot, this vast castle was the venue of magnificent receptions given by Madame Clicquot and later by her granddaughter, the Duchess of Uzès.

Continue to Vaucienes and turn left onto D 22 towards N 3.

The road offers fine **views★** of the Marne Valley, the village of Damery and the Montagne de Reims.

③ Round tour from Château-Thierry

60km/37mi – allow 4hr

The Aisne vineyards which follow the River Marne between Crouttes and Trélou (near Dormans) belong to the Champagne wine-growing region.

The *pinot meunier* vines thrive on the Marne Valley soil and grow on half the area covered by the Champagne vineyards.

Leave Château-Thierry SE along D 969 which follows the meanders of the river.

Essômes-sur-Marne – The **Église St-Ferréol★** ⏱ is the former Augustinian abbey church dating from the 13C. The **interior★** is characteristic of Lancet-Gothic architecture. Note the elegant triforium with its narrow twin openings.

Make a detour via Montcourt then turn left onto D 1400.

The road runs through vineyards, offering, between Mont-de-Bonneil and Azy, an interesting **panorama** of a meander of the Marne with the wooded Brie region in the background.

Rejoin D 969 in Azy and continue past Saulchery to Charly.

Charly – This is the most important wine-growing centre of the Aisne *département*.

Follow D 11 to Villiers-Saint-Denis and turn left onto D 842 to Crouttes.

The road offers a wide view of the deep meander of the Marne to the south.

Crouttes – This wine-growing village owes its name to its cellars dug out of the rock. Leave the car near the town hall and walk up to the church picturesquely perched above the village.

Return to Charly along D 969 and cross the river; turn left onto D 86 to Nogent-l'Artaud.

Nogent-l'Artaud – Very little remains of the former abbey of the Poor Clares Order.

Between Nogent and Chézy, the road overlooks the Marne and offers fine views of the slopes planted with vines.

Chézy-sur-Marne – There are fine walks along the banks of the Dolloir, a tributary of the Marne which flows through this village.

Follow D 15. The road runs under D 1 to Étampes-sur-Marne and joins N 3 in Chierry.

Between Chierry and Blesmes, the road offers a fine panorama of the valley. Turn left onto a minor road 1.5km/0.9mi beyond Blesmes.

Fossoy – The Déhu cellars, run by the seventh generation of a wine-growing family, welcome tourists along this Route du Champagne. Former stables have been turned into a small museum.

Le Varocien: musée de la Vigne et du Vin ⏱ – There are explanations about the three types of vines used in the area and displays of tolls and machinery traditionally used by wine-growers. Note the refractometer dating from 1863, used for measuring alcoholic concentration.

Continue along the minor road to Mézy.

Église de Mézy – This 13C Gothic church is remarkable for its homogeneous style. Inside, note the triforium with its arcades concealing a circular gallery.

Cross the River Marne and turn left onto D 3 which runs along the north bank.

Mont-St-Père – The paintings of Léon Lhermitte (1844-1925), a native of this village, were inspired by rural life and landscapes (*Harvesters' Payday* can be seen in the Musée d'Orsay in Paris).

On its way to Château-Thierry, the road skirts the Bois de Barbillon.

Return to Château-Thierry via D 15 and D 1.

★COTEAUX SUD D'ÉPERNAY

④ Round tour south of Épernay

See ÉPERNAY: Excursion

CHARLEVILLE-MÉZIÈRES

Conurbation 67 213
Michelin map 53 fold 18 or 241 fold 10 – Local map see p 199

Charleville and Mézières, lying on the banks of the River Meuse, have each retained their specific character in spite of having been united since 1966.
The middle-class and commercial city of **Charleville** stretches along the north bank of the river overlooked by Mount Olympus, whereas **Mézières**, an administrative and military centre, nestles inside a meander of the Meuse.

HISTORICAL NOTES

A Gallo-Roman city destroyed in the 5C by Barbarian invaders stood on the site of Montcy-St-Pierre; the market town of **Arches** developed on the site of Charleville from the 9C onwards and acquired a royal palace while Mézières, founded around the year 1000, was just a village; in the 13C, the two neighbouring towns belonged to the Count of Rethel and Nevers.
In 1565, Louis de Gonzague, who belonged to the House of the dukes of Mantua, acquired the duchy of Nevers and the earldom of Rethel through his marriage to Henrietta of Cleves. **Charles de Gonzague** (1580-1637) succeeded his father in 1595. In 1606, he decided to turn Arches into the main city of a principality and named it after himself. Louis XIII granted Charleville the right of free trade with France and the building of the town was completed in 1627, under the supervision of the architect Clément Métezeau.
In 1590, a citadel was built to reinforce the strategic position of Mézières and in 1815 the Prussian advance was stopped here for 45 days. During the First World War, Mézières was the headquarters of the German forces and Kaiser William II stayed in Charleville on several occasions.

In Rimbaud's footsteps

A native of Charleville, **Arthur Rimbaud** (1854-91) was a brilliant student at the local college and one of his most famous poems, *Le Bateau ivre* (The Drunken Boat) dates from his student days. Unhappy at home, he became a rebel and often ran away to Charleroi and Paris where he met Verlaine. He followed the older poet to Belgium and London and, in 1873, he wrote another of his famous poems, *Une Saison en Enfer* (A Season in Hell). He later abandoned literature to travel to the Red Sea and the Far East. Repatriated for health reasons at the age of 37, he died in Marseille's hospital and was buried in the old cemetery of his home town.
The poet's childhood house (7 quai Rimbaud) and his college, now the local library (4 place de l'Agriculture) can be seen near the museum; his birthplace (12 rue Bérégovoy) is situated south of place Ducale and his grave near the entrance of the old cemetery (avenue Charles-Boutet); a bust of Rimbaud was erected on square de la Gare in 1901. *Also see p 62, 431.*

STROLL THROUGH CHARLEVILLE

★★ **Place Ducale** – Designed by **Clément Métezeau** (1581-1652), the square is characteristic of the Henri IV-Louis XIII architectural style and shows numerous similarities with place des Vosges in Paris, which is attributed to Louis Métezeau, Clément's brother.

Place Ducale

Eating out

MODERATE

Le Val Fleuri – *25 quai Arthur-Rimbaud* – ☎ *03 24 59 94 11* – *closed Sat lunchtime and Sun evening* – *61/141F.* This restaurant on the first floor of a building bordering the Meuse is decorated in pastel tones and run by a pleasant couple. Among the local specialities, don't miss the *t'chu nous*, a white sausage from Haybes.

La Côte à l'Os – *11 cours A.-Briand* – ☎ *03 24 59 20 16* – *closed Sun evening* – *82/195F.* You can be sure of a warm welcome in this town-centre restaurant, situated in an avenue of horse chestnut trees. The terrace is pleasant in summer. Traditional regional specialities are on the menu.

Le Balard – *10 r. Tivoli* – ☎ *03 24 33 60 06* – *closed Aug, Sat lunchtime and Sun* – *95/170F.* On entering this restaurant you will find it decorated with authentic Paris-metro decor from the past: benches, white tiles, luggage racks and enamelled advertisements. The only thing missing is the vibration from the rails!

Where to stay

MODERATE

Hôtel de Paris – *24 av. G.-Corneau* – ☎ *03 24 33 34 38* – *closed 24 Dec-1 Jan* – *28 rooms 240/420F* – ⌣ *37F.* This hotel, with its classic early-20C façade, is situated on a busy avenue near the station. The light, simple rooms are well insulated against noise. Pleasant, helpful staff.

Camping Base de Loisirs Départementale – *08800 Haulmé – 22km/13.75mi NE of Charleville on D 74* – ☎ *03 24 32 81 61* – *reservation advisable Jul-Aug* – *405 plots 48F.* The agreeable setting of this camp site in the meandering Semoy Valley makes it a good choice. Tennis and volleyball courts, canoes and kayaks, bikes. Children's play area.

Camping Départemental Lac des Vieilles Forges – *08500 Les Mazures – 17km/10.6mi NW of Charleville on D 989 and D 88* – ☎ *03 24 40 17 31* – *reservation advisable Jul-Aug – 300 plots 53F.* The camp site is laid out in shady terraces overlooking the lake, and offers modern, comfortable facilities. Children's play area. Beach, table tennis, chalets for hire.

On the town

La Petite Brasserie Ardennaise – *25 quai Arthur-Rimbaud* – ☎ *03 24 37 53 53* – *Mon-Sat 3pm-1am in summer, 5pm-1am in winter.* The micro-brewery offers a large selection of beers. In the back room seven varieties of beer are brewed, including one called *oubliette* – which you are not likely to forget, despite its name – and which may be enjoyed *blonde* (pale), *ambrée* (dark) or *stout.*

Le Mawhot – *Quai Charcot* – ☎ *03 24 33 54 35* – *Wed-Mon 4pm-1am.* The Mawhot is a legendary reptile from the Ardennes region. Your host, Philippe, pays homage to this beast by telling wonderful tales of the legendary Aymon brothers and their black steed Bayard. Drink in the stories while sipping a home-made brew.

Showtime

Institut International de la Marionnette – 🎭 – *7 pl. Winston-Churchill* – ☎ *03 24 33 72 50.* Run by the pupils of the National College of Puppetry, the institute's theatre offers a high-quality programme that will appeal to young and old alike. Courses, workshops and meetings are also organised. Note the giant automat which recites the local legend of the four Aymon brothers in twelve short plays.

The square (126m/138yd long and 90m/98yd wide) is still spectacular in spite of the replacement of the duke's palace by the Hôtel de Ville in 1843. As originally planned, a fountain stands in the centre; the square is lined with arcades surmounted by pink brick and ochre-coloured stone pavilions topped by slate-covered pitched roofs, forming a harmonious and colourful ensemble. Several of these pavilions have been skilfully restored and their dormer windows fitted with mullioned windows. Each of the four corners of the square was decorated with a dome similar to that at no 9.

Charleville-Mézières, the capital of puppets

An amateur puppet theatre, known as the Petits Comédiens de Chiffons, has been staging shows in the town since 1941. To celebrate its 20th anniversary, the company invited puppeteers from France and other countries. This is how the first international puppet festival in France was born. As it became more and more famous, the festival took the name of **Festival mondial des Theâtres de Marionnettes**, which takes place every three years (the next one is due in 2003) for 10 days, in late September and early October. Courses intended to teach the technique of making puppets have been organised since 1981 and in 1987 the École supérieure nationale des Arts de la Marionnette, a higher education college, was inaugurated. The Union internationale de la Marionnette also has its headquarters in Charleville-Mézières.

A. Nozay/CDT Ardennes

A public passageway *(same opening times as the museum)*, which crosses the museum courtyard, links place Ducale and place Winston-Churchill.

Horloge du Grand Marionnettiste – *Place Winston-Churchill*
Incorporated into the façade of the Institut international de la Marionnette, this 10m/33ft high brass automaton is the work of Jacques Monestier; its head and eyes are moved by clockwork every hour between 10am and 9pm, a short puppet show depicts an episode of the legend of the Four Aymon Brothers, the 12 scenes being enacted every Saturday at 9pm.

Rue de la République – Each pavilion contains two homes under a large slate-covered roof. Shops occupy the ground floor on either side of the main door, according to the plans drawn by Charles de Gonzague. There are other similar houses in **rue du Moulin**.

Vieux Moulin – The former ducal mill looks more like a monumental gate than a mill, which is not surprising since it was designed to match the Porte de France in the south and to close the main axis of the city. Its imposing Henri IV-Louis XIII façade is decorated with Ionic Italian-style columns. It houses the Musée Rimbaud.

STROLL THROUGH MÉZIÈRES

Basilique Notre-Dame-d'Espérance – Although it was remodelled over several centuries, this basilica is essentially in Flamboyant-Gothic style, except for the belfry-porch erected in the 17C. The interior is grandiose: the central nave is flanked with double aisles and surmounted by lierne and tierceron vaulting with pendants *(see illustration p 40)*. Light pours in through some beautiful abstract stained-glass windows★, made between 1955 and 1979 by René Dürrbach who found his inspiration in a text by Henri Giriat on the theme of the Virgin Mary.
In the 19C, the basilica was dedicated to Notre-Dame-d'Espérance, a black statue of the Virgin standing on top of an altar situated to the right of the chancel.

Ramparts – Part of the medieval ramparts are still standing: Tour du Roy, Tour de l'École, Tour Milart, Porte Neuve, Porte de Bourgogne.

Préfecture – The administrative offices are housed in the buildings of the former Royal Engineers School (17C-18C).

SIGHTS

★**Musée de l'Ardenne** ⊙ – This modern museum is housed in a group of buildings constructed over 400 years, linked by covered passages and footbridges. The collections are devoted to regional archaeology, history and ethnography.
The archaeology department, which is the most important, illustrates the first human settlements in the Ardennes, particularly during the Iron Age, the Roman period (stele, 2C mill, ceramics) and the Merovingian period (jewellery and weapons found in the graves of Mézières chieftains).

The first-floor rooms display weapons made in the royal weapon manufacture between 1688 and 1836, documents about the foundation of Charleville (17C relief maps) and an important collection of coins and medals.

The pharmacy (1756) with its 120 earthenware jars decorated with blue motifs, was originally in the former Hôtel-Dieu (hospital) and was still in use 25 years ago.

The top floor houses collections devoted to folk art and traditions: tools used by blacksmiths and slate-quarry workers (in Monthermé, Fumay or Rimogne), nails made in the area during the 18C and 19C, reconstruction of a typical Ardennes interior.

The fine arts section includes sculptures by Croisy *(Fours Seasons)* and 19C paintings by Couvelet, Damas and Gondrexon.

Musée Rimbaud ⊘ – Housed inside the old mill, the museum contains mementoes of the poet Arthur Rimbaud: photographs, letters, personal objects, various documents and a portrait by Fernand Léger. *For a brief biography of the poet, see In Rimbaud's footsteps above.*

A footbridge, situated behind the museum and overlooking the River Meuse, gives access to Mount Olympus.

EXCURSIONS

Mohon – *Drive S out of town towards Reims.*
This industrial town has a 16C church, **Église St-Lié** ⊘, where pilgrims used to flock to see the relics of St Lié. The early-17C west front is decorated with *trompe-l'oeil* motifs.

Warcq – *3km/1.9mi W along avenue St-Julien and D 16.*
The fortified **church** ⊘ has a tower which looks like a keep. Inside it is a hall church and contains a statue of St Hubert dating from the 18C *(pillar on the left of the altar).*

Parc animalier de St-Laurent ⊘ – *6km/3.7mi Drive E along D 979.*
⊡ Several marked round tours offer a pleasant walk through this **zoological park** covering 45ha/111 acres, where wild boars, deer, roe-deer, goats and moufflons (not forgetting numerous species of birds) roam almost freely.

★**Vallon d'Élan** – *8.5km/5.3mi S. Drive out of Mézières along D 764 to Flize and continue S along D 33 to Élan.*
Although close to the River Meuse, the Vallon d'Élan, with its pasture-covered steep slopes, looks like a mountain valley. The Cistercian abbey, founded in 1148, became quite wealthy during the Middle Ages but its prosperity had considerably declined at the time of the Revolution. The Gothic abbey church, with its 17C Classical west front, forms a harmonious architectural ensemble with the abbey manor flanked with elegant turrets (beautiful chestnut timber-work).

At the end of the valley, the 17C **Chapelle St-Roger** stands on the spot where the first abbot, St Roger, liked to meditate. There is a spring nearby.

The **Forêt d'Élan**, covering 872ha/2 006 acres, includes beautiful specimens of oaks and beeches.

CHÂTEAU-THIERRY

Population 15 312
Michelin map 56 fold 14 or 237 fold 21

Château-Thierry lies on both banks of the River Marne and on the slopes of an isolated hill crowned by the former castle; the progress of wine-growing in this part of the Marne Valley has strengthened its links with the Champagne-producing area further east; however, Château-Thierry is mainly renowned as the birthplace of the French poet and world-famous fable-writer, **Jean de la Fontaine**.

TOUR OF THE TOWN

Start from place de l'Hôtel-de-Ville and walk up rue du Château to Porte St-Pierre.

Porte St-Pierre – This is the only one of the four town gates still standing. The main façade is flanked with two round towers.

Château – Go in through Porte St-Jean and note the embossed decoration which is characteristic of the late-14C style. The former garrison town was razed almost to the ground and the castle turned into a pleasant walking area offering fine **views** of the town, the Marne Valley and the monument on top of Cote 204 *(see Excursions below).*

From the Tour Bouillon, where a carved-stone map of the old castle can be seen, a staircase leads down to the lower watch-path.

Follow it round to rue J.-de-la-Fontaine.

La Fontaine and Château-Thierry

Born in 1621, La Fontaine was more inclined towards rambling than studying. However, he thought he had a religious vocation and entered a seminary, soon discovering that he had made a mistake. He then became a lawyer, came back to Château-Thierry and got married, but he remained a daydreamer and neglected both his work and his wife. Then one day he heard an officer recite a poem and had a revelation: he had to become a poet himself. At the age of 36, he became Fouquet's official poet and received a regular income from him. After Fouquet's arrest, he settled in Paris where he was widely acclaimed until his death in 1695. *Also see p 62, 431.*

Jean de La Fontaine

Maison natale de La Fontaine ⊙ – This 16C mansion was partly remodelled and now houses the museum devoted to La Fontaine.

🖻 In addition to private documents, it contains magnificent editions of the *Fables* and *Tales*, including those illustrated by Oudry in 1755 and Gustave Doré in 1868; there is also a collection of various objects decorated with scenes from the *Fables*.

Walk back along Grande Rue, a lively street lined with old houses.

ADDITIONAL SIGHT

Caves de champagne Pannier ⊙ – *23 rue Roger-Catillon to the W of the town.* An audio-visual presentation and a tour of the cellars located in 13C stone quarries enable visitors to follow the process of Champagne-making.

EXCURSIONS

★Vallée de la Marne – This Route du Champagne meanders through woods or across vineyards along the hillsides overlooking the River Marne *(see Routes du CHAMPAGNE).*

Condé-en-Brie – *16km/10mi SE along N 3 to Crézancy then D 4.* This small market town has retained an interesting covered market with Doric columns and a **castle** ⊙ rebuilt in the 16C then remodelled in the 18C. It belonged to the Condé family, a junior branch of the House of Bourbon who reigned over France almost continually from the advent of Henri IV (1589) to the abdication of Louis-Philippe (1848).

Where to stay

MODERATE

Chambre d'hôte M. et Mme Leclère – *1 r. de Launay – 02330 Connigis – 12km/7.5mi E of Château-Thierry on N 3 and D 4 –* ☎ *03 23 71 90 51 – closed 24 Dec-1 Jan –* ⊟ *– 5 rooms 180/300F – evening meal 90F.* The owners are Champagne producers and will make you welcome in their 16C home, set in a park and surrounded by vineyards. This old farm has retained its simple country style.

MID-RANGE

Île de France – *Rte de Soissons – 2 km/1.2mi N of Château-Thierry on D 967 –* ☎ *03 23 69 10 12 –* **P** ⊙ *– 50 rooms 270/350F –* ⊇ *38F – restaurant 98/248F.* In this large, modern hotel set in the hills on the outskirts of the town, opt for one of the rooms at the front, which are more comfortable and equipped with cane furniture.

Shopping

Caves de champagne Pannier – *23 r. Roger-Catillon –* ☎ *03 23 69 51 33 – chppannier@aol.com – Mon-Sat 9am-12.30pm, 2-6.30pm; Jul-Aug: Tue-Sat.* Discover how Champagne is made with the aid of an audio-visual presentation and a visit of the cellars, which are to be found in 13C stone quarries. Tasting with commentary.

Condé-en-Brie

The interior has retained its 18C decoration and furniture. The **Grand Salon★** is particularly noteworthy with its still-life paintings by Oudry and 17C fresco. *Trompe-l'œil* canvases by Servandoni hang in the music room. The main staircase was also designed by him. The west wing was decorated by Watteau and his students.

Monument de la Cote 204; Bois Belleau – *16km/10mi NW; allow 2hr. Drive west out of Château-Thierry along N 3 and turn left at the top of the hill along the avenue leading to Cote 204.*
Cote 204 was a very strong position held by the Germans in June 1918. It took both a French and an American division more than five weeks to dislodge them. An American monument stands at the top.
Enjoy the fine **view** of Château-Thierry, the castle and the Marne Valley.
Return to N 3 and, at the crossroads, continue straight on along D 9 to Belleau.

Bois Belleau – These woods were taken by the Marines in June 1918. The vast **American cemetery** houses 2 350 graves. The commemorative chapel, looking like a topless Romanesque tower, bears the names of all the missing soldiers. An American aircraft carrier was given the name Bois Belleau to commemorate the fierce fighting which took place here. The ship was sold to France in 1953.
The **German cemetery** is situated 500m/547yd further on.

Return to the crossroads where the American cemetery is located and turn right onto a narrow road marked Belleau Wood.

The monument dedicated to the Marines is inside the wood which was the cause of such fierce fighting.

CHAUMONT

Population 27 041
Michelin map 62 fold 11 or 241 fold 43

Chaumont-en-Bassigny, which occupies a natural defensive position on the edge of a steep plateau separating the River Suize and the River Marne, has retained part of its medieval character illustrated by the keep of the former feudal castle and the hexagonal 13C Tour d'Arse. Approaching Chaumont from the west along D 65, one immediately spots the magnificent 600m/656yd long **viaduct★**, towering 52m/171ft above the valley. It consists of 50 three-storey arches; the first storey is a pedestrian walkway offering a fine view of the Suize Valley, the second storey is intended for repair work and the third storey carries the railway line into town.

Chaumont owns an important collection of old and contemporary posters and organises several annual events including the Festival international de l'Affiche (International Poster Festival) and Rencontres internationales d'Arts Graphiques (International Festival of Graphic Arts).

OLD TOWN

Start from square Philippe-Lebon.

From the square there is a view of the keep, of the ramparts, of the towers of the Basilique St-Jean, of the steeple of the Jesuits' chapel and of the small dome of the town hall.

The "Grand Pardon de peine et de coulpe", initiated by Jean de Montmirel (1409-79) to ward off plague, famine and war, has been celebrated ever since, every time midsummer's day falls on a Sunday, that is to say every five, six or eleven years; the next celebrations will take place in 2001 with processions in the streets, floral decorations in the town centre, theatre performances...

Walk down rue de la Tour-Chartron on the right which runs along the former ramparts.

Tour d'Arse – Hexagonal 13C tower.

Walk up rue Monseigneur-Desprez to place St-Jean.

Note the house with its corbelled turret over a low arched door on the right and, opposite, a mansion dating from 1723.

Follow rue du Palais leading to place du Palais and walk up the steps to the esplanade surrounding the keep (view of the Suize Valley). The former tanners' district lies below.

Tour d'Arse

Ph.Gajic/MICHELIN

Donjon ⊙ – This square keep, built in the 12C, is all that remains of the former castle of the counts of Champagne; temporary exhibitions and cultural events are held inside.

From the top, there is a fine view of the town and the valley of the River Suize.

Follow rue Hautefeuille on the left.

Rue Guyard (fine Renaissance mansion) and rue Gouthière have retained some old houses with corbelled turrets containing spiral staircases and a few square towers.

Continue along rue Hautefeuille then take rue Decrès.

Note the lovely bartizan and, at no 17, the Louis XIV doorway.

Walk round the north side of the Basilique St-Jean and admire the flying buttresses and gargoyles.

Rue St-Jean – No 22 boasts the highest turret in town. Note the lovely early-17C dormer windows decorated with caryatids and 18C ones adorned with scrolls.

Turn left onto rue Girardon.

Two mansions with splendid doorways stand on a small square: Hôtel de Grand on the left is in Louis XIII style with a semicircular pediment whereas Hôtel de Beine on the right, in true Louis XIV style, is surmounted by a broken pediment decorated with a grotesque.

Walk along rue Damrémont then rue Bouchardon.

Rue Bouchardon – Note the mansion at no 6 in characteristic Louis XVI style and, a little further on, the bartizan crowned by a dome clad with shingles.
Rue St-Jean leads to place de la Concorde overlooked by the town hall.

Hôtel de ville – Built in the 18C, the town hall was designed by François-Nicolas Lancret, a nephew of the artist Nicolas Lancret.

Return to square Philippe-Lebon via rue Laloy, rue Toupot-de-Beveaux and rue de Verdun.

SIGHTS

★**Basilique St-Jean-Baptiste** – The edifice dates from the 13C and 16C. In the 15C, it became a collegiate church and retained its chapter of canons until the Revolution.
The west front, surmounted by two towers dates from the 13C. The **Portail St-Jean**, which opens on the south side, is protected by a stone porch. A fine Virgin with Child is bonded to the upright post; admire the carved door leaves. The tympanum is decorated with a low-relief sculpture depicting the Life of St John the Baptist (*Zachary visits the Temple, Birth of St John the Baptist,* his *Christening* and his *Beheading*) and surrounded by an archivolt adorned with angels.
Inside, the chancel and transept, decorated at the time of the Renaissance, are the most interesting parts of the church, in particular the upper gallery forming a succession of loggias and the keystone pendentives decorating the vaulting.
In the chapel situated at the west end of the nave, on the left-hand side, there is a highly realistic **Entombment**★ (1471). The expression and attitude of the 11 life-size characters in polychrome stone are remarkable.
The basilica also contains various paintings and sculptures from the School of Jean-Baptiste Bouchardon, including a high altar in gilt carved wood, a pulpit and a bench from the early 18C.

Musée ⊘ – Housed in the vaulted rooms of the former palace of the counts of Champagne, the museum displays archaeological collections (bronze armour from the 8C BC, Gallo-Roman altar and mosaic, Merovingian sarcophagi), paintings from the 16C to the 19C (works by Paul de Vos, Sébastien Stosdopff, Nicolas Poussin, François Alexandre Pernot) and sculptures (recumbent effigy of Jean l'Aveugle de Châteauvillain, altarpiece from the Basilique St-Jean and above all fragments of the funeral monument of Antoinette de Bourbon and Claude de Lorraine by Dominique Florentin). A room is devoted to the Bouchardon family.
The **Salon des expositions** (an annexe of the museum situated near the basilica) exhibits a collection of **crèches**★ (nativity scenes with figurines) from the 17C to the 20C, made from a variety of materials including wax, wood, glass, terracotta; don't miss the surprising collection of 18C crèches from Naples.

Les silos, Maison du livre et de l'affiche ⊘ – The former grain silos have been turned into a multi-purpose cultural centre housing a library, a reference library with multimedia facilities and a poster museum which contains more than 10 000 posters including works by Jules Chéret (1836-1932), Théophile Alexandre Steinlen (1859-1923) and Henri de Toulouse-Lautrec (1864-1901). Themed exhibitions are organised regularly.

Chapelle des Jésuites ⊘ – The chapel of the former Jesuits' college contains an altarpiece depicting the Assumption of the Virgin by Bouchardon (at the back of the high altar in gilt carved wood).
As you come out of the chapel, look out for the fountain on the left; it is decorated with a bust of Bouchardon.

EXCURSION

Prez-sous-Lafauche – *38km/23.6mi NE along N 74.*
▣ In this village of the upper Marne Valley, there is a **Zoo de bois** ⊘, an unusual museum of "found art" – a collection of tree branches which resemble people and animals and have been placed in funny situations.

On 25 June 1115, St Bernard settled with 11 monks in the remote Val d'Absinthe and founded one of the four major houses of the new Cistercian Order. The Abbaye de Clairvaux, whose name means "clear valley", acquired considerable influence throughout the Middle Ages, becoming one of the main religious centres.

Difficult times alternated with times of spiritual renewal until the abbey was confiscated and sold in 1792, then bought by the State in 1808 to become a prison. Today, it still belongs to the Ministry of Justice and several 18C buildings are used for administrative purposes. However, Clairvaux was partly reopened to the public in 1985.

St Bernard (1090-1153)

Bernard de Fontaine (later known as Bernard de Clairvaux), a young aristocrat from the Bourgogne region, should have become a soldier to comply with his family's wishes. Yet, at the age of 21, he entered the Abbaye de Cîteaux together with his brothers and several uncles and cousins whom he had persuaded to follow him. He was only 25 when Étienne Harding, the abbot of Cîteaux, sent him away with the mission of founding Clairvaux. Being both a mystic and a fine administrator, Bernard soon embodied the Cistercian ideal: the strict observance of the rule of St Benedict (prayer and work) which had, according to him, been relaxed by the Benedictine Order.

Deprived of everything, the young abbot encountered immense difficulties: the harshness of the climate, diseases, physical hardship. For his monks and himself, he set the hardest tasks; "they ate boiled vegetables and drank water, slept on pallets, had no heating in winter and wore the same clothes day and night". Yet this new form of spirituality and Bernard's reputation attracted many enthusiasts and the success of the new abbey was immediate.

The young mystic wanted to reform the whole religious life of his time and he played a part in many of its aspects: the election of bishops, various councils, the papal schism, the second crusade which he preached in Vezelay in 1146. His moral ascendancy gave him a considerable influence in European courts as well as in Rome where he pushed for the election of Pope Innocent II (1130-43) and then Eugene III, a former monk at Clairvaux who was elected Pope in 1145.

Shocked by the failure of the crusade (1148) and by the rise of heretic beliefs, which he fought without success, he died in 1153 and was canonised in 1174. St Bernard was one of the strongest personalities of medieval times; his authoritarian behaviour was inspired by his passionate faith ("the way to love God is to love him without limit or measure", he said) combined with his taste for simplicity and voluntary deprivation.

St Bernard and Cistercian architecture – Simplicity and voluntary deprivation naturally led to a plain and austere architectural style. St Bernard strove to fight against the sumptuosity of so many abbey churches (excessive size, a wealth of ornamentation and interior decoration) and imposed drastic rules: no carved capitals, no stained glass and no steeples. These principles were, of course, applied to Clairvaux: the abbey church, built between 1135 and 1145 then extended from 1154 to 1174, was demolished between 1812 and 1819. Its plan was copied by all the Cistercian houses founded subsequently and in particular by Fontenay in Burgundy. Shaped like a Latin cross, the abbey church was about 100m/328ft long; the nave and the aisles ended in a flat east end lit by three high windows and flanked by four chapels opening onto a vast transept.

Clairvaux and the art of illumination – The abbey workshop produced a wealth of illuminations (almost all of them have been preserved – 1 400 manuscripts – in Troyes' municipal library, see p 357) steeped in the Cistercian ideal. The principle of austerity so dear to St Bernard was also applied to the art of illumination: bright colours and imaginative motifs were banned in favour of geometric forms and palmettes in more subdued colours such as blue, green, pale red and ochre. However, St Bernard's Bible is not totally devoid of fantasy: it includes some picturesque scenes often depicted with shimmering colours.

In the 12C, the Clairvaux manuscripts had an impact on the artistic renewal of the Champagne region comparable to that of the School of Reims. They were copied by monks from all over Europe. It is estimated that, at the end of the 12C, the abbey owned 340 large volumes and that the skins of 300 sheep had been used in the making of the Great Bible alone!

TOUR OF THE ABBEY ⏱ *allow 2hr*

A high wall, 2.7km/1.6mi long, which encloses an area of 30ha/75 acres, has replaced the fortified wall built by the monks in the 14C.

The way into the estate is through the Porte du Midi. Immediately to the left is the former Hostellerie des Dames and, beyond, the houses and kitchen gardens of Petit Clairvaux; opposite stand the austere monastic buildings of Haut Clairvaux.

Hostellerie des Dames – When Clairvaux was a monastery, women were not allowed to enter the enclosure; therefore the wives of the abbey's visitors had to stay in this building, which is today an information and exhibition centre.

Petit Clairvaux – The site where Bernard de Clairvaux built his *monasterium vetus* in 1115 is occupied today by the living quarters of the personnel of a nearby penal establishment. The original spring is still visible in the middle of a clump of trees. A few sections of the old walls remain though to remind people that the first monastery was not built of wood as legend would have it.

Along the northern part of the surrounding wall stands the 18C Chapelle Ste-Anne which was reserved for outsiders.

Haut Clairvaux – In view of the expansion of the abbey and in spite of the unfavourable advice of Bernard de Clairvaux, Prior Geoffroy de la Roche Vaneau undertook, between 1135 and 1145, the construction of a new monastery at a distance of 300m/328yd from the first. His project was supported by the Count of Champagne, Thibaut II. The lodge of this "new" monastery is today that of the penal establishment. It gives access to the main courtyard which led to the abbey church and the 50 buildings which made up the great Cistercian abbey. It is possible to go into the courtyard and admire the beautiful 18C façades. A small doorway then leads to the lay brothers' courtyard and the buildings of Haut Clairvaux.

★**Bâtiment des convers** – The lay brothers' building is all that remains of Clairvaux II. It comprises a basement cellar and a dormitory in the upper part; both are divided into three naves of 12 bays each. No decoration was allowed to distract the occupants' mind from God. The groined vaulting of the upper floor offers a very sobre white-stone outline whereas the ribbed vaulting of the cellar is supported by octagonal pillars. The building dates from 1140 to 1160. Note the marks left by stonemasons on the arcading.

Grand cloître – Next comes the wash-house, which has been turned into a canteen. The River Aube was diverted to bring water to the abbey. Further on are the buildings of the new abbey built from 1740 onwards by Abbot Pierre Mayeur round a vast cloister (each side is 50m/164ft long) after the major part of the medieval abbey was demolished (except for the abbey church and lay brothers' building).

Clairvaux as a prison – When the abbey became state property in 1808, considerable work was undertaken to turn it into a prison, the largest of its kind in France. The abbey church which had survived the Revolution was almost entirely

Clairvaux – Lay brothers' building

demolished in 1812 then disappeared completely in 1819. The lay brothers' building became a workshop. The abbot's and prior's mansions lining the main courtyard were used to house the directors. The vast cloister was split into several dormitories which can be seen between the ground floor and the upper floor; there, some of the cubicles, designed to give the prisoners some privacy, are still visible.

The tour ends with the monks' refectory, a huge hall (35m/115ft long, 13m/43ft wide and 12m/40ft high) with wood panelling on the walls.

This dining room served as a prison chapel until 1971; it could hold 1 500 prisoners (standing of course!). Among the famous prisoners held at Clairvaux were the socialist and revolutionary Louis-Auguste Blanqui (1872), members of the Paris Commune, Philippe d'Orléans (1890) and Prince Protopkine (trial of the anarchists from Lyon), deserters from Verdun (1917), many members of the Resistance (1940-44) of whom 21 were shot, several ministers of the Vichy government (after the Liberation of France) and insubordinate generals during the Algerian War of Independence.

COLMAR★★★

Conurbation 83 816
Michelin map 87 fold 17 or 242 fold 31 – Local map see Route des VINS

The great appeal of Colmar lies in the typical Alsatian character of it streets lined with picturesque flower-decked houses and of its Little Venice district unaltered by time and wars... and that is not all! Situated at the heart of the Alsatian vineyards, Colmar is the starting point of numerous excursions along the Route des Vins and the town proudly hosts the international festival of gastronomy (Festiga), which gathers many culinary talents and presents excellent food products from all over the world *(the next one will be held in 2002)*.

HISTORICAL NOTES

Idyllic beginnings – A Frankish town developed in the Rhine Valley, on the banks of the River Lauch, a tributary of the Ill. Emperor Charlemagne, and his son after him, often came to stay. Labourers and craftsmen lived round the royal villa. In its centre stood a tower with a dovecote which is said to have given its name to the future city: Villa Columbaria (*colombe* means dove in French), contracted to Columbra and eventually Colmar.

A heroic mayor – In spite of these peaceful beginnings, Colmar had a troubled history and often had to fight for its freedom. In 1261 the son of a tanner, **Roesselmann**, became the local hero when he bravely led the town militia against the bishop of Strasbourg's soldiers and paid for the city's freedom with his life.

A ruthless tyrant – Two centuries later, Colmar, together with other Alsatian towns, temporarily came under the rule of the Duke of Burgundy, Charles le Téméraire, and his cruel bailiff, Pierre de Hagenbach. When the latter was at last defeated and taken prisoner, he was condemned to death and the executioner of Colmar was chosen to carry out the sentence. The sword he used is still kept in the Musée d'Unterlinden.

Natives of Colmar – Colmar is the birthplace of several famous artists, among them, **Martin Schongauer** (1445-91) whose paintings (altarpieces) and engravings were admired by Dürer and Venetian artists of the Renaissance, and **Auguste Bartholdi** (1834-1904) whose works include the famous Statue of Liberty.

Between 1870 and 1914, when Alsace was occupied by Germany, a talented caricaturist and watercolour artist, Jean-Jacques Waltz, better known as **Hansi**, stimulated the town's passive resistance to German influence and kept alive the traditional image of Alsace with his humoristic drawings of grotesque-looking German soldiers and good-natured, likeable peasants and villagers in regional costume.

★★★MUSÉE D'UNTERLINDEN ⊙

This museum, situated on place d'Uthrough, though which flows the Logelbach canal, is housed in a former 13C convent whose name means "Under the lime trees". The convent changed from the observance of the rule of St Augustin to that of St Dominic and, for 500 years, its nuns were famous for their mysticism and austere way of life. The community was dissolved and the convent turned into barracks before becoming a museum in 1849. Today it is the town's most famous museum.

Eating out

MODERATE

Winstub La Krutenau – *1 r. de la Poissonnerie* – ☎ *03 89 41 18 80 – closed 15 Dec-31 Jan and Sun out of season* – *30/40F.* At this wine bar beside the River Lauch you can go boating in Little Venice and eat a *tarte flambée* on the flower-decked terrace beside the canal in summer. A fun way, with no obligations, to learn about this lovely part of Colmar – recommended.

Enopasta Bradi – *14 r. des Serruriers* – ☎ *03 89 23 58 01 – closed 28 Oct-20 Nov, Sun, Mon, public holidays and evenings* – *80/120F.* This 16C restaurant in the heart of old Colmar has retained part of its original painted ceiling, a pleasing detail in an otherwise modern decor. Lunchtime meals of delicious home-made pasta and other tasty Italian dishes. Terrace in the square in summer.

Chez Hansi – *23 r. des Marchands* – ☎ *03 89 41 37 84 – closed Jan, Wed evening and Thu* – *98/260F.* A taste of pure Alsace in the heart of the old town. Sauerkraut is served by staff wearing traditional costume in a rustic dining room furnished in local style. Some see it as a tourist trap, others are thrilled to discover this fascinating place.

Chez Bacchus – 🏠 – *2 Grand'Rue* – *68230 Katzenthal* – *5km/3mi NW of Colmar, Kaysersberg direction, then D 10* – ☎ *03 89 27 32 25 – closed 3 weeks in Jan, 1 week in Jul, 1 week in Nov, lunchtime (except Sun), Mon and Wed 1 Oct-14 Jul and Tue – booking advisable weekends* – *90/135F.* A lovely, friendly atmosphere in this wine bar dating from 1789 in a winemaking village. Massive exposed beams and helpings of Alsatian cuisine to match – guaranteed to satisfy the healthiest appetites. Automated puppets will entertain the children with a lively show.

La Taverne Alsacienne – *99 r. de la République* – *68040 Ingersheim* – *4km/2.5mi NW of Colmar on N 83* – ☎ *03 89 27 08 41 – closed 24 Jul-14 Aug, Sun evening and Mon except public holidays* – *100/140F.* On the main street of Ingersheim, this 1900s house is a must for gourmets visiting the town. The same family has run it since 1964; today the younger generation has taken over the cooking and the management. The food is rich, tasty and nicely served.

MID-RANGE

L'Auguste – *20 pl. de la Cathédrale* – ☎ *03 89 24 93 88 – closed 15-30 Nov, Tue evening and Wed* – *125/185F.* If you pay attention while visiting the Collégiale St-Martin, you may discover this restaurant with its pink granite arcade. Inside the decor is mostly white, unless you choose the intimate little terrace. Classic, seasonally inspired cooking.

Winstub Brenner – *1 r. de Turenne* – ☎ *03 89 41 42 33 – closed 13-20 Feb, 19-29 Jun, 15-29 Nov, Tue and Wed* – *135/250F.* The terrace by the Lauch in Little Venice is very popular on fine days. Not surprising, as the setting is ideal and the cooking, though simple, is copiously served. All Colmar meets here with obvious enjoyment.

La Maison des Têtes – *19 r. des Têtes* – ☎ *03 89 24 43 43 – closed during Feb school holidays, Sun evening and Mon* – *170/360F.* Don't miss this restaurant near the Unterlinden museum. The famous Maison des Têtes has a sumptuous 19C dining room with honey-coloured wood panelling and a wonderful terrace courtyard in summer. The cuisine is locally inspired and the rooms are elegant.

Where to stay

MODERATE

Chambre d'hôte Les Framboises – *128 r. des Trois-Épis* – *68230 Katzenthal* – *5km/3mi NW of Colmar, Kaysersberg direction then D 10* – ☎ *03 89 27 48 85 – closed 1 week in Jun and 1 week in Nov.* – 🛏 – *3 rooms 200/270F.* Leave Colmar behind and head for the open countryside and this village among the vines. The proprietor distils his own marc (grape brandy) from Gewürztraminer and provides accommodation in wood-panelled attic rooms. Don't miss the puppet show in the mornings!

Hôtel Au Moulin – *Rte d'Herrlisheim – 68127 Ste-Croix-en-Plaine – 10km/6.2mi S of Colmar on A 35 and D 1 – ☎ 03 89 49 31 20 – closed 5 Nov-31 Mar –* **P** *– 17 rooms 240/510F –* ⊑ *45F.* This old mill deep in the country is perfect for those seeking peace and quiet. Its spacious rooms are all the same but nicely arranged. A small museum of old local objects has been created in a neighbouring building.

MID-RANGE

Hôtel Turenne – *10 rte de Bâle – ☎ 03 89 41 12 26 –* **P** *– 83 rooms 320/400F –* ⊑ *48F.* On the edge of the old town, this hotel occupies a large, pleasing building with a pink and yellow façade. Its rooms have been nicely renovated and are well soundproofed. A few neat and reasonably priced single rooms are available.

Hôtel Le Colombier – *7 r. de Turenne – ☎ 03 89 23 96 00 – closed Christmas holidays – 24 rooms 450/1200F –* ⊑ *65F.* This lovely 15C house in old Colmar combines old stone and contemporary decor by retaining elements from its past, such as the superb Renaissance staircase. Contemporary furniture, modern paintings and carefully arranged rooms.

On the town

Country Bar – *9 rte d'Ingersheim – ☎ 03 89 41 48 47 – daily except Tue 4pm-3am.* A magnificent saloon bar, with totem pole, life-sized horses and murals evoking the Wild West. In fact you could almost be there, and the country and western music and American beers add to the illusion. Good restaurant in the basement. A good place for all the family.

Le Kikuyu – *1-3 r. Mercière – ☎ 03 89 23 52 12 – daily 7pm-3am, Tue and Thu until 2.30am.* A place to dream of the West Indies while you sip your drink. This cocktail bar with a tropical decor and a torrid atmosphere has no less than 80 varieties to choose from, and organises theme evenings (rum and straw hats, salsa, karaoke on Wed and Sun) and rock concerts.

Le Haricot Rouge – *6 pl. de la Cathédrale (Galerie Bartholdi) – 68000 Ingersheim – ☎ 03 89 41 74 13 – Tue-Sat 7pm-3am.* A 19C former coaching inn which has conserved its lovely paintings of Greek gods, and which is now the biggest bar in Colmar. With the help of the 13 draught beers, there is an atmosphere of excitement, especially around the games of darts and billiards and on Thursday theme nights (with DJ, West Indian or reggae) and Wednesday karaoke evenings.

Shopping

Caveau Robert-Karcher – *11 r. de l'Ours – ☎ 03 89 41 14 42 – www. vins-karcher.com – daily 8am-noon, 1-7pm.* This winemaker presses his grapes and makes his wines right in the town centre, in a cellar which dates from 1602. You can taste his entire production, including Riesling, sparkling Alsace and Gewürztztraminer.

Fortwenger – *32 r. des Marchands – ☎ 03 89 41 06 93 – Mon-Fri 9.30am-12.30pm, 1.30-7pm, Sat 9.30am-12.30pm, 1.30-6.30pm, Sun 10am-12.30pm, 1.30-6pm.* Gingerbread specialists.

Maison des Vins d'Alsace – *12 av. de la Foire-aux-Vins – ☎ 03 89 20 16 20 – civa@civa.fr – Mon-Fri 9am-noon, 2-5pm.* Four important local organisations concerned with Alsace wines are based in this centre. The visitor can study a 6m/20ft-long map, showing all the winemaking villages and *grands crus*, as well as learn about the process of winemaking from hands-on models and a film.

★**Cloître** – The cloister was built in the 13C of pink sandstone from the Vosges mountains. Half way down the western gallery, one of the arches is larger than the others and more profusely decorated. It stands over what used to be the lavabo; the basin is still visible. In a corner stands an unusual Renaissance well.

The ground-floor rooms surrounding the cloister are devoted to art from the Rhine Valley. There are rich collections of late-medieval and Renaissance painting and sculpture, as well as minor art forms, stained glass, ivories, tapestries... Primitive art from the Rhine region is represented by Holbein the Elder, Cranach the Elder, Caspar Isenmann and Martin Schongauer (copper engravings). *It is advisable to visit rooms 1, 3 and 4 as a preliminary step to the discovery of the Retable d'Issenheim which remains the prize exhibit.*

GIRAUDON

The Issenheim Altarpiece

★★★**Retable d'Issenheim (Issenheim Altarpiece)** — It is displayed in the chapel together with works by Martin Schongauer and members of his school (24-panel altarpiece depicting the **Passion★★**). The gallery of the former Dominican chapel (early-16C sculpture) makes a good viewpoint, enabling visitors to have an overall view of the different panels and fully appreciate the composition of the famous polyptych.

Painted by **Matthias Grünewald** at the beginning of the 16C for the high altar of the monastery at Issenheim, it was taken to Colmar in 1793. Founded in 1298, the monastery was devoted to the cure of patients suffering from ergotism (also known as St Anthony's Fire). Around 1500, the prior had the church decorated by the greatest artists of his time. Very little is known about the artist's life, but his expressionist style, his daring colours and light effects, his realism and imagination, the poetry and humour that pervade his paintings are generally acknowledged.

Taken apart during the Revolution, the polyptych was only put together again in 1930. It is made up of a carved central part, two fixed panels, two pairs of opening panels and a lower part which also opens. In order to preserve this unique work of art, the different parts were dismantled and are now displayed separately in the chancel. Several models with opening panels have been fixed to the chapel's walls to enable visitors to understand how the altarpiece opened out.

First floor — The collections on this floor concern the history of Colmar and the region, Alsatian art, furniture, weapons, pewter, gold plate, wrought iron, 18C porcelain and earthenware (Strasbourg). There are also reconstructions of various interiors including the Gothic room, with wood panelling on the walls and ceiling, and the English ladies' drawing room (18C) with its splendid **ceiling**, painted in *trompe-l'œil* as was the fashion during the Baroque period.

Basement — The Gallo-Roman room contains fragments of the Bergheim mosaic (3C AD). Further on, the two barrel-vaulted naves of the former **cellar** of the convent (13C), admirably preserved, house the archaeological collections, from prehistory to the Merovingian period. Two rooms are devoted to 20C paintings by Renoir, Rouault, Picasso, Vieira da Silva, Nicolas de Staël and Poliakoff.

★★OLD TOWN

① Round tour starting from place d'Unterlinden

Walk along rue des Clefs.

The Hôtel de Ville is on the left; this 18C building with pink-sandstone ties belonged to the Abbaye de Pairis.

When you reach place Jeanne-d'Arc, turn right onto Grand'Rue.

Temple protestant St-Matthieu ⊘ – This former Franciscan church, which is now a Protestant temple, is decorated with fine 14C and 15C **stained-glass windows**. The most remarkable of them, known as the **Vitrail de la Crucifixion★** (15C) and believed to be the work of Pierre d'Andlau, is located at the top of the south aisle.

Turn left along the side of the temple to reach place du 2-Février and look at the old hospital.

The façade of the 18C **Ancien Hôpital** is surmounted by a sloping roof with Alsatian dormer windows.

Return to Grand'Rue and turn left.

Admire along the way the Renaissance Maison des Arcades★, framed by two octagonal turrets and the **Schwendi Fountain.**

Walk past the **Maison du Pèlerin** (1571) to reach place de l'Ancienne-Douane.

Schwendi Fountain

Place de l'Ancienne-Douane – This is one of the town's most picturesque squares, lined with timber-framed houses such as the **Maison au Fer Rouge**.

The world's longest walk

The **Paris-Colmar** walk through 171 municipalities and eight *départements* has, since 1981, been a hard test for some 50 of the best hikers in the world. They cover the 540km/234mi in about 70hr (an average of 7.5kph/4.6mph) to arrive on the picturesque place de l'Ancienne-Douane in Colmar where great festivities take place in their honour.

The women's event is a walk from Châlons-en-Champagne to Colmar (360km/220mi). Rendez-vous late May, or follow the race on www.paris.colmar.free.fr.

★Ancienne Douane or "Koïfhus" – This former customs house is the most important civilian edifice in Colmar. There are two separate buildings. The main one dates from 1480. The ground floor was used as a warehouse to stock goods subject to municipal tax. The great hall of the first floor, known as the Salle de la Décapole (the union formed by 10 Alsatian cities), was the meeting place of the representatives of those cities. The second building was added at the end of the 16C.

It is an attractive building decorated with a wooden gallery and flanked by a stair turret with canted corners; on the ground floor, three arches underline the opening and form a passage. Walk through to the other side and admire the fine outside staircase.

Take rue des Marchands opposite the customs house.

★★Maison Pfister – A hatter from Besançon had this house built in 1537; decorated with frescoes and medallions, it is the loveliest house in the old town.

The arcaded ground floor is surmounted by an elegant wooden gallery interrupted on the corner by an oriel window topped by a pyramidal roof.

Next to the Maison Pfister, at no 9, stands a fine house (1609) adorned with a wooden gallery and a corner sculpted figure representing a merchant.

On the left of rue des Marchands, the 15C **Maison Schongauer**, also known as **Maison de la Viole**, belonged to the painter's family.

Note the small house opposite, known as the **Maison au Cygne**, where Schongauer is said to have lived from 1477 to 1490.

Walk through the arcades opposite the Musée Bartholdi (see SIGHTS below), to place de la Cathédrale.

On the square stand the oldest house in Colmar, **Maison Adolphe** (1350), and the **Ancien Corps de garde** (1575). The town's magistrate took the oath from the lovely Renaissance loggia decorating the façade and infamous sentences were also proclaimed from there.

COLMAR

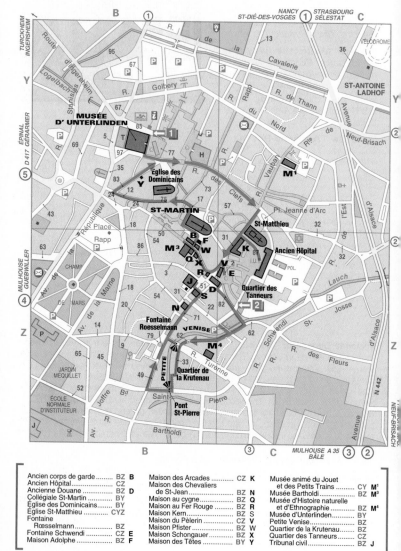

Opposite the former guard-house stands the collegiate church of St-Martin, known as the cathedral.

★Collégiale St-Martin – This imposing edifice covered with glazed tiles and decorated with red-sandstone projections was built in the 13C and 14C on the site of a Romanesque church.

The west doorway is flanked by two towers. The south tower is decorated with a sundial bearing the inscription *Memento Mori* (think of death). **St Nicholas' doorway**, which gives access to the south transept, is decorated with 13 small statues; the fourth one on the left is the representation of the builder who signed in French, Maistres Humbert.

Inside, note a 14C **Crucifixion★** in the axial chapel and a magnificent 18C organ loft by Silbermann.

Leave place de la Cathédrale along rue des Serruriers.

Église des Dominicains ⊙ – Work began on the chancel in 1283, but the main part of the edifice was only completed in the 14C and 15C. Inside, the absence of capitals adds to the impression of loftiness; altars and stalls date from the 18C; but the magnificent **stained-glass windows★** are contemporary with the construction of the church (superb effigy of King Solomon above the south doorway).

The famous painting by Martin Schongauer, the ***Virgin of the Rose Bower★★***, can be seen at the entrance of the chancel; it was painted in 1473. The Virgin and Child form a charming picture against a golden background decorated with white and red rose bushes full of birds.

Walk along rue des Boulangers then turn right onto rue des Têtes.

The fine Renaissance **Maison des Têtes★** *(no 19)* owes its strange name to the numerous carved heads decorating the façade. The graceful gable is underlined by rows of scrolls; oriel windows over two storeys complete the elaborate ornamentation *(see p 48)*.

Return to place d'Unterlinden.

"House of the Heads"

★"PETITE VENISE" (LITTLE VENICE)

② Round tour starting from place de l'Ancienne-Douane

From the square, follow rue des Tanneurs which runs along the canal.

Quartiers des tanneurs – The tanners' district owes its name to its inhabitants who, being near the river, could tan hides and wash them. This activity was discontinued in the 19C. The renovation of the district, completed in 1974, was very successful, in particular along rue des Tanneurs and "petite" rue des Tanneurs (at no 3, lovely house with ashlars underlining the openings). Timber-framed houses were narrow but very high as they had a loft for drying the skins.

Cross the River Lauch to enter the **Krutenau district**, once a fortified outlying area, where many market gardeners lived; it has retained its picturesque character. These market gardeners used flat-bottomed boats, similar to Venitian gondolas, to glide along the river.

Turn right along quai de la Poissonnerie.

Cross the next bridge to the corner of rue des Écoles and rue du Vigneron, where the **Fontaine du Vigneron** stands, it was designed by Bartholdi as a celebration of Alsatian wines.

Continue along quai de la Poissonnerie then rue de la Poissonnerie lined with picturesque fishermen's cottages. It runs into rue de Turenne, the former rue de Krutenau, once the site of the vegetable market.

Take rue de la Herse then turn right onto a narrow street leading to the river.

Pleasant stroll along the bank to **Pont St-Pierre**. From the bridge, there is a lovely **view★** of the Petite Venise and the Old Town.

Below the bridge, **boat trips** ⊙ are available to explore the district further.

Turn right onto rue du Manège leading to place des Six-Montagnes-Noires.

The **Fontaine Roesselmann**, another of Bartholdi's works, stands on the square. It is dedicated to the town's hero *(see HISTORICAL NOTES above)*.

Walk towards the bridge on the right: the river, lined with willow trees, flows between two picturesque rows of old houses.

Continue along rue St-Jean.

A quiet canal in old Colmar

On the left stands the **Maison des Chevaliers de St-Jean**, a fine Renaissance building decorated with superposed galleries (1608).
A little further, place du Marché-aux-Fruits is lined with the **Maison Kern**, in Renaissance style, the lovely Classical façade (in pink sandstone) of the **Tribunal civil★** to the left and the Ancienne Douane across the square.
Return to place de l'Ancienne-Douane.

SIGHTS

Musée Bartholdi ⊙ – The house where **Frédéric-Auguste Bartholdi** (1834-1904) was born, right in the town centre, is now a museum dedicated to the sculptor who acquired worldwide fame on account of his Statue of Liberty standing at the entrance of New York harbour.
The downstairs rooms have been turned into a museum of local history.
On the first floor, Bartholdi's private quarters, furnished exactly as they were when he lived here, celebrate the artist's life and works from the Lion of Belfort to his Vercingétorix in Clermont-Ferrand.
The second floor is exclusively devoted to his most famous Statue of Liberty. The last room displays a collection of Jewish art.
Bartholdi's works in Colmar
– Statue of General Rapp, place Rapp
– Monument to Admiral Bruat, place du Champ-de-Mars
– Schwendi Fountain, place de l'Ancienne-Douane
– Wine-grower's Fountain, corner of rue des Écoles and rue du Vigneron.

Musée animé du Jouet et des Petits Trains ⊙ – 🖼 Housed in a former cinema, the museum's collections include numerous railway engines (including the Britannia, British model Pacific 213), trains, dolls in many different materials; collectors will recognize some rare items. One window is given over to a circus theme, with automated figures and funfair rides; in another Cinderella's carriage is pulled by four horses using 22 electric motors. Trains run around landscaped tracks – guaranteed to appeal to the child in us all.

Muséum d'Histoire naturelle et d'Ethnographie ⊙ – Housed in a 17C building, the natural-history collections of the city of Colmar give a general idea of the region's fauna and forest environment.
The important geology section illustrates more than a billion years of intense activity, which explains the great diversity of the region's landscapes.
An Egyptian room and an ethnographical collection (in particular from the Marquesas Islands) complete the tour.

EXCURSION

Neuf-Brisach – *15km/9.3mi SE of Colmar. Leave by ② on the town plan and drive along N 415.*
This octagonal stronghold built by Vauban, Louis XIV's military engineer and architect, has retained its austere 17C character *(see illustration p 48)* in spite of the damage incurred during the 1870 siege and the Second World War.

The area within the 2.4km/1.5mi long walls is split into regular plots by a network of streets intersecting at right angles. In the centre stands the Église St-Louis and the vast place d'Armes (parade ground) with a well in each of its four corners.

It is possible to walk along the ditch from the Porte de Belfort (south-west) to the Porte de Colmar (north-west). This pleasant stroll (about 30min) reveals the main elements of the fortifications: bartizaned bastions, ravelins etc.

The **Porte de Belfort**, no longer used as a gate, houses the **Musée Vauban** ⊙ which contains a relief map of the stronghold with a *son et lumière* show.

Slightly further east *(5km/3mi)*, at **Vogelgrün**, the border-bridge over the Rhine offers a fine **view★** of the river, the hydroelectric power station *(see Vallée du RHIN)* and Vieux-Brisach (Breisach) across the border.

FROM THE FIELD TO YOUR TABLE

La Petite Palette – ☎ *03 89 72 73 50* – *closed 1-12 Aug, Sun evening, Tue evening and Mon* – *155/490F.* For those who appreciate good meat, this is the place to go. In a main shopping street in the town centre, this restaurant belongs to a butcher who serves meat from his shop and which is raised by his parents in the Savoie. Various menus.

COLOMBEY-LES-DEUX-ÉGLISES

Population 660
Michelin map 61 fold 19 or 241 fold 38

Situated on the edge of the Champagne region and on the borders of Burgundy and Lorraine, Colombey has, since time immemorial, been a stopover on the road from Paris to Basle. However, it became famous through its most illustrious citizen, **Charles de Gaulle**, who had his home at La Boisserie from 1933 until his death in 1970. He is buried in the village cemetery, near the church.

In his *Memoirs*, De Gaulle talks about the Champagne landscapes he loved so much: "steeped in sadness and melancholy... former mountains drastically eroded and resigned... quiet, modest villages whose soul and location has not changed for thousands of years...".

In the village, eight informative panels bear some of his quotes.

La Boisserie ⊙ – During the Second World War, La Boisserie was severely damaged by the Germans: part of the roof was destroyed by fire and a wall collapsed.

General de Gaulle only returned with his family in May 1946 after having had some work done to the house (a corner tower and a porch were added). It has not changed since that time and continues to preserve the memory of its owner who found it relaxing and conducive to deep thinking about important decisions.

COUNTRY INN

Auberge de la Montagne – *17 r. Argentolles* – ☎ *03 25 01 51 69* – *closed mid-Jan to mid-Feb, Mon evening and Tue* – *125/400F.* A peaceful inn just outside this famous village. Traditional cooking and a decor of stone walls and exposed beams. The rooms overlook the Champagne countryside.

Silence fills my house. From the corner room where I spend most of the day, I embrace the horizon towards the setting sun. No house can be seen over a distance of 15 kilometres. Beyond the plain and the woods, I can see the long curves sloping down towards the Aube Valley and the heights rising on the other side. From a high point in the garden, I behold the wild forested depths. I watch the night enveloping the landscape and then, looking at the stars, I clearly realise the insignificance of things.

Charles de Gaulle,
Mémoires de guerre

PIX

Konrad Adenauer was the only politician ever to be invited to La Boisserie. In order to secure Franco-German reconciliation, De Gaulle invited him to his home in September 1958, while the German Chancellor was on a State visit to France.

The public is allowed in the downstairs drawing room, full of mementoes, books, family portraits and photographs of contemporary personalities, in the vast library and the adjacent study where General de Gaulle spent many hours and in the dining room.

Mémorial ⊘ – Inaugurated on 18 June 1972, the memorial stands on the "mountain", which overlooks the village and surrounding forests (including the Clairvaux Forest where St Bernard founded his famous abbey in the 12C) from the great height of 397m/1 302ft.

Route des CRÊTES★★★

Michelin map 87 folds 17-19 or 242 folds 31 and 35.

This strategic road was built during the First World War at the request of the French High Command, in order to ensure adequate north-south communications between the various valleys along the front line of the Vosges.

The magnificent itinerary, which continually follows the ridge line, enables motorists to admire the most characteristic landscapes of the Vosges mountains, its passes, its *ballons* (rounded summits), its lakes, its *chaumes* (high pastures where cattle graze in summer) and offers wide panoramas and extended views.

Between the Hohneck and the Grand Ballon, the road is lined with *fermes-auberges* (farmhouses turned into inns during the season) where snacks and regional dishes are served from June to October. In winter the snowfields offer miles of cross-country tracks, in spring cattle leave for the high pastures dotted in summertime with yellow gentians and Vosges pansies.

The Route des Crêtes is generally closed between the Hohneck and the Grand Ballon from mid-November to mid-March.

Eating out

The Route des Crêtes is dotted with farm restaurants where snacks and meals made from local produce are served from June to October. It is best to reserve on Sundays and public holidays. To escape the crowds and the tourist buses, avoid the peak summer season.

MODERATE

Ferme-auberge du Molkenrain – *Rte des Crêtes – 68700 Wattwiller – 4km/2.5mi S of Vieil-Armand on D 431, then minor road –* ☎ *03 89 81 17 66 – closed Jan-Mar, 15 Nov-31 Dec and Mon – booking essential – 75/92F.* A farm built in 1926 in a fantastic setting above the Route des Crêtes, overlooking Vieil-Armand and the Alsace plain. Enjoy the view from the terrace or the welcoming dining room while you sample local dishes made from potatoes, onions and regional cheeses.

Auberge La Chaume de Schmargult – *Rte des Crêtes – La Bresse – 88400 Gérardmer – 1km/0.5mi S from the foot of Hohneck by a minor road –* ☎ *03 29 63 11 49 – closed Nov-Mar and if roads are blocked by snow, Mon evening and Tue – 85/120F.* You're guaranteed to feel close to nature in this big mountain house. Skiing is available in winter, Munster tasting and an opportunity to see the cheese being made. Restaurant with a view of the ski slopes and simple rooms.

FROM COL DU BONHOMME TO THANN

83km/52mi – allow half a day

Col du Bonhomme – Alt 949m/3 114ft. The pass links the two neighbouring regions of Alsace and Lorraine.

Beyond the pass, the road offers fine vistas of the Béhine Valley to the left, with the Tête des Faux and the Brézouard towering above. Further on, the Col du Louchbach affords a beautiful view of the valley of the River Meurthe to the south.

Turn right at Col du Calvaire.

★**Gazon du Faing** – *45min on foot there and back.*

R.Mattes/MICHELIN

Summer pastures above the tree-line

As you reach the summit (1 303m/4 275ft), climb up to a large rock from where an extended panoramic **view** is to be had. In the foreground, the small Étang des Truites, changed into a reservoir by a dam, lies inside the Lenzwasen glacial cirque. Further afield, one can see, from left to right, the Linge, the Schratz-maennele and the Barrenkopf; more to the right, beyond the Fecht Valley and the town of Munster, a long ridge slopes down from the Petit Ballon; to the right of this summit, the silhouette of the Grand Ballon (alt 1 424m/4 672ft) rises in the distance; the twin summits of the Petit Hohneck (alt 1 288m/4 226ft) and Hohneck (alt 1 362m/4 469ft) can be seen further to the right.

Lac Vert – A path starting near the 5km/3mi mark from the Col de la Schlucht leads to the Lac Vert, also known as the Lac de Soultzeren. Lichens floating in the water give the lake its characteristic colour.

Col de la Schlucht – Alt 1 135m/3 360ft. The pass links the upper valley of the River Meurthe (which takes its source 1km/0.6mi away from the pass) with that of the River Fecht. Situated at the intersection of the Route des Crêtes and the Gérardmer to Colmar road, La Schlucht is one of the busiest passes of the Vosges mountains. It is also a popular ski resort with a chair-lift to the summit of the Montabey.

Jardin d'Altitude du Haut-Chitelet ⊙ – *Alt 1 228m/4 029. 2km/1.2mi from the Col de la Schlucht towards Le Markstein, on the right-hand side of D 430.*
These botanical gardens cover an area of 11ha/27 acres and include a beech wood and a peat bog. Rockeries spreading over more than 1ha/2.5 acres shelter 2 700 species of plants from the main mountain ranges of the world.
Further on, the road offers a fine **view★** of the Valogne Valley, of Lake Longemer and Lake Retournemer. The village of Xonrupt and the suburbs of Gérardmer can be seen in the distance *(viewpoint)*.

★★★**Hohneck** – *The steep access path starts from the Route des Crêtes, 4km/2.5mi S of the Col de la Schlucht; do not follow the private path which starts closer to the pass (3km/1.9mi) as it is in bad condition. Beware of freezing winds near the summit.*
This is one of the most famous and one of the highest summits of the Vosges mountains (alt 1 362m/4 469ft). It is the highest point of the ridge which, before the First World War marked the border between France and Germany.
A splendid **panorama★★★** *(viewing table)* unfolds, encompassing the Vosges from the Donon to the Grand Ballon, the Plaine d'Alsace and the Black Forest. In clear weather, the summits of the Alps are visible.
The road runs through high pastures, known as *chaumes*. The Lac de Blanchemer can be seen on the right, framed in a beautiful wooded setting. Further on there is a magnificent view of the Grande Vallée de la Fecht, followed by the lake and valley of the Lauch with the Plaine d'Alsace in the distance.

Le Markstein – *See GUEBWILLER: Guebwiller Valley.*
As you drive along the cliff road, there are alternate views of the Thur Valley and Ballon d'Alsace massif on one side and of the Lauch Valley and Petit Ballon on the other. The small **Lac du Ballon** lies inside a funnel-shaped basin.

★★★**Grand Ballon** – *Leave the car by the hotel and follow the path on the left (30min on foot there and back).*

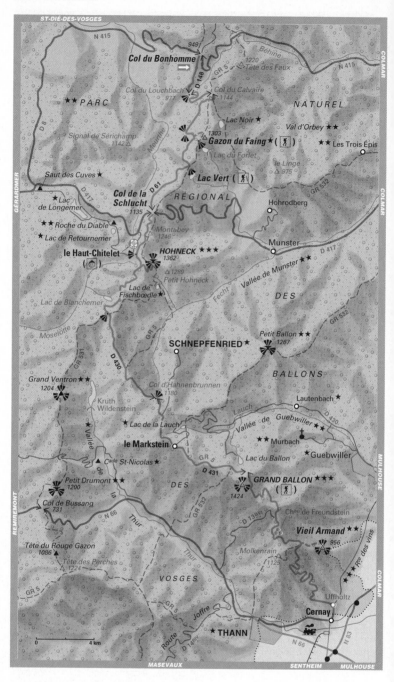

There is a radar station at the summit. The Grand Ballon, also known as the Ballon de Guebwiller, is the highest summit (alt 1 424m/4 672ft) of the Vosges mountains. Just below the summit, the Monument des Diables Bleus was erected to commemorate the various regiments of *chasseurs* (mountain troops). From the summit of the Grand Ballon, the **panorama**★★★ embraces the southern Vosges, the Black Forest and, when the weather is clear, the Jura mountains and the Alps.

On the way down, there are superb views and a chance to see the ruins of Freundstein Castle.

★★**Vieil-Armand** – The name was given by the soldiers of the First World War to the foothills of the Vosges (Hartmannswillerkopf) which slope steeply down to the Plaine d'Alsace. This strategic position was one of the most bloody battlefields along the Alsatian front (30 000 French and German soldiers killed). In 1915, attacks and counter attacks were repeatedly launched on its slopes laid waste by the artillery, and the summit, which was turned into a real fortress, was taken time and again.

The **Monument national du Vieil-Armand** ⊙ was built over a crypt containing the remains of 12 000 unknown soldiers; a bronze altar, decorated with the emblems of major French towns, stands on a vast platform.

🏃 The **summit** can be reached on foot *(1hr there and back)*. Walk through the cemetery situated behind the national monument, which contains 1 260 graves and several ossuaries. Follow the central alleyway and the path beyond it. Walk towards the summit of Vieil-Armand (alt 956m/3 136ft) surmounted by a 22m/72ft high luminous cross which marks the limit of the French front. Turn right towards the iron cross erected on a rocky promontory to commemorate the volunteers from Alsace-Lorraine. A wide **panorama**★★ can be had of the Plaine d'Alsace, the Vosges mountains, the Black Forest and, in clear weather, the Alps. Several commemorative monuments are located here including the monument to the Diables Rouges of the 152nd infantry regiment and the monument to the German mountain troops. Sections of trenches and shelters, mostly German can be visited.

On the way down to Uffholtz, the road affords views of the Plaine d'Alsace and of the Black Forest.

Cernay – This small industrial town lies at the foot of Vieil-Armand. It has retained traces of its medieval fortified wall, including the Porte de Thann which houses a small **museum** ⊙ illustrating the wars of 1870, 1914-18 and 1939-45.

🚂 From St-André, south of Cernay, it is possible to go on a **tour** ⊙ of the Doller Valley aboard a **steam train**, over a distance of 14km/8.7mi to Sentheim.

Drive W along D 35.

★**Thann** – See THANN.

Lac du DER-CHANTECOQ★★

Michelin map 61 fold 9 or 241 fold 34

Created in 1974, this artificial lake, the largest in France (4 800ha/11 861 acres, 1.5 times the area of the Lac d'Annecy), was intended to regulate the flow of the River Marne; a feeder canal, 12km/7.5mi long, diverts two-thirds of the flow when the river is in spate and another canal supplies the Paris region when the water level is low. The lake fills up slowly during the winter months and empties during the autumn. The level is at its highest in June and at its lowest in November.

This low-lying area was chosen because of the waterproof qualities of its clay soil. Part of the Der Forest (whose name means oak in Celtic) disappeared beneath the surface of the lake together with the three villages of Chantecoq, Champaubert-aux-Bois and Nuisement. However, the churches of the last two villages were spared.

Where to stay

MODERATE

Chambre d'hôte Au Brochet du Lac – *15 Grande-Rue – 51290 St-Remy-en-Bouzemont – 6km/3.75mi W of Arrigny on D 57 and D 58 – ☎ 03 26 72 51 06 – aubrochetdulac@libertysurf.fr – closed 24 Dec-3 Jan – 5 rooms 210/260F – evening meal 90F.* This lovely timber-framed house offers rooms with country furniture and a big common room with a fireplace and traditional floor tiles. The perfect place from which to explore the lake and surroundings. Mountain bikes and canoes for hire.

MID-RANGE

Le Cheval Blanc – *21 r. du Lac – 51290 Giffaumont-Champaubert – ☎ 03 26 72 62 65 – closed 1-23 Jan, 4-26 Sep, Sun evening and Mon – 🅿 – 14 rooms 280/340F – ⊑ 35F – restaurant 130/350F.* Simple, bright rooms in this peaceful lakeside resort. Varied, attractive menus. Summer terrace.

DRIVE ROUND THE LAKE *83km/52mi – allow 3hr*

Start from Giffaumont where the Maison du Lac (tourist office of Lake Der-Chantecoq) is located.

Giffaumont-Champaubert – The marina can accommodate up to 500 boats. **Boat trips on the lake** ⊙ are organised in summer.

Opposite *(access on foot along the dyke)*, Champaubert Church stands alone on a piece of land jutting out into the lake.

Grange aux abeilles ⊘ – An exhibition and an audio-visual show enable visitors to appreciate the work accomplished by bees and bee-keepers.

Follow D 13, then D 12 towards Montier-en-Der.

Ferme de Berzillières ⊘ – This entirely restored farmhouse contains a museum of agriculture with 400 pieces of machinery and agricultural tools.

Go back along D 12 and, 500m/547yd further on, turn left towards Troyes then right towards Châtillon-sur-Broué.

Châtillon-sur-Broué – This village is characteristic of the Der area, with its square church steeple and its timber-and-cob houses.

Continue towards the lake.

The road skirts the dyke and runs past the small harbour of Chantecoq.
Opposite the harbour, a path *(parking area at the beginning)* leads to the Maison de l'Oiseau et du Poisson.

Maison de l'Oiseau et du Poisson ⊘ – This nature museum is housed in the timber-framed Ferme des Grands Parts, characteristic of the Champagne scenery.
◙ It shows various specific environments such as subaquatic life, the four seasons of the lake, migrating birds, with the help of reconstructions, interactive terminals and sound effects. Two roads run along dykes to allow visitors to spot passing cranes. West of the lake, a peaceful area has been set aside as a bird sanctuary.

Continue along D 13.

Arrigny – There is a fine timber-framed church in the village.

When you reach the village square, turn left onto D 57 towards St-Rémy-en-Bouzemont. In St-Rémy, take D 58 towards Drosnay. The Ferme aux Grues is located in the hamlet of Isson.

Ferme aux Grues ⊘ – This farm is open in the winter months *(Oct-Mar)* when the cranes are in residence.
◙ There are explanations about the work undertaken for the preservation of migrating cranes and the study of their migratory habits. An observatory enables birdwatchers to watch cranes feeding on crops and meadows.

Return to Arrigny and follow D 57 towards Eclaron, then turn right in Blaise-sous-Hauteville.

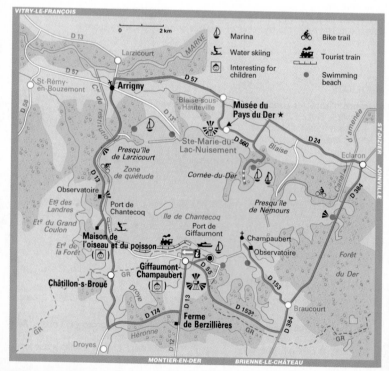

Cranes' migratory habits

Every year in autumn, cranes leave Scandinavia and travel to milder climates in Spain or Africa. They fly over Champagne in successive waves, usually by night, and give out an impressive loud cry. Some of these cranes remain in the region throughout the winter and show a particular liking for meadows situated near a lake. They fly back north in the spring. Thousands of them stop by the **Ferme aux Grues**, near the Lac du Der-Chantecoq, where grain is purposely spread over a large area to attract them.

This large grey bird, with its long neck and long legs, has a wing span of 2m/6.5ft and weighs 4-7kg/9-15lb. It feeds on grain, grass and young shoots as well as insects, molluscs and worms.

★**Musée du Pays du Der (Ste-Marie-du-Lac-Nuisement)** – This place is a village and a museum *(Village-musée)* at the same time, made up of several timber-framed buildings saved from flooding when the lake was created, including the church of Nuisement-aux-Bois, the school-town hall, the smithy's house where refreshments are available, a dovecote and the Machelignots' barn containing exhibitions on traditional aspects of the Der area: costumes, models of timber-framed houses, reconstructions of workshops. A video-film illustrates the different stages of the creation of the reservoir.

Château d'eau panoramique ⊘ – In Ste-Marie-du-Lac-Nuisement as in Giffaumont-Champaubert, the water tower stands 20m/66ft high and affords views of the lake *(viewing table, telescope and audio-guide)*.

Road D 560 leads to the Cornée du Der, a wooded peninsula jutting out into the lake.

Return to D 24 and turn right to Éclaron, then right again onto D 384.

The road offers a fine view of the lake before entering the Der Forest.

In Braucourt, it is possible to turn right onto D 153 leading to Champaubert Church at the tip of the peninsula of the same name.

Turn right 1.5km/0.9mi beyond Braucourt onto D 153[A]. Continue along D 55 to return to Giffaumont-Champaubert.

Massif du DONON★★

Michelin map 87 folds 14 and 15 or 242 folds 23 and 27

The Donon is recognisable from afar with its two-tier summit marking the boundary between Alsace and Lorraine. Geographically, the Donon massif forms the southern part of the sandstone Vosges mountains, reaching their highest point at the Donon summit (alt 1 009m/3 311ft). Numerous streams taking their source near the summit radiate across the splendid forests which cover the massif. A road runs alongside each valley and there are cross-country skiing tracks and ski lifts.

Celts, Romans, Franks and all the Germanic tribes travelling west came through the Donon pass and there is evidence that an ancient god, probably Mercury, was worshipped on the mountain. Finds excavated on the site of the Donon pass are exhibited in the archaeological museums of Strasbourg and Épinal.

THE SARRE ROUGE AND SARRE BLANCHE VALLEYS

Round tour from the Col du Donon – *55km/34mi – allow 2hr*

Col du Donon – Alt 718m/2 356ft.

Donon – Alt 1 009m/3 311ft. *About 1hr 30min on foot there and back.*

🚶 *It is possible to leave the car at the Donon pass and follow the footpath starting on the right of Hôtel Velléda; alternatively, one can drive for 1.3km/0.8mi along the road branching off D 993 on the right, 1km/0.6mi from the pass; leave the car in the parking area (barrier) and walk the last 2km.*

There are two viewing tables on the summit. The **panorama**★★ includes the Vosges mountain range, the Lorraine plateau, the Plaine d'Alsace and the Black Forest. A small temple built in 1869 stands between the two viewing tables and there are Gallo-Roman ruins scattered on the slopes.

A television relay is located 50m/164ft below the summit.

Atop Donon

From the Col du Donon, the itinerary follows the **Vallée de la Sarre Rouge** or Vallée de St-Quirin then goes across the Lorraine plateau.

Continue straight on along D 145 and then D 44, ignoring the Cirey-sur-Vezouze road on your left. The itinerary enters the Lorraine region.

The road winds its way down through picturesque scenery, along the narrow wooded valley of St-Quirin, keeping close to the Sarre Rouge which is more of a mountain stream than a river.

Grand Soldat – This hamlet is the birthplace of Alexandre Chatrian (1826-90), who collaborated with Emile Erckmann (1822-99) to write a series of novels inspired by Alsatian traditions and legends. They became extremely popular after the annexation of Alsace-Lorraine by Germany in 1871.

Abreschviller – A small **forest train** ⊘, steam or diesel-powered, leads to Grand Soldat *(6km/3.7mi).*

3km/1.9mi further on, turn left onto D 96^F towards St-Quirin.

Vasperviller – Camped on the first foothills of the Donon, this village offers amateurs of modern sacred art an interesting discovery: a remarkable little church designed in 1968 by the architect Litzenburger, the **Église Ste-Thérèse**.

The interior, plain yet subtle in design, is lit by lovely stained-glass windows (Tree of Jesse). The top of the campanile is accessible via an unusual double staircase (75 steps) lined with the Stations of the Cross. Pleasant view of the village and the valley along which runs the St-Quirin road.

St-Quirin – This low-lying village, surrounded by meadows, is overlooked by a Romanesque chapel where a pilgrimage has taken place for centuries. The 18C priory church is surmounted by two towers and a pinnacle crowned by onion-shaped domes. It houses a restored organ made in 1746 by Silbermann.

Drive W out of St-Quirin along D 96 and, 2km/1.2mi further on, turn left onto D 993.

The road follows the **Vallée de la Sarre Blanche** through lovely forests. The area is sparsely populated – with only a few sawmills and forest lodges along the road – but the beauty of the landscape retains the full attention of visitors.

At the end of the tour, you are back in Alsace as you leave the Abreschviller road on your left to return to the Donon pass.

THE PLAINE VALLEY

From the Col du Donon to Badonviller *60km/37mi – 2hr 30min*

Col du Donon – Alt 718m/2 356ft.

On the way down from the pass, the picturesque road runs through a splendid forest of fir trees then offers views of the twin villages of Raon-sur-Plaine and Raon-lès-Leau (note the memorial to escaped prisoners of war and their guides inside the bend to the right).

Raon-sur-Plaine – The village lies amid green meadows, within sight of the Donon. A small road leads up the mountain (4km/2.5mi) to a well-preserved **Roman way** running underwoods over a distance of approximately 500m/547yd.

Vallée de la Plaine or Vallée de Celles – Red-roofed houses dotted about on the edge of the forest add to the charm of the mainly green landscape.

Lac de la Maix – *1hr on foot there and back, starting from Vexaincourt; follow a narrow forest road on the left.*

A path runs round this dark green lake overlooked by a chapel.

Between Allarmont and Celles-sur-Plaine, the former **Scierie de la Hallière** ⊘ houses a folklore museum displaying tools and equipment once used for sawing *(demonstrations in summer)* and for woodwork; interesting waterwheel.

Celles-sur-Plaine is close to the two lakes of Pierre Percée.

The **Lac de la Plaine** (36ha/89 acres) has been turned into a leisure and water sports centre (swimming, sailing, rowing, canoeing...).

After the Plaine dam, turn right onto the scenic road to Badonviller (D 182A).

The drive through forests of firs affords fine views during the first part of the climb. The **road**★ leads to the tiny village of **Pierre-Percée**. The town hall has an **exhibit area and shop** devoted to "Art, crafts and regional produce from Lorraine".

The road then climbs up to the foot of a ruined castle *(parking area)* perched on top of a knoll, which has retained a 12C keep. From there, extended **views**★ of the lake in its romantic setting of hills and forests can be had.

Lac de Pierre-Percée – *Parking area near the Vieux-Pré dam. Walk towards the viewpoint where the construction of the dam is explained on several panels.*

A boat trip aboard the **Vedette Cristal** ⊘ offers varied views of the surrounding mountains.

The nature trail of the Roche aux Corbeaux and a **birdwatching post** offer the opportunity of discovering the forest environment *(access by the scenic road)*.

Return to D 182 and continue to Badonviller.

Badonviller – This small industrial town, partly destroyed in August 1914, was, 30 years later, one of the first towns to be liberated by the French second armoured division during the battle of Alsace which began in November 1944.

Return to the Col du Donon along D 992 then D 183 via the Col de la Chapelotte, Vexaincourt and Raon-sur-Plaine.

ÉCOMUSÉE D'ALSACE★★

Michelin map 242 fold 35 – 9km/5.6mi south-west of Ensisheim, in Ungersheim

Some 50 traditional old houses scattered over an area of almost 25ha/50 acres give an insight into housing in the different rural areas of Alsace.

The wish to preserve the regional heritage was at the origin of this open-air museum: old houses from the 15C to 19C, doomed to be demolished, were patiently located all over Alsace, then carefully taken apart and rebuilt in the new village. The museum, inaugurated in 1984 and continually expanding, has now turned to the region's industrial heritage with the renovation of the various buildings of the potash mine Rodolphe (1911-1930) adjacent to the museum.

Traditional architecture in the Écomusée d'Alsace

Tour of the museum ⊙ – *It is intended that visitors should walk through the museum's vast area and take as much or as little time as they wish, although half a day seems to be the minimum; in addition, activities centred on Alsatian life are organised in the evening, particularly in summer.*

⊡ Timber-framed Alsatian houses with their courtyards and gardens, grouped according to their original area, Sungdau, Ried, Kochersberg, Bas-Rhin, illustrate the evolution of building techniques and give an insight into social life in traditional Alsatian villages. These fine buildings have one thing in common, the *stube* or living room, the focus of family and social life (meals, Sunday receptions, evening gatherings). It also sometimes served as the master bedroom, but, most important, it contained an imposing earthenware stove! You will see several such stoves during your visit of the museum.

Other buildings house exhibitions or shows on such themes as the Alsatian headdress, water and fire in the home, fishing, and recurring feasts. Several workshops are operating: a blacksmith's, a potter's with an impressive wood oven, a cartwright's, a distillery, an oil-mill.

Natural environment – Ancient plant species can be seen growing in their recreated natural environment and there are demonstrations of traditional farming methods. There are beehives, an apple orchard, as well as cowsheds and stables sheltering domestic animals, and storks return regularly to nest on the weathered roofs.

Merry-go-rounds – A section of the museum is devoted to funfairs; note in particular the merry-go-round, Eden-Palladium, the last of the great Belle Epoque merry-go-rounds in France (1909).

Eating out

MODERATE

La Taverne – *At the Écomusée* – ☎ *03 89 74 44 49 – 98/198F.* The decor is that of an old Alsatian inn, with beams and roof timbers, while the hearty cooking includes pork, sauerkraut and other typical regional dishes. A nice way of discovering more about the traditions mentioned in the museum, with a good atmosphere as well.

Where to stay

MID-RANGE

Hôtel Les Loges de l'Écomusée – *At the Écomusée* – ☎ *03 89 74 44 95 –* 🅿 *– 30 rooms 335/370F –* ☕ *34F.* Right next to the museum, this hotel consists of small, locally inspired buildings, and the effect is attractive. It has been designed as a village, and offers simple, modern rooms with mezzanines or split-level apartments. Independent studio apartments.

EGUISHEIM ★

Population 1 530
Michelin map 87 fold 17 or 242 fold 31 – Local map see Route des VINS

This ancient village is today a lively wine-growing centre; it developed round its 13C castle which has retained part of its surrounding wall forming an octagon.
Surrounded by 300ha/741 acres of vines and lying at the foot of three ruined towers, used as sundials by workers in the plain below, the village has hardly changed since the 16C. Two famous wines are produced locally. The wine-growers festival takes place during the fourth weekend in August. Visitors can follow the wine trail *(1hr on foot; guided tours of cellars with wine-tasting included).*

Grand'Rue – The picturesque houses lining this street have wide doorways adorned with coats of arms and inscribed with the date. Note also the two lovely Renaissance fountains.

Tour of the ramparts – The marked itinerary follows the former watch-path. The narrow paved streets are lined with old houses offering a wealth of architectural features (balconies, oriels, timber frames, pointed gables).

Church – Inside the modern church, to the right of the entrance, there is a chapel beneath the steeple. It contains the old doorway with its 12C tympanum illustrating Christ between St Peter and St Paul; the procession of Wise Virgins and Foolish Virgins forms the lintel. Beautiful modern stained-glass windows illustrate scenes of the Life of Léon IX. Fine 19C organ by Callinet.

Cobblestone streets of the old town

★ROUTE DES CINQ CHÂTEAUX

20km/12.4mi round tour including five castles, plus about 1hr 45min on foot.

Drive to Husseren (see p 377) along D 14. As you come out of the village, turn right onto the forest road, known as the Route des cinq Châteaux; 1km/0.6mi further on, leave the car in the parking area and walk to Eguisheim's three castles (5min uphill).

Donjons d'Eguisheim – Three massive square keeps built of red sandstone and known as Weckmund, Wahlenbourg and Dagsbourg, stand at the top of the hill. They belonged to the powerful Eguisheim family and were destroyed by fire following a 15C war between the burghers of Mulhouse and the aristocracy of the surrounding area *(see MULHOUSE)*. Pope Léon IX was most probably born here *(see WANGENBOURG: Excursions).*

Return to the car and drive on for about 6km/3.7mi.

The narrow road offers fine viewpoints all the way.

Château de Hohlandsbourg ⊘ – The imposing castle stands on the left; built c 1279, it first belonged to the powerful House of Hapsburg. It was bought in 1563 by Lazare de Schwendi, Emperor Maximilian's personal advisor, who modernised it; it was eventually destroyed during the Thirty Years War. Restored in the 16C, it was adapted to the use of artillery and could accommodate many guns.

Eating out

MID-RANGE

La Grangelière – *59 r. du Rempart-Sud* – ☎ *03 89 23 00 30* – *closed Feb and Thu* – *135/390F.* This Alsatian house near the ramparts is slightly off the tourist trail. But you won't regret making the detour: the chef, who has worked in some major establishments, offers cooking that is both contemporary and very tempting.

Le Caveau d'Eguisheim – *3 pl. du Château-St-Léon* – ☎ *03 89 41 08 89* – *closed 3 Jan-12 Feb, Thu lunchtime and Wed* – *booking essential* – *175/375F.* Only regional wines are on offer in this pretty local-style restaurant situated in the village square. Fortunately they go very well with the young chef's inventive cooking, which combines regional dishes and contemporary flavours, making eating here a pleasure.

Where to stay

MID-RANGE

Hostellerie du Château – *2 r. du Château* – ☎ *03 89 23 72 00* – *closed 3 Jan-12 Feb* – *12 rooms 410/780F* – ☞ *55F.* This old building on the village square has been completely renovated by the architect owner. Its stylish modern decor offers charming, light, pleasant rooms with old-fashioned bathrooms.

There is a magnificent view of the Pflixbourg keep and Hohneck summit to the west, the Haut-Kœnigsbourg to the north, and Colmar and the Plaine d'Alsace to the east.

Donjon de Pflixbourg – *A path, branching off to the left 2km/1.2mi further on, leads to the keep.*

⚔ The fortress, which was the former Alsatian residence of the representative of the Holy Roman Emperor, came into the possession of the Ribeaupierre family during the 15C. A vaulted water tank can be seen next to the keep. There is a fine view of the Fecht Valley to the west and of the Plaine d'Alsace to the east.

As you rejoin D 417, turn right towards Colmar.
On leaving Wintzenheim (see Route des VINS: From Châtenois to Colmar), turn right onto N 83 then right again onto D 1bis to return to Eguisheim.

ENSISHEIM

Population 6 164
Michelin map 87 fold 18 or 242 fold 35

Excavations undertaken south of the town have revealed that the site was inhabited as far back as the fifth millenium BC. The name of Ensisheim, however, was mentioned for the first time in a document dating from 765. The city acquired fame and became prosperous when it became the capital of the Hapsburgs' territories in Alsace. It even remained the capital of western Austria until 1648. More than 200 aristocratic families lived in Ensisheim when it was at the height of its fame and to this day the town has retained some fine Gothic and Renaissance mansions including the Palais de la Régence.

MEDIEVAL CHARM

La Couronne – *47 r. de la 1ʳᵉ-Armée-Française* – ☎ *03 89 81 03 72* – *closed 14-18 Aug, Sat lunchtime, Sun evening and Mon* – *230/420F.* This 17C listed building has plenty of charm, notwithstanding the prison opposite. Medieval decor and a lovely terrace where it's a pleasure to eat; there is also a simple cellar restaurant, Le Thaler. Fairly plain rooms.

SIGHTS

Palais de la Régence – This fine Gothic edifice erected in 1535 was decorated in Renaissance style. On the ground floor, the vaulting of the arcade is decorated with emblems bearing the coat of arms of several Alsatian towns. The façade on the church side is flanked with an octagonal stair turret.

Musée de la Régence ⊙ – In the first room of the museum is exhibited a meteorite which fell on Ensisheim on 7 November 1492. It is believed to be the first fall of a meteorite ever recorded and its size is said to have been impressive (150kg/331lb) but it was gradually reduced to about a third of its original size through the generosity of the town as every important visitor was given a piece of it.
The most recent archaeological finds are also displayed: ceramics, tools and a child's grave dating from the first period of the Neolithic Age, objects from the Bronze Age and the Gallo-Roman period.

Hôtel de la Couronne – It is housed in an elegant building dating from 1609, decorated with scrolled gables and a two-storey carved oriel. Turenne, Louis XIV's great general, stayed here in 1675 before his victory at the battle of Turckheim, which led to the Peace of Nijmegen and the final union of France and Alsace.

EXCURSION

★★Écomusée d'Alsace – *9km/5.6mi SW along D 4 bis to Ungersheim, then D 44 towards Feldkirch Bollwiller; turn left onto D 200 and left again onto D 430 to the open-air museum (see ÉCOMUSÉE D'ALSACE).*

Population 26 681
Michelin map 56 fold 16 or 241 fold 21

Épernay is with Reims, the main wine-growing centre of the Champagne region and the meeting point of three major wine-growing areas: the Montagne de Reims, the Côte des Blancs and the Marne Valley. The town is well provided with green open spaces including the Jardin de l'Hôtel de Ville laid out in the 19C by the Bühler brothers (who also designed Lyon's famous Parc de la Tête d'Or). There are many opulent 19C buildings in neo-Renaissance or Classical style, particularly in the district around the avenue de Champagne where you will see the great names of the famous sparkling wine: Moët et Chandon, Mercier...

Eating out

MID-RANGE

Chez Pierrot – 16 r. de la Fauvette – ☎ 03 26 55 16 93 – closed during Feb school holidays, 5-20 Sep, 24-31 Dec, Thu lunchtime Mar-Oct and Wed – 160/270F. This town-centre restaurant has tasty cooking and an original decor. One room is decorated with pictures and knick-knacks, while a glass-covered inner courtyard creates a winter garden. Reasonably priced lunchtime menus.

La Table de Kobus – 3 r. du Dr-Rousseau – ☎ 03 26 51 53 53 – closed 8-16 Apr, 1-22 Aug, Sun evening and Mon – 140/240F. The attractive, contemporary yet unpretentious dishes are served in a large, high-ceilinged room, decorated in bistro style. This modern restaurant is popular with groups, for you are welcome to bring your own wine, at no extra charge.

Auberge St-Vincent – 51150 Ambonnay – 20km/12.5mi E of Épernay on D 201, D 1 and D 37 – ☎ 03 26 57 01 98 – closed Sun evening and Mon – 140/360F. A pretty, regional-style inn with a flower-decked façade. The decor is a happy combination of traditional and modern. Big fireplace in the main dining room. The cuisine uses traditional recipes and the rooms are simple and practical.

Where to stay

MODERATE

Hôtel St-Pierre – 14 av. P.-Chandon – ☎ 03 26 54 40 80 – closed Feb – 15 rooms 120/205F – ☑ 29F. This small, modest hotel in a quiet area, slightly away from the town centre, offers simple, comfortable rooms at reasonable prices. Pleasant family atmosphere.

Chambre d'hôte M. et Mme Tarlant – R. de la Coopérative – 51480 Œuilly – 13km/8mi W of Épernay on N 3 (Dormans road) – ☎ 03 26 58 30 60 – 4 rooms 210/280F. By staying with this wine producer, you will have the opportunity to visit his cellar and taste his Champagne. Although the house itself doesn't have a lot of character, the spacious rooms overlook the vineyard, the atmosphere is peaceful, and the welcome warm.

Chambre d'hôte La Boursaultière – 44 r. de la Duchesse-d'Uzès – 51480 Boursault – 9km/5.5mi W of Épernay on N 3 and D 222 – ☎ 03 26 58 47 76 – ⌂ – 4 rooms 240/320F. This hospitable bad and breakfast in the village is built around a pretty garden courtyard. The rooms are decorated with fabrics printed with medieval and Renaissance patterns. A rather unique place to stay if you plan to explore the vineyards.

MID-RANGE

Les Berceaux – 13 r. des Berceaux – ☎ 03 26 55 28 84 – 29 rooms 390/490F – ☑ 50F – restaurant 140/450F. A warm welcome and high-quality service in this hundred-year-old hotel. The façade is pleasing and flower-decked, the modern rooms are soundproof. Indulge your taste buds with the restaurant's classic, refined cuisine, or have a lighter meal in the wine bar.

Chambre d'hôte Manoir de Montflambert – 51160 Mutigny – 7km/4.3mi NE of Épernay on D 201 – ☎ 03 26 52 33 21 – closed Nov-Easter – 7 rooms 420/650F. This old hunting lodge dates from the 17C. Overlooking the Marne plain and the vineyards, it stands proudly on the edge of the forest. The prices in this charming bed and breakfast are justified by the open fireplaces, the lovely wood panelling, the imposing staircase leading to the bedrooms and the peace and quiet.

On the town

La Marmite Swing – *160 av. Foch* – ☎ *03 26 54 17 72* – *bar: Tue-Sat 10am-midnight* – *cabaret: Tue-Thu midnight-4am, Fri-Sat midnight-5am, evenings before public holidays: midnight-5am* – *closed first 3 weeks of Aug.* Three ingredients add up to an original mix: a brightly coloured bistro with hanging tables and swing chairs; a dining room/cabaret which offers paella with flamenco, or couscous with Arabic/Andalusian music; a concert room (jazz, blues, rock, world music) which turns into a nightclub after midnight. Rum and Afro-West Indian evenings are a speciality.

Le Progrès – *5 pl. de la République* – ☎ *03 26 55 22 72* – *Mon-Fri 6am-midnight, Sat-Sun 7am-midnight*. This spacious, bright bar with its modern feel and large terrace is one of the most popular places in town. A nice way to finish off a day of visiting Épernay's Champagne cellars.

Shopping

Beaumont des Crayères – *64 r. de la Liberté* – *51530 Mardeuil* – ☎ *03 26 55 29 40* – *Mon-Fri 8am-noon, 1.30-6pm, Sat 8am-noon, 2-5pm, Sun 10am-noon, 2-6pm*. This Champagne museum includes among its exhibits the biggest champagne bottle in the world. You can also taste and buy.

Chocolat Thibaut – *Pôle d'activités St-Julien* – *51530 Pierry* – *2km/1.2mi S of Épernay on D 11* – ☎ *03 26 51 58 04* – *Mon-Sat 9am-noon, 2-7pm*. This chocolate craftsman will make his specialities while you watch: chocolates in the shape of Champagne corks, filled with regional liqueurs (ratafia, grape brandies). You can taste and buy the produce in the shop next door.

**CHAMPAGNE CELLARS

The main Champagne firms, some of them going back to the 18C, line both sides of the avenue de Champagne, above the limestone cliff riddled with miles of galleries which remain at a constant temperature of 9-12°C/48-54°F.

Some of these firms organise tours during which visitors can observe the various stages that Champagne must go through to reach perfection.

Moët et Chandon ⊙ – *18 avenue de Champagne*. Moët et Chandon was the first Champagne firm; its story is linked to that of Hautvillers Abbey *(see MONTAGNE DE REIMS: Hautvillers)* which it owns and to Dom Pérignon whom it honoured by naming its prestigious Champagne after him.

The founder of the firm, Claude Moët, began producing Champagne in 1743. His grandson, Jean Rémy, a close friend of Napoleon, welcomed the emperor several times (one of Napoleon's hats is kept on the premises). Jean Rémy's son-in-law, Pierre Gabriel Chandon, added his name and the firm became known as Moët et Chandon. In 1962, the family concern was made into a limited company (the Moët-Hennessy-Louis Vuitton group).

The 28km/17.4mi long cellars, contain the equivalent of 90 million bottles. During the tour, which is very thorough, visitors can observe the various stages Champagne goes through, including *remuage* (moving the bottles round) and *dégorgement* (releasing the deposit).

A historic cask

Mercier ⊙ – *73 avenue de Champagne*. In 1858, Eugène Mercier merged several Champagne firms under his own name. He then had 18km/11.2mi of galleries dug. To celebrate the 1889 World Exhibition, he asked a sculptor from Châlons, named Navlet, to decorate a huge tun with a capacity of 215 000 bottles and placed it on a cart drawn by 24 oxen and 18 horses acting as support in uphill sections of the journey. This exceptional convoy travelled from Épernay to Paris in 20 days; some bridges had to be reinforced and walls demolished along the way. One hundred years later the huge tun, weighing 34t, was put on display in the main hall.

Mercier is the second Champagne producer after Moët et Chandon and it belongs to the same group.

A panoramic lift takes visitors down to the cellars for a ride in a small automatic train along galleries decorated with carvings by Navlet.

De Castellane ⊘ – *57 rue de Verdun.* The 10km/6mi long cellars, the tower and the museum can be visited. The **tower**, which is 60m/197ft high, is used as an exhibition area devoted to the story of the Castellane family – including the famous art collector Boni de Castellane who married the American millionairess Anna Gould – and of the Mérand family; there is a collection of posters and bottles.

A climb of 237 steps leads to the top which affords an extended view of Épernay and the surrounding vineyards.

The **museum** is devoted to the evolution of the Champagne-making process. Two rooms contain scenes illustrating various aspects of wine-growing such as the cooper's work, looking after the vines, grape-harvesting and pressing. In addition, various sections present printing techniques, regional fauna, posters having a connection with Champagne, several crafts (basketwork, glass-making...) and a rich collection of labels.

ADDITIONAL SIGHTS

Musée municipal ⊘ – *First floor.* This museum is housed in the former Château Perrier, a copy of a castle in the Louis XIII style built in the mid 19C by a wine merchant.

Vin de Champagne – Two rooms illustrate the life and work of a wine-grower and a person in charge of a cellar. Collection of bottles and labels.

Archéologie – An important **archaeological collection**★ is displayed on the upper floor: funeral objects found in various local cemeteries, reconstructions of graves, remarkable pottery, glassware, weapons and jewellery.

★COTEAUX SUD D'ÉPERNAY

Round tour south of Épernay

28km/17.4mi – allow 1hr – local map see Routes du CHAMPAGNE

The Épernay hills form the edge of the Île-de-France cuesta.

Leave Épernay along RD 51.

The road follows the Cubry Valley with vineyards on both sides of the river.

Pierry – *See Routes du CHAMPAGNE.*

As you come to Moussy, look left towards the church of Chavot (13C), perched on a peak.

Turn right 1km/0.6mi beyond Vaudancourt onto D 951.

Château de Brugny – The castle overlooks the Cubry Valley. Built in the 16C, it was remodelled in the 18C. The square stone keep, flanked by round brick-built bartizans, looks particularly attractive.

In Brugny, take D 36 leading to St-Martin-d'Ablois.

There are interesting **views**★ of the glacial Sourdon cirque, with the church of Chavot on the right, Moussy in the centre and Épernay Forest on the left.

Turn left onto D 11 towards Mareuil-en-Brie.

Parc du Sourdon ⊘ – The Sourdon takes its source under a pile of rocks then flows through the park planted with fine trees and forms a series of small pools where trout flourish.

Drive back to D 22 and turn left. The road runs through Épernay Forest (private property) and the village of Vauciennes then reaches N 3. Turn right towards Épernay.

ÉPINAL★

Conurbation 50 909
Michelin map 62 fold 16 or 242 fold 30

Épinal, which occupies a favourable position at an important crossroads, spreads along both banks of the River Moselle. Its famous prints and cotton industry (now declining) once brought prosperity to the town, which today offers visitors its bright flower-decked streets, squares and embankments. The surrounding forested area covers 3 600ha/8 896 acres.

Épinal prints – The enormous success of the Épinal prints lasted for almost two centuries. Most popular prints used to depict religious subjects at the time when Jean Charles **Pellerin** began to illustrate secular subjects such as traditional songs, riddles, La Fontaine's fables and scenes of traditional French life; towards the end of the 19C, the firm even took an interest in publicity. Several well-known artists (Caran d'Ache, O'Galop, Benjamin Rabier...) contributed to this immensely popular form of art.

Once it had been carved on wood (generally pear tree wood), the picture was printed on a Gutenberg type of press. The different colours were applied by hand using stencil-plates, a technique which is still used today.

The two world wars and new printing techniques caused the decline of this prosperous business which, however, has survived.

Eating out

MODERATE

Le Bagatelle – *12 r. des Petites-Boucheries* – ☎ *03 29 35 05 22* – *closed 16-29 Jul and Sun* – *65/200F.* On a little island between two branches of the River Moselle, this spruce 1940s restaurant is the best place for watching the canoeing/kayak competitions, as well as for enjoying inspired cooking in its bright dining room with modern furniture.

Ferme-auberge des 7 Pêcheurs – *28-32 r. de la Division-Leclerc* – *88220 Méloménil-Uzemain* – *15km/9.3mi SW of Épinal on D 51 (via Chantraine)* – ☎ *03 29 30 70 79* – *closed Jan and Wed out of season* – ⊡ – *95/130F.* The dining room is an 18C forge, which has retained a good feeling of authenticity with old beams, exposed stone walls and an open fireplace. There are bedrooms to let and a large, simply furnished holiday cottage for those who want to enjoy the peace and quiet of this old farm. A good area for lovely walks.

MID-RANGE

Le Calmosien – *88390 Chaumousey* – *10km/6.2mi W of Épinal on D 36 and D 460* – ☎ *03 29 66 80 77* – *closed Sun evening* – *115/290F.* In the village centre, this 1900s building is reminiscent of a school, with its white façade, brick-edged windows and steeply sloping roof. The old-fashioned decor and garden terrace are the setting for contemporary cooking, either fixed menus or à la carte.

Where to stay

MODERATE

Hôtel Azur – *54 quai des Bons-Enfants* – ☎ *03 29 64 05 25* – *closed 23 Dec-3 Jan* – *20 rooms 185/310F* – ☐ *35F.* This town-centre hotel borders the Moselle. Behind its modest façade, the rooms are simple but well kept and clean. It is also good value.

MID-RANGE

Hôtel Kyriad – *12 av. du Gén.-de-Gaulle* – ☎ *03 29 82 10 74* – *closed 23 Dec-2 Jan* – ⓟ – *48 rooms 320/480F* – ☐ *39F.* This hotel opposite the station is a good place to stay: the rooms are spruce, well kept and welcoming, as well as soundproof. Friendly staff and good value for money.

On the town

Daval – *44 r. Léopold-Bourg* – ☎ *03 29 35 60 60* – *www.chocolat-daval.fr* – *Tue-Sat 8.30am-7pm, Mon 2-7pm, Sun 8.30am-12.30pm* – *closed 1 May, Easter Monday and Pentecost.* This town-centre cake shop and tearoom is a good place to stop for a quiet break. Excellent pastries, coffee and tea.

Le Cartoon – *25 r. de la Maix* – ☎ *03 29 34 35 33* – *Mon-Thu 10.30am-1am, Fri-Sat 10.30am-2am.* Decorated with strip cartoons, this bar is a popular meeting place among the young of Épinal. The district is being done up; there's a nice atmosphere and theme evenings every fortnight.

Pâtisserie du Musée – *2 quai du Musée* – ☎ *03 29 82 10 73* – *Tue-Fri 7.30am-7pm, Sat-Sun 7.30am-12.30pm, 2-7pm.* This cake shop and tearoom must be one of the nicest in town, in its leafy setting near the museum. Unless you are totally single-minded, it's practically impossible to choose between a *desir des Îles,* a Mirabelle or Edelweiss delight, the aniseed-flavoured bread and the famous *charbonettes des Vosges* (a chocolate praline speciality). Eat here or take away.

The Wellington – *11 r. Chipotte* – ☎ *03 29 64 03 78* – *daily from 11am.* A pleasant, British-style pub with a friendly atmosphere. Spacious terrace which gets lively towards the end of the evening.

Brasserie-écomusée "La Vosgienne" – *48 r. de Mirecourt* – *88270 Ville-sur-Illon* – *5km/3mi from Dompaire, between Vittel and Épinal.* – ☎ *03 29 36 58 05 / 03 29 36 53 18 / 03 29 36 63 11* – *www.ecomusee-vosgien-brasserie-asso.fr* – *15 Jun-Sep: Tue-Sun 2.30-6pm; by reservation rest of year.* Ville-sur-Illon is famous for the purity of its water, and has manufactured beer since 1627. In 1887 an Alsatian brewer, Jacques Lobstein, founded a Bavarian-style industrial brewery which continued production until 1975. This unique establishment has been converted into a museum, but specialist beers are still brewed here and can be sampled on the spot or bought to take away.

Parks, Zoos, Attractions

Fraispertuis City – ⧉ – *50 r. de la Colline-des-Eaux* – *88700 Jeanménil* – *S of Baccarat on D 935, D 435 and D 32.* – ☎ *03 29 65 27 06* – *variable opening times, depending on school holidays.* A leisure park with around 20 attractions based on a Wild West theme (goldmine train, adventure river, buffalo shooting, Grand Canyon), guaranteed to please young and old alike. Restaurant.

ÉPINAL

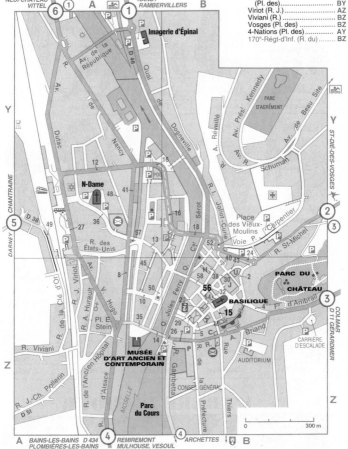

SIGHTS

Imagerie d'Épinal ⓥ – *42 bis quai de Dogneville.*
In 1984, this firm took over from the former Imagerie Pellerin, founded in 1796, which remained in the hands of the Pellerin family for nearly 200 years. The tradition of the famous Épinal prints is being maintained.

In the basement, the **Galerie Pinot**, an exhibition gallery and shop, displays reprints of old favourites, print albums and contemporary prints.

In addition, the **Écomusée** offers an insight into the techniques used by the firm, supported by demonstrations on some of the equipment (colouring machine dating from 1898).

PELLERIN & Cᵉ, imp.-édit. ## L'ILLUSTRE FAMILLE DES JEAN, IMAGERIE D'ÉPINAL. Nᵒ 1337

Jeanfesse! — J'enseigne. — J'embrasse. — J'embrouille. — Jean pêche.

Jean jean. — Jean rage!! — Ô J'empeste! — Jean chante. — J'emmaillotte.

J'embroche. — J'enfonce. — J'embellis. — Ô J'enlaidis! — J'empoche.

J'empiffre. — J'engraisse. — J'embaume. — J'embête. — J'enfourne.

L'ARBRE D'AMOUR

★Old town

★Basilique St-Maurice – Its architecture denotes various regional influences.
The west front has a belfry-porch characteristic of the Meuse region.
The 15C doorway on the north side, known as the Portail des Bourgeois, is the main entrance; it is preceded by a deep porch, characteristic of the architectural style of the Champagne region.
The 13C nave is typical of Burgundian churches with its three storeys, arcades, triforium and high windows separated by moulded string-courses; it is prolonged beyond the transept by the bright 14C chancel *(choeur des chanoinesses)*, whose elegant lines are characteristic of Champagne art.
The most noteworthy works of art are a 15C entombment in the south transept and a 14C statue of the Virgin of the Rose in the adjacent chapel.

Walk to the right of the basilica.

Rue du chapitre – This street has retained a group of houses built for the canonesses in the 17C and 18C. From there, it is easy to reach the medieval defence wall: the base of the towers and part of the red-sandstone wall can now be seen.

Walk back past St-Maurice Basilica.

Place des Vosges – This former market square, lined with arcaded houses, has a definite provincial charm. The 17C former bailiff's house, adorned with a loggia, now an art gallery, stands between a bookshop and a café.

Walk to the river and turn left along quai Jules-Ferry towards place Foch.

Parc du Cours – In this vast public park, laid out on the east bank of the River Moselle, exotic trees, sometimes more than 100 years old, mingle with typical trees of the Vosges region.

ADDITIONAL SIGHTS

★Musée départemental d'Art ancien et contemporain ⊘ – Located at the tip of an island in the River Moselle, the Museum of Ancient and Contemporary Art is built round the remains of the former 17C Hôpital St-Lazare.
It houses Gallo-Roman finds dug out from archaeological sites in Grand, Soulosse and the Donon as well as from the Merovingian necropolis in Sauville. There is an important collection of coins from the Celtic period onwards.
The paintings department is devoted mainly to the French School of the 17C and 18C and to the Northern School (Gellée, La Hyre, Vignon, **La Tour** and his *Job mocked by his Wife*, Brueghel, Van Goyen, Van Cleeve and, of course, **Rembrandt** and his *Mater Dolorosa*). 18C drawings and watercolours. The contemporary art section, one of the most important in France, is represented by Minimal Art (Carl André, Donald Judd), Arte Povera (Mario Merz) and Pop Art (Andy Warhol).
The history of **prints**, from the origin of wood engraving to today, illustrates political, social, religious and military life. The prints come from various French towns, in particular Épinal (the Imagerie Pellerin is the only printing works of its kind still operating in Europe) and from abroad.

A pleasant park and garden for an outdoor break

R.Mattès/MICHELIN

141

★**Parc du Château** ⊙ – This wooded park, one of the largest in France, covers an area of 26ha/64 acres. It occupies the site of the former castle, on top of the wooded sandstone hill which stands in the town centre. The medieval gardens have been relaid round the ruins.

⊡ In the park there is a mini zoo, a playground and a plane to climb on – a perfect place for kids who need to let off steam!

Église Notre-Dame ⊙ – Rebuilt between 1956 and 1958, the church has doors decorated with *cloisonné* enamel on a red-copper base, depicting a cross framed by the emblems of the four evangelists above a rainbow and the symbols of the seven planets.
Inside, light pours into the chancel through a huge stained-glass window dedicated to the glory of the Virgin Mary.

EXCURSIONS

Fort d'Uxegney ⊙ – *6km/3.7mi NW by ⑥ on the town plan (D 166 to Dompaire).* Uxegney, overlooking the Avière Valley, was one of the last forts built round Épinal. It was originally stone built (1882-84) but was later strengthened by the addition of reinforced concrete. This type of fortification is halfway between a bastion, such as those built by Vauban, and the buried fortifications which made up the Ligne Maginot. Since it was never damaged by war, the fort is still intact. From the top, the domes of the various gun turrets can be seen and a vast panorama unfolds.

Cimetière et Mémorial américains – *7km/4.3mi S along D 157. The path leading to the cemetery (0.5km/0.3mi) starts on the right 1.8km/1.1mi beyond Donizé.*
The cemetery, which occupies a vast area (20ha/49 acres) on top of a wooded plateau overlooking the River Moselle, houses the graves of 5 255 American soldiers killed during the Second World War. White-marble crosses and Jewish stelae line up on impeccably trimmed lawns behind a chapel and a memorial dedicated to the dead soldiers.

FISMES

Population 5 295
Michelin map 56 fold 5 or 237 fold 10

Situated at the confluence of the River Vesle and the River Ardre, Fismes was a traditional stopoff for the kings of France on their way to be crowned in Reims. The town has retained part of its ramparts although a pleasant promenade has replaced the moat filled in during the 18C.

"THE GOLDEN BALL"

La Boule d'Or – *11 r. Lefèvre* – ☎ *03 26 48 11 24 – closed Sun evening and Mon –* 🅿 *– 8 rooms 250/280F –* ⌇ *35F – restaurant 90/170F.* This little roadside house is cheerfully decorated in red and white. The newly refurbished rooms are functional but colourful, too. Traditional cooking is offered in the simple dining room.

SIGHTS

Musée – A small museum of local history, housed on the first floor of the tourist office, contains fossils and sharks' teeth found in the area, old postcards and porcelain made by the Vernon family between 1853 and 1860.

Église Ste-Macre – The church was built in the 11C on the site of an ancient oratory to receive the remains of the saint. The massive tower and the rectangular apse are the only original features.

ROMANESQUE CHURCHES OF THE ARDRE VALLEY

Round tour of 52km/32mi – allow half a day

Stocky yet harmonious, the Romanesque churches in this area are similarly constructed; each is shaped like a basilica, without transept, with a flat east end and, usually, with a belfry-porch as well.

Leave Fismes S along D 386 towards Épernay.

The road follows the River Ardre, a favourite haunt of anglers, through rural scenery. Quarries, which can be seen on the edge of the plateau, provided stone for Reims' religious buildings.

Crugny – This is the most important village of the Ardres Valley. The nave of the **Église St-Pierre** dates from the 11C whereas the transept and the flat east end are Gothic. Inside there is a polychrome wooden statue of Christ and a 12C stoup.

Savigny-sur-Ardres – The **Église St-Pierre** has retained its Romanesque tower which used to stand over the crossing. The 16C door leaves probably came from Montazin Abbey.

It was from Savigny that General de Gaulle (who was only a colonel at the time) broadcast his first appeal to the French people on 28 May 1940 (plaque on the house opposite the church).

Beyond Faverolles and Tramery, the road runs beneath the A4 motorway.

Poilly – Dedicated to St Rémy, the **church** dates from the 11C and 12C, whereas the chancel is from the 13C. The Romanesque arches of the crossing rest on columns with carved capitals similar to those in Courville.

Turn right onto D 980 to Verneuil.

As you drive through **Chambrecy**, note the massive **church** with its imposing square tower.

Ville-en-Tardenois – The 12C **church** is surmounted by an elegant tower with a characteristic saddleback roof.

Romigny – The small church has retained its Romanesque doorway; note the decorated capitals of the two columns and the rounded archivolt.

Turn right onto D 23 to Lhéry.

Lhéry – The church, dating from the late 12C, marks the transition from the Romanesque to the Gothic style with its pointed arches resting on cruciform pillars.

Lagery – On the village square stands a fine 18C covered market next to a picturesque wash-house. The church, also representative of Early Gothic style, has a doorway framed by slender ringed columns; note the capitals decorated with acanthus leaves.

Next to the church, the **manor** buildings form a large quadrangle with a dovecote in one of the corners.

Drive W along D 27 towards Coulonges-Cohan.

Abbaye d'Igny – This Cistercian monastery was founded by St Bernard in 1128 in a remote valley. The buildings were rebuilt in the 18C and again after the First World War in neo-Gothic style.

Return to the intersection with D 25 and turn left.

Arcis-le-Ponsart – This village, which lies in a picturesque site overlooking a small valley, has a 12C church and a ruined 17C castle enclosed within a fortified wall.

Continue N along D 25 to Courville.

Courville – In medieval times, the archbishop of Reims had a castle here. Excavations have unearthed the lower part of the 12C keep. The presence of the archbishop explains the size of the Romanesque **Église St-Julien** ⊘ overlooking the village.

The ancient capitals indicate that the nave dates from the 11C whereas the crossing which supports the high saddleback-roofed tower, the chancel and the side chapel date from the 12C. The original timber-work was replaced by a barrel vault in the 19C.

Turn left onto D 386.

St-Gilles – The present church is all that remains of the former priory built on high ground.

The **Église St-Pierre**, surmounted by an octagonal tower, is mainly Romanesque with a Gothic chancel.

RD 386 leads back to Fismes.

Parc Naturel Régional
de la FORÊT D'ORIENT★★

Michelin map 61 folds 17and 18 or 241 folds 37 and 38

Created in 1970 round the artificial Lac d'Orient, the nature park covers an area of 70 000ha/172 977 acres and comprises 50 municipalities, including Brienne-le-Château *(see BRIENNE-LE-CHÂTEAU)* and Vendeuvre-sur-Barse. It lies on the border of two contrasting areas known as *Champagne crayeuse* and *Champagne humide (see p 26)* and it consequently offers visitors a great variety of landscapes. The park aims to preserve the natural environment, in particular the fauna and flora, as well as the cultural and architectural heritage and to promote the economic, social and touristic development of the area with a wide choice of outdoor activities, hiking, boat trips, water sports, fishing, swimming, diving...

NATURAL ENVIRONMENT

Forêt d'Orient – Once part of the vast forested Der region stretching from the Pays d'Othe in the south-west to St-Dizier in the north-east, the Forêt d'Orient today covers 10 000ha/24 711 acres of wetlands dotted with lakes. It gets its name from the Knights Hospitallers and Knights Templars, known as the Chevaliers d'Orient (Knights from the East), who once owned the area. Following the damages caused to the forest during the Second World War, new species such as the forest pine, spruce and silver fir were introduced. However, oaks are still the main species in this regularly planted forest with varied undergrowth *(see the educational trail running through the forest).*

🚶 Two long-distance footpaths and several short-distance ones run through the forest which has become popular with hikers and cyclists alike: itineraries totalling 140km/87mi are detailed in a topo-guide available from the Maison du Parc.

Lakes – The park includes three lakes used to regulate the flow of the River Seine and of the River Aube. The oldest (1966) and largest of the lakes, **Lac d'Orient** covers 2 500ha/6 178 acres and offers many leisure activities such as

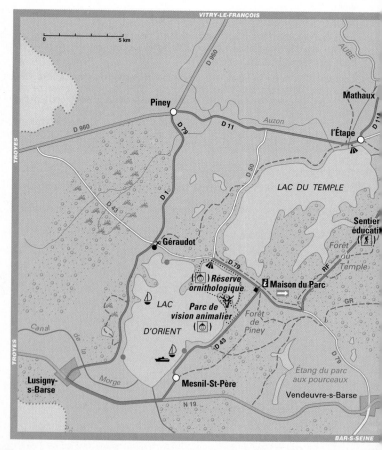

Eating out

MID-RANGE

Auberge du Lac Au Vieux Pressoir – *5 r. du 28-Août-1944 – 10140 Mesnil-St-Père – ☎ 03 25 41 27 16 – closed 13 Nov-1Dec, Sun evening out of season and Mon lunchtime – 170/305F.* In a large, attractive half-timbered house on the edge of the Orient Forest, you can sample fine cooking prepared with good produce. Plain but comfortable rooms.

Where to stay

MODERATE

Chambre d'hôte Mme Jeanne – Les Colombages Champenois – *33 r. du Haut – 10270 Laubressel – 7km/4.3mi NW of Lusigny-sur-Barse on N 19 and D 186 – ☎ 03 25 80 27 37 – ⊟ – 6 rooms 150/230F.* Two lovely local-style half-timbered guest houses offering comfortable rooms with exposed beams. At the dinner table, you will sample farm produce, sitting in front of the fire if it's chilly, or out on the terrace overlooking the meadows on a warm summer night. Holiday cottage nearby.

MID-RANGE

Bungalows Loisirs des Deux Lacs – *14 bis r. Raymond-Poincaré – 10270 Lusigny-sur-Barse – ☎ 03 25 43 80 95 – bungalows.loisirs@wanadoo.fr – closed Nov-Feb – ⊟ – 2 650F per week, sleeps 5.* These 12 modern self-catering bungalows set around the swimming pool and garden are practical and well equipped, although there is nothing quaint about them. A nice, family holiday atmosphere.

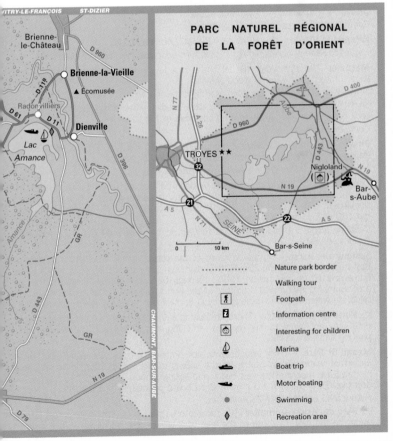

sailing and scuba diving. There are two marinas and three sand beaches in Géraudot, Lusigny-sur-Barse and Mesnil-St-Père. A scenic road runs round the lake, affording fine views, particularly between Mesnil-St-Père and the Maison du Parc.
The **Lac du Temple**, created in 1991 and covering an area of 2 300ha/5 684 acres, is the rendezvous of anglers and canoeists.
The **Lac d'Amance**, the smallest lake with an area of only 500ha/1 236 acres, is reserved for motorised water sports such as speedboat and motor-boat racing.
The last two lakes, linked by a canal 1.6km/1mi long, occupy the natural basins of three tributaries of the River Aube, the Amance, the Auzon and the Temple.
Angling is allowed in all three lakes except in the north-east creek of the Lac d'Orient which is a bird sanctuary.

TOUR OF THE LAKES

64km/40mi – allow half a day – Start from the Maison du Parc

Maison du Parc ⊙ – This fine traditional timber-framed house was taken apart and rebuilt in the Forêt de Piney. It is both an information centre about the park and an exhibition area.

Drive along D 79 for 3km/1.9mi towards Vendeuvre-sur-Barse then turn left onto the Route forestière du Temple.

This road running through the Forêt du Temple guides visitors among the various species of trees with the help of informative panels.

🚶 A forest trail starting opposite Lusigny beach introduces visitors to a dozen species characteristic of the Larrivour-Piney State forest.

Continue along the forest road to Radonvilliers then turn right onto D 11 towards Dienville.

Port Dienville – Situated on the outskirts of the town, this leisure and water-sports centre on the edge of Lake Amance attracts amateurs of speedboat and motor-boat racing. The residential complex, shaped like an ocean liner is framed by a marina and a bathing and canoeing area *(boats for hire on Lake Amance).*

Dienville – This small town, lying on the banks of the River Aube, has an impressive stone-built **covered market** and an unusual **church** with a pentagonal apse and a massive square tower surmounted by a dome. The interior is in a bad state of repair; however, note the wrought-iron chancel railing (1768) made by Mathieu Lesueur, the locksmith of Clairvaux Abbey.

Continue northwards to Brienne-la-Vieille.

Brienne-la-Vieille – See *BRIENNE-LE-CHÂTEAU: Excursions.*

Return to Radonvilliers along D 11^B then turn right onto D 61 towards Mathaux.

Mathaux – In this small village, there is a lovely timber-framed **church** with a square tower covered with wood shingles.

Drive along D 11^A to L'Étape, then bear right towards Piney (D 11).

Shortly after **L'Étape**, you will see the canal feeding water from the Lac du Temple back to the River Aube. There are wide **views** of the lake.

Continue to Piney.

Piney – The most noteworthy monument here is the fine 17C wooden **covered market**. The church has retained a late-17C allegorical painting.

Leave Piney by D 79 then follow D 1 to Géraudot.

Géraudot – The village **church** has a wooden porch; the nave dates from the 12C and the chancel from the 16C. The high altar is adorned with a fine Renaissance **altarpiece** in polychrome stone, depicting the Crucifixion and the Resurrection. Note the 16C stained-glass windows.

Continue along D 1 and 1km/0.6mi further on turn left onto the road leading to Lusigny-sur-Barse.

Lusigny-sur-Barse – At the entrance of the village stands a sculpture (a galvanised-steel-and-wood arch, 25m/82ft in diameter spanning the Barse canal) by Klaus Rinke erected on this site in 1986. Through this work, Klaus Rinke, who is the professor of Constructivist sculpture at the Kunstakademie in Düsseldorf, wished to celebrate water, a theme illustrated by G Bachelard in his essay *Water and Dreams.*

🖼 **Musée des Automates** ⊙ – These fascinating automata come to life in front of you: note the monkey with his top hat, smoking a cigarette and the wine-grower pouring himself a drink!

Mesnil-St-Père – This village, with its timber-and-brick houses, is the most important water sports centre on the shores of the Lac d'Orient; it comprises a marina (300 moorings), a vast beach and sailing schools.
Boat trips ⊙ on the lake are organised on board panoramic motor boats.

Follow D 43 back to the Maison du Parc.

🖼 **Parc de vision animalier** ⊙ – Located on a peninsula (89ha/220 acres) jutting out from the eastern shore of the lake, this **wildlife observation area** enables visitors to discover some of the local fauna.

Two observation points on the edge of the forest offer good views of wild boars, deer and roe-deer roaming around freely. The former eat acorns, roots, rodents and insects; they remain active day and night, which makes it easier to encounter them. Deer and roe-deer on the other hand are plant eaters and are mainly active at night, which means waiting patiently and silently if you wish to see them.

Go past the Maison du Parc and turn left onto D 79 towards Géraudot.

🔊 **Réserve ornithologique** – This area has been set aside as a **bird sanctuary** for waterfowl. An observation point makes it possible to watch moorhens, ducks, black-headed gulls, cranes, herons and wild geese who stop by the lake during their annual migrations in October-November and February-March.

Nature lovers know:
– not to pick flowers, fruit or plants, or gather fossils;
– to take all rubbish and empty cans out of the protected zone;
– to leave pets, particularly dogs, at home because they might frighten young wild animals;
– to stay on the paths, because hillside shortcuts cause erosion.

GÉRARDMER ★

Population 8 951
Michelin map 62 fold 17 or 242 fold 31

Gérardmer owes its fine reputation to its magnificent **setting ★ ★**, its lake, its dark forested mountains and its textile industry. Destroyed by fire in November 1944, a few days before it was liberated, the town has been completely rebuilt. Today, it is a popular winter and summer resort, with numerous facilities, hotels and villas scattered among the greenery, and the starting point of many excursions. The tourist office, created in 1865, is the oldest in France.

Eating out

MODERATE

Ferme Équestre de Liézey – *9 rte de Saucefaing – 88400 Liézey – 9.5km/6mi W of Gérardmer on D 417 and D 50 –* ☎ *03 29 63 09 51 – closed 15 Nov-15 Dec and Mon except during school holidays – 88/148F.* In the snow or among the pine forests, depending on the season, this spacious chalet-farm, dating from 1799, offers hearty meals using produce from neighbouring farms. Horse-riding in summer. Seven simple rooms.

À la Belle Marée – *88400 Bas-Rupts – 4km/2.5mi S of Gérardmer on D 486 –* ☎ *03 29 63 06 83 – closed 26 Jun-8 Jul, Tue out of season and Mon – 95/280F.* To get away from it all and for a taste of the sea, head for this seafood restaurant tucked away in the Vosges mountains. Its dark wood decor is lit by portholes, as well as picture windows overlooking the countryside. There is a covered terrace in summer.

Where to stay

MID-RANGE

Hôtel Le Chalet du Lac – *1km/0.5mi W of Gérardmer on D 417 (Épinal road) –* ☎ *03 29 63 38 76 – closed Oct –* 🅿 *– 11 rooms 320/410F –* 🍽 *45F – restaurant 100/330F.* This large chalet overlooks the lake. Run by two couples, it has a pleasant small family hotel feel to it, with simple but well-kept rooms, and a wood-panelled dining room with unpretentious regional cooking – and a lovely view.

Hôtel Les Vallées – *31 r. P.-Claudel – 88520 La Bresse – 14km/8.75mi S of Gérardmer on D 486 –* ☎ *03 29 25 41 39 –* 🅿 *– 54 rooms 360/490F – 🍽 42F – restaurant 93/260F.* In this central hotel, you can relax in the pleasant modern rooms and enjoy the indoor swimming pool. Studio apartments to let. Explore the mountain paths in summer or ski in winter, either way there's plenty to do at La Bresse.

LUXURY

Hôtel Le Manoir au Lac – *1km/0.5mi W of Gérardmer on D 417 (Épinal road) –* ☎ *03 29 27 10 20 –* 🅿 *– 7 rooms from 800F – 🍽 80F.* This chalet dating from 1830 is a real gem, in its peaceful lakeside setting. It was a favourite haunt of Maupassant, and all of its lovely rooms with their evocative names are tastefully furnished and cosy, regardless of size. Terrace and fine library/lounge.

On the town

Casino du Lac – *3 av. de la Ville-de-Vichy* – ☏ *03 29 60 05 05* – *daily from 1pm for one-armed bandits – closed Tue and Jan for main games.* This leisure centre includes fruit machines and traditional games (boule, roulette, black jack), a cinema-theatre and a seasonal restaurant with a lakeside terrace.

Les Rives du Lac – *1 av. de la Ville-de-Vichy* – ☏ *03 29 63 04 29* – *daily from 9am – closed 31 Oct-31 Jan.* This is one of the nicest cafés in town, and it's easy to see why, once settled on the terrace, with the sound of the water and the view of the blue lake and surrounding mountains.

Shopping

La Saboterie des Lacs – *25 bd de la Jamagne* – ☏ *03 29 60 09 06* – *Mon-Fri 10am-noon, 2-5pm.* A clog maker's workshop where you can watch clogs being manufactured from start to finish, complete with explanations. You can also buy all types of clogs, from utility to decorative, all made out of maple wood.

Le Jacquard Français (1) – *45 bd Kelsch* – ☏ *03 29 60 95 65.* Table linen, bath and beach towels.

Le Jacquard Français (2) – *35 r. Charles-de-Gaulle* – ☏ *03 29 60 82 50* – *summer: daily 10am-noon, 2-7pm; out of season: Tue-Sat.* Table linen, bath and beach towels.

Les Petits Crus Vosgiens – *10 chemin de la Scierie – Le Beillard – coming from Gérardmer on D 417, take the 1st left after passing D 50* – ☏ *03 29 63 11 70 – daily 2-7pm.* Daniel Villaume, proprietor of this former sawmill, will let you sample the fruit and flower wines that he makes from red and blackcurrants, rhubarb, cherries, apples, dandelion and elder flowers. These specialities of the Vosges can be drunk as an aperitif or a dessert wine.

Linvosges – *6 pl. de la Gare* – ☏ *03 29 60 11 00 – www.linvosges.com* – *daily 9am-noon, 2-7pm.* If you want to know more about the production of linen tea-towels or table napkins, visit the Linvosges factory and shop.

Marché artisanal – *Pl. du Vieux-Gérardmer – Sat 8am-7pm.* This weekly market of local craftsmen and producers is one of the most popular in the region.

Distillerie Lecomte-Blaise – *10 r. Gare-Nol – 88120 Le Syndicat – in Le Syndicat, take D 43 (La Bresse direction) for 4km/2.5mi, then turn right towards Nol* – ☏ *03 29 24 71 04 – Tue-Sat 8am-noon, 2-6pm.* This family business was founded in 1820 and produces a wide range of liqueurs, made from fruits (pear, apricot, raspberry, plum) and wild berries (rosehip, blueberry, elderberry, whitebeam and hawthorn) gathered in the forests and orchards of the Vosges. You can see the manufacturing process, taste and buy.

Jean-Louis Claude – *3 chemin du Pré-d'Anis – 88400 Liézey – take D 30 between Le Tholy and Gérardmer, Liézey direction. After passing the bus stop, follow the road on the left for 500m/0.3mi (marked route)* – ☏ *03 29 61 84 84 – daily 10am-noon, 2-7pm, 6pm in winter.* Wooden toys are made in this workshop in the middle of the forest. Jean-Louis Claude, the master craftsman, will happily demonstrate, sawing, sanding and cutting the various designs out of pine.

Maison de l'artisanat – *17 rte de Saucéfaing – 88400 Liézey – 7km/4.3mi NE of Gérardmer on D 50* – ☏ *03 29 63 16 50 – Apr-Nov: Sun 2.30-6.30pm, daily 3-6pm during school holidays.* More than 50 local craftsmen and producers exhibit their wares in this old farm: wooden toys, enamels, embroidery, lace, honey, jam, sweets, brandies, regional liqueurs, stone and leatherwork.

Sport

Fantasticable – *La Mauselaine – Chalet ESF, at the bottom of the ski slopes, approximately 1km/0.5mi S of Gérardmer on the chemin de Rayée* – ☏ *03 29 60 09 10 – www.fantasticable.com – daily 8.30am-noon, 1.30-7pm.* Once securely strapped in, let yourself glide along a cable 1km/0.5mi long, which crosses the Basse des Rupts over 100m/110yd above the pine trees. It only lasts a minute, but at a speed of 100kph/60mph, it is an unforgettable experience!

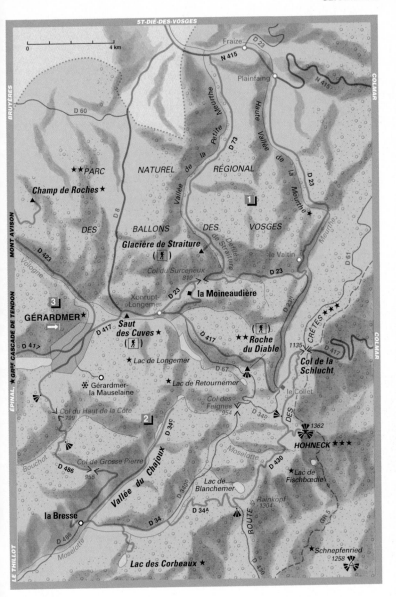

LAKES

Lac de Gérardmer – This is the largest lake of the Vosges region (2.2km/1.3mi long, 0.75km/0.45mi wide and 38m/125ft deep); *(for information about angling, see Practical information)*. A **tour**★ round the lake *(6.5km/4mi)* either on foot or by car is a pleasant excursion offering varied views of the lake framed by mountains. A **boat trip** ⊘ is a fun excursion; in addition, sailing boats, canoes and pedalos are available for hire.

★**Lac de Longemer** – This lake (2km/1.2mi long, 550m/0.3mi wide and 30m/98ft deep) is surrounded by meadows dotted with low farmhouses with relatively flat roofs *(for information about angling, see Practical information)*.

★**Lac de Retournemer** – This small lake, fed by the waterfalls of the Vologne, is set inside a green basin; its remarkably clear deep-blue waters reflect the trees growing along its shores *(for information about angling, see Practical information)*.

SKI RESORTS

✳**Gérardmer-la Mauselaine** – The ski resort enjoys good snow cover which enhances the appeal of its 40km/25mi of ski runs (including the longest run of the Vosges massif: 4km/2.5mi) accessible to beginners as well as experienced skiers; snow-cannon equipment is used on some of the runs and there is also a special run for night skiing. The first Nordic ski area of the Vosges massif, the Domaine des Bas-Rupts is only 2.5km/1.5mi out of Gérardmer. Cross-country tracks totalling 100km/62mi run through the forest forming loops of various levels of difficulty located within the municipalities of Gérardmer, La Bresse and Xonrupt. These cross-country tracks, situated at altitudes in the 800m/2 625ft-1 100m/3 609ft bracket are completed by snowshoeing tracks.

La Bresse-Hohneck – This is the largest ski area of the Vosges region. It is equipped with 200 snow cannon and includes 36 ski runs spread over three main areas, between the Hohneck and La Bresse, around the Lac de Retournemer and near the Col de la Schlucht. From a family resort, La Bresse has thus become a true ski resort which has produced several champions mainly in Alpine skiing and biathlon.

EXCURSIONS

The Gérardmer region was deeply marked by glaciers which once covered the Vosges massif. One of these, which came down from the Hohneck, filled the valley now occupied by Lake Retournemer and Lake Longemer and joined up with the Moselotte and Moselle glaciers near Remiremont. When it withdrew, it left behind a certain amount of morainic debris which retained the water of the Vologne streaming down the mountain. Downstream from Lake Longemer, the river tried to find an exit through another valley: it dug the gorge known as the Saut des Cuves and flowed towards the Moselle through the Vallée des Granges.
Trapped behind a moraine forming a natural dam, the waters of Lake Gérardmer were diverted and formed the River Jamagne, a tributary of the Vologne.

★VALLEYS OF THE MEURTHE AND PETITE MEURTHE

1 Round tour north-east of Gérardmer

55km/34mi – allow 2hr

Leave Gérardmer NE along D 417.

★**Saut des Cuves** – *Leave the car near the Saut des Cuves Hotel. Take the path starting upstream of the bridge and leading to the River Vologne spanned by two footbridges which give access to a short tour.*
The mountain stream cascades down over huge granite rocks in a succession of waterfalls; the most important of these is known as the Saut des Cuves.

Turn left onto D 23 and drive for 2km/1.2mi then turn right.

La Moineaudière – The signposted road leads to the **Domaine de la Moineaudière** ⊙ in a picturesque site on the edge of a spruce forest. There are cacti and other succulent plants, shells, insects, fossils and above all a rich collection of rocks including a quartz from Brazil weighing 650kg/1 433lb. Note also the collection of masks and primitive art.

Continue downwards along the forest road which leads to D 417: turn right to return to the intersection with D 23 and turn right again.

The road runs through the forest before reaching the River Meurthe at Le Valtin. The slopes of the **upper valley of the Meurthe** are covered with pastures and forests. Downstream from Le Rudlin, the valley gets narrower and goes through a picturesque gorge. The river supplies several sawmills.

In Plainfaing, turn left onto N 415 then left again onto D 73.

On the way back to Gérardmer, the road follows the **valley of the Petite Meurthe**, which, at first, is fairly wide with cultivated fields on both sides but then becomes narrower and forested with sawmills dotted along the river banks. The road then goes through the Straiture gorge whose steep sides are planted with firs.

Glacière de Straiture – *A small road branches off to the right; 0.7km/0.4mi beyond this intersection, a path to the south-east allows one to cross the river and reach the Glacière.*
A pile of rocks which gets its name from the pieces of ice which can be found between the rocks at the height of summer.

At the end of the gorge, the road crosses the Petite Meurthe, leads to the Col du Surceneux and back to Gérardmer.

★★★LA BRESSE – HOHNECK – COL DE LA SCHLUCHT

② Round tour south-east of Gérardmer

54km/34mi – allow 2hr 30min

Leave Gérardmer S along D 486.

The road rises through the woods then runs down towards the green valley of the River Bouchot to rise again towards the Col de Grosse Pierre. There are lovely views of the upper valley of the Moselotte and of its tributary, the Chajoux. The slopes, which have been cleared of brushwood, form a picturesque landscape.

La Bresse – This ancient little town scattered across a picturesque valley has always been economically self-supporting thanks to its cheesemaking traditions and textile industry; as a result, it remained independent until 1790. Almost completely destroyed in 1944, La Bresse had to be entirely rebuilt.

The **Église St-Laurent**, rebuilt in the 18C, has retained its Gothic chancel. The modern **stained-glass windows** of the nave illustrate the Apostles and the Prophets, whereas those of the chancel depict the Crucifixion with the Assumption on one side and St Laurent on the other. Four windows are devoted to the destruction of La Bresse.

Vallée du Chajoux – D 34^C runs north-east from La Bresse along a fish-abounding stream lined with wooded slopes and dotted with waterfalls and lakes.

★**Lac des Corbeaux** – *A road, branching off to the right near the Hôtel du Lac, leads to this remote lake (23m/75ft deep). It occupies the centre of a glacial cirque with densely forested slopes.*

🚶 A footpath runs all the way round it *(30min on foot).*

Return to D 34 and turn right along the Moselotte Valley. Cross the river, ignoring D 34^D on the left, and 2km/1.2mi further on, after a bend to the right, leave the Col de Bramont road and follow the twisting D 34^A, known as the Route des Américains.

As you reach the high pastures, the view extends to the right over the upper valley of the Thur, Wildenstein village and the Kruth-Wildenstein dam.

Turn left onto the Route des Crêtes (D 430) which goes round the Rainkopf summit.

Down on the left, you can see the **Lac de Blanchemer**, lying deep inside a wooded basin and surrounded by meadows *(for information about angling, see Practical information).*

The road then reaches the *chaumes* (high pastures) of the Hohneck.

★★★**Hohneck** – *See Route des CRÊTES.*

Beyond the Hohneck, there are glimpses of Lake Longemer in the distance to the left and later on there are splendid **views**★ of the Valogne Valley, Lake Retournemer and Lake Longemer.

Col de la Schlucht – *See Route des CRÊTES.*

★★**Roche du Diable** – *15min on foot there and back. Leave the car near the Retournemer tunnel and follow a steep path leading to the viewpoint.*

🚶 The **view**★★ extends to the Valogne Valley, carpeted with lush grass, between Lake Retournemer and Lake Longemer.

★**Saut des Cuves** – *See ① above.*

Vologne Valley from the Roche du Diable

R.Mattes/MICHELIN

151

VALLEYS OF THE TENDON AND OF THE VALOGNE

③ Round tour north-west of Gérardmer

61km/38mi – allow 2hr

Leave Gérardmer W along D 417.

At the entrance of Le Tholy, turn right onto D 11 towards Épinal and drive for 5km/3mi. Turn left 200m/219yd before the Grande Cascade Hotel and follow the road down to the waterfall (800m/875yd).

★Grande cascade de Tendon – This double waterfall drops 32m/105ft in several steps through dense firs.

Further on, as you reach Faucompierre, turn right towards Bruyères along D 30 and D 44. In Bruyères, take the street to the left of the cemetery (towards Belmont), which leads to the foot of mount Avison. Leave the car.

Tour-belvédère du mont Avison – *45min on foot there and back.*

🏃 This 15m/49ft high tower, standing on the summit (alt 601m/1 972ft) of one of the hills surrounding Bruyères, overlooks the town lying at the intersection of several valleys. From the platform *(82 steps, viewing table)*, the wide **panorama**★ extends to the Tête des Cuveaux, Hohneck and Donon summits.

Champ-le-Duc – The 12C village **church**, built of red sandstone, is a fine example of primitive Romanesque art from the Rhine region, in spite of being burnt down by the Swedes in 1635. Note the pillars, alternately massive and slim, beneath the relieving arches, the thick rolls of the vaulting over the crossing, and the oven vaulted apse with its three small rounded windows. According to tradition, one of the carved capitals of the crossing depicts a meeting between Emperor Charlemagne and his son Charles in 805.

In Granges-sur-Vologne, an industrial town with textile factories, turn left onto D 31 then right in Barbey-Seroux onto the forest road (second crossroads) which runs through the Vologne Forest. 2.4km/1.5mi further on, you come to another crossroads with a house standing nearby; turn left and leave the car 150m/164yd further on.

★Champ de roches de Granges-sur-Vologne – This horizontal moraine, 500m/547yd long, cuts through the forest like a petrified river. Its vegetation-free surface is made up of tightly packed rounded boulders of similar size, which give the moraine its uniform, almost artificial aspect.

Return to Barbey-Seroux and Granges, then follow D 423 back to Gérardmer.

GIVET

Population 7 775
Michelin map 53 fold 9 or 241 fold 2 – Local map see Vallée de la MEUSE

This border town, guarded by the Charlemont fortress, lies on the banks of the River Meuse, at the northern extremity of the Ardennes *département* jutting out into Belgian territory. **Givet Notre-Dame**, on the east bank, is a former industrial district whereas **Givet St-Hilaire**, on the west bank, is the old town nestling round a church built by Vauban and described by Victor Hugo in derisive terms: "the architect took a priest's or a barrister's hat, on this hat he placed an upturned salad bowl, on the base of the salad bowl he stood a sugar basin, on the sugar basin a bottle, on the bottle a sun partly inserted on the neck and finally on the sun he fixed a cock on a spit".

The St-Hilaire district is also a commercial centre as far as place Méhul, prolonged by the Bon Secours district leading to the Belgian border.

Givet is the birthplace of the composer, **Étienne Méhul** (1763-1817), essentially known for his operas, which denote Gluck's influence, and for his patriotic songs composed during the Revolution.

From the bridge over the River Meuse, there is a fine overall **view** of the old town, the Tour Victoire and the Fort de Charlemont.

MODERN HOTEL IN THE OLD TOWN

Val St-Hilaire – *7 quai des Fours – ☎ 03 24 42 38 50 – closed 20 Dec-5 Jan – 🅿 – 20 rooms 295/345F – ☟ 45F – restaurant 90/250F.* This large building on the Meuse quayside has comfortable rooms, furnished in contemporary style (second floor rooms are under the sloping roof). Pleasant terrace in the summer in an inner courtyard.

SIGHTS

Tour Victoire ⊙ – In summer, the former keep of the Comtes de la Marck's castle (14C-15C) houses various exhibitions under its pointed vault.

Centre européen des métiers d'art ⊙ – This centre is intended to promote handicraft. It is possible to watch craftsmen at work. Local products are sold in the vaulted cellar, a former 17C custom house.

★**Fort de Charlemont** ⊙ – *The fort is accessible via a narrow road on the left, which rises through the woods before the first entrance of the military camp.*
This small citadel fortified by Emperor Charles V and named after him, was redesigned by Vauban as it formed part of the Haurs ring meant to defend Givet. Vauban's idea was to cordon off the plateau with bastions, reinforced by ravelins and prolonged by fortified wings, but the project was never completed. Since 1962 however, the fort has been used as a commando training centre. In spite of their ruined state, several buildings have retained an imposing aspect. *Closed for restoration.*

Pointe Est du Fort – From the east end of the fort, there are fine **views**★ of Givet, the Meuse Valley, the Mont d'Haurs and the Belgian hills with the Château d'Agimont, which once belonged to the Comte de Paris. The tour includes a long gallery with 5m/16ft thick walls, the casemate with its sophisticated ventilation system, the vast magazine with its pointed brick-built vault and the two 16C bastions.

Fort du Mont d'Haurs – Located on the east bank, this stronghold formed part of the project conceived by Vauban in 1697 at the request of Louis XIV who wanted to defend the bridge at Givet and the fortress of Charlemont on the opposite bank. This fort could accommodate 16 000 to 20 000 men and 2 000 to 3 000 horses. It is the only fortified camp still complete with its monumental gate.

Chemin de fer des Trois Vallées ⊙ – The train overlooks the Meuse Valley between Givet and Dinant in Belgium. It runs past the gardens of the Château de Freyr, through the Moniat tunnel and then across the Anseremme viaduct before reaching Dinant.

EXCURSIONS

Grottes de Nichet ⊙ – *4km/2.5mi E.* Situated near the village of **Fromelennes**, these caves comprise some 12 chambers on two levels, containing numerous concretions (sound effects).

★**Site nucléaire de Chooz** ⊙ **(nuclear power stations)** – *8km/5mi S along N 51.* It consists of two nuclear power stations, **Chooz A** which stopped producing electricity in 1991 after 24 years and **Chooz B**, situated inside the meander of the river and completed in 1996, which comprises two units producing 1 450 million watts each. Chooz B will eventually produce, together with the power station at Nogent, almost 10% of the total French needs. Technological innovations include an entirely computerised control room and a new, very powerful turbine called Arabelle.
An information office, situated at the entrance of the site, has a display of explanatory panels and models about the production of electricity and nuclear energy.

VALLÉE DE LA MEUSE

South of Givet *23km/14.3mi*

Leave Givet by N 51 which runs along black-marble quarries.

Hierges – The village, which has retained a few 17C houses and a 13C mill, is overlooked by the ruins of a castle built between the 11C and the 15C, once the seat of a barony. The austerity of its fortress-like aspect is tempered by its Renaissance features (brick ornamentation of the towers).
Some 2km/1.2mi further on, turn right onto D 47 to Molhain.

Ancienne collégiale de Molhain – Built over a 9C-10C crypt and remodelled in the 18C, this former collegiate church has interesting interior decoration (Italian stuccowork, furniture). Note the 17C altarpiece over the high altar, depicting the Assumption, a 16C Entombment, 14C-16C statues, and 13C-18C tombstones.
Return to N 51 which leads to Vireux-Molhain.

Vireux-Molhain lies in a pleasant setting at the confluence of the Meuse and the Viroin. Excavations on Mount Vireux have revealed a Gallo-Roman and medieval site. Part of the medieval walls and a 14C bread oven can be seen.
Continue S along N 51 then cross the river 2km/1.2mi beyond Fépin.

Haybes – From Haybes bridge there is a lovely view of this attractive resort which offers numerous walks, in particular to the viewpoint at **La Platale** *(2km/1.2mi from Haybes along the scenic Morhon road: picnic area)*, which affords a close-up view of Fumay, and to the viewpoint of **Roc de Fépin** *(8km/5mi E along D 7; access signposted)*.

Return to N 51 which follows a deep meander of the Meuse to Fumay.

Fumay – The old town, with its twisting narrow streets, occupies a picturesque position on a hillside within a deep meander of the Meuse. From the bridge there is a pleasant view of this group of old houses.

The **Musée de l'Ardoise** ⊘ (Fumay is known for its blue slate), housed in the former Carmelite convent, illustrates the hard work of miners extracting schist during the past 800 years. The last two mines closed down in 1971.

The low-relief sculpture *(avenue Jean-Jaurès)*, dedicated to the memory of these miners, is the work of Georges-Armand Favaudon.

GUEBWILLER ★

Population 10 942
Michelin map 87 fold 18 or 242 fold 35
Local maps see Route des CRÊTES and Route des VINS

Lying on the south bank of the River Lauch, this small town, situated along the Route des Vins, has retained a wealth of architectural features which testify to its lively past. Throughout the Middle Ages, vineyards were the main source of wealth of the city and the surrounding area. After a period of industrial prosperity during the 19C, wine-growing became once again the main economic activity and today the surrounding area produces four great wines, Kitterlé, Kessler, Saering and Spiegel, by the most modern methods.

As the administrative centre of the former territory owned by the nearby Abbaye de Murbach, Guebwiller developed from the 8C onwards under the control of the abbots and, in 1275, the city was granted its own charter and allowed to build its own fortifications.

St Valentine's Day

These fortifications turned out to be very useful in 1445, on St Valentine's day, when the Armagnacs (opposed to the Burgundians and the English during the Hundred Years War) tried to take the town by surprise by crossing the frozen moat. A townswoman named Brigitte Schick gave the alarm; her shrieks were so loud that the attackers thought the whole population had been warned and they ran away, leaving their ladders behind. These are still kept in the Église St-Léger.

Eating out

MID-RANGE

Auberge Jean-Luc Wahl – *58 rte de Rouffach – 68500 Issenheim – 3km/1.8mi E of Guebwiller on D 430 and a minor road* – ☎ *03 89 76 86 68 – closed 3-9 Mar, 15 Jul-8 Aug, Sat lunchtime and Mon – 120/410F.* This village-centre 18C Alsatian-style building is particularly pleasant, with its dark wood panelling, knick-knacks and carefully arranged tables. But the inventive cooking is the main attraction, making a visit more than worthwhile.

Where to stay

MID-RANGE

Hostellerie St-Barnabé – *68530 Murbach – 5km/3mi NW of Guebwiller on D 40II* – ☎ *03 89 62 14 14 – closed 14 Jan-15 Mar, 23-26 Dec, Sun evening Nov-Apr, Mon lunchtime and Wed lunchtime* – **P** – *27 rooms 450/1100F – ☑ 65F – restaurant 158/398F.* This pink-washed house, flower-decked in summer, is tucked away in a valley. It is peaceful, surrounded by a garden, and its rooms are modern and light, particularly those in the annexe. The pleasant restaurant has a choice of menus. Heed the opening times.

SIGHTS

★**Église Notre-Dame** – Built between 1760 and 1785 by the last prince-abbot of Murbach, this church looks particularly impressive. Its neo-Classical west front is decorated with statues representing the theological and cardinal virtues. The lofty **interior**★★ is reminiscent of Roman pomp. The three semicircular apses forming the end of both transepts and of the chancel are characteristic of Baroque style. But the most striking feature is the high-relief sculpture of the high altar by Sporrer, representing the **Assumption**★★ (1783). Note also, by the same artist, the refined decoration of the stalls and the organ loft.

Place Jeanne-d'Arc – Other buildings, erected by the abbots of Murbach in the 18C, surround the church: the former canons' residence (Musée du Florival), a few other canons' houses and the Château de la Neuenbourg, the former residence of the prince-abbot.

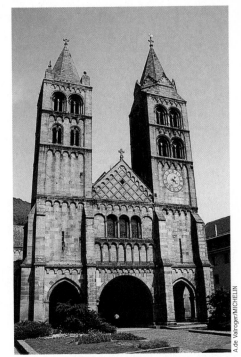

Guebwiller – Église St-Léger

Walk along rue de la République.

Place de la Liberté with its fountain is on the right.

★**Hôtel de ville** – Built in 1514 for a wealthy draper, the edifice has mullioned windows and a five-sided Flamboyant Gothic oriel. A 16C statue of the Virgin shelters inside a corner recess on the right.

Continue to the Église St-Léger.

★**Église St-Léger** – This church is a good example of Late Romanesque architecture of the Rhine region. The **west front**★★, flanked by two tall towers, has a porch open on three sides; like the nave, the transept and the aisles, it dates from the 12C and 13C.

Walk round the church.

The former bailiff's court of justice is located in a fine house dating from 1583 (no 2 rue des Blés). Next comes a lovely **tithe cellar** and last is the **former 16C town hall**.

★**Musée du Florival** ⊘ – The museum, housed in the former 18C residence of aristocratic canons from the chapter of Murbach Abbey, displays its collections on five levels; these illustrate the geology and history of the Florival Valley, its wine-growing and handicraft traditions and its industrial past. However, the museum no doubt owes its originality to its display of the **works**★ of **Théodore Deck**, including the decoration of a bathroom and a veranda with glazed tiles, vases coloured in a special blue named after the artist, dishes with a gilt background...

Ancien couvent des Dominicains ⊘ – This convent was founded in 1294. The buildings, which had witnessed so many historic events were sold during the Revolution and became a factory warehouse and then a hospital before being bought by the administrative council of the Haut-Rhin *département* and turned into the **Centre polymusical des Dominicains de Haute-Alsace** (music centre). The Jazz Cellar organises jazz sessions from September to June, on Fridays and Saturdays.

Église St-Pierre-et-St-Paul – Erected between 1312 and 1340, this Gothic church, which belonged to the convent, contains a very fine group of frescoes dating from the 14C and 16C. The acoustics are famous and the nave is the venue of prestigious concerts of classical music.

Théodore Deck (1823-91)

This native of Guebwiller was a potter and ceramist of genius. His research led him to discover in 1874 the lost formula of the turquoise blue characteristic of Persian ceramics; this blue was henceforth known as the *Bleu Deck*. Deck also found the secret of the famous Chinese celadon, he reproduced oriental *cloisonné* and succeeded in decorating his ceramics with a gilt background. In his book, *Ceramics*, published in 1887, he disclosed his formulae and offered anyone interested in the subject the benefit of his experience. He was put in charge of the Manufacture nationale de Sèvres and spent the last years of his life perfecting his art and creating new types of porcelain. His funeral monument in Montparnasse cemetery in Paris, where he is buried, was carved by his friend Frédéric Auguste Bartholdi who sculpted the famous Statue of Liberty.

★★GUEBWILLER VALLEY

From Guebwiller to Le Markstein *30km/17mi – allow 2hr*

Local map see Parc naturel régional des BALLONS DES VOSGES

The **Lauch Valley** or Guebwiller Valley is known as Florival (literally flower valley) because of its pleasant colourful aspect. Art lovers will find a lot to admire in the lovely Romanesque churches of Murbach and Lautenbach whereas hikers will appreciate the *zone de tranquillité* or quiet area *(no cars allowed)* situated at the end of the valley, on either side of D 430.

Drive out of Guebwiller along D 430 towards the Route des Crêtes and Le Markstein.

The road follows the River Lauch; the picturesque Murbach Valley can be seen on the left.

★★Église de Murbach – *See MURBACH.*

★Lautenbach – The village, which goes back to the 8C, developed round a Benedictine abbey. Today, only the **church★** remains surrounded by several canons' houses dating from the days when it was a collegiate church.

The Romanesque porch is divided into three parts surmounted by primitive ribbed vaulting. Inside, note the remarkable 15C stalls (note the detail on the historiated misericords) surmounted by an 18C canopy.

⌖ The **vivarium** of the Moulin de Lautenback-Zell houses some fascinating insects.

Just beyond Linthal, the Lauch Valley becomes narrow and wild.

★Lac de la Lauch – This artificial lake, where angling is allowed, lies inside a wooded glacial cirque.

The road enters the forest and rises in a series of hairpin bends, offering glimpses of the valley and of the Grand Ballon.

Le Markstein – This winter-sports resort is situated at the intersection of the Route des Crêtes and of the upper Lauch Valley. Some of the Alpine World Championship events took place here in 1983 and 1987. Hikes and pony rides through forested areas are popular activities in summer.

HAGUENAU★

Population 27 675
Michelin map 87 fold 3 or 242 fold 16

Haguenau lies on the banks of the River Moder, on the edge of the vast Haguenau Forest, planted with forest pines, oaks, hornbeams, beeches, and ashes, which offers nature lovers a choice of marked footpaths and cycle tracks running through ferns and bilberry bushes. According to legend, **St Arbogast**, entrusted by the king of the Franks with the christianisation of northern Alsace, stayed in this forest, which was thereafter known as the **holy forest** until the end of the Middle Ages.

The town prospered in the shadow of the massive castle, a favourite residence of Frederick I **Barbarossa** (Redbeard) of the House of Hohenstaufen, who ruled the Holy Roman Empire from 1152 to 1190.

The verses by Longfellow quoted here are part of a poem set in Haguenau; it tells the story of a local cobbler.

Haguenau was, for a long time, second only to Strasbourg as a prosperous member of the league of defence known as **Decapolis**, formed by 10 Alsatian cities within the Holy Roman Empire *(see MULHOUSE)*.

> ... A quiet, quaint and ancient town
> Among the green Alsatian hills,
> A place of valleys, streams and mills,
> Where Barbarossa's castle, brown
> With rust of centuries still looks down
> On the broad, drowsy land below ...
>
> *Henry Wadsworth Longfellow*

Eating out

MODERATE

Au Bœuf – *48 Grand'Rue – 67620 Soufflenheim – 15km/9.3mi E of Haguenau on N 63 – ☎ 03 88 86 72 79 – 98/128F.* The village is well known locally for its potters; this restaurant in the centre, with its balcony and flower-decked terrace, is also famous in its own way. Good beef features prominently on the menu, along with Alsatian dishes and *tartes flambées*. Nice 17C-style painted ceiling.

Where to stay

MODERATE

Chambre d'hôte Krumeich – *23 r. des Potiers – 67660 Betschdorf – 15km/9.3mi NE of Haguenau, Wissembourg direction on D 263 and D 243 – ☎ 03 88 54 40 56 – 3 rooms 210/320F.* You can learn how to make salt-glazed stoneware from the owner of this house, who descended from an old family of Betschdorf potters. Or you can simply stay in one of the pretty rooms, furnished in old-fashioned style, and enjoy the garden.

Sport

Ferme Charles Dangler – *Lieu-dit Haul – 67110 Gundershoffen – 6km/3.75mi SE of Niederbronn, Haguenau direction on D662 – ☎ 03 88 72 85 73 – daily 10am-noon, 2-8pm.* Despite the fact that there are 360km/225mi of way-marked tracks surrounding the town, it's almost impossible to find a bike to hire. A good excuse to try riding instead, on one of this farm's ten horses. Accompanied treks from one to eight hours, depending on your ability.

Parks, Zoos, Attractions

Nautiland – 🖻 – *8 r. des Dominicains – ☎ 03 88 90 56 56 – closed 1 week in Mar, 1 week in Sep.* A water leisure centre offering cascades, springs, slides, sauna and Turkish bath.

SIGHTS

★**Musée historique** ⊘ – The history museum is housed in an imposing edifice built at the beginning of the 20C, partly in neo-Gothic and partly in neo-Renaissance style.

It contains an important collection of Bronze and Iron-Age objects found in the region (Haguenau Forest, Seltz).

There is also a collection of Alsatian coins and medals, many of them minted in Haguenau, and written works printed in Haguenau during the 15C and 16C.

On the first floor are the collections of ceramics, in particular those produced by the Hannong factory *(see STRASBOURG p 327)*.

Église St-Georges – This 12C and 13C church harmoniously combines the Romanesque and Gothic styles. The crossing is surmounted by an octagonal steeple which houses the two oldest bells in France (1268). The buttress of the south transept bears a series of grooves representing the standard measures of length once used in Haguenau.

Inside, the vast nave has retained its Romanesque aspect; it is separated from the aisles by rounded arches resting on massive round pillars. However, the intricate ribbed vaulting and the elegant Gothic chancel, completed in the 13C by sculptors of the Œuvre Notre-Dame in Strasbourg *(see STRASBOURG p 334)*, soften the impression of austerity of the interior. It contains an elegant Flamboyant **tabernacle**, which rises up to the vaulting.

Several works of art are noteworthy: the stone **pulpit**, dating from 1500 and, opposite, the wooden crucifix carved in 1487, as well as the superb **altarpiece**★ representing the Last Judgement.

Église St-Nicolas – This Gothic church was founded by Emperor Frederick Barbarossa in 1189. The tower is the only part of the original edifice still standing. The chancel and the nave date from c 1300.

The remarkable 18C **woodwork**★ *(switch on the light to the left of the chancel)* decorating the pulpit, the organ loft and the choir stalls, was brought to St-Nicolas from the former Abbaye de Neubourg after the Revolution. The other statues superbly carved in wood, which stand at the entrance of the chancel, are fine examples of the Baroque style; they represent the Doctors of the Church: St Augustine, St Ambrose, St Gregory and St Jerome.

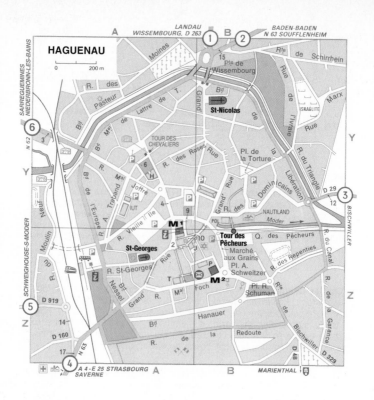

HAGUENAU

Angels and emblems

Musée alsacien ⊘ – The façade of this building is embellished with traditional motifs and regional coats-of-arms. The museum inside the restored 15C chancellery displays various local collections, including paintings mounted under glass, known as *canivets*, old costumes, a reconstructed potter's workshop and a peasant's home with its kitchen and living room or *stube*.

EXCURSIONS

Gros Chêne – *6km/3.7mi E of Haguenau. Leave by ② on the town plan.*
This ancient oak or rather what is left of it, stands near a small modern chapel dedicated to St Arbogast; it is the starting point of an interesting botanic trail, a fitness itinerary and walks through the forest *(marked paths). Playground for children.*

Soufflenheim –*14km/8.7mi E. Leave Haguenau by ② on the town plan.*
This industrial town is famous for its **ceramic workshops** ⊘ which produce typically Alsatian ceramics with floral decoration against a plain background: oval terrines, dishes, salad bowls, cake tins, jugs etc.
In the former fortified cemetery overlooking the Grand'Rue, you can see a life-size sculpture of the **Last Supper** after the painting by Leonardo da Vinci; it was modelled in clay by Léon Elchinger and Charles Burger (1871-1942).

Betschdorf – *16.5km/10mi NE by ① on the town plan.*
This lovely village with its timber-framed houses is famous for its art pottery of grey sandstone with blue decoration: jugs, pots, vases etc. The objects are hand-made and, once dry, they are decorated with a paint brush dipped in cobalt blue, fired at a temperature of 1 250°C/2 282°F and then glazed.
A **museum** ⊙, housed in an old farmhouse, displays an interesting collection of this pottery from the Middle Ages to the present time. There is a reconstructed workshop in the barn.

Hatten – *22km/13.7mi NE. Leave Haguenau by ① on the town plan. Drive to Hatten via Betschdorf.* The **Musée de l'Abri and Casemate d'infanterie Esch** is in the village; the **casemate** is situated on the left, 1km/0.6mi beyond Hatten on the way to Seltz *(see Ligne MAGINOT p 187).*

Walbourg – *10km/6.2mi N of Haguenau by ① on the town plan.*
The peaceful village of Walbourg, pleasantly situated at the heart of rolling countryside, owes its name to the foundation in 1074 of a Benedictine abbey dedicated to St Walburga, an English nun who helped to convert Germany to Christianity.
The 15C abbey church is the only part of the abbey still standing. The chancel, surmounted by an intricate ribbed vaulting is lit by five luminous 15C windows.

Morsbronn-les-Bains – *11km/6.8mi north by ① on the town plan (D 27).*
The hot-water (41.5°C/106.7°F) springs of this small spa resort contain sodium chloride.
◙ Nearby is **Fantasialand** ⊙, a leisure park for children with all kinds of attractions including rafts, mine trains, pirate ship and cinema with a 180-degree screen.

Sessenheim – *21km/13mi E.* This charming Alsatian village, was the setting of a romance between **Goethe** and **Friederike**. In October 1770, Goethe who was studying law in Strasbourg, accompanied one of his friends to the house of the pastor of Sessenheim. He fell in love with the clergyman's younger daughter and, over the next few months, the two young lovers took long walks through the countryside and spent idyllic hours under the bower of the presbytery. In August 1771, however, Goethe went back to Frankfurt leaving Friederike shattered. Eight years later, the now famous poet stopped in Sessenheim on his way to Switzerland but the past idyll was not rekindled by this meeting. Later on, Goethe immortalized Friederike in his *Memoirs.*
Inside the **Église protestante**, note the pastor's stall (Pfarrstuhl) where Goethe and Friederike used to sit side by side to listen to her father preaching. On the left of the Protestant church stands the **Auberge Au bœuf** ⊙, a typical Alsatian inn, where prints, letters and portraits relating to Goethe and Friederike are displayed.
The **Mémorial Goethe**, situated next to the presbytery, was inaugurated in 1962.

Château du HAUT-BARR ★

Michelin map 87 fold 14 or 242 fold 19
Local map see Parc naturel régional des VOSGES DU NORD

Solidly camped on three huge sandstone rocks overlooking the valley of the River Zorn and the Plaine d'Alsace, the 12C castle was completely remodelled by Bishop Manderscheidt of Strasbourg who, according to legend, founded the Brotherhood of the Horn dedicated to drinking Alsace wine out of the horn of an aurochs!

Access – *5km/3mi. From Saverne, follow D 102 which offers views of the Black Forest. Turn onto D 171 winding through the forest. Park the car near the entrance of the castle.*

SUNDAY TREAT

Au Bain – *7 r. du Mar.-Leclerc – 67700 Haegen – 6km/3.75mi S of Château du Haut-Barr on D 10 and D 102 – ☎ 03 88 71 02 29 – closed Mon – 100/175F.* The younger generation of proprietors has transformed this old village bistro into a restaurant. It is simply decorated, with paper tablecloths and a classic menu, except on Sunday nights, when it's *tarte flambée* for everyone.

Château du HAUT-BARR

Château du Haut-Barr

TOUR OF THE CASTLE *about 30min*

A paved ramp leads from the main gate to a second gateway, beyond which you
can see the restored Romanesque chapel on the right and the Restaurant du
Haut-Barr on the left. Past the chapel, there is a terrace *(viewing table)*, from
which the **view**★ extends towards Saverne, the Kochersberg's hills and the Black
Forest in the distance, beyond the Rhine Valley.
A metal staircase *(64 steps)*, fixed to the rock face, gives access to the first rock
offering similar views.
Return to the restaurant and, immediately beyond it, go up 81 steps to reach the
second rock linked by a footbridge, known as the Pont du Diable, to the third rock.
From there, the **view**★★ is even better as it offers a 360° panorama including the
Vosges mountains, the Zorn Valley (through which flows the canal linking the
Marne and the Rhine), the Lorraine plateau and, in clear weather, the spire of
Strasbourg Cathedral.
A reconstruction of **Claude Chappe's telegraph tower** ⊙ stands on its original site,
200m/219yd south of the castle: it consists of a relay tower of the famous optical
telegraph invented in 1794 by the engineer Chappe and used between Paris and
Strasbourg from 1798 to 1852. There is an audio-visual presentation in the small
museum.

Château du HAUT-KŒNIGSBOURG★★

Michelin map 87 fold 16 or 242 fold 27
Local map see Route des VINS

The castle *(see illustration in Architecture and art)*, which is mentioned for the first
time in 1147, was built by the Hohenstaufens on a promontory overlooking the Plaine
d'Alsace, at an altitude of more than 700m/2 297ft.
This exceptional position enabled the occupants to withdraw easily and to watch all
roads leading to Lorraine or crossing Alsace from north to south.
In 1479, it became the property of the Hapsburgs, who had it rebuilt, extended and
equipped with a modern defence system. However, 150 years later, these defences did
not withstand the attack of the Swedish artillery. The castle was sacked, then burnt
down and abandoned for two centuries but its ruins remained imposing until the end
of the 19C.
In 1899, the castle was offered by the town of Sélestat to Kaiser William II who had it
restored by Bodo Ebhardt, an architect from Berlin. The restoration work, which
lasted from 1900 to 1908, was carried out scientifically with the help of archaeological finds and archives. The castle was returned to France 10 years later.

Access – *The road leading to the castle (2km/1.2mi) branches off D 159 at the intersection of the latter with D 1ᴮ¹, near the Haut-Kœnigsbourg Hotel; 1km/0.6mi further on,
follow the one-way road on the right, which goes round the castle (it is possible to leave
the car on the left).*

Where to stay

MODERATE

Relais du Haut-Kœnigsbourg – *Rte du Haut-Kœnigsbourg* – *67600 Orschwiller* – ☎ *03 88 82 46 56* – *lerelais@calixo.net* – *closed Jan* – 🅿 – *26 rooms 190/300F* – ⌑ *40F* – *restaurant 102/214F.* This hotel-restaurant is worth a visit for its setting: just 5min from the castle, it commands superb views over the forest. The 1960s decor is in need of sprucing up, and only a few rooms have been redecorated; choose one of these if you are staying. Folk evenings.

MID-RANGE

Auberge La Meunière – *68590 Thannenkirch* – *5km/3mi SW of the castle on D 159 and D 42* – ☎ *03 89 73 10 47* – *closed 21 Dec-24 Mar* – 🅿 – *23 rooms 320/430F* – ⌑ *40F* – *restaurant 100/195F.* Although situated in the village centre, some of the best rooms in this brick and wood-built inn have views over the countryside with a distant glimpse of the castle. The restaurant's terrace enjoys the same view.

TOUR OF THE CASTLE ⏱ *about 1hr*

Beyond the gate and the portcullis, lies the lower courtyard surrounded by the buildings enabling the castle to be self-supporting and withstand a siege: the inn (restaurant, shop and bookshop), the stables, the forge and the mill. A ramp leads to the lions' doorway (**1**) and to the moat separating the seigneurial residence from the rest of the castle. A fortified well (**2**), 62m/203ft deep, is located on the edge of the rocky promontory, near the residence. On the ground floor of the latter, there is a cellar (**3**) on the west side and kitchens (**4**) on the north side.

From the inner courtyard, two spiral staircases lead to the upper floors with two balconies on the south side. The apartments (living room and bedroom) are on the north and south sides. The reception rooms are on the west side: great hall, Lorraine room and guard-room. The keep stands on the east side; its upper levels have been restored. The furniture and weapons (15C-17C) were bought at the beginning of the 20C in order to restore the atmosphere of a castle. Note the frescoes by Léo Schnug, an expert in perspective painting; one of them, decorating the Great Hall, depicts the siege of the castle in 1462.

★★**Panorama** – Walk across the upper courtyard to the great bastion for panoramic views including; to the north, the ruins of Franckenbourg, Ramstein and Ortenbourg castles; to the east, across the Rhine, the heights of Kaiserstuhl with the Black Forest behind; to the south, the Hohneck and, on the horizon, the Grand Ballon and Route des Vins; about 200m/218yd to the west, you can see the ruins of Œdenbourg or Petit-Kœnigsbourg.

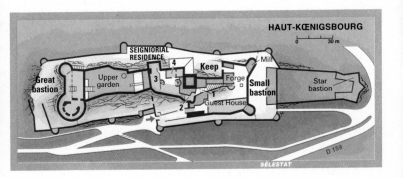

Le HOHWALD★★

Population 400
Michelin map 87 folds 5 and 15 or 242 folds 23 and 27

This secluded resort surrounded by splendid fir and beech woods offering fine walks, is the starting point of a variety of drives through a picturesque region of forests, vineyards and charming villages, which bears the same name.

There are many traces of the area's ancient past, such as the pagan wall round Mont Ste-Odile, believed to have been built by the Celts and reinforced by the Romans, as well as the numerous ruined castles and monasteries scattered about the countryside.

Vineyards manage to cohabit with the superb forest where raspberries and bilberries grow in abundance. Vines cover the hillsides right up to the villages, and the loess deposits found in the Barr area are ideal for tobacco-growing; further north, hopfields are a familiar sight and the numerous rivers and streams which crisscross the region have favoured the development of sawmills, weaving and spinning mills. This diversity accounts for the traditional prosperity of the region.

Eating out

MODERATE

Ferme-auberge Lindenhof – *11 rte du Kreuzweg* – *2km/1mi W of Hohwald on D 425* – ☎ *03 88 08 31 98* – *closed Wed evening 1 Oct-30 Jun and Thu* – 🍴 – *booking advisable* – *95/120F.* Farm cooking is served on the large veranda of this rather ordinary-looking building, situated on the edge of the forest. The home produce includes *fromage blanc*, Munster, Gruyère and butter, as well as poultry and rabbit. Alsace cuisine to order.

Where to stay

MODERATE

Chambre d'hôte Tilly's Inn – *28 r. Principale* – ☎ *03 88 08 30 17* – 🍴 – *3 rooms 203/326F* – 🛏 *50F* – *evening meal 130F.* The appealing red façade of this building, with its naïve drawings, is an invitation to enter. You won't be disappointed: the rooms are original, as is the wooden horse and surrounding knick-knacks in the breakfast room. Two apartments.

Shopping

Pain d'épice Lips – *Pl. de la Mairie* – *67140 Gertwiller* – ☎ *03 88 08 93 52* – *shop: Mon-Sat 8am-noon, 1.30-7pm, Sun 2-6pm; museum: Jul-15 Sep: Mon, Wed and Fri 2-6pm, Tue and Thu 9am-noon; rest of year: Sun 2-6pm – closed 1st fortnight in Jan (shop), Jan-Feb (museum).* At the beginning of the 20C there were nine gingerbread makers in the small winemaking village of Gertwiller, near Barr. You can visit the old tithe barn to learn more (the museum of gingerbread and old-fashioned sweets). Watch gingerbread being made, and taste it!

Sport

École de parapente Grand Vol – *Ferme Niedermatten* – *67220 Breitenbach* – *Villé direction on D 425* – ☎ *03 88 57 11 42* – *www.sxb.rte.fr/gv* – *weekend Mar-Nov; the hang-gliding site is accessible all year.* Qualified instructors to teach hang-gliding and monitor your progress. Special rates for beginners. Minimum age: 12.

★★NORTH HOHWALD

① Round tour starting from Le Hohwald

91km/56.5mi – allow one day

Leave Le Hohwald along D 425, which follows the wooded Andlau Valley dotted with sawmills.

The ruins of Spesbourg and Haut-Andlau castles can be seen high up on the left.

★**Andlau** – *See ANDLAU.*

Between Andlau and Obernai, the road runs through a hilly area covered with vineyards.

Mittelbergheim village and vineyard

Mittelbergheim – This is a picturesque village clinging to the hillside. Place de l'Hôtel-de-Ville is lined with lovely Renaissance houses with porches and window frames of typical sandstone from the Vosges region. Wine-growing is a long-standing tradition going back to Roman times and the wines of this area are famous.

Barr – *See Route des VINS p 374.*

Beyond **Gertwiller**, famous for its wine and its glacé gingerbread, Landsberg Castle can be seen on the foothills of the Vosges with, on the right, the convent of Ste-Odile and, lower down, the ruins of Ottrott's two castles.

★★**Obernai** – *See OBERNAI.*

Ottrott – Lying at the heart of vineyards which produce one of the good Alsatian red wines, this village is proud of its two castles, the 12C Lutzelbourg Castle with its square building and round tower, and the 13C Rathsamhausen Castle, larger and more elaborate than the first.

▣ Coming out of Ottrott towards Klingenthal, you will see, on the site of a former spinning mill, a large aquarium known as **Les Naïades** ⊘, containing more than 3 000 fish from all over the world. A specific natural environment has been recreated in each of the aquarium's tanks (caves, mountain streams, rivers, lakes, estuaries) where you can see exotic species swimming around: shark, piranhas, electric eels, as well as crocodiles from the Nile...

Klingenthal – This small village was once famous for its weapons factory founded in 1776, which produced fine swords and bayonets.

▣ *Drive through the forest along D 204 as far as the Fischhütte inn and leave the car; 150m/164yd further on, a path to the right leads (6km/3.7mi there and back) to the ruins of Guirbaden Castle.*

In spite of being destroyed in the 17C, the 11C **Château fort de Guirbaden** has retained the outer shell of its seigneurial residence and its keep. It offers an extended view of the surrounding forest, of the Plaine d'Alsace and of the Bruche Valley. In summer, the scenery is partly concealed by the luxuriant vegetation.

★**Signal de Grendelbruch** – *15min on foot there and back.*

▣ The wide **panorama**★ encompasses the Plaine d'Alsace to the east and, to the west, the Bruche Valley and the Vosges mountain range with the Donon in the foreground, crowned by a small temple.

The road continues towards the picturesque Bruche Valley *(see SCHIRMECK).*

Schirmeck – *See SCHIRMECK.*

In Rothau, turn left onto D 130 which follows the Rothaine Valley for 3km/1.9mi then veers suddenly left before reaching the Struthof, which has been turned into an important memorial dedicated to victims of the Second World War.

Le Struthof – During the Second World War, the Nazis built a death camp on this site. The platforms on which the huts stood were built by the prisoners who brought the building materials up from the bottom of the valley on their backs; around 10 000 of them died fulfilling this task. The camp received various convoys of prisoners from occupied countries.

Ancien camp de concentration ⊘ – Parts of the former concentration camp still stand, such as the double fence of barbed wire, the main gate, the crematorium, the prisoners' cells and two huts (a dormitory and the old kitchen) now turned into museums.

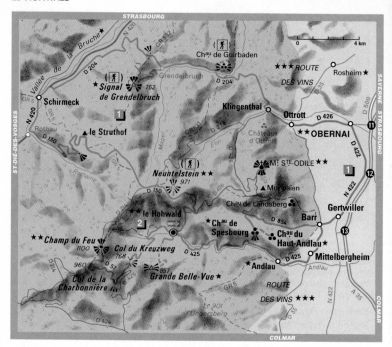

The **necropolis** situated above the camp contains the remains of 1 120 prisoners. In front stands the **memorial**, a kind of huge truncated column, hollowed out and engraved on the inside with the tall silhouette of a prisoner.
The base is the tomb of an unknown French prisoner.

The road goes across a plateau, enters the forest and runs down towards La Rothlach.

Leave the car 1.5km/0.9mi beyond La Rothlach and follow a path on the left leading to the Neuntelstein viewpoint.

★★Rocher de Neuntelstein – *30min on foot there and back.*
  There is a splendid **view★★** of Mont Ste-Odile, the Ungersberg, Haut-Kœnigsbourg and the Champ du Feu. Those who wish to practise rock-climbing can join the Rocher de Neuntelstein School *(information available from the tourist office in Le Hohwald)*.

Continue along D 130 and, at the intersection with D 426, turn right towards Le Hohwald. A left turn at that point would lead you to Mont Ste-Odile (see Mont STE-ODILE).

★★MONT STE-ODILE

② Itinerary north-east of Le Hohwald

24km/15mi – allow 1hr
From Le Hohwald drive E along D 425 then D 426 (see Mont STE-ODILE).

★★CHAMP DU FEU

③ Itinerary south-west of Le Hohwald

11km/6.8mi – about 30min

★★Le Hohwald – *See round tour ②.*
Drive W out of Le Hohwald along D 425.

Col du Kreuzweg – From the pass (alt 768m/2 520ft), the view extends over the valleys of the River Breitenbach and River Giessen framed by mountains and, beyond, over the Liepvrette Valley.
The road *(D 57)* climbs towards the Charbonnière pass, offering superb views of the Villé Valley, the Plaine d'Alsace and the Black Forest. Frankenbourg Castle and Haut-Kœnigsbourg Castle can be seen from afar, camped on their respective promontories overlooking the plain.

Col de la Charbonnière – Beyond the heights overlooking the Villé Valley, one can see the Plaine d'Alsace with the Black Forest in the distance.
On reaching the pass, turn right onto D 214 which goes round the Champ du Feu.

★★Champ du Feu – The vast **panorama★★** unfolding from the top of the observation tower includes the Vosges mountains, the Plaine d'Alsace, the Black Forest and, when the weather is clear, the Swiss Alps. The slopes all around are a popular ski area.

North of the tower, 1km/0.6mi to the left, D 414 leads to the Chalet Refuge and ski slopes of La Serva open in winter.

HIKES

★Haut-Anlau and Spesbourg castles – *1hr 30min on foot there and back. Drive W along D 854 then, 1.5km/0.9mi beyond Holzplatz, continue on a surfaced path to the left which leads to Hungerplatz forest lodge. Leave the car there and follow the path running along the mountain ridge to the ruins.*

The **Château du Haut-Andlau★**, built in the 14C and restored in the 16C, was lived in until 1806. Today, the imposing ruins include two massive towers and sections of walls with gaping Gothic windows. From the terrace, one can see the vineyard-covered hills, the Plaine d'Alsace and the Black Forest in the distance.
The **Château de Spesbourg★** had an unusually short life for a castle: built of pink granite in the 13C, it was destroyed in the 14C. The square keep overlooks the high walls of the seigneurial residence with its fine twinned windows.

★Grande Belle-Vue (Viewpoint) – *1hr 30min on foot there and back.*
After a few minutes, you will get a clear view of Le Hohwald and the surrounding area.

As you reach the former Belle-Vue inn (1km/0.6mi), take a path on the left and climb for 3km/1.9mi through the forest before reaching the high pastures.

From the summit *(100m/110yd to the left)*, the **view★** extends to Le Climont on the right, the Villé Valley in the foreground and Haut-Kœnigsbourg further ahead.

★Col d'Urbeis –This mountain pass is a favourite of local hiking clubs, who maintain the trails well. The view is splendid, encompassing the valleys of the Fave and Giessen rivers. The **observation tower★** at le Climont provides an exceptional panorama.

1hr 30min on foot there and back. North of Climont, near the church, there is a sign pointing the way to the trail (marked in yellow). It is steep climb.
You can continue the itinerary southward on D23 to Provenchères-sur-Fave.

Provenchères sur-Fave – This town on the northern edge of the Parc Naturel Régional des Ballons de Vosges *(see map p 82)* straddles de River Fave. It is a good place to set out on a bike excursion into the nature park.

Champ du Feu

JOINVILLE

Population 4 754
Michelin map 61 fold 10 or 241 fold 35

This small town nestles between the River Marne, dotted with mills, and a hill crowned by the ruins of a feudal castle which once belonged to the dukes of Guise.

One of the most prominent lords of this barony, established in the 11C, was the famous 13C chronicler, **Jean de Joinville** (1224-1317), a loyal companion of King Louis IX, better known as St Louis, whom he followed to Egypt in 1248 to take part in the seventh crusade. He related the events in a chronicle dedicated to St Louis which he wrote when he was already over 80 years old. A 3m/10ft high statue of Joinville, holding a book and a quill pen, by Lescornel, was erected in 1861 in rue Aristide-Briand; the low-relief sculptures depict his departure for the crusade, St Louis passing judgement under the oak in Vincennes Forest and the battle of Mansourah in Egypt.

Eating out

MODERATE

La Poste – *Pl. de la Grève* – ☎ *03 25 94 12 63 – closed 10 Jan-1 Feb, Sun evening Oct-Mar – 80/220F.* This family-run establishment in the town centre offers traditional cooking and small, functional rooms for a simple stay.

Where to stay

MODERATE

Le Soleil d'Or – *9 r. des Capucins* – ☎ *03 25 94 15 66 – closed 19-25 Feb, 31 Jul-6 Aug, 30 Oct-5 Nov and Sun evening –* **P***– 17 rooms 230/440F –* 🛏 *55F – restaurant 100/300F.* This late-17C house will charm you with its traditional decor of stone and exposed beams, artfully combined with contemporary materials, especially glass. Comfortable rooms. Classic menu or more elaborate cooking.

Camping La Forge de Ste-Marie – *52230 Thonnance-les-Moulins – 13km/8mi E of Joinville on D 427* – ☎ *03 25 94 42 00 – open May-Sep – booking advisable 15 Jul-15 Aug – 185 plots 150F – restaurant.* Lying between countryside, forest and a lake, the buildings of this former 18C forge have been turned into holiday accommodation. The forge itself contains a heated indoor pool with a terrace. Shady camping areas. Indoor tennis court, golf course, fishing, boating, jacuzzi, cabaret and children's club.

Chambre d'hôte Le Moulin – *Rte de Nancy – 52300 Thonnance-lès-Joinville – 5km/3mi E of Joinville on D 60* – ☎ *03 25 94 13 76 – jean.geeraert @wanadoo.fr –* 🛏 *– 4 rooms 200/240F – evening meal 80F.* This former mill by a small river on the edge of a forest is the ideal place to relax and enjoy yourself, with its garden, fishing lake and many walks possible in the region. The rooms are plain but quite comfortable.

SIGHTS

★**Château du Grand Jardin** ⊘ – The castle owes its name to the fact that it stands at the centre of a large garden. Built by Claude de Lorraine, head of the House of Guise, and Antoinette de Bourbon at the beginning of the 16C, it comprises an elegant edifice surmounted by a high roof and surrounded on three sides by a moat.

It was here that, in 1583, during the Wars of Religion, King Philip II of Spain signed an alliance with the heads of the French Holy League, a Catholic extremist group.

The façades are richly decorated with carvings, probably by Ligier Richier and Dominique Florentin, also known as Riconucci, a sculptor from Florence who studied with Primaticcio.

The castle has been restored to its Renaissance splendour. In the 16C Chapelle St-Claude, note the lovely stone coffered ceiling decorated with floral motifs.

Jardin – The gardens have been recreated as they were in Renaissance times according to written accounts and drawings and now offer pleasant walks. The ornamental beds planted with lavender, santolina or medicinal and aromatic herbs, flower beds, an orchard containing more than 70 varieties of fruit trees and a maze are particularly attractive features.

Château du Grand Jardin

Auditoire ⊙ – This seigneurial tribunal erected in the 16C also served as a prison. Note the model of Joinville around 1650 showing the feudal castle, the walled town, the suburbs and the Château du Grand Jardin. The tour starts with the Chambre des Pailleux for poor prisoners who slept on straw (*paille* means straw), followed by the Pistole accessible to prisoners who could pay a *pistole* (ancient gold coin) for their keep, then the women's quarters. The tribunal and Claude de Lorraine's funeral chamber are on the second floor together with Jean de Joinville on horseback in full fighting gear. A spiral staircase leads to the loft where the amount of grain tax owed to the local lord was kept: many characters in period dress recreate the atmosphere of the city when it was flourishing.

Église Notre-Dame ⊙ – The church dates from the late 12C and early 13C. Damaged by fire and restored in the 16C, it was partly rebuilt in primitive style in the 19C. It has retained its original nave (although the vaulting was rebuilt in the 16C) and its 13C aisles.
Note the modillions decorating the lower part of the roof and the 13C doorway under the 19C belfry-porch. The south side has a Renaissance doorway with Corinthian columns and capitals.
The church houses a 16C sepulchre denoting a Mannerist influence, an alabaster sculpture in high relief and a reliquary containing St Joseph's belt brought back by Jean de Joinville from the Holy Land in 1252.

Chapelle Ste-Anne ⊙ – The chapel (1504) stands in the centre of the cemetery; light pours in through lovely stained-glass windows: red and blue are the main colours used to depict scenes from the life of the Virgin, of St Anne and of St Laurence. Note the 15C **Christ in bonds** in polychrome wood.

EXCURSIONS

Blécourt – *9km/5.6mi S along N 67 to Rupt then right onto D 117.*
This pleasant village has a beautiful Gothic church built in the 12C and 13C whose proportions are remarkable. It contains a Virgin and Child in carved wood dating from the 13C (Champagne School); it was already a place of pilgrimage in Merovingian times and was later mentioned in the chronicles of Jean de Joinville.

Lacets de Mélaire – *19km/11.8mi there and back. Follow D 60; 4km/2.5mi beyond Thonnance-lès-Joinville, take the small road on the right which runs through the woods.*
These hairpin bends with steep slopes offer good views of the wide valley below and the village of Poissons.

Poissons – The village has retained a number of old houses and there are fine views from the banks of the River Rongeant which flows through it. The 16C Église St-Aignan is preceded by a monumental doorway with delicately carved arching forming a beautiful Renaissance ensemble. There is a lovely rood beam inside.
Return to Joinville along D 427 which follows the Rongeant Valley.

KAYSERSBERG ★★

Kaysersberg is a small charming city with flower-decked houses and a quaint medieval character; it is built on the banks of the Weiss, at the point where the river runs into the Plaine d'Alsace, and is surrounded by famous vineyards.

From the ruins of the medieval castle *(30min on foot there and back)*, there is a lovely general view of the town.

In Roman times, it was already called *Caesaris Mons* (the emperor's mountain) because of its strategic position along one of the most important routes linking ancient Gaul and the Rhine Valley. The appropriateness of this name was confirmed throughout the town's rich history, as it was fortified, protected and developed by more than one emperor: Frederick II in the 13C, then Rodolph of Hapsburg and Adolph of Nassau who declared it a free city. In 1353, Kaysersberg joined the Decapolis, an alliance between 10 free Alsatian cities *(see MULHOUSE)*. Emperor Charles V encouraged its development and Maximilian nominated **Lazarus von Schwendi** (1522-84) as imperial bailiff. He presented the town with a few vine plants he had brought back from his campaigns in Hungary. These vines from Tokay later contributed to make Kaysersberg one of the finest wine-growing areas in Alsace.

Albert Schweitzer

Born in Kaysersberg on 14 January 1875, Albert Schweitzer became a clergyman, a theologian, a famous organist, a musicologist, a writer and a missionary doctor. After the First World War, he spent most of his life in West Africa where he founded a hospital, occasionally returning to Europe to give organ concerts. He was awarded the Nobel Peace Prize in 1952 and died in 1965 in Lambaréné (Gabon) where his work lives on. He had a house built in Gunsbach, where he spent his childhood during the time his father was the village pastor.

Eating out

MODERATE

Du Château – *38 r. du Gén.-de-Gaulle* – ☎ *03 89 78 24 33* – *closed Wed evening Nov-Jul and Thu* – *94/185F.* This Alsatian village-centre restaurant is very simple, but will suit passing gourmets: its mouth-watering local dishes are very reasonably priced. Modest dining room and a few rooms.

MID-RANGE

La Vieille Forge – *1 r. des Écoles* – ☎ *03 89 47 17 51* – *closed 18 Feb-14 Mar, 2-26 Jul, Tue and Wed* – *119/290F.* It's well worth seeking out this discreet restaurant just off the main street. The cooking is delicious and reasonably priced, with some Alsatian dishes, and is much appreciated by the local inhabitants, with good reason.

Le Couvent – *1 r. Couvent* – ☎ *03 89 78 23 29* – *125/285F.* Another unassuming restaurant that is worth finding. You won't be disappointed: run by a young couple, it has a good local reputation and is much frequented by winemakers. Alsace dishes and traditional cuisine.

Where to stay

MID-RANGE

Hôtel Les Remparts – ☎ *03 89 47 12 12* – **P** – *42 rooms 320/460F* – ⚏ *42F.* This fairly quiet hotel is a little way from the town centre. If possible, choose one of the modern rooms in the recently built Alsatian-style annexe: some have balconies.

Shopping

Caveau des Vignerons de Kientzeim-Kaysersberg – *20 r. du Gén.-de-Gaulle* – ☎ *03 89 47 18 43* – *Easter to mid-Nov and Christmas holidays: Wed-Mon 10am-noon, 2-6pm.* Wine tasting and sales, including sparkling Alsace.

Pâtisserie Lœcken – *46 r. du Gén.-de-Gaulle* – ☎ *03 89 47 34 35* – *Tue-Sun 8am-6.30pm, Jul-Aug 8am-7pm* – *closed 25 Dec-1 Jan.* Cake shop in a superb 16C wood-shingled house.

TOUR OF THE TOWN

★Hôtel de ville – Built in a certain form of Renaissance style characteristic of the Rhine region, the town hall has a lovely façade, a peaceful courtyard and a picturesque wooden gallery.

★Église Ste-Croix – Kaysersberg parish church was built between the 12C and 15C. It stands beside a small square adorned with a 16C fountain, restored in the 18C and surmounted by a statue of Emperor Constantine. The Romanesque west doorway has unusual capitals decorated with pelicans and sirens with two tails, characteristic of Lombard ornamentation. Inside, the most striking feature is a large group in polychrome wood representing the Crucifixion, carved in the 15C. The left window of the west front is decorated with beautiful 15C stained glass by Pierre d'Andlau, depicting Christ on the Cross flanked by the two thieves.

The chancel contains, above the high altar, a wooden **altarpiece★★** in the shape of a triptych, a magnificent work by Jean Bongartz, the master from Colmar (1518). The central panel depicting the Crucifixion, is surrounded by 12 carved panels illustrating the Stations of the Cross; below, Christ can be seen blessing the people as his disciples surround him. On the reverse side, 17C paintings depict the discovery and glorification of the Holy Cross.

The north aisle shelters a damaged Holy Sepulchre dating from 1514; the most remarkable part is the group representing the holy women, a masterpiece by Jacques Wirt. According to an Alsatian tradition, a slit in Christ's chest is intended for the host during Holy Week.

Chapelle St-Michel – The two-storey chapel was built in 1463. The lower level was turned into an ossuary and contains a stoup decorated with a skull. The upper chapel is adorned with frescoes dating from 1464. Note the unusual 14C crucifix in the chancel, to the right of the altar.

Cimetière – The soldiers who died during the liberation of the town are buried in this cemetery. Stone fragments strewn around make it look like an archaeological museum. A 16C wooden gallery provides a shelter for the unusual cross, known as the plague cross, dating from 1511.

★Vieilles maisons – There are many old houses along rue de l'Église, rue de l'Ancien-Hôpital, rue de l'Ancienne-Gendarmerie and rue du Général-de-Gaulle (also called Grand-Rue). The Renaissance well dating from 1618, situated in the courtyard of no 54 Grand-Rue, bears a humorous inscription.

Continue towards the River Weiss.

Hostellerie du Pont – Standing on the corner of rue des Forgerons, lined with old houses, this elegant and sturdy hostel has been restored. It was the former baths.

★Pont fortifié – The fortified bridge built in the 15C and 16C is located in a charming setting with old houses all round; an oratory stands on top.

The **Maison Brief**, dating from 1594, is an elaborately carved timber-framed house with covered gallery.

KAYSERSBERG

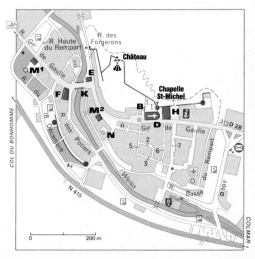

MUSEUMS

Musée communal ⊘ – Housed in a Renaissance dwelling with a double roof and a stair turret, the museum exhibits medieval religious art (rare 14C opening statue of the Virgin, Christ with branches of palms from the 15C), neolithic axes from Bennwihr, various objects connected with a cooper's craft etc.

Musée Albert-Schweitzer ⊘ – Standing next to Albert Schweitzer's birthplace, the museum displays documents, photos, personal mementoes and souvenirs retracing the life of the great humanist.

Kaysersberg is attractive and inviting

LANGRES★★

Population 9 981
Michelin map 66 fold 3 or 241 fold 47

A promontory of the Langres plateau forms the remarkable **setting★★** of this ancient city which was one of the three capitals of Burgundy under the Gauls. Later on it became a bishopric and an advanced post defending the kingdom of France. It is one of the gateways of Burgundy and a tourist stopoff on the north-south European route (A5, A31). The town is near the source of three rivers, the Marne, the Seine and the Aube and four reservoirs supplying the Marne-Saône canal.

Langres is the birthplace of **Denis Diderot**, the 18C philosopher, of **Jeanne Mance**, the missionary who founded Canada's first hospital in Montreal in the mid 17C, and of **Claude Gillot** (1674-1722), the painter who was one of Watteau's masters.

HISTORICAL NOTES

Gallo-Roman city – The Lingons, a Gaulish tribe who gave their name to Langres, became Caesar's allies and the town prospered under Roman occupation. However, when Nero died in AD 70, one of their chiefs, by the name of **Sabinus**, tried to usurp the supreme power but failed and, according to legend, he found refuge in a cave close to the source of the Marne *(see p 175)*. He remained there for nine years but was eventually discovered and taken to Rome where he was executed with his wife who wished to share his fate.

St Didier – The city was christianised in the 3C AD and became a bishopric in the 4C. According to legend, St Didier, who was the third bishop of Langres was made a martyr for having defended the town: after he was beheaded, he picked up his head, left on horseback and died on the spot where a chapel was later built in his honour (now part of the new museum).

Royal stronghold – During the Middle Ages, the bishops of Langres became dukes and peers of the realm and some of them were among the king's close advisors.
When Champagne was united with France in 1284, Langres became a royal fortress and played a strategic role on the border of Burgundy, Lorraine and Franche-Comté, a role it resumed in the 19C when the walls were restored (1843-60) and a citadel built (1842-50), reinforced by eight independent forts (1868-85).

Eating out

MODERATE

Aux Délices – Pâtisserie Henry – *6 r. Diderot –* ☎ *03 25 87 02 48 – 30/60F.* Treat yourself to a little break in this tearoom during your visit of the old town of Langres. The stone building dates from 1580. The delicious quiches, meat pies and pastries will make you forget the rather impersonal decor.

Auberge des Voiliers – *Au Lac de la Liez – 4km/2.5mi E of Langres on N 19 and D 284 –* ☎ *03 25 87 05 74 – closed during Feb school holidays, autumn half-term, Sun evening except Jul-Aug, and Mon – 100/250F.* Liez Lake is well known by sailors and windsurfers, and this lakeside inn is ideal for weekend breaks or short holidays. The rooms are simple and the cooking varied and appetising.

Auberge des Trois Provinces – *52190 Vaux-sous-Aubigny – 25km/15.5mi S of Langres on N 74 –* ☎ *03 25 88 31 98 – closed 17 Jan-7 Feb, Sun evening and Mon – 98/138F.* The decor in this little inn is decidedly modern, with beams and painted ceilings and brightly coloured frescoes. Only the stone walls give it a country feel. The helpings are generous enough to satisfy the biggest appetites.

Le Parc – *1 pl. Moreau – 52210 Arc-en-Barrois –* ☎ *03 25 02 53 07 – closed Feb, Sun evening and Mon 7 Mar-31 May, Tue evening and Wed Sep-Jan – 100/160F.* After visiting the attractions in the Haute-Marne, you can enjoy regional specialities in this peaceful restaurant. Large, light dining room, enclosed terrace with flowers. Functional rooms.

MID-RANGE

Auberge du Palais Abbatial – *52160 Auberive –* ☎ *03 25 84 33 66 – closed Mon Oct-Mar – 130/160F.* This extraordinary restaurant is in a converted abbey dating back to the 12C. Impressive fireplaces, a bread oven, local stone, massive beams and old candlesticks add up to a decor from the past. Not to be missed.

Where to stay

MODERATE

Auberge de la Fontaine – *Pl. de la Fontaine – 52210 Villiers-sur-Suize – 19 km/11.8mi NW of Langres on N 19 and D 254 –* ☎ *03 25 31 22 22 – closed 1-15 Mar and 15-30 Sep – 7 rooms 230/270F –* ⌑ *35F – restaurant 98/160F.* Nature-lovers in search of peace and quiet will appreciate this hotel, where the typical regional architecture is emphasized by the way the rooms have been given local names, rather than numbers. Dinner is served in the neighbouring inn, with local specialities, while breakfast is eaten right next to the village grocery store!

Chambre d'hôte L'Orangerie – *Pl. de l'Église – 52190 Prangey – 16km/10mi S of Langres on N 74 and D 26 –* ☎ *03 25 87 54 85 –* ▱ *– 3 rooms 240/320F.* This charming ivy-clad bed and breakfast stands in a rural setting, between the castle and the village church. Its comfortable rooms have a romantic atmosphere.

MID-RANGE

Le Cheval Blanc – *4 r. Estres –* ☎ *03 25 87 07 00 – closed 22-30 Nov – ▫ – 22 rooms 320/420F –* ⌑ *48F – restaurant 140/180F.* Some of the bedrooms have vaulted ceilings in this 9C abbey church, which was converted into a hotel in 1793. Behind the house, opposite the town ramparts, the remains of the old buildings enhance the pretty summer terrace. Traditional menu and nicely presented tables.

OLD TOWN

A **slanting elevator** links the Sous-Bie parking area, situated outside the walls, to the town centre, offering a panoramic view of the town, of the Lac de la Liez and of the Vosges mountains.

Within the ramparts, visitors strolling along the twisting medieval streets will discover the Cathédrale St-Mammès and a few beautiful old houses as well as numerous decorative features including recesses (15C-19C) which testify to the religious fervour of the town's inhabitants.

Langres and its ramparts

P.Lemoine/CDTT, Chaumont

Rue Diderot – Lined with shops, the town's high street runs past the **theatre** housed since 1838 inside the former Chapelle des Oratoriens (1676).

Collège – This vast edifice is the former 18C Jesuit college. The Baroque façade of the chapel is surmounted by flame vases.

Place Diderot – This is the town's main square; situated right in the centre, it is adorned with a statue of Diderot by Bartholdi famed for the Statue of Liberty. A plaque has been fixed on the wall of his birthplace located on the corner of rue de la Boucherie.

Denis Diderot (1713-84)

The son of a cutler, Denis Diderot was a brilliant pupil of the local Jesuit college and he seemed destined for a religious career, but he went on to study in Paris instead and only came back to Langres five times during his life. However he spoke about his native town in his *letters* to Sophie Volland and in his *Journey to Langres*.

Interested in many subjects, he wrote numerous works, including essays such as *Letters about the blind for the attention of those who can see*, for which he was imprisoned in Vincennes, novels *(The Nun)*, satires *(Jacques the Fatalist)*, and philosophical dialogues *(Rameau's Nephew)*. He was also an art critic *(Salons)*. Yet his name is first and foremost linked with that of the *Encyclopaedia*, a monumental work which he undertook to write with D'Alembert in 1747 and to which he devoted 25 years of his life. Completed in 1772, the 35-volume *Encyclopaedia* represents the sum total of scientific knowledge and philosophical ideas during the Age of Enlightenment.

As you walk down rue du Grand-Cloître, admire the view of the Lac de la Liez. Note the 15C timber-framed house at the beginning of rue Lhuillier and, on the corner of rue du Petit-Cloître, a 15C-16C house decorated with a bartizan covered with shingles.

Walk along the south side of the cathedral.

Cloître de la cathédrale ⊘ – The cloister, dating from the early 13C, has retained only two galleries which have been restored and glassed-in and now house the municipal library. Inside, the ribbed vaulting rests on slender columns decorated with crocket or leafed capitals.

Walk across place Jeanne-Mance.

The bronze statue of **Jeanne Mance** (1606-73) by Jean Cardot stands in the centre of this charming square.

Maison Renaissance – This Renaissance house built in the mid 16C has a splendid façade overlooking the garden, adorned with small Ionic and Corinthian columns and friezes representing bucranium motifs, draperies and fruit. An openwork balustrade surrounds the courtyard with a central well.

LANGRES

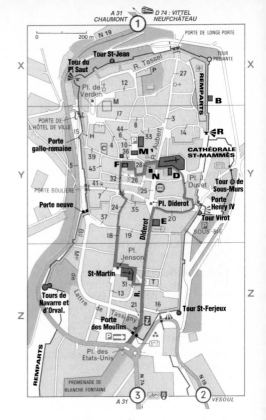

Follow the side passage *(spiral staircase)* ending rue Cardinal-Morlot and turn left after admiring another Renaissance house with twin columns on your right. Covered passages gave access to interior courtyards and could also be used as a shortcut from one street to the next.

Continue along rue Lambert-Payen and rue Gambetta leading to the charming place Jenson.

Église St-Martin – This 13C church, remodelled in the 18C following a fire, is surmounted by an elegant campanile of the same period.

★★WALK ALONG THE RAMPARTS *4km/2.5mi – about 1hr 30min*

🔆 The watch-path offers a pleasant walk round the town and a magnificent panorama including; to the east the Marne Valley, the Lac de la Liez and the Vosges mountains when the weather is clear; to the north the Colline des Fourches crowned by a chapel; to the west the slopes of the Bonnelle Valley and further afield the Plateau de Langres and its wooded slopes. The ramparts have retained seven gates and 12 towers showing the evolution of fortifications from the Hundred Years War to the 19C.

Start from place des États-Unis south of the old town.

Porte des Moulins (1647) – This is the monumental entrance to the city; its style is characteristic of Louis XIII's military architecture and it is surmounted by a dome covered with shingles of chestnut wood. The ornamentation includes an allegorical representation of French victories at the end of the Thirty Years War: chained enemies, helmets and trophies.

Tour St-Ferjeux (c 1469-72) – Specially adapted to artillery warfare, its terrace can accommodate heavy guns. The two vaulted rooms with walls 6m/20ft thick house eight casemates. From the platform, the view extends to the surrounding countryside and there are beautiful vistas of the ramparts. A polished-steel sculpture by the Dutch artist Eugene Van Lamsweerde, entitled *Air*, dedicated to the philosopher Gaston Bachelard, stands on the tower.

Tour Virot – This semicircular tower used to defend the Sous-Murs district, an area below the walls of the city (hence its name) where many tanners used to live. It was surrounded by its own wall reinforced by the **Tour des Sous-Murs** (1502), which can still be seen.

Porte Henri IV (1604) – This gate, which gave access to the Sous-Murs district, has retained traces of its defence system (ditch, drawbridge, portcullis).

Viewing table – From this point, the view encompasses the Sous-Murs district below, surrounded by its own wall, and the ramparts on either side; the Lac de la Liez and the Vosges mountains can be seen in the distance.

Tour St-Jean – Built on a rocky spur, this former gun tower was fitted as a military dovecote in 1883.

Tour du Petit-Sault (c 1517-21) – This elongated gun tower with very thick walls, contains two vaulted rooms linked by a large staircase. From the terrace *(viewing table)*, there is a view of the Bonnelle Valley and of the Plateau de Langres.

Porte gallo-romaine (1C AD) – Set within the walls, this gate was used as a tower in medieval times.

Porte Neuve or Porte des Terreaux (1855) – This is the most recent of the gates; it is crowned with neo-Gothic machicolations and there are traces of the drawbridge.

Tours de Navarre et d'Orval ⊘ – The former gun platform of the Tour de Navarre was covered with chestnut timberwork in 1825; it is the most powerful of them all. It is reinforced by the Tour d'Orval whose spiral ramp enabled soldiers to wheel heavy guns up to the summit of the Tour de Navarre.

SIGHTS

★**Cathédrale St-Mammès** – The cathedral (94m/308ft long and 23m/75ft high) was built during the second half of the 12C but it was subsequently remodelled many times. The primitive west front (12C-13C), destroyed by major fires, was replaced in the 18C by a three-storey Classical façade.

The vast interior is in Burgundian Romanesque style, the nave with its ribbed vaulting marking the transition towards Gothic style.

The first chapel along the north aisle (second bay) has a splendid coffered ceiling and houses an alabaster Virgin and Child by Évrard d'Orléans (1341); note that the bishop who donated the statue is standing next to it. The third bay is decorated with low-relief sculptures representing the Passion, embedded into a fragment of the rood screen built c 1550 by Cardinal de Givry.

Two tapestries displayed in the transept depict the legend of St Mammès. During the 3C, this saint from Cappadocia preached the gospel to wild animals and when Roman guards came to martyr him, these same wild animals protected him. The cathedral of Langres received from Constantinople some relics of the saint including his head.

The chancel and the apse, built between 1141 and 1153, are the most remarkable parts of the edifice.

The capitals of the triforium in the apse are richly decorated with supernatural animals and characters, as well as floral motifs. A 16C sculpture in low relief situated in the ambulatory illustrates the transfer of the saint's relics during a solemn procession round the walls of the city.

Trésor ⊘ – The treasury houses many objets d'art: a reliquary from Clairvaux Abbey, believed to contain a piece of the True Cross, a reliquary bust of St Mammès in vermeil and a small 15C ivory statue of the saint, an enamel evangelistary plate dating from the 13C, a chased-silver box (1615), which is all that remains of the bishop's chapel destroyed during the Revolution.

Tour sud ⊘ – *227 steps.* From the top of the **South tower** (45m/148ft), there is a panoramic view of the town and a vast surrounding area.

Musée d'Art et d'Histoire ⊘ – The museum is housed in the Romanesque Chapelle St-Didier, where the town's collections have been kept since 1842, and in a vast glass-and-concrete edifice purposely built to display the collections acquired later.

The department of prehistory and ancient history includes items discovered during excavations made in the region (Farincourt, Cohons...); note the enigmatic Celtic heads from Perrogney.

The **Gallo-Roman department★** displays fragments of stone from various buildings. The *Togatus* or *Consul* is a headless marble statue discovered in Langres during the 17C. The numerous stelae and sculptures testify to the importance of this civilization. Note in particular *Bacchus' Altar* in white marble, found in St-Geosmes, the *Wine-harvest cart*, the *Horse's head* from Isômes, the *Cobbler's stela*, the *Barducucullus' statue* (named after the hooded coat) and the semicircular *Engagement stela* with four characters.

The Bacchus mosaic was uncovered on the museum site in 1985

Painting from the 17C, 18C and 19C is represented by local artists such as Jean Tassel, Edmé Bouchardon, Courbet, Corot...

EXCURSIONS

Source de la Marne – *4km/2.7mi and 15min on foot there and back. Leave Langres along N 74 then follow D 122 on the left towards Noidant-Chatenoy; 2.5km/1.5mi further on, turn left onto D 290 towards Balesmes-sur-Marne; drive for another 1km/0.6mi and turn right towards the parking area; a path on the left leads down to the source of the River Marne (400m/437yd).*

The Marne springs from a kind of vault closed by an iron door. Nearby, you can see the cave where Sabinus hid for nine years. Footpaths meander through the rocks. Picnic area.

You can turn left 1km/0.6mi beyond Balesmes-sur-Marne onto D 17 which crosses the Marne-Saône canal.

Inaugurated in 1907, the canal makes it possible to travel across France along various waterways from Dunkerque to Marseille. A **tunnel** (4.8km/2.5mi long) had to be built to negotiate the watershed between north and south. You can watch the canal disappear into the tunnel, which is so narrow that an alternating traffic system has been installed.

Faverolles, Mausolée gallo-romain – *10km/6mi along N 19 to Rolampont, then left along D 155 and D 256.* The ruins of this mausoleum were discovered in 1980 in the forest, 3.5km/2.2mi outside the village *(it is possible to visit the excavation site during the course of a walk through the forest).*

Erected in 20 BC, it was more than 20m/66ft high and comprised three tiers of the Corinthian order. By its shape and function (it is a cenotaph dedicated to a deceased person), it is comparable to the mausoleum situated in St-Rémy-de-Provence.

Fragments of the mausoleum are displayed in an **Atelier archéologique** ⊘: sculpture in high relief representing a bird of prey, two rampant lions, funeral masks...

Château du Pailly ⊘ – *12km/7.5mi along N 74 and D 122 to Noidant-Chatenoy then left onto D 141.* An elegant Renaissance residence was built in 1560 round a feudal castle by Marshal de Saulx-Tavannes. Only three of the four buildings have survived. The most remarkable parts are the balconied façade overlooking the main courtyard and, to the left, the spiral staircase with an openwork turret.

The **Salle dorée** of the 15C keep has a superb French-style ceiling and two monumental fireplaces.

Fort du Cognelot ⊘ – *10km/6.2mi SE along D 17.* This is one of eight forts built round Langres after the 1870 war to defend France's eastern border. It was built between 1874 and 1877. Casemates for 600 men were grouped round two courtyards together with magazines, stores for food supplies, equipment and artillery.

Tuffière de Rolamport

Cascade de la Tuffière – *14km/8.7mi along N 19 to 1km/0.6mi beyond Rolampont then left onto D 254; follow the arrows.*

🚶 The cascade on this site has been formed over time as mineral spring water, rich in calcium, has made the rock porous through the deposit of microscopic algae and moss, creating a kind of petrified waterfall. The water runs down this natural stairway in the woods. A footpath winds round it.

Fayl-Billot – *26km/16mi SE along N 19.* Situated on the border of the Plateau de Langres and Plateau de Haute-Saône, this large farming village lies on the edge of a lovely forested area which offers pleasant walks (Forêt de Bussières). Cane furniture and wickerwork are a speciality of Fayl-Billot. The national school, which houses three **exhibition rooms** ⊘ displaying the creations of the students, upholds handicraft traditions.

The basket-maker's house, where the tourist office is located, has objects on display during the season. The centre of the village has retained a few workshops where craftsmen can be seen at work.

Bussières-les-Belmont ⊘ – *5km/3mi from Fayl-Billot.* The local association of willow growers presents a video on willow growing and wicker work; there is also a display of finished articles.

LAND OF THE FOUR LAKES

Four reservoirs were created at the end of the 19C and beginning of the 20C in order to supply the Marne-Saône canal. They offer relaxation, pleasant walks in wooded surroundings and a choice of water sports as well as fishing for pike, carp and perch.

During the summer, the surface of these reservoirs may shrink and the extremities are then turned into reedy marshland sheltering interesting fauna and flora.

Lac de la Liez – *5km/3mi E of Langres.* This is the largest of the four lakes (270ha/667 acres); it is possible to walk along its earth dyke (460m/503yd long and 16m/53ft high) which affords views of the fortified town of Langres.
A footpath runs round the lake.

Lac de la Mouche – *6km/3.7mi W of Langres.* This is the smallest of the four lakes (94ha/232 acres); it is overlooked by two villages, St-Ciergues in the north and Perrancey-les-Vieux-Moulins in the south, linked by a scenic road which runs over the dyke (410m/448yd long and 23m/75ft high).

Lac de Charmes – *8km/5mi N of Langres.* The earth dyke here is 362m/395yd long and 17m/56ft high and the elongated lake covers 197ha/487 acres.

Lac de la Vingeanne – *12km/7.5mi by* ③ *on the town plan along N 74.* A footpath (8km/5mi) runs all the way round this lake (190ha/250 acres) which has the longest dyke (1 254m/1 371yd). A great number of migrating birds nest or just rest in the reedy marshland.

HAUTE VALLÉE DE L'AUBE

Itinerary from Langres to Chaumont

94km/58mi – 4hr

The Plateau de Langres is covered with forests and heathland and dotted with caves, dolines and numerous resurgent springs owing to the underground layers of clay. The watershed between the Paris Basin, the Rhine Valley and the Rhône Valley is situated on this plateau and the Seine, the Aube, the Marne and the Meuse all have their source in the area.

Leave Langres southwards along N 74.

Sts-Geosmes – The 13C **church**, dedicated to three saints martyred on this site, is built over a 10C crypt with three naves.

Follow D 428 towards Auberive.

Beyond the village of Pierrefontaines, the road runs near the Haut-du-Sec (alt 516m/1 693ft), the highest point of the Plateau de Langres, before entering the Forêt d'Auberive.

A few miles further on, turn left onto the Acquenove forest road. The source of the River Aube is signposted.

Source de l'Aube – The Aube wells up in a pastoral setting with picnic facilities.

Drive to Auberive along D 20 then D 428.

Auberive – An ancient Cistercian abbey, founded in 1133 by St Bernard and mostly rebuilt in the 18C, stands in a wooded setting near the source of the Aube *(not open to the public)*. From the abbey square, one can see through the railings on the right the chancel of the abbey church (1182), which is the only Romanesque feature left apart from the doorway of the chapter-house.
A shaded alleyway runs between the Aube and the canal.

Along the road to Châtillon *(D 428)*, one can see the façade of the abbey through the elegant 18C wrought-iron railing by Jean Lamour, who also made the railings of place Stanislas in Nancy *(see NANCY)*.

On the way out of Auberive, turn right onto D 20 which follows the River Aube.

★**Cascade d'Étufs** – *Leave the car in the parking area.* Soon after Rouvres-sur-Aube, an alleyway branches off D 20 on the left and leads to a private property; go round the right side of it to reach the waterfall. Water wells up from the hillside in a lovely shaded site and forms several successive waterfalls.

Continue on D 20 to Aubepierre-sur-Aube then turn right onto D 159 towards Arc-en-Barrois.

Arc-en-Barrois – Nestling at the bottom of a valley and surrounded by forests, this small town is a lovely place to stay in.
The Église St-Martin was altered in the 19C and one has to go round the edifice to discover the old 15C doorway: the tympanum, located under a three-lobed arch, is decorated with a representation of Christ on the Cross between the church and the synagogue. The chapel situated on the right of the entrance houses a 17C sepulchre. Note the unusual cast-iron Stations of the Cross.

Take D 3 on the left then turn right onto D 65 to Châteauvillain.

Châteauvillain – In the 18C, Châteauvillain was surrounded by a wall fortified by 60 towers; three gates led in and out of the town. Parts of these fortifications dating from the 14C to the 16C (Tour St-Marc, Tour des Malades) have survived. The outline of the castle is clearly visible but only the Tour de l'Auditoire still stands; it is now used for temporary exhibitions *(mid-July to mid-September)*.
The west front of the **Église Notre-Dame de l'Assomption**, rebuilt after 1770, is believed to have been designed by the architect Soufflot (who also designed the Panthéon in Paris). The tower is the only remaining part of the original church.
Opposite the church stands the **Hôtel de ville** (town hall) designed in 1784 by Lancret.
Note the pointed arch over the gate of the former **provost's house** which has retained its stone ties and gargoyles.
Porte Madame (14C), the only remaining gate, gives access to the **Parc aux daims** (deer park) where animals are allowed to roam freely.

Return to Chaumont along D 65.

Parc naturel régional de LORRAINE

Population 60 000
Michelin map 241 folds 23, 24, 27 and 28 or 242 folds 14, 15, 18 and 19

Straddling the three *départements* of the Meurthe-et-Moselle, Meuse and Moselle, close to the towns of Nancy and Metz, this nature park offers visitors the wonderful variety of its natural environment from the Ste-Croix Safari Park to the numerous lakes home to thousands of migrating birds, perfectly in tune with the adjacent rural areas; meadows, vineyards and orchards are dotted with many villages whose inhabitants strive to preserve the fragility of the different ecosystems and to promote the harmonious economic and social development of the area as a whole.

Created in 1976, the Parc naturel régional de Lorraine extends over two distinct geographical zones on either side of the River Moselle.

The **western part** is enclosed within a perimeter defined by the towns of Verdun, Metz, Commercy and Toul. The hilly countryside (Côtes de Meuse and Côtes de Moselle) is planted with vines and fruit trees and the plateaux are furrowed with deep valleys. The Woëvre Plain with Lac de Madine in its centre, is noticeably more humid.

More irregular in shape, the **eastern part** extends from Château-Salins to Fénétrange and Sarrebourg, between the Seille Valley to the west and the foothills of the Vosges to the east. It is dotted with a myriad of small lakes, which are the habitat of many species of birds, some of them extremely rare.

🔲 **Nature trails** – The area is crisscrossed with marked footpaths with explanatory panels: forest trails of the Forêt de la Reine, Forêt de Bride-et-Kœking and Forêt de Fénétrange, salt-marsh trail in Marsal, limestone-meadow trail in Génicourt-sur-Meuse, trails of the Étang de Lindre and Étang des Essarts, vineyard trail in Lucey. In the traditional hemp-growing area around Toul, a special trail enables visitors to discover the processes used for extracting the fibre from the stem.

Birdwatching – Observatories have been set up near the Étang de la Chaussée, Étang de Lindre and Neuf Étang.

SIGHTS

Maison des Arts et Traditions rurales ⊙ – *Hannonville-sous-les-Côtes, western part of the nature park, N of Lac de Madine (map 241 fold 23).* Reconstruction of the interior of a wine-grower's house in the 1850s. Exhibitions about wine-growing, hemp, cooperage....

Maison du Pays des Étangs ⊙ – *Tarquimpol peninsula, Étang de Lindre, eastern part of the nature park (map 242 fold 18).* Jutting out into the Étang de Lindre, home to more than 250 bird species, the peninsula has retained traces of a Gallo-Roman settlement. Models, slide shows with sound and interactive games enable visitors to discover the natural and archaeological site.

Lac de Madine – *W of Pont-à-Mousson, western part of the nature park (map 242 fold 13).* Nonsard, on the north-east shore of the lake lies 25km/15mi W of Pont-à Mousson along D 958 to Flirey (15km/9.3mi) then right onto D 904 to Pannes (7km/4.3mi) and left onto D 133 (3km/1.9mi).
This large lake covering an area of 1 100ha/2 718 acres and its surroundings form a vast outdoor leisure park offering many nautical activities (boating, swimming, sailing, pedalo rides) and other sporting activities (tennis, golf, riding...) as well as the opportunity to relax in a pleasant country setting (catering, accommodation and camping).
It is also possible to take a 20km/12.4mi walk or bike ride round the lake.

▣ **Parc animalier de Ste-Croix** ⊙ – *Rhodes, 12km/7.5mi NW of Sarrebourg along D 27, eastern part of the nature park.* This safari park shelters 50 European species including wolves, lynxes, foxes, storks and deer. A traditional farm breeds endangered species such as four-horned sheep, woolly pigs, dwarf goats and donkeys from Poitou.

★CÔTES DE MEUSE

Itinerary from Verdun to St-Mihiel

83km/52mi – allow 2hr 30min
Leave Verdun by D 903 towards Metz and Nancy.

Soon after leaving Verdun, look to the right for a fine view of the Meuse Valley and its wooded rolling countryside.

7km/4.3mi beyond the intersection of D 903 and D 964, turn right onto DST 31, signposted Les Éparges, Hattonchâtel, then right again onto D 154.

Les Éparges – This outcrop overlooking the Woëvre Plain was the cause of fierce fighting during the First World War.

🔲 **Site des Éparges** – Marked footpaths running through a dense forest of fir trees, lead from the Le Trottoir national cemetery to the site of the fighting. The ground still bears the scars left by the mines.

Turn back and drive to D 908 via St-Rémy-la-Calonne and Combres-sous-les-Côtes. In St-Maurice-sous-les-Côtes, turn right onto D 101 then left onto the narrow DST 31 to Hattonchâtel.

★**Hattonchâtel** – This once fortified village, built on a promontory, owes its name to a 9C castle belonging to a bishop of Verdun named Hatton. The collegiate chapter rebuilt the **church** and erected the chapel and the cloister (1328-60). Walk through the courtyard of the cloister to the chapel which contains a magnificent **altarpiece** in polychrome stone dating from 1523, believed to be by Ligier Richier, which depicts three biblical scenes separated by Renaissance pilasters: the Bearing of the cross and St Veronica on the left, the Crucifixion and the Fainting Virgin in the centre and the Entombment on the right. Note the modern stained-glass windows by Gruber.

The neo-Romanesque town hall houses the **Musée Louise-Cottin** ⊘ containing about 100 paintings by this artist (1907-74) who excelled at portrait, still-life and genre painting.

Situated at the end of a promontory, the former **castle** ⊘, dismantled in 1634 by order of Richelieu, was restored in 15C style between 1924 and 1928. The view extends as far as Nancy.

Follow D 908 S to Woinville then turn left onto D 119 to Montsec.

American monument at the Butte de Monsec

★★**Butte de Montsec** – *19km/12mi E of St-Mihiel along D 119.*
The **monument**★ standing at the top of an isolated hill (alt 275m/902ft) was erected by the Americans to commemorate the offensive of September 1918 which enabled the American First Army to break through the St-Mihiel bulge and take 15 000 prisoners. From the memorial, the **view**★★ embraces the Woëvre Valley and Côtes de Meuse to the west and Lake Madine to the north.

From Montsec drive SW along D 12 until the road joins D 907 and turn right to St Mihiel.

★**St-Mihiel** – *See ST-MIHIEL.*

LUNÉVILLE★

Population 20 682
Michelin map 62 fold 6 or 242 fold 22

Lunéville spreads its wide streets, its vast park and its beautiful monuments, designed in the 18C, between the River Meurthe and its tributary, the Vezouze. The ceramic factory, which King Stanislas promoted to the rank of royal manufacture, specialises in tableware. At the beginning of the 18C, the duke of Lorraine, **Leopold**, often stayed in the town. He greatly admired Louis XIV and commissioned Germain Boffrand, a student of Mansart, to build the castle using Versailles as his model. The duke enjoyed dancing, gambling and the theatre as well as hunting and he attracted to his small-scale Versailles the aristocracy of Lorraine.

Later on, Lunéville was the favourite residence of King Stanislas *(see NANCY)* who remodelled the park and redecorated the castle. Writers and artists, among them Voltaire, Montesquieu, Saint-Lambert and Helvetius flocked to his court. Stanislas died in the castle on 23 February 1766.

★CHÂTEAU

This imposing castle surrounds a vast courtyard open on the west side *(see Introduction: Architecture and art)* which has in its centre the equestrian statue of General de Lasalle killed at the battle of Wagram. The central building has two monumental staircases and is flanked by two small wings separated by porticoes from the larger wings lining the main courtyard. The **chapel** ⊙ is modelled on its counterpart in Versailles.

Eating out

MODERATE

Les Bosquets – *2 r. des Bosquets* – ☎ *03 83 74 00 14* – *closed 1-15 Aug, Wed evening, Thu evening and Sun evening* – *89/199F.* This small family restaurant is frequented by the locals and proposes several menus, including one for children. The fixed-price lunch is particularly good value and the three simple dining rooms are often full.

Where to stay

MODERATE

Hôtel des Pages – *5 quai des Petits-Bosquets* – ☎ *03 83 74 11 42* – **P** – *30 rooms 250/320F* – ⌷ *36F* – *restaurant 98/130F.* A good place to stay if you are visiting the castle. Most of the rooms have been renovated in contemporary style, and these are the ones to choose. Bistro cooking is available at the Petit Comptoir restaurant.

Musée ⊙ – The museum houses an important collection of ceramics from Lunéville and St-Clément, the pharmacy of Lunéville's hospital, terracotta statuettes by Paul-Louis Cyfflé, a unique collection of ink portraits by Jean-Joseph Bernard (18C), Flemish painted-leather hangings (17C) and Art Nouveau objects dating from c 1900 (glassware from the Muller Brothers' glassworks).

The works of Georges de la Tour, painted in Lunéville between 1620 and 1652 are illustrated in an audio-visual programme.

★**Parc des Bosquets** – Laid out at the beginning of the 18C by Yves des Hours, the park was successively embellished by Leopold and Stanislas. When the latter died, the castle and the park were taken over by the army and most of the pools were filled in. In 1936, it became the property of the town. In 1946, the groves were given back their original 18C design with flower beds, statues and fountains; at the same time, the terrace reappeared.

Lunéville ceramic "Bébé", King Stanislas's dwarf

B.Kaufmann/MICHELIN

ADDITIONAL SIGHTS

Église St-Jacques – This Baroque abbey church was built between 1730 and 1747 by Boffrand and Héré. The façade is flanked by two round towers surmounted by statues of St Michael *(left)* and St John Nepomucenus *(right)*, the chaplain of Emperor Wenceslas who had him drowned for refusing to reveal the empress' confession.

Inside, note the Regency **woodwork**★ (tambour of the main doorway, choir stalls, pulpit), a *Pietà* in polychrome stone dating from the 15C *(on the left of the chancel)* and fine works by Girardet. Before leaving, do not miss the attractive gallery and organ loft (cleverly concealing the pipes) designed by Héré in 1751.

Musée de la Moto et du Vélo ⊙ – This museum houses more than 200 different types of bicycles and motorbikes with two or three wheels, the oldest dating from 1895. Some are quite rare like the motorbike of an English parachutist (1943) weighing only 43kg/95lb, the bicycle fitted with an auxiliary diesel engine of 18cc (1951), or the bike with a wooden frame dating from 1910.

LUXEUIL-LES-BAINS ✝

Population 8 790
Michelin map 66 fold 6 or 242 fold 38

Luxeuil is a well-known spa resort offering visitors a wide choice of activities (concerts, casino, tennis, golf, swimming).

The town has a wealth of red-sandstone architecture and a former abbey founded by **St Columba**, an Irish monk who arrived in France in 590 with 12 companions. Having lectured the duke of Burgundy about his dissolute life, he was expelled from the country and forced to take refuge in Bobbio (Italy).

> **MORNING DIP**
>
> **Hôtel Beau Site** – *18 r. G.-Moulimard –* ☎ *03 84 40 14 67 –* ◻ *– 32 rooms 180/380F –* ⌣ *40F – restaurant 85/160F.* This imposing building is set in a flower garden a little way from the town centre, near the baths. Spacious rooms. Eat breakfast on the terrace in fine weather, after a morning dip in the swimming pool.

The town is proud of its lace-making tradition, an internationally successful activity in the 19C. An association for the preservation of Luxeuil lace has opened up on Place de l'Abbaye. There is a fine example of the craft in St-Colomban church *(see below)*.

A 4km/2.5mi long footpath, known as the "path of the Gauls", starts from the baths and enables visitors to discover the history of the town and its monuments *(information available from the tourist office)*.

SIGHTS

★**Hôtel du cardinal Jouffroy** – Abbot of Luxeuil, then archbishop of Albi and finally cardinal, Jouffroy was King Louis XI's favourite until the end of his life. His house (15C), the finest in Luxeuil, successfully combines the Flamboyant-Gothic style (windows and gallery) with the Renaissance style (16C corbelled turret surmounted by a lantern). Madame de Sévigné, who described life at the court of Louis XIV in famous letters to her daughter, and the Romantic poet Alphonse de Lamartine lived in this house.

Note the carving on the third keystone under the balcony: it illustrates a group of three rabbits; the artist has carved only three ears in all yet each rabbit appears to have two ears.

★**Maison François I** – This Renaissance edifice is not named after the king of France but after one of the abbots of Luxeuil Abbey.

★**Ancienne abbaye St-Colomban** ⊙ – The present basilica was built in the 13C and 14C on the site of an 11C church. The west tower is the only one left of the three original towers; rebuilt in 1527, it was raised in the 18C. The apse was remodelled by Viollet-le-Duc in 1860.

From place St-Pierre, one can see the north side of the church and the modern statue of St Columba. A doorway in the Classical style gives access to the interior in the Burgundian Gothic style. Note the impressive **organ case**★ supported by a telamon resting on the floor, decorated with splendid carved medallions. The pulpit with its refined Empire-style decoration contrasts with the general architectural style of the church; it dates from 1806 and was originally in Notre-Dame Cathedral in Paris. In the south transept, one can see the reliquaries of St Columba.

Cloître – Three of the four red-sandstone galleries have been preserved: the bay with three windows surmounted by an oculus dates from the 13C, the others were rebuilt in the 15C and 16C.

Conventual buildings – They include the 17C-18C monks' building, situated south of the church, and the 16C-18C abbot's palace on place St-Pierre, which is now the town hall.

Unique lacework

181

Maison du Bailli – This building dates from 1473. The courtyard is overlooked by a Flamboyant stone balcony and a crenellated polygonal tower.

★**Musée de la Tour des Échevins** ◷ – The museum is housed in an imposing 15C crenellated building whose general appearance is in striking contrast with the exterior decoration and the elegant loggia in the Flamboyant-Gothic style. On the ground floor and first floor are displayed several splendid stone funeral monuments from the Gallo-Roman period, when the town was called Luxovium, as well as votive **stelae**★, inscriptions, a Gaulish ex-voto, sigillate pottery etc. The second and third floors house the **Musée Adler** with paintings by J Adler, Vuillard and Pointelin. From the top of the tower *(146 steps)*, there is an overall **view** of the town and of the Vosges, Jura and Alps in the distance.

Ligne MAGINOT ★

Michelin map 56 and 57 or 241 and 242

Between the two world wars French people put all their pride and trust in this mighty north-eastern shield which did not, as we know, fulfil the mission assigned to it by the war minister Paul Painlevé and his successor André Maginot (1877-1932).

The new frame of mind of France's politicians, who concentrated purely on defence and the need to protect the territories regained as a result of the First World War, led, as early as 1919, to the elaboration of a defensive perimeter skirting the new borders. Modern warfare with tanks, aircraft and the use of gas ruled out a defence system based on isolated strongholds or forts and a network of open trenches. Instead, plans were drawn to divide the length of the border into fortified areas consisting of a continuous frontline, 20-60km/12-37mi long, and underground fortifications adapted to modern warfare. Once completed, the Maginot Line consisted of mixed large works, infantry or artillery small works, shelters, strings of casemates and, behind a flood zone, simple pillboxes linked by barbed wire, minefields or anti-tank ditches and supporting one another by crossfire.

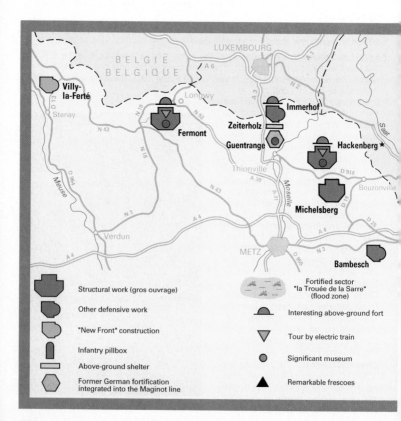

Troops were meant to fill in the gaps between these fortified areas. The project was launched on 14 January 1930 when France's economy began to recover.

France's eastern wall – The number of works built in less than 10 years is amazing: 58 works along the north-east border, including 22 large works, and 50 in the Alps; in addition, there were about 410 casemates and shelters for the infantry; 152 revolving turrets; 1 536 fixed cupolas with special armour-plating crowning the superstructures in reinforced concrete, the only parts of the fortifications which could be seen. Beneath those there were 100km/62mi of underground galleries.

From the very beginning however, the project was cut back owing to lack of funds; the number of works built was considerably reduced and infantry weapons often replaced the artillery initially planned.

From 1935 onwards, it was clear that the original purpose was being thwarted: several large works were replaced by pillboxes and casemates, artillery from the First World War, deemed too costly, was substituted for ultra-modern technology, and there were too few anti-tank guns.

Overground blocks were built of reinforced concrete; the thickness of their back walls turned out to be insufficient when they were attacked from the rear in 1940. Underground structures, below 20m/66ft, were built of stone, which was less costly.

Large works were linked to an ammunition dump by electrified railway lines, today used by visitors along the galleries.

The size of the garrison, known as the crew, depended on the size of the fortified work: around 15 men for a small casemate such as that of Dambach-Neunhoffen and nearly 1 100 men for Hackenberg or Guentrange. They were elite troops, created in 1933, specially trained to man forts.

Defeat – By 1939 the Maginot Line, which did not extend along the northern border of France for political as well as economic reasons, had aged and it was sadly under-equipped with modern anti-tank and anti-aircraft weapons; moreover, it was not used as a base from which to launch an offensive during the Phony War and was even deprived of part of its troops at the crucial moment, when the German onslaught came in May-June 1940. It is therefore not surprising that it did not fulfil the task assigned to it by its promoters.

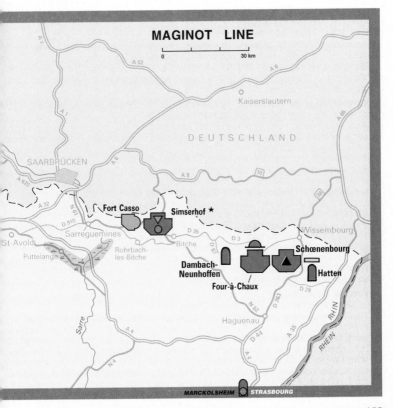

Eating out

MODERATE

Auberge de la Tour – *3 r. de la Gare – 57230 Bitche – 4km/2.5mi E of Simserhof on D 35 –* ☎ *03 87 96 29 25 – closed 1-15 Jul, Mon evening and Tue – 75/260F.* The Belle Epoque style of one of the dining rooms makes this an attractive restaurant, while the other room is rather old-fashioned. Regional cooking is the order of the day.

Where to stay

MODERATE

Hôtel de la Canner – *57920 Kedange-sur-Canner – 8km/5mi S of Hackenberg on D 60 and D 2 –* ☎ *03 82 83 00 25 –* **P** *– 15 rooms 230/260F –* ☕ *36F – restaurant 99/220F.* A good place to stay to visit the Maginot Line. The building is modern and rather characterless, but the rooms are comfortable and practical. Lorraine-style cooking features prominently in the restaurant.

SIGHTS

The various works are described from the north-west to the south-east, from the Ardennes to the Rhine.
Visits often last 2hr. Wear warm clothing and walking shoes.
During the cold war, some of the existing structures formed part of NATO's defence system. In 1965, the French army decided to stop maintaining the whole of the Maginot Line. Some of the works were ceded to private owners, associations or municipalities who restored them and opened them to the public.

Petit ouvrage de Villy-la-Ferté ⊙ – *18km/11mi NW of Montmédy along N 43 and D 44.*
This is one of the new front constructions built from 1935 onwards and including technical improvements such as zigzag entrances, revolving firing positions offering more protection, mixed-gun cupolas equipped with machine guns and extremely precise anti-tank guns. Villy was meant to be the main western work of the Maginot Line, defending the Chiers Valley; however, it was eventually reduced to a couple of infantry blocks linked by a gallery running more than 30m/98ft below ground and flanked by two artillery casemates (one of these stands on the side of the road opposite the access path).
On 18 May 1940, the fort, which was no longer defended from the outside was encircled by German sappers; the whole crew (more than 100 men), who took refuge in the badly ventilated underground gallery, died of suffocation.
Outside, close to the field of anti-tank obstacles, a monument recalls the sacrifice of these men. The overground constructions bear the mark of the attack: damaged cupolas, turret overturned by an explosion.

Gros ouvrage de Fermont ⊙ – *13km/8mi SW of Longwy along N 18 and D 172 to Ugny, then right onto D 17ᴬ and left onto D 174.*
This large work occupying the most western position along the Maginot Line comprised two entrance blocks and seven combat blocks, including three equipped with artillery. In front of the fort, there is a monument dedicated to the fortress troops and a shed housing a museum of heavy equipment.
Ammunition elevators and small electric trains convey visitors to Block 4, an imposing artillery casemate covered with a concrete slab (3.5m/11.5ft thick which represents the maximum protection along the Maginot Line) and fitted with 75mm/3in guns. The tour of the barracks is very interesting: it has been left as it was in 1940 and consists of kitchens, a bakery, a cold room, a sick bay, dormitories, NCOs' and officers' quarters, showers, soldiers' quarters etc. The tour of the overground installations includes revolving turrets, cupolas with periscopes and automatic rifles, cupolas equipped with grenade-launchers and casemates. Damage caused by fighting which took place in 1940 is clearly visible: submitted to heavy shelling, then attacked by assault troops from 21 June onwards, Fermont did not suffer defeat but was compelled to surrender six days later by the French high command.

Fort de Guentrange ⊙ – *2km/1.2mi NW of Thionville. Leave town along allée de la Libération then turn right towards Guentrange.*
This former German stronghold, built between 1899 and 1906 and occupied by French troops in 1918, was integrated into the Maginot Line in 1939-40 as a support work for the Thionville fortified area. Some of its technical advantages were adopted throughout the Maginot Line: electrical machinery, telephone transmissions etc. Besides the power station and its eight diesel engines, still in working order, the most spectacular feature of the fort is the 140m/153yd long barracks on four levels, suitable for 1 100 men. Note that the revolving turrets fitted with 105mm/4in guns were not retractable. Several rooms contain detailed information about the fort.

Abri du Zeiterholz  – *14km/8.7mi N of Thionville. Drive towards Longwy then turn right onto D 57. Go through Entrange and follow the signposts from the chapel.*
The Zeiterholz is the only shelter along the Maginot Line that can be visited; it was built of reinforced concrete on two levels as an overground shelter, quite different from cave shelters in which men were accommodated in underground areas. Its occupants were entrusted to the defence of pillboxes scattered between the larger works and casemates. The barracks, which have been well preserved, are being gradually refitted and reconstructed scenes are displayed throughout.

Petit ouvrage de l'Immerhof – *From the Zeiterholz shelter, go to Hettange-Grande via Entrange-Cité then turn left onto D 15 (signpost) which leads to the Immerhof.*
This is one of only two works along the Maginot Line *(and the only one open to the public)*, which were built overground owing to the lie of the land and completely covered with concrete. Bedrooms, sick bay, washrooms etc are in excellent condition because the fort was, for a long time, used by NATO as one of its headquarters. During the tour of overground structures, note the false cupolas intended to deceive the enemy.

★**Gros ouvrage du Hackenberg** – *20km/12.4mi E of Thionville. Leave the town by D 918. The route is signposted from Metzervisse.*
The largest fort of the Maginot Line lies hidden at the heart of a forest covering 160ha/395 acres, near the village of Veckring. With its two block-houses at the entrance and another 17 spread around, it perfectly illustrates the definition of fan-shaped forts given by André Maginot, "forts split into several parts placed at strategic points". The fort could accommodate 1 200 men and its power station could supply a town of 10 000 inhabitants. As for its artillery, it could fire more than 4t of shells per minute!
On 4 July 1940, the crew manning the fort was forced to surrender to comply with the orders brought by the liaison officer of the French government whose members had retreated to Bordeaux.

Block 9 – Armour-plated airlock and railway

Everything here is monumental, which tends to make Hackenberg rather special: the massive blastproof door, the high-vaulted central station, miles of empty galleries and the huge power station all suggest a useless, abandoned metropolis... The lively atmosphere of the brightly shining kitchens, of the impressive sickbay or of the firing headquarters is reconstructed with the help of dummies. The extensive **museum** displays all kinds of weapons, including a rich collection of machine guns and tommy guns of the two world wars, as well as uniforms of units having taken part in the Battle of France. A small electric train and an elevator lead you to artillery blockhouse no 9, fitted with guns able to fire bombs with a 135mm/5.3in diameter. The gun-turret demonstration is first followed from inside and then from outside, among firing or observation posts and casemates.
In order to understand the strategic importance of the fort, whose defence works overlooked both the Nied Valley and the Moselle Valley, drive up (or walk up if the weather is fine) to the fort chapel surrounded by ancient graves *(2.5km/1.5mi along the road starting from the end of the parking area; in front of the men's entrance, take the surfaced path on the left).* One can see the two observation towers emerging from the Sierck Forest. Behind the chapel, a path leads to a concrete escarpment (700m/765yd long), a unique defence line reinforced by five blockhouses.

Gros ouvrage du Michelsberg – *22km/13.7mi E of Thionville along D 918 (access from the village of Dalstein). From Hackenberg, drive E along D 60, turn right onto D 60^B then left onto D 118^N to Dalstein.*
The fort successfully withstood the attack launched against it on 22 June 1940 thanks to its own fire-power and crossfire from nearby forts, in particular Hackenberg situated 6km/3.7mi away. The crew only left Michelsberg on 4 July by order of the French high command and was granted military honours.

The medium-size fort includes an entrance block, two infantry and three artillery blocks. Artillery block no 6 comprises the famous turret fitted with a 135mm/5in gun which smashed the German attack on 22 June 1940; the gun, which weighs 19t and is still in good condition, was the largest gun along the Maginot Line.

Petit ouvrage du Bambesch ⊙ – *9km/5.6mi W of St-Avold along N 3.*
This is a good example of a work which was gradually modified owing to the shortage of funds: the number of blocks was reduced as was the artillery and the flanking support... The fort, thus limited to three infantry blocks, was attacked from the rear with heavy guns on 20 June 1940 and the cupolas were burst open. The crew, having heard of the tragedy of Villy-la-Ferté, chose to surrender.
The galleries, situated 30m/98ft below ground, are reached by a staircase. The tour includes the barracks and combat blocks. The machine-gun turret is particularly narrow. Block no 2 bears the marks of the German assault of June 1940.

Zone inondable de la Trouée de la Sarre – Situated between two large fortified sectors of the Maginot Line, that of Metz and that of the Lauter, the area extending from Barst to Wittring and limited in the north by the Sarre region under French administration, was not defended by fortified works but by a flood zone controlled by a system of dyked reservoirs. When the Saarland became German once more in 1935, this system was reinforced by a network of pillboxes and anti-tank obstacles.
Drive from St-Avold along N 56 to Barst (8km/5mi), turn right past the church then twice left onto rue de la Croix and the first path.
The path is lined with a variety of characteristic pillboxes (about a dozen in all), of the type built after 1935.
Leave the path and take the next one on the right; park the car.
Some 50m/164ft below the level of the lake, the concreted railway carriage is the last anti-tank obstacle of the Trouée de la Sarre.
Drive E out of Barst.
Between Cappel and Puttelange-aux-Lacs, the road overlooks some of the reservoirs which were used to flood the area.

Fort Casso ⊙ – *Rohrbach-lès-Bitche, 18km/11mi E of Sarreguemines along N 62. Turn left onto D 84 1km/0.6mi before Rohrbach.*
This new front work *(see characteristics under Villy-la-Ferté above)*, named after one of its defenders, Lieutenant Casso, who became a general in the Paris fire-brigade, has some interesting features: roughcast buildings, hammocks in the dormitories, a mixed-weapon turret (the structure dates from the First World War) and machine-gun turret in working order.
The well-preserved structures are gradually being refitted: firing station, telephone exchange etc.

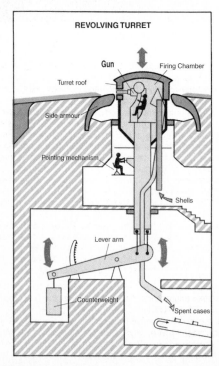

REVOLVING TURRET

Gun

Firing Chamber

Turret roof

Side armour

Pointing mechanism

Shells

Lever arm

Counterweight

Spent cases

Attacked on 20 June 1940, Fort Casso was able to resist with the support of the guns of Simserhof and to avoid the fate of Villy-la-Ferté but the crew was eventually ordered to surrender.

★**Gros ouvrage du Simserhof** ⊙ – *4km/2.5mi W of Bitche along D 35 then the military road starting opposite the former barracks of Légeret.*
A tour of this structural work, which was one of the most important along the Maginot Line, leads visitors to the discovery of a very specific type of fortification whose role in 1940 remains largely unknown.

The only parts visible from the outside are the south-facing entrance block, with its 7t armoured door and its flankers, and the firing or observation cupolas surmounting the combat blocks scattered over several miles so as to overlook the plain below (a few can be seen from D 35A, Hottwiller road, 1km/0.6mi from D 35).

The underground part of the work is in two sections: the service section at the back and the combat section in front, both on the same level and linked by a 5km/3mi gallery fitted with a railway line. The total length of the Simserhof galleries is 10km/6mi. The munitions store has been turned into a museum (periscopes, diascopes, episcopes, photographs).

Casemate de Dambach-Neunhoffen ⊘ – *Between Neunhoffen and Dambach, 20km/12.4mi E of Bitche along D 35, then right onto D 87 and D 853.*
This very basic model, consisting of a small concrete block on one level, defended one of the 12 dykes of the flooding system of the Schwarzbach Valley.
Note the ventilation system, hand operated (or by pedalling) since the fort was not equipped with electricity.

Four à Chaux de Lembach ⊘ – *15km/9.3mi W of Wissembourg along D 3 then D 27 on the way out of Lembach.*
This medium-size artillery work (6 combat blocks and 2 entrances, crew: 580 men) is still in good condition and has retained its original equipment: barracks, HQ, telephone exchange, power station, central heating and hot-water supply...
The fort has an original feature; an inclined plane fitted with a rack, used for the transport of small trucks between the fort and the entrance of the ammunition dump below. A museum, housed in the former munition yard, is fitted with a video room.
Outside, visitors can see part of the anti-tank obstacles.

Lembach

Ouvrage d'artillerie de Schœnenbourg ⊘ – *12km/7.5mi S of Wissembourg along D 264. Follow the signposts.*
This fort was one of the main components of the Haguenau fortified sector; its design took into consideration the experience gained at Verdun from 1916 to 1918. When it was completed in 1935, it was considered that no known weapon could have the advantage over this type of fort. The tour takes visitors round some of the underground structures: communications galleries (totalling more than 3km/1.9mi, running 18-30m/59-125ft below ground), kitchen, power station, air-filtering system, barracks and HQ, as well as an artillery block with its revolving turret.
On 20 June 1940, Schœnenbourg, having withstood the assault of a German division, was attacked by bombers and heavy mortars. No other work was submitted to such fire power, yet this fort managed to hold on until the armistice was signed.

Hatten – *22km/13.7mi NE of Haguenau along D 263 then right onto D 28. From Schœnenbourg (14km/8.7mi), drive to Soultz-sous-Forêts along D 264 then turn left onto D 28.*
Musée de l'Abri ⊘ – The half-buried casemate provided shelter for the troops defending areas situated between fortified works of the Maginot Line: soldiers' sleeping quarters, officers' room, food-supply storeroom, kitchen... Some of the rooms display French, American and German military equipment (uniforms, weapons, photos). There is also an open-air display of vehicles including a T34 Russian tank, a Sherman tank, some jeeps, lorries...
Casemate d'infanterie Esch ⊘ – This casemate was situated at the heart of the battle which took place in January 1945 between American and German tanks, devastating Hatten and the nearly villages.

187

The reconstruction of the soldiers' quarters, a firing chamber and a small museum (uniforms, weapons, various equipment...) are a lively illustration of the Maginot Line's defensive system. The section of a model of an artillery block with a revolving turret helps to explain how the main underground forts worked.

Mémorial et Musée de la Ligne Maginot du Rhin ⊙ – *Marckolsheim, 15km/9.3mi SE of Sélestat along D 424. Leave Marckolsheim by D 10.*
On the esplanade, there is a display of a Soviet gun, a Sherman tank, a machine-gun truck and a half-track. Inside the eight compartments *(beware of the metal steps)* of the casemate, there are weapons and objects connected with the battle of 15-17 June 1940 when the casemate was bravely defended by 30 men. Hitler visited it after the battle.

MARMOUTIER ★

Population 2 234
Michelin map 87 fold 14 or 242 fold 19 – 6km/3.7mi south of Saverne

Marmoutier's former abbey church is one of the most remarkable examples of Romanesque architecture in Alsace.
From **Sindelsberg** *(1.5km/0.9mi NW along the old Saverne road and a small surfaced road on the left)*, there is a lovely bird's-eye view of Marmoutier.
The abbey was founded by St Leobard, a disciple of St Columba *(see LUXEUIL-LES-BAINS)*. Endowed with royal possessions, the abbey soon acquired fame and in the 8C it was named Maurmunster after one of its abbots, Maur. In the 14C, the abbots had an enormous spiritual and worldly influence. Craftsmen and farmers lived in the shadow of the abbey and one of the oldest Jewish communities in Alsace was most probably called in by the abbots to deal with the abbey's trading activities. In 1792, during the Revolution, the abbey was abolished and the monks dispersed.

SIGHTS

★★**Abbey church** – The **west front**★★ *(see Introduction: Architecture and art)* is the most interesting part of the edifice. Built in local red sandstone, it consists of a heavy square belfry and two octagonal corner towers.
The porch has a central ribbed vault with a barrel vault on either side.
The narthex, surmounted by several domes, is the only Romanesque part of the interior.
The transept houses some funeral monuments built in 1621 and the chancel contains beautiful carved wooden furniture: stalls in Louis XV style with charming angels and four canopies surmounted by foliage and branches. The organ, built by Silbermann in 1710, is one of the finest in the whole of Alsace.
Traces of a **Merovingian church** were found beneath the transept *(access through the crypt; entrance in the south transept)*.

Musée d'Arts et Traditions populaires ⊙ – The folk museum is housed in a timber-framed Renaissance building. The collections illustrate Alsatian rural life in the past: reconstructions of interiors *(stube, kitchen...)*, craftsmen's workshops (blacksmith, cooper, stone mason...). In addition, there is a large collection of terracotta cake pans as well as numerous Jewish religious objects.

Part of the façade of the abbey church

MARSAL

Population 284
Michelin map 57 fold 15 or 242 fold 18

Situated in the western part of the Parc naturel régional de Lorraine, an area once liable to flooding, this village has retained numerous Gallo-Roman ruins and a section of its defensive wall fortified by Vauban in the 17C, including an elegant gate, the Porte de France, which has been restored.

Maison du Sel ⊙ – Housed in the Porte de France, part of Vauban's fortifications, the salt museum relates the history of this precious commodity, gathered since Antiquity in the salt mines of the Seille Valley.

⊠ A marked footpath leads to the nearby salt ponds.

Ancienne collégiale – This 12C collegiate church, built without a transept, like a basilica, has a Romanesque nave and a Gothic chancel.

EXCURSIONS

Vic-sur-Seille – *7km/4.3mi W along D 38*. The administration of the diocese of Metz and the residence of the bishop were established here from the 13C to 17C. Visitors can still see the ruins of the bishop's castle. Vic was a prosperous little town in the 15C-16C thanks to its salt mines and it is well known by art lovers as the birthplace of **Georges de La Tour** (1593-1652). A few of the artist's works are displayed in the Musée d'Art et d'Histoire housed in the town hall.
The 15C Gothic Maison de la Monnaie (mint) and the former Carmelite convent dating from the 17C stand on place du Palais.
Note, on the north side of the 15C-16C church, an interesting doorway with a lintel illustrating the legend of a hermit known as St Marian.

▣ The Base de loisirs de la Tuilière (leisure park), situated close to Vic-sur-Seille, offers fishing, swimming etc.

METZ ★★

Population 193 117
Michelin map 57 folds 13 and 14 or 242 folds 9 and 10

Situated between the Côtes de Moselle and the Plateau Lorrain, Metz occupies a strategic position at the confluence of the Seille and the Moselle, which temporarily divides into several arms as it flows through the town. Metz is therefore a major junction at the heart of Lorraine (railway lines, roads and motorways, waterways and air traffic).
In the past, Metz played an important role as a religious centre (with nearly 50 churches) and a military stronghold; the wealthy medieval city has become an administrative and intellectual centre, with its university founded in 1972 and its European Ecological Institute, but it is, above all, a large commercial town.
Metz is also an attractive tourist centre with a choice of pleasant walks in the pedestrianised historic district and interesting monuments, including one of the finest Gothic cathedrals in France, enhanced at night by special light effects.
The poet **Paul Verlaine** (1844-96) paid homage to his native town in the *Ode to Metz* written in 1892, shortly before his death.

HISTORICAL NOTES

In the 2C AD, Metz was already an important Gallo-Roman trading centre with 40 000 inhabitants and a 25 000-seat amphitheatre. It soon became a bishopric and, in 275, fortifications were built round the city to ward off Germanic invasions.
According to legend, **St Livier**, a local nobleman, fought the Huns then tried to Christianise them but Attila had him beheaded; the saint then picked up his head and climbed a mountain where he was buried. Later on the city became one of the favourite residences of Emperor Charlemagne.
In the 12C, Metz became a free city and the capital of a republic whose citizens were so wealthy that they often lent money to the dukes of Lorraine, the kings of France and even the Holy Roman emperors.
In 1552, the French king, Henri II, annexed the three bishoprics of Metz, Toul and Verdun. The Holy Roman Emperor, Charles V, then besieged Metz but all his attempts to take the city were thwarted by the young intrepid François de Guise.
During the 1870 war with Prussia, part of the French army was encircled in Metz and eventually surrendered, its general being booed by the population.

Eating out

MODERATE

La Migaine – 1-3 pl. St-Louis – ☎ 03 87 75 56 67 – closed during Feb school holidays, 15-31 Aug, evenings and Sun – 60/95F. You can eat at any time from morning to the end of the afternoon in this tearoom in a pretty square surrounded by arcades. It serves copious breakfasts, meat pies and quiche Lorraine, cakes and tea; the choice is yours. Terrace in summer.

Restaurant du Pont-St-Marcel – 1 r. du Pont-St-Marcel – ☎ 03 87 30 12 29 – 98/168F. A 17C restaurant not far from St Étienne's cathedral, standing on piles beside a branch of the Moselle. Inside, an amusing contemporary fresco depicts a 17C fairground scene, complete with acrobats and theatre. The staff wear costumes to serve the local cuisine.

MID-RANGE

Maire – 1 r. du Pont-des-Morts – ☎ 03 87 32 43 12 – closed Wed lunchtime and Tue – 150/380F. There is a superb view of the Moselle from this town-centre restaurant. You will enjoy the young chef's carefully prepared dishes, whether in the salmon-pink dining room with its pale wood furniture or on the attractive terrace.

L'Écluse – 45 pl. de la Chambre – ☎ 03 87 75 42 38 – closed 6-14 Mar, 8-25 Aug, Sun evening and Mon – 165/300F. A taste of Brittany, near the cathedral. The chef's enthusiasm for the region is evident in the decor, inspired by the Breton coast, with blue chairs and a menu that includes seafood served in an attractive, bright dining room.

Restaurant du Fort – Allée du Fort – 57070 St-Julien-lès-Metz – 8km/5mi NE of Metz, Bouzonville direction on D 3, then a minor road – ☎ 03 87 75 71 16 – closed 1-12 Jan, 23 Jul-9 Aug, Sun evening and Wed – booking advisable at weekends – 135F. At the end of a forest track you will be amazed to discover this 1870 fort, evidence of the Moselle's turbulent history. Part of it has been restored to create a restaurant offering Lorraine cuisine.

Where to stay

MODERATE

Chambre d'hôte Bigare – 23 r. Principale – 57530 Ars-Laquenexy – 9km/5.6mi E of Metz, Château-Salins direction then D 999 – ☎ 03 87 38 13 88 – 🗇 – 3 rooms 180/220F – evening meal 85F. If the bustle of city life doesn't suit you, a short journey will bring you to this village and this friendly local house. You will be made to feel welcome for the evening meal through to breakfast time. Simple rooms and reasonable prices.

MID-RANGE

Hôtel de la Cathédrale – 25 pl. de la Chambre – ☎ 03 87 75 00 02 – 20 rooms 360/490F – ☑ 55F. A charming hotel, situated in a lovely 17C house which was completely restored in 1997. The attractive rooms have cast-iron or cane beds, old floorboards and furniture, some of which is oriental. Most rooms face the cathedral, just opposite.

Hôtel Royal Bleu Marine – 23 av. Foch – ☎ 03 87 66 81 11 – 62 rooms 395/900F – ☑ 65F – restaurant 128/157F. In an old building in the station area, this hotel has been completely renovated. Its rooms are modern, spacious and well soundproof. Two restaurants, one of which is a bistro, Le Caveau, with a blackboard menu and wine by the glass. Gym and sauna.

Hôtel du Théâtre – 3 r. du Pont-St-Marcel – ☎ 03 87 31 10 10 – www.port-saint-marcel.com – 🄿 – 36 rooms 450/990F – ☑ 55F – restaurant 98/168F. This city-centre hotel is ideally situated on the banks of the Moselle, facing the cathedral. There are only three en-suite rooms in the original 17C house; the rest of the rooms are modern and overlook the port or the river. Swimming pool, Turkish bath and sauna.

On the town

Irish Pub – *3 pl. de Chambre* – ☎ *03 87 37 01 38* – *daily 5.30pm-2.30am, until 3.30am weekends.* Typical small Irish pub, frequented by its regulars, including many English speakers. Specialities: 11 draught beers including Guinness, and 42 whiskies. Traditional Irish music concerts on last Wednesday of month.

Le Jehanne-d'Arc – *Pl. Jeanne-d'Arc* – ☎ *03 87 37 39 94* – *Mon-Thu 11am-2am, Fri 11am-3am, Sat 3pm-3am.* One of the most famous cafés in Metz, for its decor, which still includes Roman stones, 13C frescoes and 17C stencils. Terrace in the attractive square, where jazz concerts are organised in summer. Discreet regular clientele, including students and intellectuals.

Le Pierre qui mousse – *24 r. du Palais* – ☎ *03 87 75 25 52* – *Sun and Mon 3pm-midnight, Mon-Sat 11am-2am.* Despite its exposed beams, real tree trunks and rustic stools, this isn't the haunt of Tyrolean woodcutters but one of the trendiest places in Metz. Warm, friendly atmosphere, with an impressive choice of beers.

Oscar Bar – *1 r. Paul-Bezanson* – ☎ *03 87 36 65 82 / 06 09 75 51 03* – *Mon-Thu noon-2.30am, Fri-Sat noon-3.30am.* If you're bored and there doesn't seem to be anything going on in Metz, there's only one solution: the Oscar. This music bar organises weekly concerts: jam sessions on Tue, rock, blues, soul or salsa on Wed, Thu, Fri or Sat. Terrace in St-Étienne square in summer.

Showtime

L'Arsenal – *Av. Ney* – ☎ *03 87 39 92 00* – *Ticket sales: box office Tue-Sat 1-5.30pm, by phone Tue-Fri 9am-noon, 2-5pm.* Built to a 1989 design by Ricardo Bofill within the walls of a former 19C arsenal, this concert hall is said to be the finest in Europe, with "fantastic acoustics", according to Rostropovitch. Apart from the main hall, which can seat 1 354, there is another hall seating 352, an exhibition gallery, and a museum/shop. With nearly 200 events each year, the programme is far-ranging, from contemporary dance to classical music, and from jazz to world music.

Shopping

Boucherie-charcuterie-traiteur Éric Humbert – *8 r. du Grand-Cerf* – ☎ *03 87 75 09 38* – *Mon-Thu 7.45am-12.40pm, 2.30-7pm, Fri-Sat 7.15am-12.40pm, 2.15-7pm – closed Jul and 1 week in Feb.* Éric Humbert has been honoured by an award from a major design magazine, which is explained by the fact that this butcher/delicatessen/caterer is equally talented as a designer as he is in the culinary domain. He himself designed the avant-garde counters in his otherwise traditional shop, adding a visual treat to that in store for the taste buds, with his chicken and pistachio sausage, or his foie gras in aspic with Riesling.

On 19 November 1918, French troops entered the town after 47 years of German occupation.

In 1944, Metz was at the heart of heavy fighting once more as it lay on the path of the advancing American third army. It was bitterly defended for two and a half months by the German forces stationed in the town; the surrounding forts were pounded by heavy allied artillery but the town was spared in memory of La Fayette who commanded the garrison in 1777. American troops eventually entered Metz on 19 November 1944, 26 years to the day after French troops had entered the town at the end of the First World War.

★★★CATHÉDRALE ST-ÉTIENNE ⊘ *1hr 30min*

The entrance of the cathedral in on **place d'Armes**. From the square, there is a fine view of the south side of the cathedral.

One is impressed by the harmonious proportions of the cathedral, built of yellow stone from Jaumont like several other edifices in Metz. The north and south sides are most remarkable. In order to appreciate the south side, it is better to stand on the pavement running along the town hall on the opposite side of the square.

The Protestant church and the Cathedral on either side of the Moselle

The church is flanked by two symmetrical towers, the chapter tower on the north side and the Tour de Mutte on the south side; both built from the 13C onwards. The **Tour de Mutte** owes its name to the famous bell known as Dame Mutte, dating from 1605 and weighing 11t; the name is derived from the verb *ameuter* which originally meant "to call for a meeting". The bell used to ring for all major events and even today, it sounds the 12 strokes of midday and every quarter hour on election days.

Enter through the Virgin's doorway, located to the left of the Tour de Mutte.

The sides of the Notre-Dame-la-Ronde portal (second bay on the north side) are decorated with carved draperies and small 13C low-relief sculptures: note the supernatural animals on the left, which are reminiscent of medieval bestiaries and, on the right, the scenes from the Life of King David, St Margaret and St Stephen. The portal is dedicated to the small primitive church which stood on this site.

Inside the cathedral, the most striking feature is undoubtedly the height of the nave (41.77m/137ft), dating from the 13C and 14C. The impression of loftiness is enhanced by the fact that the aisles are rather low. This nave is, with that of Amiens Cathedral and after the chancel of Beauvais Cathedral, the highest of any church in France. Light pours generously into the nave, the chancel and the aisles.

A frieze decorated with draperies and foliage runs all the way round the edifice, between the triforium and the impressively large high windows.

Note the overhanging 16C choir organ (**1**) situated at the end of the nave, on the right-hand side. Its unusual position enhances its outstanding acoustic features.

★★★**Stained-glass windows** – They form a splendid ensemble covering more than 6 500m²/7 774sq yd. They are the work of famous as well as anonymous artists, completed or renewed through the centuries: 13C (**2**) and 14C (Hermann from Munster), 16C (Theobald from Lyxheim **3**, followed by Valentin Bousch **4**), 19C and 20C (Pierre Gaudin, Jacques Villon, Roger Bissière **5**, Marc Chagall **6** and **7**).

The west front is adorned with a magnificent 14C rose-window by Hermann from Munster, which unfortunately lost its base part when the large doorway was built in 1766.

The openwork design of the edifice is even more apparent in the **transept** built at the end of the 15C and beginning of the 16C. The stained-glass window in the north part of the transept (**3**) is decorated with three roses; that in the south part of the transept (**4**) is by Valentin Bousch, an artist from Strasbourg. These two windows light up the cathedral in a remarkable way.

The eastern wall of the south part of the transept has the oldest stained-glass windows (**9**) which illustrate six scenes from the Life of St Paul (13C).

Note the starlike vaulting of the middle part of the transept.

The stained-glass window in the western wall of the north part of the transept, designed by Chagall in 1963, depicts scenes from the Garden of Eden (**6**).

In the ambulatory, two more stained-glass windows by Chagall can be seen above the sacristy door and the door leading to the Tour de la Boule d'Or on the left. Designed in 1960, they illustrate scenes from the Old Testament (Jacob's Dream, Abraham's Sacrifice, Moses and David).

Crypt ⊙ – It was adapted in the 15C to preserve some elements from the 10C Romanesque crypt, the damaged tympanum of the 13C Virgin's doorway as well as various objects, carvings and reliquaries from the treasury. Note in particular a 16C **Entombment**, originally in the church of Xivry-Circourt, and, hanging from the vaulting, the famous Graoully, the legendary dragon slain by St Clement which used to be carried in procession round the town until 1785. In the chancel, St Clement's episcopal throne (**8**), carved out of a cipolin-marble column, dates back to Merovingian times.

Treasury ⊙ – It is housed in the 18C sacristy. The most remarkable items include St Arnoult's gold ring (primitive Christian art), a 12C enamel reliquary, 12C and 13C ivory crosiers, Pope Pius VI's mule, precious religious objects etc.

The Gueulard, a 15C carved-wood head, originally decorating the organ, used to open its mouth (hence its name) when the lowest note was sounded.

During the storm of December 1999, a pinnacle weighing several tonnes was torn off, fell through the roof and lodged itself in the ceiling of the sacristy.

CATHÉDRALE ST-ÉTIENNE

Former church N.-D.-la-Ronde

Rue du Vivier

N

Ambulatory

Tour de la Boule d'Or — 7 — CHANCEL — Tour de Charlemagne

Treasury (large sacristy) — 7 — 8 — Crypt — 9

Place d'Armes

3 — TRANSEPT — 4

6 — 1

NAVE

Chapelle du Saint-Sacrement

St-Étienne

Tour du Chapitre — 5 — 5 — Tour de Mutte

Chapelle Notre-Dame

Portail de N.-D.-la-Ronde

Place

2 — Portail de la Vierge

Grand Portail

Place de la Cathédrale

0 — 15m

★★MUSÉE DE LA COUR D'OR ⊙

The museum is housed in the buildings of the former Couvent des Petits Carmes (17C), of the Grenier de Chèvremont (15C) and in several rooms which link or prolong this monumental ensemble. Elements of the antique baths are displayed in situ in the basement.

Extended in 1980, the museums were organised along the most modern lines and offer a unique journey into the past.

★★★**Section archéologique** – The exhibits, which were mostly found during excavations in Metz and the surrounding region, testify to the importance of the city, a major road junction in Gallo-Roman times and a thriving cultural centre during the Carolingian period.

Social life during the **Gallo-Roman period** is illustrated by remains of the large baths, of the town wall and of the drainage system as well as by objects of daily life (meals, garments, jewellery, trade).

Various glass-cases are devoted to the methods of producing ironwork, bronzework, ceramics and glasswork.

Metz was the capital of Austrasia during the **Merovingian period** illustrated by graves, sarcophagi and tombstones bearing Christian emblems, jewels and objects of daily life (crockery), and damascened metal objects.

In the rooms devoted to **paleo-Christian archaeology**, there is an important ensemble dating from the early Middle Ages, surrounding the chancel of St-Pierre-aux-Nonnains. This stone screen comprises 34 carved panels admirably decorated and extremely varied.

Architecture et cadre de vie – Exhibits in this section illustrate daily life, building techniques and decorative styles in the past, up to the Renaissance period. There are reconstructed façades including the front of a house decorated with four busts. Several mansions and ordinary houses have been reconstructed round the museums' courtyard.

La Cour d'or, Musées de Metz

Grenier de Chèvremont

*Grenier de Chèvremont – This well-preserved edifice dating from 1457 was once used to store the tithe taken on cereal crops.

Note in particular the beautiful collection of regional religious art: *Pietà*, Virgin lying down, 15C statues of St Roch and St Blaise.

Beaux-Arts – *First and second floors*. Interesting paintings of the French School (Delacroix, Corot, Moreau), of the German, Flemish and Italian Schools. The School of Metz (1834-70) is mainly represented by its leading exponent, the painter, pastellist and stained-glass artist Laurent-Charles Maréchal.

The modern-art gallery contains works by Bazaine, Alechinsky, Dufy, Soulages...

Collection militaire – Gathered by Jacques Onfroy de Bréville (JOB), who specialised in the illustration of school manuals and history books, this collection consists of weapons, uniforms and accessories from the late 18C and from the 19C.

*ESPLANADE

This is a splendid walk laid out at the beginning of the 19C on the site of one of the citadel's moats: from the terrace, there is a fine view of Mount St-Quentin crowned by a fort and of one of the arms of the River Moselle.

Palais de Justice – Built in the 18C, during the reign of Louis XVI, this edifice was intended to be the military governor's palace but the Revolution changed all that. Sentry boxes on either side of the entrance remind visitors of the military origins of the building. In the courtyard, there are two interesting low-relief sculptures: one shows the Duc de Guise during the 1552 siege of the town, the other celebrates the 1783 peace treaty between England, France, the USA and Holland.

Walk across the gardens to the arsenal.

Arsenal – The walls of the 19C arsenal were partially used to build this ultra-modern centre dedicated to music and dance.

Designed by Ricardo Bofill, the large hall fitted with a central stage was intended for a variety of shows. Its special shape and its elaborate acoustics were inspired by the Musikverein in Vienna. Surrounded by warm wood panelling, the 1 500 spectators get the impression that they are at the centre of a huge musical instrument.

OLD TOWN

*Place St-Louis – Situated at the heart of the old town, the rectangular place St-Louis is lined on one side with buttressed arcaded buildings dating from the 14C, 15C and 16C, which once housed the money-changers' shops. At the end, on the corner of rue de la Tête-d'Or, note the three golden Roman heads protruding from the wall, which gave its name to the street.

Follow rue de la Tête-d'Or to the River Moselle.

*Moyen Pont – Pleasant view of the arms of the River Moselle, of the islands, of the neo-Romanesque protestant church (1901) and of the two small bridges reflected in the water.

Walk to place de la Comédie.

The 18C **theatre** overlooking place de la Comédie, is the oldest in France; opposite stands the **Hôtel du Département**, also dating from the 18C.

Walk round to the back of the Hôtel du Département and along rue du Pont Moreau then rue St-Georges and finally rue St-Vincent.

Église St-Vincent ⊘ – The Gothic chancel of the church, flanked by two elegant steeples, is in striking contrast with the west front, rebuilt in the 18C and reminiscent of that of St-Gervais-St-Protais in Paris *(closed for restoration).*

Walk back to the Hôtel du Département and cross the river.

METZ

Place d'Armes – The square was designed in the 18C by Jacques François Blondel on the site of the former cloister. The **town hall** (**H**), facing the south side of the cathedral, has an elegant Louis XVI façade with two pediments. The two remaining sides of the square are lined with the district hall, a former guard-house whose pediment is decorated with trophies, and with the regional parliament, now a residential building.

View of the Moyen Pont, quai Vautrin and St-Étienne

Follow rue En-Fournirue to the right of the town hall then turn left onto rue Taison. Turn right when you get to place Ste-Croix.

The **Ancien couvent des Récollets** (former convent) now houses the European Ecological Institute. The 15C cloister has been restored.

Follow rue d'Enfer opposite and turn left onto rue En-Fournirue to place des Paraiges then continue along rue des Allemands.

Église St-Eucaire – The fine square belfry dates from the 12C and the west front from the 13C. The small 14C nave with its huge pillars looks out of proportion. The aisles, lined with low arcades, lead to unusual 15C chapels, surmounted by pointed vaulting converging on carved corbels.

★**Porte des Allemands** – This massive fortress, which formed part of the town walls running along the Moselle and the dual-carriageway ring road south and east of Metz, straddles the River Seille. It gets its name from an order of German hospitallers established nearby in the 13C.

There are in fact two gates: the first one, dating from the 13C and standing on the town side, is flanked by two round towers topped with slate pepper-pot roofs; the other tower, facing the opposite way, dates from the 15C and has two large crenellated towers. A 15C arcaded gallery links the four towers. The edifice was remodelled in the 19C.

North of the Porte des Allemands, the fortified wall continues for another 1.5km/0.9mi, with numerous towers at regular intervals: Tour des Sorcières (Witches' Tower), Tour du Diable (Devil's Tower), Tour des Corporations (Guilds' Tower). A path follows the ramparts, first along the Seille then along the Moselle.

Walk along boulevard Maginot and turn onto the fourth street on your right.

★**Église St-Maximin** – A fine carved head of Christ decorates the central pillar at the entrance. The beautiful chancel is decorated with stained-glass windows by Jean Cocteau. Note also the 14C-15C Chapelle des Gournay, named after a prominent local family, which opens onto the south transept through two basket-handled arches;

Follow rue Mazelle to place des Charrons. Cross rue Haute-Seille and walk along a street which runs under a bridge, then turn left onto rue de la Fontaine and right onto rue Lasalle.

Église St-Martin – A Gallo-Roman wall, once part of the town's fortifications, forms the base of the church; it is visible on both sides of the entrance. The most attractive feature of this 13C church is its very low **narthex**★ whose three sections, covered with pointed vaulting resting on four Romanesque pillars surrounded by colonnettes, open onto the lofty nave. The 15C transept and chancel have stained-glass windows dating from the 15C, 16C and 19C, an organ case in Louis XV style, various tombstones and a fine sculpture representing the Nativity (in the north transept).

Walk past the church and turn right onto rue des Parmentiers which runs onto rue de la Chèvre.

Église Notre-Dame-de-l'Assomption – This Jesuit church was erected in 1665 but the west front was completed in the 18C. The interior, decorated in the 19C, is lined with rich wood panelling. The Rococo confessionals come from the German city of Trier, as does the Baroque organ built by Jean Nollet.

Continue along rue de la Chèvre then turn right onto rue de la Tête-d'Or to return to place St-Louis.

MODERN TOWN

After 1870, William II wanted to turn Metz into a prestigious German city. He entrusted his plan to Kröger, an architect from Berlin, who used pink and grey sandstone, granite and even basalt. Strangely enough, the new district does not clash too much with the old district and it gives the town a sense of spaciousness it would have otherwise lacked. The new district includes the wide avenue Foch, the chamber of commerce, the old station built in 1878, the post office etc.

★**Place du Général-de-Gaulle** – The **station** (1908) a huge neo-Romanesque edifice (300m/328yd long), profusely decorated (capitals, low-relief sculptures), is one of several buildings erected by the Germans at the beginning of the 20C to assert the power of their empire. The vast pedestrianised semicircular area in front of the station is lit by lamp posts designed by Philippe Stark.

Église Ste-Thérèse-de-l'Enfant-Jésus – *Entrance along avenue Leclerc-de-Haute-clocque.* Consecrated in 1954, this large church, topped by a 70m/230ft mast known as the pilgrim's staff, has an imposing nave and fine stained-glass windows by Nicolas Untersteller.

ADDITIONAL SIGHTS

★**Église St-Pierre-aux-Nonnains** ⊘ – Around 390, during the reign of Emperor Constantine, a **palæstra** or gymnasium was built on this site. When Attila plundered the town in 451, the edifice was partially destroyed, but the walls built of rubble stones reinforced at regular intervals by ties of red bricks were spared and used again in the building of a chapel c 615. The nuns settled here. Fragments of the **chancel** added to the edifice at that time, which are fine examples of Merovingian sculpture, are kept in the Musée de la Cour d'Or. Around 990, the abbey, which followed the Benedictine rule, was reorganised and the vast chapel was split into three naves by rounded arcades. During the Gothic period, the naves were covered with pointed vaulting and an elegant cloister (one side of which is still standing) was added to the conventual buildings in the 15C.
Excavations undertaken in the 20C enabled archaeologists to reconstruct the history of this ancient building which is believed to be the oldest church in France. Important repair work has made it possible to restore the volume of the original building.

Chapelle des Templiers ⊘ – This chapel, built at the beginning of the 13C by the Knight Templars established in Metz since 1133, marks the transition between the Romanesque and Gothic styles. The building is shaped like an octagon, each side except one having a small rounded window; the last side opens onto a square chancel prolonged by an apse. Buildings of this type are rare and this chapel is, in fact, the only one of its kind in Lorraine. The paintings are all modern except one which decorates a recess on the right (14C).

EXCURSIONS

Scy-Chazelles – *4km/2.5mi W along D 157A then turn right.*
Robert Schuman's house ⊘ is located in the village, near the 12C fortified church where the "father of Europe" (1886-1963) is buried. This austere building, characteristic of Lorraine, conveys an impression of calm and serenity which this generous and modest man found conducive to meditation. His library, his diplomas and decorations are among Schuman's personal mementoes.
In the park, beyond the terrace, there is a sculpture by Le Chevallier entitled The European Flame.

Vallée de la Canner ⊘ – *Departure from Vigy, 15km/9mi NE along D 2 then D 52.* From Vigy to Hombourg *(12km/7.5mi)*, a small tourist train, pulled by a real steam engine, follows the remote Canner Valley through a densely forested part of the Lorraine plateau.

Château de Pange ⊘ – *10km/6mi E along D 999, D 70 and D 6.*
Built between 1720 and 1756 on the site of an ancient fortress, along the banks of the Nied, a small tributary of the Moselle, the castle has retained its plain Classical façade.
The dining room in Louis XV style is still decorated with green wood panelling and a primitive regional stove.

Groupe fortifié de l'Aisne ⊙ – *14km/8.7mi S along D 913*. The former Wagner Fortress, built by the Germans between 1904 and 1910, formed part of the outer defences of Metz. Renamed Aisne after 1918, it was not, unlike Guentrange, incorporated into the Maginot Line *(see Ligne MAGINOT)*; during the Second World War, it was only used to store torpedo heads.

This type of fortified complex replaced massive fortresses at the end of the 19C; it consisted of several works linked by underground galleries. The Aisne for instance comprises four infantry blocks with up to three levels of underground barracks, three artillery blocks fitted with revolving turrets suitable for heavy guns and about 15 armor-plated observatories.

Sillegny – *20km/12.5mi S along D 5*.
This village of the Seille Valley has a small 15C **church**, which looks unassuming but is entirely covered with **murals★** dating from 1540. Note the warmth of the colours and the great number of naive details of these murals representing the Apostles, the Evangelists, the Tree of Jesse (in the chancel on the right), the Last Judgement above the entrance and the huge St Christopher, 5m/16ft high.

Gorze – *18km/11mi SW along D 57, then right onto D 6^B*.
This village, which developed round a Benedictine abbey founded in the 8C, has retained a number of old Renaissance residences dating from the 17C and 18C. The surrounding forest offers a choice of fine walks along a network of marked paths.

The **Maison de l'Histoire de la Terre de Gorze** ⊙ relates episodes of Gorze's prosperous past, in particular the harnessing of the springs by the Romans during the 1C AD, the construction of a bridge-aqueduct (model) and the Benedictine foundation.

The **Église St-Étienne** is Romanesque on the outside and Early Gothic (late 12C and early 13C) inside, with characteristic features of the Rhine region. The central belfry dates from the 13C; note the absence of flying buttresses and the narrow windows. The tympanum of the north porch is decorated with a 13C Virgin between two praying figures. Note the large wooden crucifix, attributed to Ligier Richier, on the inside of the north doorway. The tympanum of the small adjacent doorway shows a late-12C Last Judgement. The chancel is decorated with fine woodwork and 18C biblical paintings.

The former **abbatial palace**, built in 1696, is a Baroque edifice designed by Philippe-Eberhard of Lowenstein and Bavaria; note the staircase and the fountains decorated with mythological scenes, as well as the chapel adorned with Baroque motifs.

Aqueduc romain de Gorze à Metz – *12km/7.5mi SW. Drive along N 3 to Moulins then continue along D 6 to Ars-sur-Moselle*.
Seven arches of this 1C AD Roman aqueduct, which spanned the Moselle, are still standing alongside D 6, south of **Ars-sur-Moselle** (west bank). Excavations have revealed pipes and sections of masonry. In **Jouy-aux-Arches** (east bank), another 16 arches, in a better state of preservation, span N 57.

Parc d'attractions Walibi-Schtroumpf – *See AMNÉVILLE: Excursions*.

Méandres de la MEUSE

Michelin maps 53 folds 8 and 18 or 241 folds 2, 6 and 10

The River Meuse takes its source in the foothills of the Plateau de Langres, not far from Bourbonne-les-Bains, at an altitude of only 409m/1 342ft; it flows into the North Sea 950km/590mi further on, forming with the Rhine a common delta along the coast of the Netherlands where it is known as the Maas.

The course of this peaceful river often changes, for instance when it flows along the bottom of the ridge known as the Hauts de Meuse, or crosses a large alluvial plain (beyond Dun-sur-Meuse), or meanders through the Ardennes.

The section from Charleville-Mézières to Givet is the most picturesque part of the river's journey through France: the Meuse has dug its deep and sinuous course through hard schist, which is sometimes barren and sometimes forested (hunting for wild boar and roe-deer is a favourite pastime in the area). The railway line linking Charleville and Givet follows the river which is linked to the Aisne by the Canal des Ardennes dug in the mid 19C. River traffic is reduced to barges not exceeding 300t because the rate of flow is insufficient and the river bed not deep enough in places, whereas downriver from Givet, the river has been adapted to allow barges of up to 1 350t through.

Cruises and boat trips are organised from Charleville-Mézières, Monthermé and Revin *(see Practical information)*.

IN THE FOOTSTEPS OF THE FOUR AYMON BROTHERS

① Round tour from Charleville-Mézières

57km/35mi – allow 4hr
Leave Charleville along D 1 which soon follows the Meuse.

Nouzonville – This industrial centre (metalworks and mechanical industries), situated at the confluence of the Meuse and the Goutelle, follows a long-standing nail-making tradition introduced in the 15C by people from Liège running away from the duke of Burgundy, Charles the Bold.

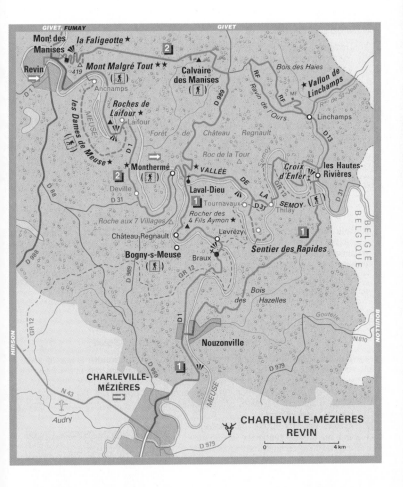

Bogny-sur-Meuse – Bogny-sur-Meuse, which stretches for 10km/6mi along the river, evolved in 1967 from the merging of three villages, Braux, Levrézy and Château-Regnault. There are several marked footpaths starting from the tourist office.

The **Sentier Nature et Patrimoine du Pierroy** (the Pierroy Nature and Heritage Trail) leads past typical geological features (conglomerate and schist) and the remains of quartzite quarries, offering fine views of the Meuse Valley.

Continue along D 1 to Braux.

Église de Braux – The former collegiate **church** has retained its Romanesque apse, chancel and transept but the nave and the aisles date from the 17C and 18C. Note the rich 17C marble altars with low-relief sculptures and above all the fine 12C christening font, carved out of blue stone from Givet and decorated with grotesques.

Cross the River Meuse.

From the bridge, there is an interesting vista on the left of the Rocher des Quatre Fils Aymon.

Levrézy – A former factory houses the **Musée de la Métallurgie** ⊘ which illustrates the making of nuts and bolts with tools and machines still in working order (forge, planing and milling machines...).

199

Château-Regnault – Once the main centre of a principality, Château-Regnault had its castle razed to the ground by Louis XIV. The village lies at the foot of the **Rocher des Quatre Fils Aymon★** whose outline formed by four sharp points suggests the legend of the Four Aymon Brothers escaping from Charlemagne's men on their famous horse Bayard.

The **Centre d'exposition de minéraux** ⊙ displays rocks from the Ardennes region together with fossils from various parts of the world.

Where to stay and eating out

MODERATE

Debette – *Pl. de la Mairie – 08320 Aubrives – ☎ 03 24 41 64 72 – closed 29 Jan-4 Feb, Christmas holidays, Sun evening and Mon lunchtime – 75/250F.* This restaurant opposite the town hall has a large, bright dining room and classic, unpretentious cooking. Attic rooms under the sloping ceiling on the second floor.

MID-RANGE

Le Moulin Labotte – *52 r. Edmond-Dromard – 08170 Haybes – ☎ 03 24 41 13 44 – moulinlabotte@wanadoo.fr – closed Sun evening and Mon – 120/160F.* From your table you can admire the fine restored machinery of this old watermill, which stands on the edge of a river surrounded by woods. Game features prominently on the menu. A few rooms are available.

Platelle des Quatre Fils Aymon – This artificial ledge fitted as a play area is overlooked by the monument of the Four Aymon Brothers. There is a view of the meanders of the Meuse, of the factories lining its course, of workers' housing estates and of private mansions.

Continue along D 1 which runs beneath the railway line before crossing the Semoy which flows into the Meuse at Laval-Dieu.

Four Brothers and their Legendary Steed

The deep and impenetrable Ardennes Forest is the favourite haunt of wild animals, of pagan spirits and fantastic creatures. Among the many legends which flourish in the thick woods, the most famous is undoubtedly the legend of *The Four Aymon Brothers*, sometimes called *The Tale Renaud de Montauban*, which relates the feats of four brave knights astride their mighty horse, **Bayard**.

Aymon was the Duke of Dordogne and an ardent supporter of Charlemagne. In a complicated dispute, the duke's brother killed a son of Charlemagne, and was then killed himself by supporters of the king. Aymon's four sons, handsome and valiant (as legend must have it), could not suffer their uncle's murder and finally had to flee; their mother thoughtfully provided them with the family treasury. They established themselves in the thick forest of the Ardennes in a castle, Montfort, built into the rocky cliff above the Meuse.

S.Sauvignier/MICHELIN

This epic can be compared to the *Chanson de Roland*, the earliest masterpiece of the French *chansons de gestes* (songs of deeds), which formed the core of the Charlemagne legends. Numerous episodes were gradually added to the simple story which, in the 13C, became a poem intended to be read. The 15C prose version is a precursor of the novel form.

Precious manuscripts, incunabula and old editions of this work are kept with the archives of the *département*, and many place names recall the brothers' heroic exploits.

Laval-Dieu – This industrial suburb of Monthermé grew round an abbey of Premonstratensians established here in the 12C. The former abbey church stands on a peaceful wooded site. The massive 12C square belfry, built of schist, contrasts with the elegant late-17C west front, brick built with stone surrounds. Note the flat east end, decorated with Lombardy banding, the only one of its kind in the region.

Turn right onto D 31 to Thilay.

The road follows the Semoy Valley (see Vallée de la SEMOY).

Return to Charleville along D 13 which runs through the Bois de Hazelles.

MONT MALGRÉ TOUT

② Round tour from Revin

40km/25mi – allow 2hr 30min including 1hr 15min on foot

Revin – Revin occupies an exceptional position within two deep meanders of the Meuse; the old town nestles round its 18C church, inside the northern meander whereas the southern meander shelters the industrial district with its factories specialising in the production of domestic appliances and bathroom units. There are a few 16C timber-framed houses along quai Edgar-Quinet; note in particular the **Maison espagnole** ⊘ on the corner of rue Victor-Hugo, which has been turned into a museum holding a yearly exhibition about traditions and customs of the Ardennes. A building situated on the edge of the **Parc Maurice-Rocheteau** ⊘ houses a **Galerie d'art contemporain** ⊘ (contemporary art gallery) including works by Georges Cesari (1923-82).

On the outskirts of Revin, the winding Route des Hauts-Buttés branches off D 1 and rises 300m/984ft in a series of hairpin bends to the Monument des Manises standing on the roadside.

Monument des Manises – The monument is dedicated to the members of the Maquis des Manises resistance group. Bird's-eye view of Revin and the surrounding area.

★**Point de vue de la Faligeotte** – The viewing-platform of La Faligeotte also offers an interesting **view** of Revin and of the meanders of the Meuse.

The road reaches the edge of the plateau.

★★ **Mont Malgré Tout** – *Park the car 400m/437yd from a signpost bearing the inscription "Point de vue à 100m". The footpath begins here (1hr on foot there and back).*
🔼 The steep path leads to a television relay. From there it is possible to walk through a thicket of birch and oak trees and reach a higher viewpoint (alt 400m/1 312ft) offering a wide **view** of Revin, the meanders of the Meuse, the Dames de Meuse across the river to the south and the Vallée de Misère to the west.

Drive 6km/3.7mi along Route des Hauts-Buttés to the signpost marked Calvaire des Manises, and park the car.

Calvaire des Manises – 15min on foot. A path leads to the clearing where 106 members of the Resistance were massacred: calvary, monuments and common grave.

Continue along the same road to the intersection with D 989 and turn right.
The road runs through the Château-Regnault Forest.

★**Monthermé** – *See MONTHERMÉ.*

In Monthermé, the road (D 1) crosses back to the west bank, running close to the hill topped by the Roche aux Sept Villages (see MONTHERMÉ) and goes through Deville before reaching Laifour.

Meander of the Meuse at Monthermé

★**Roches de Laifour** – This promontory rises 270m/886ft above the river bed; its schist slopes dropping steeply towards the river are a striking feature of this wild landscape.

From the bridge, there is an impressive **view**★★ of the Roches de Laifour and Dames de Meuse.

★**Dames de Meuse** – This ridge line sloping steeply down to the river, forms a black gullied mass whose curve follows the course of the Meuse; it reaches an altitude of 393m/1 289ft at its highest point and rises 250m/820ft above the river bed.

According to legend, it owes its name to three unfaithful wives turned to stone by God's wrath.

🚶 A **path** branches off D 1 south of Laifour, climbs to the Dames de Meuse refuge and reaches the edge of the ridge *(2hr on foot there and back)*; the walk affords a fine **view**★★ of the valley and the village. From there, another path follows the top of the ridge and leads to Anchamps *(about 2hr 30min on foot)*.

Drive along D 1 which crosses the Meuse and offers impressive views of the Dames de Meuse before reaching Revin.

MOLSHEIM ★

Population 7 973
Michelin map 87 folds 5 and 15 or 242 folds 23 and 24
Local map see Route des VINS

IN THE HAYLOFT

Auberge Vigneronne Dr. Winschnutzer – *12 pl. de la Liberté* – ☎ *03 88 38 55 47* – *closed 25-30 Dec* – *booking essential* – *75/ 215F.* This Molsheim farm is easily recognised, thanks to its mural painting. It serves local wine, of course, but also natural fruit juice and home-grown vegetables with Alsatian dishes, in the former hayloft.

This quiet old town lies in the Bruche Valley, at the heart of a wine-growing area which produces the famous Bruderthal wine. The Messier-Bugatti factory, specialising in landing gear *(not open to the public)* is located on the outskirts of town, along the Sélestat road.

Of its past as religious capital of Alsace, Molsheim has retained the imposing Jesuit church, which once belonged to the university transferred to Strasbourg, and part of the Carthusian monastery, the only one ever to be built in a town.

TOWN WALK

★**Église des Jésuites** – The church belonged to the famous Jesuit university founded in 1618 by Archduke Leopold of Austria, who was the bishop of Strasbourg at the time. The fame of this university, which included a faculty of theology and philosophy spread far and wide. The Cardinal de Rohan transferred it to Strasbourg in 1702 in order to counteract the influence of the town's protestant university.

Although it was built between 1615 and 1617, the edifice was designed in the Gothic style. The harmonious proportions of the interior, the wide gallery and the fishnet vaulting draw the visitor's attention. The two **transept chapels** are adorned with stuccowork, gilt ornamentation and 17C-18C paintings depicting the Life of St Ignatius and of the Virgin. St Ignatius' chapel contains white-sandstone fonts dating from 1624 as well as several early-15C tombstones. The Virgin's chapel contains a fine polychrome recumbent effigy of Jean de Durbheim, who was the bishop of Strasbourg from 1306 to 1328.

The pulpit (1631) and the doorways (1618), particularly the sacristy doorway, are decorated with fine carvings. The Silbermann organ dates from 1781.

The north entrance houses the Carthusian Cross, a beautiful stone cross dating from the late Middle Ages.

Follow rue Notre-Dame on the left of the building.

Tour des Forgerons – This 14C fortified gate, located in rue de Strasbourg, houses one of the oldest bells in Alsace, dating from 1412. The tower was flanked c 1650 by a toll-house and a guard-house.

Rue de Strasbourg on the right leads to place de l'Hôtel-de-Ville.

La Metzig

★La Metzig – This graceful Renaissance building was built in 1525 by the butchers' guild whose meetings were held on the first floor, the ground floor being occupied by butchers' shops. It looks typically Alsatian with its scrolled gables and its double flight of steps leading to the belfry-loggia. On either side of the jack clock (1537), two angels strike the hours. An elegant carved-stone balcony runs along the façade and the sides at first-floor level.

The centre of the square is decorated with a fountain consisting of two superposed basins and an impressive lion bearing the arms of the city.

Take rue Jenner starting on the left of the square.

Note the two Renaissance canon's houses at nos 18 and 20, dating from 1628.

Follow rue des Étudiants on the right which runs past the Musée de la Chartreuse (see description below) then turn right onto rue de Saverne.

Maison ancienne – A beautiful timber-framed Alsatian house with wooden oriel (1607) and finely decorated windows can be seen along rue de Saverne.

Continue along rue de Saverne and rue des Serruriers across rue du Mar.-Foch. Turn left onto rue de la Boucherie then right onto rue St-Joseph. Rue du Mar.-Kellermann on the right leads back to the Église des Jésuites.

MUSEUM

Musée de la Chartreuse ⓥ – The priory of the former Carthusian monastery (1598-1792) houses a museum devoted to the history of Molsheim and its region, from prehistoric times to today.

Objects discovered on the archaeological sites of Dachstein, Achenheim and Heili-genberg-Dinsheim (sigillate ceramics) testify to the presence of man from the Paleolithic period to Merovingian times. With the arrival of Jesuits, Capuchins and above all Carthusian monks in the 17C, the town soon became the religious capital of Alsace. A general map dating from 1744 shows the importance of the Carthu-sian monastery which spread over 3ha/7.4 acres within the town. Part of the cloister has been restored and two monks' cells, divided into three rooms each, have been reconstructed with the original furniture.

In another building, the **Bugatti Foundation** displays mementoes of the family and a few models of cars built here between the two world wars.

Ettore Bugatti

A native of Italy, Ettore Bugatti (Milan 1881-Neuilly 1947) gave up his fine arts studies to devote himself to mechanical engineering. At the age of 17 he was engaged as an apprentice in a cycle factory. At the age of 20 he designed his first car which was awarded the major prize of the town of Milan. He next worked with Baron de Dietrich in Niederbronn and then became the partner of Mathis with whom he built the Hermès Simplex in 1904. In 1909, he founded his factory in Molsheim and produced the prestigious models which brought him fame, including the 1926 Royale.

Parc naturel régional de la
MONTAGNE DE REIMS ★★

Michelin map 56 folds 16 and 17 or 241 fold 21

The Montagne de Reims is a picturesque massif covered with vineyards and woods and offering a wide choice of pleasant drives.

Forest and vines – The Montagne de Reims is a section of the Ile-de-France cuesta jutting out between the Vesle and the Marne towards the plain of Champagne. The Grande Montagne (high mountain) extends east of N 51 whereas the Petite Montagne (small mountain) spreads to the west of N 51. The highest point of the massif (287m/942ft) is located south of Vezy but, apart from Mont Sinaï (alt 283m/928ft) and Mont Joli (alt 274m/899ft), there are no distinct summits. The Montagne de Reims would be more appropriately described as an uneven limestone plateau covered with sand and marl deposits, with occasional depressions filled by lakes or chasms leading to the formation of underground rivers.

Wild boars and roe-deer roam freely through the vast forest of oaks, beeches and chestnuts, which covers an area of 20 000ha/49 422 acres. The north, east and south slopes, gullied by erosion, are covered with 7 000ha/17 298 acres of vineyards producing some of the best Champagnes.

Eating out

MID-RANGE

La Maison du Vigneron – *51160 St-Imoges – 8km/5mi N of Épernay on N 51 – ☎ 03 26 52 88 00 – closed 2-14 Jan, Sun evening and Wed – 130/280F.* You can sample local wines and Champagnes in the cellar bar of this large house in the middle of the woods. Local dishes are served in the dining room, with exposed beams and an open fireplace. The staff are friendly and the terrace very pleasant in summer.

LUXURY

Le Grand Cerf – *51500 Montchenot – 3km/2mi W of Rilly-la-Montagne on D 26 – ☎ 03 26 97 60 07 – closed during Feb school holidays, 8-31 Aug, Sun evening and Wed – 285/470F.* This local inn on the main road offers carefully prepared, refined dishes and is well known among local gourmets. The pleasant veranda-style dining room opens onto a terrace and a pretty garden.

Where to stay

MID-RANGE

Hôtel du Cheval Blanc – *51400 Sept-Saulx – 20km/12.5mi SE of Reims on N 44 and D 37 – ☎ 03 26 03 90 27 – closed 22 Jan-20 Feb – ▣ – 22 rooms 350/810F – ☕ 50F – restaurant 180/540F.* This peaceful former coaching inn is well off the beaten track. The spruce, flowery courtyard has been converted into a terrace. A branch of the River Vesle winds through the attractive park, where you can play tennis, volley-ball and golf, or just simply relax in fine weather.

Shopping

Forget-Chemin – *15 r. Victor-Hugo – 51500 Ludes – 3.5km/2mi W of Mailly-Champagne on D 26 – ☎ 03 26 61 12 17 –* This fourth-generation vineyard owner and wine producer offers tastings enhanced by an initiation into winemaking.

Serge Pierlot – *10 r. St-Vincent – 51150 Ambonnay – 6.5km/4mi SE of Louvois on D 34 and D 19 – ☎ 03 26 57 01 11 – Mon-Fri 9am-noon, 2.30-6.30pm, Sat 9am-noon, 2.30-6pm, Sun 9am-noon.* In his shop at the end of an alley, Serge Pierlot exhibits an 18C winepress and other vine-growing and winemaking implements from his family. Tasting and sales.

Soutiran-Pelletier – *13 r. St-Vincent – 51150 Ambonnay – 6.5km/4mi SE of Louvois on D 34 and D 19 – ☎ 03 26 57 07 87 – Mon-Fri 8.30am-noon, 1-6pm, Sat 8am-noon, 2.30-6pm.* In this typical village, the Soutiran-Pelletier establishment will take you to see its presses, vats and cellars, as well as explain the techniques used in winemaking. Tasting and sales.

Parc naturel régional de la Montagne de Reims – Created in 1976, the nature park extends over an area of 50 000ha/123 555 acres between the towns of Reims, Épernay and Châlons-en-Champagne and includes 68 villages and hamlets of the Marne *département*. The forest, consisting essentially of deciduous trees, covers more than a third of the park's area; part of it, south of Verzy, is a biological reserve.

There are numerous possibilities and facilities for exploring the park: footpaths starting from Villers-Allerand, Rilly-la-Montagne, Villers-Marmery, Trépail, Courtagnon and Damery; walks along the canal running alongside the Marne, picnic areas, viewpoints in Ville-Dommange, Hautvillers, Dizy, Verzy and Châtillon-sur-Marne.

In addition to the sights listed in the itinerary, **Olizy** has a small **Musée de l'Escargot de Champagne** ⓥ (snail museum) and offers a tour of a snail farm.

The Maison du Parc in **Pourcy** organises numerous cultural and outdoor activities every year. There are other information centres about the park in **Hautvillers** and **Châtillon-sur-Marne**.

CHAMPAGNE KINGDOM

Round tour starting from Montchenot

100km/62mi – allow one day

Drive out of Montchenot along N 51 then follow D 26 towards Villers-Allerand.

The road, which follows the northern ridge of the Montagne de Reims, winds its way through vineyards and the prosperous villages of the Champagne countryside.

Rilly-la-Montagne – A number of wine-growers and Champagne merchants have brought prosperity to this village. In the church, note the 16C stalls carved with motifs connected with wine-growing.

From Rilly there are fine walking possibilities on the slopes of **Mont Joli** through which goes the railway tunnel (3.5km/2.2mi long) of the Paris-Reims line.

Mailly-Champagne – 1km/0.6mi beyond Mailly-Champagne, whose vineyards slope down into the plain, there is an interesting **Carrière géologique** ⓥ (geological quarry) showing a complete cross section of the Tertiary formations of the eastern Paris Basin.

From the road, one can spot, at the top of the hill to the right, a contemporary sculpture by Bernard Pages celebrating the Earth.

Verzenay – A windmill can be seen among the vines just before the village. From the esplanade on the roadside, there is a **view**★ of the vast expanse of vineyards with Reims and the Monts de Champagne beyond.

Verzy – This ancient wine-growing village developed under the protection of the Benedictine abbey of St-Basle, founded in the 7C by the archbishop of Reims, St Nivard, and destroyed in 1792.

★**Faux de Verzy** ⓥ – *In Verzy, take D 34 towards Louvois. On reaching the plateau, turn left onto the Route des Faux. From the parking area, follow the path over a distance of about 1km/0.6mi.* No tours in feb.

🚶 The Faux (from the Latin *fagus* meaning birch) are twisted and stunted birches. This is the result of a genetic phenomenon, probably reinforced by natural layering. The site is now a biological reserve with footpaths, a playground and picnic area.

Faux de Verzy

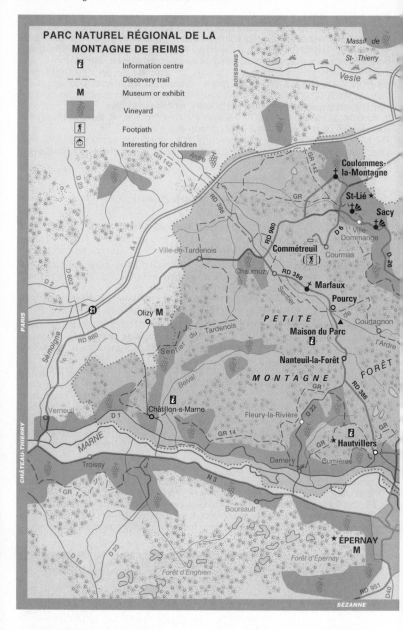

Mont Sinaï – *Parking area on the other side of D 34. Walk along the forest road and, 200m/219yd further on, turn right onto a very wide path (30min there and back).*

🔲 A casemate situated on the edge of the ridge marks the observation post from which General Gouraud studied the positions and the terrain during the battle of Champagne in 1918. There is an extended view of the area towards Reims and the Champagne hills.

Return to D 34 and continue towards Louvois.

Louvois – Erected by Mansart for Louis XIV's minister, the **castle** *(not open to the public)* became the property of Louis XV's daughters. This splendid residence surrounded by a park designed by Le Nôtre was for the most part demolished between 1805 and 1812. From the gate of the park, one can see the present castle which consists of a pavilion partly rebuilt in the 19C.

Drive N along D 9 to Neuville-en-Chaillois then turn left onto D 71 which goes through the forest.

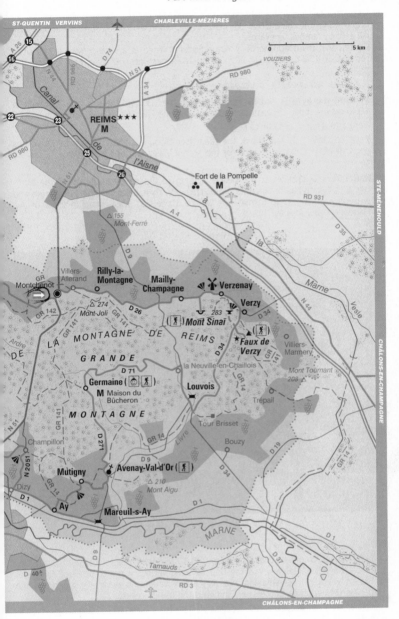

Germaine – ▣ A small museum, the **Maison du bûcheron** ⊙, created by the nature park, is devoted to all the aspects of forestry (marking, clearing, cutting, felling, carrying) and its corresponding skills. Nearby, there is a nature trail through the forest.

Follow D 271 to Avenay-Val-d'Or.

Avenay-Val-d'Or – The **Église St-Trésain** ⊙, dating from the 13C and 16C, has a fine Flamboyant west front, a 16C organ in the south transept and pictures from a Benedictine abbey destroyed during the Revolution. A discovery trail starting from the station *(brochure available from the Maison du Parc)*, enables visitors to discover a rural community.

Follow D 201 opposite the station and immediately after the railway line, take the small road which climbs through the vineyards to Mutigny.

Mutigny – Stand near the simple rural church, situated on the edge of the ridge, to get a good **view** of Ay and the Côte des Blancs on the right, Châlons and the plain straight ahead.
On the way down to Ay, there are glimpses of Épernay and the Côte des Blancs.

Ay – This ancient city, well-known in Gallo-Roman times and well liked by several French kings including Good King Henri (IV), lies in a secluded spot at the foot of a hill among famous vineyards.

Gosset, the Champagne firm whose founder is listed as a wine-grower in the city's records of 1584, prides itself in being the oldest firm in the whole Champagne region.

In Ay, turn left onto D 1 to Mareuil-sur-Ay.

Mareuil-sur-Ay – The castle was erected in the 18C and the estate was bought in 1830 by the duke of Montebello who created his own make of Champagne.

Return to Ay and continue to Dizy.

Between Dizy and Champillon, the road rises through endless vineyards. There is a good **view**★ of those vineyards, of the Marne Valley and of Épernay from a terrace on the side of the road.

★**Hautvillers** – This attractive village clinging to the southern slopes of the Montagne de Reims has retained its old houses with their basket-handled doorways and wrought-iron signs. It forms part of the three top wine-growing areas of Ay, Hautvillers and Avenay.

Worth a thousand words

According to tradition, **Dom Pérignon** (1638-1715), who was in charge of the cellars of the Benedictine abbey, was the first to blend various wines to produce a vintage. His knowledge of winemaking was very extensive and he eventually supervised the double fermentation process and initiated the use of corks.

Former abbey church – Founded in 660 by St Nivard, a nephew of King Dagobert, the abbey became one of the finest artistic centres in Western Europe: the most beautiful manuscripts of the **École de Reims** were produced within its walls. An alleyway at the end of the village leads to the abbey church. Particularly noteworthy is the 17C-18C chancel decorated with carved oak panels, late-18C stalls and large religious paintings including two remarkable works from the School of Philippe de Champaigne: *St Benedict helping St Scholastic* and *St Nivard founding Hautvillers Abbey*. A vast chandelier made up of four wheels from winepresses hangs over the high altar. Dom Pérignon's tombstone is located at the entrance of the chancel.

Nanteuil-la-Forêt – There was once a Templars' priory in this remote place hidden inside a narrow vale and surrounded by a forest.

Pourcy – The **Maison du Parc** ⊘, built in the Ardre Valley, houses the offices of the nature park as well as an information centre. Designed by Hervé Bagot, it is reminiscent of farm buildings surrounding an enclosed courtyard.

Marfaux – The church boasts fine capitals carved with acanthus leaves and small characters.

Beyond Chaumuzy, turn right onto RD 980 then, as you reach Bouilly, turn left onto D 206 to Coulommes-la-Montagne.

Coulommes-la-Montagne – In this flower-decked village, there is a fine Romanesque **church**; note the tower with just one opening and the foliage decoration of the capitals in the transept and chancel.

Turn right to rejoin D 980 vial Pargny-les-Reims; l.5km/0.9mi further on, turn left towards St-Lié, then right onto D 6 to Courmas.

Continue to the parking area known as Aire de l'Étang, at the entrance of Courmas. The **Domaine de Commetreuil**, which belongs to the nature park, offers many fine walks.

Turn back.

★**Chapelle St-Lié** – This chapel, dating from the 12C, 13C and 16C, stands on a mound near Ville-Dommange, at the centre of a copse which was probably a holy grove in Gallo-Roman times. Note the wrought-iron cross on the edge of the wood. Dedicated to a 5C hermit, the chapel is surrounded by its cemetery.
There is an extended **view**★ of Ville-Dommange, the ridge, Reims and its cathedral and the plain as far as the St-Thierry massif.

Sacy – The Église St-Rémi has an 11C east end and a 12C square belfry. From the adjoining cemetery there is a fine view of Reims.

MONTHERMÉ ★

Population 2 866
Michelin map 53 fold 18 or 241 fold 6 – Local map see Vallée de la MEUSE

Situated just beyond the confluence of the Semoy and the Meuse, this lively little town is the ideal centre from which to explore the Ardennes region. The old town *(vieille ville)* and new districts are separated by the River Meuse; from the bridge linking them, there is a fine overall view of Monthermé.

Vieille ville – A long street lined with old houses runs through the old town and leads

to the fortified **Église St-Léger** ⊙ (12C-15C), built of fine stone from the Meuse region. Inside there are 15C frescoes, a Romanesque christening font and an 18C pulpit.

EXCURSIONS

★**Roche à Sept Heures** – *2km/1.2mi along the Hargnies road then left at the top of the hill onto the tarmacked path.* From this rocky spur, there is a bird's-eye **view**★ of Monthermé and the meander of the Meuse with Laval-Dieu upstream and, further away, Château-Regnault and the Rocher des Quatre Fils Aymon.

★★**Longue Roche** – *The tarmacked path continues beyond the Roche à Sept Heures for a further 400m/437yd to a parking area. From there, you can walk to the viewpoint (30min there and back).*

⛰ This is another rocky spur (alt 375m/1 230ft) overlooking the Meuse. A path running along the ridge offers bird's-eye views of the valley from different angles. The **panorama**★★ is wilder and sharper than that of the Roche à Sept Heures.

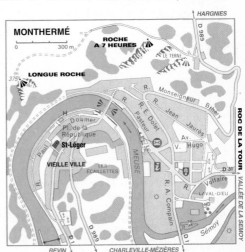

★★Roc de la Tour – *3.5km/2.2mi E then 20min on foot there and back. The access road branches off D 31 on the left as you leave Laval-Dieu; it rises through the wooded vale of a stream (the Lyre). Leave the car and follow the footpath.*

🚶 This ruin-like quartzite spur surrounded by birches stands in a dramatic setting overlooking the Semoy and affords a panoramic **view★★** of the wooded heights of the Ardennes massif.

★★Roche aux Sept Villages – *3km/1.9mi S. Follow the Charleville road (D 989).*
As the road rises, the view gradually extends over the valley.
Steps climb this rocky peak rising above the forest. From the top there is a remarkable **view★★** of the meandering River Meuse lined with seven villages from Braux to Deville. Next to Château-Regnault stands the jagged Rocher des Quatre Fils Aymon.

The road continues to climb beyond the Roche aux Sept Villages; at the top, a path leads to the viewpoint of the Roche de Roma.

★Roche de Roma – Alt 333m/1 093ft. **View★** of the meander of the Meuse between Monthermé and Deville.

VALLÉE DE LA SEMOY

From Monthermé to Linchamps *19km/11.8mi – 1hr 30min*

From the Belgian border to the Meuse, the River Semoy (called Semois in Belgium) meanders across pastureland between steep slopes covered with forests of oak, fir and birch trees and inhabited by roe-deer and wild boars. The green secluded valley is the paradise of anglers fishing for trout and of anyone yearning for solitude.

Leave Monthermé along D 31.

The road runs below the Roc de la Tour.

Follow the forest road for 4km/2.5mi.

Sentier des Rapides – *1hr on foot there and back.*
🚶 The path starts at the end of the parking area and follows the tumultuous river flowing through wild scenery as far as Tournavaux.

Return to D 31.

The road rises to the top of the cliff offering bird's-eye **views★** of Tournavaux nestling in a slightly widened part of the valley.
The road runs down to Thilay then crosses the Semoy. Beyond Naux, lying inside a deep meander of the river, the itinerary crosses the Semoy once more.

Les Hautes-Rivières – This is the largest village along the French section of the River Semoy. It extends over 2km/1.2mi to Sorendal.

Drive S along D 13 towards Nouzonville, climbing 1.5km/0.9mi to the beginning of the path leading to the Croix d'Enfer.

Croix d'Enfer –*30min on foot there and back.*
🚶 View of the valley, of the village of Les Hautes-Rivières and of the Vallon de Linchamps.

★Vallon de Linchamps – *N of Hautes-Rivières along D 13.* Beautiful remote area.
The rural, isolated village of **Linchamps** is the starting point of walks through the **Ravin de l'Ours** and **Bois des Haies**, across a hilly area reaching altitudes in excess of 500m/1 640ft.

MONTIER-EN-DER

Population 2 023
Michelin map 61 fold 9 or 241 fold 34

Destroyed by intensive shelling in June 1940, Montier-en-Der was completely rebuilt and now boasts pleasant public gardens.
The town developed round a Benedictine monastery established on the banks of the River Voire. It is the capital of the **Der**, a low-lying area of sand and clay, covered with oak forests (Der means oak copse in Celtic language) until medieval monks undertook to deforest it; the Der Forest in the north-east is all that remains of the original forests. Pastures where horses and cattle graze alternate with woods and lakes where wildlife abounds. Villages set in ancestral orchards have retained their characteristic features: low timber-framed houses with cob walls, the church steeple rising to a shingled point above one and all.

SIGHTS

Église Notre-Dame – This is the former church of the monastery founded in Montier in 672, which followed the rule of St Columba (an Irish monk who founded Luxeuil Abbey, *see LUXEUIL-LES-BAINS*). The present edifice was built between the 10C and 13C. Damaged by fire in June 1940, it was remarkably well restored. The conventual buildings were razed in 1850.

The **nave** (36.50m/120ft long) is the oldest part of the building: eight rounded arches rest on low rectangular piers. The timber vaulting is a copy of the 16C vaulting.

The **chancel★** (12C-13C) is a splendid example of Early Gothic in the Champagne region. It consists of four-storey elevations:

– main arcades resting on twinned columns decorated with strange grotesques;

– upper gallery with twinned arches surmounted by an oculus;

– triforium with trefoil arches;

– clerestory windows separated by colonnettes.

The soaring chancel of Notre-Dame church

A row of columns separates the radiating chapels from the ambulatory; the deep apsidal chapel is surmounted by an elegant ribbed Gothic vault.

Haras ⊙ – This stud farm, situated on the site of the former abbey, on the left of the church, looks after some 40 stallions and 15 horses for various riding clubs.

★TIMBER-FRAMED CHURCHES

Round tour starting from Montier-en-Der

60km/37mi – allow 4hr

The Lac du Der-Chantecoq *(see Lac du DER-CHANTE-COQ)* and the timber-framed churches are the

---

Horse Sense

The Ardennes horse is one of most sought-after breed of draught horses in France. This small, tough, calm and docile horse is essentially bred in north-east France, that is Champagne, Ardennes, Lorraine and Alsace. It is extremely useful on farms, in the fields and in forests but is also used for leisure activities (riding, barouche trips, horse-drawn caravanning, touring along bridle paths).

A competition, which takes place in Sedan every September, brings together the best representatives of the Ardennes breed.

---

two main attractions of the Der region. The name Der, from the Celtic *dervos* meaning forest, is a reminder of the forests which once covered the area and provided timber for building many a church, in a region where stone was hard to find. Most of these are decorated with stained glass from the Troyes School.

Churches are floodlit every night from May to September and at weekends only during the rest of the year. Other churches and some edifices situated round the Lac du Der-Chantecoq are also floodlit: Éclaron, Giffaumont, St-Rémy-en-Bouzemont, Larzicourt, Arrigny and the museum-village of Ste-Marie-du-Lac-Nuisement.

Drive out of Montier-en-Der along the Brienne road.

Ceffonds – The **Église St-Rémi**, rebuilt round its Romanesque belfry at the beginning of the 16C, stands in the disused cemetery which has retained a 16C stone cross. The church is entered through a Renaissance doorway added to the west front in 1562. Note, on the inside wall, the interesting 16C mural depicting St Christopher and, in the first chapel on the south side, the unusual stone christening fonts; on the north side, the Holy Sepulchre chapel contains a 16C Entombment including 10 polychrome stone statues.

The transept and the chancel are decorated with fine 16C **stained-glass windows★** made in the famous workshops of the city of Troyes: in the chancel, you can see from left to right St Rémi's legend, Christ's Passion and Resurrection and the

Creation; in the transept, to the left of the chancel, the legend of St Crépin and St Crépinien, patron saints of tanners and cobblers who made a present of the stained glass to the church; in the transept, to the right of the chancel, a Tree of Jesse.

Turn back towards Montier-en-Der then left onto D 173.

Puellemontier – Timber-framed houses are scattered in the fields. The **church** is surmounted by a slender pointed steeple; the nave dates from the 12C but the chancel is more recent (16C); in the south transept, two 16C statues of St Cyre and St Flora stand on either side of a stained-glass window representing a Tree of Jesse (1531), one of several fine stained-glass windows made in the workshops of Troyes in the 16C.

Continue along D 173 then D 62 to Lentilles.

The road runs close to the peaceful **Étang de la Horre** (250ha/618 acres), lined with tall grass.

Village church in Lentilles

*Lentilles – This is a typical Der village with a well-ordered street plan and low timber-framed houses. The **church** is a fine 16C edifice whose timber frame is strengthened by horizontal and oblique beams. The pointed octagonal spire is covered with shingles and the wooden porch is surmounted by a statue of St James.

Follow D 2 to Chavanges.

Chavanges – The church, dating from the 15C and 16C, has a 12C doorway; it contains several interesting 16C stained-glass windows and statues from the 14C to 16C.

Opposite the church, there is a splendid 18C timber-framed house flanked by a square turret.

Drive E along D 56 to Bailly-le-Franc.

Bailly-le-Franc – Hardly restored during the past centuries, the **church** has remained the simplest and most authentic of all the churches of the Der region.

Follow D 127 to Joncreuil.

Joncreuil – The church, surmounted by an imposing timber-framed steeple, has a Romanesque nave and a 13C chancel.

Arrembécourt – Note the carved doorway of the **church** and, inside, the stained-glass window depicting the Crucifixion.

Continue along D 6 then D 58.

Drosnay – This village has retained a few timber-framed buildings including some houses and the church which contains a carved-wood altarpiece over the high altar.

Drive along D 55 to Outines.

Outines – This is a typical Der village with its timber-framed cob-wall houses and its church surmounted by a pointed steeple covered with shingles.

Châtillon-sur-Broué – *See Lac du DER-CHANTECOQ.*

Droyes – The brick-built church comprises a Romanesque nave and a 16C chancel.

Take D 13 to return to Montier-en-Der.

MONTMÉDY

Population 1 943
Michelin map 57 fold 1 or 241 fold 15

There are two towns in one: Montmédy-Bas (lower town), on the banks of the River Chiers, and Montmédy-Haut (upper town), fortified during the Renaissance and remodelled by Vauban, which has retained its ramparts. Montmédy belonged to the duke of Burgundy, to the Hapsburgs and to Spain before being ceded to France in 1659. It was then that Vauban altered the town's defence system.

The town organises two lively festivals: the Fête des Remparts involving jugglers, clowns and tightrope walkers, which takes place on the first Sunday in May, and the Fête des Pommes centred on a busy market, exhibitions and tasting sessions, which takes place on the first Sunday in October.

MONTMÉDY-HAUT

The upper town is perched on an isolated peak. On the north side, two successive gates fitted with drawbridges and an archway lead inside the walled town.

★Citadelle ⊘ – A walk along the ramparts, past glacis, curtain walls, bastions and underground passages, gives a good idea of the complexity and ingenious design of the citadel's defence system, modernised after 1870. From the top of the ramparts, the **view** extends over the lower town, the Chiers Valley and numerous surrounding villages.

Musées de la Fortification et Jules Bastien-Lepage ⊘ – Situated at the entrance of the citadel, these museums are devoted respectively to the history of fortifications (models, historic documents, audio-visual presentation) and to the life and work of a native of the region, the painter Jules Bastien-Lepage (1848-84).

Église St-Martin – This vast church dating from the mid 18C has retained its stalls and woodwork decorating the chancel.

EXCURSIONS

Louppy-sur-Loison – *14km/8.7mi S. Leave Montmédy by N 43 towards Longuyon then turn right in Iré-le-Sec.*
The **castle** ⊘ built at the beginning of the 17C by Simon de Pouilly, who was the governor of Stenay (*see Vallée de la MEUSE*), is still owned by his descendants. The tour of the exterior enables visitors to admire the dovecote, the chapel and some richly carved doorways.
Ruins of the original fortress can be seen near the church.

Marville – *12.5km/7.8mi SE along N 43.*
Founded in Gallo-Roman times under the name of Major villa, Marville is situated on a promontory jutting out between the valleys of the Othain and the Crédon. It was under Spanish rule during the first half of the 17C while being granted the privileges of a free city. There are a few 16C and 17C houses to be seen along the Grand'Rue.
In the **Église St-Nicolas**, note the early-16C balustrade of the organ loft.

Cimetière de la chapelle St-Hilaire ⊘ – *The tarmacked path leading to the cemetery branches off N 43.* Situated at the top of the hill, the cemetery of the former Église St-Hilaire contains a walled ossuary said to house 40 000 skulls. In the chapel, note, in particular, a Christ in bonds and above all a beautiful *Pietà* with the statues of the Apostles decorating the base, believed to be the work of the Ligier Richier School.

★★Avioth – *8.5km/5.3mi N along D 110. See Basilique d'AVIOTH.*

Montmédy citadel

MONTMIRAIL

Population 3 812
Michelin map 56 fold 15 or 237 folds 21 and 22

The low roughcast houses of this once fortified town cling to the slopes of a promontory overlooking the rural valley of the Petit Morin.
Paul de Gondi, who later became the famous **Cardinal de Retz**, was born in Montmirail Castle in 1613. After the death of Cardinal Richelieu and Louis XIII, this dangerous schemer used his ecclesiastical influence to destabilise the regency of Anne of Austria during Louis XIV's childhood.

CHÂTEAU

The 17C brick-and-stone castle was acquired in 1685 by one of Louis XIV's ministers, the **Marquis de Louvois**, who remodelled it, had French-style gardens laid and invited the king. His great-granddaughter married the Duc de La Rochefoucauld whose descendants still own the castle.

EXCURSIONS

Colonne commémorative de la bataille de Montmirail – *4km/2.5mi NW along RD 933.* A column surmounted by a gilt eagle (1867) commemorates one of the last battles won by **Napoleon** in 1814 over Russian and Prussian troops.
A century later, in September 1914, the German army commanded by Von Bülow was attacked here by French troops under the command of Foch and Franchet d'Esperey who managed to stop the German advance.

Verdelot – *15km/9.3mi W along D 31.* The imposing **church** ☉, dating from the 15C-16C, stands on the hillside. Note the intricate vaulting and the height of the aisles almost level with the chancel vaulting. On either side of the chancel, there are small statues of St Crépin and St Crépinien, patron saints of cobblers, to whom the church is dedicated. A sitting Virgin in carved walnut (Notre-Dame-de-Pitié de Verdelot), forming part of a 19C altarpiece, is reminiscent of 12C or 13C representations of the Virgin carved in the Auvergne and Languedoc regions.

Jardins de Vieils-Maisons – *12km/7.5mi W along D 933.* A park surrounding a castle and covering 5ha/12.5 acres, contains 2 000 different plant species displayed in the French-style garden (roses and medicinal plants), in the English-style garden (bushes and perennials) and in symbolic gardens (heather, hydrangeas, different varieties of grass).

VALLÉE DU PETIT MORIN *24km/15mi – allow 1hr*

This 90km/56mi long tributary of the Marne, which takes its source in a marshland area east of Montmirail *(see Marais de ST-GOND)*, flows through undulating meadows, marshy in places, dotted with groves and rows of poplars. Traditional houses, with roughcast walls underlined by brickwork and roofs covered with flat brown tiles, nestle round village churches.
The road *(D 43)*, which follows the Petit Morin upriver, goes through charming villages.

Abbaye du Reclus – A holy hermit called Hugues-le-Reclus, retired to this remote vale (c 1123) and gave it his name. In 1142, St Bernard founded a Cistercian abbey which was partly destroyed during the Wars of Religion and then rebuilt. Parts of the 12C abbey (east gallery of the cloister, chapter-house, sacristy) were discovered beneath the present monastery building.
Beyond Talus-St-Prix, turn left towards Baye.

Baye – This village lies in the valley of a tributary of the Petit Morin. St Alpin, a native of Baye who became bishop of Châlons, was buried in the 13C church. The 17C castle has retained a 13C chapel believed to have been designed by Jean d'Orbais. Baye is the birthplace of Marion Delorme (1611-50) who, like Ninon de Lenclos, was famous for her numerous love affairs; her legend inspired Victor Hugo to write a drama entitled *Marion Delorme* in 1831.

MOUZON ★

Population 2 637
Michelin map 56 fold 10 or 241 folds 10 and 14

This small town, lying on an island formed by the River Meuse and the Canal de l'Est, was originally a Gaulish trading centre (Mosomagos) then a Roman military post. The Frankish king Clovis offered it to St Remi (who had christened the king c 498), and it later became a favourite residence of the archbishops of Reims. United with France in 1379, Mouzon was besieged by the Holy Roman Emperor Charles V in the 16C, by the Spaniards and by Condé in the mid 17C. The fortifications were demolished in 1671 except for the 15C **Porte de Bourgogne**. The last factory to produce industrial felt is based in Mouzon.

SIGHTS

★**Église Notre-Dame** – The construction of this ancient abbey church, started at the end of the 12C and was completed in just over 30 years, except for the towers, which were built in the 15C (north tower) and 16C (south tower). The west-front central doorway is richly carved.
The interior *(see p 43)* is imposing. The nave and the chancel rest on massive round piers, as in Laon Cathedral on which Mouzon is modelled. The upper gallery goes all the way round the nave and the chancel, and above the ambulatory and the radiating chapels. The 18C furniture is noteworthy, in particular the organ and the carved-wood organ case (1725), the only remaining example of the work of Christophe Moucherel in northern France.
The late-17C conventual buildings, situated to the left of the church, have been turned into a pensioners' home. The French-style gardens offer a pleasant walk.

Musée du Feutre ⊙ – The Felt Museum, housed in one of the abbey's former farmhouses, is devoted to the history and manufacture of felt from its traditional use in daily life (carpets and coats of nomadic stockbreeders in Turkey and Afghanistan) to its industrial use (floor coverings, filters) or its more current use (hats, slippers, decorative objects). The reconstruction of a production line (on a reduced scale) helps visitors to understand the manufacturing process. There is an exhibition of contemporary designs as well as workshops for children and adults.

Musée de la Tour de la Porte de Bourgogne ⊙ – This small museum illustrates 2 000 years of local history and includes finds from the Flavier archaeological site.

EXCURSIONS

Site gallo-romain du Flavier – *4km/2.5mi SE on D 964 to Stenay.*
The remains of a Gallo-Roman sanctuary, discovered on this site in 1966, include the foundations of three small temples *(information panels).*

The River Meuse and Canal de l'Est

67km/41mi drive S of Mouzon.

Leave Mouzon SE along D 964 and turn right onto D 222 9km/5.6mi further on (just before Inor). Cross the river at Pouilly-sur-Meuse and turn right onto a minor road leading to D 30; turn right again to Beaumont-en-Argonne then left onto D 4.

★**Parc de vision de Belval** ⊙ – Situated in the grounds of a former Augustinian monastery, this wildlife park covers 600ha/1 483 acres of meadows, woods and lakes at the heart of the Belval Forest.
⌖ All the animals live or used to live in this natural environment a few hundred years ago: wild boars, deer, roe-deer and also moufflons, bisons and bears which have now disappeared. During the 6km/3.7mi drive round the park, it is possible to stop, go on short hikes and watch the animals roaming around almost freely from watchtowers and hidden observation points. Mallards and herons live on the lakes.

Return to Beaumont-en-Argonne and turn right onto D 30 towards Stenay.

Stenay – This former stronghold, situated on the east bank of the river and of the canal, lies at the heart of beer country.

The vast **Musée européen de la Bière** ⊙ (European Beer Museum) is housed in the former supply stores of the 16C citadel turned into a malt factory in the 19C. Explanatory panels, maps, models, objects and tools help to inform visitors about the history and technique of beer-brewing since ancient times. The uninitiated discover how brewers make beer from simple ingredients such as spring water, barley turned into malt and hops which give beer its characteristic bitter flavour.

Stenay – Musée de la Bière

The 16C residence of the former governor of the citadel, situated on the edge of town, houses the **Musée du pays de Stenay** ⊙ which contains collections of archaeology as well as arts and crafts *(temporarily closed)*.

Drive S along D 964 and cross the canal and the river 10km/6.2mi from Stenay. In Sassey-sur-Meuse turn left to Mont-devant-Sassey.

Mont-devant-Sassey – The village lies at the foot of a hill on the west bank of the river. An interesting 11C church, remodelled later, stands on the hillside. During the 17C wars, it was turned into a fortress. The building, characteristic of the Rhine region, has square towers over the transept and a raised east end built over a crypt. Preceded by a Gothic porch decorated with statues in naive style, the monumental 13C doorway, dedicated to the Virgin, is similar in design to those of the great Gothic cathedrals: a damaged bearing shaft supports a tympanum consisting of three historiated bands, framed by four recessed arches decorated with carved characters.

Return to Sassey-sur-Meuse, cross the river and the canal and turn right onto D 964 to Dun-sur-Meuse.

Dun-sur-Meuse – The oldest part of this small town is built on a picturesque hilltop, on the edge of the Lorraine plateau. From the open space in front of the 16C church, there is an extended view of the Meuse Valley.

MULHOUSE★★

Population 223 856
Michelin map 87 folds 9 and 19 or 242 fold 39

Situated on the northern foothills of the Sungdau, Mulhouse has several attractive features including its rich past as an independent republic, its strong industrial tradition and its prestigious museums.

This modern and dynamic town has, since 1975, been the seat of the Université de Haute-Alsace, which specialises in high technology, working on the principle of close links between training, research and industry.

From the top of the Tour de l'Europe *(tearoom, revolving restaurant)*, there is a good overall **view** of the town and the surrounding area.

Born in Mulhouse in 1859, **Alfred Dreyfus**, a captain in the intelligence service, was wrongly accused and convicted in 1894 of having passed on military secrets to the German attaché in Paris. He spent several years in Cayenne before his case was reviewed following pressure from the press and in particular from the famous open letter by Émile Zola entitled *J'accuse* which earned its author one year's imprisonment and a heavy fine.

MULHOUSE: CITY AND REPUBLIC

A passion for independence – From the 12C onwards, Mulhouse strived to liberate itself from its feudal bonds and in 1308 it acquired the status of an imperial city, thus becoming a virtually independent republic, acknowledging the Holy Roman Emperor as its sole suzerain. Encouraged by the latter, Mulhouse formed, with nine other imperial cities, a league of defence against the power of the nobility, known as **Decapolis**.

Eating out

MODERATE

Aux Caves du Vieux Couvent – *23 r. du Couvent – ☎ 03 89 46 28 79 – closed Sun evening and Mon – 57/150F.* An Alsace tavern in the city centre. The dining room has a vaulted ceiling and its walls are decorated with murals. The rustic style of its solid wood benches and chairs goes well with the regional cuisine, which is served in a cheerful atmosphere.

Zum Saüwadala – *13 r. de l'Arsenal – ☎ 03 89 45 18 19 – closed Mon lunchtime and Sun – 98/145F.* You can't miss this restaurant, with its typical façade in the centre of old Mulhouse. Beer mugs hang from the ceiling, the tablecloths are gingham, and the cuisine is genuine Alsace. Several menus, including one for children.

MID-RANGE

Auberge de Frœningen – *68720 Frœningen – 9km/5.6mi SW of Mulhouse on D 8^{BIII} – ☎ 03 89 25 48 48 – closed 7-29 Jan, 14-28 Aug, Sun evening and Mon – 140/360F.* Warm red colours and shining copperware set the tone: this flower-decked village inn serves rich rustic local cuisine in a comfortable setting. One of the dining rooms is decorated in Alsatian style, and is the most welcoming. A few well-kept rooms.

LUXURY

Hostellerie Paulus – *4 pl. de la Paix – 68440 Landser – 11km/6.8mi SE of Mulhouse in the direction of the zoo, Bruebach, D 21 and D 6^{B} – ☎ 03 89 81 33 30 – closed 30 Jul-14 Aug, 24 Dec-8 Jan, Sat lunchtime, Sun evening and Mon – booking essential – 235/365F.* This red-painted establishment in a country village not far from Mulhouse is renowned among gourmets. The two modern dining rooms are slightly austere, but the cooking is both creative and daring, with interesting menus.

Where to stay

MODERATE

Hôtel St-Bernard – *3 r. des Fleurs – ☎ 03 89 45 82 32 – stber@evhr.net – 21 rooms 170/290F – ☕ 38F.* This small, functional hotel is well situated, near the attractive place de la Réunion and the town hall. Just for a laugh, ask for one of the two rooms with a waterbed, or the one with a painted ceiling, for sweet dreams. Free Internet access available at reception and bikes can be hired, for the active.

MID-RANGE

Hôtel Bristol – *18 av. de Colmar – ☎ 03 89 42 12 31 – P – 70 rooms 320/650F – ☕ 45F.* A little way from the old town, this early-20C hotel has been completely renovated. Its many rooms are spacious and well equipped. Some bathrooms have corner baths. A good place to stay in Mulhouse.

Chambre d'hôte Le Clos du Mûrier – *42 Grand-Rue – 68170 Rixheim – 6km/3.75mi E of Mulhouse, Bâle direction – ☎ 03 89 54 14 81 – 5 rooms 300/350F – ☕ 40F.* This 16C Alsatian house in the centre of Rixheim has been attractively restored. Spacious rooms with exposed beams and stylish modern decor. All have kitchenettes. Pretty garden.

On the town

Charlie's Bar – *26 r. de Sinne – ☎ 03 89 66 12 22 – daily 9am-1.30am.* The Hôtel du Parc's piano bar is a classy spot, much frequented by businessmen and the Mulhouse bourgeoisie. In this lovely setting you can hear music worthy of the best jazz clubs: nightly piano concerts from 7pm, with duets on Thu, Fri and Sat (from 10pm). The cocktails are irresistible!

Glen Cœ – *143 av. de Colmar – ☎ 03 89 43 00 22 – daily 7pm-1.30am – closed 24, 25 and 31 Dec.* A larger-than-life Scottish pub: the owner lived among the moorland mists and lakes of Scotland for ten years, and even got married there. All the staff are in kilts, and there are no less than 100 whiskies and nine draught beers. Folk and rock concerts at weekends. Meals available on ground floor.

Le Blash – *41 r. de la Sinne – ☎ 03 89 45 55 71 – Tue-Thu 8pm-1.30am, Fri-Sat 8pm-3am – closed Aug.* Its dance floor and theme evenings (French songs, fashion shows) make this the latest place to go in Mulhouse. Don't miss trying a Caipirinha, a punch made from Cachaça and honey.

In the mid 15C, the town's guilds became politically powerful; they installed a kind of oligarchic government and the Republic freed itself from imperial control. In 1515, under threat from the Hapsburgs' territories which completely surrounded it, Mulhouse left Decapolis and entered into an alliance with the **Swiss cantons**, an inspired decision which placed the town under the protection of the kingdom of France: the intervention of Henri IV in favour of his allies and the cession to France of the Hapsburgs' possessions in Alsace under the treaty of Westphalia (1648) enabled the Republic to retain its independence. Even the revocation of the Edict of Nantes in 1685 did not really threaten this bastion of Calvinism which remained the only Alsatian territory not under French control after the Sun King had annexed Strasbourg in 1681.

In the 18C, low custom duties imposed on goods entering France and the possibility for Mulhouse to trade freely with foreign states, favoured the town's commercial activities and encouraged it to launch into industrial expansion.

Calvinist citadel – In 1524, the Republic's government adopted the principles of the Reformation and a little later on adhered to Calvinism. As a consequence, theatrical performances were banned, inns had to close at 10pm and the citizens' clothing had to be discreet in style and colour. However, the spirit of the new religion also had its positive aspects: it spurred industrial development and prompted original social and cultural initiatives.

Union with France – In 1792, the new French Republic imposed a commercial blockade on Mulhouse and the town opted for union with France. During the union festivities, which took place in 1798 on place de la Réunion, the flag of the city was rolled inside a case bearing the colours of the French flag and the following inscription was written on the case: *La République de Mulhouse repose dans le sein de la République française* (the Republic of Mulhouse rests in the bosom of the French Republic).

Together with the rest of Alsace, Mulhouse was German from 1870 to 1918 and from 1940 to 1944. It took the French first armoured-car division two months to completely liberate the town.

INDUSTRIAL MUSEUMS

***Musée national de l'Automobile: collection Schlumpf** ⊙ – *Entrance along avenue de Colmar.*

🖸 This fabulous collection of 500 vintage cars (not all of them are on permanent display) was gathered with passionate enthusiasm over a period of 30 years by the Schlumpf brothers, who owned a wool-spinning mill in the Thur Valley upstream of Thann.

The textile recession, social unrest, the unwise acquisition of many expensive cars led to bankruptcy and a legal judgement enabled an association to acquire the museum which was opened to the public in 1982.

The collection illustrates more than 100 years of motor-car history, from the steam-driven Jacquot of 1878 to the Citroën Xenia of the year 2000; 98 European makes and some rare, even unique specimens are displayed over an area of

Vintage cars in the car museum

17 000m²/22 322sq yd. The models are usually in working order and several belonged to celebrities such as President Poincaré (Panhard X26), King Leopold of Belgium (Bugatti 43 roadster sport) or Charlie Chaplin (Rolls Royce Phantom III limousine).

Cars are exhibited along alleyways lined with turn-of-the-century lamp-posts; many of them can be regarded as authentic works of art such is the refinement of their bodywork (Peugeot 174 saloon, 1924), the smoothness of their aerodynamic lines (Bugatti Model 46, streamlined saloon, 1933), the finish of their wheels and hubs (Gardner-Serpollet), the design of their radiator grill (Alfa Romeo saloon, 1936), the elegance of their radiator stoppers (Hispano-Suiza's stork) and the quality of their accessories (Renault NM small coupé, 1924).

The Bugatti section is something of a collection within the collection. Bugatti who settled in Molsheim in 1909 was extremely demanding regarding quality, reliability and finish (hence his 340 patents and 3 000 racing victories); this is illustrated by some 120 racing cars, sports cars and luxury cars.

The gems of this outstanding collection are two Bugatti Royales: a limousine and the Napoleon coupé, Ettore Bugatti's personal car, sometimes considered as the most prestigious car of all time.

Other makes include Panhard et Levassor (the 1893 model was the first car to be presented in a catalogue with options), Mercedes, Alfa Romeo, Rolls-Royce, Porsche, Ferrari, Gordini... The museum also follows the evolution of the three major French manufacturers before the Second World War and gives details of all the other makes which disappeared owing to the tendency to concentrate which characterized the car industry (Ravel from Besançon, Zedel from Pontarlier, Vermorel from Villefranche-sur-Saône, Clément-Bayard from Mézières).

★★★**Musée français du Chemin de fer** ⊘ – *Situated in the western part of the town.*
◉ Before starting on a tour of the railway museum, visitors can get acquainted with railways at the **Musée-express**, through models, games and interactive programmes.

The French Railways (SNCF) collection, splendidly displayed, illustrates the evolution of railways from their origin until today. Apart from engines and rolling stock, there is an important section devoted to various equipment: signals, rails, automatic coupling, shunting, level-crossing keeper's hut, swing bridge etc. The main hall invites visitors to get personally involved by means of video films, animated presentations; foot-bridges offering a view in-

Mulhouse – French Railway Museum

Musée français du Chemin de fer, Mulhouse

side carriages, pits making it possible to walk beneath engines, driver's cabins open for inspection...

The panorama of steam engines which spans more than 100 years includes famous engines such as the Saint-Pierre, built of teak, which ran between Paris and Rouen from 1844 onwards, the very fast Crampton (1852) which already reached speeds of around 120kph/75mph and the 232 U1 (1949), the last operating steam engine. The museum also boasts the drawing-room carriage of Napoleon III's aides-de-camp (1856) decorated by Viollet-le-Duc and the French President's carriage (1925) decorated by Lalique and fitted with a solid-silver washbasin... In striking contrast, the bottom of the range includes one of the fourth-class carriages of the Alsace-Lorraine line.

◉ **Musée du Sapeur-Pompier** – Housed under the same roof, the Fire Brigade Museum, devoted to the history of this dangerous and prestigious profession, displays some 20 hand pumps, the oldest dating from 1740, steam-powered fire engines, others dating from the early 20C, uniforms, weapons and a big collection of helmets. There is also a reconstruction of the fire brigade watchtower in Mulhouse and of the telephone exchange of the former fire station.

★**Electropolis: musée de l'Énergie électrique** ⊘ – *Situated in the western part of the town, Électropolis shares a vast parking area with the Musée du Chemin de Fer; a combined ticket for both museums is available.*
◉ A large masonry cube and an elliptical gallery surrounding it are the unusual setting of the exhibition showing the different stages of the production of electricity and its various uses. Many themes are dealt with: music, domestic

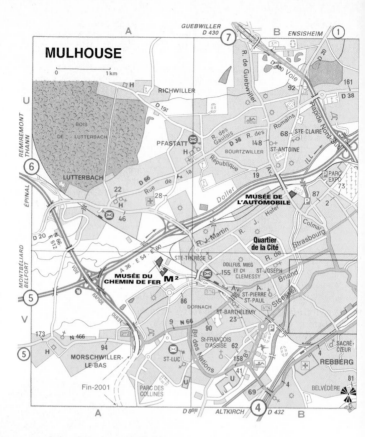

MULHOUSE

Index of street names and sights on the town plans of Mulhouse

appliances, computer science, laser, electronic toys, radio, satellites... Experiments and interactive games help to introduce the amazing world of electricity to visitors. The Maison de l'Électricité occupying one of the pavilions in the garden, gives visitors an insight into tomorrow's comfort.

★**Musée de l'Impression sur étoffes** ⊘ – The Museum of Printed Fabric is housed in a former industrial building, which once belonged to the Société Industrielle de Mulhouse. Founded in 1825 by 22 industrialists, including Koechlin, Schlumberger, Dollfus, Zuber, the **Société Industrielle de Mulhouse** aimed at promoting and spreading industrial development also set out to play a role in the intellectual and artistic life of the town by creating museums and to further education with the opening of

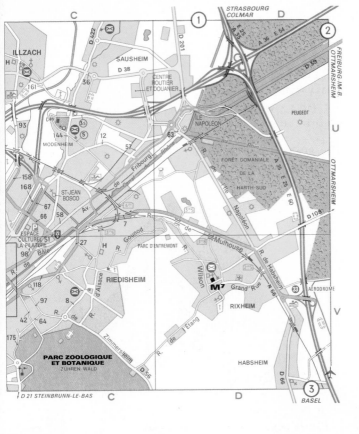

schools of chemistry, weaving, spinning and commerce (the first one of its kind in France). The Museum of Industrial Design (later to become the Museum of Printed Fabrics) was created as early as 1857; next came the Natural History Museum, the zoo, the Fine Arts Museum...

The Museum of Printed Fabric illustrates the birth and development of the industry: engraving and printing techniques are explained, and impressive machines used throughout the ages are employed for regular demonstrations.

The museum shop which reprints original motifs offers a choice of tablecloths, shawls, scarfs, handkerchiefs and various accessories, along with books and stationery. This museum and its lovely shop are a must for anyone interested in fashion or interior design or the history of decorative arts.

*Musée du Papier peint ⊘ – *In Rixheim, 6km/3.7mi E towards Basle; see town plan above.*

The Wallpaper Museum is housed in the right wing of the former headquarters of an order of Teutonic knights where, c 1790, Jean Zuber set up a wallpaper factory, which brought fame to his family. The superb **collection**** of panoramic wallpaper was exported throughout the world (but mainly to North America) during the 19C. Vast landscapes painted with fresh colours include views of Switzerland, Algeria or Bengal.

*PLACE DE LA RÉUNION, the historic centre of Mulhouse

**Hôtel de ville – Erected in 1552 of Renaissance style characteristic on the outside by artists from the Swiss cantons, which is unique in France. The either side of the cov- entrance, are a re- ties linking the Confederation. by an architect from Basle in a kind of the Rhine region and decorated the Constance area, this edifice shields bearing the arms of decorate the façade on ered steps leading to the minder of the historic city and the Swiss

Painted Façade of the Town hall in Mulhouse

On the right side of the building, you can see a grinning stone mask similar to the Klapperstein or gossips' stone weighing 12-13kg/26-28lb, which was tied to the neck of slanderers condemned to go round the town riding backwards on a donkey. This punishment was used for the last time in 1781.

The entrance of the history museum *(see OTHER MAIN SIGHTS)* is located at the foot of the steps on the right. The **council chamber** on the first floor, once the council chamber of the Republic's government, is now the municipal council chamber.

On the left side of the square, note the Poêle des Tailleurs, a building once used by the tailors' guild, and, a little further on along rue Henriette, the Poêle des Vignerons, a 16C house used by the wine-growers' guild.

Temple St-Étienne ⊘ – This neo-Gothic building has retained several 14C **stained-glass windows*** from the previous church demolished in 1858, said to be the finest in all Alsace.

Walk diagonally across the square.

On the corner of rue des Boulangers stands the oldest pharmacy in Mulhouse (1649).

Leave place de la Réunion and follow rue des Bouchers; turn right onto rue des Bons-Enfants then take the first turning on the left, rue des Franciscains.

MULHOUSE

Ancien hôtel de ville .... FY **H¹**
Musée des Beaux-Arts... FY **M⁴**
Musée de l'Impression sur étoffes .... FZ **M⁶**
Société industrielle .... FZ **N**

Index of street names and sights, see page 221-222

On your left you will see the mansion built by the Feer family (1765-70). Halfway along the street are the manufactures of printed calico, the most famous being the Cour des Chaînes inaugurated in 1763 in a 16C building. There is an interesting wall decorated by Fabio Rieti, a contemporary artist, which illustrates the history of Mulhouse.

Continue along rue de la Loi.

Note to your right and on the corner of rue Ste-Claire, a manufacturing complex dating from the 18C, which replaced, as it is often the case in Mulhouse, an older property owned by local aristocrats.

Take passage des Augustins then the first street on the right followed by rue Henriette on the left; go through passage Teutonique on the right and turn left onto rue Guillaume-Tell where the Musée des Beaux-Arts is situated. The street leads back to place de la Réunion.

THE INDUSTRIAL TOWN

The Nouveau Quartier – *SE of the historic centre, beyond place de la République.* A new residential complex intended for young industrialists was built from 1827 onwards on the edge of the old town centre. Known as the **Nouveau Quartier**, it consists of arcaded buildings modelled on those of rue de Rivoli in Paris, surrounding a central triangular garden, the square de la Bourse; the building of the Société Industrielle de Mulhouse, erected in 1827 and intended to house the chamber of commerce and the stock exchange, stands along the small side of the triangle.

Working-class garden-cities – *On both sides of the Ill diversion canal.* Social urban planning launched by the Société Industrielle was a novelty in Europe. From 1855 onwards, the Cité de Mulhouse and the Nouvelle Cité were built on both sides of the Ill diversion canal. Each family had lodgings with a separate entrance and a small garden. A leasing system enabled workers to become property owners. The availability of public services was remarkable for the time. The Quartier de la Cité, which has been preserved round the Église St-Joseph, is worth a visit; rue des Oiseaux is the main street with passages branching off. The small houses (although many have been transformed and enlarged) and their carefully tended plots are an eloquent illustration of the ideals which once united industrial growth and popular welfare.

OTHER MAIN SIGHTS

★★Musée historique ⊙ – Housed in the former town hall, the rich and varied collections of this museum, carefully displayed to take into account the building and its past, illustrate the history of the town and daily life in the region over the past 6 000 years (archaeological collections). The first floor, which was the official floor of the government of the Republic, houses the medieval collections.

On the second floor, there are various objects of historic interest: paintings, manuscripts, weapons, furniture... including the original Klapperstein and the **silvergilt cup** offered by the town to the representative of the French government in 1798 when Mulhouse was united with France. Daily life in the 18C and 19C is illustrated by the reconstruction of various drawing rooms; note an unusual bed concealed as a painted cabinet and a large blue-and-white-ceramic stove.

◙ The former **corn loft** (access from the second floor across a footbridge built in the 18C) contains a collection of toys: dolls' houses, outfits, crockery, games. The folk-art gallery houses reconstructions of regional interiors (kitchen and bedroom from the Sungdau area), pottery, woodcarvings etc. Note the monumental mechanical piano dating from the beginning of the 20C and an 18C sledge.

Musée des Beaux-Arts ⊙ – *Just off place de la Réunion.*
The Fine Arts Museum contains works by Brueghel the Younger, Teniers, Ruysdael, Boucher and other 17C and 18C painters; 19C landscapes and mythological scenes (Boudin, Courbet, Bouguereau); paintings by Alsatian artists (nudes and portraits by **Henner** 1829-1905, landscapes and still-life paintings by **Lehmann** 1873-1953, bright compositions by **Walch** 1896-1948).

★★Parc zoologique et botanique ⊙ – *S of the town centre, on the edge of the Rebberg district.*
◙ This zoological and botanical garden, covering an area of 25ha/62 acres and sheltering more than 1 000 animals, aims at preserving, breeding and studying rare and endangered species by collaborating with other zoos and various agencies. This policy was launched with the arrival in 1980 of lemurs from Madagascar, followed by Prince Alfred's deer, of which only a small number had survived on two Philippine islands, then white-backed tapirs, wolves, panthers and rare primates from South America (tamarins, capuchins) housed in a building specially adapted for them in 1993.

Gibbons from China and Vietnam are a typical example of an endangered species placed under the protection of the park. The spectacular regression of this primate in its natural environment can be explained by deforestation and excessive hunting. These agile animals, with their characteristic cry, are extremely popular inmates of the zoo. Other interesting animals include sea-lions, jackass penguins, pythons... The large botanical collection is an array of rare species in beautifully landscaped areas.

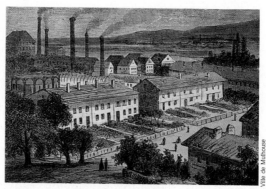

19C Garden city

Population 5 000
Michelin map 87 folds 5 and 15 or 242 fold 31

Irish monks arrived in the area in the 7C to complete the Christianisation of Alsace and founded an abbey which gave its name to the village growing in its shadow (Munster comes from the Latin word for monastery). The village developed into a town, freed itself from the authority of the abbots and formed, with neighbouring villages, a cultural as well as a geographical entity spanning the Grande Fecht and Petite Fecht valleys and known as the Munster Valley. The region lives on its traditional cheese industry and on the textile industry introduced in the area in the 18C by André Hartmann.

Further up the Fecht Valley, to the south of Munster, the rounded summit of the Petit Ballon, also known as **Kahler Wasen**, stands in an area of high pastures where herds spend the summer and Munster cheese is made.

Eating out

MODERATE

Restaurant des Cascades – *6 chemin de Saegmatt – 68140 Stosswihr – 6km/3.75mi W of Munster on D 417 and minor road –* ☎ *03 89 77 44 74 – closed Jan, 1 week in Oct, Mon except Jul-Aug and Tue – 100/200F.* Tucked away by a stream on the route des Crêtes, this restaurant is well known locally for its *tartes flambées*, cooked on a wood fire, which attract crowds at weekends. Large garden with animals.

Where to stay

MID-RANGE

Hôtel La Verte Vallée – *10 r. A.-Hartmann – parc de la Fecht –* ☎ *03 89 77 15 15 – closed 5-25 Jan –* 🅿 *– 107 rooms 460/630F –* ☎ *63F – restaurant 95/270F.* A relaxed stay is guaranteed is this modern hotel, whether lazing by the two indoor pools, getting fit in the gym, relaxing in the sauna or bronzing in the solarium – and all this in a peaceful setting. Carefully prepared cuisine and a friendly welcome.

TOWN WALK

The Grand'Rue is a lively shopping street with attractive boutiques. The fine Protestant church was built in the 1920s in neo-Romanesque style.

The only remaining wing of the former abbots' palace, situated south of the market square, is now the headquarters of the **Parc naturel régional des Ballons des Vosges**. The **Maison du Parc** ⊙ suggests various activities to discover this fascinating environment and presents a permanent exhibition covering 600m^2/718sq yd and illustrating the main feature of the park with the help of models, dioramas, video films and interactive terminals.

★★VALLÉE DE MUNSTER

5 Round tour from Munster

55km/34mi – allow 3hr – local map see Parc naturel régional des BALLONS DES VOSGES

From Munster drive NW along D 417 then turn right onto D 5bis which winds its way up to Hohrodberg.

Hohrodberg – This summer resort spreads along sunny slopes which afford an extended **view**★★ to the south-west of Munster, its valley and, from left to right, the summits rising in the background from the Petit Ballon to the Hohneck.

🚶 During the climb, stop by the picnic area and walk along the road as far as the bend to admire the surrounding area. A brochure available from the tourist office suggests three marked footpaths: **Sentier de Rosskopf** (fauna and flora), **Sentier de Katzenstein** (landscapes and economic life) and **Sentier du Barrenkopf** (traces of the First World War).

Le Collet du Linge – On the right-hand side of the road lies a German military cemetery.

Le Linge – *30min.* Memorial and museum.
In 1915, following fierce fighting, French troops secured their position on the western slopes of the Linge and Schratzmaennele, close to German troops which occupied the summit. Walk to the right to reach the summit of the Linge, quite close, through what is left of the German position and of the trenches dug out of sandstone.
Continue along D 11 which soon overlooks the Orbey Valley.

Col du Wettstein – The cemetery contains the graves of 3 000 French soldiers.
D 48 then runs down into the valley of the Petite Fecht and joins up with D 417 near Soultzeren.

The road winds up towards the Col de la Schlucht offering better and better views first of the Fecht Valley and then of the Petite Fecht Valley. The Hohneck can be seen to the south. The road leading to Lac Vert *(see Route des CRÊTES)* branches off on the right just before a bend. The road then runs through a forested area, affording glimpses of the Plaine d'Alsace and of the Black Forest and finally overlooks the splendid glacial cirque where the Petite Fecht takes its source.

Col de la Schlucht – At the pass, D 417 joins up with the Route des Crêtes *(see Route des CRÊTES).*

Jardin d'altitude du Haut-Chitelet – *See Route des CRÊTES.*

★★★**Le Hohneck** – *See Route des CRÊTES.*

Le Markstein – *See GUEBWILLER: Guebwiller Valley.*
Turn left onto the Route des Crêtes.

As you pass beneath a ski lift, you will catch a glimpse of the Lac de la Lauch below, of the Guebwiller Valley and of the Plaine d'Alsace in the distance.

Turn back and follow D 27.

After a short climb, the road leaves the high pastures and offers a fine view on the left of the Hohneck massif. The road runs down through the forest where beeches take over from firs.

★**Schnepfenried** – This popular winter sports resort is equipped with several ski lifts. There is a beautiful **panorama**★ of the Hohneck massif to the north with the Schiessrothried dam and lake lower down on the slopes of the mountain; Munster can also be seen to the right.

⬛ From the summit of Schnepfenried (alt 1258m/4 127ft), just south of the resort, which is accessible on foot *(1hr there and back)*, there is a panoramic **view**★ of the range from the Grand Ballon to the Brézouard, of the Fecht Valley, of the Black Forest and, when the weather is perfectly clear, of the Bern Oberland.

In Metzeral, take D 10^{VI}; turn right 1km/0.6mi further on, cross the river and leave the car.

The footpath *(3km/1.9mi, about 1hr)* rises through the wild glacial valley of the Wormsa and reaches the Lac de Fischbœdle.

★**Lac de Fischbœdle** – Alt 790m/2 592ft. This almost circular lake, barely 100m/328ft in diameter, is one of the most picturesque lakes of the Vosges region. It was created c 1850 by Jacques Hartmann, the Munster industrialist. Rocks and firs reflecting in the water form a splendid setting. The Wasserfelsen stream supplying the lake forms a lovely waterfall at the time of the thaw.

The River Fecht winds through the valley

Schiessrothried Lake

Lac de Schiessrothried – *1hr on foot there and back along the winding path starting on the right as you reach Lake Fischbœdle. It is directly accessible by car from Muhlbach along D 310.*

The lake, which covers 5ha/12 acres, now a reservoir, lies at an altitude of 920m/3 018ft, at the foot of the Hohneck summit.

Return to Metzeral and turn left onto D 10.

Muhlbach-sur-Munster – The **Musée de la Schlitte** ⊘ stands on the village square, opposite the train station; which shows a reconstruction of the traditional natural environment in which sledges would carry timber from the dense forests of the Vosges mountains.

Luttenbach-près-Munster – Voltaire stayed here several times in 1754, right at the heart of the forest.

Return to Munster along the D 10 which follows the River Fecht.

VALLÉE DE LA FECHT

⑥ From Munster to Colmar

20km/12.4mi – local map see Parc naturel régional des BALLONS DES VOSGES

From Munster drive E along D 10.

Gunsbach – Albert Schweitzer spent part of his childhood in this village where his father was the vicar until his death in 1925. Schweitzer regularly came back here and had a house built after he won the Goethe prize in 1928; this is now a **museum** ⊘ housing furniture, books, photos, music, sermons and other mementoes of the great man.

There is an interesting **walking itinerary** *(4km/2.5mi, about 2hr 30min)* on the theme of "water" along the banks of the Flecht lined with explanatory panels. The southern slopes of the Flecht Valley are entirely forested.

In Wirh-au-Val, cross the Fecht and D 417.

Soultzbach-les-Bains – This peaceful medieval city, known for its spa, has a wealth of timber-framed flower-decked houses. A **historic trail** *(2km/1.2mi, 1hr 30min, brochure available from the tourist office)*, lined with 16 information panels, acquaints visitors with the history and traditions of the village.

The 17C **Chapelle Ste-Catherine** contains two interesting paintings (1738) by Franz-Georg Hermann, *Our Lady of Solace* and *St Nicholas of Tolentino*. The isolated parish **church** ⊘, extensively restored, houses three remarkable gilt **altars**★★ in carved wood made between 1720 and 1740. In the chancel, on the left, there is a fine 15C tabernacle carried by St Christopher. The Callinet organ dates from 1833.

Turn left onto D 10 towards Turckheim.

★**Turckheim** – See Turckheim.

★★★**Colmar** – *See COLMAR.*

★MASSIF DU PETIT BALLON

⑦ From Munster to Le Markstein

40km/25mi – about 4hr 30min – local map see Parc naturel régional des BALLONS DES VOSGES

Drive out of Munster along D 417 towards Colmar then turn right 5km/3mi further on and follow D 40.

Beyond Soultzbach, a scenic road *(D 43)* on the right follows the verdant pastures and forests of the Krebsbach Valley.

In **Wasserbourg**, turn onto a forest road leading to an inn *(Auberge Ried)* where there is a fine view of the Hohneck summit. After going through a wood, the road comes out into the open again. The Kahler Wasen farm-restaurant stands on pastureland and the **view★** extends down the Fecht Valley towards Turckheim and, beyond, across the Plaine d'Alsace.

★★**Petit Ballon** – Alt 1 267m/4 157ft. *1hr 15min on foot there and back from the Kahler Wasen farm-restaurant.*

🔲 The **panorama** is superb: the Plaine d'Alsace, the Kaiserstuhl hills and the Black Forest to the east; the Grand Ballon massif to the south; the valleys of the two Fecht rivers to the north and west.

Drive down via the Boenlesgrab pass and forest road.

The road runs steeply down, offering a fine view of the Lauch Valley on the right. Beware of the two hairpin bends just before Lautenbach.

> **SAY CHEESE**
>
> **Ferme-auberge Kahlenwasen** – *68380 Metzeral – at the foot of Petit Ballon* – ☎ *03 89 77 32 49 – closed Nov-Easter and Wed* – 🍴 – *88F.* This farm has a good reputation. The simple building dates from the 1920s, and the dining room is pleasant in summer and decorated with old agricultural tools, and the terrace has a lovely view over the Alsace plain. Cheese is the house speciality. A few plain rooms.

★**Lautenbach** – *See GUEBWILLER: Guebwiller Valley.*

Le Markstein – *See GUEBWILLER: Guebwiller Valley.*

THE VOSGES SUMMITS
Le Donon 1 009m/3 310ft
Champ du Feu 1 100m/3 609ft
Ballon de Servance 1 216m/3 990ft
Ballon d'Alsace 1 250m/4 101ft
Petit Ballon or Kahler Wasen 1 267m/4 157ft
Le Hohneck 1 362m/4 469ft
Grand Ballon or Ballon de Guebwiller 1 424m/4 672ft, highest summit.

Église de MURBACH★★

Michelin map 87 fold 18 or 242 fold 35

The village of Murbach, lying in a remote wooded valley, nestles round the former abbey church of the famous Murbach Abbey, whose Romanesque style is characteristic of the Rhine region.

Founded in 727 the abbey was generously endowed by Count Eberhard, a powerful Alsatian lord and by the 9C it was already rich and famous; its library was remarkable and it owned property in more than 200 places from Worms to Lucerne. "As proud as the Murbach hound" soon became a popular saying, referring to the black hound decorating the coat of arms of the abbey. From the 12C onwards, the abbots of Murbach were also princes of the Holy Roman Empire and the monks were all aristocrats. Considering the number of castles under its control, the abbey was certainly a powerful feudal lord and its mint worked from 1544 to 1666. In 1789, the peasants of the St-Amarin Valley, wishing to shake off the abbey's authority, plundered the castle at Guebwiller, where the abbey had been transferred in 1759.

> **GOOD VALUE**
>
> **Auberge de l'Abbaye** – *20 r. de Guebwiler – 68530 Murbach* – ☎ *03 89 74 13 77 – closed Feb, Tue evening and Wed – 90/ 130F.* The dining room is reached by a staircase decorated by firebacks. The menu is classic rather than regional, but *tartes flambées* are served on Friday and Sunday evenings. Terrace and garden.

CHURCH *15min*

The 12C church is now reduced to the chancel and the transept surmounted by two towers, the nave having been demolished in 1738.

The **east end**★★ is the most remarkable part of the edifice. Its flat wall, which projects slightly, is richly decorated in its upper section. A gallery with 17 different colonnettes can be seen above two tiers of windows.

The tympanum of the south doorway, with its low-relief carvings depicting two lions facing each other framed by palmettes and foliated mouldings, is reminiscent of certain oriental works. Inside, in the chapel situated to the left of the chancel, lies the sarcophagus of the seven monks killed by Hungarians in 926. A recess in the south transept contains the 14C recumbent figure of Count Eberhard.

On leaving the abbey church, walk (note the Stations of the Cross below) to the Chapelle Notre-Dame-de-Lorette (1693) to enjoy views of the church and the surroundings through trees and shrubs.

EXCURSION

Buhl – *3km/1.9mi E along D 40*. The large neo-Romanesque **church** of this lively village (metalworks and plastics) houses one of the few sizeable painted triptychs in Alsace (7m/23ft wide) to be found outside a museum. The **Buhl altarpiece**★★ was probably made c 1500 by artists from the Schongauer School *(see COLMAR: Musée d'Unterlinden)*. The superb central Crucifixion is framed by four scenes depicting Christ's Passion. On the other side, the Last Judgement is represented between episodes of the Virgin's life.

The church in Murbach

NANCY ★★★

Conurbation 310 628
Michelin map 62 folds 4 and 5 or 242 folds 17 and 18

The former capital of the dukes of Lorraine offers visitors the elegant harmony of its 18C town planning, its aristocratic architecture and beautiful vistas, including the most famous place Stanislas, a World Heritage site since 1983. In addition, the town has retained a remarkable ensemble of buildings erected at the turn of the 20C, which are fine examples of the decorative style of the **École de Nancy** *(see p 233)*.

Nancy is also an important intellectual centre with several scientific and technical institutes, its higher school of mining engineering, its national centres of forestry research and study, as well as its cultural centre and theatre housed in a former tobacco manufacture.

HISTORICAL NOTES

Medieval beginnings – The foundation of Nancy goes back to the 11C. The site chosen by Gérard d'Alsace, the first hereditary duke of Lorraine, to build his capital was a piece of land flanked by two marshes where he had a fortress erected. Nancy's only real advantage was that it was located at the centre of the Duke's land. At first the new capital consisted of the ducal castle and a few monasteries.

In 1228, Nancy was destroyed by fire and rebuilt almost immediately. In the 14C, what is now the old town was surrounded by a wall of which only the Porte de la Craffe has survived.

In 1476, Charles the Bold, Duke of Burgundy, occupied Lorraine which was lying between Burgundy and Flanders (both belonging to him) but the following year, Duke **René II** returned to Nancy and stirred up a rebellion. Charles then lay siege in front of the town; he was killed at St-Nicolas-de-Port *(see ST-NICOLAS-DE-PORT)* and his body was found later in a frozen lake, half eaten by wolves.

Croix de Lorraine – The distinctive Croix de Lorraine, with two crosspieces, was a reminder of Duke René's illustrious ancestors, his grandfather good King René, Duke of Anjou and Count of Provence, and a more remote ancestor and founder of the dynasty, the brother of Godefroy de Bouillon who led the first crusade and became king of Jerusalem. Used as a distinguishing mark by René II's troops on the battlefield of Nancy, the cross later became a patriotic symbol *(see Colline de SION-VAUDÉMONT)*. In July 1940 it was adopted as the emblem of the Free French Forces.

The dukes of Lorraine and their city – Gradually becoming more powerful, the dukes of Lorraine set out to develop their capital city. A new palace was erected and, at the end of the 16C, Duke Charles III built a new town south of the old one. At the same time, Nancy became an important religious centre and, in the space of 40 years, 13 monasteries were founded. However, the **Thirty Years War** stunted Nancy's economic growth as illustrated by **Jacques Callot**'s engravings entitled Misfortunes of War. When peace returned, Duke Leopold undertook the building of the present cathedral designed by **Germain Boffrand** (1667-1754), who also built several mansions north of place Stanislas.

The gateway (porterie) of the Ducal palace

Stanislas the Magnificent – In the 18C, François III exchanged the duchy of Lorraine for the duchy of Tuscany. Louis XV, King of France, seized the opportunity and gave Lorraine to his father-in-law, **Stanislas Leszczynski**, the deposed king of Poland, on the understanding that the duchy would naturally become part of the kingdom of France after Stanislas' death. Stanislas was a peaceful man who devoted himself to his adopted land, embellished his new capital and made it into a symbol of 18C charm and elegance with the magnificent square which bears his name in its centre. He chose artists of genius such as Jean Lamour, who made Nancy's superb wrought-iron railings.

Eating out

MODERATE

Les Nouveaux Abattoirs – *4 bd Austrasie* – ☏ *03 83 35 46 25* – *closed 1-22 Aug, Sat, Sun and public holidays* – *96/270F.* This rather sombre-looking restaurant in a dull area away from the city centre has dark, old-fashioned dining rooms – but don't let all this put you off! The meat is of excellent quality, which is what gives this authentic restaurant its high reputation.

Les Pissenlits – *25 bis r. des Ponts* – ☏ *03 83 37 43 97* – *closed 1-15 Aug, Sun and Mon* – *99/148F.* There's always a crowd in this bistro near the market, and with good reason: the atmosphere is relaxed, the cuisine innovative and diverse, and the decor is very pleasant, with its closely packed tables, Majorelle furniture and daily specials on the blackboard. Join the crowd!

MID-RANGE

Le V Four – *10 r. St-Michel* – ☏ *03 83 32 49 48* – *closed 23 Dec-3 Jan, Mon lunchtime and Sun* – *booking advisable* – *103/154F.* It may be small, but this restaurant in the heart of the old city is popular among the locals, who appreciate its simple modern decor. The cooking is also contemporary. Terrace.

Le Foy – *1 pl. Stanislas* – ☏ *03 83 32 21 44* – *closed mid-July to beginning Aug, Sun evening, Tue evening and Wed* – *120/180F.* Climb the lovely stone staircase to reach this first-floor restaurant above the café-brasserie of the same name in place Stanislas. The food is good and served in generous portions. Rustic decor with exposed beams.

Excelsior Flo – *50 r. H.-Poincaré* – ☏ *03 83 35 24 57* – *159F.* One of the bastions of the Nancy school of decorative arts, whose artists were asked to design its early-20C decor. The result is a remarkable example of its kind, not to be missed, and the dining room is a listed monument. Brasserie-style cooking and efficient service.

Le Gastrolâtre – *1 pl. Vaudémont* – ☏ *03 83 35 51 94* – *closed 1 week at Easter, 13-31 Aug, 1 week at Christmas, Sun and Mon* – *185/300F.* This popular bistro just behind place Stanislas is run with a master's hand by a media boss. Its mouth-watering menu and colourful cuisine combine local flavours with those from the south of France.

LUXURY

Le Capucin Gourmand – *31 r. Gambetta* – ☏ *03 83 35 26 98* – *closed 1-22 Aug, February school holidays, Sun evening Sep-Jun, and Mon* – *220/320F.* This restaurant near place Stanislas has had a complete facelift under its young owner: the decor is decidedly modern and fairly spectacular, with its superb chandelier, its blue walls and round tables. Much appreciated by the chic clientele of Nancy.

Where to stay

MODERATE

Chambre d'hôte Ferme de Montheu – *54770 Dommartin-sous-Amance* – *10 km/6.25mi NE of Nancy, Sarreguemines and Agincourt direction* – ☏ *03 83 31 17 37* – ⊱ – *5 rooms 200/250F* – *evening meal 85/95F.* This working farm in the middle of the country has lovely uninterrupted views, apart from a nearby high-tension power line. But that's soon forgotten in the peace of the simple rooms with their old furniture. Evening meal by arrangement.

MID-RANGE

Hôtel Crystal – *5 r. Chanzy* – ☏ *03 83 17 54 00* – *closed 29 Dec-2 Jan* – *58 rooms 400/530F* – ⊐ *48F.* This entirely renovated hotel near the station is a good place to stay in Nancy. Its modern, spacious rooms have been nicely arranged and decorated, and feel welcoming.

LUXURY

Grand Hôtel de la Reine – *2 pl. Stanislas* – ☏ *03 83 35 03 01* – *48 rooms from 830F* – ⊐ *80F* – *restaurant 180/370F.* A superb 18C palace on place Stanislas which has retained all its former splendour: mouldings, parquet floors, superb chandeliers and old furniture all contribute to the luxury. Even if some find its decor a little outdated, it remains nevertheless the best hotel in town.

On the town

Blitz Café – *76 r. St-Julien* – ☎ *03 83 32 77 20* – *Mon 2-9pm, Tue 11am-9pm, Wed-Sat 11am-2am – closed Aug, 25 Dec and 1 Jan.* An extraordinary place, born out of the marriage between a trendy fashion boutique and a former café, where the chairs are on the ceiling and the bar is made out of old shoes. Friday and Saturday evenings are hosted by a DJ, and various theme evenings take place at other times each month.

L'Arquebuse – *13 r. Héré* – ☎ *03 83 32 11 99* – *Tue-Sun 6.30pm-4am, until 5am Fri and Sat.* This high-class bar with a refined decor has a good view of place Stanislas. A wide choice of cocktails with atmospheric music and disco, attracting a mixed clientele of smart students and businessmen.

L'Échanson – *9 r. de la Primatiale* – ☎ *03 83 35 51 58* – *Tue-Fri noon-2.30pm, 4.30-9.30pm, Sat 10am-9.30pm – closed Sun and Mon.* A pleasant little wine bar which also serves as the local bistro. A dozen or so wines are available by the glass, which can be accompanied by a savoury snack, and the cellar comprises 250 different wines for sale.

Le Pierre qui mousse – *5 terrasse de la Pépinière* – ☎ *03 83 30 68 79* – *Sun and Mon 3pm-1am, Tue-Thu 11am-1am, Fri 11am-2am, Sat 3pm-2am – closed 25 Dec and 1 Jan.* A maze of passages among a tangle of beams and tree trunks with rustic wooden stools add up to a fairy-tale atmosphere in this bar. There is an impressive selection of beers from all over the world, in particular from Belgium. Shaded terrace in summer, with seating for over 150.

Le Vertigo – *29 r. de la Visitation* – ☎ *03 83 32 71 97* – *Mon-Thu 11am-4am, Fri-Sat 11am-5am – closed Aug and public holidays.* A fashionable bar which organises café-theatre evenings (stand-up comics, impressionists) and concerts (hip-hop, groove, rock). It is often packed, and the drink flows freely, mainly beer and cocktails.

Shopping

Maison des Sœurs Macarons – *21 r. Gambetta* – ☎ *03 83 32 24 25* – *Mon-Sat 9am-noon, 2-7pm.* The secret recipe for macaroons has been handed down within the family since the 18C. Other Lorraine specialities are available here: *bergamots* (a sweet made with essence of bergamot), *Berg'amours* (crystallized fruits), *perles de Lorraine* (crystallized fruits with plum liqueur centres), *Babas du Roi*, gingerbread etc.

Modern times – Between 1871 and 1918, Nancy welcomed refugees from the nearby regions occupied by the Germans and a modern town developed next to the three already existing – the old town, the dukes' town and Stanislas' town. The new industrial town expanded rapidly and its population doubled in the space of 50 years.

In 1914, Nancy was narrowly saved from occupation but was shelled and bombed throughout the war.

Occupied in 1940, Nancy was liberated in September 1944 by General Patton's army, with the help of the Résistance.

LORRAINE'S CAPITAL CITY

★★★**Place Stanislas** – The collaboration between the architect, **Emmanuel Héré**, and the craftsman who made the railings, **Jean Lamour**, resulted in a superb architectural ensemble (1751-60) characterised by the perfect harmony of its proportions, layout and detail. Place Stanislas forms a rectangle with canted corners, measuring 124m/136yd by 106m/116yd. Louis XV's statue which stood in its centre was destroyed during the Revolution and in 1831 a statue of Stanislas replaced it and the square was renamed after him.

Wrought-iron craftsmanship on Place Stanislas

R.Mattes/MICHELIN

The partly gilt wrought-iron **railings**, a model of delicacy and elegance, decorate the canted corners of the square as well as the beginning of rue Stanislas and rue Ste-Catherine. Each railing on the north side forms a triple portico framing the Poseidon and Amphitrite fountains by Guibal, a sculptor from Nîmes.

The square is surrounded by five tall **pavilions** and two one-storey pavilions; this emphasises the impression of space and harmony. The façades designed by Emmanuel Héré are elegant, graceful and symmetrical without being monotonous. The wrought-iron balconies by Lamour enhance the richness and elegance of the ensemble.

★**Arc de Triomphe** – This deep triumphal arch, built between 1754 and 1756 in honour of Louis XV, is modelled on Septimus Severus' arch in Rome. The decoration of the main façade facing place Stanislas is a glorification of war and peace, both aspects of Louis XV's reign.

On the park side, to the right, there is a monument dedicated to Héré and on the left a monument dedicated to Callot.

Place d'Alliance – Designed by Héré, the square is lined with 18C mansions and adorned with a fountain by Cyfflé, commemorating the alliance signed by Louis XV and Maria-Theresa of Austria in 1756.

Hôtel de ville ⊘ – The town hall was erected between 1752 and 1755. The pediment is decorated with the coat of arms of Stanislas Leszczynski: Polish eagle, Lithuanian knight, Leszczynski buffalo.

The staircase is enhanced by a handrail and banisters by Jean Lamour. It leads to the Salon Carré adorned with frescoes by Girardet then to the Grand Salon, inaugurated by Empress Eugénie in 1866, followed by the Salon de l'Impératrice. These rooms offer a splendid vista which includes place Stanislas, place de la Carrière and the Palais du Gouvernement.

★**Place de la Carrière** – This elongated square dates from the time of the dukes of Lorraine; originally used for cavalry drills, it was remodelled by Héré and is now lined with beautiful 18C mansions. Fountains decorate the corners and at each end there are railings by Lamour, adorned with lanterns.

★**Palais du Gouverneur** – Facing the Arc de Triomphe across place du Général-de-Gaulle and place de la Carrière, this edifice is the former residence of the governors of Lorraine. The peristyle is linked to the other buildings of the square by an ionic **colonnade**★ surmounted by a balustrade decorated with vases. The columns are separated by busts of mythological characters.

★★**Palais ducal** – Dating from the second half of the 13C, the palace was in ruins when René II had it rebuilt after his victory over Charles the Bold of Burgundy.

In the 16C, Duke Antoine had the Porterie (gateway) completed together with the Galerie des Cerfs (Deer Gallery). In 1792, the palace was ransacked and skilfully restored in 1850. The northern part was entirely rebuilt.

The plain façade overlooking Grande-Rue enhances the elegant and rich decoration of the **Porterie**★★. Above this remarkable gate, in a mixture of Flamboyant-Gothic and Renaissance style, stands the equestrian statue (reconstructed) of Antoine de Lorraine surmounted by a Flamboyant gable.

At first-floor level, three balconies decorated with a Flamboyant balustrade are supported by carved corbels.

The former Ducal palace houses the very interesting Historical Museum of Lorraine.

★**Église Notre-Dame-de-Bon-Secours** – *Avenue de Strasbourg.*
Built in 1738 for Stanislas by Emmanuel Héré, on the site of René II's chapel commemorating his victory over Charles the Bold (1476), this church is a well-known place of pilgrimage. Note the Baroque west front.

The richly decorated interior includes carved confessionals in Louis XV style, railings by Jean Lamour and a splendid Rocaille pulpit. The chancel contains **Stanislas' tomb**★ and the monument carved by Vassé for the heart of Marie Leszczynska, Louis XV's wife, on the right-hand side and, on the left, the **mausoleum of Catherine Opalinska**★, Stanislas' wife.

ÉCOLE DE NANCY

★★**Musée de l'École de Nancy** ⊘ – Housed in an opulent residence from the turn of the 20C, this museum offers a remarkable insight into the renewal movement in the field of decorative arts which took place in Nancy between 1885 and 1914 and became known as the **École de Nancy** *(see p 57)*. Finding its inspiration in nature, this movement blossomed under the leadership of **Émile Gallé**.

The museum contains an important collection of exhibits characteristic of this movement: carved and inlaid furniture by Émile Gallé, Louis Majorelle, Eugène Vallin, Jacques Gruber and Émile André; book bindings, posters and drawings by Prouvé, Martin, Collin and Lurçat; glassware by Gallé, the Daum brothers and Muller; ceramics also by Gallé as well as by Bussière and Mougin; stained glass by Gruber.

NANCY

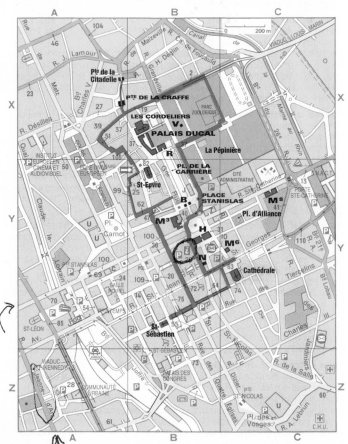

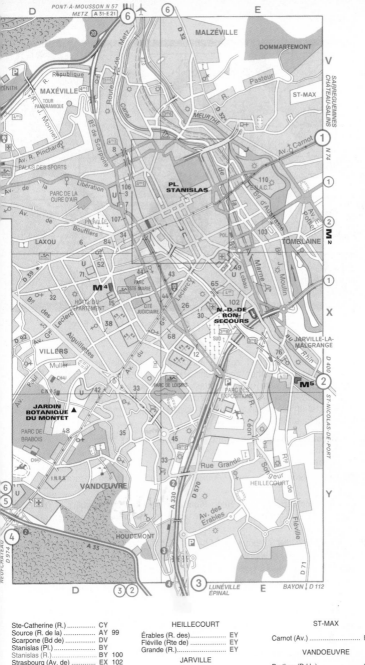

D.Thierry/DIAF

Musée de l'École de Nancy – Art Nouveau window by Henri Bergé

Several complete furnished rooms, including a splendid **dining room** by Vallin (painted ceiling and leather wallcovering with delicate floral motifs by Prouvé) show the changing styles of middle-class interiors at the turn of the 20C. On the first floor, there is an interesting bathroom decorated with ceramics by Chaplet, a businessman's office comprising leatherwork with floral motifs, seats, a bookcase and a monumental filing cabinet.

Art Nouveau architecture in Nancy – Much of Nancy's architecture (commercial buildings, villas, houses) was influenced by the Art Nouveau movement. Interesting examples are listed below:

– **Brasserie Excelsior** *(70 rue Henri-Poincaré)*, built in 1910 and decorated by Majorelle.

– **Chamber of commerce** *(40 rue Henri-Poincaré)*, designed by members of the École de Nancy in 1908, with wrought-iron work by Majorelle and stained glass by Gruber.

– **Maison Weissenburger** *(1 boulevard Charles V)*, built for himself by the architect in 1904 with decorations and wrought-iron work by Majorelle.

– **House** *(86 rue Stanislas)* built in 1906 by Eugène Vallin.

– **Building of the regional newspaper** *L'Est Républicain (5 avenue Foch)*, dating from 1912.

– **BNP bank** *(9 rue Chanzy)*, built in 1910, wrought-iron work by Majorelle.

– **Shop** *(2 rue Bénit)*, dating from 1900-01, the first metal-framed building to be erected; the stained glass is the work of Gruber.

– **Block of flats** *(42-44 rue St-Dizier)* built in 1902 by Georges Biet and Eugène Vallin.

– **Crédit Lyonnais building** *(7 bis rue St-Georges)* with stained glass by Gruber (1901).

– **Semi-detached houses** *(92-92 bis quai Claude-le-Lorrain)* built by Émile André in 1903.

– **Villa Majorelle** *(1 rue Louis-Majorelle – not open to the public)*.
This house, originally named Villa Jika, was designed in 1899 by the Parisian architect Henri Sauvage (1873-1932) and built in 1901 for Louis Majorelle. Originally, it stood in a large park on the edge of town. It is possible to walk through the garden surrounding the villa.

– **House of the printer Jules Bergeret** *(24 rue Lionnois)*, built in 1903-04 and decorated with stained glass by Gruber and Janin.

A brochure entitled "École de Nancy, itinéraire Art Nouveau" *(available from the tourist office)* suggests five itineraries which will help you discover the town's architectural heritage. Audio-guided tours of Art Nouveau districts are also available *(apply to the tourist office, cost 35F, deposit 300F)*.

OLD TOWN AND NEW TOWN

The Old Town is the historic heart of the city, centred on place St-Epvre. When it extended outside its original gates, the New Town was born. *Brochures are available from the tourist office to help you make the most of your tour of the town.*

Basilique St-Epvre – Built in the 19C, in neo-Gothic style, this imposing church is dedicated to a 6C bishop of Toul. Its elegant west front is preceded by a monumental staircase (a present from the emperor of Austria). The roof was blown off during the severe storm of December 1999.

Turn right onto rue de la Charité then right again onto rue du Cheval-Blanc.

The **Hôtel de Lillebonne** *(no 12 rue de la Source)*, with its fine Renaissance staircase, houses the American library. Next door at no 10, note the unusual doorway of the Hôtel du Marquis de Ville, decorated with a bearded head. Rue de la Monnaie on the left (the Hôtel de la Monnaie at no 1 was built by Boffrand) leads to place de La-Fayette adorned with a statue of Joan of Arc by Frémiet, a replica of the statue which can be seen in Paris.

Follow rue Callot to Grande-Rue: on the corner note the 17C turret. Retrace your steps and turn left. Follow rue St-Dizier then turn right on place Henri-Mengin.

Église St-Sébastien – This hall-church is the masterpiece of the architect Jenesson; consecrated in 1732, it has a striking concave Baroque façade★ decorated with four large low-relief carvings. Inside, the three naves are surmounted by unusual flattened vaulting resting on massive Ionic columns. Eight huge windows let light into the church. The chancel has retained some elegant woodwork. The side altars are the work of Vallin (École de Nancy).

Walk back and take rue de la Primatiale opposite, which leads to place Mgr-Ruch on the left.

Cathédrale – This imposing edifice was erected during the first half of the 18C. Inside, the superb railings of the chapels are the work of Jean Lamour and François Jeanmaire, and the graceful Virgin and Child which can be seen in the apse was carved by Bagard in the 17C. The sacristy houses the **treasury** ⊙ containing, among others, the ring, the chalice, the paten, the comb and the evangelistary of St Gauzelin, who was bishop of Toul during the first half of the 10C.

Follow rue St-Georges on the left and turn right onto rue des Dominicains.

Maison des Adam – *57 rue des Dominicains.*– This is the elegant home of the Adam family, who were renowned sculptors in the 18C and decorated the house themselves.

Walk to place Stanislas then along the Pépinière on your right.

La Pépinière – This fine 23ha/57 acre open space includes a terrace, an English garden, a rose garden and ⊡ a zoo. Note the statue of the artist, Claude Gellée, known as Le Lorrain, by Rodin.

On leaving the park, turn left onto rue Sigisbert-Adam then continue along rue Braconnot and turn right towards the Porte de la Craffe.

★**Porte de la Craffe** – This gate, which formed part of the 14C fortifications, is decorated with the thistle of Nancy and the cross of Lorraine (19C). The opposite façade is in Renaissance style. The gate was used as a prison until the Revolution.

To the north stands the **Porte de la Citadelle** which used to secure the old town. This Renaissance gate is decorated with low-relief sculptures and trophies by Florent Drouin.

Retrace your steps then turn right onto rue Haut-Bourgeois.

Private mansions – Admire the Hôtel de Fontenoy *(no 6)* designed by Boffrand at the beginning of the 18C, the **Hôtel Ferrari** *(no 29)* also by Boffrand with an emblazoned balcony, a monumental staircase and Neptune fountain in the courtyard, the Hôtel des Loups *(no 1 rue des Loups)* again by Boffrand and the Hôtel de Gellenoncourt *(no 4)* with a Renaissance doorway.

Porte de la Craffe, the oldest of the city gates still standing

Walk across place de l'Arsenal (16C arsenal at no 9, decorated with trophies) *towards rue Mgr-Trouillet.*

Admire the Renaissance **Hôtel d'Haussonville** *(no 9)* with its outside galleries and Neptune fountain.

Continue to place St-Epvre adorned with the equestrian statue of Duke René II by Schiff.

ADDITIONAL SIGHTS

★★**Musée des Beaux-Arts** ⊙ – The Museum of Fine Arts, housed in one of the pavilions of place Stanislas prolonged in 1936 by a modern pavilion and extended again between 1996 and 1998, contains rich collections of European art from the 14C to the present day. Completely refurbished, the museum displays its collections in a definitely modern, sometimes unconventional way with a departure from a strict chronological order which makes them particularly attractive.

The most remarkable paintings of the 17C French School include *Love taking its revenge* by Vouet, *Pastoral Landscape* by Claude Lorrain and *Charity* by Philippe de Champaigne.

The Modern Art collection, housed in the contemporary extension, is essentially represented by Manet, Monet, Henri Edmond Cross, Modigliani, Juan Gris, Georg Grosz, Picasso... and a few early-20C artists from Lorraine: Julien Bastien-Lepage, Émile Friant, Étienne Cournault, Francis Gruber, the son of the stained-glass artist Jacques Gruber. Sculptures include works by Rodin, Duchamp-Villon, Jacques Lipchitz, César...

Italian painting is well represented by the Primitives as well as Perugino, Tintoretto, Pietro da Cortona, Caravaggio, Volterrano and Cigoli. Also noteworthy are the landscapes and still-life paintings by Joos de Momper, Jan II Bruegel and Hemessen as well as *The Transfiguration* by Rubens which testify to the importance of the Northern School.

18C painting, housed in the Emmanuel Héré pavilion, includes works by Jean-Baptiste Claudot, Desportes, François Boucher and Carle Van Loo.

The department of **graphic art** holds remarkable collections of prints by Jacques Callot (787 engravings) and drawings by Grandville (1 438 drawings).

The Daum collection, a magnificent group of 300 pieces of glassware and crystal is housed in what remains of the 15C-17C fortifications found during the building of the extension.

★★★**Musée historique lorrain** ⊙ – *Housed in the Palais Ducal; entrance: no 64 Grande-Rue.* The museum contains a wealth of exceptional documents illustrating the history of Lorraine, its artistic production and its folklore, displayed on three floors.

On the first floor, the Galerie des Cerfs, 55m/180ft long, contains mementoes of the House of Lorraine, from the 16C to the mid 18C, as well as tapestries from the early 16C, paintings by Jacques Bellange, **Georges de La Tour** *(Woman with a Flea, Discovery of St Alexis' Body, Young Smoker, St Jerome reading)*, Charles Mellin and Claude Deruet.

The pavilion at the bottom of the garden houses an **archaeological gallery** concerned with prehistory, the Celtic period, Gallo-Roman and Frankish times. *Walk across the garden.*

The collections, displayed in the vaulted vestibule and gallery at the entrance of the main building, illustrate the history of Lorraine from the Middle Ages to the 16C (sculptures).

The history of Lorraine during the lifetime of dukes Charles V, Leopold and Francis III is brought to life by numerous paintings, documents, miniatures, ceramics from eastern France (Niederviller, Lunéville, St-Clément), biscuits and terracottas and sculptures by Clodion.

A large area is devoted to Lorraine and Nancy during the lifetime of Stanislas: his foundations, his creations including the square which bears his name, as well as to political, military and literary history from the Revolution to the Empire.

★**Église and Couvent des Cordeliers** ⊙ – The Franciscan convent and the adjacent church were erected in the 15C on the initiative of Duke René II; after being restored, they partially regained their original aspect.

★**Église** – The church has only one nave as is usual for the church of a mendicant order. All the dukes are buried in the crypt. Most of the funeral monuments are the works of three great Renaissance artists, native of Lorraine: Mansuy Gauvain, Ligier Richier and Florent Drouin.

A chapel on the left-hand side contains the **recumbent figure of Philippa of Gelderland**★★, René II's second wife, carved in a fine tuffa, one of the finest works of Ligier Richier. Against the south wall (near the high altar), note the funeral recess of **René II's funeral monument**★, carved by Mansuy Gauvain in 1509. The effigy of Cardinal de Vaudémont (d 1587) is the work of Florent Drouin. The latter is also the author of a remarkable Last Supper, a low-relief sculpture after the famous painting by Leonardo da Vinci. The chancel contains a carved altarpiece over the high altar (1522), 17C stalls and an 18C wrought-iron lectern bearing the emblems of Lorraine. Paintings include Notre-Dame-de-Lorette believed to be the work of Guido Reni and works by R Constant, a native of Lorraine.

★**Chapelle ducale** – On the left of the chancel. Built from 1607 onwards over the tomb of the dukes of Lorraine, the octagonal chapel was modelled on the Medici Chapel in Florence at the request of Charles III. Its walls are framed by 16 columns in front of which are seven black-marble cenotaphs. On each of these are placed the emblems of sovereignty. Jean Richier, a nephew of Ligier, and the Italian artist Stabili were responsible for the building; the coffered cupola is the work of Florent Drouin.

Couvent – The cloister and some of the rooms of the former monastery were restored and now house a rich **Musée d'Arts et Traditions populaires** (Museum of Folk Art and Traditions) which contains reconstructions of interiors (kitchen and bedroom) furnished in regional style and a wealth of objects of daily life, craftsmen's tools, kitchen utensils, lighting and heating equipment (enamelled ceramic tiles), models, maps, photos and paintings.

★**Jardin botanique du Montet** ⊘ – Situated in a vale, near the university's college of science, the botanical gardens cover an area of 25ha/62 acres including hot houses extending over 2 000m²/2 392sq yd. The gardens contain some 15 thematic collections (Alpine, ornamental, medicinal plants, an arboretum etc) and 6 500 species grow in the hot houses: orchids, insect-eating and succulent plants... In their role as National Botanical Conservatory, the gardens also contribute to the preservation of endangered species in the Alsace-Lorraine region and in the French overseas territories.

Maison de la Communication ⊘ – The museum illustrates the history of telecommunications over the past 200 years with the help of objects, documents, reconstructions of historic scenes, technical demonstrations... 1793 saw the advent of Chappe's aerial telegraph and 1876 the birth of the telephone. The museum also exhibits models of telephone exchanges in working order, the reconstruction of a post office of the 1920s, submarine telegraph and telephone cables, toys and old documents.

Musée-aquarium de Nancy ⊘ – ⬚ On the ground floor is the **tropical aquarium**★ which comprises 70 ponds full of numerous species of fish, from Asia, Africa, the Red Sea, the Indian and Pacific oceans and the Amazone Basin.
The first floor houses a collection of over 10 000 stuffed animals.

Excelsior Flo, Art Nouveau and traditional cooking

EXCURSIONS

Musée de l'Histoire du fer ⊘ – Located in **Jarville-la-Malgrange**, the museum is housed in a building which illustrates the role of metallic architecture in contemporary design.
The museum illustrates the evolution of iron-working from prehistoric times to the present, including techniques used to make weapons during the Gaulish period, as well as various processes such as Merovingian damascening. Cast-iron and iron art works.

Chartreuse de Bosserville – *5km/3mi. Leave Nancy by ② on the town plan. In Laneuville, immediately after the bridge on the Marne-Rhine canal, turn left onto D 126. The road veers to the right, offering a fine overall view of the Chartreuse de Bosserville before crossing the Meurthe. Turn left onto D 2; 1km/0.6mi further on, an alleyway lined with plane trees leads to the Chartreuse de Bosserville. Not open to the public.*

Founded in 1666 by Duke Charles IV, this former Carthusian monastery is now occupied by a technical college. Built on a terrace overlooking the Meurthe, the edifice, with the chapel in its centre, comprises a long imposing 17C-18C façade flanked by two perpendicular wings. A splendid stone staircase leads up to the terrace. Bosserville was used as a military hospital from 1793 to 1813 and many French and foreign soldiers died there. Hundreds of bodies were deposited in the former lakes of Bois Robin.

Château de Fléville ⊘ – *9km/5.6mi SE. Leave Nancy along A 330 and continue to the Fléville exit (8km/5mi).* The present edifice, erected in the 16C, replaced a 14C fortress of which only the square keep remains.

Once across the former moat, you are in the main courtyard. A balcony with a balustrade runs along the beautiful Renaissance façade of the central building. The tour of the interior includes the dukes of Lorraine's hall, Stanislas' bedroom, the 18C chapel, as well as several bedrooms decorated with paintings and furnished in the Louis XV, Regency or Louis XVI styles.

After the visit, take a walk round the outside of the castle through the landscaped park.

Parc de loisirs de la forêt de Haye – *9km/5.6mi W. Leave Nancy by ⑤ on the town plan and continue along D 400. There is an information centre near the entrance on the right.*

🎣 This leisure park lies at the heart of the Haye Forest, a vast area of rolling hills covering 9 000ha/22 240 acres, used as hunting grounds by the dukes of Lorraine. Mostly planted with beeches, the park includes several sports grounds, tennis courts, playgrounds, picnic areas, and marked itineraries for walking or running. It is also the starting point of long hikes, as well as riding and mountain-bike tours *(130km/81mi of paths and trails)* through the forest.

Musée de l'Automobile ⊘ – The museum houses about 100 vehicles of different makes, dating from 1898 (such as the Aster of 1900) to 1989; note the collection of GT saloon cars of the 1960s, radiator stoppers and advertising posters.

NEUFCHÂTEAU

Population 7 803
Michelin map 62 fold 13 or 242 fold 25

Situated at the confluence of the Meuse and the Mouzon, this ancient town has retained a number of old houses, mainly from the 17C and 18C round place Jeanne-d'Arc and along the adjacent streets. Neufchâteau owes its name to the former castle of the dukes of Lorraine destroyed together with the 18C fortifications. Having received its charter in 1123, it became the first free city of the duchy of Lorraine and enjoyed considerable prosperity from the 13C to 15C. This thriving market town also became a busy industrial city specialising in period furniture and food-processing. Its annual fair, which takes place in mid-August, is one of the oldest fairs in the Vosges region.

SIGHTS

Hôtel de ville – This late-16C edifice, has retained a fine Renaissance doorway; inside, there is a beautiful, richly decorated **staircase★** dating from 1594 and 14C cellars with pointed vaulting.

Église St-Nicolas ⊘ – The church stands on the mound where the dukes of Lorraine's castle also stood and, because of the difference in ground level, it consists of two superposed churches.

The doorway and tower of the upper church are modern, but the nave dates from the 12C and 13C.

The side chapels contain funeral monuments of wealthy 15C and 16C burghers; note the late-15C polychrome **stone group★** representing the anointing of Christ.

Église St-Christophe ⊘ – Part of the church goes back to 1100, but most of it dates from the 13C: the arcading of the west front resting on slender colonnettes denotes a Burgundian influence. On the south side, the christening-font chapel, originally a funerary chapel, was added in the 16C; admire the beautiful lierne and tierceron vaulting.

EXCURSIONS

St-Élophe – *9km/5.6mi N. Leave Neufchâteau along N 74.*
The church, standing on the edge of a plateau, at the end of the village, was remodelled several times. The massive belfry dating from the 13C contrasts with the early-16C nave, lit by the tall windows of the apse and containing the recumbent figure of St Élophe, who evangelised Lorraine and was martyred in the 4C. The monumental statue (7m/23ft) of the saint, which used to stand on top of the belfry, dates from 1886.
From the square in front of the church, there is a fine view of the Vair Valley, of Bois-Chenu Basilica and of Bourlémont Castle. It is possible to take a **walk** in the footsteps of St Élophe to the fountain where he washed his head after having been decapitated.
A small **museum** ⊘ housed inside the town hall also recalls St Élophe.
A pilgrimage takes place every year on the third Monday in October.

★**Domrémy-la-Pucelle** – *9km/5.6mi along D 164. See VAUCOULEURS: Excursions.*

Pompierre – *12km/7.5mi S along D 74 then left onto D 1.*
The **Église St-Martin**, rebuilt on the roadside in the 19C, has retained its 12C Romanesque **doorway★**. Superbly carved recessed arches frame the three historiated bands of the tympanum depicting: the Massacre of the Innocents, the Flight to Egypt, the Message brought to the Shepherds, the Adoration of the Magi and Jesus entering Jerusalem. The capitals and colonnettes are also elaborately decorated.

Roman amphitheatre in Grand

Grand – *22km/13.7mi W. Drive N out of Neufchâteau along D 53 then turn left onto D 3 to Midrevaux. From there, D 71^E leads directly to Grand.*
In Roman times, Grand, which was then called Andresina, was a kind of water sanctuary dedicated to Apollo Grannus; the healing and oracular powers of this god attracted crowds of pilgrims including one or two emperors such as Caracalla in AD 213 and Constantine in AD 309.
Excavations have revealed some 60 different kinds of marble from all over the Empire, which testify to the splendour of the town's equipment.
Several miles of piping brought fresh water to the sacred pool, over which the present parish church stands. However, a **section of piping** ⊘ (80m/88yd long) gives a good idea of what this intricate network was like.
The **amphitheatre** ⊘, built c AD 80 in the shape of half an oval, could contain 17 000 spectators who came to watch gladiators fight; it was abandoned at the end of the 4C but part of the walls and some arcades were saved; tiers have recently been rebuilt so that the amphitheatre can be used once more.
A huge **mosaic** ⊘ (224m²/268sq yd), dating from the first half of the 3C AD, one of the best-preserved Roman mosaics ever found, was discovered in Grand; it used to pave the ground of a basilica. In the centre are two characters sometimes thought to represent a pilgrim and a priest of Apollo Grannus. Various animals decorate the corners and the apse is adorned with geometric motifs.

The 1 760m/1 925yd long **rampart** surrounding a sacred area reserved for the local deities, was fortified with 22 round towers and with gates, including a monumental one, every 80m/88yd.

NEUWILLER-LÈS-SAVERNE★

Population 1 116
Michelin map 87 fold 13 or 242 fold 15
Local map see Parc naturel régional des VOSGES DU NORD

Situated on the forested foothills of the northern Vosges mountains, this pleasant village has retained several fine balconied houses and two interesting churches, including the Romanesque abbey church of one of the richest abbeys in Alsace.

★ÉGLISE ST-PIERRE-ET-ST-PAUL *allow 30min*

The original church was remodelled in the 9C to receive the relics of the bishop of Metz, St Adelphus. The oldest part is the crypt. The chancel, the transept and the first bay of the nave were built in the 12C. There are two doorways on the north side facing a vast square surrounded by canons' houses: on the right, a 13C doorway, framed by the statues of St Peter and St Paul, and on the left a 12C doorway with a fine tympanum depicting Christ giving his blessing.

Interior ⊙ – The gallery and the organ situated at the extremity of the nave date from 1773 to 1777.

At the west end of the south aisle, the 13C tomb of St Adelphus rests on top of eight tall columns, which enabled the congregation to pass beneath the saint's tomb. Walk up the south aisle to the south transept which contains a 15C sitting **Virgin★**.

The north transept houses a polychrome Holy Sepulchre dating from 1478. Above the group formed by the three Marys carrying perfume vases and surrounding Christ's body, the recess of a Flamboyant Gothic gable contains a 14C statue of the Virgin.

★**Superposed chapels** – They were both built in the 11C and their plans are identical. Round piers support the vaulting. The base of the columns are similar in both chapels; however, the cubic-shaped capitals of the lower chapel are plain whereas those of the upper chapel, dedicated to St Sebastian, are carved with beautiful motifs. In addition, this chapel houses remarkable **tapestries★★**. The four panels dating from the 15C depict St Adelphus' life and the miracles he accomplished.

ADDITIONAL SIGHT

Église St-Adelphe ⊙ – This church, characteristic of the transition between the Romanesque and Gothic styles (12C-13C), now belongs to the Lutheran Church.

At the time of the Reformation, in 1562, St-Adelphe was the first church to adopt the *simultaneum*, which consisted in sharing the premises between Catholics and Protestants; in this case Catholics were allowed to use the chancel and Protestants the nave. Today the church is used solely for Protestant services.

NIEDERBRONN-LES-BAINS✚✚

Population 4 372
Michelin map 87 fold 3 or 242 fold 16
Local map see Parc naturel régional des VOSGES DU NORD

This spa is an excellent holiday resort and the ideal starting point of hikes and excursions in the nature park of the northern Vosges region *(see Parc naturel régional des VOSGES DU NORD)*.

Lying at the heart of a hilly area, the town grew up around the mineral springs. Founded by the Romans c 48 BC and destroyed in the 5C AD, when barbarian tribes swept across Western Europe, it was restored in the 16C by Count Philip of Hanau; his work was continued in the 18C by the Dietrich family.

During the second half of the 19C, the resort became quite popular and as many as 3 000 people took the waters in 1869. The Dietrich metalworks prospered during the same period and today, they are the city's main job provider.

There are two springs:

– the **Source Romaine** (Roman spring) which gushes forth in the town centre, in front of the municipal casino, recommended for various forms of rheumatism;

– the **Source Celtic** (Celtic spring) relatively low in mineral content, bottled since 1989.

SIGHTS

Maison de l'Archéologie ⊙ – Modern display of local archaeological documents. One room is devoted to cast-iron stoves, which have been the speciality of Niederbronn for over 300 years.

Château de Wasenbourg – *W of the town. 1hr 15min on foot there and back. Start from the station and follow the alleyway lined with lime trees.*

Walk under the bypass and turn left onto the sentier promenade et découvertes *(discovery trail).*

▮ It leads to the ruins of the 13C castle. Fine view of Saverne to the south-west and of the south-eastern part of Alsace.

Nearby there are traces of a Roman temple.

Eating out

MID-RANGE

Anthon – *67510 Obersteinbach – 14km/8.75mi N of Niederbronn on D 653 and D 53 – ☎ 03 88 09 55 01 – closed Jan, Tue and Wed – 155/380F.* This pretty red-painted house is a lovely place to stay in a small picturesque village in the Vosges. Its lovely rotunda dining room has large French windows leading into the garden, where you can eat in summer. There are two interesting rooms with Alsatian box-beds.

Where to stay

MODERATE

Hôtel Cully – *R. de la République – ☎ 03 88 09 01 42 – closed Feb, Tue evening and Wed – 𝐏 – 40 rooms 250/340F – ⌣ 49F – restaurant 120/250F.* In a busy street not far from the town centre, this hotel consists of two buildings separated by a lovely flower-decked terrace. The spacious, well-kept rooms in the main building are the best. Alsace cuisine served outdoors in summer.

On the town

Casino de Niederbronn-les-Bains – *10 pl. des Thermes – ☎ 03 88 80 84 88 – alsace-casino.com – Sun-Thu 11am-2am, Fri-Sat 11am-3am.* The only casino in Alsace, comprising 135 slot machines and a room for traditional games. Three restaurants, including an Alsace brasserie.

Le Parc (at the Casino de Niederbronn) – *Pl. des Thermes – ☎ 03 88 80 84 84 – www.casinodeniederbronn.com – Fri-Wed (daily Jul-Aug) noon-midnight – closed Feb.* In summer the casino orchestra plays daily on the terrace of this restaurant; there are also tea-dances. Enjoy the music while relaxing in the brasserie. Evening concerts every night in Jul-Aug.

NOGENT-SUR-SEINE

Population 5 500
Michelin map 61 folds 4 and 5 or 237 fold 33

This small town, lying on both banks of the Seine and on an island linked to the river bank by a watermill, is overlooked by mills, silos and the cooling towers of the nuclear power station.

SIGHTS

Église St-Laurent – Built in the 16C, the church offers a pleasant blend of Flamboyant Gothic and Renaissance styles. An imposing tower rising on the left of the main doorway is decorated in the Renaissance style and surmounted by a lantern which supports the statue of St Laurence holding the grid on which he was roasted alive.

Château de la Motte-Tilly

Eating out

MODERATE

Beau Rivage – *R. Villiers-aux-Choux* – ☎ *03 25 39 84 22* – *closed during Feb school holidays, Sun evening and Mon, except public holidays* – *100/205F.* Near the castle of La Motte-Tilly, this small, bright, modern establishment with its white façade offers a riverside terrace beside the Seine, making it a charming rural place to stop and eat. Home-style cooking and functional rooms.

MID-RANGE

Hostellerie du Moulin – *At La Chapelle-Godefroy – 3km/2mi E of Nogent-sur-Seine on N 19* – ☎ *03 25 39 88 32* – *closed Tue evening and Wed* – *140/288F.* If you don't want to go too far off the beaten track, stop off in this imposing old building, where you will appreciate the riverside terrace and the shady park in the summer. Traditional cuisine and children's menus.

Where to stay

MID-RANGE

Chambre d'hôte Péniche la Quiétude – *2 r. Île-Olive* – ☎ *03 25 39 80 14* – *http://perso.wanadoo.fr/quietude* – ✉ *– 5 rooms 250/400F – evening meal 100/ 150F.* Enjoy the peace of river life on this barge moored on the Seine near Nogent's old watermills. The cosy little cabins are an invitation to take to the water; cruising holidays are organised in summer.

The Renaissance aisles have large windows and the buttresses are adorned with carved capitals and gargoyles. Note the fine pediment of the south doorway. Inside, the Renaissance chapels contain a few works of art.

Musée Paul-Dubois-Alfred-Boucher ⊙ – The archaeological collection consists of finds excavated in the area: Gallo-Roman pottery found in Villeneuve-au-Châtelot, coins... On the first floor, there are paintings and plaster casts by regional artists including the two sculptors after whom the museum is named.

Note in particular a landscape painted in 1764 by Joseph Vernet, entitled *Le Livon*. The painting was believed to have been lost until it was found in Great Britain and bought in London in 1996. It forms a pair with another painting owned by the Fine Arts Museum in Berlin.

EXCURSIONS

Centre nucléaire de production d'électricité de Nogent-sur-Seine ⊙ – *4km/2.5mi NE.* Situated upriver from Nogent, this nuclear power station comprises two production units (pressurised-water reactor) of 1 300MW. The information centre offers explanations with the help of a model.

★**Château de la Motte-Tilly** ⊙ – *6km/3.7mi SW along D 951.*
The castle was opened to the public following the bequest of the Marquise de Maillé (1895-1972), an archaeologist and art historian. The family furniture was restored and added to with a preference given to the 18C.
Although simple in style, the edifice has a certain nobility. Designed by François Nicolas Lancret, a nephew of the artist Nicolas Lancret, it was built in 1754 on a natural terrace overlooking the Seine by the Terray brothers; one of them, a priest (1715-78), was one of Louis XV's finance ministers.
The main features of the south façade, facing the road from Nogent-sur-Seine to Bray, are the unusually high roofs and the arcading linking the main building to the pavilions. The ground-floor reception rooms are beautifully furnished and decorated with painted woodwork which adds to the impression of intense luminosity and refined atmosphere. Two rooms on the first floor recall the benefactress, her bedroom with its green decoration and the Empire-style bedroom of her father, the Count of Rohan-Chabot.
Dangerous Liaisons by Milos Forman was filmed in the castle in 1989.
After the tour of the castle, walk to the north side with its characteristic stone-built central part and admire the park with its beautiful ornamental lake and canal.

Ancienne abbaye du Paraclet ⊙ – *6km/3.7mi SE along N 19 and D 442.*
Abélard retired to this remote place with one of his companions after the Church had condemned his teaching in 1121. He built a modest oratory with reeds and straw and was soon joined by a group of students who camped round the oratory and helped rebuild it in stone. **Héloïse** became the abbess of Le Paraclet in 1129.

There is nothing left of the abbey except a cellar located beneath some farm buildings. Behind the chapel, an obelisk marks the site of the crypt where Abélard and Héloïse were buried. Moved in the 15C to the main church of Le Paraclet, their remains were taken away during the Revolution and now rest together in a grave in the Père-Lachaise cemetery in Paris.

Villenauxe-la-Grande – *15km/9.3mi N along D 951.*

This small town is situated on the Île-de-France cuesta *(see p 26)* among rolling hills of fertile soil with outcrops of white limestone. The **church**, built of local sandstone, is plain on the outside. The 16C tower rises above the north aisle and the badly damaged Flamboyant doorway is decorated with the effigies of St Peter and St Paul. The most striking part of the interior is the Gothic chancel and its 13C ambulatory. The panelled vaulting is supported by tall arcades resting on round piers. The **ambulatory★** is lit by twin windows surmounted by five-foiled oculi. The arcades of the nave are wider and less elaborately decorated than those of the chancel and the pointed vaulting is loftier. The south aisle has fine pendentives.

OBERNAI★★

Population 9 610
Michelin map 87 fold 15 or 242 folds 23 and 24
Local maps see Région du HOWALD and Route des VINS

Nestling beneath Mont Ste-Odile, at the heart of wine-growing country, Obernai is a pleasant holiday resort. The old town, with its narrow winding streets lined with rows of pointed gables, its shop signs and its well, is still partly surrounded by ramparts. Don't miss the Hans em Schnokeloch folk festival in July and the harvest festival in October.

TOWN WALK

Place du Marché – The golden hues of the buildings surrounding it add to the charm of the picturesque market square; in its centre, a fountain dating from 1904 is surmounted by a statue of St Odile.

★Ancienne Halle aux blés – The old covered market dates from 1554.

★Tour de la Chapelle – This 13C belfry was the tower of a chapel now reduced to its chancel. The last storey, dating from the 16C, is Gothic; the spire, which soars 60m/197ft into the sky, is flanked by four openwork bartizans.

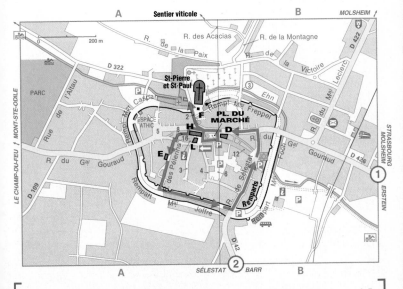

Eating out

MID-RANGE

La Cour des Tanneurs – *Ruelle du Canal-de-l'Ehn* – ☎ *03 88 95 15 70* – *closed 22 Dec-3 Jan, Tue evening and Wed – 125/185F.* In a tiny narrow street in the town centre, this neat, recently redecorated restaurant serves regional cooking in a family atmosphere. A simple place with reasonable prices to satisfy the appetites of hungry walkers.

Winstub O'Baerenheim – *46 r. du Gén.-Gouraud* – ☎ *03 88 95 53 77* – *closed Wed – 130/165F.* This courtyard restaurant in Obernai's main street with open-air tables is a good place to have an inexpensive lunch. Notice the barrel-making tools over the doorway. Typical decor and cuisine.

Where to stay

MID-RANGE

Hôtel La Diligence – *23 pl. de la Mairie* – ☎ *03 88 95 55 69* – **P** – *40 rooms 265/430F* – ⌑ *52F.* An attractive Alsatian building, well situated on the main square of Obernai. Its pleasant, spacious rooms are decorated in rustic local style. Light meals are available in the cosy tearoom.

On the town

L'Athic – *6 pl. de l'Étoile* – ☎ *03 88 95 50 57* – *Easter-Nov: daily 11am-3am; rest of year: 15pm-3am.* This elegant cocktail bar, furnished with velvet arm-chairs and a piano for customers' use, has several different rooms: a billiard room on the first floor, and another bar with a pewter counter and old marble-topped tables. Large terrace in summer.

Shopping

Aux Caves d'Obernai – *14 r. du Marché* – ☎ *03 88 95 36 94* – *Mon 2-6.30pm, Tue-Sat 9.30am-noon, 2-6.30pm, 6pm Sat – closed 10 Jan-1 Feb.* The wines of Clos Ste-Odile, whose vines surround the town, are on sale in this shop: Riesling, Tokay, Gewürztraminer, Pinot Noir, sparkling *blanc de blanc*, liqueurs, raspberry and plum brandies.

Maison du Vin – Seilly – *1 r. de la Paille* – ☎ *03 88 95 46 82 / 55 80* – *seilly.com* – *daily 8.30am-noon, 2.30-7pm except some weekends – closed Jan-Easter.* Situated in a building dating from 1628, this former draper's shop is now a wine store, run by the wine-grower Seilly. Among other treats, you can sample the *vin de pistolet*, which gets its name from an amusing local story of an encounter between Ferdinand I and the impudent mayor of Obernai, which is explained to you in the shop.

Market square in Obernai

★**Hôtel de ville** – The town hall has retained some features from the 14C-17C in spite of being remodelled and extended in 1848; the façade is adorned with an oriel and a beautifully carved balcony, both added in 1604.

Puits aux six seaux – This elegant Renaissance well is surmounted by a baldaquin resting on columns and crowned by a weather cock dating from 1579. Six pails hang from the three pulleys.

Église St-Pierre-et-St-Paul – This imposing neo-Gothic church, built in the 19C, houses, in the north transept, a Holy Sepulchre altar (1504) and a reliquary containing the heart of the bishop of Angers, Charles Freppel, a native of Obernai, who died in 1891 and asked in his will that his heart be returned to the church of his native town once Alsace became French again. His wish was fulfilled in 1921. Note also the four stained-glass windows dating from the 15C, believed to be the work of Pierre d'Andlau or his pupil Thibault de Lyxheim.

★**Maisons anciennes** – Most of them are to be found near the town hall, the old market, or along rue du Marché and round place de l'Étoile.
In rue des Pèlerins, there is a three-storey stone house dating from the 13C (**L**). At the back of the town hall, the picturesque rue des Juifs is worth the detour. On the corner stands a fine timber-framed house with a wooden footbridge.

Ramparts – It is pleasant to walk along the ramparts lined with a double row of trees. The best-preserved part of the inside wall, once reinforced by more than 20 towers, is the Maréchal-Foch section.

ORBAIS-L'ABBAYE

Population 602
Michelin map 56 fold 15 or 237 fold 22

An important Benedictine abbey was founded here in the 7C. The village makes a pleasant outing and can also be the starting point of excursions through the Surmelin Valley and Vassy Forest.

★CHURCH ☉

It includes the chancel and transept of the former abbey church as well as two bays from the original nave (one being used as a porch, the other forming part of the interior). The other bays and the west front flanked by two towers were destroyed in 1803. The building of the church (end of the 12C and 13C) was most probably supervised by Jean d'Orbais, one of the master builders of Reims Cathedral.
As you walk round the edifice, note the unusual positioning of the flying buttresses of the transept and of the apse which meet on the same abutment; the slender spire surmounting the crossing date from the 14C.

Interior – The chancel★, with its ambulatory and radiating chapels, is considered as the prototype of that of Reims Cathedral; the sanctuary is remarkably well designed: pointed arcades supporting a lofty triforium and clerestory windows surmounted by oculi.
The entrance to the transept, which replaces the nave, is furnished with early-16C stalls: the parcloses are decorated with representations of the Apostles except the first two which depict a Tree of Jesse on the right and the Virgin on the left. The misericords and cheeks are carved with amusing figures. The axial chapel contains a 13C stained-glass window illustrating scenes from the Old Testament.
The well-preserved **monastery buildings** include a fine 13C hall, used as a winter chapel.

EXCURSIONS

Église de Fromentières – 6km/3.7mi S. The village church contains a monumental Flemish altarpiece, carved and painted at the beginning of the 16C, which was bought by the vicar in 1715 for a very modest sum. The signature, a severed hand, is the legendary emblem of Antwerp.
The **altarpiece**★★ is behind the high altar. The paintings decorating the side panels depict episodes of the New Testament whereas the central panel comprises three tiers of delicately carved scenes; the refined expressive figures, originally painted with bright colours against a gilt background, illustrate Christ's Life and Passion.

Montmort-Lucy – 9.5km/6mi SE. Occupying a pleasant site overlooking the River Surmelin, Montmort is the ideal starting point for excursions through the valley and the surrounding woodland area dotted with picturesque lakes.

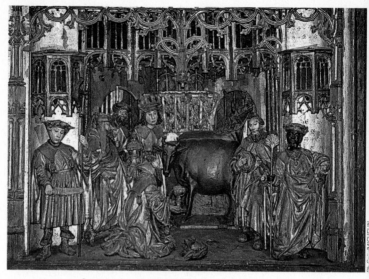

Scene on the magnificent 16C altarpiece in Fromentières

Château ⊙ – Standing on high ground, the castle occupies a commanding position above the Surmelin Valley. Some parts date from the 12C, but the castle was rebuilt at the end of the 16C. It belonged at one time to Pierre Rémond de Montmort (1678-1719), an esteemed mathematician who published an essay on games of chance. In 1914, it was here that General von Bülow ordered the retreat from the Marne *(see MONTMIRAIL)*.

The edifice, which shows a fine brick bond with white-stone facing, still retains a certain feudal aspect with its 14m/46ft deep moat. During the tour, the well-preserved bread oven, a beautiful Renaissance doorway (1577), the guard-room and the kitchens can be admired. The lower part of the castle can be reached by a ramp designed for horses, similar to that in the château at Amboise.

Église – Still surrounded by a cemetery, the church has an interesting porch, a Romanesque nave, a 13C transept, a second transept and an early-16C chancel (stained-glass windows of the same period). In the nave there is an 18C pulpit.

Étoges – *16km/10mi SE along D 11 to Mareuil-en-Brie, then D 18.*
Étoges is a wine-growing village close to the Côte des Blancs. There is a fine view of the elegant 17C castle from the bridge spanning the moat: pink-brick buildings with white-stone ties and facings, high French-style roofs covered with pale-purple slates. The edifice was restored in 1991 and turned into a hotel.

The 12C **church** ⊙, remodelled in the 15C and 16C, has a Gothic rose-window and a Renaissance doorway; it contains several 16C recumbent figures.

Val d'ORBEY★★

Michelin map 87 fold 17 or 242 fold 31

The round tour of the Val d'Orbey starts from the northern extremity of the Route des Crêtes *(see Route des CRÊTES)*. It is one of the finest excursions in the Trois-Épis area, which takes in the austere landscapes of the Lac Noir and the Lac Blanc contrasting with the picturesque valleys of the River Béhine and the River Weiss and leads to Le Linge, one of the most dramatic battlefields of the First World War. This is Welche country, a kind of French enclave (linguistically speaking) in Alsace. Welche is a Romance dialect, derived from vulgar Latin.

ROUND TOUR FROM LES TROIS-ÉPIS

57km/35mi – allow 4hr

★★**Les Trois-Épis** – This resort is the ideal starting point of numerous hikes and drives for those who are keen to explore the mountains or visit interesting towns, castles and battlefields. An event which took place in 1491 led to a famous pilgrimage which is at the origin of Les Trois-Épis. The Virgin Mary appeared to a blacksmith on his way to market; in her left hand she held a piece of ice as a symbol of a hardened heart and in her right hand she had three ears of corn *(épis de maïs)* as a symbol of divine mercy and blessing.

★★Le Galz – *1hr on foot there and back.*

🚶 At the summit a huge monument by Valentin Jæg commemorates the return of Alsace to France in 1918. The view extends over the Plaine d'Alsace, the Black Forest, the Sundgau and the Jura mountains.

Sentier de la forêt de St-Wendelin – *1hr 30min on foot (brochure available from the tourist office). Start from the car park on place des Antonins and follow the green markings indicated by a squirrel.*

🚶 This forest trail explores the flora covering the Val d'Orbey slopes.

From Les Trois-Épis drive W along D 11 for 3km/1.9mi then turn left onto D 11^{VI}.

The road follows the ridge separating the Val d'Orbey and the Munster Valley, offering fine views of both. It then runs through the forest right round the Grand Hohneck.

Le Linge – *See MUNSTER p 226.*

Turn right at Collet du Linge then, leaving the Glasborn path on your left, continue to the Col du Wettstein (war cemetery) and turn right again.

★Lac Noir – *Parking space by the lake.* The Lac Noir (alt 954m/3 130ft) lies inside a glacial cirque. A moraine reinforced by a dam retains the water on the east side; the lake is otherwise surrounded by high granite cliffs which contribute to the austerity of the landscape.

🚶 **Tour of the lake** *(1hr there and back along a path marked with yellow crosses). Start from the parking area and follow a path on the left which rises towards a rocky promontory.* From there, the **view★** embraces the whole lake and extends towards the Pairis Valley and the Plaine d'Alsace. The path then continues to rise among the cliffs affording more fine views of the glacial cirque filled by the lake.

Lac Blanc

R.Mattes/MICHELIN

★Lac Blanc – Alt 1 054m/3 458ft. The road skirts the Lac Blanc, offering beautiful views of the glacial cirque which forms the setting of the lake (area: 29ha/72 acres, depth: 72m/236ft). A strange rock, shaped like a fortress and known as the **Château Hans**, overlooks the lake. The high cliffs surrounding it are partly forested.

The road joins the Route des Crêtes at the Col du Calvaire. Turn right; the road enters the forest.

The road affords glimpses of the Béhine Valley, over which towers the Tête des Faux, before reaching the Col du Bonhomme.

Col du Bonhomme – Alt 949m/3 114ft. This pass links Alsace and Lorraine via the Col de Ste-Marie in the north and the Col de la Schlucht in the south *(see also Route des CRÊTES)*. The twisting road leading down from the pass into the Béhine Valley offers fine views of the valley with the Brézouard summit in the distance and the Tête des Faux quite near to the right, then passes beneath a rocky spur topped by the ruins of Gutenburg Castle.

Le Bonhomme – This is the beginning of Welche country. Streams rush down the slopes to form the River Béhine.

Eating out

MODERATE

Restaurant Pays Welche – *2 r. de la Rochette – 68240 Fréland –* ☎ *03 89 71 90 52 – closed mid-Feb to mid-Mar and Wed – 80/250F.* After visiting the museum and learning about the history of the Pays Welche, come and eat in this old restaurant, decorated with agricultural tools, bellows and a cart suspended from the roof timbers. Classic cooking.

Where to stay

MID-RANGE

Chambre d'hôte Ferme du Busset – *33 r. du Busset – 68370 Orbey – 1km/0.5mi E of Orbey on a minor road –* ☎ *03 89 71 22 17 –* 🖂 *– 6 rooms 270/290F.* A chance to enjoy the peace and fresh air on a working farm in the countryside near Orbey. Wood-panelled bedrooms, but also two holiday cottages and accommodation for walkers. Before you leave, stock up with cheese, *charcuteries* and home-made jam.

Gîte rural Le Forêt – *3 Le Forêt – 88230 Plainfaing – 14km/8.75mi N of the Col de la Schlucht on D 23 and D 23^H –* ☎ *03 89 47 51 24 –* 🖂 *– 1 cottage sleeping 6/7: 2 000F per week.* This late-19C Vosges farm has been converted into well-equipped holiday accommodation, overlooking a wooded meadow where sheep graze. View over the valley and mountains. Open fireplace in the spacious dining room.

Shopping

Confiserie des Hautes-Vosges (CDHV) – 🖼 *– 44 Habeaurupt – 88230 Plainfaing – on the Valtin road, coming out of Plainfaing –* ☎ *03 29 50 44 56 – www.cdhv.fr – shop: Mon-Sat 9am-noon, 2-6.30pm – guided tours: Mon-Sat 10am-noon, 2-6pm.* Sugar, honey from the Vosges mountains, natural flavourings and even essential oils are the ingredients of these old-fashioned sweets, which are cooked in copper cauldrons on open fires while you watch. You can taste and buy *bonbons des Vosges, bergamotes de Nancy,* blueberries, violets, poppies.

Lapoutroie – In this village there is a small **Musée des Eaux-de-Vie** ⊘ (liqueurs and traditional distillery), housed in a former posting house dating from the 18C.

Continue along N 415 towards Kaysersberg, past the intersection with D 48 (roundabout), then turn immediately left onto D 11^{IV} leading to Fréland.

Fréland – The name means free land; miners from Ste-Marie-aux-Mines *(see Parc naturel régional des BALLONS DES VOSGES: Val d'Argent)* enjoyed the right to cut timber.

Maison du Pays Welche ⊘ – *2 rue de la Rochette.* Local people have gathered objects illustrating the region's traditions and displayed them in a former presbytery dating from the 18C. The setting and the local way of life are carefully recreated.

Musée de la Forge ⊘ – Here you can see an old water-powered smithy with its water-wheel in working order.

Return to N 415 and to the roundabout where you turn left onto D 48 towards Orbey.

Orbey – This village, which includes several hamlets, stretches along the green valley of the River Weiss; the heights overlooking the valley, crisscrossed by paths, are ideal hiking country.

Beyond Orbey, the road *(D 11)* rises up a narrow valley past Tannach then, after a deep bend, it winds its way up offering fine views of the Weiss Valley overlooked by the Grand Faudé.

Further on it continues along a different slope revealing the Walbach Valley ahead with Le Galz and its monument behind and the Plaine d'Alsace in the distance. Leaving **Labaroche** on your left, you will soon notice the Grand Hohneck straight ahead and, quite close on your right, the conical summit of Petit Hohneck.

Les Trois-Épis lies 3km/1.9mi beyond the intersection of D 11 and D 11^{VI}.

OTTMARSHEIM

Population 1 897
Michelin map 87 fold 9 or 242 fold 40

This village, situated on the edge of the vast Harth Forest, acquired fame through its church, a unique example of Carolingian architecture in Alsace. Nowadays, Ottmarsheim is also known for its hydroelectric power station, the second of eight such power stations along the Grand Canal d'Alsace (see VALLÉE DU RHIN).

★**Église** – The church, consecrated by Pope Leo IX c 1040, is a very unusual octagonal edifice, characteristic of Carolingian architecture. All the measurements are divisible by three, the figure symbolising the Holy Trinity. For a long time, it was thought to be a kind of pagan temple or baptistery when, in fact, the Ottmarsheim building is the church of a Benedictine abbey founded in the mid-11C. The upper part of the belfry dates from the 15C as does the rectangular chapel on the south-east side, whereas the Gothic chapel was built in 1582 on the left side of the apse.
The **interior** is designed in the shape of an octagon surmounted by a cupola. To the left of the square apse, a wrought-iron gate gives access to the Gothic chapel: above the entrance are seven 18C funeral medallions.
The church has retained some 15C murals depicting St Peter's Life and Christ in Glory presiding over the Last Judgement.

★**Centrale hydro-électrique** ⊙ – The Ottmarsheim hydroelectric power station, the reach and the locks, built between 1948 and 1952, form the second section of the Grand Canal d'Alsace, which was the first stage of the harnessing-of-the-Rhine project between Basle and Lauterbourg.

Locks – They are of equal length (185m/202yd) but of different widths (23m/75ft and 12m/40ft). They are closed by angled gates upstream and by lifting gates downstream.
The control room overlooks the two locks.
The whole operation takes less than half an hour: 11min in the small lock and 18min in the large lock.

Power station – The engine room is vast and light. The four units have a total output of 156 million watts and produce an average of 980 million kWh every year.

La PETITE-PIERRE ★

Population 623
Michelin map 87 fold 13 or 242 fold 15
Local map see Parc naturel régional des VOSGES DU NORD

Situated at the intersection of several major routes, La Petite-Pierre, also known as Lützelstein or Parva Petra, prospered during the Middle Ages, was later fortified by Vauban, Louis XIV's military engineer, and then no longer maintained as a stronghold after 1870. Today, it is a popular summer resort at the heart of the forested massif of the low Vosges and the starting point of more than 100km/62mi of marked footpaths.
🚶 Information panel inside the town hall.

OLD TOWN

Walk up a steep path past an outwork and follow the high street.

Église – The belfry and the nave were rebuilt in the 19C, but the Gothic chancel dates back to the 15C. It is decorated with **murals** of the same period depicting the Coronation of the Virgin, the Temptation of Adam and Eve, the Last Judgement etc. Since 1737, the church has been used for Catholic and Protestant offices.

Maison des Païens – This Renaissance house, situated in the gardens of the town hall, was built in 1530 on the site of a Roman watchtower.

WEEKEND BREAK

Auberge d'Imsthal – *At Imsthal Lake – 3.5km/2mi SE of La Petite-Pierre on D 178 – ☎ 03 88 01 49 00 – closed Jan and Tue 15 Sep-31 Mar – 🅿 – 23 rooms 290/660F – ⌑ 50F – restaurant 140/235F. This half-timbered inn on the edge of a lake is a lovely place for a weekend stay, in a peaceful country setting. Choose one of the newer rooms, which are more spacious. Sauna, Turkish bath and solarium.*

R.Mattes/MICHELIN

Looking for a
knight in shining armour?

Chapelle St-Louis – Built in 1684 and once reserved for the garrison (funeral monuments of former governors and military chiefs), the chapel now houses the interesting **Musée du Sceau alsacien** ⊙ (Museum of Alsatian Heraldry), illustrating the history of Alsace through numerous reproductions of seals which used to be the distinguishing marks of cities, stately homes, important people or families, crafts or guilds, religious orders or chapters etc.

Château et maison du Parc – Built in the 12C, the castle was remodelled several times, in particular in the 16C, at the instigation of Georg Hans von Veldenz, the Count Pala-

tine of the Rhine region. Today the castle houses the **Maison du parc** ⊙. Skilfully displayed (reconstructions, games, slide shows) in six thematic multimedia rooms, the **permanent exhibition** entitled Nouveaux Espaces (New Spaces) helps visitors to discover the historic, cultural and technical heritage of the **Parc naturel régional des Vosges du Nord** as well as its natural diversity (fauna and flora). Nature park management issues (protection of the environment, fight against pollution) are also explained.

Follow rue des Remparts which offers views of the surrounding countryside and forested heights.

Magazin ⊙ – This former 16C warehouse, which forms part of the ramparts, houses a small **Musée des Arts et Traditions populaires**; the museum of folk art and customs displays an interesting collection of tins for specific cakes such as *springerle* (aniseed cake) and *lebkuche* (gingerbread).

Continue along rue des Remparts leading back to the high street.

EXCURSION

Parc animalier du Schwarzbach – *Access via D 134, by the Loosthal forest lodge, between La Petite-Pierre and Neuwiller.*

This wildlife park offers the opportunity to observe red deer (one of the most interesting large species of the northern Vosges) in their natural surroundings. Visitors enjoy the view from an observation tower.

Further on, a **nature trail** reveals the diversity of the northern Vosges environment (trees, ecological forestry, geology, fauna). There are two separate itineraries: one is 1.8km/1mi long *(45min)*, the other is 4km/2.5mi long *(2hr)*; both offer fine views of the surrounding area.

PFAFFENHOFFEN

Population 2 285
Michelin map 87 fold 3 or 242 fold 16

Once the main centre of the bailiwick of Hanau-Lichtenberg, Pfaffenhoffen was fortified in the 15C to guard the south bank of the River Moder and became in the 16C one of the rallying points of rebellious peasants *(see SAVERNE)*. Today the small industrial town (shoes, metalworks) has retained part of its fortifications enclosing lovely timber-framed houses as well as an interesting museum of hand-painted pictures which testifies to one of the oldest artistic traditions in Alsace.

*Musée de l'Imagerie populaire ⊙ – *17 rue du Dr-Albert-Schweitzer (high street) on the first floor.*

The museum illustrates the long-standing Alsatian tradition of picture-painting through rich collections of hand-painted pictures (on paper or vellum, on the back of glass plates or on objects) by ordinary people or by local painters.

Regimental memento

There are religious pictures intended to encourage prayers, to protect houses, cattle and crops and memento pictures illustrating important events in peoples' lives.

Among the exhibits, there are pictures mounted under glass; most are very old yet note how bright the colours are. There is also a collection of pictures, known as *églomisés*, with black backgrounds and gilt decorations and texts. They are intended to adorn oil-lamp or candle-lit rooms and date from the Second Empire (1852-70).

Note the variety of memento pictures (17C-19C) on display next to decorated notarial deeds, as well as the minutely executed paper cut-outs, ex-votos, pictures of patron saints, banners, small religious pictures, some dating back to the 17C, and reliquaries.

Other rooms house a collection of Goettelbriefe or christening wishes, one of the oldest traditions in Alsace, which lasted for nearly 400 years.

Hôtel de ville – The façade is adorned with a medallion of Dr Schweitzer, who was made a freeman of the city. In the hall there is an exhibition of the work (sculpture, figurative painting in the style of Impressionism) of a native of Strasbourg, Alfred Pauli (1898-1988).

Maisons anciennes – The town has retained many half-timbered houses dating from the 16C to 19C, particularly in rue du Docteur-Schweitzer and rue du Marché.

Synagogue – dating from 1791, this is the oldest Alsatian synagogue to have remained intact. The imposing yet discreet edifice testifies to the importance of Jewish society in the late 18C. Note the Kahlstub (communal room) and the room reserved for occasional guests.

EXCURSION

Cimetière juif d'Ettendorf – *6km/3.7mi SW along D 419A and D 25, first road on the right. Drive through the village and follow a small road running parallel to the railway line which leads to the cemetery (500m/547yd).*

This is the oldest Jewish cemetery in Alsace; it spreads over a large area, on the hillside, blending perfectly well with the landscape.

Continue NW along D 735 to Buswiller (2km/1.2mi).

Buswiller – The village has retained some fine timber-framed houses. In the high street, note the carved gable of no 17, painted in cobalt blue; the house, dated 1599, was spared by the Thirty Years War.

CHOOSE THE MENU

Ferme-auberge Galipette – *27 r. Principale – 67350 Kindwiller – 2km/1.2mi N of Pfaffenhoffen on a minor road –* ☎ *03 88 07 01 18 – closed 20 Dec-early Feb – open weekdays by reservation and Sun –* ✉ *– booking essential – 120F.* Home-made charcuterie, roast kid, slowly simmered lamb, Alsace-style rabbit, chicken cooked in Riesling, beef stew, *bäeckeoffe*, sauerkraut, garden vegetables, goats' cheese... all hard to resist. The first person to book gets to choose the menu!

PLOMBIÈRES-LES-BAINS‡‡

Population 2 084
Michelin map 62 fold 16 or 242 fold 34

Plombières stretches along the narrow and picturesque valley of the River Augronne. It is a renowned spa and a pleasant holiday resort. Water from the mineral spring is used in the treatment of diseases of the digestive system and various forms of rheumatism.

A fashionable spa – The Romans built imposing baths in Plombières and the spa flourished until it was destroyed by barbarians during the great wave of invasions from the east. Revived in the Middle Ages, the resort has steadily developed and welcomed many a famous person.
The dukes of Lorraine were, of course, regular visitors. Montaigne took the waters in 1580 and Voltaire spent several summers there. Louis XV's daughters stayed in Plombières for two consecutive seasons accompanied by a great many followers. Napoleon's wife Josephine and her daughter Queen Hortense also spent some time in Plombières. In 1802, an American engineer named Robert Fulton gave a demonstration of the first steamship on the River Augronne, in front of the Empress. Napoleon III stayed in Plombières several times and decided to embellish the town. In 1858, he met the Italian minister, Cavour, and together they planned Italy's future and agreed on Nice and the Savoie being united with France.

PLOMBIÈRES-LES-BAINS

Église (Pl. de l')	3
Français (Av. Louis)	4
Franche-Comté (Av. de)	5
Gaulle (Av. du Gén.-de)	8
Hôtel-de-Ville (Rue de l')	9
Léopold (Av. du Duc)	10
Liétard (R.)	13
Stanislas (R.)	16

Musée Louis-Français **M**

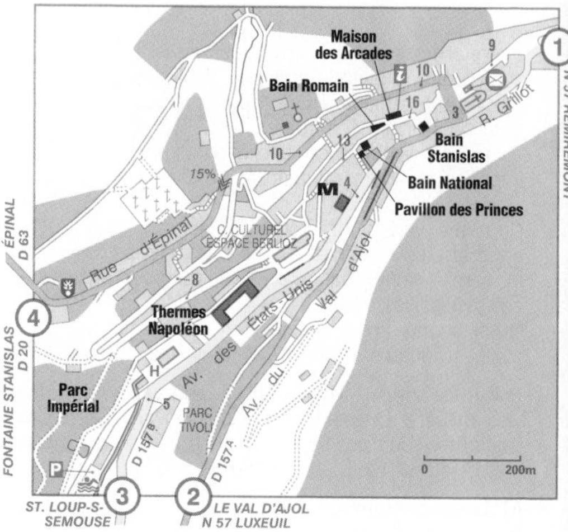

SPA TOWN

Spa town – The historic baths and thermal establishments can be seen along the town's lively high street, rue Stanislas and rue Liétard.
The **tour** ⓥ begins with the **Bain Stanislas**, built between 1733 and 1736.

Étuve romaine ⓥ – The Roman steam room was discovered during excavations in 1856. Nearby is the **Bain romain**, in a basement, which can also be visited *(staircase at the end of the square)*; the vestibule shaped like a rotunda has retained important traces of the Roman pool (tiers and statue of Emperor Augustus).

Maison des Arcades – This is one of the finest 18C houses (note the wrought-iron balconies), built in 1762 by Stanislas Leszczynski whose coat of arms is carved on the façade. On the ground floor, beneath the arcades and behind a wrought-iron railing, the Crucifix spring was, for a long time, a public fountain.

Bain national ⓥ – Built at the request of Napoleon (bust of the emperor) and rebuilt in 1935, the baths have retained their façade in the First Empire style (1800-14). In the hall, the pump room is still in use.

LOVELY SETTING

Hôtel de la Fontaine Stanislas – *4km/2.5mi W of Plombières on D 20 – ☎ 03 29 66 01 53 – closed 16 Oct-31 Mar –* **P** *– 16 rooms 165/330F – ☕ 40F – restaurant 98/220F.* A good night's sleep is guaranteed in this early-20C hotel surrounded by a garden, on the edge of a forest overlooking the Plombières Valley. Its strongest point is the setting, as the decor is slightly outdated, but it is nevertheless well kept. Veranda dining room.

Thermes Napoléon ⊙ – They were erected by Napoleon III, whose statue decorates the entrance. The vast hall (55m/180ft long) is reminiscent of the Caracalla Baths in Rome.

Parc impérial – The park was laid by Baron Haussmann. It contains beautiful trees and some rare species.

ADDITIONAL SIGHTS

Musée Louis-Français ⊙ – The museum contains paintings by Louis Français, a native of Plombières, and his friends from the Barbizon School: Corot, Courbet, Diaz, Harpignies, Monticelli, Troyon...

Plombières ice cream

This ice cream, flavoured with kirsch and glacé fruit, was supposed to have been invented accidentally in 1858 by a chef preparing a dessert ordered by Napoleon III for his guests during his famous visit to Plombières. The cream having turned out wrong, the chef added the kirsch and fruit to save the day and the guests were delighted. It so happened that, in 1798, an Italian confectioner was already serving a similar kind of ice cream in the Paris region; it was called Plombières because it was left to set in lead *(plomb)* moulds. The name was originally spelt without an "s" but it was eventually confused with the name of the town where it became a speciality.

The tradition lives on at Fontaine Stanislas where the ice cream is still handmade.

Pavillon des Princes ⊙ – Built during the Restoration (1814-30) for members of the royal family, the pavilion houses an exhibition devoted to the Second Empire. It is here that Napoleon III secretly met Cavour to decide on military action against the Austrians who had invaded the north of Italy. In 1859, the French and the Italians together won the battles of Magenta and Solferino.

EXCURSIONS

Fontaine Stanislas – *3.5km/2.2mi SW. Leave Plombières by ④ on the town plan, along D 20; 1km/0.6mi further, turn left twice.*

Very pleasant drive through the beech forest.

1.5km/0.9mi after the last turn, take the path on the left leading to the Fontaine Stanislas.

From the terrace of the hotel, there is a fine view of the valley where fields and woods alternate. Nearby, a small spring gushes forth from a rock covered with inscriptions dating from the 18C and beginning of the 19C.

✦ **Bains-les-Bains** – *23km/14mi NW.* This spa resort lies on the banks of the Bagnerot, at the heart of a forested region; there are many walks and cycle tours in the surrounding area. Water gushing forth from 11 springs, at temperatures varying from 25-51°C/77-124°F, is mainly used in the treatment of rheumatism and cardiovascular diseases. The **Bain romain**, rebuilt in 1845, stands on the site of the springs harnessed by the Romans, whereas the **Bain de la Promenade**, dating from 1880 and remodelled in 1928, houses the pump room. From the Chapelle Notre-Dame-de-la-Brosse, situated 500m/550yd east along D 434, there is a pleasant **view** of the hills overlooking the Bagnerot Valley.

★AUGRONNE AND SEMOUSE VALLEYS

33km/21mi round tour – allow 1hr

Leave Plombières along D 157bis.

Vallée de l'Augronne – The road follows the river through pastureland and forested areas.

In Aillevillers-et-Lyaumont, drive N along D 19 to la Chaudeau then turn right onto D 20 which follows the Semouse Valley upstream.

★**Vallée de la Semouse** – This green and peaceful valley with densely forested slopes is deep and sinuous and barely wide enough for the river to flow through although there are here and there a few narrow strips of pastureland. Wireworks, rolling mills and sawmills once lined the river, making use of its rapid flow (only one of those mills has survived at Blanc Murger).

Turn right onto D 63 which leads back to Plombières.

The road runs rapidly down towards Plombières, offering a fine view of the town.

VALLÉE DES ROCHES *47km/29mi round tour – allow 2hr*

Leave Plombières along N 57 towards Luxeuil.

The road soon leaves the picturesque Augronne Valley to climb onto the plateau marking the watershed between the Mediterranean and the North Sea, it then runs down towards Remiremont and the Moselle Valley.

Remiremont – *See REMIREMONT.*

Drive S out of Remiremont along D 23.

The road rises through a green vale then enters the forest.

3.5km/2.2mi further on, turn left onto D 57.

Just beyond La Croisette d'Hérival, turn right onto a surfaced forest road which winds its way through the Hérival Forest dotted with rocks.

Shortly after leaving the road to Girmont and an inn on your left, you will reach the Cascade du Géhard.

★**Cascade du Géhard** – The waterfall is situated below the level of the road, to the left. Foaming water cascades down into a series of potholes. The effect is particularly striking during the rainy season.

Continue past the forest lodge on your left and the path to Hérival on your right and turn left onto the road which follows the Combeauté Valley, also known as the Vallée des Roches.

Vallée des Roches – The deep narrow valley is framed by magnificent forested slopes.

Shortly after entering the village of Faymont, turn right near a sawmill and leave the car 50m/55yd further on; continue on foot along a forest road leading to the Cascade de Faymont (300m/328yd).

Cascade de Faymont – The waterfall, set among coniferous trees and rocks, forms a remarkable picture.

Le Val-d'Ajol – The municipality of Le Val-d'Ajol includes more than 60 hamlets scattered along the Combeauté Valley and Combalotte Valley which have retained their traditional industrial activities (metalworks, weaving, sawmills).

Turn right towards Plombières.

Continue 1.8km/1.1mi beyond a hairpin bend to the right, and take in the fine view of the valley on your right.

Soon after, a path branching off on the left climbs up to La Feuillée Nouvelle (100m/109yd).

La Feuillée Nouvelle – From the platform there is a fine bird's-eye **view**★ of Le Val-d'Ajol.

Continue past the swimming pool at Le Petit Moulin on your left and follow N 57 back to Plombières.

PONT-À-MOUSSON ★

Population 14 647
Michelin map 57 fold 13 or 242 fold 13

Pont-à Mousson developed from the 9C onwards round the bridge built across the Moselle, beneath a knoll crowned with a fortress. This strategic position accounts for the heavy shelling which the town was subjected to between 1914 and 1918 and in 1944.

Pont-à-Mousson's industrial activity centres round a foundry of the St-Gobain group.

The town is the headquarters of the **Parc naturel régional de Lorraine** and the convenient starting point of hikes and excursions through protected wide open spaces.

For a fine view of Pont-à-Mousson and the Moselle Valley, climb up to the **Signal de Xon**: drive N out of Pont-à-Mousson along N 57 and turn right onto D 910 then left 3km/1.9mi further on towards Lesménils and left again at the top of the hill. Continue for 1km/0.6mi and leave the car to reach the Signal de Xon on foot.

SIGHTS

★Ancienne abbaye des Prémontrés ⓥ – *Allow 1hr*. The former Premonstratensian abbey is a rare example of 18C monastic architecture. In 1964 it became a **cultural centre** and it is also now the headquarters of the European Centre of Sacred Art.

The old abbey is a now a cultural centre

Conventual buildings – Several rooms formerly used by the monks surround a lovely cloister: warming-room, refectory, chapter house, sacristy, former chapel etc. The three **staircases★** lead to the conference rooms, bedrooms and library: the small spiral-shaped staircase, situated in a corner of the cloister near the warming-room, is very elegant; on the other side of the chapel (used as a concert hall), the oval Samson staircase is one of the finest features of the abbey; as for the great square staircase, located on the right of the sacristy, it is concealed by a beautiful wrought-iron handrail and matching banisters.

Ste-Marie-Majeure – The Baroque interior of the former abbey church has been preserved including the slightly curved piers supporting the vaulting.

Musée de Pont-à-Mousson ⓥ – The University of Lorraine, based in Pont-à-Mousson from 1572 to 1768, attracted printers, engravers and booksellers to the town. The museum shows their work and displays a remarkable collection of objects made of papier mâché.

Eating out

MODERATE

Ferme-auberge Les Verts Pâturages – *14 r. St-Christophe – 54610 Éply – 14km/8.75mi E of Pont-à-Mousson on D 910, D 110¹ and D 70 – ☎ 03 83 31 30 85 – ⌷ – booking essential – 95/150F.* Why not stop for lunch in this peaceful village and enjoy a meal based on home produce, or stay a night in one of the rooms in a separate house, with a small garden. The attic room is the largest.

Ferme-auberge de la Petite Suisse – *124 r. de l'Église – 54380 Martincourt – 12km/7.5mi SW of Pont-à-Mousson on D 958 and D 106 – ☎ 03 83 23 10 70 – open Sat and Sun lunchtime – closed 4th weekend of each month – ⌷ – booking essential – 100/140F.* In this little village in the lush countryside you can enjoy the home-raised barbecued lamb, served with garden vegetables. Rustic decor and old objects.

TOWN WALK

★Place Duroc – The square is surrounded by 16C arcaded houses. In its centre stands a monumental fountain dating from 1931, offered to the town by the American ambulance service. There are several remarkable buildings in the vicinity including the **Maison des Sept Péchés Capitaux** (House of the Seven Deadly Sins), adorned with lovely caryatides representing the various sins and flanked by a Renaissance turret, where the dukes of Lorraine used to stay, and the town hall.
Follow rue Clemenceau at the back of the Maison des Sept Péchés Capitaux.

Maisons anciennes – The house at no 6 rue Clemenceau has a picturesque inner yard, restored to its original appearance, with a Renaissance well, a balcony and regional furniture.

Continue along rue Fabvier then along rue St-Laurent running parallel to it.

No 9 rue St-Laurent has a balcony overlooking the courtyard; no 11 has a brick façade with stone ties; no 19 is a Renaissance house built in 1590 and no 39 is the birthplace of General Duroc, one of Napoleon's faithful generals.

Église St-Laurent – The chancel and the transept date from the 15C and 16C. The central doorway and the first two storeys of the tower date from the 18C, the rest of the west front being completed in 1895.

Inside, note the polychrome triptych of a 16C altarpiece from Antwerp and a statue of Christ carrying his cross by Ligier Richier; the chancel is decorated with fine 18C woodwork.

Return to place Duroc.

Hôtel de ville ⊙ – This 18C edifice decorated with a pediment is surmounted by a monumental clock supported by two eagles; one of these wears the cross of Lorraine round its neck. The interior is adorned with fine tapestries.

Walk across Pont Gélot to the Église St-Martin.

Église St-Martin – *Guided tours by appointment with the tourist office.* The church was built in the 14C and 15C and extended by means of side chapels in the 17C and 18C. The 15C west front is flanked by two dissimilar towers.

Inside, note a Flamboyant Gothic funerary recess containing two medieval recumbent figures. In the north aisle, you can admire an Entombment comprising 13 characters by early-15C artists from Champagne and Germany (note the dress of the three soldiers asleep in the foreground); Ligier Richier was probably influenced by this work when he made the St-Mihiel Entombment half a century later.

As you come out of the church, turn right along rue St-Martin.

Ancien Collège des Jésuites – This former Jesuit college is now a secondary school. The edifice originally housed the university founded in the 16C; when it was transferred to Nancy in the late 18C, it was replaced by a royal military school. The fine courtyard has regained its original 16C-17C appearance.

Cross the river to return to place Duroc or continue to the former Abbaye des Prémontrés.

EXCURSIONS

★**Butte de Mousson** – *7km/4.3mi E then 15min on foot there and back. Drive N out of Pont-à-Mousson along N 57 for 200m/219yd then turn right onto D 910 and, 3km/1.9mi further on, turn left towards Lesménils in order to reach D 34 and the village of Mousson.*

A modern chapel stands at the top of the knoll as do the ruins of the feudal castle of the counts of Bar. From the viewpoint *(parking area)*, there is a fine **panorama** ★ of Lorraine and Moselle.

Vallée de l'Esch – *17km/10.6mi SW. Drive S out of Pont-à-Mousson along N 57. In Blénod, take the second road on the right after the church. It leads to Jezainville.*

As you enter Jezainville, turn round to catch a glimpse of the Butte de Mousson right behind you and of the Blénod power station on the right, with four units of 250 million watts each.

The road enters the charming Esch Valley, at the heart of an area known as Little Switzerland. The narrow road sometimes runs level with the small river winding its way across pastures and at other times climbs up a hill offering views of the pleasant green scenery.

Prény – *13km/8mi N. Leave Pont-à-Mousson along D 958 then turn right onto D 952. In Pagny-sur-Moselle, turn left onto D 82.*

The substantial ruins of a 13C castle dismantled by order of Richelieu stand on a hill (365m/1 197ft) overlooking the village. The towers linked by a high curtain wall formed an imposing fortress. It was the residence of the dukes of Lorraine before they moved to Nancy. The castle was finally abandoned at the beginning of the 18C. From the ruins, there is a fine view of the Moselle Valley.

Vallée du Rupt de Mad – If you have an hour to spare, you can prolong this excursion by continuing along D 952 then turning left to Arnaville, Villecey-sur-Mad and beyond, along the picturesque Rupt de Mad Valley, past the Château de Jaulny and as far as Thiaucourt-Regniéville.

PROVINS★★

Population 11 608
Michelin map 61 fold 4 or 237 fold 33

Whichever way one approaches the medieval town of Provins, the outline of the Tour César and the dome of the Église St-Quiriace can be seen from afar. The lower town lies on the banks of the Voulzie and the Durteint, beneath the promontory on which stand the romantic ruins celebrated by Balzac and painted by Turner. The formidable ramparts are the backdrop for medieval festivals and demonstrations in the summer months.

Clay from the Provins Basin, extracted from open quarries since time immemorial, supplies potters as well as brick and tile manufacturers with a complete range of raw materials.

HISTORICAL NOTES

The lower town developed from the 11C onwards round a Benedictine priory built on the spot where the relics of St Ayoul (or Aygulf) were miraculously found.

Under the leadership of Henri I (1152-81), Count of Champagne, known as the Liberal, Provins became a prosperous trading town and one of the two capital cities of the Champagne region.

The Provins fairs – The two fairs, held in Provins from May to June and from September to October, were, with those of Troyes, the most important of the Champagne fairs. There were three stages to each fair: first of all there was the display during which traders showed their merchandise, comparing prices and quality; next came the sale during which goods changed hands; the payment of the goods came last and, for this operation, sellers and buyers needed the help of money changers, notaries and **fair keepers**. The latter were initially police officers responsible for the prevention of theft and fraud, but by the 13C they had acquired real judicial power.

During the fair, the city looked like a huge market hall full of a colourful crowd of people from northern regions as well as from the Mediterranean. Transactions were made in local currency, hence the growing importance of Italian bankers who could calculate complex exchange rates; by the end of the 13C, they had taken control of the fairs and money changing took precedence over the sale of goods. The first annual fair, which was the most important, took place on the hilltop, near the castle, the second near the Église St-Ayoul.

Medieval town – Two separate towns developed simultaneously: the Châtel or upper town and the Val or lower town. They were later included within the same fortifications. In the 13C the city already had a large population of more than 10 000 inhabitants. Apart from numerous merchants, there were weavers, fullers, dyers, cloth-makers, shearers, without forgetting money changers, guards entrusted with police duties and other judicial representatives of the counts of Champagne. Numerous inns, shops and a thriving Jewish community added to the town's cosmopolitan atmosphere.

The counts of Champagne stayed in Provins for long periods and were surrounded by a lively court. Thibaud IV (1201-53), known as the Chansonnier, encouraged the arts and wrote songs which range among the best 13C literature.

In the 14C, the town's activities declined and the fairs were supplanted by those of Paris and Lyon. The Hundred Years War confirmed the end of economic prosperity for Provins.

Roses – According to tradition it was **Thibaud IV** the Troubadour who brought roses back from Syria and grew them successfully here in Provins. Edmund Lancaster (1245-96), brother of the King of England, married Blanche of Artois and was for a while suzerain of Provins, at which time he introduced the red rose into his coat of arms.

June is the best month to visit the rose beds at the **Pépinières et Roseraies Vizier** ⊙, rue des Prés.

★★UPPER TOWN

It is advisable to park in the car park near Porte St-Jean. This is the location of the tourist office and the departure point for the small tourist train which tours the Upper Town and then returns to the Lower Town.

Porte St-Jean – St John's Gateway was built in the 13C. This stocky construction is flanked by two projecting towers which are partially hidden by the buttresses which were added in the 14C to support the drawbridge.

Follow allée des Remparts which overlooks the old moat.

BN - Paris

Common Rose of Provins

PROVINS
VILLE HAUTE

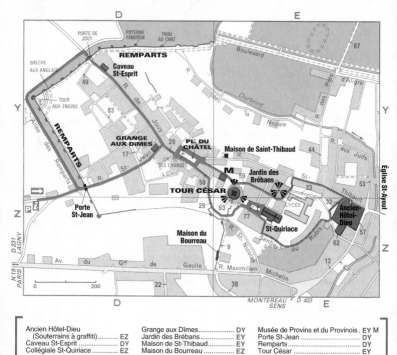

★★ **Remparts** – The town walls were built in the 12C and 13C along an existing line of defence, then altered on several occasions. They constitute a very fine example of medieval military architecture. A house straddling the curtain wall was the home of the Provins executioners. The last one to live here was Charles-Henri Sanson who executed Louis XVI. The most interesting part of the ramparts runs between Porte St-Jean and Porte de Jouy. The Tour aux Engins, on the corner, links the two curtain walls; it derives its name from a barn nearby in which engines of war were housed.

In summer, on a space behind this tower, within the ramparts, the falconers of the "Aigles de Provins" company put on a **show** of birds of prey; other birds of prey are displayed in shelters.

Beyond the 12C Porte de Jouy take rue de Jouy, which is lined by picturesque low houses with long tiled roofs or an overhanging upper storey. **Caveau St-Esprit** *(open during special events)* was once the store of an old hospital which was destroyed by fire in the 17C.

Place du Châtel – This vast, peaceful square, rectangular in shape, is bordered by attractive old houses: the 15C Maison des Quatre Pignons (south-west corner), the 13C Maison des Petits-Plaids (north-west corner), the Hôtel de la Coquille to the north. The remains of Église St-Thibault (12C) stand on the north-east corner.

In the centre, next to an old well with a wrought-iron cage, stands the Croix des Changes, where the edicts of the Counts of Champagne were posted.

Walk past the **Musée du Provinois**, housed in one of the town's oldest buildings, the "Maison Romane" (Romanesque house).

Église St-Quiriace – The church was begun in the 11C. The transept and nave date from the 13C, the dome from the 17C. On the square in front of the church stands a Cross on the site of the old bell-tower which collapsed in 1689.

★★**Tour César** ⊙ – This superb 12C keep, 44m/144ft high and flanked by four turrets, is the emblem of the town. It was once part of the walls of the upper town. The pyramidal roof was built in the 16C.

The revetment wall which encloses the base of the keep was added by the English during the Hundred Years War, in order to house the artillery.

The guard-room on the first floor is octagonal and 11m/36ft high; it is topped by vaulting formed of four arcades of pointed arches ending in a dome and pierced by an orifice through which the soldiers on the floor above were passed supplies. The gallery encircling the keep at the

Tour César

height of the turrets was originally roofed over. One **view**★ extends over the town and the surrounding countryside.

A very narrow stairway leads to the upper level. Under the fine 16C wooden roof are the bells of St-Quiriace, which have hung here since the church lost its bell-tower.

Return to Porte St-Jean via place du Châtel then rue St-Jean on the left.

Eating out

MODERATE

Petit Écu – *9 place du Châtel – ☎ 01 64 08 95 00 – closed Jan and evenings from Oct to Apr except Sat-Sun – 98/115F.* On a charming square in the old city of Provins stands this fine half-timbered house offering traditional French cuisine during the week. Alternatively, try the unusual weekend formula consisting of buffets based on a medieval theme...

Where to stay

MID-RANGE

Hôtel Aux Vieux Remparts – *3 rue Couverte – ☎ 01 64 08 94 00 – **P** – 25 rooms 420/750F – ⊆ 55F – restaurant 150/360F.* This modern building dating from the 1980s, located in the Cité des Roses, contains simple but comfortable rooms. French regional cooking. The peaceful, shaded terrace is especially popular in the summer months.

Chambre d'Hôte Clos Thibaud de Champagne – *1 rue du Souci, 77520 Cessoy-en-Montois – 16km/10mi south-west of Provins by N 19 then D 75 – ☎ 01 60 67 32 10 – ⊟ – 4 rooms 350/450F – meal 150F.* In a small village, this beautifully restored former Briard farmhouse has retained its authentic character. The garden commanding nice views of the surrounding landscape adds to the charm of the blissfully quiet bedrooms.

On the town

Auberge du Chatel – *2 rue Couverte – ☎ 01 64 08 97 34 – daily 9am-1am.* The slightly eccentric decoration of this bar lends it an old-fashioned touch with the odd reference to advertising. It is also an art gallery as the pictures and statuettes on display are for sale. Shaded courtyard with terrace.

Le Jardin Saint-Ayoul – *6 place St-Ayoul – ☎ 01 64 00 38 75 – www. tishase.aol.com – Tues-Sun 9.30am-1am.* This modest, unassuming café stages a number of interesting activities you can buy books at reduced prices, surf on the Internet or take part in weekend discussions centring on poetry or philosophical issues. If you have musical skills, why not settle at the piano and tease the keys while sipping your drink...

Showtime

À l'Assaut des Remparts – Tournoi de Chevalerie – ⬚ – *Office de Tourisme, chemin de Villecran* – ☎ *01 64 60 26 26* – *www.provins.net* – Near the Porte Saint-Jean, at the back of the moat, you will be plunged into the Dark Ages thanks to two remarkable shows of startling realism. First, there is a demonstration of military equipment and defensive weapons, then you will attend a jousting tournament in which competitors fight with swords or lances and sometimes even with their feet!

Les Aigles des Remparts – ⬚ – *Rue de Jouy* – ☎ *01 64 60 26 26* – *www.provins.net* – One of the favourite pastimes of medieval lords was to observe the antics of birds of prey gliding through the skies. After the demonstration, the falconer takes those who wish around the aviary.

ADDITIONAL SIGHTS

★**Grange aux Dîmes** ⊘ – *Rue St-Jean*.
This massive 13C building belonged to the canons of St-Quiriace, who hired out the space to merchants during the major fairs. When the fairs went into decline the barn became a store for the tithes *(dîmes)* levied on the harvests of the peasants.
The atmosphere of the town's famous fairs is realistically recreated in a permanent exhibition entitled, "**Provins au temps des foires de Champagne**".

Musée du Provinois ⊘ – This local museum is housed in one of the oldest buildings in the town, "The Romanesque House".
On the ground floor are displayed **the sculpture and ceramic collections★**, valuable works of local medieval and Renaissance art.
Exploiting the underground clay quarries enabled potters to produce pieces now noted for their remarkable variety and timelessness.

Église St-Ayoul – In 1048 Thibaud I, Count of Troyes and Meaux (and also Count of Blois under the name Thibaud III), grand protector of the abbeys, installed the monks from Montier-la-Celle in the St-Ayoul district in the Lower Town.
The three doorways project far beyond the line of the gable on the west front. Missing parts of the **central doorway** were replaced with new pieces by the sculptor Georges Jeanclos, who was responsible for the bronze **statues★** with antique patina which now harmonise well with the medieval reliefs.
Inside, in the north aisle, stand 16C **statues★★**: a graceful if rather affected Virgin Mary and two **musician angels** with wonderfully draped clothes.

Souterrains à graffiti ⊘ – *Entrance in rue St-Thibault, left of the doorway to the Ancien Hôtel-Dieu*. There is a substantial network of underground passages around Provins, some marked with ancient graffiti. The section which is open to the public runs through a layer of a tufa which lies parallel to the base of the spur on which the Upper Town stands. The entrance is through a low-roofed chamber with ribbed vaulting in the old hospice.

Provins – Portail de l'église St-Ayoul

This ancient university town lying on the banks of the River Vesle is famous for its magnificent cathedral, where French kings were traditionally crowned, as well as the Basilique St-Remi. Reims is also, together with Épernay, the capital of Champagne and most cellars are open to the public.

The town, surrounded by a ring of boulevards laid out in the 18C, has, since then, considerably expanded and some of its vast suburbs stretch as far as the edge of the vineyards.

Allow at least one day to see the city's main sights.

HISTORICAL NOTES

Ancient times – The origins of Reims go back to pre-Roman times when it was the fortified capital of a Gaulish tribe, the Remes. After the Roman conquest, it became a thriving administrative and commercial city with many public buildings. The **Porte de Mars** and the **Cryptoportique** are the only two to have survived to this day. From the 3C onwards its strategic position increased its military importance as the Romans desperately tried to stop invading hords from the east. At the same time, Reims became a Christian city and the first cathedral was built.

Clovis' christening – Then came the conversion of **Clovis**, the proud king of the Franks, who was baptised by the bishop of Reims, **Remi** (440-533), on Christmas day shortly before the year 500. The whole population rejoiced and led a procession from the former imperial palace to the baptistery situated near the cathedral. According to legend, a dove brought a phial containing holy oil used by Remi to anoint Clovis. This phial was carefully preserved and used for the coronation of every king of France from the 11C to 1825, the most famous being that of Charles VII in 1429, at the height of the Hundred Years War, in the presence of Joan of Arc.

Medieval Reims – From the end of the 5C and during the whole medieval period, Reims was an important religious, political and artistic centre **(École de Reims)**. The powerful arch-bishops of Reims played the role of arbiters between kings and princes who came to stay at the Abbaye de St-Remi. One of the archbishops, **Gerbert**, became Pope in 999.

During the 11C, 12C and 13C, the town expanded and acquired some splendid edifices such as the abbey church of St-Remi and the cathedral. **Guillaume aux Blanches Mains**, who was archbishop from 1176 to 1202, contributed to the prosperity of the town by granting it a charter and, by the beginning of the 13C, Reims had doubled in size.

Modern times – Badly damaged during the First World War when 80% of the town's buildings were destroyed, Reims was spared during the Second World War. The capitulation of the German forces on 7 May 1945 was signed in Reims where General Eisenhower had his headquarters.

Today the textile industry, which brought prosperity to the town as early as the 12C, has practically disappeared but the production of Champagne remains one of the town's main activities. The city's artistic tradition is also being maintained by the famous stained-glass workshops which once employed the talents of Villon, Chagall, Braque and Da Silva.

★★CHAMPAGNE CELLARS

The famous Champagne firms are gathered in the Champ de Mars district and along the limestone slopes of St-Nicaise hill, full of galleries known as *crayères*, often dating from the Gallo-Roman period. The depth and extent of the galleries makes them ideal Champagne cellars.

Pommery ⊘ ✗ Founded in 1836 by Narcisse Gréno and Louis Alexandre Pommery, it was expanded by the latter's widow who inaugurated Brut Champagne and had the present buildings erected in the Elizabethan style in 1878. She also linked the Gallo-Roman *crayères* by building 18km/11mi of galleries and acquired many vineyards so that Pommery now owns 300ha/731 acres of the finest Champagne vines.

The tour enables visitors to discover the different stages of Champagne-making through galleries decorated with 19C sculptures and to see a 75 000l/16 500gal tun by Émile Gallé, dating from 1904.

◉ Nearby, the 22ha/54-acre **Parc Pommery** ⊘ includes a playground and various sports grounds.

Taittinger ⊘ – In 1734, the Fourneaux family of wine merchants launched into the production of sparkling wine made according to Dom Pérignon's methods. In 1932, Pierre Taittinger took over the management of the firm which was renamed after him. Today, the Taittinger vineyards extend over 250ha/618 acres and the firm owns 6 grape-harvesting centres on the Montagne de Reims, the Château de la Marquetterie in Pierry, the Hôtel des Comtes de Champagne in Reims *(see TOWN CENTRE below)* and superb cellars.

This mosaic shows vinters turning bottles, removing sediment and blending

Visitors can enjoy a fascinating tour of the cellars among 15 million bottles maturing in the cool Gallo-Roman galleries and in the crypts of the former 13C Abbaye St-Nicaise, destroyed during the Revolution.

Veuve Clicquot-Ponsardin ⊘ – This firm, founded in 1772 by Philippe Clicquot, was considerably expanded by his son's widow whose maiden name was Ponsardin. In 1816, she introduced *remuage (see p 69)* into the process of Champagne-making. Today, Veuve Clicquot-Ponsardin, which owns 265ha/655 acres of vines and exports three quarters of its production, is one of the best-known Champagne firms outside France. *Reserve 1 wk in advance*

Ruinart ⊘ – Founded in 1729, this Champagne firm prospered during the Restoration period (1814-30) and again after 1949, having gone through years of decline during the two world wars. Today Ruinart, which belongs to the Moët-Hennessy group, specialises in top-quality Champagne. Its Gallo-Roman galleries are particularly interesting. *By appt, free*

Piper-Heidsieck ⊘ – The firm was founded in 1785. The various stages of Champagne-making are explained by means of an audio-visual presentation and visitors can afterwards tour the cellars, extending 16km/10mi underground, in a gondola car. *Closed T+W. 30-min tour 9-11:45 2-5:15 €6.90*

Mumm ⊘ – After its creation in 1827, this firm prospered throughout the 19C in Europe and in America; today, it owns 420ha/1 038 acres of vines and its cellars *(open to the public)* extend over a total distance of 25km/16mi. *9-11 2-5 €3.81*

TOWN CENTRE *allow 2hr*

From the square in front of the cathedral, walk along rue Rockefeller and turn right onto rue Chanzy.

The itinerary takes you past the Musée des Beaux-Arts housed in the former 18C Abbaye St-Denis.

Continue along rue Chanzy then turn left onto the lively pedestrian rue de Vesle.

Note the small doorway which used to give access to the south transept of the Église St-Jacques.

Turn right onto rue Max-Dormoy.

Église St-Jacques ⊘ – The 13C-14C Gothic nave with a traditional triforium is prolonged by a Flamboyant Gothic chancel (early 16C) framed by two Renaissance chapels (mid-16C) with Corinthian columns. The modern stained-glass windows were designed by Vieira da Silva (side chapels) and Sima (chancel).

Place Drouet-d'Erlon – Named after one of Napoleon's generals, this lively pedestrianised space lined with cafés, restaurants, hotels and cinemas is the heart of the city.

Walk up to the Fontaine Subé, erected in 1903, turn right onto rue de l'Étape and continue as far as rue de l'Arbalète.

Eating out

MODERATE

Le Forum – *32-34 pl. du Forum* – ☎ *03 26 47 56 87* – *closed 15-30 Aug, 25 Dec-2 Jan, Mon evening and Sun* – *80/134F.* Advertising posters from the 1930s, old toys and a collection of objects evoking cars and motorbikes all contribute to a pleasant atmosphere in this bistro. A nice spot, not far from place Royale. Terrace.

Continental – *95 pl. Drouet-d'Erlon* – ☎ *03 26 47 01 47* – *99/193F.* Right in the centre of the Champagne capital, this restaurant proposes classic cooking served in an old dining room with beams and panelling.

Brasserie Le Boulingrin – *48 r. Mars* – ☎ *03 26 40 96 22* – *closed Sun* – *100/150F.* This Art Deco style restaurant dating from 1925 has become an institution in Reims life. The owner is much in evidence, overseeing the operations and creating a congenial atmosphere. The menu is inventive and the prices reasonable.

MID-RANGE

Café du Palais – *14 pl. Myron-Herrick* – ☎ *03 26 47 52 54* – *closed Sun* – *150F.* This lively café near the cathedral was founded in 1930. With its original glass roof and a warm red decor, the generous portions of salad and other daily dishes are much appreciated, as are the home-made pastries. You can also enjoy a reasonably priced glass of Champagne.

Le Vigneron – *Pl. P.-Jamot* – ☎ *03 26 79 86 86* – *closed 1-20 Aug, 24 Dec-3 Jan, Sat and Sun* – *booking essential* – *180/360F.* Here, a century of Champagne-making is celebrated, with posters from 1850 to 1950 decorating the walls of the warm and welcoming dining room. A small museum exhibits the winemaker's clothing and tools, and of course the regional menu includes Champagne, too!

Where to stay

MID-RANGE

Grand Hôtel du Nord – *75 pl. Drouet-d'Erlon* – ☎ *03 26 47 39 03* – *49 rooms 260/320F* – ☲ *35F.* Comfortable rooms with floral decor in a 1920s building set in a pedestrianised square. The rooms facing the back are quieter. After a busy tour of the town centre, you can relax in one of the sitting rooms.

Hôtel La Cathédrale – *20 r. Libergier* – ☎ *03 26 47 28 46* – *17 rooms 265/350F* – ☲ *40F.* This smart but welcoming hotel stands in one of the streets which lead to the cathedral. The small rooms have comfortable beds and are bright and cheerful, while the breakfast room is decorated with old engravings.

Hôtel Continental – *93 pl. Drouet-d'Erlon* – ☎ *03 26 40 39 35* – *closed 22 Dec-7 Jan* – *50 rooms 330/620F* – ☲ *50F.* An imposing 19C town house next to the cathedral. The large entrance hall opens onto a high-ceilinged salon with beams, sculptures and a period chandelier. Comfortable rooms under the roof on the second floor.

Hôtel Porte Mars – *2 pl. de la République* – ☎ *03 26 40 28 35* – *24 rooms 340/395F* – ☲ *50F.* A 1920s building where it's a pleasure to drink tea near the fire in the cosy sitting room, or enjoy a drink in the sophisticated bar. Breakfast is also particularly good, served in the glass-roofed dining room. Attractive decor with photographs and old mirrors. Comfortable, personal rooms.

LUXURY

Boyer "Les Crayères" – *64 bd Vasnier* – ☎ *03 26 82 80 80* – *closed 23 Dec-12 Jan* – 🅿 – *16 rooms, from 1480F* – ☲ *130F* – *restaurant 990/1090F.* Enjoy the exceptional setting of the Count of Polignac's castle, in a 7ha/17-acre park. Three dining rooms, with a particularly lovely table in the rotunda, a cosy bar with glass roof, and superbly decorated rooms combine to offer peace, luxury and especially fine cooking.

On the town

Arrigo's Bar – *35 r. Buirette* – ☎ *03 26 47 02 27* – *Tue-Sat 6pm-2am.* This high-class American bar is run by an Italian. Ask to see the sumptuous reception rooms designed by Degermann. The house specialities include cocktails and Italian ice cream.

Bar de l'Hôtel de la Paix – *9 r. Buirette* – ☎ *03 26 40 04 08* – *daily 4pm-1am*. The bar of this three-star hotel is a favourite of the inhabitants of Reims, especially among the many wine-growers and restaurateurs who gather here. The terrace leads out onto a garden with a swimming pool. Specialities: cocktails and Champagne.

Baradaz – *79 bd du Gén.-Leclerc* – ☎ *03 26 47 83 33* – *Mon-Thu noon-12.30am, Fri noon-1.30am, Sat-Sun 7am-1.30am* – *closed public holidays*. Popular with a trendy, younger crowd, this unusual bar has a huge dragon suspended over the customers' heads. Musical events are organised on a regular basis, including concerts and DJ-hosted evenings (rock, jazz, groove).

Café du Palais – *14 pl. Myron-Herrick* – ☎ *03 26 47 52 54* – *Mon-Sat 8am-8.30pm*. The Vogt family, who have owned this magnificent café since the 1930s, have decorated it tastefully with paintings, sculptures and clocks acquired over the years through their travels and friendships. It may appear starchy at first glance, but you will soon find the atmosphere very friendly. Sip a glass of reasonably priced Champagne under the Art Deco glass roof by Jacques Simon (from the family which for generations has worked to restore the windows in Reims Cathedral) or enjoy the terrace opposite the law courts.

L'Apostrophe – *59 pl. Drouet-d'Erlon* – ☎ *03 26 79 19 89* – *daily 8-1am* – *closed 24-25 Dec*. A hot-spot of Reims nightlife, this modern ground-floor bar has a restaurant upstairs. Specialities: beers and cocktails. Variety concerts on Fridays.

L'Aquarium – *93 bd du Gén.-Leclerc* – ☎ *03 26 47 34 29* – *Sun-Thu 10pm-4am, Fri-Sat 10pm-5am*. This fashionable discotheque always draws a crowd. Varied programme of music: disco, house.

La Chaise au Plafond – *190 av. d'Épernay* – ☎ *03 26 06 09 61* – *Mon-Sat 7am-8pm* – *closed 2 weeks in Feb and 3 weeks in Aug*. Founded in 1910, this bar and tobacconists is famous for the chair which has remained stuck to the ceiling ever since a shell hit the establishment on 12 September 1914. Terrace in summer. Small selection of Cuban cigars.

Le César's Club – *17 r. Lesage* – ☎ *03 26 88 24 80* – *Mon-Fri noon-3am, Sat-Sun 2pm-3am*. Two former national billiards champions run this attractive club, which offers 21 tables in all (snooker, pool, French billiards). Tournaments on Monday evenings at 8pm. Occasional regional competitions and exhibitions.

Shopping

Champagne Piper-Heidsieck – *51 bd Henry-Vasnier* – ☎ *03 26 84 43 44* – *daily 9-11.45am, 2-5.15pm* – *closed Tue, Wed 1 Jan-28 Feb and 25 Dec*. Founded in 1785. The cellars are visited by boat. Tasting and sales after the visit.

Champagne Pommery – *5 pl. du Gén.-Gouraud* – ☎ *03 26 61 62 56* – *Mar-Nov: daily 10am-18pm; Nov-Mar: Mon-Fri 10am-6pm*. Founded in 1836. 18km/11mi of underground passages link 120 former Roman chalk pits. The establishment owns 300ha/740 acres of vineyards and a reserve of 75 000l of wine.

Fossier – *25 cours Langlet* – ☎ *03 26 47 59 84* – *Mon 2-7pm, Tue-Sat 9.30am-7pm*. Founded in 1845, the biscuit and chocolate maker Fossier creates the ultimate in Reims confectionery (*biscuits roses* and *croquignoles*).

Science, Techniques, Tradition

Mumm – *29 r. du Champ-de-Mars* – ☎ *03 26 49 59 70*. Founded in 1827, this establishment owns 420ha/1 037 acres of vineyards and 25km/15.5mi of cellars.

Ruinart – *4 r. Crayères* – ☎ *03 26 77 51 51*. Created in 1729, this establishment has been producing top-quality Champagne ever since.

Taittinger – *9 pl. St-Nicaise* – ☎ *03 26 85 45 35*. Founded in 1734, this establishment owns 250ha/617 acres of vineyards. In its cellars 15 million bottles are gradually ageing.

★ **Hôtel de la Salle** – This Renaissance edifice, built between 1545 and 1556, is the birthplace of **Jean-Baptiste de la Salle** *(see below)*. The harmonious façade, adorned with Doric pilasters at ground-floor level and Ionic ones at first-floor level, is flanked by a pavilion whose carriage entrance is decorated by statues of Adam and Eve on either side.

An elaborately carved frieze runs across the façade.

A picturesque openwork stair turret rises in a corner of the courtyard.

Jean-Baptiste de la Salle and schooling for the poor.

Small schools intended for children of poor families began to open in Reims from 1674 onwards, at the instigation of Canon Roland. His work was continued by Jean-Baptiste de la Salle.

Born in Reims in 1651, Jean-Baptiste de la Salle belonged to a rich aristocratic family who intended him to pursue a brilliant career within the Church. However, the young canon decided instead to devote his energies and his wealth to educating the poor. He began by founding the Communauté des Sœurs du Saint Enfant Jésus, which spread throughout the countryside. The nuns ran schools, and catechism classes but they also taught adults. A few years later, Jean-Baptiste de la Salle founded the Communauté des Frères des Écoles Chrétiennes, which expanded considerably.

In 1695, he published a work entitled *The Running of Schools*, in which he explained his theories about teaching: he was in favour of collective teaching and wanted French to replace Latin. However, his ideas, which were revolutionary at the time, only triumphed long after his death (Rouen 1719).

Turn left onto rue du Dr-Jacquin.

Hôtel de ville – The imposing 17C façade was saved from the fire which destroyed the building in 1917. The pediment is decorated with an equestrian low-relief sculpture representing Louis XIII.

Follow rue du Général-Sarail on the left.

Basses et Hautes Promenades – These vast shaded areas were designed in the 18C to replace the moat and glacis of the old fortifications. They provide a useful parking area close to the town centre. A fun fair invades the Hautes Promenades at Christmas and Easter. A remarkable wrought-iron **railing**, made in 1774 for the coronation of Louis XVI, stands at the end of the Basses Promenades.

Not far from there, along boulevard du Général-Leclerc, stand two 19C buildings, the **Cirque** (1 100 seats) and the **Manège** (600 seats) where various events are held.

★ **Porte Mars** – This triumphal arch (height: 13.5m/44ft) of the Corinthian order was erected in honour of the Roman Emperor Augustus some time after the 3C AD. During the Middle Ages, it was included in the ramparts and used as a town gate. It consists of three arches decorated inside with low-relief sculptures depicting Jupiter and Leda, as well as the founders of Rome, Romulus and Remus.

Walk along rue de Mars.

Rue de Mars – The façade of no 6 is decorated with mosaic panels illustrating the Champagne-making process.

Hôtel des Comtes de Champagne – This Gothic mansion belongs to the Taittinger Champagne firm.

The Maison des Musiciens, whose first storey has been reconstructed and exhibited in the Musée St-Remi, was located next door.

The street leads to place du Forum, formerly place des Marchés.

Cryptoportique gallo-romain ⊘ – This large half-buried Gallo-Roman monument, dating from the 2C AD, stands on the site of the ancient city's forum.

Walk along rue Colbert to place Royale.

★ **Place Royale** – The square, designed by Legendre in 1760, is characteristic of the Louis XVI style: arcades, roofs edged by balusters. The former Hôtel des Fermes, on the south side, houses administrative offices. The statue of Louis XV by Pigalle, which used to stand in the centre of the square, was destroyed during the Revolution and the holy coronation phial was smashed on the pedestal; another statue by Cartellier replaced the original during the Restoration (1814-30).

Follow rue Carnot on the right.

Porte du Chapitre – This 16C gate, flanked by two corbelled turrets, formed the main entrance of the chapter-house.

Walk through the gateway to return to the cathedral.

REIMS

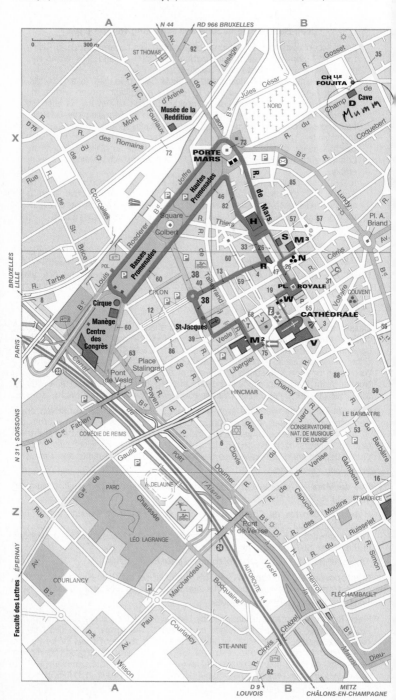

***CATHÉDRALE NOTRE-DAME

Owing to its homogenous architectural style, its superb sculptures and its spiritual role over more than a 1 000 years of French and European history, the Cathédrale Notre-Dame undoubtedly deserves to be considered as one of the finest cathedrals in Christendom.

In 1210, Archbishop Aubry de Humbert decided to build a Gothic cathedral (the third to be erected on this site) modelled on those which were being built at the time in Paris (1163), Soissons (1180) and Chartres (1194). The edifice was designed by Jean d'Orbais and five successive architects followed the original plans, which accounts for the extraordinary homogeneity of the cathedral. Their names were inscribed on the original paving stones which unfortunately disappeared in the 18C. Jean d'Orbais built the chancel, Jean le Loup the nave and the west front which Gaucher de Reims decorated with statues and three portals, Bernard de Soissons designed the rose-window and the gables and finished the nave vaulting. By 1285, the interior had been completed. The towers were erected in the 15C; others were planned but a severe fire, which damaged the roof structure in 1481, halted the project.

The cathedral was regrettably altered in the 18C (suppression of the rood screen, of some stained glass and of the labyrinth), but it was not damaged during the Revolution. Unfortunately, a long restoration programme had just been completed when, in September 1914, heavy shelling set fire to the timber framework causing the bells and the lead of the stained glass to melt and the stone to split. More shell damage occurred throughout the First World War and a new restoration programme was launched, partly financed by the Rockefeller Foundation. The damaged timber framework was replaced by a concrete roof structure. The cathedral was finally reconsecrated in 1937.

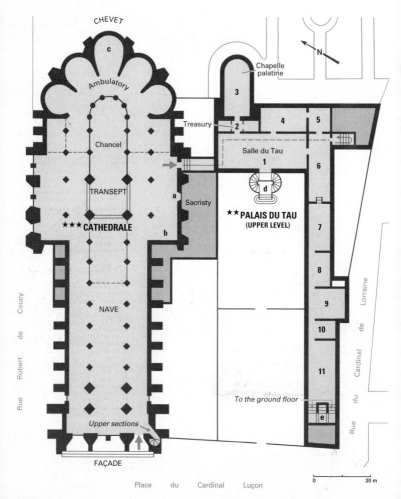

Exterior

A wealth of statues decorate the outside of the cathedral, more than 2 300 in fact. Some of them, however, which were badly damaged by war and bad weather, are now exhibited in the Palais du Tau and have been replaced by copies.

West front – Best seen in the setting sun, the west front of Reims Cathedral is reminiscent of Notre-Dame in Paris but here the vertical lines are emphasized by the pointed gables and pinnacles, the slender colonnettes and the tall statues decorating the kings' gallery.

The **three doorways**, in line with the three naves, are surmounted by elaborately carved gables contrasting with the openwork tympanums. The 13C statues adorning the doorways are from four workshops employed successively.

Central doorway (the Virgin's portal) – It is composed of several elements starting with, against the upright post, the smiling Virgin; on the right, the Visitation and the Annunciation; on the left, Jesus at the Temple; on the gable, the Coronation of the Virgin (copy).

Situated above the rose-window and the scene depicting David slaying Goliath, the kings' gallery includes 56 statues (4.5m/15ft high and weighing 6-7t); in the centre, Clovis' christening.

Walk along the north side of the cathedral.

The north side of the cathedral has retained its original features: the **buttresses** are surmounted by recesses containing a large angel with open wings.

North transept – The façade has three doorways decorated with statues which are older than those of the west front. The right doorway comes from the Romanesque cathedral: the tympanum is adorned with a Virgin in glory framed by foliage beneath a rounded arch. The upright post of the middle portal is decorated with a statue of Pope Calixtus. The embrasures of the left doorway have retained their six fine statues representing the Apostles and the tympanum is carved with picturesque scenes of the Last Judgement.

East end – From cours Anatole-France, there is a fine view of the east end of the cathedral with its radiating chapels surmounted by arcaded galleries and its superposed flying buttresses.

Interior ⊘

Inside, the cathedral is well lit and its proportions are remarkable (138m/151yd long and 38m/42yd high); the impression of loftiness is enhanced by the narrowness of the nave in relation to its length and by the succession of very pointed transverse arches.

The three-storey elevations of the **nave** consist of the main arcading supported by round piers, a blind triforium (level with the roofing of the aisles) and tall clerestory windows, divided into lancets by mullions. Capitals are decorated with floral motifs.

The **chancel** has only two bays but the space used for services extends into the nave as there was always a large number of canons and a lot of space was needed for coronations. The chancel used to be closed off by a rood screen on which the royal throne was placed. Pillars get gradually narrower and closer together, thus increasing the impression of height. The radiating chapels are linked by a passage typical of the region's architectural style.

The **inside of the west front**★★ was the work of Gaucher from Reims. The large rose-window (12m/40ft in diameter) is located above the triforium arcading backed by stained-glass windows of similar shape. A smaller rose decorates the doorway. On either side, a number of recesses contain statues. Floral motifs, similar to those of the nave capitals, complete the decoration. The inside of the central doorway is very well preserved: on the left the Life of the Virgin is represented and on the right scenes from the Life of John the Baptist.

Western façade of Reims Catehdral

★★Stained glass – The 13C stained-glass windows suffered considerable damage: some were replaced by clear glass in the 18C, others were destroyed during the First World War. Those of the apse are still intact: in the centre is the donor with suffragan bishops on either side. The great 13C rose-window, dedicated to the Virgin, looks its best in the setting sun.

Jacques Simon, a member of the family of stained-glass makers who have been restoring the cathedral for generations, was able to repair some of the damaged ones and even to reconstruct the missing ones from drawings his ancestors made before the First World War. Note in particular the wine-growers' window (**a**). His daughter Brigitte Simon-Marcq made a series of abstract windows including one entitled the River Jordan to the right of the christening font (**b**) in the south transept.

In 1974, Marc Chagall decorated the apsidal chapel (**c**) with luminous blue-based stained-glass windows. They were made in the Simon workshop: in the centre, Abraham's Sacrifice and the Crucifixion; on the left, a Tree of Jesse and on the right, great events which took place in the cathedral such as Clovis' christening and St Louis' coronation.

The cathedral has retained a 15C astronomical clock. Each hour struck starts two processions: the Adoration of the Magi and the Flight to Egypt.

★★PALAIS DU TAU ⊘

The archbishops' palace, first built on this site in 1138, owes its strange name to its T shape which resembles ancient episcopal croziers; it contains the cathedral treasury and some of the original statues. The present building, designed in 1690 by Robert de Cotte and Mansart, has retained a 13C chapel and the 15C great hall known as the Salle du Tau. Severely damaged in September 1914, at the same time as the cathedral, it was restored over a considerable number of years.

Access from the south transept of the cathedral.

Stairs lead to the Gothic **lower room** covered with ribbed vaulting, where stone fragments were stored. An exhibition shows the evolution of the cathedral site and of the canons' district which has disappeared. From there, the stone fragments (part of the rood screen) housed in the lower chapel can be seen.

Walk upstairs and through the Salle du Goliath.

Reliquary of St Ursula

The **Salle du Tau** (**1**) was used for the festivities which followed coronations. Lined with cloth bearing fleurs-de-lis, the symbol of French royalty, and decorated with two huge 15C tapestries from Arras illustrating the story of Clovis, it is covered with an elegant vault shaped like a ship's hull.

The **treasury** (**2**) is exhibited in two rooms: the left-hand one, lined with blue velvet, houses royal presents preserved during the Revolution such as Charlemagne's 9C talisman, which contains a piece of the True Cross, the coronation chalice, a 12C cup, the reliquary of the Holy Thorn, carved out of an 11C crystal, the 15C reliquary of the Resurrection and the reliquary of St Ursula, a delicate cornelian vase decorated with statuettes enamelled in 1505.

The right-hand room contains ornaments used for the coronation of Charles X: the reliquary of the Holy Phial, a large offering vase and two gold and silver breads, the necklace of the Order of the Holy Spirit worn by Louis-Philippe and a copy of Louis XV's crown.

The doorway of the **chapel** (**3**), built between 1215 and 1235, is surmounted by the Adoration of the Magi. The altar is decorated with the cross and six gilt silver candelabra made for the wedding of Napoleon and Marie-Louise.

The **Salle Charles X** (**4**) is devoted to the coronation of 1825. It contains the royal cloak as well as garments used by heralds and a painting of *Charles X in regal dress* by Gérard.

The **Antichambre des appartements du roi** (**5**), which illustrates the restoration of the cathedral's sculptures, leads to the Musée de l'Œuvre de la Cathédrale.

The **Salle du Goliath** (**6**) contains monumental statues of St Paul, St James, Goliath (5.4m/18ft) wearing a coat of mail, as well as allegorical representations of the Synagogue (blindfolded) and the Church, damaged by shelling.

The **Salle des petites sculptures** (**7**) houses refined heads from the north transept and Passion doorways, the statues of Abraham and Aaron from the south doorway, two wingless angels and a 17C tapestry from Brussels depicting the story of Clovis (Battle of Tolbiac).

Note, in the **Salle du Cantique des Cantiques** (**8**), four precious 17C hand-embroidered pieces of cloth made of wool and silk.

The **Salon carré** (**9**) is adorned with 17C tapestries, depicting scenes from Christ's childhood, woven in Reims. Two large statues of Magdalene and St Peter originally decorated the west front.

The **Salle du roi de Juda** (**10**) contains large statues including that of Judah (14C, kings' gallery) and three tapestries illustrating the Life of the Virgin.

Nine more sections of this tapestry are in the **Galerie du couronnement de la Vierge** (**11**) together with three kings from the north transept, three kings from the south transept and the statue of the Pilgrim from Emmaus which used to stand on the right of the great rose-window.

The Coronation of the Virgin (**e**) originally decorating the gable of the central doorway, overlooks the staircase.

Before leaving the courtyard, note the 15C angel (**d**) used as a weathervane.

★★BASILIQUE AND MUSÉE ST-REMI

★★**Basilique St-Remi** – Remi was buried in 533 in a small chapel dedicated to St Christopher. Shortly afterwards, a basilica was constructed. Then the Abbaye de St-Remi was founded in the 8C by a group of Benedictine monks. Work on the present basilica began c 1007, but the project was deemed too ambitious and abandoned. The Carolingian church was demolished and the new basilica was erected during the course of the 11C. The chancel was built over the grave of St Remi. The church was consecrated by Pope Leo IX in 1049.

However the building was remodelled at the end of the 12C and the Gothic basilica we see today dates from that period. A few minor changes occurred in the 16C and 17C. Used as a barn during the Revolution, the church was restored in the 19C and again after the First World War. Many archbishops of Reims and the first kings of France were buried inside; the Holy Phial was kept in the church.

★★**Interior** – The basilica is very narrow (26m/85ft) in relation to its length (122m/400ft) and dimly lit, which makes it look even longer. The 11C nave consists of 11 bays with rounded main arcades resting on piers whose capitals are decorated with animals and foliage. Note the crown of light symbolising the life of St Remi, a copy of the original destroyed during the Revolution.

The four-storey Gothic chancel is closed off by a 17C Renaissance screen and lit by 12C stained-glass windows depicting the Crucifixion, the Apostles, Prophets and archbishops of Reims.

Behind the altar, **St Remi's grave**, rebuilt in 1847, has retained its 17C statues located in the recesses and representing St Remi, Clovis and the 12 peers who took part in the coronation.

Colonnades surrounding the chancel separate the ambulatory from the radiating chapels whose entrance is marked by two isolated columns. The polychrome motifs decorating the capitals are the original ones and the statues date from the 13C and 18C. The 45 stone slabs, inlaid with lead (biblical scenes), which can be seen in the first bay of the north aisle, come from the former Abbaye St-Nicaise.

The south transept houses an Entombment dating from 1530 and the altarpiece of the Three Christenings (1610) showing Christ between Constantine and Clovis.

★★**Musée St-Remi** ⊙ – The museum is housed in the former royal abbey of St-Remi, consisting of a remarkably well-restored group of 17C and 18C buildings which have retained part of the medieval abbey such as the 13C parlour and the chapter-house.

The museum contains regional art collections from the origins until the end of the Middle Ages, with two exceptions, the military history section and the St-Remi tapestries.

Ground floor – The main courtyard leads to a building with an imposing façade in the Louis XVI style. The cloister, designed by Jean Bonhomme, dates from 1709; it leans against the basilica whose flying buttresses overlap into one of the galleries.

The **chapter-house** is adorned with a series of magnificent Romanesque capitals. The former 17C refectory and kitchen contain the Gallo-Roman collections illustrating the ancient city of Durocortorum which later became Reims. Note the fine mosaics, the large relief map (1:2 000) and **Jovin's tomb★**, a splendid 3C and 4C Roman sarcophagus.

First floor – A superb staircase, dating from 1778, leads to the gallery where the **St-Remi tapestries★★** are exhibited; commissioned by Archbishop Robert de Lenoncourt for the basilica, they were made between 1523 and 1531. Each one consists of several scenes depicting various episodes of St Remi's life and the miracles he accomplished.

Musée St-Remi – Tapestry illustrating St Remi's life (1531)

On the left of the staircase, three small rooms are devoted to the history of the site on which the abbey was built: 12C stone and bronze sculptures, 17C enamel work from the Limoges area illustrating the lives of St Timothy, Apollinarius and Maurus.

Follow the regional archaeological trail round the cloister from the Paleolithic and the Neolithic periods (tools and funeral objects) through to the Protohistoric period (Bronze Age to the Roman conquest, including a wealth of objects discovered in chariot graves and in the large Gaulish necropolises) and up to Gallo-Roman times (handicraft, agriculture, clothing, jewellery, medicine, games, household items). The Merovingian period is represented by jewellery, pottery, glassware and weapons found in nearby necropolises. The exhibits displayed in the flying-buttress gallery were seized during the Revolution: St Gibrien's crozier, the 14C Virgin's triptych, carved out of ivory.

The next gallery shows the evolution of medieval sculpture from the 11C to the 16C; note the delicately carved tympanum and the carved-wood console representing Samson and the Lion.

The Gothic room contains fragments of religious or lay monuments which have disappeared: carvings from the Église St-Nicaise, reconstruction of the façade of the 13C Maison des Musiciens (House of Musicians), adorned with five statues.

A large room contains uniforms, military gear, weapons, documents etc illustrating the main events of the city's **military history**; note in particular the glass cabinets devoted to the Champagne regiments, to the famous battles of the Revolutionary period, or to the military parade which took place on the occasion of Charles X's coronation in 1825.

ADDITIONAL SIGHTS

★**Musée des Beaux-Arts** ⊙ – The Fine Arts Museum, housed in the former 18C Abbaye St-Denis whose church was destroyed during the Revolution, covers the period from the Renaissance to the present times.

Ground floor – Exhibits include:

– 13 portraits (16C) of German princes by **Cranach the Elder** and **Cranach the Younger**; these are extremely realistic drawings enhanced by gouache and oil paint.

– 26 landscapes by **Corot** (1796-1875) and the portrait of a seated Italian youth, painted by Corot during his stay in Rome in 1826.

– ceramics produced by the most important French and foreign manufacturers as well as a few sculptures by René de Saint-Marceaux (1845-1915), a native of Reims.

First floor – The first room contains some strange *grisaille* works enhanced by colours, painted during the 15C and 16C, which include four series of picturesque scenes *(the Apostles, Christ's Vengeance* and *Christ's Passion).* They may have been used as sets for mystery plays or lined along the way from St-Remi Basilica to the cathedral on coronation days.

The following rooms are devoted to French painting from the 17C to the present day.

★**Musée-hôtel Le Vergeur** ⊙ – This mansion, dating from the 13C, 15C and 16C, offers a picturesque façade with a timber-framed upper part over a stone base and overlapping gables. A Renaissance wing, built at right angles and overlooking the garden, has an interesting frieze carved with warring scenes.

The 13C great hall and the floor above it contain paintings, engravings and plans concerning the history of Reims and the splendour of coronation ceremonies.

The living quarters, decorated with woodwork and antique furniture, recall the daily life of Baron Hugues Krafft, a patron of the arts who lived in the mansion until his death in 1935 and bequeathed it together with all his possessions to the Friends of Old Reims.

One of the drawing rooms contains an exceptional collection of engravings by Dürer including the Apocalypse and the Great Passion.

Ancien collège des Jésuites ⊙ – In 1606, the Jesuits were allowed by King Henri IV to found a college in Reims; they then erected the chapel (1617-78) which now stands on place Museaux and the buildings surrounding the courtyard. Clinging to one of the walls and still giving grapes is a 300-year-old vine, brought back from Palestine by the Jesuits. The college prospered until the Jesuits were expelled from France in 1764; it was then turned into a general hospital.

The tour includes the **refectory**, decorated with 17C woodwork and paintings by Jean Helart depicting the Life of St Ignatius Loyola and St Francis-Xavier. Note the magnificent table top carved out of one single piece of oak; a branch of the same tree was used to make the table of the public prosecutor's office upstairs.

A Renaissance staircase leads to the **library★**, elaborately adorned with Baroque woodwork and a coffered ceiling supported by garlands, scrolls and cherubs. It was the setting chosen by Patrice Chéreau for his film *La Reine Margot* with Isabelle Adjani and Daniel Auteuil, in which Margot, the wife of the future Henri IV, condemns the St Bartholomew massacre initiated in 1572 by her mother, Catherine de' Medicis. Note the small reading cubicles and the table with hoof-shaped feet.

The tour of the underground galleries (refreshing in summer) includes a 17C cellar, a 12C gallery and a Gallo-Roman gallery.

Planétarium et Horloge astronomique ⊙ – The former Jesuit college houses a planetarium and an astronomical clock made between 1930 and 1952 by Jean Legros, a native from Reims.

★**Chapelle Foujita** ⊙ – Designed and decorated by **Léonard Foujita** (1886-1968) and donated by the Champagne firm Mumm, the chapel was inaugurated in 1966. It celebrates the mystical inspiration felt by the Japanese painter in the Basilique St-Remi. Foujita, who belonged to the early-20C school of art known as the École de Paris, converted to the Christian faith and was baptized in Reims Cathedral.

The interior of the chapel is decorated with stained glass and frescoes depicting scenes of the Old and New Testaments.

Salle de Reddition ⊙ – *12 rue Franklin-Roosevelt.* General Eisenhower established his headquarters in this technical college towards the end of the Second World War and this is also where the German capitulation act was signed on 7 May 1945. The Salle de la Signature (Signing Room) has remained as it was at the time with its maps etc.

Musée automobile de Reims-Champagne ⊙ – Created in 1985, this car museum houses a collection of 100 vintage cars and prototypes in excellent condition including famous makes such as Delahaye, Salmson, Porsche, Jaguar, a Sizaire-Berwick limousine dating from 1919 and a Messier coupé from 1929. Models, pedal cars and posters are also displayed.

Citroën Type A, 1919

Musée automobile de Reims-Champagne

EXCURSIONS

Fort de la Pompelle – *9km/5.6mi SE; leave Reims along avenue H.-Farman.*
The fort sits on top of a hill rising to 120m/394ft. It was built between 1880 and 1883 as part of the defence system of the city of Reims. At the beginning of the First World War, it was under constant German attack but its resistance contributed to the victory of the Battle of the Marne.
From the lower parking area, a path leads to the fort which has remained in the state it was in at the end of the war. Guns are displayed in front of the fort and trenches and casemates are visible on the south side.
The **museum** ⊙ houses mementoes of the First World War (decorations, uniforms, weapons and a rare **collection of German helmets★**).

MASSIF DE ST-THIERRY

50km/31mi round tour – allow 1hr 30min
Leave Reims along avenue de Laon, N 44 and turn onto the first road to the left (D 26) after La Neuvillette.

The road rises along the slopes of the Massif de St-Tierry, which, like the Montagne de Reims, is a section of the Île-de-France cliff jutting out towards the plain of Champagne. The area has a wealth of Romanesque churches preceded by a porch.

St-Thierry – This village lying on the foothills overlooking the plain of Reims has a 12C **church** with a porch. Archbishop Talleyrand, the uncle of the famous early-19C minister, had a **castle** built at the end of the 18C on the site of an abbey founded in the 6C by St Thierry.

Chenay – Views of the Montagne de Reims.
In Trigny, turn right onto D 530 leading to Hermonville.
Asparagus and strawberries are grown in this sandy area.

Hermonville – An imposing arcaded porch extends across the whole width of the west front of the **church** (late 12C). The doorway recess shelters an 18C statue of the Virgin. The Early Gothic interior offers a striking contrast with the 18C baldaquined altar.
Drive W along D 30 across the highest point of the Massif de St-Thierry. In Bouvancourt, turn left onto D 375.
Just before reaching Pévy, enjoy the charming bird's-eye view of the village nestling inside the valley with the Vesle Valley beyond.

Pévy – This village has an interesting **church** whose Romanesque nave contrasts with the Gothic chancel surmounted by a belfry with a saddleback roof. The interior houses a Romanesque font and a 16C stone altarpiece.
Follow D 75 down to the River Vesle and cross over at Jonchery; N 31 leads back to Reims.

REMIREMONT

Population 9 068
Michelin map 62 folds 16 and 17 or 242 folds 30 and 34

The small town of Remiremont, situated in the deep and densely forested upper valley of the River Moselle, was once the seat of a famous abbey.
The **Promenade du Calvaire** offers an overall view of the town and of the Moselle Valley to the north.

The chapter of the Ladies from Remiremont – In 620, a nobleman named Romaric founded a convent on a height overlooking the confluence of the Moselle and the Moselotte. However, the convent soon settled in the valley below and acquired a rich and powerful chapter under the direct control of the Pope and the Holy Roman Emperor. The canonesses, who were all aristocrats of ancient lineage, lived in mansions surrounding the convent. The mother superior, who had the title of Princess of the Holy Empire, and her two assistants were the only ones to take their vows; the other nuns were free but had to attend services.
This chapter was, for centuries, one of the most important in the western world. The Revolution ended its prosperity.

ABBATIALE ST-PIERRE *allow 15min*

The former abbey church, surmounted by an onion-shaped belfry, is, for the most part, Gothic but the west front and the belfry were rebuilt in the 18C. Note the beautiful 17C marble ornamentation of the chancel which includes a monumental altarpiece intended for the display of reliquaries. The statue of Notre-Dame-du-Trésor, located in the right-hand chapel, dates from the 11C.
Beneath the chancel, there is an 11C **crypt★** with groined vaulting resting on monoliths.
The former 18C **abbatial palace**, adjacent to the church, has a beautiful façade. A few of the 17C and 18C mansions inhabited by the canonesses still surround the church and the palace.

Eating out

MODERATE

Le Clos Heurtebise – *13 chemin des Capucins by r. Capit.-Flayelle* – ☎ *03 29 62 08 04* – *closed 8-22 Jan, 13-20 Jun, 9-23 Oct, Sun evening, Wed evening and Mon* – *95/265F.* In a former textile manufacturer's residence in the upper part of the town, this restaurant's terrace overlooks the valley and the forest in fine weather. Fish is a house speciality, and the menus combine regional and traditional flavours.

MID-RANGE

Le Chalet Blanc – *34 r. des Pêcheurs (opposite the shopping centre)* – *88200 St-Étienne-lès-Remiremont* – *2km/1.2mi E of Remiremont on D 417, Gérardmer road* – ☎ *03 29 26 11 80* – *closed 15 Aug-1 Sept, Sun evening and Mon* – *115/340F.* A large, white modern building reminiscent of a chalet. Much frequented by the locals, who appreciate the good cooking. Dining room decorated with light-coloured wood, and pretty, reasonably priced bedrooms.

Where to stay

MODERATE

Hôtel du Cheval de Bronze – *59 r. Ch.-de-Gaulle* – ☎ *03 29 62 52 24* – 🅿 – *35 rooms 180/350F* – 🍽 *37F.* The façade of this former town-centre post office is decorated with arcades. The atmosphere and standard of comfort are slightly outdated, but it is a good place to stay for a night.

ADDITIONAL SIGHTS

★**Rue Charles-de-Gaulle** – This picturesque arcaded street with flower-decked pillars is a fine example of 18C town planning.

Musée municipal ⊙ – The town museum is housed in two different buildings.

Fondation Ch.-de-Bruyère – *70 rue Ch.-de-Gaulle.* The collections of the foundation are devoted to local history and handicraft from Lorraine; precious manuscripts and tapestries from the former abbey are displayed together with Gothic sculpture from the Lorraine region, 18C ceramics and 17C paintings from northern countries (Rembrandt's School).

Fondation Charles-Friry – *12 rue du Général-Humbert.*
This section of the town museum, housed in one of the former canonesses' mansion (18C and 19C), contains collections of documents, statues, objets d'art etc connected with the Ladies from Remiremont or with local and regional history, as well as numerous 17C-18C paintings, including *Le Vielleur à la sacoche* (the Hurdy-gurdy Player) by Georges de La Tour, prints by Goya and Callot and furniture from various periods.
The garden, which partly recreates the Grand Jardin of the abbey, is decorated with two ornamental fountains and a few other features from the abbey.

★UPPER VALLEY OF THE MOSELLE

Downriver from Remiremont

27km/16.8mi – allow 30min
Leave Remiremont N along D 42 which follows the east bank of the Moselle.

Forêt de Fossard – The road runs between the river and the forest which bears traces of ancient religious settlements going back to the 7C. It is crisscrossed by marked footpaths ideal for hiking.

★**Tête des Cuveaux** – *30min on foot there and back. Follow the road leading to the ridge line marked by a spruce forest and leave the car in the parking area (picnic area).*
🚶 Walk to the right along the ridge line to a viewpoint *(viewing table at the top).* There is a beautiful **panoramic view**★ of the Moselle Valley, the Plateau Lorrain and the Vosges mountains.

Éloyes – This small town has thriving textile and food-processing industries.

Arches – Arches is known for its traditional paper industry; a paper mill was already operating here in 1469. **Beaumarchais**, the famous playwright, author of *The Barber of Seville* and *The Marriage of Figaro*, bought the mill in 1779 in order to produce the necessary paper for the complete edition of Voltaire's works. As most of the great philosopher's writings had been banned in France, he set up a printing press in Kehl (across the Rhine from Strasbourg). This resulted in two editions, both known as the Kehl editions, which are today much sought after by book lovers.

★**Épinal** – *See ÉPINAL.*

Upriver from Remiremont

50km/31mi – allow 2hr

A lovely drive upstream to the source of the Moselle at the heart of the Vosges mountains.

La Beuille – *Drive 6km/3.7mi along D 57 then turn left onto a tarmacked path leading to the parking area overlooking the Chalet de la Beuille.* From the terrace-viewpoint at the chalet, there is a fine **view**★ of the Moselle Valley and of the Ballon d'Alsace in the distance.

At Col des Croix, turn NE onto D 486 to Le Thillot, ignoring D 16 which winds its way past the Ballon de Servance down to Plancher-les-Mines.

Le Thillot – Many tourists go through this lively industrial centre (weaving, spinning, tanning, industrial woodwork) on their way to visit the surrounding area and the highest summits of the Vosges mountains.

St-Maurice-sur-Moselle – *See BALLON D'ALSACE p 79.*

Between St-Maurice and Bussang, morainic deposits at the bottom of the valley have created a landscape of rolling hills crowned by wooden-gabled farmhouses.

Bussang – Bussang, lying in a picturesque setting near the source of the River Moselle, is both a summer and winter resort.

The **Théâtre du Peuple** (folk theatre) founded in 1895, consists of a mobile stage using nature as its background and can seat 1 100 spectators. The actors, many of them local inhabitants, give performances of folk plays as well as plays by Shakespeare, Molière etc.

★★**Petit Drumont** – *15min on foot there and back. Turn onto the forest road branching off D 89 just before the Col de Bussang.*
🏃 At that point, you are barely 100m/110yd from the **source of the Moselle** (alt 715m/2 346ft – monument by Gilodi, 1965).
Leave the car near the inn and follow the path which rises through high pastures.
At the summit of Petit Drumont (alt 1 200m/3 846ft), there is a viewing table forming two semicircles. The **panorama**★★ extends from the Hohneck to the Ballon d'Alsace.

Col de Bussang – At the pass (alt 727m/2 388ft) stands the monument marking the source of the Moselle, which at this point is no more than a small stream. It soon swells to a powerful torrent to reach the size of an impressive river by the time it flows through Rupt-sur-Moselle. Having become definitely tamer, it then meanders through wooded hills towards Remiremont and Épinal.

RETHEL

Population 7 923
Michelin map 56 fold 7 or 241 fold 13

Rethel lies on the banks of the River Aisne and of the Canal des Ardennes. The town had to be almost completely rebuilt after being destroyed during May and June 1940.
The French poet, **Paul Verlaine**, spent several quiet years in Rethel during the 1870s teaching literature, history, geography and English.

Église St-Nicolas ⊙ – This unusual Gothic edifice, standing on top of a hill, in fact consists of two churches built side by side and of an imposing tower.
The left-hand church (12C-13C) acquired new vaulting in the 16C; it was used by monks from a Benedictine monastery.
The right-hand church (15C-16C) was the parish church. Characteristic features include a wide aisle lit by Flamboyant Gothic windows and a richly decorated doorway completed in 1511, a fine example of Flamboyant Gothic ornamentation: note the statue of St Nicholas bonded to the upright post and the Assumption decorating the gable, reminiscent of the Coronation of the Virgin on the central doorway of Reims Cathedral.

Boudin blanc

This white sausage made from fresh pork meat and containing no preservatives is a gastronomic speciality of Rethel with the Ardennes de France seal as a guarantee of its quality. It comes in different sizes, large or cocktail sausages, and can be prepared in different ways: in a pastry case, barbecued or as a tasty stuffing for *crêpes* (pancakes).
A fair takes place every year during the last weekend in April.

EXCURSIONS

Asfeld – *22km/13.7mi SW along D 18 then D 926*. In this village, lying on the south bank of the River Aisne, which once belonged to the counts of Avaux, Jean-Jacques de Mesmes built an unusual Baroque church.

★**Église St-Didier** – This church is unique: designed in 1683 by the Dominican priest, François Romain, who built the Pont-Royal in Paris, it was entirely brick built in the shape of a viol. Its vestibule leading to a rotunda is surmounted by a flattened cupola and flanked by four semi-oval chapels. On the outside, a brick colonnade links the oval peristyle and the rotunda. Inside, sturdy columns support the dome of the cupola whereas, in the upper part, small columns decorate the galleries running all round the building. Passages, known as *tournelles* make it possible to walk round the church without going across it.

Wasigny – *16km/10mi N along D 10*.
On the way, the road goes through **Séry** where a 3km/1.9mi **botanic trail** allows nature lovers to discover the local flora: orchids as well as plants and bushes characteristic of fields where sheep used to graze.
Wasigny Castle (16C-17C), is situated at the entrance of the village, in pleasant surroundings, by the riverside. A fine 15C covered market stands in the village centre.

Vallée du RHIN★★

Michelin map 87 folds 3-10 or 242 folds 16, 20, 24, 28, 32, 36 and 40

Marking the border between France and Germany, the wide River Rhine is flanked on the French side by the foothills of the Vosges, along which runs the Route des Vins, and on the German side by the dense Black Forest. From time immemorial men have attempted to harness its fast impetuous flow and its fearsome spates by building dykes, cutting its arms off and gradually forcing it to follow an artificial course. In spite of this, the "Vater Rhein" is still there, ready to welcome you along part of its fabulous journey to the North Sea.

Barges on the Rhine

Vallée du RHIN

Story of a river – With a total length of 1 298km/807mi, including 190km/118mi along the Franco-German border, the Rhine is the seventh longest European river. The spates of the Rhine were fearsome; this is the reason why no town, not even Strasbourg, settled on its banks. When the water level rose, local people took turns to watch the dykes day and night. In spite of this, catastrophes were frequent and many an Alsatian village was destroyed by flooding. One of its branches even flowed through Strasbourg; rue d'Or now marks its former route and the rebuilt Ancienne Douane (former custom house) is a reminder of the time (not so long ago) when river craft went through the town.

In the 8C and 9C, boatmen from Strasbourg sailed downriver to the North Sea in order to sell wine to the English, the Danes and the Swedes. At the end of the Middle Ages, these boatmen controlled the Rhine between Basle and Mainz and theirs was the most powerful guild in Strasbourg. Some 5 000 wagoners, with 20 000 horses at their disposal, carried inland goods unloaded in Strasbourg.

Harnessing of the Rhine – Water transport was at its height under Napoleon I and in 1826, the first steamships, operating regular sailings along the Rhine, called at Strasbourg. Unfortunately, dykes built along the Rhine during the 19C to control the river flow caused the river bed to become deeper by 6-7cm/2-3in per year. This, in turn, uncovered rock lying at the bottom of the river and rendered navigation impossible when the water level was low. Water transport consequently declined. In order to bring boats and barges back on the Alsatian section of the Rhine, the French decided in 1920 to divert part of the river flow between Basle and Strasbourg to a low-gradient canal. Begun in 1928 and completed in the 1960s, the Grand Canal d'Alsace offers, in addition, the possibility of tapping the river's considerable potential of hydroelectric power.

A walk along the banks of the Rhine gives visitors an insight into the importance of the international river traffic.

**GRAND CANAL D'ALSACE AND HARNESSING OF THE RHINE

From Kembs to Strasbourg

Barrage de Kembs – *9km/5.6mi S of Kembs.* The dam was the only one built along the first four reaches; it diverts the major part of the river flow towards the Grand Canal d'Alsace. A hydroelectric power station uses the remaining flow.

★Hydroelectric power station – Built between 1928 and 1932, the power station was damaged during the Second World War but repaired in 1945. Today, it produces 938 million kWh every year.

★Bief de Kembs – Situated downriver from the dam, the reach includes the canal and a recently modernised double lock.

Petite Camargue alsacienne – *9km S of Kembs along D 468. Parking area near the stadium in St-Louis-la-Chaussée.* Three marked footpaths, one all the way round the large marsh *(3km/1.9mi)*, offer the opportunity of observing many species of fauna and flora through reedy marshes, copses, ponds, marshland and heaths.

River traffic

Rhine barges are between 60m/197ft and 125m/410ft long, and between 8m/26ft and 13m/43ft wide. Among these, there are many self-propelled barges with a capacity of 3 000t for carrying gas. Navigable between Basle and Rotterdam, the Rhine carries more than 10 000 boats every year and these in turn transport 190 million tonnes of freight. It is interesting to note that water transport on the Canal d'Alsace uses only a fourth of the energy required on the Rhine. Strasbourg is France's second largest river port after Paris.

The Canal de Huningue branches off near Niffer towards Mulhouse. The canal and its access lock form the first section of the Rhine-Rhône link.

Each of the following reaches along the Grand Canal d'Alsace comprises a hydro-electric power station and a double lock, which attracts many curious observers when in operation.

★**Bief d'Ottmarsheim** – *See OTTMARSHEIM.*

★**Bief de Fessenheim** ⊙ – Situated less than 1km/0.6mi from the Fessenheim lock, it is the first French **nuclear power station** to have used a high-water-pressure reactor; it consists of two units of 900 million watts *(an information centre is open to visitors)*.

The reach is about 17km/11mi long and includes locks similar to those of Ottmarsheim: they have the same length (185m/202yd) but different widths (23m/75ft and 12m/39ft).

The **Maison de l'Hydraulique** ⊙, situated near the power station, displays models of various water-powered works as well as turbines and other machinery.

★**Bief de Vogelgrün** – 1959. The characteristics of the power station are roughly the same as those of Ottmarsheim and Fessenheim; the reach is 14km/9mi long with locks similar to those of the Fessenheim reach.

Downstream from Vogelgrün, the harnessing of the river includes four more reaches; each one comprises a dam on the river, a feeder canal supplying water to the power station and navigation locks and another canal returning the diverted flow to the Rhine.

The power station is decorated (on the side overlooking the road and on the side overlooking the Rhine) with a huge fresco (1 500m²/1 794sq yd) by Daniel Dyminski from Mulhouse, entitled *Nix from Vogelgrün*, and with a large bronze allegorical sculpture by Raymond Couvègnes, entitled *Electricity*.

Bief de Gerstheim – 1967. The power station produces 818 million kWh per year. It was built at the same time as the tidal power station of the Rance estuary in northern Brittany.

Bief de Strasbourg – 1970. The annual production of the power station amounts to 868 million kWh. A regulating reservoir forms a lake covering 650ha/1 606 acres with a water sports centre at Plobsheim.

The Pont de l'Europe is, of course, a must for anyone visiting Strasbourg *(see STRASBOURG)*, but it is also easy to get close to the Rhine between Lauterbourg and Strasbourg, by following one of the roads branching off D 468.

The harnessing of the Rhine was prolonged beyond Strasbourg by a Franco-German project, the two countries sharing the power produced by the **Gambsheim** power station, situated on the French side and inaugurated in 1974, and the **Ifferzheim** power station, situated on the German side and completed in 1977.

RIBEAUVILLÉ ★

Population 4 774
Michelin map 87 fold 17 or 242 fold 31 – Local map see Route des VINS

Ribeauvillé lies in a picturesque site at the foot of the Vosges mountains crowned with old castles. The small town is renowned for Riesling and Gewurztraminer, famous Alsatian white wines made in the area. A wine festival takes place in July.

Pfifferdaj – The "day of the fifes" is one of the last traditional festivals in Alsace, whose origin goes back to ancient times. It takes place on the first Sunday in September. Travelling musicians used to gather in the town to pay homage to their suzerain. The statutes of their powerful corporation were recorded by Colmar's Council. Today, the Pfifferdaj or **Fête des Ménétriers** is a folk festival with a historic procession and free wine tasting at the Fontaine du Vin, place de l'Hôtel-de-Ville.

★★GRAND'RUE

Two old towers, standing at the town's southern and eastern entrances, are surmounted by stork nests.
Start from the tourist office housed in the former guard-house (1829).
The street is lined with picturesque timber-framed flower-decked houses.

Pfifferhüs (Restaurant des Ménétriers) – *No 14.* Two statues standing on a loggia above the door illustrate the Annunciation.

Halle au Blé – *Place de la 1ʳᵉ-Armée.* Once the site of a weekly granary exchange, the old covered market sits atop a secret passageway.

Eating out

MID-RANGE

Winstub Zum Pfifferhüs – *14 Grand-Rue* – ☎ *03 89 73 62 28* – *closed 7 -8 Mar, 3-13 Jul, Wed and Thu* – *booking essential* – *180F.* This is the place to come for a typical *winstub* meal. An authentic, pretty 14C village restaurant with dark-wood decor, dried flowers and local-style furniture. The appealing cooking is simple but very carefully prepared.

LUXURY

Chez Norbert – *68750 Bergheim* – *4km/2.5mi NE of Ribeauvillé on D 1ᴮ and minor road* – ☎ *03 89 73 31 15* – *closed Mar, 15-30 Nov, lunchtime, Mon and Tue Nov-Mar* – *250/280F.* In the village centre, a lovely flower-decked courtyard lies behind a porch, enclosed by two pretty 14C half-timbered houses. The regional-style meals are served in a room decorated with pot-bellied bottles, stained-glass windows and beams.

Where to stay

MODERATE

Camping Municipal Pierre-de-Coubertin – *E of Ribeauvillé on D 106, then turn left towards Landau* – ☎ *03 89 73 66 71* – *open Mar-15 Nov* – *260 plots 68F.* A large camp site, where you can enjoy the peace and quiet as well as the magnificent village of Ribeauvillé. The site is spaciously laid out, with pleasant plots, even if they are not well-defined. Lovely view.

MID-RANGE

Hôtel de la Tour – *1 r. de la Mairie* – ☎ *03 89 73 72 73* – *closed 1Jan-15 Mar* – 🅿 – *35 rooms 325/445F* – 🍽 *42F.* A quiet town-centre hotel with pale-blue shutters. Most of its rather plain rooms overlook a quiet street or a courtyard. Small gym for fitness fans.

Fontaine Renaissance – Built in 1536, the red-and-yellow-sandstone fountain is surmounted by a heraldic lion.

★**Tour des Bouchers** – This former belfry used to mark the separation between the upper and the middle town. The base dates from the 13C.

Beautiful 17C timber-framed house at no 78 Grand'Rue.

Place de la Sinne – This is a charming little square, lined with timber-framed houses, with a fountain (1860) in its centre.

Ribeauvillé

RIBEAUVILLÉ

Pedestrian zone in summer

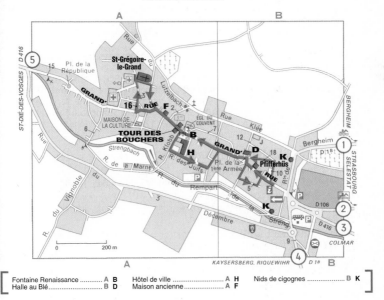

Fontaine Renaissance .... A B
Halle au Blé .... B D

Hôtel de ville .... A H
Maison ancienne .... A F

Nids de cigognes .... B K

ADDITIONAL SIGHTS

Église St-Grégoire-le-Grand – The church dates from the 13C-15C. Note the tympanum of the west doorway and the fine ironwork of the door. In the south aisle, there is a 15C carved-wood Virgin and Child, gilt and painted, wearing the local headdress; the Baroque organ was made by Rinck.

Walk back along Grand'Rue then along rue Klobb and rue des Juifs.

Maisons anciennes – 16C and 17C houses can be seen along rue des Juifs, rue Klobb, rue Flesch and rue des Tanneurs (note the openings in the roof of no 12, which helped to dry skins).

Hôtel de ville – The town hall houses a small **museum** ⊙ containing 17C gold plate and vermeil goblets having belonged to the local lords.

Walk back along rue Flesch and rue des Tanneurs.

A WALK IN THE WOODS

Leave Ribeauvillé by ⑤ on the town plan. Leave the car in the parking area situated on the roadside (D 416), about 800m/875yd out of town.

🚶 Walk up along the Chemin des Stations (20min) or the Chemin Sarassin (40min).

Notre-Dame-de-Dusenbach – This place of pilgrimage includes the Virgin's Chapel, a convent, a neo-Gothic church (1903) and a pilgrims' shelter (1913). The **Chapelle de la Vierge** has been destroyed three times since it was founded in 1221. It was rebuilt for the last time in 1894 in neo-Gothic style on the edge of a promontory towering above the narrow Dusenbach Valley. The chapel contains murals by Talenti (1938) and, above the altar, a 15C **Pietà** in polychrome wood, said to perform miracles.

Follow the Chemin Sarassin then the path leading to the castles.

Stop by the **Rocher Kahl**, at the halfway mark. From this granite scree, there is a fine bird's-eye view of the Strengbach Valley and its forested slopes.

The path leads to a major intersection of forest lanes: continue straight on along the narrow path signposted Ribeauvillé par les châteaux.

Château du Haut-Ribeaupierre – It is possible to walk through the ruins of this 12C castle *(the keep is closed to the public)*.

Retrace your steps (avoiding the direct path linking Haut-Ribeaupierre and St-Ulrich) back to the intersection and follow the marked path leading down to St-Ulrich.

★**Château de St-Ulrich** – The stairs leading to the castle start from the foot of the keep, on the left. The **castle** was not only a fortress, like most castles in the Vosges region, but also the luxury residence of the Comtes de Ribeaupierre, one of the oldest aristocratic families in Alsace. The stairs lead through the castle gate to a small courtyard which offers a fine view of the ruins of Girsberg Castle and of the Plaine d'Alsace. A door at the end of the courtyard, beyond the water tank, gives access to the Romanesque Great Hall, lit by nine twinned rounded windows, which was once covered by a timber ceiling.

Return to the small courtyard and walk up the stairs to the chapel, leaving the entrance of the 12C tower on your right.

West of the chapel stands an enormous square tower accessible via outside stairs. Retrace your steps to visit the oldest part of the castle including Romanesque living quarters, whose windows are decorated with fleurs-de-lis, another courtyard and the keep. The red-sandstone square keep, built on a granite base, towers over the rest of the castle and makes a remarkable viewpoint. From the top, reached by walking up 64 steps, the **panorama**★★ extends over the Strengbach Valley, the ruins of the **Château de Girsberg** (dating from the 12C and abandoned in the 17C), Ribeauvillé and the Plaine d'Alsace.

COL DE FRÉLAND *47km/29mi round tour – allow 5hr*

Leave Ribeauvillé by ⑤ on the town plan.

The road *(D 416)* follows the River Strengbach which flows rapidly through the beautiful Ribeauvillé Forest.

After driving 7km/4.3mi, turn left towards Aubure along a picturesque cliff road offering glimpses of the valley on the left.

Aubure – The resort is pleasantly situated on a sunny plateau and surrounded by fine pine and fir forests.

Turn left onto D 11[III]. On the way down from the Col de Fréland, 1.5km/0.9mi from the pass, turn left onto a narrow road.

It runs through a beautiful **pine forest**★, one of the finest to be seen in France. The tall straight trees (60cm/2ft in diameter and 30m/98ft high) are quite impressive.

After coming out of the forest, drive on for another 1km/0.6mi and turn back to return to D 11[III].

There is a clear view of the Weiss Valley and part of the Val d'Orbey.

Continue past Fréland and, 1.5km/0.9mi beyond the intersection with D 11[IV] to Orbey, turn left onto N 415.

★★**Kaysersberg** – *See KAYSERSBERG.*

The road joins the Route des Vins which takes you back to Ribeauvillé, through villages camped on the hillside among famous vineyards, Kientzheim, Sigolsheim, Bennwihr, Mittelwihr and Beblenheim *(see Route des VINS).*

★★★**Riquewihr** – *See RIQUEWIHR.*

Hunawihr – *See Route des VINS.*

Drive back to Ribeauvillé.

★★CASTLES OVERLOOKING THE PLAINE D'ALSACE

46km/29mi round tour – allow 2hr

Leave Ribeauvillé by ① on the town plan, D 1[B].

This round tour offers views of the castles built along the line of the Vosges mountains.

Bergheim – *See Route des VINS.*

St-Hippolyte – *See Route des VINS.*

As you enter the village, turn left towards Haut-Kœnigsbourg then right 4km/2.5mi beyond St-Hippolyte and left 1km/0.6mi further on to take the one-way road which goes round the castle.

★★**Haut-Kœnigsbourg** – *See HAUT-KŒNIGSBOURG.*

Return to D 1[B1] and turn right then right again onto D 48[I].

★**From Schaentzel to Lièpvre** – The picturesque road, lined with imposing fir trees, runs rapidly downhill, offering superb views of the Liepvrette Valley and the ruined castles towering above it to the north.

Return to D 1[B1] and turn right onto D 42.

Thannenkirch – This charming village lies in restful surroundings, amid dense forests.

The road follows the deep **Bergenbach Valley** down to the Plaine d'Alsace.

At Bergheim, turn right towards Ribeauvillé.

The ruins of St-Ulrich, Girsberg and Haut-Ribeaupierre castles stand out on the right.

RIQUEWIHR★★★

Population 1 075
Michelin map 87 fold 17 or 242 fold 31 – Local map see Route des VINS

Riquewihr is an attractive little Alsatian town lying at the heart of a wine-growing area, which has been actively engaged in the production of the famous Riesling for generations, the liveliest period being grape-harvest time. Spared by the many wars which ravaged the region, the town looks today just as it did in the 16C.

Yet life in Riquewihr was not always as peaceful; it was sold in 1324 to the duke of Wurtemberg, who remained its suzerain until the Revolution but the town suffered frequent incursions from the troops of rival feudal lords such as the bishop of Strasbourg and the duke of Lorraine. Its marvellous wine, however, consistently enabled Riquewihr to overcome the worst situations throughout its troubled past.

R.Mattes/MICHELIN

Riquewihr and its vineyards

Eating out

MODERATE

Auberge St-Alexis – *68240 St-Alexis – 6km/3.75mi W of Riquewihr on a minor road and lane –* ☎ *03 89 73 90 38 – closed Fri – 67/100F.* It's worth going deep into the forest on a dirty road to reach this 17C hermitage, as the cooking is excellent: simple, like the decor, but authentically prepared with produce from neighbouring farms.

MID-RANGE

Le Sarment d'Or – *4 r. du Cerf –* ☎ *03 89 86 02 86 – closed 3 Jan-8 Feb, 25 Jun-3 Jul, Tue lunchtime, Sun evening and Mon – 120/320F.* Pale wood panelling, copper light-fittings and huge beams create a lovely warm atmosphere in this restaurant. The cooking is original and uses good ingredients. A little expensive, but a pleasant setting.

Where to stay

MODERATE

Chambre d'hôte Schmitt – *3 chemin des Vignes –* ☎ *03 89 47 89 72 – closed Jan and Feb –* ✑ *– 3 rooms 204/270F.* A house with a garden in the higher part of the village, on the edge of a vineyard. The wood-panelled rooms have sloping ceilings. Not all the bathrooms have toilets, but the standard of cleanliness is high and the prices reasonable.

MID-RANGE

Hôtel L'Oriel – *3 r. des Écuries-Seigneuriales –* ☎ *03 89 49 03 13 – 19 rooms 370/510F –* ⌧ *49F.* This 16C hotel is easily recognised by its wrought-iron sign. The lack of straight lines in the building, combined with simple decor and old Alsatian furniture, create a romantic atmosphere.

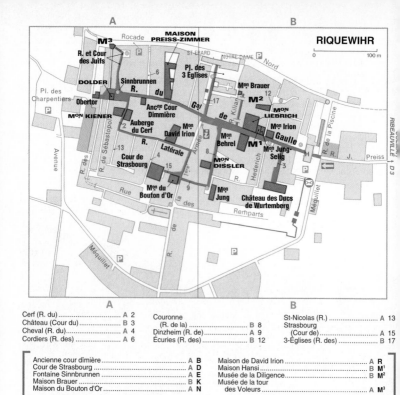

TOUR OF THE TOWN 2hr

Leave the car outside of town (parking fee). Walk through the archway of the town hall and follow rue du Général-de-Gaulle straight ahead. On the left is the Cour du Château at the end of which stands the castle.

Château – Completed in 1540, the castle has retained its mullioned windows, its gable decorated with antlers and its stair turret. A small open-air archaeological museum and the Altar of Freedom erected in 1790 can be seen on the east side.

Continue along rue du Général-de-Gaulle.

No 12, known as the **Maison Irion**, dating from 1606, has a corner oriel; opposite, there is an old 16C well. Next door, the **Maison Jung-Selig** (1561) has a carved timber frame.

★**Maison Liebrich (cour des cigognes)** – A well dating from 1603 and a huge winepress from 1817 stand in the picturesque courtyard of this 16C house, surrounded by balustraded wooden galleries (added in the 17C).
Opposite stands the **Maison Behrel** adorned with a lovely oriel (1514) surmounted by openwork added in 1709.

Take the first turn on the right and follow rue Kilian.

Maison Brauer – This house, situated at the end of the street, has a fine doorway dating from 1618.

Continue along rue des Trois-Églises.

Place des Trois-Églises – The square is framed by two former churches, St-Érard and Notre-Dame, converted into dwellings, and a 19C Protestant church.

Return to rue du Général-de-Gaulle.

★**Maison Preiss-Zimmer** – The house which belonged to the wine-growers' guild stands in the last but one of a succession of picturesque courtyards.
Further on, on the right, stands the former tithe court of the lords of Ribeaupierre.

Rue et cour des Juifs – The narrow rue des Juifs gives access to the picturesque Cour des Juifs, a former ghetto, from which a narrow passageway and wooden stairs lead to the ramparts and the **Musée de la tour des Voleurs** *(see Museums below)*. On place de la Sinn, which marks the end of rue du Général-de-Gaulle, stands an imposing gate, the Porte Haute or Dolder. Note the lovely **Fontaine Sinnbrunnen** on the right, which dates from 1580.

★**Dolder** – Erected in 1291, this gate was reinforced during the 15C and 16C.

Walk through the gate to reach Obertor.

Obertor (upper gate) – Note the portcullis and the place where the former draw-bridge (1600) was fixed. On the left, you can see a section of the ramparts and a defence tower.

Turn back, walk through Dolder and along rue du Général-de-Gaulle then turn right onto rue du Cerf.

★**Maison Kiener** – *No 2*. The house built in 1574 is surmounted by a pediment with an inscription and a low-relief carving depicting Death getting hold of the founder of the house. The rounded doorway is built at an angle to make it easier for vehicles to enter. The courtyard is very picturesque with its spiral staircase, corbelled storeys and its old well (1576). The old inn opposite, Auberge du Cerf, dates from 1566.

Continue along rue du Cerf then turn left onto rue Latérale.

Rue Latérale – The street is lined with lovely houses including the **Maison David Irion** at no 6, which has retained its oriel dating from 1551 and a lovely Renaissance doorway in the courtyard.

Turn right onto rue de la 1ʳᵉ-Armée.

Maison du Bouton d'Or – *No 16*. The house goes back to 1566. An alleyway, starting just round the corner, leads to another court known as the **Cour de Strasbourg** dating from 1597.

Retrace your steps once more then carry straight on past the Maison du Bouton d'Or along rue Dinzheim, which leads to rue de la Couronne.

Maison Jung – *No 18*. The house was built in 1683 opposite an old well, **Kuhlebrunnen**. The Maison Dissler stands further along on the left.

★**Maison Dissler** – *No 6*. With its scrolled gables and loggia, this stone-built house (1610) is an interesting example of Renaissance style in the Rhine region.

Continue along rue de la Couronne to rue du Général-de-Gaulle and turn right towards the town hall.

MUSEUMS

Musée d'histoire des PTT d'Alsace ⊘ – A stagecoach with three compartments (1835 model) is parked at the entrance. Housed inside the castle, the museum follows the evolution of means of communication in Alsace from the Gallo-Roman period to the 20C, including the history of foot messengers, ordinary mail, airmail, the telegraph and the telephone.

Musée de la Diligence ⊘ – Housed in the former seigneurial stables (16C), the museum displays various stagecoaches from the 18C (first wicker mail coach dating from 1793) to the beginning of the 20C, together with postilions' uniforms and boots, mail record-books and signs.

Musée Hansi ⊘ – This museum contains watercolours, lithographs, etchings, decorated ceramics and posters by the talented artist and cartoonist from Colmar, JJ Waltz, known as Hansi *(see COLMAR)* whose brother was a chemist in Rique-wihr.

Musée de la tour des Voleurs ⊘ – The tour includes the torture chamber, the oubliette, the guard-room and the caretaker's lodgings of this former prison.

Musée du Dolder ⊘ – The museum houses mementoes, prints, weapons and objects connected with local history (tools, furniture, locks...).

ROCROI★

Population 2 566
Michelin map 53 fold 18 or 241 fold 6

Vauban, Louis XIV's military engineer, redesigned the fortifications of this 16C strong-hold, situated on the Ardennes plateau, round a vast parade ground.
Rocroi, whose name means King's Rock, changed its name to Roc Libre (free rock) during the Révolution!

Remparts – The ramparts form a bastioned wall characteristic of military architec-ture at the time of Vauban, who was appointed *Commissaire général des fortifica-tions* in 1678. Starting from the Porte de France to the south-west, follow the tourist trail running along the east front, which gives a good idea of the complexity of the defence system.

Musée ⊘ – Housed in the former guard-house, the museum presents an inter-active audio-visual show illustrating the sequence of manoeuvres which led the young duke of Enghien, the future Grand Condé, to victory over the Spanish army at the battle of Rocroi (1643). There is also a reconstruction of the battle with tiny lead soldiers and several documents relating to the history of the stronghold.

ROSHEIM ★

Population 4 016
Michelin map 87 fold 15 or 242 fold 23 – Local map see Route des VINS

Rosheim is a small wine-growing town which has retained, within its ruined ramparts, some of the oldest buildings in Alsace, including an interesting Romanesque church. The local June festival celebrates music, art, handicraft and gastronomy.

Sculpted capital

SIGHTS

★**Église St-Pierre-et-St-Paul** – Considerably restored during the 19C, the 12C church fortunately regained its original aspect in 1968. The yellow-sandstone edifice has a massive 16C octagonal belfry surmounting the crossing. Note the flat strips decorating the west front and the walls, known as Lombardy banding because this kind of ornamentation was introduced by the Lombards (Italian bankers who shared with the Jews the monopoly of money transactions). Arcading runs along the top of the nave and the aisles and links up with the Lombardy banding. Lions devouring humans adorn the gable of the west front (another Lombardy feature). The symbols of the Evangelists are represented at the four corners of the apsidal window.

Inside, strong piers alternate with weak piers surmounted by carved capitals (note in particular the ring of small heads, all different). The restored organ by Silbermann dates from 1733.

Porte du Lion, Porte Basse and Porte de l'École – These gates formed part of the town's fortifications.

Puits à chaîne and Zittglœckel – A well dating from 1605 (used until 1906) and a clock tower stand on the town hall square.

Maisons anciennes – Numerous old houses line rue du Général-de-Gaulle and the narrow adjacent streets.

Maison païenne – Situated between no 21 and no 23 rue du Général-de-Gaulle, this house is the oldest edifice built of Alsatian stone (second half of the 12C). It has two storeys pierced by small openings.

FAMILY-STYLE

Auberge du Cerf – *120 r. du Gén.-de-Gaulle* – ☎ *03 88 50 40 14* – *closed 8-15 Jan, 25 Jun-3 Jul, Sun evening and Mon* – *85/195F.* This inn lies on the main road through Rosheim. It is simple, clean and has a nice family atmosphere. The regional dishes on the menu are reasonably priced. Recommended.

ROUFFACH ★

Population 4 303
Michelin map 87 fold 18 or 242 fold 35 – Local map see Route des VINS

Rouffach is a prosperous agricultural centre nestling at the foot of vine-covered hills. An ecological fair livens up the town during the weekend following Ascension Day.

The Holy Roman Emperor once owned a castle here (now in ruins) and the town has retained several interesting buildings from its rich medieval past: two churches, some old houses and a machicolated tower.

Rouffach was the birthplace of François-Joseph Lefebvre (1755-1820), one of Napoleon's colourful marshals, who distinguished himself during the Napoleonic Wars and became duke of Danzig, but remained unaffected by his social position and often returned to his humble origins in Rouffach. His monument stands on place Clemenceau.

12C feminists

In 1106, Emperor Henry V kidnapped a young girl and settled her in Rouffac Castle. The village women did not appreciate this behaviour and took up arms. Their husbands followed and together they attacked the castle. Pannick-stricken, Henry V fled from Rouffac leaving behind his crown, his sceptre and his imperial cloak which were placed as offerings on the Virgin's altar.

Eating out

MODERATE

Auberge au Vieux Pressoir – *68250 Bollenberg – 6km/3.75mi SW of Rouf-fach on N 83 and minor road –* ☎ *03 89 49 60 04 – closed 20-27 Dec – 95/395F.* A large winemaker's house set among vines. The typically Alsatian decor features country furniture, old objects and a collection of old weapons. Cellar for tastings and local cuisine.

Where to stay

MID-RANGE

Hôtel Relais du Vignoble – *68420 Gueberschwihr – 6km/3.75mi N of Rouf-fach on N 83 and minor road –* ☎ *03 89 49 22 22 – closed 1 Feb-5 Mar –* **P** *– 30 rooms 260/450F –* ☲ *45F – restaurant 80/250F.* A hotel among the vines, run by a family of wine-growers. The large, modern building just behind the Bellevue restaurant faces the plain, with spacious, rather fussily decorated rooms on the second floor.

SIGHTS

Église Notre-Dame-de-l'Assomption – This church was mostly built in the 12C-13C although the transept is older (11C-12C). The north and south towers were added in the 19C; the latter was never completed owing to the Franco-Prussian War of 1870.

Inside, the main arcades comprise strong piers alternating with weak ones as is the custom in 12C architecture from the Rhine region. All the columns are surmounted by crocket capitals.

Note the octagonal christening font (1492) in the south transept. An elegant staircase, leaning against the piers of the crossing, is all that remains of the 14C rood screen. On the left of the high altar, there is a lovely 15C tabernacle. A Virgin and Child surmounted by a canopy, carved c 1500, is bonded to one of the pillars of the nave on the north side.

Church tower and spire and Tour des Sorcières

ROUFFACH

Tour des Sorcières – The machicolated tower covered with a four-sided roof crowned by a stork's nest dates from the 13C and 15C and was used as a prison until the 18C.

Maisons anciennes – The old covered market (late 15C-early 16C) stands on place de la République; nearby, to the left of the Tour des Sorcières, is the Gothic Maison de l'Œuvre Notre-Dame and the former town hall with its beautiful Renaissance façade surmounted by a twin gable. There are three other interesting houses at nos 11, 17 and 23 rue Poincaré.

Église des Récollets ⊙ – The church was built between 1280 and 1300 but the aisles were remodelled in the 15C. A pulpit with an openwork balustrade is bonded to one of the buttresses. A stork's nest sits on the top.

EXCURSION

Pfaffenheim – *3km/1.9mi N along N 83.*
This wine-growing village, whose origins go back to the end of the 9C, has retained a church with a 13C apse, adorned with floral friezes and a blind gallery with slender colonnettes. Notches which can be seen in the lower part might have been made by wine-growers sharpening their pruning knives.

ST-DIÉ ★

Population 22 635
Michelin map 87 fold 16 or 242 fold 27

Situated in a fertile basin overlooked by red-sandstone ridges covered with firs, St-Dié owes its name to a monastery founded in the 7C by St Déodat shortened to St Dié.
The town was partly destroyed by fire on four occasions, the last one being in November 1944, towards the end of the Second World War.
Textile and wood industries are the town's main economic activities.
The continent discovered by Christopher Columbus was first named America, in honour of the explorer Amerigo Vespucci, in a work entitled *Cosmographiæ Introductio*, published in St-Dié in 1507 by a team of scientists who called themselves the Gymnase Vosgien. In October, the town hosts an international event devoted to the science of geography.

Where to stay

MID-RANGE

Hôtel Le Haut Fer – *88100 Rougiville – 6km/3.75mi W of St-Dié on N 420 and minor road – ☎ 03 29 55 03 48 – closed 1-10 Jan and Sun evening except Aug – 🅿 – 16 rooms 300/400F – ⊇ 38F – restaurant 120/200F.* This 1960s hotel just outside the town is built on the site of a sawmill, and is named after a saw blade for lopping branches. The rooms are rather old-fashioned but well kept. The best ones overlook the countryside.

On the town

Billard's Club – *33 r. de la Prairie – ☎ 03 29 56 07 14 – Mon-Thu 3pm-1am, Fri-Sat 3pm-2am.* One of the most popular venues in town, for at least three reasons: there are 19 billiard tables, 8 pool tables and a smart bar which gets busy towards the end of the week when there are concerts or theme evenings.

Le FBI – *82 r. d'Alsace – ☎ 03 29 55 09 81 – daily from 11am.* This bar resembles a smart pub, decorated with gleaming copperware, mahogany panelling and red-velvet seats. An intimate place, by popular accord.

Shopping

Domaine Ste-Odile – *27 r. Ste-Odile – 88480 Étival-Clairefontaine – 10km/6.25mi NE of St-Dié, Saint-Rémy direction on D 424. – ☎ 03 29 41 40 83 – Tue-Sun 8am-8pm. Closed 2nd fortnight in Jan.* A fish farm which raises rainbow and Fario trout, char, pike, pikeperch, eels, crayfish and carp, and which creates all kinds of wonderful dishes from these fish: trout pâté with plums, trout mousse with herbs, aniseed-flavoured carp sausage, trout in aspic. Rods can be hired for those who prefer the excitement of fishing themselves.

SIGHTS

★**Cathédrale St-Dié** – The former collegiate church became a cathedral in 1777. Its imposing Classical west front dating from the early 18C is flanked by two square towers. There is a fine Romanesque doorway on the south side. The greatest part of the edifice was blown up in November 1944 but the vaulting and the east end were rebuilt as they were before the explosion.

Interior ⊘ – In the Romanesque nave, strong piers alternate with weak ones surmounted with carved **capitals**★ having miraculously been spared by the explosion. The transverse arches and ribbed vaulting of the nave date from the 13C. There is a 14C Virgin and Child against the column situated on the right of the crossing. Some 13C windows in the second chapel on the north side, illustrate episodes from the Life of St Déodat. In 1987, the cathedral acquired some fine abstract **stained-glass windows**★ made by a group of 10 artists headed by Jean Bazaine.

Cathedral cloister

★**Cloître gothique** – This former canon cloister, linking the cathedral and the Église Notre-Dame-de-Galilée, is remarkable; in the 15C and 16C, building took place but it was never completed.
Note the Flamboyant openings on the side of the courtyard and the ribbed vaulting resting on engaged colonnettes and pilasters. A 15C outdoor pulpit leans against a buttress of the east gallery.

Église Notre-Dame-de-Galilée ⊘ – The church is characteristic of Romanesque architecture in southern Lorraine. The plain west front is preceded by a belfry-porch with simple capitals. The originality of the nave lies in its groined vaulting, an unusual feature in such a large nave.

Musée Pierre-Noël – musée de la vie dans les Hautes-Vosges ⊘ – The museum, which was rebuilt on the site of the former episcopal palace (the monumental entrance alone has survived), includes an archaeological section (finds from the site of La Bure), an ornithological section (350 stuffed birds) and other sections devoted to the Vosges Forest, wood and textile crafts, agriculture and stock farming, ceramics from eastern regions and glassware.
A large room is devoted to Jules Ferry, a native of St-Dié.
There is also a Franco-German military exhibition including an important display about the pilot René Fonck, an ace of the First World War, born near St-Dié.
In addition, the museum houses the Goll collection of modern art.

Bibliothèque ⊘ – The library has a stock of 230 000 works including 600 manuscripts and 140 incunabula (early printed books). The treasury room contains a copy of the extremely rare *Cosmographiæ Introductio* and an illuminated gradual – a kind of missal – from the early 16C, with miniatures illustrating work in the mines during the Middle Ages.

Tour de la Liberté ⊘ – This entirely white edifice, made of steel, canvas and cables, rises 36m/118ft above ground and weighs more than 1 440t. Erected in Paris for the Bicentenary of the Revolution in 1989, the Tower of Liberty was moved to its present location a year later. It contains an unusual display of **jewellery** created by Heger de Lœwenfeld after paintings by Georges Braque.

From the viewpoint, there is a stunning view of the town and the blue line of the Vosges mountains.

EXCURSIONS

Camp celtique de la Bure – *7.5km/4.6mi then 45min on foot there and back. Drive out of St-Dié along N 59 and, 4km/2.5mi further on, turn right towards La Pêcherie then right again onto the forest road to La Bure and finally left onto the forest road to La Crenée.*

⬆ *Leave the car at the Col de la Crenée and take the path running along the ridge (starting behind a forest shelter) and leading to the main entrance of the camp (large explanatory panel).*

This archaeological site has revealed traces of constant human occupation beginning roughly in 2000 BC and ending in the 4C AD.

Occupying the western extremity (alt 582m/1 909ft) of a ridge known as the Crête de la Bure, the camp is elliptical and measures 340m/372yd by 110m/120yd diagonally. The outer wall consisted of an earth base (2.25m/7.5ft thick) and a wooden palisade interrupted by two gates and two posterns. The eastern approach of the camp was barred as early as the 1C BC by a wall (*murus gallicus*, 7m/23ft thick) preceded by a ditch and from AD 300 onwards by a second Roman-type rampart. There were several pools in the camp (two of them were dedicated to Gaulish goddesses) and important ironworks (two anvils weighing 11kg/24lb and 23.5kg/52lb were discovered together with 450kg/992lb of iron slag). The archaeological finds are exhibited in the St-Dié Museum.

From the camp, there are fine **views**★ *(viewing table)* of the Meurthe Valley to the west and of the St-Dié Basin to the south.

Jardins de Callunes ⊘ – *In Ban-de-Sapt, 10km/6.2mi NE of St-Dié. Drive out of town along D 49 to St-Jean d'Ormont then follow D 32.* These landscaped botanic gardens extending over 4ha/10 acres present 230 species of heather, various rhododendrons, azaleas, perennials and maple trees. The gardens are at their best in spring and autumn.

From St-Dié to the Donon pass – *43km/27mi – allow 2hr 30min. Drive out of St-Dié along N 59.*

Étival-Clairefontaine – This small town, lies on the banks of the Valdange, a tributary of the River Meurthe. A lively cheese fair takes place during the first weekend in October. The ruins of a paper mill dating from 1512 can still be seen on the riverside. The modern mill has been set up in Clairefontaine on the banks of the Meurthe. The former **church**★ ⊘ of a Premonstratensian abbey, built of sandstone from the Vosges region, has retained its nave and aisles in transitional style (Romanesque to Gothic).

Moyenmoutier – The vast abbey **church** ⊘, rebuilt in the 18C, is one of the finest religious buildings of the Baroque period in the whole Vosges region.

Senones – This small town, surrounded by forested heights, developed near a Benedictine abbey and became in 1751 the capital of the principality of Salm, a sovereign state whose inhabitants asked to become French in 1793. Senones has retained a few princely residences and 18C mansions.

Every year in July and August, a historic display staging the Prince of Salm's guard takes place on Sunday mornings.

The **former abbey** has a fine 18C stone staircase with wrought-iron banisters, which used to lead to the apartments of **Dom Calmet**, one of the last erudite abbots, and to those of Voltaire who stayed with him in 1754.

From Senones, drive N along D 424 to La Petite-Raon (2km/1.2mi) then turn left onto D 49.

The forest road, which prolongs D 49, runs along the narrow and remote valley of the River Rabodeau. The **Col de Prayé** marked the former border between France and Germany. The road reaches the **Col du Donon** (alt 727m/2 385ft; *see Massif du DONON*).

ST-DIZIER

Population 33 552
Michelin map 61 fold 9 or 241 fold 30

This modern industrial town with a concentration of smelting works, ironworks and steelworks was once a mighty stronghold with a garrison of some 2 500 soldiers. In 1544 it successfully withstood an attack by the Holy Roman Emperor, Charles V, and his army of 100 000 men. It was here that, in 1814, Napoleon won his last victory before being exiled to the island of Elba.

Besides its military activities, the town has been involved in the floating of logs down the River Marne since the 16C, and in 1900, **Hector Guimard**, one of the initiators of Art Nouveau in France, used the St-Dizier ironworks for his ornamental creations. His initiative was at the origin of a now established activity.

Eating out

MODERATE

La Cigogne Gourmande – *46 r. de l'Europe – 52100 Perthes – 10km/6.2mi W of St-Dizier on N 67 – ☎ 03 25 56 40 29 – closed during Feb school holidays, 17-30 Jul and Sun evening – 80/450F.* You will appreciate the carefully-tended setting of this country restaurant. Attractive, well-spaced tables with pretty fabrics, silver and glassware will enhance your enjoyment of the copious local cuisine. Peaceful rooms.

Where to stay

MODERATE

Chambre d'hôte M. et Mme Marsal – *4 rte d'Eurville – 52410 Chamouilley – 9km/5.6mi SE of St-Dizier on N 67 – ☎ 03 25 55 02 26 – ⊭ – 4 rooms 190/230F.* This pretty stone house is set back beside a quiet local road behind a courtyard and garden. Pleasant hosts, a good standard of comfort and attractive prices make up for a slight lack of character in the recently renovated rooms.

TOUR OF THE TOWN

In search of Guimard's cast-iron ornaments

Many houses were decorated by Guimard, outside and inside, in Art Nouveau style: balconies, window sills, palmettes, door leaves, banisters...

Start from place de la Liberté (tourist office).

At the beginning of rue de la Commune-de-Paris, no 29 has a door leaf decorated with tulips dating from 1900.

Follow rue de l'Arquebuse.

Rue de l'Arquebuse – No 1: railing, banisters and window sill dating from 1900; nos 1bis and 1ter: window sills by Guimard; no 31: window sills, door leaves, basement window by Guimard; no 33: window sills dating from 1900.

Turn left onto rue du Colonel-Raynal.

Rue du Colonel-Raynal – No 4: window sills; no 6: window sills and door leaf by Guimard; no 8: window sills.

Before turning left onto rue du Général-Maistre, note the window sills of no 39 on the right.

Rue du Général-Maistre – No 24 on the street corner: window sills; no 15: door leaves by Guimard; no 13: door leaves by Guimard and window sills dating from 1900.

Return to the square via rue Robert-Dehault.

Quartier de la Noue

This suburb was inhabited by boatmen who floated convoys of logs down the River Marne to Paris and walked back home. They lived in low houses with cob walls; every house had a yard backing onto gardens and fields. The tiny alleyways (80 in all, known as *voyottes*) lying perpendicular to avenue de la République can still be seen today.

ADDITIONAL SIGHT

Musée – The museum overlooking square W.-Churchill contains interesting paleontological collections (fossils found in the area including an 11m/36ft long iguanodon, the largest ever found in France) as well as ornithological (birds sharing the same habitat are displayed together) and archaeological collections. Some cast-iron ornaments by Guimard.

EXCURSIONS

Vallée de la Blaise – *See WASSY.*

★★**Lac du Der-Chantecoq** – *See Lac du DER-CHANTECOQ.*

Abbaye de Trois-Fontaines – *11km/6.8mi N. Drive out of St-Dizier along D 157 and continue along D 16.*
The remains of the former Cistercian abbey, founded in 1118 by monks from Clairvaux *(see Abbaye de CLAIRVAUX)*, rebuilt in the 18C and partly destroyed during the Revolution, stand at the heart of the forest. A monumental 18C doorway leads to the main courtyard and, beyond, to the park (3ha/7.5 acres) dotted with statues. The former conventual buildings and the ruins of the 12C abbey church can also be seen.

Marais de ST-GOND

Michelin map 56 folds 15 and 16, 61 folds 5 and 6 or 241 fold 29

This marshland, situated below the Île-de-France cuesta and covering more than 3 000ha/7 413 acres over an area 15km/9mi long and 4km/2.5mi wide, owes its name to a 7C coenobite. Water from the marsh is drained by the Petit Morin.
In September 1914, the area and the surrounding heights were the scene of fierce fighting between Von Bülow's second German army and **General Foch**'s 9th French army. Foch eventually succeeded in driving the Germans back to the River Marne.

MARSHLAND AND VINEYARDS

36km/22mi round tour starting from Mondement – allow 1hr 30min

This drive goes through the solitary expanses of the marshland area which has been partly drained and turned into pastures or agricultural land (maize). The south-facing slopes of the limestone hills surrounding the marsh are covered with vineyards producing a fine white wine.

Mondement – The Mondement hill (alt 223m/732ft), overlooking the marsh and commanding the way to the River Seine, was at the centre of the fighting in September 1914. The German troops eventually withdrew after suffering heavy losses. A monument commemorates these events.
The view extends over the St-Gond marsh to Mont Aimé and the Champagne hills.

Allemant – This tiny village clinging to the hillside has a surprisingly large Flamboyant Gothic church with a double transept and a high tower surmounting the crossing. From the adjacent cemetery, the view extends towards the Île-de-France cuesta on the left, the St-Gond marsh and Fère-Champenoise plain on the right.

Coizard – Charming Romanesque village church.

Villevenard – Wine-growing village. One's attention is immediately drawn to the tastefully restored 12C **church**, its harmonious proportions, its Romanesque nave with small rounded openings and its fine octagonal tower surmounting the crossing.

ST-MIHIEL ★

Population 5 367
Michelin map 57 folds 11 and 12 or 241 fold 27

Situated on the western edge of the Parc naturel régional de Lorraine, St-Mihiel has had close links with the famous Benedictine abbey of the same name since it was founded in 709 near the present town and relocated in 815 along the banks of the Meuse by one of Charlemagne's counsellors. In 1301, St-Mihiel became the main town of the Barrois region lying east of the River Meuse.
The city then prospered both economically and culturally, the 16C being a particularly brilliant period: renowned drapers and goldsmiths settled in St-Mihiel and the fame of **Ligier Richier** and his school of sculpture spread throughout eastern France. Born in St-Mihiel in 1500, Richier surrounded himself with talented sculptors and apprentices. In 1559, he was asked to decorate the town for the arrival of Duke Charles III and his wife. In later life, however, he was converted to the Protestant faith and went to live in Geneva where he died in 1567. Fine examples of his considerable output can be seen in Bar-le-Duc, Hattonchâtel, Étain and Briey.

In September 1914, the German army launched a thrust in that area in order to skirt round the powerful stronghold of Verdun. They succeeded in establishing a bridgehead on the west bank of the Meuse, known as the **St-Mihiel Bulge**, which prevented supplies and reinforcements from reaching Verdun via the Meuse Valley through the duration of the war.

TOWN WALK

Start from the tourist office.

Bâtiments abbatiaux – The vast conventual buildings, adjacent to the Église St-Michel, were rebuilt in the 17C with a façade in the Louis XIV style and are still almost intact.

Walk to place Bérain.

Église St-Michel – The abbey church was almost entirely rebuilt in the 17C, nevertheless retaining its 12C square belfry and Romanesque porch. Aisles of equal height and shallow side chapels flank the large nave, comprising five bays. The Gothic vaulting rests on massive fluted columns crowned by Doric capitals. The deep chancel is decorated with 80 beautifully carved stalls.

G. Guittot/DIAF

The finest piece in the church is the **Sépulcre★★** (Entombment of Christ) sculpted by Ligier Richier between 1554-64. The 13 figures *(in The first side chapel along the south aisle)* are life-sized: Salomé prepares the funeral bed, Joseph and Nicodemus hold the body of Christ, Mary Magdalene kisses Christ's feet. In the background, St John supports the Virgin, an angel holds the instruments of the Passion, and two guards are seen throwing the dice for Christ's tunic.

The baptismal chapel on the same side contains the Child with Death's Heads, carved in 1608 by Jean Richier, Ligier Richier's grandson. The magnificent organ case dates from 1679 to 1681.

Follow rue Notre-Dame.

Maison du Roi – *2 rue Notre-Dame.* This 14C Gothic house belonged in the 15C to King René of Anjou, who also had the title of Duc de Bar.

Falaises – The cliffs consist of seven limestone rocks, over 20m/66ft high, overlooking the east bank of the river. In 1772, Mangeot, a native of St-Mihiel, carved a representation of the Holy Sepulchre in the first rock. From the top of the cliffs, there is a fine view of the town and the Meuse Valley.

Walk back to town across the Promenade des Capucins and along rue Poincaré on the left.

Église St-Étienne – The nave of this original hall-church was built between 1500 and 1545. Note the modern stained-glass windows and the Renaissance altarpiece in the apse. But the church is above all famous for the **Sepulchre★★** or Entombment sculpted by Ligier Richier from 1554 to 1564, situated in the middle bay of the south aisle. It consists of 13 life-size figures depicting the preparations for Christ's Entombment *(light switch on the right).*

ADDITIONAL SIGHTS

Bibliothèque ⊙ – *Inside the former abbey.* The library has, since 1775, been housed in a large hall decorated with woodwork and ceilings in the Louis XIV style. It contains 9 000 works including 74 manuscripts (beautiful 15C gradual) and 86 incunabula. The prize exhibit is the first book to have been printed in Lorraine.

Musée départemental d'Art sacré ⊙ – *First floor of the south wing of the former abbey.* The museum contains more than 800 objects of religious art from the Meuse region: paintings, sculptures, gold plate, liturgical ornaments dating from the 13C to the 20C.

EXCURSIONS

Bois d'Ailly – *7km/4.3mi SE along D 907 and a signposted forest road.*
There are several reminders of the heavy fighting which took place in this wood in September 1914: a row of trenches (complete with shelters and communication trenches) starting from the memorial leads to the Tranchée de la Soif (the thirst trench) where a few soldiers held on for three days against a strong unit of the German Imperial Guard.

Sampigny, Musée Raymond-Poincaré ⊘ – *9km/5.6mi S along D 964.*
The former summer residence of Raymond Poincaré, one of the outstanding personalities of France's Third Republic, houses mementoes, objects and documents connected with the life of this exceptional politician. The opulent villa was built for Poincaré in 1906 by Bourgon, an architect from Nancy.
Raymond Poincaré (1860-1934) was a liberal republican at heart, as well as a brilliant barrister and a writer (he entered the French Academy in 1909). Re-elected without interruption for 48 years, he became in turn a regional councillor, a member of Parliament, a minister, a senator, the prime minister and the president of the Republic. As president during the First World War, he chose Clemenceau as his prime minister in 1917 at a turning point in the war.

Génicourt-sur-Meuse – *19km/11.8mi N along the River Meuse.* The **church** ⊘ is a fine example of the Flamboyant Gothic style. It contains beautiful 16C stained-glass windows by members of the School of Metz, a high altar surmounted by a retable depicting the Passion and, on its right, another altar dating from 1530. The interesting wooden statues of the Calvary are believed to be the work of Ligier Richier; 16C frescoes were discovered in June 1981.

Commercy – *18km/11.2mi S along the River Meuse.* Commercy occupied a strategic position on the west bank of the River Meuse and the number of fortified houses and churches still standing are a reminder of the constant threat of invasion the whole area lived under in the past. The town has retained an ancient metalwork tradition and a biennial exhibition of contemporary art takes place in the castle as part of a competition known as the Art du Fer. Small soft cakes called *madeleines*, a speciality of Commercy, are the product of a prosperous industry.
An imposing horseshoe esplanade precedes the **Château Stanislas** *(the interior is not open to the public)* situated along the axis formed by rue Stanislas and the alleyway lined with lime trees which leads to the Commercy Forest. Designed in 1708 by Boffrand and d'Orbay for the Prince de Vaudémont, it was used as a hunting lodge by the dukes of Lorraine before becoming the property of Stanislas Leszczynski, King Louis XV's father-in-law
The former municipal baths, dating from the 1930s, have been turned into the **Musée de la Céramique et de l'Ivoire** ⊘, which houses a fine collection of ceramics together with European and Asian ivories.
It is worth continuing south along the River Meuse for another 3km/1.9mi to **Euville** to look at the Art Nouveau town hall (École de Nancy).

ST-NICOLAS-DE-PORT★★

Population 7 702
Michelin map 62 fold 5 or 242 fold 22

The splendid Flamboyant basilica of St-Nicolas-de-Port, which looks as impressive as a cathedral, stands in the centre of this small industrial town. It has been a popular place of pilgrimage since the 11C. Pilgrims flocked to the city which became the most prosperous economic centre in Lorraine and the venue of international fairs.
In 1635, during the Thirty Years War, the town was ransacked by the Swedes and only the church, dedicated to the patron saint of Lorraine, was spared.

FAMILY FARE

Auberge de la Mirabelle – *6 rte de Nancy – 54210 Ferrières – 12km/7.5mi S of St-Nicolas-de-Port on D 115 and D 112 –* ☎ *03 83 26 62 14 – closed evenings except Sat – 120F.* As its name suggests, Léon's farm specialises in mirabelle plums. In the former cowshed which is now a restaurant, the cooking is simple family fare, much appreciated locally.

★★BASILIQUE ST-NICOLAS ⊙

The road skirting the north bank of the River Meurthe offers a fine view of the basilica. The present edifice, built as a shrine for one of St Nicholas' fingers, is a splendid specimen of Flamboyant Gothic architecture.

Knights from Lorraine brought the precious relic back from Bari in Italy and placed it in a chapel dedicated to Our Lady. There followed a series of miracles and a church had to be built to accommodate the growing number of pilgrims. Joan of Arc came to pray in the church in 1429 before embarking on her mission. The huge church dating from the late 15C and early 16C suffered fire and war damage and the roof was only repaired in 1735. It became a basilica in 1950.

Having been damaged again in 1940, this time by bombing, the church needed extensive restoration to recover its past splendour. A bequest from Madame Camille Croue-Friedman, a native of St-Nicolas-de-Port, who died in the United States in 1980, provided the answer and, since 1983, the basilica has looked like a building site once again.

The basilica from afar

Exterior – The west front features three doorways surmounted by Flamboyant gables.

The central doorway has retained the statue representing St Nicholas' miracle (in the recess of the central pillar), believed to be the work of Claude Richier, the brother of the famous sculptor, Ligier Richier.

The towers rise to 85m/279ft and 87m/285ft. Note on the north side, level with the transept and the chancel, a row of six basket-handled recesses in which traders used to set up shop when a pilgrimage was on.

There is a good view of the east end from rue Anatole-France.

Interior – The lofty nave is well lit and covered with lierne and tierceron vaulting whose highest point reaches 32m/105ft above ground level, as in Strasbourg Cathedral; its diagonal arches rest on tall columns. The aisles are similarly constructed; the transept vaulting, supported by very tall pillars (28m/92ft high, the highest in France), rises to the same height as that of the central nave, which was often the case in the Champagne region.

The stained-glass windows of the apse, dating from 1507 to 1510, are particularly remarkable; they were made by Nicole Droguet whereas those of the aisle and chapels on the north side are the work of Valentin Bousch from Strasbourg; both date from the same period. Note that the Renaissance influence can already be felt in the decorative motifs used.

The sanctuary which received St Nicholas' relic in the 11C was probably located where the **baptismal chapel** (accessible from behind the Virgin's altar) now stands. It contains interesting 16C fonts and a beautiful Early Renaissance altarpiece surmounted by openwork pinnacles. Several 16C painted wood panels illustrate scenes from the Life of St Nicholas. The **treasury** includes a silver gilt reliquary arm of St Nicholas (19C), the cardinal of Lorraine's ship (16C), a silver reliquary of the True Cross (15C), Voltaire's ivory Crucifix, and a large 19C processional cross.

ADDITIONAL SIGHTS

Musée français de la Brasserie ⌚ – The museum is housed in the brewery which closed down in 1985.
The visit begins with an audio-visual presentation which explains the brewing process. Two stained-glass panels by Jacques Gruber light up the Salle Moreau.
The Art Deco brewing tower, lit by wide windows, houses various installations: the laboratory, the malt loft, the hops storeroom, the brewing room with its fine copper vats, the room containing the refrigerating equipment and the cold room with the fermentation vats.
The visit ends with beer tasting in the basement.

Musée du Cinéma, de la Photographie et des Arts audiovisuels ⌚ – *10 rue Georges-Rémy*. The museum illustrates the evolution of animated pictures and photography from the early 19C to the birth of the cinema.

EXCURSIONS

Varangéville – *N of the town, between the River Meurthe and the Marne-Rhine canal.*
Dating from the early 15C, the Flamboyant Gothic church contains a superb forest of ribbed pillars with palm motifs and interesting statues, including a Virgin and Child dating from the early 14C and a 16C Entombment.

Dombasle-sur-Meurthe – *5km/3mi W.*
Lying between the River Meurthe and the Marne-Rhine canal, the town is an industrial centre specialising in chemicals (**Solvay** group from Belgium), mainly sodium carbonate, salt and by-products. The plant is situated on both sides of D 400; its lime kilns are among the largest in the world.
Salt, which is the raw material of this industry, has been mined from the **Haraucourt** plateau since 1904 (1 400 000t per year). The process consists in injecting fresh water into the soil in order to dissolve the salt and thus extract it. This intensive mining concerns an area of 200ha/494 acres. Huge craters are visible from D 80 and D 81.

Rosières-aux-Salines – *8km/5mi SE along D 400 then right onto D 116.* A stud farm took over the buildings of the former salt plant which closed down in 1760. The farm houses some 30 thoroughbred stallions.

Ste-MENEHOULD

Population 5 178
Michelin map 56 fold 19 or 241 fold 22

THE RED HORSE

Le Cheval Rouge – *1 r. Chanzy – ☎ 03 26 60 81 04 – closed 20 Nov-11 Dec and Mon Oct-Easter – 20 rooms 240/310F – ☕ 38F – restaurant 92/280F.* Modern, well-furnished rooms and carefully prepared, traditional cuisine. The dining room has exposed beams and a superb stone fireplace.

Situated in the Aisne Valley, on the edge of the Argonne Forest, Ste-Menehould occupies a strategic position at the entrance of the Islettes pass. The town, which was the birthplace of Dom Pérignon *(see ÉPERNAY: Excursions)*, is overlooked by a hillock known as Le Château.
In June 1791, during the Revolution, Louis XVI secretly fled Paris with his family, intending to return at the head of an army and restore his authority. However, the king was recognised at the Ste-Menehould posting house by a young boy who gave the alarm and the party was stopped at Varennes *(see ARGONNE)*. Today, the *gendarmerie* (police station) stands on the site of the former posting house.
Gourmets will enjoy the local speciality: delicious pig's trotters.

SIGHTS

Place du Général-Leclerc – Split into two by the main road *(N 3)*, the square is lined by a fine group of pink-brick buildings – including the **town hall** (1730) – with stone ties and bluish-slate roofs, designed by Philippe de la Force who rebuilt the city after the fire of 1719.

Musée ⌚ – Housed in an 18C mansion, the museum contains various regional collections: history, religious art, geology. Note the model (more than 2 000 pieces) of the Battle of Montfaucon which took place in 888 between King Eudes' army and Vikings sailing up the River Meuse.

Butte du château – *Accessible by car up a ramp or on foot along a path and up some steps.*
This is the upper town, looking like a Champagne village with its low timber-framed, flower-decked houses. From the top, there is a fine **view★** of the lower town, its roofs covered with curved tiles and the 19C Église St-Charles.
The 13C-15C **Église Notre Dame** (also called Église du Château) is surrounded by its cemetery. The walls, rebuilt in the 18C, are decorated with brick and white-stone ties.

EXCURSIONS

★**Château de Braux-Ste-Cohière** ⊙ – *5.5km/3.4mi W.* The buildings were erected in the 16C and 17C by Philippe de Thomassin, who was governor of Châlons during the reign of Henri IV; they were designed for a unit of the Household Cavalry whose uniform the king of France wore on the battlefield. In 1792, General Dumouriez made his headquarters here to prepare for the Battle of Valmy against the Prussians.

Château of Braux-Ste-Cohière

Today, the château is the headquarters of the **Association culturelle Champagne-Argonne** and is used for numerous cultural events: audio-visual show introducing the region, exhibitions, music festival.
Every year, celebrations for the Noël des Bergers de Champagne include a musical evening with a procession followed by the midnight mass.
The vast quadrangle flanked with four corner towers offers a charming view with its white-striped brick walls reflecting in the deep waters of the moat.
It is possible to walk round the main courtyard and admire the architectural style of the various buildings: the old stables covered with oak shingles supporting the tiles, the officers' quarters and its mansard, the dovecote which houses the **Musée régional d'Orientation** (geology, local history, popular art).
A charming walk takes you through several **gardens** separated by hedges made up of various species of plants and bushes. Part of the park is used for training horses.

Valmy – *12km/7.5mi W.* A decisive battle took place near this village in September 1792 between French and Prussian troops. Although there were relatively few casualties, the psychological consequences were enormous. French soldiers were ill-equipped patriotic volunteers and the fact that they withstood the attack of the Prussian army and forced it to retreat boosted the morale of the whole French nation; two days later the Republic was proclaimed.
The **Moulin de Valmy**, reconstructed in 1947, is identical to the windmill next to which stood François-Christophe **Kellermann**, the French commanding officer, at the time of the Prussian attack. Four viewing tables show the position of the two armies. The view extends over the Champagne region and the Argonne Forest.

Mont STE-ODILE★★

Michelin map 87 fold 15 or 242 fold 23
Local map see Le HOHWALD

Mont Ste-Odile is undoubtedly one of the most popular sights in Alsace: tourists are attracted by the site and the panorama, whereas the devout are inspired by the holiness of the place.

HISTORICAL NOTES

The so-called pagan wall *(Mur Païen)* which winds its way on the top of Mont-Ste-Odile testifies to human presence in the area probably dating back to prehistoric times or in any case to the Celtic or Gaulish period.

In the 7C, Hohenburg Castle was the summer residence of Duke Étichon, **St Odile**'s father. According to legend, the blind baby girl was rejected by her father, and subsequently saved and raised by her nurse. She recovered her sight miraculously and later escaped her father's determination to marry her to a knight. Her vocation became clear and her father eventually made her a present of Hohenburg where she founded her convent.

After St Odile's death, the convent became an important place of pilgrimage.

COUVENT *30min*

The forested escarpments of Mont Ste-Odile (alt 764m/2 507ft) tower over the Plaine d'Alsace. The convent is situated at the northern end of the promontory.

Pilgrims flock here all year round and particularly for the feast of St Odile.

The porch, located beneath the former hostel, gives access to the main courtyard shaded by lime trees and framed by the present hostel on the left, the church on the right and the south wing of the convent at the end.

St Odile's convent

Église conventuelle – Destroyed by fire, the monastery church was rebuilt in 1692. The three-naved building is adorned with fine woodwork (chancel) and confessionals richly carved in the 18C.

★**Chapelle de la Croix** – *Access from inside the monastery church, through a door situated on the left.* This is the oldest part of the convent, going back to the 11C. The four groined vaults are supported by a single Romanesque pillar with a carved capital. A sarcophagus housed the remains of Duke Étichon, Odile's father.

On the left, a low doorway decorated with Carolingian carvings leads to the small Chapelle Ste-Odile.

Chapelle Ste-Odile – An 8C sarcophagus contains St Odile's relics. This 12C chapel is presumed to have been built on the site of the previous chapel where St Odile died.

The nave is Romanesque and the chancel is Gothic. Two 17C low-relief carvings depict the christening of St Odile, and Étichon spared the sufferings of Purgatory by the grace of his daughter's prayers.

Terrasse – The terrace has two excellent viewpoints *(viewing tables)*, one in the north-west corner offering a view of the Champ du Feu and Bruche Valley, the other at the north-east extremity, affording a splendid **panorama**★★ of the Plaine d'Alsace and the Black Forest.

Chapelle des Larmes – This is the first of the chapels standing in the north-east corner of the terrace. It was built on the site of the Merovingian cemetery (several graves have been preserved).
A stone slab behind a railing is said to have been worn by St Odile kneeling on it daily as she prayed for her father's salvation.

Chapelle des Anges – This chapel houses a fine mosaic dating from 1947. According to a local belief, if a young woman went round it nine times, she could be sure to find a husband before the end of the year!

Fontaine de Ste-Odile – The road leading down to St-Nabor *(D 33)* runs past the spring (protected by a railing) which is said to have gushed forth from the rock at St Odile's request to quench the thirst of an exhausted blind man. It is now a place of pilgrimage for people with eye complaints.

IN THE FOOTSTEPS OF HISTORY

Mur païen – *30min on foot there and back. As you come out of the convent, walk down 33 steps on the left then follow the path starting at the foot of the stairs.*
🏃 It would take four or five hours to walk round the remains of this mysterious wall running through forests and screes over a distance of more than 10km/6mi. Its average thickness is 1.7m/5.5ft and it reaches a height of 3m/10ft in the best-preserved parts. However, seeing even a part of this monumental work is already an awe-inspiring experience; note the cavities carved in the huge blocks to insert the tenons used to join them together.
Return to the convent along the same path.
A path *(starting from the southern parking area)* offers a fine walk along the pagan wall.

Château de Landsberg – *4km/2.5mi SE along D 109, then 1hr on foot there and back down the signposted path.*
🏃 The itinerary offers a pleasant walk through the forest, past the former Landsberg inn to a platform beneath the castle which can be seen through the trees. The 13C castle is now in ruins.

SARREBOURG

Population 13 311
Michelin map 87 fold 14 or 242 fold 19

This city of Roman origin belonged to the bishops of Metz during the Middle Ages and then to the duchy of Lorraine before becoming part of the kingdom of France in the late 17C.
Today Sarrebourg is the starting point of fine excursions along the River Sarre in an area renowned for its crystal works. The town hosts an international music festival in May and in July there is a convivial soft white cheese fair!

SIGHTS

Chapelle des Cordeliers ⊙ – This deconsecrated Franciscan chapel houses the *syndicat d'initiative* (tourist office). Erected in the 13C, the edifice was rebuilt in the 17C and its west front is lit by a huge **stained-glass window**★ by Marc Chagall illustrating "peace" (12m/39ft high and 7.5m/25ft wide). It consists of 13 000 pieces of glass weighing 900kg/1 985lb. In the centre, vivid blues, reds and greens symbolize the Tree of Life in Genesis with Adam and Eve surrounded by the Serpent, Christ's cross, the Prophet Isaiah, the Lamb, the Candelabra, angels accompanying Abraham, Jesus entering Jerusalem... At the foot of the Tree, Birth, Work, Suffering and Death illustrate mankind.

Musée du Pays de Sarrebourg ⊙ – *13 avenue de France.* The museum contains regional archaeological collections: finds from the Gallo-Roman villa in St-Ulrich and from necropolises and sanctuaries of the Vosges mountains, 14C statuettes and low-relief ceramics from Sarrebourg, medieval sculpture (beautiful 15C Crucifix) as well as a remarkable collection of 18C ceramics and porcelain from nearby Niderviller.

Cimetière national des Prisonniers – *On the outskirts of town, on the right of rue de Verdun (D 27).* The cemetery contains some 13 000 graves of soldiers of the First World War. The monument facing the gate, entitled Giant in chains, was sculpted by Stoll while he was a prisoner of war.

EXCURSIONS

Réding – *2km/1.2mi NE along N 4 then left in Petit-Eich.*
In 1977, during the restoration of the **Chapelle Ste-Agathe**, 13C frescoes illustrating the emblems of the Evangelists were discovered on the chancel vaulting.

St-Ulrich, Villa gallo-romaine ⊘ – *4km/2.5mi NW.* The villa was the residence of a rich landowner and stood at the heart of a vast estate probably covering 2 000ha/4 942 acres. Built in the 1C AD, it was extended during the 2C to include more than 100 rooms, courtyards, galleries, cellars and even baths.

Hartzviller, Cristallerie ⊘ – *10km/6mi S. Drive out of Sarrebourg along D 44. As you leave Hesse, turn left onto D 96⁰ leading to Hartzviller.*
During the tour of the crystalworks, some 80 glass-blowers can be seen at work.

Fénétrange – *15km/9mi N along D 43.*
This small fortified town has retained several beautiful medieval houses and an elegant castle with a curved façade overlooking a circular courtyard. The **collegiate church of St-Remi** is a fine edifice rebuilt in the 15C with a short lofty nave covered with ribbed vaulting and a vast polygonal apse lit by stained-glass windows partially dating from the 15C.

🏃 Walking tours of the Arboretum (2hr 30min) and of the Gros-Chêne (1hr) are organised in Fénétrange Forest.

SARREGUEMINES

Population 23 117
Michelin map 57 folds 16 and 17 or 242 fold 11

A.Mertz/Ville de Sarreguemines

The Earth

This border town, situated at the confluence of the Sarre and the Blies, offers pleasant walks along the river banks. Sarreguemines used to be the seat of a feudal domain guarding the borders of the duchy of Lorraine.

Pottery – The Sarreguemines manufacture, founded in 1790, developed and acquired fame, in spite of financial difficulties and the annexation of Lorraine in 1870, through the inspired management of the De Geiger family. Production reached its peak at the turn of the 20C: more than 3 000 workers produced majolica, porcelain, dinner sets and panels. Bought by the Lunéville-St-Clément group in 1979, the pottery now essentially produces floor tiles. In 1982, it was renamed Sarreguemines-Bâtiment.

SIGHTS

Musée ⊘ – *17 rue Poincaré.* Housed in the former residence of the manager of the earthenware manufacture, the museum illustrates local history in attractive fashion. The **ceramics collection★** retraces the history and main production of Sarreguemines pottery over the past 200 years. The **winter garden★★**, designed by Paul de Geiger in 1882 is particularly remarkable. Note, on the wall facing the entrance, the monumental majolica fountain with Renaissance-style decoration offering a shimmering display of yellows, greens, ochres and browns. On either side, there are panels depicting the small pavilion (left) and the factory buildings (right). Dinner services and decorative objects placed in the centre of the room illustrate changing techniques linked to the evolution of fashion and society.

Musée des Techniques faïencières ⊘ – An interactive museum designed to explain the manufacturing process of earthenware. The machinery and tools are authentic.

Circuit de la faïence de Sarreguemines ⊘ – A **walking tour** *(3km/1.9mi)* links the main sites connected with the manufacture of earthenware in Sarreguemines *(brochure available from the tourist office or the museum).*

Behind the town hall, visitors can see the former **oven** of one of the workshops. Around 1860, there were about 30 similar conical brick-built ovens.

At the end of the tour, souvenirs are available at the pottery shop.

EXCURSION

Parc archéologique européen de Bliesbruck-Reinheim ⊙ – *9.5km/5.9mi E via Bliesbruck*. On either side of the border separating Saarland from the Moselle region, lies the site of an antique city which has been the object of Franco-German excavations since 1978. The settlement, which apparently goes back to the Neolithic period, became important after the arrival of the Celts. The grave of the princess from Reinheim (c 400 BC) dates from that period; gold jewellery and a wine service found in it are to be displayed in a reconstructed **tumulus** near the remains of a large 2C villa.

The **public baths★**, located in Bliesbruck, have been reconstructed in Siberian pine and the site is now protected by a huge glass structure. A marked itinerary dotted with explanations enables visitors to get a better appreciation of what they see. The park's souvenir shop sells replicas of pottery and stage masks.

Two areas once inhabited by craftsmen lie on either side of the main Roman way; one is open to the public, but excavations are still going on in the other.

At certain times of the year, there are demonstrations of the techniques used by Gallo-Roman craftsmen.

In Reinheim, one can see the remains of a vast villa dating from the same period as the ancient city.

SAVERNE★

Population 10 278
Michelin map 87 fold 14 or 242 fold 19

Saverne is a pleasant town situated along the Zorn Valley, at the point where the river flows into the Plaine d'Alsace. The Marne-Rhine canal also runs through Saverne and a lock operates in the lively town centre. The marina, facing the castle, can accommodate 70 boats.

The 16C peasant rebellion ended tragically in Saverne when the Duke of Lorraine besieged the town; he promised to spare the lives of the 20 000 peasants if they came out of the town unarmed, but when they did, they were massacred to the last one by the duke's soldiers in spite of his efforts to stop them.

From the 13C to the Revolution, Saverne belonged to the bishops of Strasbourg. These princes stayed in the castle and sometimes welcomed royal visitors (Louis XIV in 1681, Louis XV in 1744). One of them, **Louis de Rohan**, the famous cardinal who was mixed up in the necklace scandal involving Queen Marie-Antoinette, rebuilt the edifice destroyed by fire and led a life of luxury.

Saverne's annual rose festival includes an international competition of new varieties and a flower show. Rose-flavoured chocolate sweets and shortbread biscuits topped with rose petals have been specially created to celebrate the town's dedication to roses.

The town is the starting point of a picturesque tour through the nature park of the Vosges du Nord *(see Parc naturel régional des VOSGES DU NORD: The Hanau region)*.

Château de Saverne

SIGHTS

★Château – The fine red-sandstone building in the Louis XVI style stands in a beautiful park bound by the Marne-Rhine canal. Acquired by the town in 1814, the castle of the House of Rohan was turned into barracks between 1870 and 1944. The south façade is visible from the square but, in order to see the north façade, which is the most attractive, you will have to walk through the gate and along the right side of the castle. This **façade★★**, which is over 140m/153yd long is very impressive with its fluted pilasters and its peristyle supported by eight columns of the Corinthian order.

Musée ⊘ – The museum is housed in the right wing. The basement contains archaeological collections dating mainly from the Gallo-Roman period. The second floor is devoted to the fine arts and to the town's history: medieval sculpture, archaeological finds from the nearby castles (Haut-Barr, Geroldseck, Wangenbourg), mementoes of the House of Rohan, Louise Weiss' bequest (this politician, who died in 1983, defended feminism and Europe).

Roseraie ⊘ – Over 7 000 rose bushes representing 550 varieties grow in this splendid park situated on the bank of the River Zorn.

Eating out

MODERATE

Le Caveau de l'Escale – *10 quai du Canal* – ☎ *03 88 91 12 23* – *closed Christmas-New Year, 25 Jun-8 Jul, Sat lunchtime, Tue evening and Wed* – *76/150F.* A discreet-looking restaurant near the canal, where you can hire boats. Meals are served in the vaulted cellar, with regional cooking and *tartes flambées* in the evening. Friendly atmosphere.

Where to stay

MID-RANGE

Chez Jean – *3 r. de la Gare* – ☎ *03 88 91 10 19* – *closed 20 Dec-10 Jan* – *25 rooms 338/478F* – ⊋ *53F* – *restaurant 90/220F.* A good place to stay in Saverne. The cosy, welcoming rooms have been renovated and have wood panelling. There is a choice of cuisine, between the regional dishes in the wine bar and a more elaborate menu in the restaurant.

TOWN WALK

★Maisons anciennes à colombage – The two finest timber-framed houses (17C) including the **Maison Katz** *(see p 44)* stand on either side of the town hall. Others can be seen at no 96 Grand'Rue, on the corner of rue des Églises and rue des Pères and on the corner of rue des Pères and rue Poincaré.

Turn left onto rue du Tribunal.

Vieux château – The old castle, which was the former residence of the bishops, is now an administrative building. Note the beautiful Renaissance doorway of the stair tower.

Église paroissiale – Rebuilt in the 14C and 15C, the parish church has retained a Romanesque belfry-porch dating from the 12C. On the right of the doorway, there is a fine outside staircase. The 15C nave houses a pulpit (1495) by Hans Hammer and a 16C high-relief marble sculpture representing Mary and John mourning Christ. The chapel of the Holy Sacrament in the north aisle is adorned with a 16C *Pietà* and a large low-relief woodcarving, painted and gilt, also dating from the 16C, depicting the Assumption. The stained-glass windows of the chapel, made in the 14C, 15C and 16C, illustrate the Adoration of the Magi and scenes from the Passion.

Gallo-Roman and Frankish gravestones can be seen in the garden adjacent to the church.

Ancien cloître des Récollets – The cloister, built in 1303, has lovely red-sandstone pointed arcades and nine murals (added in the 17C, now restored) in the first gallery on the right of the entrance, which depict (from west to east) the Assumption, the Adoration of the Magi, the Annunciation, the Stigmatisation of St Francis, a Christian's Fight for the Good Cause, the Choice of True Goodness and the Last Judgement.

SAVERNE

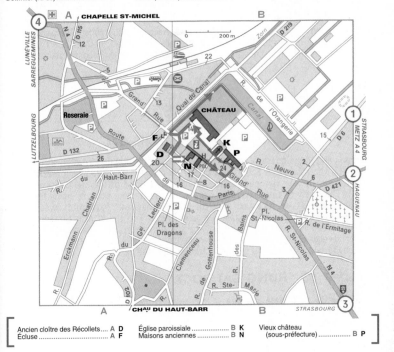

EXCURSIONS

Jardin botanique du col de Saverne ⊙ – *3km/1.9mi then 15min on foot there and back. Leave Saverne by ④ on the town plan (N 4). Drive for 2.5km/1.5mi to the parking area on the right-hand side of the road. Cross the road and follow the signpost.*

🚶 Situated at an altitude of 335m/1 099ft, inside a loop of the road, this botanical garden (2.3ha/5.7 acres) includes an arboretum, an Alpine garden, a small bog and numerous species of fern. Sixteen varieties of orchids flower during the months of May and June.

Saut du Prince Charles (Prince Charles's jump) – *From the botanical garden, walk through the forest along a forest track.*
According to legend, a prince named Charles jumped over the red-sandstone cliff with his horse. There is a fine view of the foothills of the Vosges mountains and the Plaine d'Alsace.
On the way back, follow a path to the left leading down to the bottom of the cliff. The overhang bears an inscription dated 1524, which mentions the building of the road beneath the cliff.

★Château du Haut-Barr – *5km/3mi then 30min tour of the castle. See Château du HAUT-BARR.*

St-Jean-Saverne – *5km/3mi N.* The village **church** is all that remains of an abbey for Benedictine nuns founded at the beginning of the 12C and subsequently ransacked by the Armagnacs and the Swedes. It is surmounted by an 18C belfry built over an interesting Romanesque doorway. At the entrance of the chancel, there are fine cubic-shaped capitals decorated with foliage.

Chapelle St-Michel ⊙ – *2km/1.2mi then 30min on foot there and back starting from the Église St-Jean. Follow the road going through the forest to Mont-St-Michel and turn sharply left 1.5km/0.9mi further on.*
🚶 The **chapel** dates from the same period as the abbey, but it was remodelled in the 17C and restored in 1984.
Follow a path on the right of the chapel to the extremity of the rocky spur forming a platform *(viewing table)* from which the **view★** extends over the hills of Alsace and the Black Forest in the distance. The platform forms a circular hollow known as the **École des Sorcières** (witches' school) because, according to legend, witches used to gather there at night.

Return to the chapel.

Walk down the 57 steps starting on the south side then follow a path on the left which skirts the foot of the cliff and leads to a cave; at the end of this cave, there is a narrow opening known as the **Trou des Sorcières** (witches' hole).

Phalsbourg – *11km/6.6mi W.* The **Porte de France** and the **porte d'Allemagne** are all that remains of the fortifications put in place by Vauban in the 17C. There is a museum on the upper floor of the town hall which is devoted to military items (uniforms, arms etc) and local arts and traditions.

SCHIRMECK

Population
Michelin map 87 fold 15 or 242 fold 23

This small and lively industrial town (metalworks, electronics) stretches along the River Bruche, on the road from Strasbourg to St-Dié. A lovely west front and an octagonal tower framed by four Baroque statues are all that remains of the neo-Classical church (1754). The lovely forests around Schirmeck are the starting point of many hikes.
The River Bruche takes its source near the Col de Saales and, having furrowed its way between the sandstone and crystalline massifs, flows into the Ill near Strasbourg. On the west bank, in the Wisches area, there are some porphyry quarries. The Bruche supplies several textile factories and sawmills and is partly responsible for the industrial activity which brings life to the Schirmeck and Rothau areas.

CLIMB TO "HUNG CAT ROCK"

Rocher de la Chatte pendue – *2hr on foot there and back. 5km/3mi SW of Rothau to Les Quelles, then 1km/0.6mi along an unsurfaced road (towards La Falle); a panel on the right signals the start of the marked path to La Chatte Pendue; it is possible to park at the next bend.*

🚶 The path climbs through the undergrowth to the top of the plateau (alt 900m/2 953ft) where there is a fine **viewpoint★** with a viewing table.

EXCURSIONS

In the footsteps of Oberlin

41km/25.5mi SW – allow 2hr

Fouday – Jean-Frédéric Oberlin *(see below)* is buried in the small cemetery adjacent to the Lutheran church, which has retained the groin-vaulted apse of the earlier Romanesque church.

Turn left onto D 57.

Vallon du Ban de la Roche – This small valley on the east bank of the Bruche still looks unspoilt in spite of some charming houses scattered about.
In 1767, the area was suffering from economic depression (being rather unproductive and having been ruined by several wars), when **Jean-Frédéric Oberlin** (1740-1826) became the new pastor of the small village of Waldersbach, where he remained for the rest of his life. With his wife, he set out to change the life of his parishioners. Helped by local women including **Louise Scheppler**, he created several playschools and extended the age of obligatory schooling to 16. He built roads through the valley, set up mortgage societies, developed agriculture and traditional crafts and initiated a small textile industry by acquiring several looms. Today, he is still venerated throughout Alsace.

Waldersbach – The former protestant presbytery of this charming village houses the **Musée Oberlin** ⊙, devoted to the memory of this great philanthropist.

Drive back to rejoin N 420.

Near the lively village of **St-Blaise-la-Roche**, the narrow river, lined with aspens and birches, flows tamely through a pastoral landscape.

Saales – Situated at the beginning of the Bruche Valley, Saales guards the pass of the same name which gives easy access from one side of the Vosges to the other.
Every Friday afternoon from mid-June to mid-September, the town hall's covered market is the rendezvous of farmers from the upper Bruche Valley who come to sell high-quality local produce.

★Le Climont – Alt 966m/3 169ft. *About 9km/5.6mi E of Saales.* Lovely viewpoint from the summit *(1hr 30min on foot there and back).*

★Vallée de la Bruche

29km/18mi NE – allow 30min

The road *(D 392)* follows the north bank of the Bruche as vineyards and orchards form part of the landscape.

Wisches – This small village marks the border between the French-speaking areas and those where Alsatian dialects are currently spoken.
On the way out of Urmatt, note the huge sawmill on the right.

Niederhaslach – *See WANGENBOURG.*

Framed by forested slopes, the valley gets narrower as the village of **Heiligenberg** appears perched on a promontory on the north bank.

Mutzig – This charming little city, which was once fortified, has been a garrison town for centuries. There is a lovely fountain and a 13C gate surmounted by a tower. The famous brewery dating back to 1812 closed down in 1990 but the town still hosts a beer festival on the first Sunday in September.
Antoine Chassepot, the inventor of a rifle named after him, was born in Mutzig in 1833. In 1870, the French infantry was equipped with this rifle, which was far superior to its German counterpart and should have given the French a considerable advantage but a shortage of munitions made the Chassepot useless.
Near the river, the former **Château des Rohan** (17C), named after the bishops of Strasbourg, was converted into a weapons factory after the Revolution. Today it is a cultural centre and houses the **Musée régional des Armes** ⊘ (firearms – history of the Chassepot – swords, bayonets etc).
From Mutzig to Molsheim, the road runs along the hillside, through vineyards.

★**Molsheim** – *See MOLSHEIM.*

SEDAN

Population 21 667
Michelin map 53 fold 19 or 241 fold 10

Sedan, which was rebuilt after the Second World War, lies on the banks of the River Meuse, beneath the castle and the old town. South of the town, a 13ha/32-acre artificial lake is convenient for bathing and sailing. In addition to the traditional textile industry, industrial activities include metalworks, chemicals and foodstuffs.

HISTORICAL NOTES

According to tradition, the origins of the town go back to Gaulish times but in fact the name Sedan is mentioned for the first time in 997 as belonging to Mouzon Abbey. In 1594, it became the property of the La Tour d'Auvergne family. Henri de La Tour d'Auvergne, Viscount of **Turenne** and Marshal of France (1611-75) was born in Sedan before the town was reunited with the kingdom of France in 1642. This illustrious soldier faithfully served Louis XIII and his son Louis XIV, fighting the Spaniards during the Thirty Years War and later defeating the Fronde thus consolidating young Louis XIV's throne. He had just won back the Alsace region when he was killed at the Battle of Sasbach.
The Revocation of the Edict of Nantes in 1685 was detrimental to Sedan's cloth industry, which had been developed by Protestants, it likewise put an end to the flourishing Academy of the Reformed Religion.
The capitulation of Sedan on 2 September 1870, during the Franco-Prussian War, led to the proclamation of the Third Republic in Paris on 4 September. Seventy years later, in May 1940, another defeat at Sedan tolled the end of the Third Republic.

THE CLOTH INDUSTRY

Sedan flourished as a cloth-manufacturing centre during the second half of the 17C and above all during the 18C. The manufactures usually consisted of a large house along the street, workshops in the wings and a building closing off the courtyard at the back. The technical evolution which took place in the 19C meant that these buildings were turned into dwellings. Some of them can still be seen today.

No 33 place de la Halle – This 18C mansion facing the square and backing onto the Promenoir des Prêtres, was probably used as a private house and a warehouse. The main building is prolonged by curved wings which straighten out as in the case of the Dijonval. Note the wrought-iron banisters.

No 1 rue du Mesnil – Built as a private mansion in 1626, the Hôtel de Lambermont became a royal manufacture and was granted privileges in 1726. Note the heads surmounting the windows in the first courtyard: they are believed to represent Elizabeth of Nassau, her family and friends.
Opposite stands another draper's house dating from 1747.

No 3 rue Berchet – This former dyer's workshop was acquired in 1823 by the owner of the royal manufacture.

No 8 rue de Bayle – Private mansion and cloth manufacture, whose façade is decorated at each end by a colossal order pilaster and a projecting cornice.

No 1 rue des Francs-Bourgeois – This 18C building, which was probably a draper's workshop, has openings with arched lintels, curved balconies and a staircase with wrought-iron banisters.

No 1 place Turenne – The gate giving access to the courtyard is more elaborately decorated than that which opens onto the street. Note in the courtyard the system used to lift heavy bundles.

No 1 rampe des Capucins – Former manufacture of fine cloth. At the back of the courtyard, on the right, there is an interesting staircase with wooden banisters.

SIGHTS

★★Château fort ⊘ – This fortress covering an area of 35 000m²/41 860sq yd on seven levels is the largest in Europe. It was built on a rock spur in several stages on the site of a former monastery dating from the 11C and 13C. Work began in 1424; the twin towers and the ramparts date from that period. The latter (30m/98ft high), surrounded by ditches, were completed in the 16C by the addition of bastions. The **Palais des Princes** was built in the 17C outside the walls and the original living quarters which used to stand within the ramparts were partly demolished in the 18C. Between 1642 and 1962, the stronghold was army property. The town then acquired it and undertook its restoration. From the towers and the ramparts, there are fine views of the town with its slate roofs.

The Historium in the château of Sedan

Historium – The tour of the castle *(audio-guided tours, explanatory panels)* includes a number of reconstructed scenes illustrating the lifestyle of princes, soldiers and servants in the past.

The castle also houses archaeological collections (gathered during excavations in the basement: medieval pottery, ceramics), ethnographic exhibits and documents relating to the town's history. One room is devoted to the Franco-Prussian War of 1870 and to the First World War. The 15C framework of the **Grosse tour** (large tower) is remarkable.

An audio-visual presentation completes the panorama of the castle's history.

It is possible to drive round the fortress or to walk along boulevard du Grand Jardin (benches) to the Résidence des Ardennes overlooking the town. From the esplanade, there is a superb **view★** of the Meuse Valley.

SEDAN

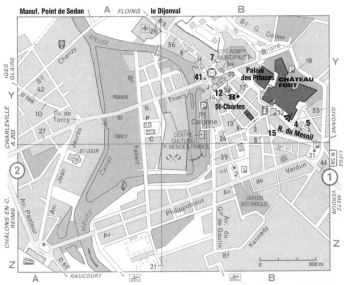

Dijonval ⊙ – *Avenue du Général-Margueritte*. This royal cloth manufacture founded in 1646 continued to operate until 1958. Its imposing 18C façade extends on either side of a central pavilion adorned with a pediment and surmounted by a campanile. On the courtyard side, the central building is flanked by curved wings prolonged by long straight ones. The windows are decorated with ovoli carved with geometric motifs. It now houses the **Musée des anciennes Industries du Sedanais** (Traditional Industries Museum).

Manufacture du Point de Sedan ⊙ – In this traditional manufacture, weavers can be seen working on looms dating from 1878; they make carpets with New Zealand wool on a linen base. The motif is drawn on graduated paper and transcribed onto a piece of cardboard (each perforation represents one stitch in the chosen colour). Several thousand spools of coloured wool are used and it takes over a month to make a carpet.

Cloth manufacturing in Sedan

Sedan's textile tradition goes back to the Middle Ages but the manufacture of cloth and lace really flourished from the end of the 16C, following the Wars of Religion and a sudden influx of Protestants. The lace stitch, imported by the Calvinist community, was called Point de Sedan by foreign buyers. When the town was returned to France in 1642, Sedan became the capital of fine woolens with the creation of the Dijonval manufacture. The industry began to decline in the 18C, however, in 1878, an industrialist and an engineer from the Ardennes region invented a device which made it possible to tie the wool stitch onto a linen warp and weft. Lacemaking is no longer one of the town's activities and the last cloth manufacture has closed down but the carpet industry carries on for prestigious clients including sovereigns and embassies.

Église St-Charles – This edifice dating from 1593 was a Calvinist church until the Revocation of the Edict of Nantes. In 1688 Robert de Cotte added a vast rotunda-shaped chancel.

Ancien hôtel de ville – The former town hall, designed by Salomon de Brosse, was built in 1613. Note the embossed façade decorated with vermicular motifs.

Where to stay

MODERATE

Château du Faucon – 08350 Doncherry – 4km/2.5mi W of Sedan on A 203, Doncherry exit, then follow signs for Vrigne-aux-Bois on D 334 – ☎ 03 24 52 10 01 – www.faucon.fr – 🅿 18 rooms 250/750F – 🚼 48F – restaurant 135/290F. The good life is even better when you're living in a castle. According to your budget, you can choose a lovely room in the 17C wing with its restaurant, or the simpler rooms in the inn with its carvery and open fire. Park, riding stables, tennis courts.

MID-RANGE

Auberge du Port – Rte de Remilly – 08450 Bazeilles – 3km/1.8mi E of Sedan on N 58 – ☎ 03 24 27 13 89 – closed 20 Dec-5 Jan – 🅿 20 rooms 280/315F – 🚼 42F – restaurant 98/250F. In the heart of the country. Idle your time away as you please between the Meuse, the garden, the shady terrace and the surrounding fields. You will enjoy the cooking in this opulent-looking inn, before sleeping peacefully in its comfortable rooms.

On the town

Au Roy de la bière – 19 pl. des Halles – ☎ 03 24 29 01 74 – daily 10am-3am closed Mon in winter. The atmosphere of this rustic-style establishment with its mixed decor (beer tankards hanging from the ceiling, old photographs) is typically reminiscent of a Belgian pub. Naturally, there is a good choice of beers.

Le Pub Forum – 35 r. du Rivage – ☎ 03 24 29 65 23 – Mon-Sat 10am-3am, Sun from 5pm. This long bar is popular among the young of Sedan, as the noise level testifies! Billiard room at the back.

Shopping

Le Maître d'Orge – 1 bis r. Carnot – ☎ 03 24 26 89 35 – Tue-Fri 10am-noon, 2-7.30pm, Sat 9am-12.15pm, 2-7.30pm closed last week in Sep and first 2 weeks in Oct except Sat. This shop offers a ray of hope for beer aficionados who aren't lucky enough to make it to nearby Belgium. Wide choice of barley beers, including the prize-winning Passe Tout, brewed by Lional Passe and much appreciated among enthusiasts.

Le Point de Sedan – 13 bd Gambetta – ☎ 03 24 29 04 60 – le.point.de.sedan@wanadoo.fr – Mon-Sat 8am-noon, 2-6pm. In this old-fashioned factory, you can see carpets woven on looms, some of which are over a hundred years old. The company can claim some prestigious former customers, such as General de Gaulle, President Kennedy and the Duchess of Windsor. Carpets of all types and styles are on sale.

Pâtisserie Jouannet – 28 pl. de la Halle – ☎ 03 24 29 09 26 – Tue-Sun 8.30am-noon, 2-7pm closed Aug. Prominently situated in one of the town's busiest squares, this chocolate shop and tearoom offers home-made specialities such as the *palet de princes* (chocolate mixed with almond paste) and *écailles d'ardoises* (chocolate-covered nougat). Pleasant little terrace.

EXCURSIONS

Aérodrome de Sedan-Douzy: Musée des débuts de l'aviation ⊙ – 10km/6mi E. The museum of early flying is devoted to the pioneer Roger Sommer (1877-1965), who not only piloted aircraft but also built them. A replica of the 1910 biplane, used for India's first air link in 1911, is exhibited together with numerous documents dating from the early 20C. In addition, there is an important collection of postcards recalling famous pilots such as Blériot and Farman. Modern aviation is illustrated by about 100 models of aircrafts.

Bazeilles – Bitter fighting took place here in September 1870, before Sedan capitulated. The **Maison de la dernière cartouche** ⊙ (House of the last round of ammunition), where a group of French soldiers resisted to their last round, is now a museum containing many French and German exhibits gathered on the battlefield together with photocopies of letters sent by Gallieni to his family giving details about the fighting. A nearby ossuary contains the remains of some 3 000 French and German soldiers.
The 18C **castle** ⊙, built in the Rococo style for a wealthy draper from Sedan, stands beyond an elegant wrought-iron gate flanked by stone lions. In the French-style gardens there are two charming pavilions, an oval-shaped orangery *(now a restaurant)* and a dovecote as well as the former stables turned into a hotel.

SÉLESTAT ★

Population 15 538

Michelin map 87 folds 6 and 16 or 242 fold 27 – Local map see Route des VINS

This ancient city, lying on the west bank of the River Ill, between Strasbourg and Colmar, has retained two fine churches and some interesting old houses. In the 15C and 16C, Sélestat was an important Humanist centre with one of the finest libraries in the world.

Martin Bucer

Born in Sélestat in 1491, Martin Bucer entered a Dominican monastery after completing his studies. His meeting with Luther in Heidelberg in 1518 changed the course of his life.

He left his monastery, converted the town of Wissembourg to the ideas of the Reformation and settled in Strasbourg as pastor of Sainte-Aurélie. Influenced by Humanism, this open-minded thinker tried, through his writings and his actions, to restore a common doctrine among all Protestants. His spiritual influence spread throughout southern Germany and the state of Hesse.

After the defeat of the Schmalkaldic League opposed to the Hapsburgs, Bucer was forced by Emperor Charles V to go into exile in 1549. He settled in Cambridge where he died in 1551.

★OLD TOWN *allow 2hr*

Start from boulevard du Général-Leclerc and turn right onto rue du Vieux-Marché-aux-Vins. Walk across place Gambetta and follow rue des Serruriers on the left.

The **Ancienne Église des Récollets**, formerly part of a Franciscan monastery, is now a Protestant church. The chancel is all that is left of the monastery.

Turn left onto rue de Verdun.

Maison de Stephan Ziegler – This Renaissance house was built in the 16C by one of the town's master builders.

Rue de Verdun leads to place de la Victoire where the former arsenal stands.

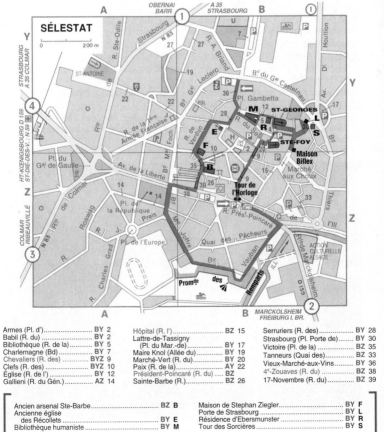

Armes (Pl. d')	BY	2
Babil (R. du)	BY	2
Bibliothèque (R. de la)	BY	5
Charlemagne (Bd)	BY	7
Chevaliers (R. des)	BYZ	9
Clefs (R. des)	BYZ	10
Église (R. de l')	BY	12
Gallieni (R. du Gén.)	AZ	14
Hôpital (R. l')	BZ	15
Lattre-de-Tassigny (Pl. du Mar.-de)	BY	17
Maire Knol (Allée du)	BY	19
Marché-Vert (R. du)	BY	20
Paix (R. de la)	AY	22
Président-Poincaré (R. du)	BZ	
Sainte-Barbe (R.)	BZ	26
Serruriers (R. des)	BY	28
Strasbourg (Pl. Porte de)	BY	30
Victoire (Pl. de la)	BZ	35
Tanneurs (Quai des)	BZ	33
Vieux-Marché-aux-Vins	BY	36
4e-Zouaves (R. du)	BZ	38
17-Novembre (R. du)	BZ	39

Ancien arsenal Ste-Barbe	BZ	B
Ancienne église des Récollets	BY	E
Bibliothèque humaniste	BY	M
Maison de Stephan Ziegler	BY	F
Porte de Strasbourg	BY	L
Résidence d'Ebersmunster	BY	R
Tour des Sorcières	BY	S

311

Arsenal Ste-Barbe – The former arsenal is an attractive 14C building; its lovely façade is adorned with a double-flight staircase leading to a small canopy preceding the entrance. The gable is crenellated and the roof is crowned by two stork nests.

Continue straight on along rue du 17-Novembre and turn right onto rue du 4ᵉ-Zouaves then left again along boulevard du Maréchal-Joffre which leads to the ramparts.

Promenade des Remparts – From these fortifications erected by Vauban, there is a fine view of the foothills of the Vosges and of Haut-Kœnigsbourg.

Walk along boulevard de Verdun then rue Poincaré.

Tour de l'Horloge – The clock tower dates from the 14C except for the upper parts which were restored in 1614.

Walk beneath the clock tower, then follow rue des Chevaliers straight ahead which leads to place du Marché-Vert.

★**Église Ste-Foy** – This fine Romanesque church (12C) built of red sandstone and granite from the Vosges, stands on the site of a Benedictine priory church. The porch is decorated with arcading, cornices and historiated capitals.

The capitals of the nave are beautifully decorated with floral motifs modelled on churches from the Lorraine region.

Come out of the church through the small door situated behind the pulpit and follow the narrow lane on the right leading to place du Marché-aux-Choux.

Maison Billex – Note the fine two-storey Renaissance oriel. In 1681, the city of Strasbourg signed its surrender to Louis XIV in this house.

Walk to the Église St-Georges.

On the way, you will get a glimpse of the **Tour des Sorcières** on the right; part of the fortifications demolished by Louis XIV, and of the **Porte de Strasbourg**, designed by Vauban in 1679.

★**Église St-Georges** – This imposing Gothic church built between the 13C and 15C was considerably remodelled, particularly in the 19C. Three doorways have retained their original door leaves with their strap-hinges.

The nave is preceded by a wide narthex which covers the whole width of the west front and opens on the south side *(place St-Georges)* through an elegant doorway. The stone pulpit was carved and gilt at the time of the Renaissance.

The musician angels on the stained-glass windows of the west front date from the late 14C or early 15C; the rose-window (14C) of the south doorway of the narthex illustrates the Ten Commandments; three stained-glass windows in the chancel, dating from the 15C, depict scenes from the lives of St Catherine, St Agnes and St Helena; the new stained-glass windows of the east end and the chancel were made by Max Ingrand.

Walk along rue de l'Église.

Résidence d'Ebersmunster – N*No 8.* This house, built in 1541, is the urban residence of the Benedictine monks. The Renaissance doorway, surmounted by ovoli, is decorated with Italian motifs.

A few yards further on, turn left onto the narrow rue de la Bibliothèque.

★**Bibliothèque humaniste** ⊙ – Towards the middle of the 15C, Sélestat's Latin school flourished into a great Humanist school which explains the extent of its splendid library housed on the first floor of the former Halle aux Blés (granary exchange) dating from 1843.

The Humanist library

The library consists of two separate collections: that of the Latin library founded in 1452 and the private collection bequeathed in 1547 by Beatus Rhenanus, a Humanist and close friend of Erasmus.

The great hall houses precious manuscripts including the Merovingian Lectionary (late 7C), the oldest work still kept in Alsace, the Book of the Miracles of St Foy (12C), the *Cosmographiæ Introductio* printed in St-Dié *(see ST-DIÉ)*. In all, the Humanist library comprises 450 manuscripts, 530 incunabula and 2 000 16C printed documents.

Eating out

MID-RANGE

Auberge de l'Illwald – *67600 Le Schnellenbuhl – 8km/5mi SE of Sélestat on D 159 and D 424 – ☎ 03 88 85 35 40 – closed 24 Dec-12 Jan, 27 Jun-12 Jul, Tue evening and Wed – 145/190F.* A pleasant inn on the road towards Germany, run by a young couple who serve simple, well-presented local dishes. The dining room is prettily decorated with wall paintings. Family atmosphere and reasonable prices.

Les Deux Clefs – *72 r. du Gén.-Leclerc – 67600 Ebersmunster – 8km/5mi NE of Sélestat on N 83, Strasbourg direction, and D 210 – ☎ 03 88 85 71 55 – closed 11-21 Jul, Christmas to end Jan, Mon evening and Thu – booking advisable at weekends – 158/175F.* This local-style building opposite Ebersmunster's lovely church used to house the convent abattoir. Today the restaurant serves *matelote* (freshwater fish stew) and fried fish, among other classic regional dishes, cooked in a traditional family style.

Where to stay

MID-RANGE

Hôtel Dontenville – *94 r. du Mar.-Foch – 67730 Châtenois – 5km/3mi W of Sélestat, towards St-Dié – ☎ 03 88 92 02 54 – closed during Feb school holidays, Sun evening and Tue – 13 rooms 265/290F – ☕ 35F – restaurant 100/150F.* A half-timbered hotel dating from 1909, which has retained the charm and simplicity of old Alsatian houses. The upper-floor bedrooms are the best, with their exposed roof beams. Regional cuisine is served in the wood-panelled dining room.

Chambre d'hôte La Romance – *17 rte de Neuve-Église – 67220 Dieffenbach-au-Val – 12km/7.5mi NW of Sélestat on N 59 and D 424, towards Villé – ☎ 03 88 85 67 09 – www.la-romance.net – 4 rooms 380/420F.* Don't give up when looking for this house in the higher part of the village: it may not be easy to find, but it is quiet and comfortable. The modern rooms have been carefully decorated, the garden is pleasant and the sauna ideal for relaxing.

On the town

L'Ami Fritz – *3 r. des Bateliers – ☎ 03 88 92 88 07 / 82 01 01 – Wed-Sun 7am-1.30am.* As soon as you cross the threshold you feel at home in this world of books. Browse while your host, known to all as *l'ami Fritz*, prepares soup or fresh fruit, depending on the season. As for his record collection, he will be happy to dig out and play you old jazz, blues or rock pieces, according to your taste. If you get talking, it's no good telling him he's a chatterbox, he knows it. Terrace in summer in the inner courtyard.

Shopping

Local produce market – *Sq. Ehm – Sat morning.*

Pâtisserie-chocolaterie Benoît Wach – *7 r. des Chevaliers – ☎ 03 88 92 12 80 – Tue-Fri 7am-7pm, Sat-Sun 8am-6pm, public holidays 7am-6pm closed one week in Jul-Aug and Sept.* In a lovely building decorated with *trompe-l'œil* mouldings and an attractive alcove above the doorway, this cake shop and tearoom offers all kinds of regional specialities: *œufs de cigogne* (storks' eggs), gingerbread, *kougelhopf* and pure butter Alsatian biscuits.

Leisure

Office du Tourisme – *Bd. Leclerc – ☎ 03 88 58 87 23 – Oct-Apr: Mon-Fri 8.30am-noon, 1.30-6pm, Sat 9am-noon closed Sun and public holidays; May-Sep: Mon-Fri 9am-12.30pm, 1.30-7pm, Sat 9am-noon, 2-5pm, Sun and public holidays 9am-3pm.* Sélestat has received an award for its 85km/53mi of cycle paths, and the tourist office can arrange the hire of new mountain bikes, which are serviced weekly.

EXCURSIONS

Château de Ramstein and Château d'Ortenbourg – *7km/4.3mi then 15min on foot. Leave Sélestat by ④ on the town plan (N 59); drive for 4.5km/2.8mi then turn right onto D 35 towards Scherwiller; 2km/1.2mi further on, turn left onto an unsurfaced path.*

🏃 *Leave the car in Huhnelmuhl, near the inn and follow the path leading to the two castles 300m/328yd apart.*

The ruins are interesting and there is a lovely view of the Val de Villé and Plaine de Sélestat.

Château de Frankenbourg – *11km/6.8mi then 1hr 45min on foot. Leave Sélestat by ④ on the town plan (N 59) and drive to Hurst then turn right onto D 167 to La Vancelle.*

🏃 *Leave the car 2km/1.2mi further on and follow the path on the right.*

From the ruins of the castle (alt 703m/2 306ft), there are fine views of the Liepvrette Valley and Val de Villé.

Parc d'animaux de Kintzheim – *8.5km/5.3mi. Leave Sélestat by ④ on the town plan (D 159).*

📷 This excursion will be of particular interest to animal lovers who will be able to visit two experimental centres for the acclimatisation of very different species such as birds of prey and monkeys.

Volerie des Aigles ⊙ – *30min on foot there and back.*

🏃 The courtyard of the ruined castle is home to about 80 diurnal and nocturnal birds of prey. Some of them take part in spectacular **training demonstrations**★ organised during the visit *(except in bad weather)*.

Return to you car and continue along the forest road then D 159; 2km/1.2mi further on, turn right onto a path leading to the electrified fence surrounding the Montagne des Singes.

Montagne des Singes ⊙ – 📷 In this large park (20ha/50 acres), planted with pine trees and laid out on top of a hill, 300 barbary apes, well adapted to the Alsatian climate, live in total freedom. View of Haut-Kœnigsbourg Castle to the SW.

Mémorial et Musée de la Ligne Maginot du Rhin – *Marckolsheim, 15km/9.3mi SE. Leave Sélestat by ② on the town plan (D 424); 1.5km/0.9mi beyond Marckolsheim, the pillbox of the memorial can be seen on the right-hand side of N 424. See Ligne MAGINOT.*

Benfeld – *20km/12.4mi NE. Leave Sélestat by ① on the town plan (N 83).* This small town has an elegant 16C **town hall** with a lovely carved doorway giving access to the polygonal turret dating from 1617, decorated with a shield bearing the town's coat of arms. The clock has three jacks striking the hours: Death, a Knight in armour and Stubenhansel, a Traitor who, in 1331, sold the city to its enemies for a purse full of gold, which he holds in his hand.

Ebersmunster – A famous Benedictine abbey once stood in this peaceful village. It was believed to have been founded by St Odile's parents, Duke Étichon and his wife *(see Mont STE-ODILE)*.

Built c 1725, the **abbey church**★ can be seen from afar, surmounted by three onion-shaped steeples. The **interior**★★ is considered as the finest example of early-18C Alsatian Baroque art. Daylight pouring in on the brightly painted decoration and stucco work enhances the refined setting and the elegantly carved furniture. However, one's attention is inevitably drawn to the imposing **high altar** (1728): decorated with numerous gilt carvings and surmounted by a huge baldaquin in the shape of a crown, it almost reaches the chancel vaulting.

Organ and choral concerts, known as "Les Heures musicales d'Ebersmunster", take place in the church every Sunday at 5pm during the month of May.

SÉZANNE

Population 5 833
Michelin map 61 fold 5 or 237 folds 22 and 34

Sézanne is a small provincial town, peacefully settled on a hillside riddled with underground galleries and cellars. A ring of wide avenues, replacing the former fortifications, surrounds the old town.

Trade fairs were frequently held in the town from medieval times onwards and today Sézanne is a lively agricultural and industrial centre. The hillside vineyards produce still white wine.

From the Épernay road to the north *(RD 951)* there is a picturesque view of the town.

Église St-Denis – This Flamboyant Gothic church flanked by a Renaissance tower, stands in the town centre, on the edge of place de la République. Small dwellings are bonded to the foot of the massive square tower (42m/138ft high). Note the clock framed by two carved friezes.

A double-flight staircase leads to a small doorway with Renaissance carved leaves which gives access to the church. The Flamboyant Gothic interior is very homogeneous and the star vaulting noteworthy.

As you leave the church, have a look at the **Doré well** facing the west front.

Mail des Cordeliers – Chestnut trees line the walkway along the former ramparts; the flattened remains of two round towers recall the castle that once stood here.

View of the hillside covered with orchards and vineyards.

Where to stay

MODERATE

La Croix d'Or – *53 r. Notre-Dame – ☎ 03 26 80 61 10 – closed 2-17 Jan and Mar –* 🅿 *13 rooms 240/350F –* ☑ *35F – restaurant 85/295F.* This spruce and charming town-centre hotel with its ivy-covered façade has standard, comfortable rooms. Fish and shellfish dishes on offer in the attractive dining room.

MID-RANGE

Chambre d'hôte Domaine Équestre Montgivroux – *51120 Mondement-Montgivroux – 8km/5mi NE of Sézanne on D 39 and D 45 – ☎ 03 26 42 06 93 – closed Nov-Feb – 6 rooms 350/400F.* Whether you're travelling on horseback, on foot or by car, this large 17C-19C Champagne farm will provide a warm welcome. The colours in the rooms are reminiscent of Africa. An ideal place for horse lovers.

EXCURSIONS

Corroy – *18km/11mi E along N 4 to Connantre, then right onto D 305.*
This village boasts a remarkable church with a 13C Champagne-style porch on the west front. The porch has twinned arcades and is covered with a 15C timber frame shaped like a ship's hull. The long nave covered with a 12C timber frame is prolonged by the chancel, the apse and two chapels built in the late 16C.

FORÊT DE TRACONNE *54km/34mi round tour – allow 2hr*

🏃 The dense Traconne Forest, covering almost 3 000ha/7 413 acres, mainly consists of hornbeam thickets beneath tall oak trees. It is crisscrossed by numerous footpaths including a discovery trail marked by signposts and panels pinned to the trees.

Drive W out of Sézanne along D 239. In Launat, turn left towards Le Meix-St-Époing and, 500m/0.3mi further on, right towards Bricot-la-Ville.

Bricot-la-Ville – This tiny village hidden at the heart of the forest has a charming little church, a manor house and a lovely pond covered with water lilies; an abbey of Benedictine nuns stood here from the 12C to the 16C.

Continue to Châtillon-sur-Morin (fortified church).

The road follows the Grand Morin Valley: clearings alternate with copses as in an English-style garden.

In Châtillon-sur-Morin, turn left onto D 86 which joins D 48. In Essarts-le-Vicomte, turn left onto D 49.

L'Étoile – On the edge of this grass-covered roundabout, which has a column surmounted by an 18C iron cross in its centre, stands a twisted stunted birch from the Bois des Faux de Verzy *(see Parc naturel régional de la Montagne de REIMS).*

Follow D 49 to Barbonne-Fayel then turn right onto D 50.

Fontaine-Denis-Nuisy – A 13C fresco of the Last Judgement, located in the north transept of the church, depicts damned souls roasting in a vast cauldron.

Drive along D 350 towards St-Quentin-le-Verger.

Shortly after Nuisy, you will see a dolmen on the right.

In St-Quentin-le-Verger, turn left onto D 351 then right onto the Villeneuve-St-Vistre road. RD 373 will lead you back to Sézanne.

SIERCK-LES-BAINS

Population 1 825
Michelin map 57 fold 4 or 242 fold 2 and 6

Sierck lies in a picturesque setting on the banks of the River Moselle, close to the German border. The old village spreads up the hill crowned by a fortress. In the 12C, the duke of Lorraine and the archbishop of Trier fought over its ownership; it was ransacked and burned down by the Swedes during the Thirty Years War and by Turenne's army in 1661.

The name alone reminds visitors that Sierck was once a spa town with three springs, but the thermal establishment was taken over by the railway station and today Sierck is the starting point of boat trips on the River Moselle and hikes through the nearby forest.

CHÂTEAU ⊙

Built on a rocky promontory, the castle has retained most of its 11C fortifications: walls, casemates, massive towers pierced with loopholes (Tour de l'Artillerie, Tour du Guet, Tour de la Redoute, Tour des Pères Récollets).

From the castle, there is a lovely **view★** of the Moselle Valley overlooked by the Stromberg whose slopes are covered with vineyards.

The nearby **Chapelle de Marienfloss**, which is all that remains of a once flourishing Carthusian monastery and important place of pilgrimage, has been restored and extended.

Contz-les-Bains on the Moselle

EXCURSIONS

Rustroff – *1km/0.6mi NE.* The village **church** stands at the end of the steep high street. Rebuilt in the 19C, it contains a beautiful 15C altarpiece in painted wood and a small *Pietà* dating from the beginning of the 16C.

🏯 **Château de Malbrouck** ⊙ – *8km/5mi NE along N 153 then right along D 64. As you come to the village of Manderen, drive up the steep lane on the left.*
The imposing 15C fortress, built on the summit of a wooded hill on the border with Luxemburg and Germany, has been restored and its history is brought to life by *son et lumière* shows, dioramas etc. In 1705, during the War of the Spanish Succession, John Churchill, **Duke of Marlborough**, used it as his headquarters.

COTEAUX DE LA MOSELLE

Round tour from Sierck-les-Bains

45km/28mi – allow 1hr 30min

Leave Sierck along D 64.

This itinerary explores the hilly countryside lying on the north bank of the Moselle and ends with a detour to Mondorf-les-Bains in Luxemburg.

Haute-Kontz – From the terrace in front of the church, which has an 11C belfry, there is a fine **view** of a meander of the Moselle and of the village of Rettel on the opposite bank.

Drive to Fixem then turn left onto D 1.

In Cattenom, you can see the 165m/541ft cooling towers of the **Centre nucléaire de production de Cattenom** which comprises four units with an output of 1 300 million watts each. The centre produces 30 billion kWh every year.

Turn right onto D 56.

Usselskirch – The cemetery stretches along the road on the right. Inside stands a solitary Romanesque tower, which is all that remains of the 12C church.

Drive to Boust along D 57.

Boust – Standing on high ground, the stone-built Église St-Maximin (1962), designed by Pingusson, has a remarkable circular nave prolonged by a long chancel flanked by a campanile.

Return to D 56 and turn left.

Roussy-le-Village – The modern Église St-Denis (1954), built of stone and concrete contains interesting carvings by Kaeppelin and stained-glass windows by Barillet.

Return to Usselskirch and turn left onto D 57 to Rodemack.

Rodemack – From its prosperous medieval past, this ancient city, situated 5km/3mi from the border between France and Luxemburg, has retained an imposing fortress restored in the 17C and a fortified gate with two round towers. The grey-roughcast village houses with arched windows, the cellars and barn entrances are all characteristic of the architectural style of the Lorraine region. The simple church, dating from 1783, contains interesting statues and furniture.

Continue along D 57 and turn left onto D 1.

Mondorf-les-Bains – This elegant spa has two hot springs (24°C/75.2F) used in the treatment of liver and bowel complaints as well as rheumatism. There is a lovely 36ha/89-acre **park★** close to the baths. Built in 1764 on a hill overlooking the old town, the Église St-Michel contains fine Louis XV-style furniture and is decorated with stuccowork and *trompe-l'œil* frescoes painted by Weiser in 1766.

Return to Sierck along CR 152.

Colline de SION-VAUDÉMONT★★

Michelin map 62 fold 4 or 242 fold 25

The horseshoe-shaped hill of Sion-Vaudémont stands isolated in front of the Côtes de Meuse. It is one of the most famous viewpoints overlooking the Lorraine region as well as a historic site called the *Colline inspirée* by Maurice Barrès, a native of the area, who celebrated it in one of his novels.

Maurice Barrès (1862-1923), born in the nearby town of Charmes, became a famous writer and a politician but he spent several months a year in his grandparents' house which he modernised. During his stay, he loved to climb the hill of Sion. His deep attachment to his native Lorraine can be felt throughout his works, particularly *La Colline inspirée*.

For 2 000 years, the hill

FRUIT AND VEG

Domaine de Sion – *R. de la Cense-Rouge – 54330 Saxon-Sion –* ☎ *03 83 26 24 36 – closed Jan and Feb – booking essential – 95/130F.* This fruit-grower has a distillery which can be visited. In the simple restaurant you can sample the home-produced fruit and vegetables in various guises. Pick up a few things for an afternoon snack!

has been a kind of mystical place for pagan worshippers and later for Christians. After the Franco-Prussian War of 1870, and after each of the two world wars, pilgrims came to pray on top of the hill. In 1973, the unveiling of the Peace monument was celebrated.

★Sion – *30min. Leave the car in the parking area and walk up to the Hôtel Notre-Dame then take the path on the left, alongside the cemetery, to reach the esplanade shaded by lime trees.*

Basilique – The basilica dates mainly from the 18C; a monumental belfry (1860) towers over the porch. The restored apse (early 14C) contains the statue of Notre-Dame-de-Sion (Our Lady of Sion), a 15C crowned Virgin in gilt stone.
A small **museum** ⊙ of local history is housed across the inner courtyard.

★Panorama – *As you come out of the church, walk to the right along the courtyard and turn right on the corner of the convent wall.* From the calvary, a vast panorama unfolds (viewing table – alt 497m/1 631ft). There is another viewpoint on the west side of the plateau; it can be reached along a lane starting on the left, at the entrance of the parking area.
Nearby, lower down, is the village of Saxon-Sion.

Colline de Sion-Vaudémont

★★Signal de Vaudémont – *30min. 2.5km/1.5mi S of Sion. As you leave Sion, ignore the path on the right leading to Saxon-Sion and, near a calvary, continue straight on along D 53, a ridge road running right across the hill.*
The **Barrès Monument** stands at the top of the Signal de Vaudémont (alt 541m/1 775ft); it is 22m/72ft high and was erected in 1928 to celebrate the memory of Maurice Barrès. There is a superb **panorama★★** of the Lorraine plateau. It is possible to continue to the village of Vaudémont on the opposite side of the hill.

Vaudémont – The ruins of Vaudémont castle, birthplace of the House of the dukes of Lorraine, stand near the church (Tour Brunehaut). The village has retained its original aspect. The Grand'Rue is lined with semi-detached houses or farms with a round-arched gateway giving access to the barn. Houses have only one storey although there is a loft under the roof and a cellar accessible from the street. Built of rubble stone, they have very little ornamentation (stone-frame round doors and windows), except for a few inscriptions, statues and relief sculpture.

★Château de Haroué ⊙ – *10.5km/6.5mi from Sion. Drive along D 913 to Tanton-ville then E for 3.5km/2.2mi along D 9 to Haroué.*
The imposing residence of the princes of Beauvau-Craon lies on the banks of the Madon; it was built from 1720 onwards by Boffrand, the architect of Duke Leopold of Lorraine. Surrounded by a moat, the edifice is preceded by a main courtyard enclosed by railings made by Jean Lamour. The statues decorating the park are the work of Guibal who, like Lamour, worked on place Stanislas in Nancy. The **tour** of the castle includes the chapel, the main staircase with banisters by Lamour and the apartments. The furniture by Bellanger dating from the Restaura-tion (1814-30) was a present from King Louis XVIII; the **tapestries★** depicting the story of Alexander the Great (17C) were woven at La Malgrange near Nancy. Portraits by François Pourbus, Rigaud and Gérard and landscapes by Hubert Robert can also be seen. The **Chinese drawing room** owes its name to its decoration including Chinese-style paintings by Pillement, dating from 1747. The **golden drawing room** was decorated by the painter Hébert in 1858-59 for Napoleon III's visit. The reception room, in which King Stanislas was received several times, contains a 17C bed which once belonged to the Medicis.

SOULTZ-HAUT-RHIN

Population 5 867
Michelin map 87 fold 18 or 242 fold 35

This ancient town grew up around a rock salt vein which still exists today. Many old houses dating from the 16C, 17C and 18C, are adorned with oriels, stair turrets, porches bearing the construction date and inner courtyards which passers-by may glimpse through open doors.
Storks are back on the town's chimney stacks to the delight of inhabitants and visitors alike.

SIGHTS

Maisons anciennes – Apart from the tourist office dating from 1575, there are several fine old houses in the historic centre:
– Maison Litty, the former Hôtel St-Michel (1622) at no 15 rue des Sœurs;
– Maison Vigneronne (wine-grower's house, 1656) at no 5 rue du Temple;
– Maison Horn (1588) at no 42 rue de Lattre-de-Tassigny;
– Maison Hubschwerlin (16C) with its lovely inner courtyard, its oriel and stair turret, at no 6 rue des Ouvriers.
In rue Jean-Jaurès stands the family mansion (1605) of the Heeckeren d'Anthès, a powerful Alsatian industrial dynasty; one of its members, Georges-Charles de Heeckeren, killed the Russian writer Pushkin in a dual near St-Petersburg in 1837.

Église St-Maurice – The church, which shows great unity of style, was built between 1270 and 1489. The tympanum of the south doorway bears a 14C representation of St Maurice on horseback, above the Adoration of the Magi. Inside, there is a fine early-17C pulpit, a large organ by Silbermann dating from 1750, a late-15C relief sculpture in polychrome wood, with St George slaying the dragon in the foreground, and a huge mural depicting St Christopher.

Valeur sûre

Metzgerstuwa – *69 r. du Mar.-de-Lattre-de-Tassigny* – ☎ *03 89 74 89 77 – closed Christmas-New Year, 3 weeks mid-June to early July, Sat and Sun – booking advisable – 100/130F.* You'll be sure to eat well here! The façade of the butcher's shop is painted red, while the restaurant is green, and the chef who runs both establishments makes everything himself: regional dishes, bread, ice creams. A treat for good food lovers.

Promenade de la citadelle (citadel walk) – This walk, on the west side of the town, follows a section of the ramparts, including the Tour des Sorcières (witches' tower).

La Nef des jouets ⊙ – This rich toy collection is displayed in the former headquarters of the Order of the Knights of the Hospital of St John at Jerusalem, the present Order of the Knights of Malta, dating from the end of the 12C. The varied collection includes toys made of clay, cardboard, wood and plastic, both popular and sophisticated.

Musée du Bucheneck ⊙ – The museum is housed in a former 11C fortress, which was the seat of the episcopal bailiff from 1289 to the Revolution. Remodelled several times, the building now contains various collections concerning the town's history, in particular a model of the city as it looked in 1838, and portraits of members of the town's leading families.

STRASBOURG★★★

Conurbation 388 483
Michelln map 87 folds 4 and 5 or 242 folds 20 and 24

This important modern city lying on the banks of the River Ill, with its busy river port and renowned university is the intellectual and economic capital of Alsace. Built round its famous cathedral, Strasbourg is also a town rich in art treasures, which has been the "capital" of Europe since 1949, for it is here that the European Parliament and the European Council are located. Moreover, the town has set an example in environmental protection with its famous tramway, and it has proudly maintained its gastronomic tradition (foie gras, Alsatian wines, chocolate and brandy) which attracts gourmets from all over the world. An important music festival takes place every year in June followed by the European Fair in early September. The historic centre of Strasbourg, which includes the cathedral, has been on UNESCO's World Heritage List since 1988.

EUROPEAN BY TRADITION

Famous oath – Argentoratum, which was but a small fishing and hunting village at the time of Julius Caesar, soon became a prosperous city and a major crossroads between Eastern and Western Europe: Strateburgum, the city of roads... This geographical position meant that Strasbourg found itself on the path of all invasions from across the Rhine and was destroyed, burnt down, ransacked and rebuilt many times throughout its history. In 842, it was chosen as a place of reconciliation by two of Charlemagne's grandsons. This oath of fidelity is the first official text written both in a Romance and a Germanic language.

Gutenberg in Strasbourg – Born in Mainz in 1395, Gutenberg had to flee his native town for political reasons and came to settle in Strasbourg in 1434. He formed an association with three Alsatians to perfect a secret process which he had invented. But their association ended in a law suit in 1439 and this is how we know that the invention in question was the printing press. Gutenberg went back to Mainz in 1448 and, with his partner Johann Fust, he perfected the invention which deeply changed our society.

Visiting celebrities – In 1725, Louis XV married Marie Leszczynska in the Cathédrale Notre-Dame. In 1770, Marie-Antoinette, arriving from Vienna to marry the future Louis XVI, was welcomed in the cathedral by Louis de Rohan. The young Mozart gave concerts in Strasbourg and Goethe was a student at the famous university.

Rouget de Lisle's Marseillaise – On 24 April 1792, the mayor of Strasbourg, Frédéric de Dietrich, offered a farewell dinner to a group of volunteers from the Rhine army. The men talked about the necessity for the troops to have a song which would rouse their enthusiasm and the mayor asked one of the young officers named Rouget de Lisle, if he would write such a song. The next morning, the young man brought him his *Chant de guerre pour l'Armée du Rhin* (War song for the Rhine Army). Shortly afterwards, volunteers from Marseille on their way north adopted the song which then became known as the Marseillaise. It was designated the French national anthem in 1795. A plaque on the Banque de France building, at no 4 rue Broglie, recalls the memory of Rouget de Lisle.

1870-1918 – On 27 September 1870, Strasbourg capitulated after being besieged and shelled by the Germans for 50 days. According to the terms of the Treaty of Frankfurt (10 May 1871), Strasbourg was to become a German city, which it remained until 11 November 1918.

European crossroads – Even before the end of the Second World War, major politicians of that period (Winston Churchill, Robert Schuman, Konrad Adenauer, Charles de Gaulle...) agreed that Strasbourg should officially assume the role it had played throughout its history and become a European crossroads. Reconciliation between former enemies would have its roots in a city that had become a symbol, Strasbourg, lying alongside a mighty river once dotted with defensive works and now acting as a major link between neighbouring countries at the heart of Europe.

The **European Council** was created on 5 May 1949; all the countries of Western Europe are members. Eastern European countries can attend as guests. The Council, which has a purely consultative role, sends recommendations to governments and establishes conventions which commit the states signing the agreements, with the object of harmonising legislation in various fields of common interest. The most famous is the European Convention for the Safeguard of Human Rights (1950).

The European Council created the **European flag** (12 gold stars arranged in a circle on a sky-blue background). It shares its chamber with the **European Parliament**, an important institution of the European Union; its members have been elected by universal suffrage since 1979; its role is consultative, financial and restraining.

Strasbourg shares with Brussels and Luxembourg the privilege of housing the main institutions of the European Union. Luxembourg houses the **Court of Justice** and the general secretariat of the European Parliament, whereas the **Council**, which has executive and legislative powers, and the **Commission**, which administers and controls, are both based in Brussels.

★★★CATHÉDRALE NOTRE-DAME ⊘

Notre-Dame is one of the finest and most original Gothic cathedrals. Enjoy the best **view**★ of it from rue Mercière. The edifice owes a great deal of its charm to the pink sandstone from the Vosges with which it was built.

The Foolish Virgins – right-hand doorway of the cathedral

B.Kaufmann/MICHELIN

Work began in 1015 on a Romanesque edifice on the site of a temple dedicated to Hercules. The cathedral architects were later influenced by Gothic art newly introduced in Alsace. In 1365, the recently built towers were joined together up to the level of the platform and then the north tower was raised. Finally, in 1439, Johann Hültz from Cologne surmounted the tower with the famous spire which confers on the cathedral its amazing outline.

The Reformation whose main spokesman was **Martin Bucer** (1491-1551), established in Strasbourg in 1523 *(see SÉLESTAT)*, was well received in Alsace.

For many years, the old and the new religions fought for supremacy in the cathedral, Luther's proposals being posted on the main door. The Protestant faith finally triumphed and the cathedral only returned to Catholicism in 1681, during the reign of Louis XIV.

No fewer than 230 statues were destroyed during the Revolution. Fortunately, 67 others decorating the west front were saved. Then there was talk of doing away with the spire until someone had the brilliant idea of dressing it with a huge bright-red Phrygian cap. Hültz's masterpiece was saved.

In August and September 1870, Prussian shells set fire to the roof and the spire was hit by 13 of them.

In 1944, allied bombing damaged several parts of the edifice which have since been restored.

Exterior

★★★**West front** – *(See illustration p 42)*. Erwin of Steinbach was the architect in charge of building to slightly above the Apostles' Gallery that surmounts the rose-window. The **central doorway** is the most richly decorated. Statues and low-relief sculptures were made at different periods. The tympanum is made of four historiated bands: the first three, dating from the 13C, are remarkably realistic; the fourth is modern. They depict scenes from the Old Testament (The Creation, the story of Abraham, Noah, Moses, Jacob Joshua, Jonas and Samson...) and from the New Testament (Judas embracing Jesus; Jesus crucified positioned above Adam's coffin, between the Synagogue and the Church collecting his blood; miracles...).

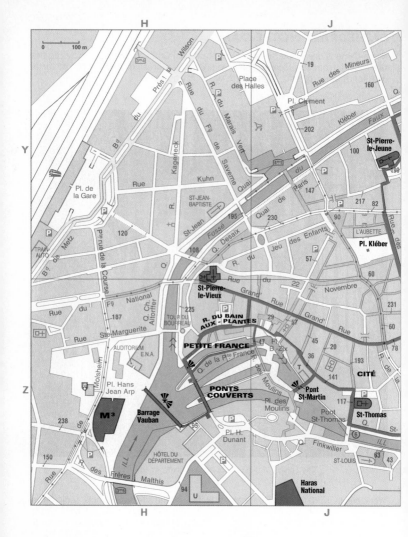

Brewery.................... 🍺

Docks

Index of street names on the town plans of Strasbourg

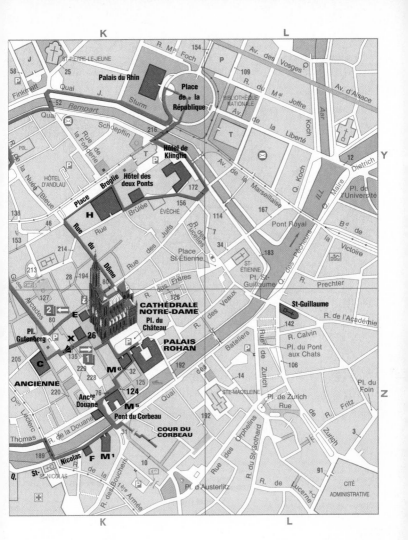

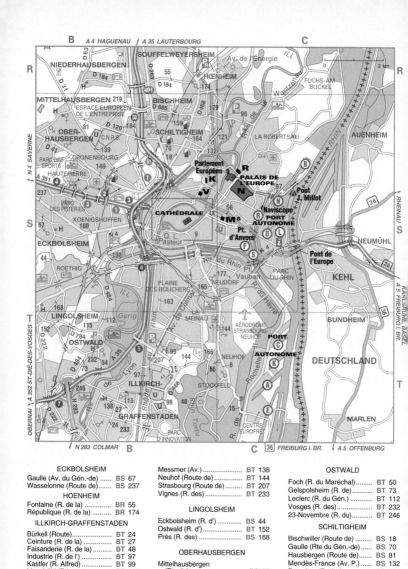

Index of sights on the town plans of Strasbourg

The decoration of the **right-hand doorway**, illustrating the parable of the Wise Virgins and the Foolish Virgins, includes several famous statues; some of them have been replaced by copies *(the original ones are in the Musée de l'Œuvre Notre-Dame)*.
The 14C statues of the **left-hand doorway** represent the Virtues. Slim and full of majesty in their long flowing gowns, they strike the Vices down.

★★★Tower ⊙ – The west-front platform is 66m/217ft high (328 steps; *30min*). The tower rises another 40m/131ft above the platform and is surmounted by a spire whose point is 142m/466ft above ground level (only 9m/30ft lower than the cast-iron spire of Rouen Cathedral).
Johann Hültz's spire, octagonal at the base, consists of six tiers of openwork turrets housing the stairs and is topped by a double cross. It is a light and graceful masterpiece.

From the platform there is a fine **view★** of Strasbourg, in particular the old town with its picturesque superposed dormer windows, of the suburbs and the Rhine Valley framed by the Black Forest and the Vosges.

South side – The beautiful 13C **Clock doorway**, the cathedral's oldest doorway, opens on the south side. It consists of two adjacent Romanesque doors separated by a statue of Solomon on a pedestal which recalls his famous Judgement. On the left of Solomon's statue, the Church, wearing a crown and looking strong and proud, holds the cross in one hand and the chalice in the other. On the right of the statue, the Synagogue, looking tired and sad, bends over in an effort to catch the fragments of her lance and the Tables of the Law which are dropping out of her hands. The band which covers her eyes is the symbol of error. The tympanum of the left-hand door depicts the **Death of the Virgin★★**. As he was dying, Delacroix loved to look at a reproduction of this carving. The figurine which Jesus is holding in his left hand represents Mary's soul.

The outside dial of the astronomical clock can be seen above the two doors.

North side – The restored **St Laurence doorway**, dating from the late 15C, illustrates the martyrdom of St Laurence (the carved group was remade in the 19C). On the left of the doorway are the statues of the Virgin, of the three kings and of a shepherd; on the right are five statues including that of St Laurence *(the originals are in the Musée de l'Œuvre Notre-Dame)*.

Interior

Nave and south aisle – Work on the nave, which consists of seven bays, began in the 13C. The stained glass of the clerestory windows and that of the aisles date from the 13C and 14C. Note the 50 or so statuettes decorating the hexagonal **pulpit★★** (1), in true Flamboyant Gothic style, designed by Hans Hammer for the Reformation preacher Geiler of Kaysersberg.

The **organ★★** (2) hanging over the nave beneath the triforium, displays its magnificent polychrome organ case (14C and 15C) across the full width of a bay. The corbelled loft is carved with a representation of Samson with, on either side, a town herald and a pretzel seller in period costume. These articulated characters would sometimes come to life during sermons to entertain the congregation.

St Catherine's chapel spreads across the two bays of the south aisle adjacent to the transept; it contains an epitaph of the Death of Mary (3), dating from 1480 and 14C stained-glass windows.

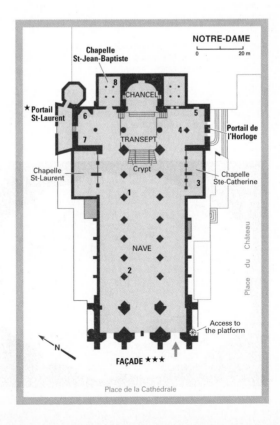

South transept – The **Angels** or **Last Judgement**★★ **pier** (**4**), erected in the 13C, stands in the centre.

The **Astronomical Clock**★ ⊙ (**5**) is the cathedral's most popular feature. It was made by Schwilgué, a native of Strasbourg, in 1838.

The seven days of the week are represented by chariots led by gods, who appear through an opening beneath the dial: Diana on Mondays, then Mars, Mercury, Jupiter, Venus, Saturn and Apollo.

A series of automata strikes twice every quarter hour. The hours are struck by Death. On the last stroke, the second angel of the Lions Gallery reverses his hourglass.

The astronomical clock is half an hour behind normal time. The midday chiming occurs at 12.30pm. As soon as it happens, a great parade takes place in the recess at the top of the clock. The Apostles pass in front of Christ and bow to him; Jesus blesses them as the cock, perched on the left-hand tower, flaps his wings and crows three times, a reminder of Peter's denial of Christ.

North transept – It contains splendid Flamboyant Gothic christening fonts (**6**). On the opposite wall, an unusual stone group represents Christ on the Mount of Olives (**7**). Carved in 1498 for the cemetery of St Thomas' Church, it was transferred to the cathedral in the 17C.

The 13C and 14C stained-glass windows depict several emperors of the Holy Roman Empire.

Chapelle St-Jean-Baptiste and crypt – The 13C chapel contains the tomb of Bishop Conrad of Lichtenberg (**8**) who began the construction of the west front. It is believed to be the work of Erwin.

★★**Tapestries** – The cathedral owns 14 very large and splendid 17C tapestries which are hung between the pillars of the nave on special occasions (certain religious holidays or for exceptional municipal or European events). The remarkable collection depicts scenes from the Life of the Virgin, designed by Philippe de Champaigne, Charles Poerson and Jacques Stella.

PALAIS DE ROHAN AND ITS MUSEUMS

★**Palais Rohan** – Designed by Robert de Cotte, the king's first architect, the palace was built in 1704 for Cardinal Armand de Rohan-Soubise. The beautiful Classical front with central pediment overlooks the main courtyard. The imposing **façade**, on the river side, is also Classical and decorated with columns of the Corinthian order. The edifice houses the rich museums of the Palais Rohan *(go to the end of the courtyard on the left)*.

★★**Musée des Arts décoratifs** ⊙ – The Museum of Decorative Arts is housed on the ground floor and in the right-hand part of the edifice *(stables wing and Hans-Hang pavilions)*. The **Grands Appartements** (official apartments) rank among the finest 18C French interiors.

The synod room, the king's bedroom, the assembly room, the cardinals' library, the morning room and the emperor's bedroom are particularly remarkable for their decoration, their ceremonial furniture, their tapestries (tapestry by Constantin after Rubens, c 1625) and their 18C pictures.

Dish from the Hannong manufacture

Musée des Arts Décoratifs

The museum, which is devoted to the **arts and crafts of Strasbourg and eastern France**, from the end of the 17C to the mid-19C, contains the famous **ceramics collection ★ ★**, one of the most important of its kind in France. The collection includes earthenware and porcelain from the Strasbourg and Haguenau manufacture, founded and run by the **Hannong** family from 1721 to 1781, and from the Niderviller manufacture, founded in 1748 by the Baron of Beyerlé, the director of Strasbourg's royal mint.

Particularly remarkable are the "blue" period pieces, polychrome ones which marked the transition, terrines shaped like animals or vegetables and above all magnificent crimson-based floral decorations which were a source of inspiration for many European manufactures after 1750.

★**Musée des Beaux-Arts** ⊘ – *The Fine Arts Museum is housed on the 1st and 2nd floors of the main building.* It contains an interesting collection of paintings mainly from the Middle Ages to the 18C.

Italian painting (primitive and Renaissance works) is very well represented by Filippino Lippi, Botticelli, Cima da Conegliano (magnificent *St Sebastian*) and by Correggio *(Judith and the Servant)*, one of his earliest paintings.

The **Spanish School** is represented by a few pictures, including works by Zurbarán, Murillo, Goya and above all a Mater Dolorosa by El Greco.

The collection of paintings from the 15C-17C **Dutch School** is particularly rich: fine *Christ of Mercy* by Simon Marmion, *Engaged Couple* by Lucas of Leyden, several works by Rubens, *St John* (portrait of the artist) by Van Dyck, *Going for a Walk* by Pieter de Hooch.

The French and Alsatian schools of the 17C-19C are illustrated by several works including *The Beautiful Woman from Strasbourg* by N de Largillière (1703).

The museum also houses an important collection of **still-life paintings** from the 16C to the 18C, among them the famous ***Bunch of Flowers*** by Velvet Brueghel.

★★**Musée archéologique** ⊘ – *Located in the basement.* The museum houses regional archaeological collections concerning the prehistory and early history of Alsace from 600 000 BC to AD 800.

The prehistory section contains Neolithic collections offering an insight into the life of the first farmers who settled in Alsace as early as 5500 BC.

There are also numerous objects illustrating the Bronze-Age and Iron-Age civilizations: ceramics, weapons and tools, jewellery, ceremonial plates and dishes imported from Greece or Italy, and the Ohnenheim funeral chariot.

The Roman section includes remarkable collections of stone carvings and inscriptions (votive and funeral sculpture) as well as fine glassware and numerous objects of daily life in Gallo-Roman times.

The Merovingian period is represented by collections of weapons and jewellery and a few outstanding items such as the Baldenheim helmet or the military decorations from Ittenheim.

Fragments from the Donon sanctuary.

THE CAPITAL OF EUROPE

★**Palais de l'Europe** ⊘ – *Leave the town centre along quai des Pêcheurs. Entrance in allée Spach.* The palace houses the **European Council**, including the council of ministers, the parliamentary assembly and the international secretariat. The new buildings, inaugurated in 1977 were designed by the French architect Henri Bernard. The palace contains 1 350 offices, meeting rooms for the various commissions and committees, a library and the largest parliamentary amphitheatre in Europe. The ceiling is supported by a 12-ribbed wooden fan, a symbol which is repeated in the palace's entrance hall.

The **Parc de l'Orangerie**, located opposite the Palais de l'Europe, is Strasbourg's largest park; it includes a lake, a waterfall and a zoo where storks are a familiar sight.

Palais des Droits de l'Homme – Nearby, on the banks of the River Ill, stands the new Palais des Droits de l'Homme, designed by Richard Rogers, which houses the European Court of Human Rights dependent on the European Council.

★★★OLD TOWN *allow one day*

The old town nestles round the cathedral, on the island formed by the two arms of the River Ill.

★**Place de la Cathédrale** – It is situated along the west front and north side of the cathedral. The **Pharmacie du Cerf** on the corner of rue Mercière, which dates from 1268, is believed to be the oldest chemist's in France.

On the north side of the cathedral, the **Maison Kammerzell ★** (1589), restored in 1954, is decorated with frescoes and splendid woodcarvings. The door dates from 1467. It is now occupied by a restaurant.

Eating out

MODERATE

Zum Strissel – *5 pl. de la Gde-Boucherie* – ☎ *03 88 32 14 73* – *closed during Feb school holidays, 1 Jul-1 Aug, Sun except public holidays and Mon* – *64/135F.* An authentic wine bar, run by the same family for three generations. Traditional cuisine and amusing decor, with wood panelling and stained-glass windows depicting Bacchus. Good value for money.

Caveau Gurtlerhoft – *13 pl. de la Cathédrale* – ☎ *03 88 75 00 75* – *89/135F.* Sample regional and traditional cooking in the lovely cellars of this 14C canonical building near the cathedral, with their splendid vaulting and massive pillars. Mouth-watering menus and fixed-price lunch, served in a leisurely way.

Les Trois Brasseurs – *22 r. des Veaux* – ☎ *03 88 36 12 13* – *closed Christmas and New Year* – *99/110F.* You can drink freshly brewed beer in this brasserie just behind the cathedral, made on the spot and not pasteurised. Probably one of the last breweries of its kind in the city, serving several buffet menus. Cellar bar at weekends, except in summer.

La Choucrouterie – *20 r. St-Louis* – ☎ *03 88 36 52 87* – *www.choucroute-rie.com* – *closed 6-30 Aug, lunchtime and Sun* – *100/185F.* This 18C coaching inn was the last place in Strasbourg to make pickled cabbage. Feast and have fun in a slightly chaotic setting, with music, cabaret or theatre dinners, as you choose. Alsace cuisine served with local white wine.

MID-RANGE

Au Renard Prêchant – *34 r. de Zürich* – ☎ *03 88 35 62 87* – *closed lunchtime on Sat, Sun and public holidays* – *130/210F.* A 16C chapel in a pedestrianised street, which takes its name from the murals decorating its walls telling the story of the preaching fox. Rustic dining room, pretty terrace in summer, and reasonable fixed-price lunches.

L'Arsenal – *11 r. de l'Abreuvoir* – ☎ *03 88 35 03 69* – *closed 29 Jul-28 Aug and Sat except evenings Sep-Jun* – *145/240F.* In the Krutenau district near the university, this restaurant serves tasty local cooking at very reasonable prices. It is frequented by the locals and the lunchtime menu is particularly good value. Wooden benches and rendered walls.

Oberjägerhof – *Chemin de l'Oberjägerhof* – *10km/6.25mi S of Strasbourg via pl. de l'Étoile, then Neuhof road and La Ganzau road* – ☎ *03 88 39 63 84* – *closed Christmas-New Year, Mon and Tue* – *145F.* This lovely half-timbered building tucked away in the Neuhof Forest is a little difficult to find, but what a pleasure when you get there! A rural setting, with a lovely terrace in summer, Alsatian dishes and an interesting cellar: the perfect way to gather strength for a walk in the surrounding countryside.

Hailich Graab "Au St-Sépulcre" – *15 r. des Orfèvres* – ☎ *03 88 32 39 97* – *closed 7-18 Jul, Sun and Mon* – *170F.* A truly authentic *winstub* with a worn façade, whose extraordinary decor, dating from the 1950s/60s, with a rough plank floor, Alsatian checked curtains and narrow tables, is as genuine as the copious helpings of food. The proprietor is a character and the customers adore him.

Le Clou – *3 r. du Chaudron* – ☎ *03 88 32 11 67* – *closed Wed lunchtime, Sun and public holidays* – *170/320F.* This small wine bar in a little street near the cathedral is always popular, with its typical decor, friendly atmosphere and good Alsace cooking, as you'd expect in a place like this. Well known locally.

Maison Kammerzell and Hôtel Baumann – *16 pl. de la Cathédrale* – ☎ *03 88 32 42 14* – *closed during Feb school holidays* – *177/295F.* You can't miss this picturesque 16C restaurant on the corner of the cathedral square. It's rather busy, the tables are close together, but the sauerkraut is home-made and the wall paintings are worth seeing.

LUXURY

La Maison des Tanneurs, known as "Gerwerstub" – *42 r. du Bain-aux-Plantes* – ☎ *03 88 32 79 70* – *closed 31 Dec-23 Jan, 28 Jul-11 Aug, Sun and Mon* – *220/405F.* A picture-postcard restaurant on the banks of the Ill, in a cobbled street in the Petite France district. Inside, the rooms are panelled with dark wood and have Alsatian furniture. Typical regional cuisine.

Where to stay

MODERATE

Chambre d'hôte La Maison du Charron – *15 r. Principale – 67370 Pfettisheim – 13km/8mi NW of Strasbourg on D 31 –* ☎ *03 88 69 60 35 –* ⌂ – *5 rooms 240/300F.* The owner of this 1858 property has done up the rooms himself, making each one individual by using different woods, while his wife's hobby is patchwork. Small garden, stabling for horses and two holiday cottages.

MID-RANGE

Hôtel des Rohan – *17 r. Maroquin –* ☎ *03 88 32 85 11 – 36 rooms 410/795F –* ⌛ *52F.* Named after the nearby Palais de Rohan, this little hotel is also near the cathedral. Its quiet, pleasant rooms are furnished in Louis XV style, and those on the south side have air conditioning.

Hôtel Pax – *24 r. du Fg-National –* ☎ *03 88 32 14 54 – closed 22 Dec-2 Jan –* ⓟ *– 106 rooms 420F –* ⌛ *45F – restaurant 95/130F.* A family hotel in a busy street on the edge of the city's old district. Its plain rooms are well kept, and its restaurant serves regional dishes. You can eat in the vine-shaded courtyard in summer.

Hôtel de la Cathédrale – *12 pl. de la Cathédrale –* ☎ *03 88 22 12 12 – 50 rooms 450/790F –* ⌛ *55F.* A modern hotel in a wonderful setting, right opposite the cathedral and the Maison Kammerzell, ideal for visiting the old city. Its rooms are well kept and equipped, and those overlooking the square are particularly romantic.

LUXURY

Hôtel Beaucour – *5 r. des Bouchers –* ☎ *03 88 76 72 00 – 49 rooms from 550F –* ⌛ *65F.* Those who like staying in lovely places will appreciate this city-centre hotel, in several old houses. Attractions include the flower-decked courtyard, cosy rooms and regional furniture in an inviting decor.

On the town

Bar des Glacières – *5 r. des Moulins –* ☎ *03 88 76 43 43 – rpf@regent-hotels.com – daily 3pm-1am.* The hotel bar of the luxurious Regent Petite France, which was a mill for 800 years, was an ice manufacturer's until the late 1980s. No effort has been spared to ensure that you spend a relaxing evening here: the fine contemporary decor, the riverside terrace, a good choice of cocktails and the best whiskies. The discreet jazzy background music adds the final touch.

Key West – *9 quai des Pêcheurs –* ☎ *03 88 37 03 03 – daily except Mon 7pm-3am.* A bar with a tropical decor frequented by well-heeled customers of all ages. Rumour has it that some of the theme evenings are slightly bizarre: the beach in winter, or Christmas in August, unless this is an illusion brought on by the house speciality, the Margarita. Meals available at weekends.

L'Opéra-café (in the public theatre) – *Pl. Broglie –* ☎ *03 88 75 48 26 – Mon-Sat 11am-4am, Sun 2-8pm – closed Aug.* The purple and gold decor in this theatre bar evokes the world of the stage. A classy setting for an intimate date over a glass of whisky or wine – or a hot chocolate with the family. Painting and photography exhibitions.

Le Bateau Ivre – *Quai des Alpes –* ☎ *03 88 61 27 17 – Thu-Sat from 10.30pm.* This bar/disco is comfortably housed in an enormous barge. The prices and the clientele match the ostentatious decor: expensive and classy. If those who are lucky enough to frequent this fashionable place are to be believed, the DJ is particularly gifted in his field.

Le Chalet (Espace J.-C. Helmer) – *376 rte de la Wantzenau –* ☎ *03 88 31 18 31 – lechalet@strasbourg-by-night.com – Tue-Sat from 9pm for the restaurant, 9.30pm for the karaoke, 10pm for the disco.* A huge leisure complex, comprising three restaurants, three bars and two discos (Planète Fête and the Solitair's Club), which has won an award for the most lively venue in France. Last but not least, there is a major karaoke event every evening for those who want to be a star for one night.

Le Festival – *4 r. Ste-Catherine –* ☎ *03 88 36 31 28 – daily 8pm-4am.* A chic American-style bar where smart attire is the rule. The barman is reputed to be an expert when it comes to mixing cocktails and giving advice on what to drink. For example, try an "Écho des Savanes", guaranteed to break the ice on a first date!

STRASBOURG

Les Aviateurs – *12 r. des Sœurs* – ☎ *03 88 36 52 69* – *daily except Sun, 8pm-4am.* There are at least two good reasons to visit this bar: as the name suggests, the original decor, on the theme of aviation, and the lively atmosphere which makes it one of the coolest bars in Strasbourg. Be prepared to use your elbows to get to the bar, though.

Les Trois Brasseurs – *22 r. des Veaux* – ☎ *03 88 36 12 13* – *daily 11.30am-1pm.* An authentic brasserie which, apart from a wide range of beers of all colours, makes its own brew, whose reputation attracts large numbers of beer drinkers from all over Strasbourg. You can also eat here, and there are rock, jazz and blues concerts on Thu, Fri and Sat evenings.

Showtime

Opéra National du Rhin – *19 pl. Broglie* – ☎ *03 88 75 48 23* – *www.opera-national-du-rhin.com* – *box office: Mon-Fri 11am-6pm, Sat 11am-4pm, and 45min before each performance* – *closed mid-Jul to mid-Aug.* The Rhine Opera cultural organisation was created in 1972 to manage operatic events in Strasbourg, Mulhouse and Colmar. Apart from the classic opera repertoire, the programme includes high quality chamber music, dance and recitals (Thomas Hampson, Peter Seiffert, Gwyneth Jones). The theatre can seat 1 142 people.

Place du Château – It is lined with the Musée de l'Œuvre Notre-Dame *(see Museums)* and the **Palais Rohan★**.
Follow rue de Rohan then turn right onto rue des Cordiers leading to the charming **place du Marché-aux-Cochons-de-Lait★** lined with old houses including a 16C house with wooden galleries. The adjacent place de la Grande-Boucherie looks typically Alsatian.

Turn left onto rue du Vieux-Marché-aux-Poissons.

The **Ancienne Douane** stands on the right; this former custom house, rebuilt in 1965, was originally a warehouse used by the town's river traffic. It houses temporary exhibitions.
Opposite, the Grande Boucherie buildings, dating from 1586, contain the Musée Historique *(see Museums)*.

Pont du Corbeau – This is the former "execution" bridge from which infanticides and parricides, tied up in sacks, were plunged into the water until they died; those condemned for lesser crimes were put inside iron cages and dipped into the river at the spot where waste water from the Boucherie flowed in.

A carriage entrance at no 1 quai des Bateliers, gives access to the Cour du Corbeau.

★Cour du Corbeau – This picturesque courtyard goes back to the 14C. Note the old well on the right dating from 1560. This former fashionable inn welcomed some illustrious guests: Turenne, King Johann-Casimir of Poland, Frederick the Great, Emperor Joseph II.

Quai St-Nicolas – The embankment is lined with some fine old houses; three of them have been turned into a museum *(Musée Alsacien: see Museums)*.
Louis Pasteur lived at no 18.

Cross the bridge and continue along quai St-Thomas.

Église St-Thomas ⊘ – This five-naved church, rebuilt at the end of the 12C, became a Lutheran cathedral in 1529. It contains the famous **mausoleum of the Maréchal de Saxe★★** (Moritz von Sachsen, Marshal of France), one of Pigalle's masterpieces (18C). The allegorical sculpture represents France weeping and holding the marshal's hand while trying to push Death aside. Strength, symbolised by Hercules, gives way to grief and Love can be seen crying as he puts out his torch. On the left, a lion (Holland), a leopard (England) and an eagle (Austria), are represented vanquished, next to crumpled flags.

Walk along rue de la Monnaie to the Pont St-Martin.

The bridge offers a fine **view★** of the Bain-aux-Plantes district *(see below)*.
The river divides into four arms (watermills, dams and locks can still be seen).
As you walk along rue des Dentelles, note the 18C house at no 12 and an older one at no 10 dating from the 16C.

The street leads to place Benjamin-Zix and the beginning of rue du Bain-aux-Plantes.

Strasbourg – La Petite France

★★ La Petite France – This is one of the most interesting and best-preserved areas of the old town, with its houses reflected in the canal. At dusk the whole district is fascinating. It was once the fishermen's, tanners' and millers' district.

★★ Rue du Bain-aux-Plantes – The street is lined with old buildings dating from the Alsatian Renaissance (16C-17C); these timber-framed corbelled houses are adorned with galleries and gables. Note, along the canal on the left, the tanners' house (Gerwerstub, no 42), dating from 1572, and on the right, no 33 on the corner of rue du Fossé-des-Tanneurs and the extremely narrow rue des Cheveux; nos 31, 27 and 25 (1651) are also noteworthy.

★ Ponts Couverts – This is the name given to three successive bridges spanning the River Ill; each bridge is guarded by a massive square tower, once part of the 14C fortifications. The three towers used to be linked by covered wooden bridges.

Turn right just before the last tower, known as the Tour du Bourreau, and walk along quai de l'Ill, the only way to reach the terrace of the Vauban dam.

Barrage Vauban ⊘ – From the panoramic terrace *(viewing table, telescope)*, covering the whole length of the casemate bridge, known as the Barrage Vauban (part of Vauban's fortifications), built right across the Ill, there is a striking **view★★** of the Ponts Couverts and their four towers in the foreground, of the Petite France district and its canals in the background, and of the cathedral on the right.

Go back over the Pont Couverts.

Follow quai de la Petite France running alongside the canal and admire the romantic **view★** of the old houses reflected in the water.

Walk across the Pont du Faisan and return to Grand'Rue.

Église St-Pierre-le-Vieux – This church consists in fact of two adjacent churches; one is Catholic and the other Protestant. The north transept of the Catholic church (rebuilt in 1866) contains 16C carved-wood panels by Veit Wagner, depicting scenes from the Life of St Peter and St Valerus. The **scenes★** from the Passion (late 15C-early 16C), which can be seen at the end of the chancel, are believed to be the work of Henri Lutzelmann, a native of Strasbourg. The south transept contains **painted panels★** by members of the Schongauer School (15C) illustrating the Resurrection and Christ's apparitions. *In order to see these works in better lighting conditions, press the switch on the left.*

Continue along Grand'Rue lined with 16C-18C houses then along rue Gutenberg to the square of the same name.

On **place Gutenberg** stand the **Hôtel de la Chambre de Commerce** (Chamber of Commerce building), a fine Renaissance edifice, and Gutenberg's statue by David d'Angers.
No 52 rue du Vieux-Marché-aux-Poissons is the birthplace of Jean Arp (1887-1966), a sculptor, painter, poet and major protagonist of modern art.

Rue Mercière takes you back to place de la Cathédrale.

OLD TOWN VIA PLACE BROGLIE

Start in front of the cathedral and follow rue des Grandes Arcades.

Place Kléber

Place Kléber – This is the most famous square in the city. On the north side is an 18C building called "l'Aubette" because the different units of the garrison came here at dawn *(aube)* to get their orders.

In the centre stands Kléber's statue, erected in 1840; he is buried beneath it. Born in Strasbourg in 1753, murdered in Cairo in 1800, **Jean-Baptiste Kléber** is one of the most illustrious natives of Strasbourg, a brilliant general of the Revolutionary period. The base of the statue is decorated with two low-relief carvings depicting his victories at Altenkirchen and Heliopolis.

Église St-Pierre-le-Jeune ⊙ – Three successive churches were built on this site. All that remains of the first church is a tomb with five funeral recesses, estimated to date from the end of the Roman occupation (4C AD); the lovely restored cloister belonged to the church built in 1031. The present Protestant church, dating from the 13C but considerably restored around 1900, contains a fine Gothic **rood screen** decorated with paintings from 1620. The organ was made in 1780.

Walk along quai Schoepfin and cross the Pont de la Fonderie.

Place de la République – The central part of this vast square is occupied by a circular garden shaded by trees; in its centre stands a war memorial by Drivier (1936); on the left is the **Palais du Rhin**, the former imperial palace (1883-88); on the right is the National Theatre, housed in the former Landtag Palace, and the National Library.

Cross the Pont du Théâtre.

Place Broglie – This rectangular open space planted with trees, was laid in the 18C by Marshal de Broglie, who was then the governor of Alsace. The south side is lined with the 18C **town hall**★ built by Massol, the former residence of the counts of Hanau-Lichtenberg and then of the Landgraves of Hess-Darmstadt.

Standing at the eastern end, the municipal theatre is decorated with columns and muses carved by Ohmacht (1820).

To the right of the theatre, the imposing **façade** of the former **Hôtel de Klinglin** (1736) can be seen on the waterside; the edifice also opens onto rue Brûlée (no 19: lovely doorway).

Rue du Dôme and adjacent streets – The district adjoining place Broglie (rue des Pucelles, rue du Dôme, rue des Juifs, rue de l'Arc-en-Ciel) used to be inhabited by the aristocracy and the upper middle class. The area has retained several 18C mansions, particularly rue Brûlée: the former **Hôtel des Deux-Ponts** (1754) at no 13, the bishop's residence at no 16, and at no 9 the town hall's side entrance; no 25 rue de la Nuée-Bleue, on the other side of place Broglie, is the former Hôtel d'Andlau dating from 1732.

19C DISTRICT

After 1870, the Germans erected a great number of monumental public buildings in neo-Gothic Renaissance style. They intended to transfer the town centre to the north-east, and include the orangery and the university. This district with its broad avenues is a rare example of Prussian architecture.

Parc des Contades – This park situated north of place de la République, was named after the military governor of Alsace who had it laid in the late 18C. On the edge of the park stands the **Synagogue de la Paix**, built in 1955 to replace the synagogue destroyed in 1940.

★**Orangerie** – The splendid park was designed by Le Nôtre in 1692 and remodelled in 1804 for Empress Josephine's stay. The Josephine pavilion, rebuilt following a fire in 1968, is used for temporary exhibitions, theatrical performances and concerts.

Maison de la Télévision FR3-Alsace – Television house was built in 1961; a monumental (30x6m/98x20ft) ceramic by Lurçat, symbolising the Creation, decorates the concave façade of the auditorium.

THE PORT AUTONOME AND THE RHINE

Situated at one of the main intersections of major European routes, Strasbourg is one of the most important ports along the River Rhine. Its impact on eastern France's economy equals that of a major maritime port because of the exceptionally good navigable conditions of the Rhine (now canalised between Basle and Iffezheim), comparable to an international sound, 800km/497mi long. The advantages of Strasbourg's geographical situation are enhanced by the network of waterways, railway lines and roads linking the whole region with Western and Central Europe.

Overall view and excursion along the Rhine – *25km/16mi round tour – allow 1hr 30min.*
This tour offers the most interesting views of the Rhine and the harbour installations.
From the Pont d'Austerlitz, follow N 4. Shortly before reaching the Pont Vauban, turn right onto rue du Havre which is parallel to the René-Graff dock.

Rue de la Rochelle, which prolongs it, leads to the southern and most modern part of the harbour, with its three main docks: Auguste-Detœuf (cereals), Gaston-Hælling and Adrien-Weirich (containers and heavy goods) as well as basin IV. The Eurofret-Strasbourg centre is located between the last two docks *(access via rue de Rheinfeld and rue de Bayonne).*

Turn back along rue de la Rochelle and rue du Havre. At the end of the latter, turn right and drive across the Pont Vauban which spans the Vauban dock. Avenue du Pont de l'Europe leads to the Rhine.

The river, which at this point is 250m/273yd wide, is spanned by the **Pont de l'Europe** (1960) consisting of two metal arches and linking Strasbourg with Kehl on the German side. This bridge replaces the famous Kehl Bridge (1861), destroyed during the war.

Turn back once more and bear right to follow rue Coulaux, then rue du Port-du-Rhin (view of the Bassin du Commerce).

From the **Pont d'Anvers**, the view embraces several docks: on the left, the entrance of the large Bassin Vauban and Bassin Dusuzeau (harbour station); on the right, the Bassin des Remparts.

Drive over the bridge and turn right onto rue du Général-Picquart skirting the Bassin des Remparts where the Naviscope is moored.

◉ This former barge-driver has been turned into a **Musée du Rhin et de la Navigation** ⊙ (Rhine Museum).

Drive along rue Boussingault then cross the Marne-Rhine canal and turn right along quai Jacoutot which follows the canal.

From the **Pont Jean-Millot**, at the entrance of the Albert-Auberger dock, the view takes in the Rhine on the left and the north entrance of the harbour. The Marne-Rhine canal and three docks (Bassin Louis-Armand, Bassin du Commerce and Bassin de l'Industrie) open into the northern outer harbour.

MUSEUMS

★★**Musée alsacien**⊙ – This museum of popular art, located in three 16C-17C houses including an aristocratic house, gives a good insight into the history, customs and traditions of the Alsace region. The tour of the museum through the maze of stairs and wooden galleries overlooking inner courtyards, enables visitors to discover a wealth of quaint little rooms. The displays include costumes, prints, ancient toys, flour-spitting masks that used to decorate old mills, and reconstructions of interiors such as the apothecary's laboratory and wood-panelled bedrooms furnished with box beds, painted furniture and monumental stoves.

Musée alsacien, Strasbourg – A.Wolf/EXPLORER

Musée Alsacien – Traditional dresser

★★**Musée de l'Œuvre Notre-Dame** ⏱ – *A tour of this museum is a must after a visit of the cathedral.*

The **Œuvre Notre-Dame** is a unique institution founded to collect donations for the building work, upkeep and improvement of the cathedral. The first recorded donation dates from 1205.

The museum is devoted to medieval and Renaissance Alsatian art; the collections are displayed in the wings of the Maison de l'Œuvre, dating from 1347 and 1578 to 1585, in the former Hôtellerie du Cerf (14C) and in a small 17C house, surrounding four small courtyards: Cour de l'Œuvre, Cour de la Boulangerie, Cour des Maréchaux and Cour du Cerf . The small medieval garden of the Cour du Cerf is planted with vegetables as well as medicinal and ornamental plants in order to recreate the *Paradisgärtlein* depicted by medieval Alsatian paintings and prints.

The hall which contains pre-Romanesque sculpture gives access to the Romanesque sculpture rooms and to the room displaying 12C and 13C stained glass, some of it originally decorating the Romanesque cathedral; note the cloister of the Benedictine nuns of Eschau (12C) and the famous **Christ's Head**★★ from Wissembourg, the oldest representational stained glass known (c 1070).

From there, one goes through the Cour de l'Œuvre, with a partly Flamboyant and partly Renaissance decoration, and enters the former meeting hall of the builders' and stone masons' guild, whose woodwork and ceiling date from 1582 and which contains the statues of the cathedral's St Laurence doorway. Next comes the main room of the Hôtellerie du Cerf where 13C works originally decorating the cathedral are exhibited.

The fine oak staircase, dating from the 18C, leads to small rooms containing 17C prints showing the cathedral at different periods and famous drawings on parchment which reveal the original intentions of the architects. The first floor houses an important collection of 15C-17C gold plate from Strasbourg.

The second floor is devoted to the evolution of Alsatian art in the 15C; stained glass on the left and on the right, and in the rooms with period woodwork and ceilings, sculpture and **paintings**★★ of the Alsatian School: Conrad Witz and Alsatian primitives, Nicolas de Leyden.

Visitors go back to the first floor by means of the fine spiral staircase dating from 1580.

In the Renaissance wing, a room is devoted to **Hans Baldung Grien** (1484-1545), a student of Dürer, who was the main representative of the Renaissance in Strasbourg.

The east wing contains displays of Alsatian and Rhenish furniture as well as 16C and 17C sculpture, a collection of 17C still-life paintings, some of them by **Sébastien Stoskopff** (1597-1657); miniatures, interiors and costumes from Strasbourg dating from the 17C, glassware.

★★**Musée d'Art Moderne et Contemporain** ⏱ – Standing on the bank of the River Ill, this modern building clad with pink granite and white concrete panels was designed by Adrien Fainsilber, the architect of the Cité des Sciences et de l'Industrie at La Villette in Paris.

A central glass nave, more than 100m/110yd long and 25m/82ft high, leads to the exhibition rooms presenting a vast panorama of modern and contemporary art.

Modern art from 1850 to 1950 – *Located on the ground floor*. The works exhibited illustrate the various artistic expressions which have left their stamp on the history of modern art, from the academic works of William Bouguereau *(The Consoling Virgin)* to the abstract works of Kandinsky, Baumeister and Poliakoff of Magneli.

Renoir, Sisley and Monet illustrate Impressionism. Paintings by Signac and a few Nabis such as Gauguin, Vuillard and Maurice Denis show that the post-Impressionists were looking for something different. Art at the turn of the last century is represented by a group of Symbolist works headed by Gustav Klimt's *Plenitude*.

Several rooms are devoted to **Jean Arp** and his wife Sophie Taeuber-Arp, who made, in collaboration with Theo Van Doesburg, a series of stained-glass panels recreating the constructivist interiors (1926-28) of l'Aubette, an 18C building situated on place Kléber. The desk designed by Arp and Sophie Taeuber's carpet are next to items connected with the Bauhaus, the De Stijl movement and the modern approach (furniture by Eileen Gray and Marcel Breuer, dining room designed by Kandinsky). One room is entirely devoted to Arp's sculpture.

Artists such as Marinot, Dufy, Vlaminck, Campendonk, connected with Fauvism and Expressionism, are adepts of pure bright colours. In striking contrast, *Still Life* (1911) by George Braque is a typical Cubist work.

As a reaction against the First World War, the Dadaists signed derisory even absurd works (Janco, Schwitters). Following in their footsteps, the Surrealists with Victor Brauner, Max Ernst and Arp tried to introduce the world of dreams into their works.

Furniture and inlaid items by **Charles Spindler**, sculpture by François-Rupert Carabin, Ringel d'Illzach and Bugatti, and early-20C stained-glass panels made in Strasbourg testify to the renewal of art and decorative arts in Alsace around 1900.

The **Salle Doré** was specifically designed for the display of the huge painting by Gustave Doré (1869), depicting *Christ leaving the prætorium*. A cabinet shows Doré's talents as a sculptor and above all as an illustrator *(Dante's Inferno)*. A balcony situated at the entrance of the restaurant makes it possible to look down into this room.

The **graphic arts** room contains rotating displays of prints and drawings from 1870 to the present day, posters from the 1880s to the 1920s and a collection of photographs.

Modern art from 1950 onwards – *Upstairs.* In the first room, works by Picasso, Richier, Pinot-Gallizio, Kudo and Baselitz reflect the uncertain times. The next room illustrates the Fluxus movement with Filliou and Brecht, and the so-called Poor Art *(Arte povera)* movement with Kounellis, Penone and Merz who strive to show the energy of the simplest objects. The 1960s and 1970s are represented by the experiments of Buren, Parmentier, Toroni, Rutault, Morellet and Lavier, which blossom in the 1980s and 1990s with Toni Grand, Miroslav Balka, Christian Boltanski, Philippe Ramette, Maurice Blaussyld and Javier Pérez. The last room exhibits the most contemporary works in quick rotation; Nam June Paik, Collin-Thiébaut *(Clandestine Museum in Strasbourg)*, Gerhard Mertz *(Dove sta Memoria)* and Sarkis are some of the artists represented, the last three having lived or worked in Strasbourg.

The panoramic terrace of the Art Café offers views of the Vauban dam and Ponts Couverts.

🖼 **Musée zoologique de l'université et de la ville** ⊙ – Housed on two partly renovated floors, this museum presents regional and world fauna in its natural environment: cold regions, the Andes, the savannah, Alsace... Rich collections of insects and stuffed birds are exhibited.

Permanent and temporary (two per year) exhibitions deal with biology and ecology.

ADDITIONAL SIGHTS

Église St-Guillaume ⊙ – The church was built between 1300 and 1307. The nave is lit by beautiful stained-glass windows (1465) by Pierre d'Andlau. However, the main attraction is the 14C two-storey tomb of the Werd brothers; Philippe, in canon's clothes, occupies the lower slab and above it, Ulrich, dressed as a knight, rests on two lions.

Haras national ⊙ – The stud farm is located near the Petite France district, in a pink-sandstone building dating from the 17C and 18C: a medieval hospital for travellers (1360), remodelled and extended into a private mansion and converted into a royal stud by Louis XV in 1763. The stables house some 30 stallions of various breeds: Arabs, English thoroughbreds, Anglo-Arabs, French saddle horses, French saddle ponies, Connemara ponies, draught horses.

SUNDGAU★

Michelin map 87 folds 9, 10, 19 and 20 or 242 folds 39, 43 and 44

The Sundgau or southernmost area of Alsace, adjacent to the foothills of the Jura mountains, stretches from north to south between Mulhouse and the Swiss border. and from east to west between the Rhine and the Largue Valley. The area has been deeply carved by the tributaries of the upper Ill; the resulting hills and limestone cliffs are crowned by forests of beeches and firs and the valleys are dotted with numerous lakes – full of carp, a local gastronomic speciality – pastures and rich crops. Flower-decked farmhouses often have timber-framed walls roughcast in an ochre colour or clad with wooden planks and are covered with long sloping roofs.

Altkirch is the only town of some importance, but many prosperous villages are scattered along the rivers or across sunny hillsides.

ROUND TOUR STARTING FROM ALTKIRCH

117km/73mi – allow half a day

Altkirch – *See ALTKIRCH.*

Drive E out of Altkirch along D 419 which follows the south bank of the Ill.

Pleasant walks can be added to this itinerary, particularly in the southern part of the area, known as the Alsatian Jura.

St-Morand – This village is a place of pilgrimage. The **church** contains the beautiful 12C sarcophagus of the area's patron saint, Morand, who converted the Sungdau to Christianity.

The road continues along the Thalbach Valley before reaching the plateau. It then runs down towards the Rhine offering views of the northern part of the Jura mountains, the Basle depression and the Black Forest.

Eating out

MODERATE

À l'Arbre Vert – *17 r. Principale – 68560 Heimersdorf – 9km/5.5mi S of Altkirch, Ferrette direction –* ☎ *03 89 07 11 40 – closed 23 Jul-12 Aug, Mon and Tue – 95/135F.* Fried carp is so famous in Sundgau that there is a route you can follow to discover more about it. This family restaurant is a good place to sample it in a friendly atmosphere.

MID-RANGE

Le Moulin Bas – *1 r. Raedersdorf – 68480 Ligsdorf – 4km/2.5mi S of Ferrette on D 41 and D 432 –* ☎ *03 89 40 31 25 – closed 1-22 Jan, Mon and Tue except public holidays – 180/360F.* This watermill near the Swiss border is a lovely place to stay, surrounded by a garden through which the Ill flows. Typical local cooking in a country decor on the ground floor, and slightly more refined cuisine upstairs. Very pleasant bedrooms.

MID-RANGE

Chambre d'hôte Moulin de Huttingue – *68480 Oltingue – 1.5km/1mi S of Oltingue on D 21^B –* ☎ *03 89 40 72 91 – closed Jan and Feb – ⊠ – 5 rooms 280/350F – evening meal 100/150F.* Beside the Ill, which is only a stream here, this former flour mill has combined part of its original interior, such as the lovely wooden pillars, with a modern decor. The superb loft room, with its roof timbers, is definitely worth booking. Pretty garden and terrace in summer. Holiday cottage.

As you enter Ranspach-le-Bas, turn off D 419 to the right. On leaving Ranspach-le-Haut, turn left towards Folgensbourg.

Revolving turrets from the Maginot Line can be seen on both sides of the road *(see Ligne MAGINOT)*.

In Folgensbourg, turn S onto D 473 then left onto D 21bis towards St-Blaise.

The itinerary offers a fine view of the Basle depression, of the town and of the Rhine flowing into the Plaine d'Alsace.

In St-Blaise, follow D 9bis to Leymen.

Château du Landskron – *30min on foot there and back.*

🏃 This castle, believed to date from the 11C, is in ruins. Reinforced by Vauban in the 17C, it was besieged and destroyed in 1814. From its privileged position on a height overlooking the border, the view embraces the small town of Leymen below and, further north, the forested Sundgau and Basle region.

Return to St-Blaise.

In Oltingue, the road joins the upper Ill Valley, overlooked in the south by the ridge of the Alsatian Jura.

Oltingue – A folk museum, the **Maison du Sundgau** ⊙, stands in the centre of this charming village. It surveys the different architectural styles of the region and contains a selection of furniture, crockery and kitchen utensils illustrating rural life in the past. Note the large bread oven in the bakery, the steps of an old staircase, each cut out of a tree trunk, cob walls, a collection of *kougelhopf* (a type of cake) tins appropriately shaped for each feast day and a series of ceramic tiles used to decorate stoves.

In Rædersdorf, continue along D 21^B towards Kiffis.

Hippoltskirch – The **chapel** ⊙ has several remarkable features including a painted coffered ceiling, a painted-wood balustrade along the gallery and ex-votos on the walls, some of them showing a naive style of painting. On the left of the nave, there is a miracle-working statue of Our Lady, once the object of a pilgrimage, to whom the ex-votos are dedicated.

Leave Kiffis on your left and follow the international road (D 21^{BIII}) which skirts the Swiss border (and even crosses it beyond Moulin-Neuf for a very short distance) along the bottom of a wooded coomb.

Lucelle – This lakeside village at the southern-most end of the Alsace region, once stood next to a wealthy Cistercian abbey.

Drive N along D 432.

*★**Ferrette** – The former capital of the Sundgau was, from the 10C onwards, the residence of independent counts whose authority extended over a large part of Alsace. This region became the property of the House of Austria in the 14C and was ceded to France in 1648 by the Treaty of Westphalia. The prince of Monaco is still entitled to be called Count of Ferrette.

The small ancient town, lying in a picturesque **site**★, is overlooked by the ruins of two castles built on an impressive rockspur rising to an altitude of 612m/2008ft.

🏃 Marked footpaths lead to the foot of the castles. From the platform, there is a fine **view**★ of the Vosges mountains, of the Rhine and Ill valleys, of the Black Forest and of the foothills of the Jura mountains. The surrounding wooded hills offer a choice of interesting walks.

Drive to Bouxwiller along D 473.

Bouxwiller – This pretty village adorned with many fountains is built across one of the slopes of the valley. The **Église** St-Jacques contains a lovely 18C gilt-wood pulpit, originally in the Luppach Monastery, and an elaborate Baroque altarpiece, decorated with columns and richly painted and gilt.

D 9bis, which follows the upper Ill Valley, leads to Grentzingen.

★**Grentzingen** – The characteristic timber-framed houses of this flower-decked village are lined up at right angles to the road. A few of them have retained their original ochre colour and their awning. Note the roofs with their canted gables.

Turn left in Grentzingen.

The road runs through **Riespach**, a village with typical regional houses.

Feldbach – The restored 12C Romanesque **church** is in two parts, one for the nuns and one for the congregation. The nave, which has successively round and square pillars, ends with an oven-vaulted apse.

D 432 runs through the green valleys of the Feldbach and the Ill back to Altkirch.

THANN★

Population 7 751
Michelin map 87 fold 18 or 242 fold 35
Local maps see Route des CRÊTES and Route des VINS

This small southern town, situated west of Mulhouse, is renowned for having the most richly decorated Gothic church in the whole of Alsace. The local wine, known as Rangen wine, has been famous since the 16C as a potent wine to be consumed in moderation and at home!

From legend to history – The foundation of Thann, like that of many Alsatian towns and villages, is steeped in legend. When Bishop Thiébaut (Theobald) of Gubbio in Umbria died in 1160, he bequeathed his episcopal ring to his most trusted servant who took it, together with the bishop's thumb, hid it inside his staff and arrived in Alsace the following year. One night, he went to sleep in a fir forest after having driven his staff into the ground. As he was about to leave in the morning, he was unable to lift his staff out of the ground. At the same time, three bright lights appeared above three fir trees; the lord of the nearby castle of Engelbourg saw the lights and having arrived promptly, he decided to build a chapel on the very site where the miracle had occurred. The chapel soon became a popular place of pilgrimage and a town grew all around. It was named Thann, which means fir tree.

Every year in June, three fir trees are burnt in front of the church to commemorate this event.

THANN

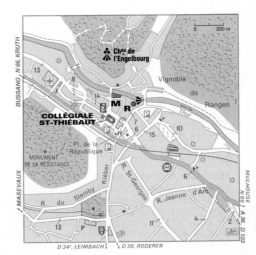

★★COLLÉGIALE ST-THIÉBAUT ⊘

The Gothic architecture of the collegiate church (14C-early 16C) shows a continuous progression towards the Flamboyant Gothic style.

Exterior – There is a remarkable **doorway★★** on the west front. It is 15m/49ft high and has an elegant tympanum surmounting two doors, each having its own smaller tympanum.

Walk round the north side of the church to admire the Flamboyant doorway adorned with fine 15C statues.

Continue towards the town hall to get an overall view of the lofty chancel with its high roof covered with glazed tiles and the belfry (76m/249ft high) surmounted by an openwork stone spire.

Interior – A polychrome wooden statue of the wine-growers' Virgin, carved c 1510, is bonded to the central buttress pier of the pentagonal chapel *(accessible from the south aisle)*. At the end of the aisle, in St-Thiébaut Chapel, a polychrome carved-wood statue of the saint dating from 1520 stands on the altar.

Chancel – The deep chancel is adorned with the 15C statues of the 12 Apostles in polychrome stone. A large crucifix (1894) in polychrome wood by Klem from Colmar hangs in the entrance. However, the outstanding feature is undoubtedly a superb group, 51 in all, of 15C oak **stalls★★**, which express all the fantasy of the Middle Ages. There is a profusion of foliage, gnomes and comic characters carved with great precision. The chancel is flooded with light pouring in through eight superb 15C **stained-glass windows★**.

Eating out

MODERATE

Hostellerie Alsacienne – *R. du Mar.-Foch – 68290 Masevaux – 15km/9.3mi SW of Thann on the Joffre road –* ☎ *03 89 82 45 25 – closed 15-28 Feb, 15 Oct-1 Nov and Mon Sep-Apr – 60/170F.* Situated in a pedestrianised street in the town centre, this rustic inn serves reasonably priced local dishes. The menu is simple but there is enough choice, and the interior is interesting, with its carved wooden panelling. A few rooms are available.

Where to stay

MID-RANGE

Hôtel Le Parc – *23 r. Kléber –* ☎ *03 89 37 37 47 –* 🅿 *– 20 rooms 450/760F – 🛏 85F – restaurant 155/280F.* This early-19C bourgeois town house is a pleasant place to stay. It has a peaceful well-kept walled garden with a swimming pool in summer, and its rooms are decorated with old furniture. Those on the first floor are more spacious. Friendly staff.

ADDITIONAL SIGHTS

Tour des Sorcières – This 15C tower surmounted by an onion-shaped roof is all that remains of the old fortifications. The most picturesque view of the tower is from the bridge across the Thur.

Œil de la Sorcière – *30min on foot there and back.*

🔳 Engelbourg Castle (the angels' castle), built by the counts of Ferrette, became the property of the Hapsburgs and, in 1648, of the king of France who, 10 years later, gave it to Mazarin whose heirs kept it until the Revolution.

In 1673, Louis XIV gave the order for it to be dismantled. During the demolition process, the lower part of the keep remained intact and the centre appeared to be overlooking the plain. Popular imagination promptly found a name for this unusual ruin, the "witch's eye".

From the ruin, there is a view of Thann, the Plaine d'Alsace and the Black Forest in the distance. A monument to the Alsatian Resistance stands on top of the Staufen, across the valley.

Musée des Amis de Thann ⊘ – Housed in the former corn exchange dating from 1519, the museum's collections spread on four levels illustrate the town's history and provide additional information about the collegiate church. The main themes dealt with are: vineyards (series of panels from the former vineyard-keepers' hut), the castle and fortifications, the collegiate church and the cult of St Theobald, furniture and popular art, mementoes of two world wars, the beginnings of the textile industry.

Under the gaze of the Witch's Eye

ROUTE JOFFRE *18km/11mi from Thann to Masevaux*

Drive NW along N 66 to Bitschwiller and turn left onto D 14^{BIV}.

This road was built by the army during the First World War to establish vital communications between the valleys of the Doller and the Thur.

Its military role was revived during the winter of 1944-45, when French troops used it to attack Thann from the north.

On the way up to the Col du Hundsrück, the road affords a magnificent **view★★** of the Thur Valley overlooked to the north by the Grand Ballon (alt 1 424m/4 672ft). The road then winds its way up to the pass through the forest.

Col du Hundsrück – Alt 748m/2 454ft. View of the Sundgau *(see SUNDGAU)* and the Jura mountains to the south and of the Plaine d'Alsace to the east.

Beyond the Col du Schirm, the road runs down towards the Doller Valley and goes through the hamlet of **Houppach**; a pilgrimage takes place in Notre-Dame d'Houppach, the village chapel also known as Klein Einseideln.

Masevaux – This small industrial and commercial town developed round an abbey founded by Mason, St Odile's nephew, in memory of his son who had drowned in the Doller. There are some lovely squares adorned with 18C fountains and surrounded by 16C and 17C houses.

THIÉRACHE ARDENNAISE

Michelin map 53 folds 17 and 18 or 241 folds 5, 9 and 10

Lying at the heart of the Champagne plain, west of Charleville-Mézières, this area of forest and meadows is ideal hiking country and its profusion of fortified churches will delight history buffs.

FORTIFIED CHURCHES

Round tour from Signy-l'Abbaye

111km/69mi – allow one day

Churches were fortified during the late 16C and throughout the 17C in an effort to protect villages from the hords of plundering mercenaries that constantly invaded the region. Tall square keeps, round towers and bartizans were added to the original 12C and 13C buildings which were intended to shelter villagers in case of need; extra accommodation was even added above the nave, which explains the presence of ceilings in most churches.

Signy-l'Abbaye – The village developed in the Vaux Valley, near a famous Cistercian abbey founded in 1134 by Bernard de Clairvaux and destroyed in 1793. The Gibergeon chasm located in the centre of the village supplies the River Vaux. Signy-l'Abbaye is a pleasant resort for walking enthusiasts.

Eating out

MODERATE

Auberge de l'Abbaye – *2 pl. Aristide-Briand – 08460 Signy-l'Abbaye* – ☎ *03 24 52 81 27 – closed 2 Jan-28 Feb, Tue evening and Wed – 80/160F.* This stone-built inn has a pleasant country feel, set in a picturesque little village. The cooking is simple and regional. Small, well-kept rooms and a welcoming atmosphere.

Where to stay

MID-RANGE

Chambre d'hôte La Cour des Prés – *08290 Rumigny* – ☎ *03 24 35 52 66 – closed Nov-Mar and Tue Jul-Aug – ☒ – 2 rooms 325/420F.* A lovely welcome awaits you in this fortified house, built in 1546 by the provost of Rumigny. Its two rooms are reminiscent of an old-fashioned private house. Visit the castle and enjoy the dinner-concerts which are open to all.

Abbaye de Sept Fontaines – *R. des Sept-Fontaines – 08090 Fagnon – 8km/5mi SW of Charleville-Mézières on D 139 and D 39* – ☎ *03 24 37 38 24 – closed 8-14 Jan – ▯ – 23 rooms 460/850F – ☐ 65F – restaurant 145/350F.* It's impossible not to feel soothed by the peace and quiet of the huge park which surrounds this majestic dwelling. Though not luxurious, the rooms have personalised colour schemes. Those on the first floor are very spacious; those on the second floor are under a sloping attic roof. Golf course.

Forêt de Signy – Signy Forest, which extends over an area of 3 535ha/8 735 acres, comprises two massifs separated by the **Vaux Valley**: the small forest (oaks and beeches) to the south-east and the damper large forest (oaks, ashes and maples) to the north-west. The forest yields quality timber.

Drive NW out of Signy along the Liart road (D 27) which follows the Vaux Valley; 5km/3mi from Signy, turn left onto the forest road (Route forestière de la Grande Terre).

🔲 The road runs past the **Fontaine Rouge** *(100m/110yd on the right)*, a ferrous spring marking the start of a 4km/2.5mi footpath, then goes through the oak forest and reaches the path *(parking area)* leading down to the **Gros Frêne**. A stump and a slice of the trunk nearby are all that remain of this imposing ash tree, fallen in 1989 *(about 45min there and back)*. Two marked footpaths, 5km/3mi and 6km/3.7mi long, start from the parking area.

Rejoin D 27 and continue NW to Liart.

Liart – The medieval west front of the **Église Notre-Dame-de-Liart★** was flanked in the 17C by a massive rectangular keep reinforced by brattices, crenels and loopholes whereas the east end was fortified by an octagonal tower with stairs leading to an attic above the chancel, used as a shelter in case of attack.

Aouste – The Église St-Rémi was built in the 17C on the ruins of a 15C church. The machicolated main doorway is reinforced by three brattices and a turret with canted corners. The square tower flanking the turret pierced with loopholes is strengthened by stone buttresses.

Turn left onto D 36 to La Férée then right onto D 236.

Ancienne abbaye de Bonnefontaine – *Private property.* Founded in 1152, this former Cistercian abbey stands in a wide open area of lush meadows. The ruins of the Gothic church are hidden by trees but the imposing silhouette of the pink-brick-built and slate-roofed 18C conventual buildings can clearly be seen.

In Blanchefosse, turn right onto D 10 to Mont-St-Jean, then right again onto D 977 to Rumigny.

Rumigny – As you enter the village, look to the right and admire the façade of the castle overlooking the garden.

Situated on the banks of the River Aube, the Renaissance **Château de la Cour des Prés** was fortified at the request of King François I. The ground floor consists of two halls with impressive fireplaces and drawing rooms with 18C wainscotting; upstairs, the bedrooms open onto the gallery decorated with family portraits.

Hannapes – Although it was not fortified, the **Église St-Jean-Baptiste** provided shelter to the village community in case of invasion.

Turn right onto D 31 starting from the south side of the church.

Bossus-les-Rumigny – The **church** features two crenellated turrets; one of these is pierced with loopholes. The room located above the chancel is also pierced with loopholes.

Turn left onto D 10 to Fligny.

Fligny – Above the chancel of the Église St-Étienne, there is a room intended as a shelter, flanked with a round tower.

Continue along D 10.

Signy-le-Petit – The imposing **church★**, fortified by brick-built corner towers, stands in the centre of a large square. The castle was rebuilt in the 18C and remodelled in the 19C.

Drive towards Rocroi and Charleville then turn right onto D 34 to Tarzy.

Fortified church in Signy-le-Petit

Tarzy – A tower with canted corners pierced with loopholes, was built to the left of the belfry of the hilltop **church**.

Antheny – In spite of being destroyed by fire several times, the village has retained 16C and 17C houses with brattices. The Église St-Remy, standing in the middle of the enclosed cemetery, features a buttressed square tower; the upper windows were blocked up in the 15C-16C as a means of defence.

Continue along D 34 via Champlin and Estrebay.

Prez – The church is dedicated to St Martin, the famous bishop of Tours. The attic above the chancel was used for defence purposes. A round tower pierced with loopholes was added in the 16C. Panels of stucco work depicting Christ's life surround the chancel.

Continue along D 34.

The road runs past **Le Malpas**, a fortified farm built by a Scottish lord. The rectangular building is flanked by four corner towers pierced with loopholes.

About 1km/0.6mi further on, turn left onto D 32 to La Cerleau then right onto D 36 to Flaignes.

Flaignes-Havys – Clovis made a present of Flaignes to St Remi when he was baptised in Reims. The **Église St-Laurent** has an unusually imposing chancel flanked by a round tower. The small nave is supported by massive buttresses.

Havys – The **Église St-Gery** features a round tower pierced all round with loopholes used not only as look-outs but also to light the winding staircase.

Continue along D 20 to Cernion then turn left to l'Échelle.

L'Échelle – The façade of the fine-looking **castle** facing the church is framed by two 16C round towers. The bartizan in the north-west corner is known as the Tour du Massacre (massacre tower) in memory of the Thirty Years War.

Opposite the castle stands the **Hôtel Beury** with its ochre-coloured stone façade. A **Centre d'art et de littérature** (cultural centre) has been housed inside since 1996. The centre comprises rooms devoted to exhibitions of contemporary art, a **literary café**, artists' living quarters and a garden.
Drive SE to Rouvroy-sur-Audry and cross D 978 to reach Servion.

Servion – Impasse St-Étienne. The deconsecrated church is now a cultural centre, but the building has retained its former fortifications: loopholes and two round towers framing the porch.

Rémilly-les-Pothées – Note the impressive square belfry of the church. The former 16C fortified house is now a pleasant residence.
Continue along D 9 then turn right onto D 39.

Ancienne Abbaye de Sept Fontaines – The former abbey, dating from the 17C, owes its name to the seven springs on the property.
Drive through **Gruyères** nestling at the bottom of a vale, with its fortified church and castle (14C-19C).
Continue along D 39 then D 3.

Launois-sur-Vence – This small village has retained a 17C **posting house**, which made communications between Amsterdam and Marseille easier, particularly after the foundation of Charleville-Mézières. The buildings surrounding the vast inner courtyard include the postmaster's house, the coach house with its beautiful timber frame, the stables, the sheep pen and the vaulted cider cellar. It is now occupied by the tourist office and a cultural centre which organises many events.
Drive NW along D 27 to Dommery.

Launois, a lively tourist centre

Third weekend in April: Festival of tourism in the Ardennes region
Last weekend in April: Regional heritage and rural dwellings fair
Weekend nearest 1 May: Ardennes' landscape gardening fair
Second weekend in May: Regional antiques fair
Whitsun weekend: North-east France gastronomic fair
Fourth weekend in June: Festival of arts and crafts in Champagne-Ardennes
Second weekend in August: Holidaymakers in Ardennes fair
Fourth weekend in September: Autumn flower show and rural market in Ardennes
First Sunday in October: Vintage car show
Third weekend in October: Gastronomic fair
First Sunday in December: St Nicholas and Christmas fair
Second Sunday of every month: Antiques market

Dommery – The village is said to owe its name, meaning house of St-Remy, to a visit of the holy bishop. Note the imposing church tower and the east-end windows which were blocked following repeated invasions.

THIONVILLE
Conurbation 132 413
Michelin map 57 folds 3 and 4 or 242 fold 5

This former stronghold is the metropolis of the iron industry, the nerve centre of the whole industrial area which extends along the west bank of the River Moselle, 100m/328ft wide at that point. The town centre has retained a few houses with lovely old façades. The former convent of the Poor Clares' Order (1629), facing the river, has beautiful arcades and now houses the town hall. Part of the town walls (retaining wall) can be seen along the Moselle. Public gardens and walks (Parc Napoléon) have been laid on top.
Four of the forts forming part of the Maginot Line are situated nearby.

HISTORICAL NOTES

A castle built in Merovingian times and called Theodonis Villa was one of Charlemagne's favourite residences. In the 13C, Thionville was a stronghold belonging to the counts of Luxemburg who built a mighty castle. The fortified town successively belonged to the House of Burgundy, the Hapsburgs, and the Low Countries then to the Spanish, who commissioned a Flemish engineer to rebuild the fortifications between 1590 and 1600. Finally, Thionville became French in 1659 by the Treaty of the Pyrenees.

SIGHTS

Tour aux Puces – This mighty 11C-12C medieval keep, also known as the Tour au Puits (Well Tower), is the most important remaining part of the feudal castle of the counts of Luxemburg. It has no fewer than 14 sides and the complexity of its interior confers a certain architectural originality to the edifice which houses the municipal museum.

Musée municipal ⊙ – The museum retraces the history of Thionville and the surrounding area from Neolithic times to the siege of 1870. There is a rich Gallo-Roman section and an important collection of stone fragments from the late Middle Ages.
The different occasions on which the town was besieged are illustrated by maps, prints, objects...

Église St-Maximin – This vast sturdy Classical church houses an 18C organ; the organ case is decorated with a profusion of bright motifs.

★**Château de la Grange** ⊙ – *N of the town along avenue Albert I then left at the intersection of route de Luxembourg and chaussée d'Amérique.*
Designed in 1731 by Robert de Cotte, the castle was erected over the base of a fortress used until the 17C as an outer defence work guarding the town's citadel. The large kitchen contains traditional Lorraine furniture; note the fireplace surmounted by a lovely basket-handled arch. In the dining room, there is a white and gold earthenware stove, almost 5m/16ft high, built for the marquis; facing the windows are two glass cases containing collections of Boch and Chantilly porcelain.

Flemish tapestries from the early 17C illustrating the theme of the Trojan War hang in the entrance hall. At the bottom of the main staircase, with its fine 18C wrought-iron banisters, there are two remarkable Chinese vases in cloisonné enamel, and two low-relief sculptures from the school of Jean Goujon. Opposite the sedan chair, an Alsatian stove from Rouffach, dating from 1804, is decorated with religious scenes.
The Empire-style bathroom contains a bath cut out of a single block of white marble, which belonged to Pauline Bonaparte (Napoleon's sister).
The large blue drawing room contains fine Louis XV furniture; note the floor inlaid with star-shaped designs. The library, located in the former chapel, houses a remarkable collection of celadon ceramics from the Far East (between the two windows).

Château de la Grange – The dining room

The original French-style gardens were replaced in the 19C by an English-style park.

IRON COUNTRY

90km/56mi round tour – allow half a day

Drive S out of Thionville along D 953.

The long string of factories starts immediately south of Thionville, past the Daspich level crossing: the industrial site of Sollac-Florange, one of the Sollac factories (Société Lorraine de Laminage continu) and a branch of the Usinor-Sacilor group, the European leader in its field.

Turn right onto D 18 to Serémange-Erzange, then left onto D 17 towards St-Nicolas-en-Forêt.

The road rises offering extended views of the **Industrial Fensch Valley** (Unimetal-Sollac Florange, Lorfonte blast furnace, Ebange cement factory).
In St-Nicolas-en-Forêt, from the Bout-des-Terres roundabout to the end of boulevard des Vosges, there is a panoramic view of the Moselle Valley.
Continue beyond Hayange – where the Sogérail factory producing rails for the TGV (high speed train) is situated – towards Neufchef.

Lorraine's iron and steel industry

The iron-ore deposits, located in the upper reaches of the Moselle, extend over a distance of 120km/75mi from the Haye Forest to Luxemburg. In just over 100 years, three billion tonnes of *minette*, a type of ore with a relatively low iron content (about 33%) have been extracted; peak production was reached in 1962 with 62 million tonnes. There was a subsequent decline owing to competition from imported ore, richer in iron content, and to a drop in traditional outlets. The mines closed down one after the other; the closure of the Roncourt mine in August 1993 put an end to the mining activity in the area, with the exception of the Bure-Tressange site *(4km/2.5mi east of Aumetz)*, which exports its ore to Luxemburg via an underground route.

Having diversified its production and invested heavily in new technology, the steel industry has now regained a certain competitiveness. Thus the Usinor-Sacilor group ranks third in the world.

The area has also turned to other industries such as the car industry and nuclear energy.

★**Musée des Mines de Fer de Neufchef** ⊙ – This hillside mine did not require the drilling of a shaft, which means that it is now more easily accessible to the public. Extracting processes of different periods, showing the evolution of mining techniques, have been recreated along a 1.5km/0.9mi-long stretch: 1820, introduction of crank-drills; 1860, tip-trucks are put into use; early 20C, the use of compressors and pneumatic drills becomes generalised; 1930s, ore-extracting machines are introduced. Above ground, a large building provides information about the formation of iron ore, deposits, a miner's job and social environment.

Beyond Neufchef, the road runs through the dense Moyeuvre Forest, split into two by the picturesque Conroy Valley.

In Avril, it is possible to turn right onto D 906 and to drive N to Aumetz.

Musée des Mines de Fer d'Aumetz ⊙ – The former Bassompierre mine was accessible by a shaft 240m/787ft deep, which had to be filled in together with all the galleries when the mine was abandoned. Above ground, the pithead frame was retained as were various buildings housing the compressor room, the forge, the huge extracting machine etc.

Drive back along the same road to Briey.

Briey – Situated at the heart of a prosperous industrial area, Briey expanded in a remarkable way during the 1950s and, in 1960, Le Corbusier built his third **Cité Radieuse** including 350 homes on a forested site north-west of the town. Today, Briey is a peaceful but lively administrative town.

The **Église St-Gengoult**, a Romanesque church extended during the Gothic period, has a main nave flanked by double aisles on either side. At the top of the north aisle, there is a 16C stone carving representing Christ in bonds and a late-15C *Pietà* in polychrome wood in the last side chapel off the south aisle; note how the Virgin is represented taking her veil to wipe her son's wounds. The chancel contains a moving **calvary**★ (behind the high altar) comprising six wooden life-size figures carved c 1530 by artists from the school of Ligier Richier, possibly by the master himself.

From the small garden located on the north side of the church, there is a panoramic view of the **Sangsue**, a vast water expanse created by the Woigot dam, which offers water sports activities and walks through the surrounding forested area.

Beyond Homécourt, the road *(D 41 then D 11)*, running through the **Orne Valley**, is lined with housing estates and factories.

From Rombas take the D 47 to Hagondange.

Hagondange – On the right-hand side of D 47 stands an interesting modern church with an isolated campanile consisting of two concrete slabs.

Driving north from Hagondange to Uckange, you will notice, on the right of D 953, the Richemont steelworks established here in 1960.

The metalworks of the Uckange industrial centre mark the beginning of the Thionville suburbs.

Vallée de la THUR ★

This large furrow carved out by ancient glaciers is a very busy industrial area.
The upper Thur Valley and the Urbès Vale have retained a charming rural character along slopes covered with forests and pastures. The lower Thur Valley is dotted with small towns which have a long-standing tradition in the textile industry.
Famous local personalities are all industrialists, connected with the metal, textile and chemical industries: Risler, Kœchlin, Kestner, Stehelin.

INDUSTRIAL VALLEY

From Thann to Husseren-Wesserling

12km/7.5mi – about 30min – local map see Parc naturel régional des BALLONS DES VOSGES.

★**Thann** – *See THANN.*

Drive NW out of Thann along N 66.

The Thur Valley narrows and widens successively. In spite of their factories, the villages are charming, set amid an undulating landscape of pastures and orchards, crisscrossed by streams and torrents.

Willer-sur-Thur – A road *(D 13^{BVI})* branches off to the right, joins up with the scenic Route des Crêtes and leads to the Grand Ballon (alt 1424m/4 672ft), the highest summit of the Vosges mountains *(see Route des CRÊTES).*

Moosch – A cemetery situated on the east slope of the valley contains the graves of almost 1 000 French soldiers killed during the First World War.

St-Amarin – The little town has given its name to this part of the Thur Valley situated between Moosch and Wildenstein. The **Musée Serret et de la vallée de St-Amarin** ⊙ is devoted to local history: old prints and pictures of the area, Alsatian headdresses, weapons, wrought-iron work and emblems of brotherhoods.

Typical village in the Thur Valley

Ranspach – A botanic trail *(2.5km/1.5mi)*, marked by a holly leaf, starts from the top of the village, beyond a factory. Panels explain the characteristics of all the trees and bushes along the path. It is an easy and pleasant walk.

Husseren-Wesserling – An important printed-fabric manufacture is located in this small town. The **Musée du Textile et des Costumes** ⊙ is housed in a former industrial building at the heart of a vast park planted with rare trees. The museum deals with three main themes: from raw material (cotton) to fabric, the history of the great industrial families from the 18C to today, and costumes (the evolution of feminine fashion, crafts and occupations connected with fashion such as florist, embroiderer, glove-maker). Reconstructed scenes illustrate 19C fashion at different times of the day.

★UPPER VALLEY

From Husseren-Wesserling to Grand Ventron

46km/29mi – about 2hr – local map see Parc naturel régional des BALLONS DES VOSGES.

The upper valley of the River Thur is dotted with granite knolls spared by the eroding action of ancient glaciers. Three of these knolls overlook **Oderen**. From the southern approach to the village, there is a fine view, ahead and slightly to the left, of the picturesque escarpments of the Fellering woods. A fourth, the forested Schlossberg, situated upstream, is crowned by the **ruins of Wildenstein Castle**.

In Kruth, turn left onto D 13[B1].

★**Cascade St-Nicolas** – The waterfall, which consists of several charming smaller ones, drops to the bottom of a lovely deep vale with densely forested slopes.

Return to Kruth.

Between Kruth and Wildenstein, the road runs to the right of the Schlossberg through a narrow passage where the Thur once flowed.
Another road runs along the other side of the Schlossberg and the **Kruth-Wildenstein dam**, an earth dike with a waterproof central core of clay, which is one of the major works of the Thur Valley's harnessing project *(the road can only be followed in the Wildenstein-Kruth direction; it is closed in winter).*
Beyond Wildenstein, the road starts rising towards the Col de Bramont, offering a beautiful vista of the Thur Valley followed by a picturesque run through the forest.

Col de Bramont – Alt 956m/3 136ft. The pass is situated on the main ridge of the Vosges mountains.

★★**Grand Ventron** – *The access road branches off from the pass. Turn left onto the forest road (8km/5mi) which goes through the Col de la Vierge on its way to the Chaume du Grand Ventron.*
From the summit (alt 1 204m/3 950ft), there is a vast **panorama**★★ of the Thur Valley and the Vosges summits, including the Hohneck, Grand Ballon and Ballon d'Alsace.

URBÈS VALE

From Husseren-Wesserling to the Col de Bussang.

11km/7mi – about 30min – local map see Parc naturel régional des BALLONS DES VOSGES.

The road *(N 66)* starts along the Thur Valley then enters the Urbès Vale blocked by morainic deposits.

See d'Urbès – *Parking on the lake shore (signpost).* The depression in which the lake (or *see*) is situated, was scooped out during the Quaternary Era by the glacier which carved the Thur Valley. The lake lies behind a moraine left by the glacier. A bog-type vegetation covers the area, progressively filling up the depression.
🚶 A marked *path (1hr 30min)*, dotted with explanatory panels about local flora, fauna and traditional activities, makes it easier to explore this remarkable place.
The road then rises gently towards the Col de Bussang, affording lovely views of the Thur Valley and the surrounding heights.

Col de Bussang – *From the pass, it is possible to drive down the upper Moselle Valley (see REMIREMONT: Upriver from Remiremont).*

TOUL★

Population 17 281
Michelin map 62 fold 4 or 242 fold 17

Situated on the banks of the River Moselle, Toul occupies a strategic position at the intersection of several main roads and waterways.
The town lies at the point where the Moselle changed its course during the Quaternary Era, suddenly veering north-east to join the Meurthe just north of Nancy.
The antique city of Tullum, which was already a bishopric by the 4C AD, soon became so prosperous that it was granted its independence in 928 under the terms of the Mainz Charter.
In 1700, Vauban, Louis XIV's military engineer, built new ramparts round the city (the Porte de Metz is all that remains today) whose fortifications were subsequently improved at regular intervals so that on the eve of the First World War, Toul was acknowledged as one of the best-defended strongholds in Europe.

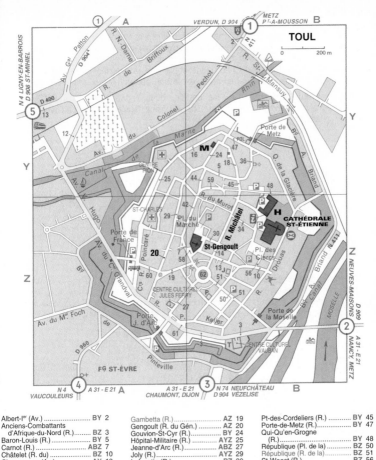

TOWN WALK

Maisons anciennes – There are Renaissance houses along **rue du Général-Gengoult** at nos 30, 28 and 26; one 14C house at no 8; the 17C is represented by nos 6 and 6bis (former Pimodan mansion) and no 4; **rue Michâtel** is also lined with a fine Renaissance house decorated with gargoyles (no 16).

★★Cathédrale St-Étienne ⊘ – *Closed for repairs (the violent storms which swept across France in December 1999 blew the roof off the cathedral).*
Work began on the chancel at the beginning of the 13C but the edifice was only completed in the 16C.
The cathedral's magnificent **west front★★**, built between 1460 and 1496, is a superb example of the Flamboyant style.
The interior shows characteristic features of the Champagne Gothic style: high and low galleries over the main arcades and the aisles, extremely pointed arcades, absence of triforium. The nave (30m/98ft high) is the most attractive part of the edifice.
Note, on the right, the fine **Renaissance chapel** surmounted by a coffered cupola.
Many **tombstones** dating from the 14C to the 18C pave the floor of the cathedral, particularly in the transept. Before leaving, have a look at the elegant Louis XV-style gallery supporting the monumental organ (1963) placed beneath the great rose-window.

Access to the cloister is through the small doorway opening onto place des Clercs.

★**Cloître** – The cloister, one of the largest in France, was built in the 13C and 14C. It only consists of three galleries with large openings forming equilateral arches; note the beautiful capitals decorated with foliage. The walls are adorned with trefoil arcading (in typical Champagne style) and interesting gargoyles. The **former chapter hall** houses an annual summer exhibition about the birth of a cathedral.

Ancien palais épiscopal – This edifice, built between 1735 and 1743, was restored and is now the town hall. The imposing **façade**★ is adorned with colossal-order pilasters.

Eating out

MID-RANGE

La Belle Époque – *31 av. Victor-Hugo* – ☎ *03 83 43 23 71* – *closed 23 Dec-5 Jan, Sat lunchtime, Mon evening and Sun* – *186F.* A small family restaurant near the station. Its small, slightly old-fashioned dining room has a zinc counter and tightly packed tables. The menu combines regional dishes and traditional cuisine. Reasonably priced lunchtime menu.

On the town

Place des Trois-Évêchés – *Pl. des Trois-Évêchés* – Most of the bars which are open in the evening are found in this central square. Sample the local speciality, the *vin gris de Toul*, so named for its pink colour which is obtained from the combination of Gamay, Pinot Noir and a third grape variety from the Auxerre region.

Leisure

Amycycles – *13 r. de la Halle* – ☎ *03 83 43 01 16* – *Tue-Fri 9am-noon, 2-7pm, Sat 9am-noon, 2-6pm.* Bikes for hire.

ADDITIONAL SIGHTS

Église St-Gengoult ⊙ – This former collegiate church, erected in the 13C and 15C, is a fine example of Champagne Gothic architecture. The west front has an elegant doorway dating from the 15C.
Inside, unusual features include the short but elegant nave and the very wide transept. Note the missing triforium and the style difference between the last two bays and of the first two which have to support the weight of the towers. The apsidal chapels open onto the chancel and the transept, a frequent occurrence in typical Champagne architecture. The chapels are lit by fine 13C **stained-glass windows**.

★★**Cloître St-Gencoult** – The cloister dates from the 16C. The Flamboyant openings confer considerable elegance to the ensemble. The outside decoration of the galleries is in Renaissance style (capitals, medallions) and gables underline the elevation of the arcades. The star vaulting has ornately worked keystones.

★**Musée municipal** ⊙ – *25 rue Gouvion-St-Cyr.* Housed on three floors in the former 18C Maison-Dieu (almshouse), the town museum contains various collections: painting, sculpture, Flemish tapestries, ceramics (Toul-Bellevue manufacture), religious art, antique and medieval archaeology (graves and Merovingian jewellery), popular art and traditions. A reconstructed drawing room in the Louis XVI style is decorated with a painting by F Boucher, *The Enjoyable Lesson.* The two world wars are illustrated by weapons, uniforms and mementoes of the main opponents' daily life. The **sick room**★ is a Gothic building of the early 13C, remodelled many times, used as a sanctuary and as a hospital ward for all kinds of sick people. The pointed vaulting is supported by six strong pillars.

Cloister of St Gencoult

EXCURSIONS

Église Notre-Dame-d'Écrouves – *4km/2.5mi W.* Built on a south-facing hillside once covered with vineyards, overlooking Toul's industrial depression, the former Église d'Écrouves, dedicated to Our Lady of the Nativity, has retained its 12C massive square belfry pierced with openings decorated with three colonnettes. The high 13C nave has had a double row of windows opening onto the roof space of the aisles since the edifice was reinforced in the 14C.

Vannes-le-Châtel – *18km S along D 960 to Blénod-lès-Toul then D 113.* This village has a long-standing tradition in the glassworks industry (Daum Crystalworks). It therefore seems only natural that a European research and training centre, known as the **Plate-forme verrière** ⊙, should have settled here. Its aim is to encourage craftsmen to create their own collection. The centre has an exhibition of contemporary works and a demonstration of various techniques including glass-blowing

Liverdun – *15km/9.3mi NE along D 90 which follows the east bank of the Moselle.* Liverdun nestles in a pleasant setting, inside a meander of the Moselle. Access to the small town on its south side is through a 16C town gate. The 13C **church** contains St Eucharius' tomb consisting of a 13C statue in a 16C frame.
Place de la Fontaine behind the church is lined with 16C arcading.
The carved door of the so-called Governor's House in **rue Porte-Haute** dates from the late 16C.
Guided tours of the town ⊙ are available.

Villey-le-Sec – *7km/4.3mi E along N 4 then D 909.*
This village, lying on top of a ridge overlooking the east bank of the Moselle, is the only example in France of a village combined with a fortified work of the late 19C.
★ **Ensemble fortifié** ⊙ – *Leave the car at the exit of the village, on the way to Toul.* Built in the space of five years, this fortified work did not play any defensive role during the First World War. The north battery with its special armour-plating, its ditch, its caponiers, its observation cupolas, its armour-plated revolving turret equipped with a 75mm/3in gun, whose firing chamber can be visited, appears like a forerunner of the later structural works of the Maginot Line.
Visitors are brought to the fort by narrow-gauge railway.
View of the south battery and south-west curtain wall.
The fort houses the ammunition stores and barracks, a museum (**Musée Séré de Rivières**) and a memorial crypt. There is also a military railway, an armour-plated turret equipped with a 155mm/6in gun in working order and an 1879 model of a Hotchkiss machine-gun.

Touring wine cellars

Société vinicole du Toulois, M. Laroppe – *253 r. de la République – 54200 Bruley –* ☎ *03 83 11 04 – 8am-noon and 2-6.30pm.* No charge for the tour and tasting.

Centre de promotion des produits des côtes de Toul – *6 r. Victor-Hugo – 54200 Bruley –* ☎ *03 83 64 55 09 – Mar-Dec: Tue-Sun 2-7pm.* Museum of vineyards and wine, tasting.

Lilièvre – *3, r. de la Gare – 54200 Lucey –* ☎ *03 83 63 81 36.* Tour of the cellars, vineyards and orchards. Tasting. The owners also sell organically grown produce and a farm-style "four o'clock" (light meal).

M. Claude Vosgien – *29 r. St-Vincent – 54113 Bulligny –* ☎ *03 83 62 50 66 – 9am-noon and 2-7pm.* Tour of the cellar and vineyards, tasting.

M. Michel Vosgien – *24 r. St-Vincent – 54113 Bulligny –* ☎ *03 83 62 50 55 – 9am-7pm.* The shop sells Côtes de Toul wine, liqueurs and cordials from Lorraine.

Coopérative des vignerons du Toulois – *54113 Mont-le-Vignoble –* ☎ *03 83 62 59 93.*

TROYES ★★★

The former capital of Champagne became a prosperous commercial city through its famous annual fairs as well as an artistic centre with a wealth of churches, museums, old houses and mansions.

The town has now expanded outside the ring of boulevards surrounding the centre, whose shape suggests a Champagne cork; it is surrounded by suburbs and industrial zones. Although Troyes has extended its industrial activities to other industries, it remains the main French hosiery centre following a long-standing tradition going back to the 16C.

HISTORICAL NOTES

St Loup and Attila – Built on the site of a Gaulish fortress, Troyes was Christianised in the 3C AD. In 451, the Huns led by Attila invaded Gaul, ransacking and destroying everything on their way. Reims was burnt down. The bishop of Troyes, St Loup, went to meet Attila in his camp and offered himself in exchange for the safety of his town. Attila was impressed and agreed to spare Troyes.

The counts of Champagne – In the 10C, the city came under the authority of the counts of Champagne. Some of them embellished it and made it prosperous. One of them, Henri I founded 13 churches, 13 hospitals – including the Hôtel-Dieu – extended the town and fully deserved his nickname, the Liberal.

His grandson, Thibaud IV, a knight-poet, founded the Champagne fairs and brought fame to the town.

When the last heiress of the counts of Champagne, Jeanne, married the king of France, Philippe le Bel, in 1284, her dowry included the Champagne region.

The shameful Treaty of Troyes – During the strife between Burgundians and Armagnacs at the height of the Hundred Years War, **Isabeau of Bavaria**, the wife of the mad French king, Charles VI, signed the shameful Treaty of Troyes disowning the dauphin (heir to the French throne) and sealing the marriage of Catherine of France with Henry V of England who was proclaimed regent pending his accession to the French throne on the death of Charles VI. Burgundian and English troops then occupied Troyes which was liberated by Joan of Arc in 1429.

Eating out

MODERATE

Salon de thé Potron Minet – *1 cours du Mortier-d'Or – ☎ 03 25 73 62 42 – closed 15 Aug-7 Sep and Mon – 68/78F.* In fine weather you can enjoy a home-made pastry or pie on the terrace, which is surrounded by lovely half-timbered buildings. Indoors, the elegant and refined decor is well suited to this tearoom in a 16C building.

Aux Crieurs de Vin – *4-6 pl. Jean-Jaurès – ☎ 03 25 40 01 01 – closed 1 week in Feb, 2 weeks in Aug, Sun and Mon – 95F.* Wine connoisseurs will appreciate this establishment. One part is a wine and spirits shop, and next to it is a bistro with an old-fashioned atmosphere. The cuisine will also please enthusiasts, with fresh produce from the market and a good choice of fish.

Bistrot Dupont – *5 pl. Charles-de-Gaulle – 10150 Pont-Ste-Marie – 3km/1.8mi NE of Troyes on N 77 – ☎ 03 25 80 90 99 – closed Sun evening and Mon – 90/150F.* Flowers and smiles from the staff provide a fine welcome. In a simple but carefully planned setting, the cheap and cheerful dishes are well adapted to the style of this bistro. Terrace in summer.

MID-RANGE

Le Bistroquet – *Pl. Langevin – ☎ 03 25 73 65 65 – closed Sun evening – 110/164F.* This restaurant is situated in the centre of the pedestrianised part of Troyes, and is reminiscent of a Parisian brasserie. The large dining room is attractively lit by a decorated glass ceiling, and has leather seats, indoor plants and a lively atmosphere. All dishes are based on fresh ingredients. Terrace with shrubs and outside lights.

Le Valentino – *Cour Rencontre – ☎ 03 25 73 14 14 – closed 2-22 Jan, 21 Aug-4 Sept, Sat lunchtime, Sun evening and Mon Oct-Easter – 110/270F.* In the pedestrianised town centre, the combination of an enthusiastic chef and an artistic proprietor results in creative cooking, in an original setting. The dining room is decorated with contemporary works of art and leads onto a veranda.

Where to stay

MID-RANGE

Hôtel de Troyes – *168 av. du Gén.-Leclerc* – ☎ *03 25 71 23 45* – **P** – *23 rooms 265/300F* – ⚏ *39F.* A useful place to stay on the outskirts of town. The rooms in this modern hotel are functional, well kept and soundproof. Pleasant lounge with glass roof and greenery.

Hôtel Le Champ des Oiseaux – *20 r. Linard-Gonthier* – ☎ *03 25 80 58 50* – **P** – *12 rooms 490/900F* – ⚏ *70F.* A lovely hotel near the cathedral, comprising three 15C-16C half-timbered houses restored by registered craftsmen. Personalised rooms with bright colours and charming furniture. Library. Garden and paved inner courtyard.

On the town

La Cocktaileraie – *56 r. Jaillant-Deschainets* – ☎ *03 25 73 77 04* – *Tue-Sat 5pm-3am, Sun 6pm-3am.* Businessmen and young lovers appreciate this high-class bar, whether discussing stock options and the Dow Jones or whispering sweet nothings. A hundred or so cocktails are on offer, around 45 whiskies and many prestigious Champagnes.

Le Bougnat des Pouilles – *29 r. Paillot-de-Montabert* – ☎ *03 25 73 59 85* – *Mon-Sat 6pm-3am.* The high-quality vintages in this wine bar are sought out by the young proprietor himself, among the smaller producers in the region. The walls are often hung with exhibitions of painting and photography. The atmosphere is very peaceful and the music an easygoing blend of jazz, blues and world music.

Le Chihuahua – *8 r. Charbonnet* – ☎ *03 25 73 33 53* – *Mon-Sat 6pm-3am.* This fashionable cellar bar also has dancing. Each Thursday a theme night takes place (tequila, techno...) and a rock concert is organised once a month. The barman's Tex-Mex cocktails are brilliant.

Le Relais St-Jean – *51 r. Paillot-de-Montabert* – ☎ *03 25 73 89 90* – *daily 24/24hr.* This three-star hotel has a classy bar, elegantly furnished in black and with subdued lighting. An ideal place to gather one's thoughts before a night at the nearby Tricasse or the Chihuahua. Specialities: cocktails and whiskies.

Le Tricasse – *16 r. Paillot-de-Montabert* – ☎ *03 25 73 14 80* – *Mon-Sat 3pm-3am.* This most famous of Troyes' nightspots is in a high-class area and offers a glorious mix of music, from jazz to salsa to house. It is frequented by students from the business school and engineers, among others. Billiards and darts. Rum is the house speciality.

Le Miami – *2 r. de la Croix-Blanche* – *10120 St-André-les-Vergers* – *SW of Troyes on N 77* – ☎ *03 25 74 73 95* – *Wed-Sat 10pm-5am.* This popular little discotheque plays music from the 1970-90s. There is a floor show (mind-reading, dancing girls...) on Thursdays or Fridays.

Shopping

Charcuterie Audry-Chantal – *Halles de l'Hôtel-de-Ville, Case 37* – ☎ *03 25 73 27 74* – *Mon 8am-12.45pm, Tue-Thu 7.30am-12.45pm, 3.30-7pm, Fri-Sat 7.30am-7pm, Sun 9am-12.30pm* – *closed 3 weeks in Jul and 2 weeks in Feb.* A good place for buying real home-made Troyes *andouillettes* (chitterling sausages).

La Boucherie Moderne – *Halles de l'Hôtel-de-Ville* – ☎ *03 25 73 32 64* – *Tue-Thu 7.30am-12.45pm, 3.30-7pm, Fri-Sat 7.30am-7pm, Sun 9am-12.30pm.* Here you can buy the famous Troyes chitterling sausages made by Gilbert Lemelle, the top manufacturer in France.

Marques Avenue – *114 bd de Dijon* – ☎ *03 25 82 00 72* – *Mon 2-7pm, Tue-Fri from 10am, Sat from 9.30am.* Marques Avenue is the biggest centre for *fins de séries* (discontinued stock) discount fashion stores in Europe. Here you will find all the big brand names, and not just French.

TROYES

Major artistic centre – The city's artistic activities multiplied from the Renaissance onwards. Ignoring the Italian influence which pervaded French artistic expression, artists continued to work along the lines of the great medieval tradition. The school of architecture was famous throughout Champagne and even in neighbouring Burgundy. Sculptors such as Jean Gailde and Jacques Julyot created a wealth of charming works. Stained-glass makers, such as Jehan Soudain and **Linard Gontier**, were also well established and, between the 14C and 17C, their workshops produced all the fine stained glass decorating the town's churches. This artistic tradition continued into the 17C with painters like **Pierre Mignard** and **François Girardon**, both native of Troyes.

Capital of hosiery – This long-standing tradition began at the beginning of the 16C, with a handful of manufacturers of hand-knitted bonnets and stockings.
In 1745, the Trinity Hospital (Hôtel de Mauroy) introduced special looms so that poor children in its care could learn to make stockings. The experiment was successful and in 1774, the hosiers' guild counted no fewer than 40 members. The industry further developed in the 19C and today it includes 250 firms employing 15 000 people.

★★OLD TOWN *allow 4hr*

In medieval times, Troyes consisted of two separate districts: the Cité, the aristocratic and ecclesiastical centre surrounding the cathedral, and the Bourg, the commercial middle-class area, where the Champagne fairs took place. In 1524, a fire swept through the town. The prosperous inhabitants took this opportunity to build the more opulent houses which you can see today as you stroll through the old town.
The timber-framed houses had cob walls and corbelled upper floors often supported by carved consoles and surmounted by pointed gables and tiled roofs. More opulent houses had walls of limestone rubble and brick in the traditional Champagne style.
The most elegant mansions were built of stone, an expensive building material in that region owing to the absence of hard-stone quarries.

Place Alexandre-Israël – The square is overlooked by the Louis XIII-style façade of the town hall. Note the motto over the porch, dating from the 1789 Revolution: Liberty, Equality, Fraternity or Death.

Start walking along rue Champeaux.

Rue Champeaux – This unusually wide 16C street was the district's main artery.
On the corner of rue Paillot-de-Montabert stands the **Maison du Boulanger** which houses the Thibaud-de-Champagne cultural centre; opposite, you can see the **Tourelle de l'Orfèvre** which owes its name to its first owner, a goldsmith. Partly clad with slates forming a chequered pattern, it is supported by caryatids and a telamon with goat's feet.
Turn round as you walk towards the Église St-Jean *(see p 356)* to admire this picturesque 16C architectural ensemble.

Walk alongside the church then follow rue Mignard which leads you back to rue Champeaux.

Half-timbered houses

Across the street stands the **Hôtel Juvénal-des-Ursins** dating from 1526. The white-stone façade is pierced by a doorway surmounted by a triangular pediment and a charming Renaissance oratory.

★**Ruelle des Chats** – A medieval atmosphere pervades this narrow lane lined with houses whose gables are so close that a cat can jump from one roof to the other. The bollards marking the entrance of the alleyway were placed there to prevent carriage wheels from hitting the walls of the houses. The street was closed by a portcullis at night.
The road widens and becomes rue des Chats.

On the left, a passageway leads to the **Cour du Mortier d'or**, a fine courtyard reconstructed with various ancient elements.

Continue along ruelle des Chats and turn left onto rue Charbonnet.

Hôtel de Marisy – Erected in 1531, this beautiful stone mansion is adorned with a charming Renaissance corner turret, decorated with figures and emblems.

Turn left onto rue des Quinze-Vingts then right onto rue de la Monnaie.

Rue de la Monnaie – The street is lined with fine timber-framed houses. At no 34 stands the 16C Hôtel de l'Élection, clad with shingles, at nos 32-36 the early-16C Hôtel de la Croix d'Or, the stone-built former residence of one of the town's mayors.

Turn left onto rue des Ursins and walk towards place Audiffred.

Note the 18C former mansion of another of Troyes' mayors, now housing the Chamber of Commerce and Industry.

Retrace your steps and continue along rue de la Monnaie.
Turn left onto rue Colbert and left again onto rue de la Bonneterie.

Place Jean-Jaurès – This is where the old Corn Exchange once stood.
The house on the corner of rue de Vauluisant is a fine example of Champagne bond (brick and limestone rubble). The corbelled upper part rests on consoles decorated with carved heads; on the corner stands a fine Virgin of the Apocalypse.

Turn right onto rue de Turenne.

On the corner, note the old house which has been erected over a modern one-storey building (the main doorway is on the first floor).

Hôtel de Chapelaines – *55 rue Turenne.* Beautiful Renaissance façade dating from 1524 to 1536.

Follow rue du Général-Saussier, then turn left onto rue de la Trinité.

★★**Hôtel de Mauroy** – This mansion is an interesting example of 16C local architecture. The façade overlooking the street shows a chequered bond typical of the Champagne region, whereas on the courtyard side (accessible during the tour of the museum), the building features a polygonal turret surrounded by timberframing, bricks, a chequered slatecladding and string-courses. Note also the Corinthian columns supporting the wooden gallery. The building was erected in 1550 by wealthy merchants and was turned into the Hôpital de la Trinité through the generosity of Jean de Mauroy. It was a home for poor children who were taught a trade during their stay. In 1745 special looms for making stockings were brought in and this marked the beginning of machine-made hosiery in Troyes. In 1966, the building was restored and turned into a museum.

Next door, on the corner of rue de la Trinité and rue Thérèse-Bordet, stands the Maison des Allemands.

Maison des Allemands – Built in the 16C and decorated in the 18C, this timber-framed house used to welcome German merchants in town for the fairs, hence its name. It is now the library of an ancient guild of craftsmen, the Compagnons du Devoir et du Tour de France.

Turn right onto rue Thérèse-Bordet, then right again onto rue Larivey leading to rue Général-Saussier.

Rue du Général-Saussier – The street is lined with fine old houses; no 26: Hôtel des Angoiselles with a pinnacled tower; a passageway leads to the picturesque inner courtyard surrounded by a gallery; no 11: 18C stone mansion where Napoleon stayed; no 3: fine stone-and-brick house roofed with glazed ceramic tiles, built during the first half of the 17C.

Retrace your steps and turn right onto rue de la Montée-des-Changes, which becomes a passageway beyond rue Émile-Zola and leads to place du Marché-au-Pain.

Place du Marché-au-Pain – During the Champagne fairs, the square was occupied by money changers. Note the fine view of the clock tower of the Église St-Jean.

Rue Urbain IV leads to place de la Libération. Cross the canal and follow rue Roger-Salengro then rue Linard-Gonthier, named after a famous 16C glass-blower.

At no 22 stands the Hôtel du Petit Louvre, the former residence of Henri de Poitiers (14C); turned into a coaching inn in 1821, it is now an international research centre.

Turn left towards place St-Pierre.

The Musée d'Art Moderne housed in the former bishop's palace and the cathedral with its doorways surmounted by elaborate gables are on the right.

Rue de la Cité – This street follows the former Roman way from Lyon to Boulogne, which intersected at right angles the road from Paris to Troyes.

Take a few steps along the peaceful rue du Paon, lined with timber-framed houses.

Across rue de la Cité is the former **Hôtel-Dieu**, dating from the 18C, now a branch of Reims University.

Cross the canal once more and walk along the north side of St-Urbain Basilica to return to place Alexandre-Israël.

Detail of the gate, Hôtel-Dieu

CHURCHES

★★Cathédrale St-Pierre-et-St-Paul – The cathedral, built between the 13C and 17C, has remarkable proportions, an exceptionally rich decoration and a beautiful nave. Martin Chambiges, who built the transept of Beauvais Cathedral and also worked on Sens Cathedral, contributed to the ornate west front (early 16C) adorned with a splendid Flamboyant rose-window. The three doorways are surmounted with richly carved gables. Sculptures and statues were destroyed during the Revolution. The cathedral was intended to have two towers, but the north tower alone *(restoration work in progress)* was completed in the 17C (height: 66m/217ft). A plaque on the base of the tower reminds visitors that Joan of Arc stayed in Troyes on 10 July 1429.

Walk along the north side of the cathedral in order to admire the north-transept doorway (13C) surmounted by a huge rose-window.

Interior – This vast sanctuary conveys an impression of power and lightness, of elegance and harmonious proportions.

The **stained-glass windows★★** date from different periods. Those of the chancel and ambulatory go back to the 13C. Note the warmth and intensity of the colours; they mainly depict isolated characters (popes and emperors) and scenes from the Life of the Virgin Mary. The windows of the nave, dating from the 16C, are completely different: they are more like real paintings on glass with red as the dominant colour. The most remarkable are, on the north side, the Story of the True Cross, the Legend of St Sebastian, the Story of Job and that of Toby; on the south side, the Story of Daniel and that of Joseph, the Parable of the Prodigal Son and a magnificent Tree of Jesse.

Mystical winepress

The rose-window of the west front by Martin Chambiges, was completed in 1546 and decorated with stained glass by Jehan Soudain: the Patriarchs surrounding God the Father. The rose is partially concealed behind the 18C organ case from Clairvaux Abbey. The fourth chapel along the north aisle is lit by the famous stained glass made in 1625 by Linard Gontier and known as the **mystical winepress**: Christ is seen lying beneath the winepress with blood coming out of the wound in his side and filling a chalice. Out of his chest grows a vine whose branches support the 12 Apostles.

★Treasury ⊘ – The cathedral treasury, exhibited in a 13C vaulted room, includes an 11C ivory box, four 11C cloisonné enamels representing the symbols of the four Evangelists, a 9C manuscript psalter with gold lettering, two missel covers inlaid with precious gems, the 12C reliquary of St Bernard, late-12C regional enamels, a 14C red cope embroidered with medallions and religious gold plate from the 16C to 19C.

★**Basilique St-Urbain** – This is a perfect example of 13C Gothic architecture from the Champagne region. It was built between 1262 and 1286, by order of Pope Urban IV, a native of Troyes, on the site of his father's workshop.

Exterior – The west front dates from the 19C but the doorway beneath the porch goes back to the 13C; the tympanum is decorated with the Last Judgement. Walk alongside the edifice to the east end to admire the graceful flying buttresses, the elegant windows, the delicate pinnacles, the gargoyles and the profusion of decorative features. The side doorways are protected by 14C porches.

Interior – One's attention is immediately drawn to the chancel, built in one go. Stained-glass windows are spread over a considerable area, a rare occurrence in Early Gothic architecture. The medallions of the low windows, the clerestory windows and high chancel windows, and the medallions of the Chapelle St-Joseph on the left of the chancel (Annunciation, Visitation, Holy Innocents) are all decorated with **13C stained-glass panels**.

The chapel on the right of the chancel contains the smiling **Virgin with the Grapes**, a fine example of 16C local sculpture.

★**Église Ste-Madeleine** – This is the town's oldest church. The original late-12C building was remodelled in the 16C; a new apse was erected between 1498 and 1501 and a Renaissance tower added to the west front.

The nave contains a remarkable stone **rood screen**★★, carved in Flamboyant style between 1508 and 1517 by Jean Gailde, a local sculptor and architect. It consists of three pointed arches underlined by delicate festoons and is decorated with a profusion of foliage and carved figurines dressed in Renaissance fashion. The work is surmounted by a balustrade with fleur-de-lis motifs; on the chancel side, a staircase, lined with grotesques, leads to the gallery. Note, on the side overlooking the north aisle, a graceful 16C Flemish sculpture in painted and gilt wood.

★**Stained-glass windows** – The east end is decorated with brightly coloured Renaissance windows: from left to right the Life of St Louis (1507), the Creation (1500), the Legend of St Eloi (1506), the Tree of Jesse (1510), the Passion (1494), the Life of Mary-Magdalene (1506) and the Triumph of the Cross.

In the south aisle, against a pillar of the nave, stands a statue of **Martha**★, by the Master of Chaource, one of the main exponents of 16C sculpture in Troyes *(see p 360)*.

Opposite, in the north aisle, there is a wooden statue of Robert de Molesme (early 15C), who founded the Cistercian Order.

As you come out of the church, note, on your left, the Flamboyant doorway of the former charnel house (1525) decorated with a salamander, the emblem of King François I, and his initial, F.

Église Ste-Madeleine – Rood screen

★**Église St-Pantaléon** – This 16C church, covered with a wooden vault in the 17C and lit by tall Renaissance windows with *grisaille* stained glass, contains an important collection of **statues**★ mostly standing against the pillars of the nave; these statues come from churches which were destroyed during the Revolution. Note, against the first pillar on the right, the statue of St James by **Dominique Florentin**, which is a self portrait and, opposite, the pulpit, a Gothic Mater Dolorosa; the pillars of the chancel are adorned with Charity and Faith by Dominique Florentin, which denote an Italian influence.

Église St-Jean – It was in this church that the marriage of Catherine de France (daughter of Charles VI and Isabeau of Bavaria) and Henry V of England was celebrated in 1420. The clock tower dates from the 14C. The Gothic nave is relatively low whereas the chancel, rebuilt at the beginning of the 16C, is quite high. The altar is surmounted by two paintings by Mignard. The marble-and-bronze tabernacle was made in 1692 after drawings by Girardon.

Église St-Nicolas ⊘ – Rebuilt after the fire of 1524, this church has a south doorway flanked by pilasters and decorated with statues by François Gentil. Inside, the gallery is markedly ornate. Take the staircase in the aisle to admire the keystone pendentives of the Flamboyant vaulting.

Église St-Remy ⊘ – Originally built in the 14C and 16C, the now-restored church has a delicate spiral steeple covered with slates and flanked by pointed pinnacles.
The interior is adorned with numerous 16C wooden panels painted in *grisaille*, as well as low-relief medallions (Death praying, Jesus and the Virgin) and a bronze crucifix by Girardon, who was one of the parishioners.

Église St-Nizier ⊘ – This 16C church covered with brightly coloured glazed tiles can be seen from afar. It contains a beautiful Entombment and a 16C *Pietà*.

MUSEUMS

★★**Musée d'Art moderne** ⊘ – In 1976, two local industrialists, Pierre and Denise Levy, donated to the State the numerous works of art they had been collecting since 1939. The town then decided to house the collection in the buildings of the former bishop's palace.

The building – Erected around a courtyard, the palace consists of a Renaissance edifice featuring brick-and-stone chequered walls, in characteristic Champagne style, and a 17C wing bearing the arms of the bishop who had it built.

The Collections – There are 388 paintings from the 19C and the early 20C, 1 277 drawings, 104 sculptures, glassware and works of African and Oceanian art.
Fauvism★★ is particularly well represented. The fauves (wild beasts) were so-called for their pure, brilliant colours applied straight from the tube in what was qualified as an aggressive style. The Levy collection includes works by Derain *(Hyde Park, Big Ben)*, Vlaminck *(Landscape in Chatou)*, Braque *(Landscape at l'Estaque)* and Van Dongen.
The first few rooms contain earlier paintings by Courbet, Degas, Seurat *(The Anglers*, a study which he used for his painting *The Grande Jatte)*, Vallotton *(Woman sewing indoors)* and Vuillard.
More recent works include paintings by Robert Delaunay before his abstract period, works by Roger de la Fresnaye, Modigliani, Soutine, Buffet, Nicolas de Staël, Balthus and numerous post-fauvist paintings by **Derain**.
There are also a number of works by Maurice Marinot, a painter who became a stained-glass maker; note his unusual Art Deco creations.
The collection of **African art** includes statues, reliquary figures, spoons, a bronze statue from Benin, and headdresses representing stylised antelopes which inspired many artists at the turn of the 20C.

★★**Maison de l'Outil et de la Pensée ouvrière** ⊘ – This museum is housed in the Hôtel de Mauroy *(see p 353)* restored by the **Compagnons du Devoir**.
An itinerary *(detailed notice available)* enables visitors to admire a great number of 18C tools used for various crafts, exhibited in large glass cases. Some of these tools were carved or engraved by the craftsman who used them.
A large room, in the courtyard on the left, contains works by master craftsmen.
The **library**, adjacent to the museum, is devoted to literature concerning the working class and includes many technical works, encyclopaedias and history books.

★Hôtel de Vauluisant ⊙ – This 16C mansion has a fine Renaissance turreted façade and 17C side buildings. Note the large reception room with its French-style ceiling and its magnificent stone fireplace. The mansion contains two museums.

★Musée historique de Troyes et de Champagne – The museum is in two sections.

The first section illustrates regional art from the Romanesque period to the end of the 16C with works by members of the famous School of Troyes: sculpture, including a Christ on the cross believed to be by the Master of Chaource, paintings and a few objets d'art.

Painting by Valton

One room, devoted to 16C local architecture, displays wood carvings, paintings and graphic documents.

Another room presents an overall view of the local school of stained-glass decoration from the late 15C to the beginning of the 17C.

Terracotta floor tiles dating from the 13C to the 17C are displayed in the vaulted cellars.

The painting by Valton reproduced above shows women in traditional local dress choosing shawls from a merchant.

Musée de la Bonneterie – This museum is devoted to hosiery, which has been the town's main activity since the 16C. Several rooms illustrate the history of hosiery and the different manufacturing processes; there is a fine collection of embroidered stockings as well as several machines and looms, the oldest dating from the 18C. The reconstruction of a 19C workshop shows the evolution of techniques.

Abbaye St-Loup ⊙ – The buildings of the former abbey, dating from the 17C and 18C and extended later, now house two museums and the library.

Musée d'Histoire naturelle – The Natural History Museum, occupying part of the ground floor, contains a collection of mammals and birds from all over the world. Skeletons, rocks and meteorites are exhibited in the cloister.

★Musée des Beaux-Arts et d'Archéologie – **Regional archaeological collections★** from prehistory to the Merovingian period are displayed in the former cellars of the abbey. Main exhibits include the Apollo from Vaupoisson, a Gallo-Roman bronze statue, and the Pouan treasury, an exceptional collection of weapons and jewellery found in a 5C Merovingian grave.

The gallery of **medieval sculpture** testifies to the creative activity of the Champagne region from the 13C to the 15C: capitals, gargoyles, 13C Christ on the cross.

The mezzanine houses the collection of **drawings and miniatures** from the 16C to the 18C, shown in rotation.

The gallery of **painting** displays works of all the major schools from the 15C to the 19C. The 17C is particularly well represented with paintings by Rubens, Van Dyck, Philippe de Champaigne, Jacques de Létrin, Le Brun, Mignard... There is also a rich collection of 18C works by Watteau *(The Enchanter* and *The Adventurer)*, Natoire, Boucher, Fragonard, Lépicié, Greuze *(Portrait of a child with a cat)*, and David and Elisabeth Vigée-Lebrun *(The countess of Bossancourt)*.

These rooms also contain sculpture (works by Girardon), 16C enamels and furniture.

Bibliothèque – Founded in 1651, the library owns more than 340 000 works, including 8 000 manuscripts and 700 incunabula from the 7C onwards. The **great hall**, which can be seen through a glass panel on the first floor of the museum, used to be the canons' dormitory.

Hôtel-Dieu-le-Comte – This 18C edifice houses a branch of Reims University. The fine wrought-iron gate opening onto rue de la Cité was made in 1760 by Pierre Delphin. The **pharmacy★** ⊙ contains a rich collection of 18C earthenware jars, 320 painted wooden boxes decorated with plant motifs and 16C and 17C bronze mortars. The former laboratory has been turned into a museum: 16C reliquary busts, pewter jugs... The chapel dates from the 18C.

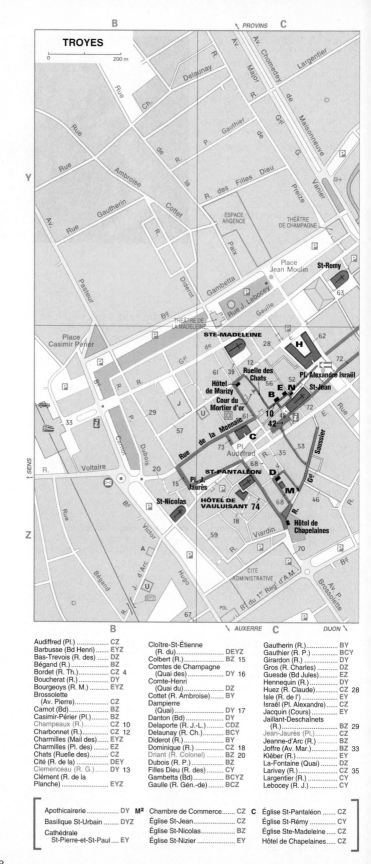

TROYES

0 — 200 m

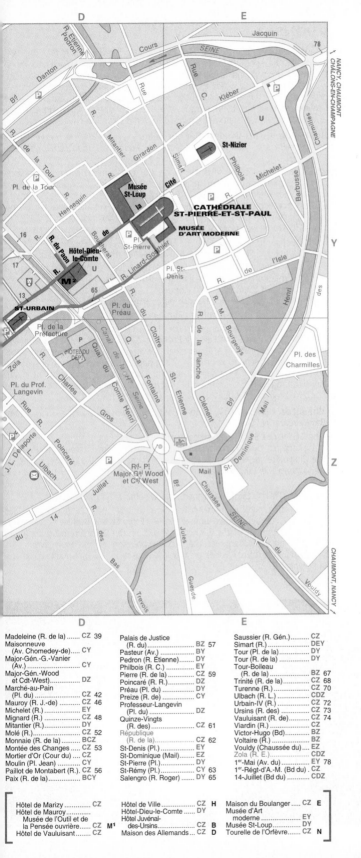

EXCURSIONS

St-Parres-aux-Tertres – *5km/3mi E along avenue du 1er-Mai and N 19.* The 16C church stands on the spot where St Parres, a 3C local martyr, is believed to be buried. The south doorway has retained its Renaissance ornamentation. Inside, note the lovely 16C stained-glass windows and many works of art: statue of St Parres in the north chapel, Virgin and Child in the south chapel. A building, known as the **Nécropole paléochrétienne**, has been purposely erected to display Gallo-Roman sarcophagi and various objects found in graves discovered near the church.

Isle-Aumont; Rumilly-lès-Vaudes; Bar-sur-Seine – *41km/25.5mi. Leave Troyes by avenue Pierre-Brossolette and drive 8.5km/5mi along N 71 then turn right onto D 444.*

Isle-Aumont – There have been settlements on the Isle-Aumont promontory since Neolithic times: pagan and Christian sanctuaries, Viking camp, necropolis, monasteries and castles succeeded one another and the site still bears traces of all of them. Several edifices preceded the present **church** ⊙ which has retained the 10C semi-circular apse beneath the present chancel. A Gothic nave was added, in the 15C to 16C, to the 12C Romanesque nave which now contains sarcophagi, capitals and a statue of Martha. In the Gothic nave on the right, note the fine 13C wooden crucifix.

Return to N 71 and drive SE to St-Parres-lès-Vaudes then turn right onto D 28.

Rumilly-lès-Vaudes – Fine 16C church with a richly carved doorway, containing a splendid polychrome-stone **altarpiece★** dating from 1533 and a few 16C stained-glass windows, some of them by Linard Gontier.
The elegant castle, flanked by turrets, also dates from the 16C.

Return to N 71, turn right and continue to Bar-sur-Seine.

Bar-sur-Seine – From its prosperous past (16C-17C), this small town has retained a fine ensemble of old houses. The **Église St-Étienne** is a mixture of Gothic and Renaissance styles. The **interior★** offers an interesting set of *grisaille* stained-glass windows typical of the local 16C school. Four low-relief sculptures in the south transept are believed to be the work of Dominique Florentin. The alabaster panels of the north transept, illustrating the Life of the Virgin, together with the statues of St Anne and St Joseph are by François Gentil.

Bouilly; Chaource – *34km/21mi. Leave Troyes along boulevard Victor-Hugo, boulevard de Belgique and N 77.*

Bouilly – The 16C **Église St-Laurent** ⊙, restored in the 18C has a remarkable Renaissance stone altarpiece over the high altar, representing scenes from the Passion; beneath the altarpiece, note the delicate low-relief carving depicting the legend of St Laurence; among the 16C statues, there is an interesting St Sebastian and a fine St Margaret.

Continue along N 77 for 5.5km/3.4mi then turn left onto D 34 to Chaource.

★**Chaource** – This village, which has given its name to a famous creamy cheese, has retained a few 15C timber-framed houses. In the **Église St-Jean-Baptiste★**, the semi-basement chapel on the left of the 13C chancel contains an **Entombment★★** carved in 1515 by the Master of Chaource; the facial expression of the Holy Women is extremely moving. The third chapel on the left houses a 16C **gilt-wood crib** in the shape of a polyptych.

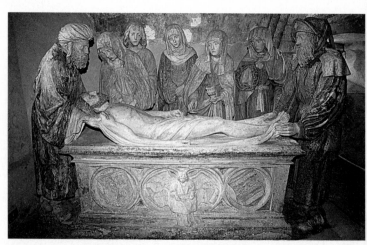

The Entombment, in St-Jean-Baptiste church

Maisons-lès-Chaource – *6km/3.7mi S along D 34*. This building houses an interesting **Musée des Poupées d'antan et de la Tonnellerie** ⊙ (Museum of antique dolls and cooperage), which displays a collection of fine dolls with porcelain heads next to the reconstruction of a cooper's workshop. The visit ends with a convivial cheese tasting and a glass of the local aperitif.

Pont-Ste-Marie; Ste-Maure; Fontaine-lès-Grès – *46km/29mi. Drive E out of Troyes along avenue du 1er-Mai*.

Pont-Ste-Marie – The 16C **church** ⊙ has a fine west front adorned with three monumental doorways; the central doorway is Flamboyant whereas the other two are fine examples of the Renaissance style. Beautiful stained-glass window by Linard Gontier.

Follow D 78 NW to Ste-Maure.

Ste-Maure – 15C **church** ⊙ with Renaissance chancel containing the tomb of St Maure (9C sarcophagus).

Continue along D 78 to Rilly -Ste-Syre and turn left to Fontaine-lès-Grès.

Fontaine-lès-Grès – The **Église St-Agnès**★ was erected in 1956 by the architect Michel Marot. This triangular church is surmounted by a slender steeple. Inside, light filters through an opening concealed in the steeple and falls onto the high altar, lighting a 13C wooden crucifix of the Spanish School.

Follow N 19 back to Troyes.

★★**Parc naturel régional de la Forêt d'Orient** – *10km/6.2mi East of Troyes*. This nature park offers a choice of outdoor activities on and around its lakes *(see Parc naturel régional de la FORÊT D'ORIENT)*.

TURCKHEIM★

Population 3 567
Michelin map 87 fold 17 or 242 fold 31 – Local map see Route des VINS

This ancient little town lying just outside Colmar, on the north bank of the River Flecht, has retained its fortifications and its long-standing traditions: every evening at 10pm *(from May to October)*, Alsace's last night watchman walks through the streets, wrapped in his great coat and carrying his halberd, his lamp and his horn. He stops and sings at every street corner.

It was here that **Turenne**, France's 17C military genius, won one of his most famous battles against a far-superior imperial army from across the Rhine, during the Alsatian campaign of 1674-75 which cost him his life.

To catch the most picturesque view of the town with its ancient roofs, colourful church tower and stork nests, it is best to arrive from the north along the scenic road running from Niedermorschwihr to Turckheim across famous vineyards.

SIGHTS

The town, shaped like a triangle, had three main gates.

Porte de France – Facing the river embankment, it consists of a massive 14C quadrangular tower crowned by a stork nest.

Eating out

Place Turenne – The square is surrounded by ancient houses: on the right is the former guard-house with a fountain in front. Across the square is the brightly painted town hall surmounted by a Renaissance gable; behind it stands the old church with its partly Romanesque tower.

Grand'Rue – The street is lined with numerous late-16C and early-17C houses. Note the timber-framed house *(on the right as you walk away from place Turenne)* with its oriel resting on a wooden pillar.

Porte de Munster – Named after the nearby town and a famous local cheese, this is another of the town's main gates.

Hôtel des Deux-Clefs – This is the former town hostel, renovated in 1620, a charming Alsatian house adorned with an elegant loggia and carved beams.

VAUCOULEURS

Population 2 401
Michelin map 62 fold 3 or 242 fold 21

Pleasantly situated opposite the hills stretched along the east bank of the River Meuse, Vaucouleurs has retained part of its 13C fortifications. The peaceful little town offers visitors boat trips on the Marne-to-Rhine canal and hikes through the forested Parc naturel régional de Lorraine.

In May 1428, a young shepherdess from Domrémy *(19km/12mi south)* arrived in Vaucouleurs to see the governor and told him that God had sent her to save France. Robert de Baudricourt's first reaction was to send her back to her village but Joan of Arc persisted and after several months, urged by public enthusiasm, Baudricourt gave in and agreed to help. In February 1429, Joan left Vaucouleurs with a small escort by the Porte de France on her way to meet the king of France and her destiny which would eventually lead her to Rouen where she died on 30 May 1431.

SIGHTS

Porte de France – Joan of Arc and her escort left Vaucouleurs through this gate. Very little remains of the original gate.

Site du château – Excavations were undertaken to expose the ruins of the castle where Joan was received by Baudricourt in 1428. All that is left is the upper part of the Porte de France rebuilt in the 17C and an arch of the main doorway. A neo-Gothic church was built on the site. A huge lime tree is believed to date back to Joan of Arc's time.

Église – The vaulting of the 18C church is decorated with frescoes. The church-wardens' pew and the pulpit (1717) are elaborately carved.

Place de l'Hôtel de ville – On this square stands a statue of Joan of Arc brought back from Algiers.

Chapelle castrale ⊙ – The chapel was built over the 13C crypt of the former castle chapel consisting of three separate chapels. The central chapel contains the statue of Notre-Dame-des-Voûtes before which Joan used to pray during her stay in Vaucouleurs.

Musée Jeanne d'Arc ⊙ – Housed in the right wing of the town hall, this museum is devoted to local history and archaeology.

The most remarkable exhibit is the **Christ de Septfonds**, a magnificent oak crucifix from a nearby chapel where Joan of Arc went to pray for guidance when, at first, Baudricourt refused to take her seriously.

EXCURSION

★**Domrémy-la-Pucelle** – *19km/12mi S along D 964 then D 164.*
This humble village is the birthplace of Joan of Arc (1412-31), the pious peasant girl who heard voices ordering her to deliver France and the king from the English. An important annual pilgrimage takes place on the second Sunday in May, Joan of Arc's feast day, in Bois-Chenu Basilica *(see below)*.

The **church**, which Joan of Arc knew, was remodelled in the 15C and extended in 1825. The entrance is now situated where the former chancel stood. However, it has retained of few objects which were familiar to the young girl: a stoop on the right as you go in, a statue of St Margaret (14C) against the first pillar on the right, the font over which she was christened in the transept.

★**Maison natale de Jeanne d'Arc** ⊙ – The house in which Joan of Arc was born is that of a comfortable peasant family; the walls are thick and the door is surmounted by the emblem of the family next to the arms of the kingdom of France. A recess houses a copy of a 16C statue of Joan kneeling (the original is in the museum).

Birthplace of Joan of Arc

On the left-hand side of the house, a small museum contains maps, documents, prints concerning the history of the region and Joan of Arc's youth and mission.

Basilique du Bois-Chenu – *1.5km/0.9mi along D 53 towards Coussey.*
Consecrated in 1926, the basilica stands on the site where Joan heard the voices of St Catherine, St Margaret and St Michael telling her about her mission. Start with the crypt *(entrance on the left)*; statue of Notre-Dame-de-Bermont before which Joan prayed every Saturday. Walk up the fine staircase decorated with the emblems of the towns where Joan stayed. The basilica contains frescoes illustrating Joan's life. The mosaics decorating the chancel and the cupola depict Joan being sent on her mission and entering the Kingdom of Glory.
Leave by the side door. The Stations of the Cross lead to the adjacent wood.

VERDUN★★

Population 20 753
Michelin map 57 fold 11 or 241 fold 23

This ancient stronghold occupies a strategic position on the west bank of the Meuse, which flows between well-defined hills. The upper town – cathedral and citadel – is camped on an outcrop overlooking the river.

HISTORICAL NOTES

Verdun started out as a Gaulish fortress, then became a Roman fort under the name of Virodunum Castrum. In 843, the treaty splitting the Carolingian Empire into three kingdoms was signed in the city which was ceded to the kingdom of Lorraine. In 1552, Verdun was seized by Henri II and became part of the French kingdom.
Occupied briefly by the Prussians in 1792, it was liberated following the French victory at Valmy in the Argonne *(see STE-MENEHOULD: Excursions)*.
In 1870, the town was again besieged by the Prussians and was forced to capitulate. The occupation lasted three years.
At the start of the First World War, Verdun was, together with Toul, the most powerful stronghold in eastern France. The famous and extremely bloody Battle of Verdun, took place all round the town between February 1916 and August 1917.

The Battle of Verdun

German troops had, since 1914, been trying in vain to skirt round Verdun and then to take it. Verdun nevertheless remained a formidable obstacle with its powerful citadel, its ring of forts and its gullied wooded plateaux. Yet this is where the German army, led by General von Falkenhayn, decided to strike a heavy blow in February 1916 in the hope of weakening the French army, lifting their own morale and thwarting the offensive which they suspected the Allies to be preparing (it actually came in July on the Somme). The Crown Prince Emperor William II's own son, was entrusted with the operation.
The German offensive, masterfully orchestrated, took the French high command by surprise.

363

German offensive (February-August 1916) – It began on 21 February, 13km/8mi north of Verdun, with the heaviest concentration of shelling ever experienced. The resistance was stronger than expected but the Germans progressed slowly and the Fort de Douaumont soon fell, thus becoming a threat to the city. General Pétain, who was made commander in chief of the Verdun forces, began to organise the defence of the city. Reinforcements and supplies were brought in via the only available route, Bar-le-Duc to Verdun, nicknamed the **sacred way**.

The frontal attack was finally stopped on 26 February and, in March and April, German troops widened the front on both banks of the Meuse but failed to take several key positions.

There followed a savage war of attrition: forts, ruined villages or woods were taken over and over again at a terrible cost in human lives.

On 11 July, German troops finally received the order to remain on the defensive.

The Russian offensive and the Franco-British offensive on the Somme put an end to any hope the Germans may have had of taking the advantage at Verdun.

French counter-offensive (October 1916-October 1917) – Three brilliant but costly offensives enabled French troops to take back all lost ground:

– the **Bataille de Douaumont-Vaux** (24 October-2 November 1916) on the east bank,

– the **Bataille de Louvemont-Bezonvaux** (15-18 December 1916), also on the east bank, which cleared the Vaux and Douaumont sectors once and for all.

– the **Bataille de la Cote 304 et du Mort-Homme** (20-24 August 1917) on the west bank; German troops were forced back to the positions they held on 22 February 1916 and tried in vain to counter-attack until well into October. The pressure on Verdun was released but it was only in September-October 1918, following the Franco-American offensive, that the front line was pushed back beyond its position of February 1916.

Eating out

MODERATE

Le Forum – 35 r. des Gros-Degrés – ☎ 03 29 86 46 88 – closed 23 Jul-12 Aug, Wed evening and Sun – 90/150F. The owner has changed careers, from accountant to restaurateur and occasional painter. His wife does the cooking while he welcomes the customers in the two vaulted dining rooms, which are decorated with his works. A good place to eat, not far from the town centre.

Where to stay

MID-RANGE

Chambre d'hôte Château de Labessière – 55320 Ancemont – 15km/9.3mi S of Verdun on D 34 (St-Mihiel road) – ☎ 03 29 85 70 21 – rene.eichenauer@wanadoo.fr – closed Christmas and New Year – ☞– 3 rooms 400/450F – evening meal 150F. An 18C castle which has miraculously survived unscathed through the last two wars. Its charming rooms are not too large and contain old furniture, and the dining room is stylish. A pretty garden and swimming pool add to the pleasure of your stay.

On the town

Havana Club – 42 r. des Rouyers – ☎ 03 29 86 73 44 – xana.cardoso@wana-doo.fr – daily 5pm-4am. An elegant bar with ochre-coloured walls, where the wreaths of cigar smoke mingle with the discreet sound of Latin-American music. Sink into a superb leather armchair and enjoy the atmosphere of this club, while sipping a glass of wine, a whisky or beer, and sampling a Cuban cigar.

L'Estaminet – 45 r. des Rouyers – ☎ 03 29 86 07 86 – Mon-Sat 2pm-3am. A friendly pub, decorated with murals, old posters and dolls dressed as witches, who watch over the bar. A good choice of unusual beers and cigars to sample, to a background of old jazz. Billiard table on the first floor.

Shopping

Dragées Braquier – 3 r. Pasteur – ☎ 03 29 86 05 02 – Tue-Sat 9am-noon, 2.30-7pm. This old-fashioned little shop is the place to find the famous dragées de Verdun, the sweets that Goethe bought after the town was captured by the Prussians in 1792. Other regional specialities include madeleines from Commercy and the famous redcurrant jam from Bar-le-Duc, deseeded with the help of a goose feather.

★VILLE HAUTE *1hr 30min*

Start from the tourist office. Walk across the bridge.

Porte Chaussée – This 14C building used to guard the entrance of the town and served as a prison; it is flanked by two round towers with crenellations and machicolations; the protruding front part was added in the 17C. It formed part of a thick wall surrounding the town and skirting the west bank of the River Meuse.

Take rue des Frères-Boulhaut on the right, walk round the left side of place Vauban to reach rue St-Paul.

★**Cathédrale Notre-Dame** – Standing at the highest point of the town, the Romanesque cathedral was built between 990 and 1024 in characteristic Rhenish style, with two chancels and two transepts. The west chancel is typically Rhenish, the east chancel (1130-40), denotes the Burgundian influence. The nave was covered with pointed vaulting in the 14C.

After the fire of 1755 which destroyed the Romanesque towers, it was decided to introduce the Baroque style when doing repair work. On the west side, two balustraded square towers were erected on the base of the former belfries; in the nave, the existing Gothic vaulting was replaced by rounded vaulting and the pillars were decorated with mouldings; the high altar was surmounted by an imposing baldaquin with twisted columns; the crypt was filled in and the Romanesque doorways concealed. The Romanesque part of the edifice was fortunately restored following the shelling of 1916. The 12C crypt was excavated and the **Portail du Lion** (Lion's doorway) brought to light, with its fine tympanum illustrating Christ in glory inside a mandorla, surrounded by the symbols of the four Evangelists. All the stained glass destroyed in 1916 has been replaced.

Crypt – Note the beautiful capitals decorated with acanthus leaves along the aisles. The new capitals are carved with scenes illustrating Life in the trenches, Suffering and Death.

★**Cloître** – The cloister, built on the south side of the cathedral, consists of three galleries: one of these, on the east side has retained three 14C arched openings which once led to the chapter-house; the other two galleries were built in the Flamboyant style between 1509 and 1517 and covered with network vaulting.

Walk along the north side of the cathedral to place Châtel.

Porte Châtel – The 13C gate, crowned by 15C machicolations, leads to place de la Roche offering a fine view of the town.

Palais épiscopal

★**Palais épiscopal** – The bishop's palace was built in the 18C by Robert de Cotte on a rock spur overlooking the Meuse. The courtyard, shaped like an elongated semicircle precedes the main building. The town's library is located in the west wing. The other part of the palace houses the Centre mondial de la Paix.

Walk back along rue de Rû to place du Maréchal-Foch.

Hôtel de ville – This former private mansion dating from 1623 is a fine example of Louis XIII style.

Musée de la Princerie ⊙ – The museum is housed in the former residence of the Princier or Primicier who was the most important ecclesiastical dignitary after the bishop. The edifice is an elegant mansion with a 16C arcaded courtyard. The rooms are devoted to prehistory, to the Gallo-Roman and Merovingian periods, to the Middle Ages and to the Renaissance. Note the 12C carved-ivory comb (first room), several medieval statues, ancient earthenware from the Argonne region and paintings by local artists such as Jules Bastien Lepage and Louis Hector Leroux.

VERDUN

Alsace-Lorraine (Av.)	CZ 2	Douaumont (Av. de)	CY 6
Beaurepaire (R.)	CZ 3	Foch (Pl. Mar.)	CY 7
Belle-Vierge (R. de la)	BY 4	Fort de Vaux (R. du)	CZ 8
Chevert (Pl.)	CZ 5	Frères-Boulhaut (R. des)	CY 9
		Lattre-de-Tassigny	
		(Av. Mar. de)	CY 10
		Mautroté (R.)	BY 13

Mazel (R.)	CY 14
Prés.-Poincaré (R.)	CZ 17
République (Q. de la)	CY 18
Rû (R. de)	BZ 19
St-Paul (R.)	CY 20
St-Pierre (R.)	BY 21
Soupirs (Allée des)	BY 24

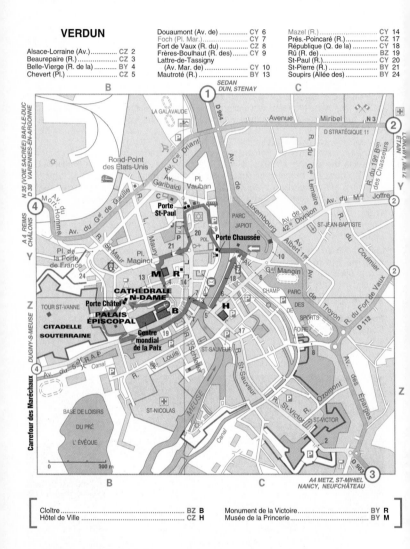

Cloître	BZ B	Monument de la Victoire	BY R
Hôtel de Ville	CZ H	Musée de la Princerie	BY M

WAR AND PEACE

In town

★**Citadelle souterraine** ⊙ – *30min.* The citadel was built on the site of the famous Abbaye de St-Vanne, founded in 952. One of the abbey's 12C towers was retained by Vauban when he rebuilt the citadel.

In 1916-17, the citadel was used as a rest area for troops taking part in the Battle of Verdun. The 7km/4.3mi of galleries were equipped to fulfil the needs of a whole army: arsenal, telephone exchange, hospital with operating theatre, kitchens, bakery (nine ovens could turn out 28 000 rations of bread in 24 hours), butcher's and cooperative.

A self-guided vehicle takes visitors on a **round tour**★★ of the citadel where the soldiers' daily life during the Battle of Verdun is recreated through sound effects, lively scenes, virtual pictures (HQ, bakery) and reconstructed scenes, in particular "Life in the trenches".

On 10 November 1920, during a ceremony staged in the Salle des Fêtes (meeting hall), in the presence of the French war minister, André Maginot, the youngest volunteer, a soldier in the 132nd infantry regiment, named Auguste Thin, was asked to choose among eight coffins, that of the unknown soldier, who would be laid to rest beneath the Arc de Triomphe. He added the figures of his regiment and chose the sixth coffin.

Carrefour des Maréchaux – Large statues of marshals and generals of the French Empire, of the war of 1870 and of the First World War stand inside the fortification ditches, some 0.8km/0.5mi from the citadel.

Centre mondial de la Paix ⊙ – The permanent exhibition of the World Peace Centre is divided into seven sections: war, the earth and its frontiers, from war to peace, Europe, the United Nations for peace, human rights, peace concepts.
The centre, which has a specialised information department, welcomes groups of school children.

Monument de la Victoire ⊙ – Seventy three steps lead to a terrace on which stands a high pyramid surmounted by the statue of a warrior wearing a helmet and leaning on his sword, as a symbol of Verdun's defence.
The **crypt** beneath the monument bears the list of all the ex-servicemen who were awarded the medal of Verdun.

★★★The battlefields

Thousands of visitors come every year and wander through the battlefields where fierce fighting took place from 21 February 1916 to 20 August 1917 in what is now known as the **Battle of Verdun**.
In less than two years, this battle, which unfolded along a 200km/124mi front, involved several million soldiers and caused the death of 400 000 Frenchmen and almost as many Germans as well as several thousand American soldiers.
Several decades later, a huge area covering some 200km^2/72sq mi on both banks of the Meuse still bears the marks of the fighting.

East bank of the Meuse

21km/13mi – about 3hr. Michelin map 241 folds 19 and 23

This was the main sector of the battle, where the decisive turning point occurred.

Drive E along avenue de la 42e-Division then avenue du Maréchal-Joffre and leave Verdun by ② on the town plan, N 3 towards Étain.

Cimetière militaire du Faubourg-Pavé – Drive through Faubourg-Pavé; on the left, there is a cemetery containing the graves of 5 000 soldiers.

Turn left past the cemetery onto D 112 towards Mogeville.

On the right, 6km/3.7mi further on, stand the **Monument Maginot** and Souville Fort.

At the intersection of D 112 and D 913, turn right onto D 913 towards Verdun then left onto D 913^A towards the Fort de Vaux.

The terrain is in a complete upheaval. On the right, slightly off the road, stands the **Monument des Fusillés de Tavannes**, a reminder of an episode of the Second World War *(it is possible to drive along the path to the monument).*

Fort de Vaux ⊙ – Thirst drove the garrison to surrender on 7 June 1916 after two months' heroic resistance; the fort was reoccupied by the French five months later. The tour enables visitors to see a number of galleries. From the top, there is a good view of the ossuary, cemetery and fort of Douaumont, the Côtes de la Meuse and Plaine de la Woëvre.

Return to D 913 and turn right towards Fleury and Douaumont.

On the left, Souville Fort, the last bastion guarding Verdun, can barely be seen. At the Chapelle Ste-Fine crossroads, the Monument du Lion marks the most forward position reached by the Germans.

Mémorial de Verdun ⊙ – Video films, an illustrated map and slide shows explain the various stages of the battle and a collection of uniforms, weapons, pieces of equipment and documents illustrate the fierce fighting which took place.
A little further on, a stela marks the site of the former village of **Fleury-devant-Douaumont**, which was taken 16 times.

Turn right onto D 913^B leading to Douaumont.

Fort de Douaumont ⊙ – The fort was stone built on a height in 1885, (388m/1 273ft) which accounted for its strategic importance. Reinforced several times, it was covered with a layer of concrete 1m/3ft thick resting over a layer of sand also 1m/3ft thick. Taken by surprise at the beginning of the German offensive, it was recaptured by the French at the end of October.

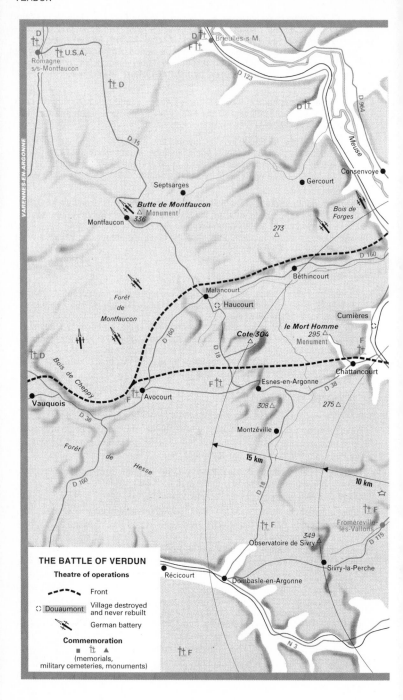

The tour takes visitors through galleries, casemates and arsenals which show the importance of this fortress. A chapel marks the site of the walled-up gallery where 679 German soldiers, killed in the accidental explosion of an ammunition dump, were buried on 8 May 1916.

From the top of the fort, there is an overall view of the 1916 battlefield and of the ossuary.

Slightly further on, to the right, a chapel stands on the site of the village church of **Douaumont** completely destroyed during the initial German attack.

Return to D 913 and turn right.

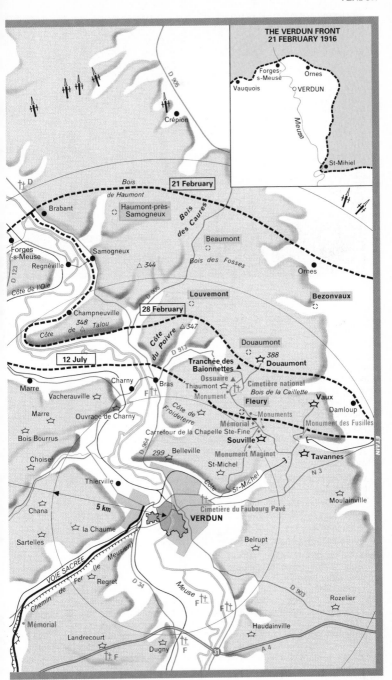

**THE VERDUN FRONT
21 FEBRUARY 1916**

Forges-s-Meuse
Ornes
Vauquois
VERDUN
St-Mihiel
Meuse

21 February

28 February

12 July

Bois de Haumont
Brabant
Haumont-près-Samogneux
Bois des Caures
Beaumont
Forges-s-Meuse
Samogneux
Regnéville
Côte de l'Oie
△ 344
Bois des Fosses
Ornes
Crépion
Louvemont
Bezonvaux
Champneuville
Côte de Talou
348 △
△ 347
Côte du Poivre
Douaumont
388 ☆ Douaumont
Charny
Bras
Tranchée des Baionnettes
Ossuaire ▲ Thiaumont
Cimetière national
Bois de la Caillette
Marre
Vacherauville
Monument
Fleury
Vaux
Marre
Ouvrage de Charny
Côte de Froideterre
Monuments
Damloup
Monument des Fusillés
Bois Bourrus
Carrefour de la Chapelle Ste-Fine
Mémorial
Choisel
299
Belleville
Souville
Tavannes
Thierville
St-Michel
Monument Maginot
Moulainville
Chana
5 km
Côte St-Michel
N 3
la Chaume
Cimetière du Faubourg Pavé
VERDUN
Sartelles
Belrupt
VOIE SACRÉE
Chemin de Fer (le Meusien)
Regret
Rozelier
Mémorial
Meuse
Landrecourt
Haudainville
Dugny
31
A 4

Ossuaire de Douaumont ⊘ – The ossuary, which was erected to receive the unidentified remains of some 130 000 French and German soldiers killed during the battle, is the most important French monument of the First World War. It consists of a long gallery (137m/150yd) comprising 18 bays, each housing two granite sarcophagi. The Catholic chapel is located beneath the main vault. At the centre of the monument stands the Tour des Morts (Tower of the Dead), 46m/151ft high, shaped like a shell and carved with four crosses. The first floor of the tower houses a small war museum. At the top *(204 steps)*, viewing tables enable visitors to spot the different sectors of the battlefield through the windows.

The 15 000 crosses of the **national cemetery** are lined up in front of the ossuary.

Douamont ossuary

A small path starting on the left of the parking area, leads to the **Ouvrage de Thiaumont**, taken many times during the battle.

Tranchée des Baïonnettes – A massive door leads to the monument built over the trench where, on 10 June 1916, two companies of the 137 infantry regiment were buried following intense shelling. The tip end of their rifles showing above ground was the only sign of their presence.

West bank of the Meuse

40km/25mi – about 2hr. Michelin map 241 folds 19, 22 and 23

The fighting was just as fierce on the west bank. In September 1918, American troops led by General Pershing played a key role in this sector.

Drive out of Verdun NW along D 38 to Chattancourt and turn right towards Le Mort-Homme.

Le Mort-Homme – This wooded height was the site of fierce fighting. All the German attacks of March 1916 were halted on this ridge.

Return to Chattancourt, turn right onto D 38 and right again onto D 18 shortly after Esnes-en-Argonne; 2km/1.2mi further on, a path on the right leads to the Cote 304.

La Cote 304 – For nearly 14 months the Germans met unflinching resistance from the French who knew the considerable strategic importance of this site.

Butte de Montfaucon – This is the highest point of the area (336m/1 102ft); the village which stood at the top was fortified and used by the Germans as an observation point.

A **monument** ⊙ was erected by the American government to commemorate the victory of the 1st American army during the offensive of September-November 1918. A monumental staircase leads to a column (57m/187ft high, 235 steps) surmounted by a Statue of Liberty. From the top, there is an overall **view★** of the battlefield north-west of Verdun, including the Butte de Vauquois and Cote 304 with the Douamont beacon in the distance. The ruins of the village of Montfaucon can be seen near the monument; the village was totally destroyed and rebuilt 100m/110yd further west.

Cimetière américain de Romagne-sous-Montfaucon – The American cemetery extending over 52ha/128 acres contains more than 14 000 graves in strict alignment in a setting of shaded lawns, a pond and flower beds. In the centre stands the chapel and the side galleries bear the names of the missing soldiers (954); in the right-hand gallery, a map showing the area of the battlefield has been engraved in the stone.

EXCURSIONS

Étain – *20km/12.4mi NE along N 3.* This large village was entirely rebuilt after the First World War. The church, dating from the 14C and 15C, has been restored. Note the carved arch leading to the Flamboyant chancel, lit by modern stained-glass windows by Gruber, and the carved keystones of the chancel.

Along the south aisle, the chapel of the Sacred Heart contains a group depicting Mary gazing at her dead Son, believed to be by Ligier Richier.

Senon – *9.5km/6mi N along N 18 then left onto D 14 via Amel-sur-l'Étang.*
The **church** ⊙ was built during the transition period from the Gothic to the Renaissance (1526-36) styles. It consists of three naves of equal height and has retained some beautiful Renaissance capitals.

Dugny-sur-Meuse – *7km/4.3mi S of Verdun along the Dugny road.* In the village, there is a fine 12C Romanesque **church** ⊙, now deconsecrated; this edifice of moderate proportions is surmounted by a massive square belfry decorated with a row of arcading resting on colonnettes and topped by timber hoarding. Inside, the large square pillars of the nave not surprisingly support timber vaulting (a common practice in the Rhine region) since, in the mid-12C, Lorraine formed part of the Holy Roman Empire.

VIGNORY★

Population 335
Michelin map 61 fold 20 or 241 fold 39

The picturesque village nestles inside a vale overlooked by the ruins of a 13C keep and 15C castle.

★Église St-Étienne – Built c 1000 by the lord of Vignory, this church is a rare example of mid-11C Romanesque architecture.
The rectangular belfry is adorned with a storey of blind arcading surmounted by two storeys of twinned openings and topped by a stone cone covered with an octagonal roof.

★Interior – Although remodelled, the church has retained its original aspect with a nave extending over nine bays and separated from the aisles by three-storey elevations: main arcading at ground level resting on rectangular piers, triforium above consisting of twinned openings separated by columns with carved capitals, and clerestory at the top.
The chancel, linked to the nave by a high triumphal arch, is divided into two parts: a forward area with two-storey elevations and an oven-vaulted apse separated from the ambulatory by seven columns; some of these are surmounted by capitals elaborately carved with lions, gazelles etc.
The church contains a wealth of sculpture from the 14C, 15C and 16C. Note the 14C monumental statue of the Virgin carrying Jesus who is holding a bird in his hand. However, the most remarkable sculpture is to be seen in the first chapel off the south aisle: it consists of an altar front featuring the Coronation of the Virgin between St Peter and St Paul and an altarpiece illustrating scenes from the Passion. The same regional workshop (late 14C, 15C) produced a series of small Nativity scenes to be found in the fourth chapel.

Castle ruins – The ruins are accessible by car up a narrow road leading to the keep. From the esplanade laid out as a picnic area, there is a fine view of the town.

An unusually decorative washhouse

Route des VINS★★★

Michelin map 87 folds 14-19 or 242 folds 19, 23, 27, 31 and 35

The 180km/112mi itinerary, known as the Route des Vins (the Wine Road), winds its way from Marlenheim to Thann, the northern and southern gateways to Alsace where there are information centres about Alsatian vineyards and wines. The well-signposted road runs along the foothills of the Vosges crowned by old towers and ruined castles. The numerous flower-decked villages dotted along the route, nestling round their church and town hall, are one of the most charming aspects of the Alsace region, no doubt enhanced as far as visitors are concerned by convivial wine-tasting opportunities.

Alsatian vineyards – A tour of the vineyards at harvest time is a fascinating experience. The animation is at its height and tourists can fully appreciate the lifestyle of the local people deeply committed to their wine-growing activities. Wine-growing in Alsace goes back to the 3C AD; since then, the region has been concerned with looking after its vineyards to the exclusion of any other form of agriculture. The landscape is characterised by terrace cultivation, with high stakes and low walls climbing the foothills of the Vosges. In the region entitled to the *appellation contrôlée* (label of origin), seven types of vines are grown: Riesling, Gewürztraminer, Sylvaner, Pinot Blanc, Tokay Pinot Gris, Muscat d'Alsace and Pinot Noir. These in turn give their name to the wines made from their grapes.

THE BAS-RHIN REGION

① From Marlenheim to Châtenois

68km/42mi – allow 4hr

Between Marlenheim and Rosheim, the road stays clear of the foothills of the Vosges.

Marlenheim – Renowned wine-growing centre (information available about Alsatian wines).

Eating out

MODERATE

À la Truite – *17 r. du 25-Janvier – 68970 Illhaeusern – ☎ 03 89 71 83 51 – closed during Feb school holidays, Tue evening and Wed – 89/210F.* This 1950s waterfront restaurant has a terrace in summer beside the river. The staff are friendly, and you have the choice of eating outside or in the colourful dining room. Simple, no-frills cooking with a reasonably priced lunchtime menu.

MID-RANGE

L'Auberge du Cabri – *67520 Nordheim – 3km/1.8mi N of Marlenheim on D 220 – ☎ 03 88 87 56 87 – fermecabri@wanadoo.fr – closed 24 Dec-17 Jan, 1-8 Jul, Thu evening except Jul-Aug, Mon and Tue – 110/190F.* Goats are raised on this farm, so goats' cheese and kid are on the menu, as well as *charcuterie* and other regional dishes. Nice view over the countryside from the veranda.

Auberge du Père Floranc – *68000 Wettolsheim – 4,5km/2.8mi W of Colmar on D 417 and D 1bis II – ☎ 03 89 80 79 14 – closed 7 Jan-12 Feb, 29 Jun-14 Jul, Sun evening out of season, Tue lunchtime and Mon – 120/390F.* This discreet-looking inn on the edge of the village of Wettolsheim, on the wine route, has a large dining room whose walls and ceilings are covered in wood carvings. Genuine traditional cooking is served here, or in the garden in summer.

Where to stay

MODERATE

Chambre d'hôte Maison Thomas – *41 Grand-Rue – 68770 Ammerschwihr – ☎ 03 89 78 23 90 – http://thomas.guy.free.fr – ☐ – 4 rooms 245/285F.* A village house with large, functional rooms, each with its own kitchenette and some with a mezzanine. There is also an apartment for rent. There is a peaceful garden and a courtyard near a fortified doorway surmounted by a tower.

MID-RANGE

Domaine Bouxhof – *R. du Bouxhof – 68630 Mittelwihr – ☎ 03 89 47 93 67 – 3 holiday cottages sleeping 3/7: 2200/3500F per week.* This 17C house with square towers, set among vines, is a nice place to stay a few days. The holiday homes are spacious, and there are two impeccable new bed and breakfast rooms. Breakfast in the 15C chapel is a memorable experience.

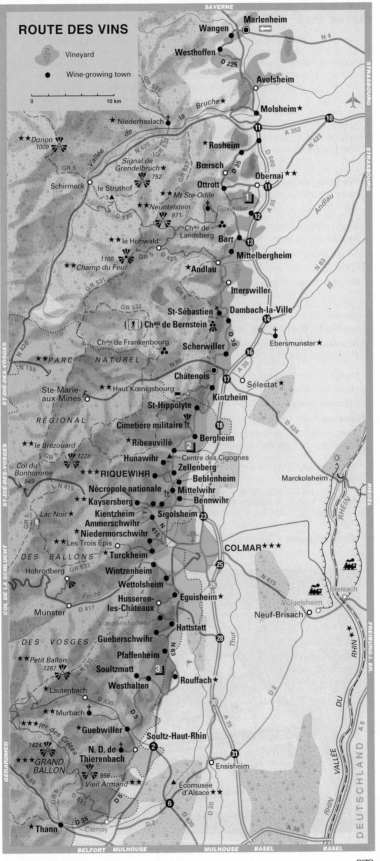

ROUTE DES VINS

Vineyard

● Wine-growing town

0 ─────────── 10 km

SAVERNE

Marlenheim
★ Wangen
★ Westhoffen
D 225
★ Avolsheim
Molsheim ★

N 4
STRASBOURG
STRASBOURG

★ Niederhaslach
★★ Donon 1009
Signal de Grendelbruch ★ 752
Schirmeck
le Struthof
★★ Mt Ste-Odile
★★ Neuntelstein 971
★★ le Hohwald
1100
★★ Champ du Feu
★★ PARC

★ Rosheim
Bœrsch
Ottrott
Obernai ★★
Ch^au de Landsberg
Barr
Mittelbergheim
★ Andlau
Itterswiller
St-Sébastien ★ Dambach-la-Ville
(🏃) Ch^au de Bernstein
Ch^au de Frankenbourg
Scherwiller
Ebersmunster ★

Ste-Marie-aux-Mines
NATUREL
★★ Haut Kœnigsbourg
Châtenois
Sélestat ★
Kintzheim
St-Hippolyte
Cimetière militaire ★★
Bergheim
★ Ribeauvillé
★★ le Brézouard 1228
Col du Bonhomme 949
Hunawihr
Centre des Cigognes
Zellenberg
★★★ RIQUEWIHR
Beblenheim
Nécropole nationale
Mittelwihr
★★ Kaysersberg
Bennwihr
Lac Noir ★
Kientzheim
Sigolsheim
Ammerschwihr
Niedermorschwihr
★★ Les Trois Épis
DES BALLONS
★ Turckheim
Hohrodberg
Wintzenheim
Wettolsheim
Husseren-les-Châteaux
Eguisheim ★
Munster
Voegtlinshofen
Hattstatt
DES VOSGES
Gueberschwihr
★★ Petit Ballon 1267
Pfaffenheim
Soultzmatt
Westhalten
Rouffach ★
Lautenbach
★★ Murbach
★★★ Rte des Crêtes
★ Guebwiller
1424
GRAND BALLON
N. D. de Thierenbach
Soultz-Haut-Rhin
956
Vieil Armand ★★
Écomusée d'Alsace ★★
Ensisheim
★ Thann
Cernay

RÉGIONAL
ST-DIÉ-DES-VOSGES
ST-DIÉ-DES-VOSGES
COL DE LA SCHLUCHT
GÉRARDMER

COLMAR ★★★
Marckolsheim
Neuf-Brisach
Breisach
Vögelsheim

RHEIN
RIEGEL
FREIBURG-I. BR.
DEUTSCHLAND
VALLÉE DU RHIN
A 5

BELFORT MULHOUSE   MULHOUSE   BASEL   BASEL

Wangen – Wangen is a typical wine-growing village with twisting lanes lined with old houses and arched gates. Until 1830 the villagers had to pay St Stephen's Abbey in Strasbourg an annual tax calculated in litres of wine. The Fête de la Fontaine (Fountain Festival) is a reminder of this ancient custom: on the Sunday following 3 July, wine flows freely from Wangen's fountain.

Westhoffen – Typical wine-growing village with 16C and 17C houses and a Renaissance fountain.

Avolsheim – This village has retained an old baptistery and, 500m/547yd south, a famous church believed to be the oldest sanctuary in Alsace.

The **Chapelle St-Ulrich** is a former baptistery built c 1000 in the shape of a clover leaf, containing fine 13C **frescoes** depicting the Trinity, the four evangelists and scenes from the Old Testament.

The **Église St-Pierre**, known also as Dompeter *(ad Dominum Petrum)*, stands in rural surroundings, at the centre of a small cemetery. Although partly rebuilt in the 18C and 19C, the church, surmounted by an octagonal belfry, is a moving example of Early Romanesque architecture (the edifice was consecrated by Pope Leo IX in 1049). Original features include the base of the belfry-porch with the interesting narthex and doorway, the side doorways with carved lintels and, inside, the massive square piers supporting heavy rounded arcades.

★**Molsheim** – *See MOLSHEIM.*

★**Rosheim** – *See ROSHEIM.*

Driving out of Rosheim, note *(ahead and slightly to the left)* the ruins of Landsberg Castle crowning the first foothills of the Vosges. The road runs through hilly terrain offering numerous viewpoints across the Plaine d'Alsace, with castles perched on promontories (Ottrott, Ortenbourg, Ramstein).

Boersch – This typical Alsatian village has retained three ancient gates and a picturesque **square**★ lined with old houses, the most remarkable being the town hall dating from the 16C. A Renaissance well marks the entrance of the square. Leave Boersch via the Porte du Haut (upper gate). Stop at the **Marquetry workshop** ⊙ to see an exhibition and an audio-visual presentation of its work.

Ottrott – *See Le HOHWALD: Drive* 1️⃣.

★★**Obernai** – *See OBERNAI.*

Barr – Barr is an industrial town (famous tanneries) and an important wine-growing centre producing quality wines: Sylvaner, Riesling and above all Gewürztraminer. The annual wine fair is held in the town hall, a fine 17C building decorated with a loggia and a carved balcony; go into the courtyard to admire the rear part.

A former partly seigneurial and partly middle-class residence known as the **Folie Marco** ⊙, houses a **museum** containing 17C-19C furniture, porcelain, pewter and mementoes of local history; a section is devoted to *la schlitte (see MUNSTER: Muhlbach).*

Mittelbergheim – *See Le HOHWALD: Drive* 1️⃣.

Dambach-la-Ville

★**Andlau** – *See ANDLAU.*

Itterswiller – The flower-decked houses of this charming wine-growing village climbing up the hillside are lined along the high street. Note the partly Gothic tower of the church which contains a 13C or 14C mural.

🅱 A footpath leads visitors on a tour of the vineyards *(about 1hr, viewpoint)*.

Dambach-la-Ville – This renowned wine-growing centre (Frankstein vintages) lies in a picturesque setting overlooked by wooded heights. The attractive town centre with its flower-decked timber-framed houses was once surrounded by ramparts, of which three town gates are still standing. An annual wine fair takes place on 14 and 15 August.

Turn left 400m/437yd beyond the Porte Haute (upper gate).

At the top of the road, turn right onto a path which rises to the **Chapelle St-Sébastien**. Extended view of the Plaine d'Alsace and the vineyards. Inside, the late-17C Baroque altar in carved wood illustrates the Holy Family.

🅱 The path continues *(2hr on foot there and back)* to the ruined **Château de Bernstein** (12C-13C), built on a granite ridge (residential building, pentagonal keep). There is a fine view of the Plaine d'Alsace.

Scherwiller – Lying at the foot of Ortenbourg and Ramstein castles, this village has retained its former guard-house (note the oriel) and fine 18C timber-framed houses, as well as its old wash-house along the River Aubach. Art, handicraft and Riesling fair during the third weekend in August.

Châtenois – Note the unusual Romanesque belfry, surmounted by a spire and four timber bartizans, and the picturesque 15C gatehouse known as the Tour des Sorcières (witches' tower) crowned by a stork's nest.

THE HAUT-RHIN REGION

② From Châtenois to Colmar

54km/34mi – allow 5hr

As far south as Ribeauvillé, the road is overlooked by numerous castles: the imposing mass of Haut-Kœnigsbourg, the ruins of Kintzheim, Frankenbourg, St-Ulrich, Girsberg and Haut-Ribeaupierre.

Kintzheim – *See SÉLESTAT: Excursions.*

St-Hippolyte – This village is most attractive with its numerous flower-decked fountains and its lovely Gothic church dating from the 14C and 15C.

Bergheim – The Porte Haute, a 14C fortified gate, leads inside this wine-growing village shaded by an old lime tree believed to date back to 1300. The northern section of the medieval wall, which protected Bergheim from the Burgundians in 1470, is still standing with three of its original round towers. The village has many old houses and a picturesque market square adorned with a lovely fountain and decorated with flowers in summer.

The red-sandstone **church** ⓥ has retained 14C features (apse, chancel and lower part of the belfry); the rest dates from the 18C as does the town hall.

Cimetière militaire allemand – *1.2km/0.7mi N of Bergheim along a road branching off D 1⁸ on the left.* Built on a hillside, the cemetery contains the graves (facing the fatherland) of German soldiers killed during the Second World War. From the cross standing at the top, the fine **view**★ extends westwards to the heights of the Vosges, northwards to Haut-Kœnigsbourg Castle and eastwards to Sélestat and the Plaine d'Alsace.

★**Ribeauvillé** – *See RIBEAUVILLÉ.*

Beyond Ribeauvillé, the road rises half way up the hillsides offering a wider panorama of the Plaine d'Alsace. The heart of the Alsatian wine-growing centre is situated here, between Ribeauvillé and Colmar. Charming villages and famous wine-growing centres are scattered across the rolling hills lying on the edge of the Vosges.

Hunawihr – The square belfry of the church is as massive as a keep. The church is surrounded by a 14C wall which had only one entrance defended by a tower. The six bastions flanking the wall can still be seen. From the church, there is a good view of the conical Taennchel summit, of the three castles of Ribeauvillé and of the Plaine d'Alsace.

The church is used for Catholic and Protestant church services, which explains the way the nave looks. The chancel has been reserved for Catholic parishioners since the reign of Louis XIV. The chapel situated on the left of the chancel contains 15C-16C frescoes depicting the Life of St Nicholas, the miracles he accomplished and the canonization of St Huna.

A centre devoted to the return of storks (**Centre de réintroduction des cigognes** ⓥ) has been trying to encourage these birds to remain in Alsace throughout the winter and to nest at the centre or in nearby villages. More than 200 storks are fed and looked after in the centre. Every afternoon, there is a show involving various animals who are particularly clever at fishing: cormorants, penguins, sea-lions and otters. In 1991, a centre for the safeguard and reproduction of otters was created. The **Jardin des Papillons exotiques vivants** ⊘ includes more than 150 species of exotic butterflies of all sizes and colours, flying about freely inside a hothouse full of luxuriant vegetation (orchids, passion flowers).

A short distance from Hunawihr, at the top of a hill, stands the small village of **Zellenberg** overlooking Riqhewihr and the vineyards. A **historic trail** *(40min, booklet available from the town hall or the tourist offices of Ribeauvillé and Riquewihr)* leads visitors round the most interesting old buildings.

★★★ **Riquewihr** – *See RIQUEWIHR*.

Beblenheim – The village, which boasts a 15C Gothic fountain, lies close to the Sonnenglantz (Sunshine), a famous hillside producing high-quality wines on its 35ha/86 acres of vineyards (Alsatian Tokay, Muscatel and Gewürztraminer).

Mittelwihr – At the southern end of the village stands the Mur des Fleurs Martyres, a wall which, throughout the German occupation was decked with blue, white and red flowers as a token of Alsatian loyalty.

The hillsides all around enjoy a microclimate which causes almond trees to flower and yield ripe fruit. The reputation of the Riesling and Gewürztraminer made in this area is steadily growing.

Benwihr – This is another famous wine-growing village, with a monumental fountain in its centre. The modern **church** is brightly lit by a colourful stained-glass window stretching right across the south side. Note the soft tones of the stained glass decorating the chapel on the left.

Sigolsheim – This is supposed to be the place where, in 833, the sons of Louis the Meek, Charlemagne's son, met before capturing their father to have him imprisoned.

The Église St-Pierre-et-St-Paul dates from the 12C. The Romanesque doorway is adorned with a tympanum carved in a style similar to those of Kaysersberg and Andlau.

Follow rue de la 1ʳᵉ-Armée (the main street) leading, beyond the Couvent des Capucins, to the national necropolis.

Nécropole nationale de Sigolsheim – *5min on foot there and back from the parking area; 124 steps.*

The necropolis, standing on top of a hill and surrounded by vineyards, contains the graves of 1 684 French soldiers killed in 1944. From the central platform, there is a splendid **panorama**★ of the nearby summits and castles, as well as of Colmar and the Plaine d'Alsace.

Kientzheim – This wine-growing village has retained several interesting medieval buildings, fortifications, old houses, squares, wells and sundials.

The **Porte Basse** is a fortified gate surmounted by a grinning head which was placed there as a warning to attackers that they did not stand a chance to get past this mighty tower. The medieval **castle**, remodelled in the 16C, is the headquarters of St Stephen's Brotherhood, the official body controlling the quality of Alsatian wines. Housed in an outbuilding, the **Musée du Vignoble et des Vins d'Alsace** ⊘ is devoted to all aspects of wine-growing from vineyards to wines. Note the monumental winepress and some rare tools, no longer in use.

Inside the church, next to a 14C statue of the Virgin (north-side altar), are the **tombstones**★ of Lazarus von Schwendi (d 1583), who brought Tokay vines back from Hungary, and of his son *(see KAYSERSBERG)*.

The **Chapelle Sts-Felix-et-Régule** contains naive paintings on canvas and on wood, dating from 1667 to 1865.

★★ **Kaysersberg** – *See KAYSERSBERG*.

Ammerschwihr – Situated at the foot of vine-covered hills, Ammerschwihr was destroyed by fire following the bombings of December 1944 and January 1945. The town was rebuilt in traditional Alsatian style but it has nevertheless retained one or two interesting old buildings: the Gothic **Église St-Martin** with its chancel lit by modern stained glass, the old town hall with its Renaissance façade, two fortified towers and the **Porte Haute**, on the western edge of the town; the gate's square tower, crowned by a stork's nest, is decorated with the arms of the town and a painted sundial.

★ **Niedermorschwihr** – This lovely village set among vineyards has a modern church with a 13C spiral belfry. The high street is lined with old houses adorned with oriels and wooden balconies.

★ **Turckheim** – *See TURCKHEIM*.

Wintzenheim – This famous wine-growing centre (Hengst vintage) is a pleasant city, fortified in 1275, which has retained a few old houses (rue des Laboureurs) and the ancient manor of the Knights of St John, now the town hall.

★★★ **Colmar** – *See COLMAR*.

Vineyard and village of Ammerschwir

③ From Colmar to Thann

59km/37mi – allow 3hr

★★★**Colmar** – *See COLMAR.*
Leave Colmar by ⑤ on the town plan, along D 417.

Wettolsheim – This village claims the honour of being the birthplace of Alsatian wine-growing, which was introduced here during the Roman occupation and later spread to the rest of the country. A wine festival takes place during the last weekend in July.

★**Eguisheim** – *See EGUISHEIM.*
The picturesque road is overlooked by the ruins of the three castles of Eguisheim and the view extends over a wide area of the Plaine d'Alsace.

Husseren-les-Châteaux – This is the highest point of the Alsatian vineyards (alt 380m/1 247ft). Husseren is the starting point of a tour of the three castles of Eguisheim *(see EGUISHEIM: Route des Cinq Châteaux)* towering above the village.

Hattstatt – This once-fortified old village has an early-11C church with a 15C chancel containing a stone altar of the same period. The baptistery also dates from the 15C. Note the fine Renaissance calvary on the left-hand side of the nave. The pulpit and the altarpiece are Baroque.

Gueberschwihr – A magnificent Romanesque belfry (all that remains of an early-12C church) overlooks this peaceful village, camped on a hillside and surrounded by vineyards.

Pfaffenheim – *See ROUFFACH: Excursion.*

★**Rouffach** – *See ROUFFACH.*
Shortly beyond Rouffach, the Grand Ballon *(see Route des CRÊTES: Drive ②)* comes into view.

Westhalten – Picturesque village surrounded by vineyards and orchards, with two fountains and several old houses.

Soultzmatt – Charming city lying along the banks of the Ohmbach. The local Sylvaner, Riesling and Gewürztraminer are highly rated as are the mineral springs. There is a wine festival in early August.
The **Château de Wagenbourg** stands nearby.

★**Guebwiller** – *See GUEBWILLER.*

Soultz-Haut-Rhin – *See SOULTZ-HAUT-RHIN.*
Turn right onto D 51.

Basilique Notre-Dame de Thierenbach – The onion-shaped belfry can be seen from afar. The basilica was built in 1723 in the Austrian Baroque style by the architect Peter Thumb. An important pilgrimage, going back to the 8C and dedicated to Notre-Dame-de-l'Espérance takes place in the church. The basilica contains two *Pietà*: the miracle-working Virgin dating from 1350 and the Mater Dolorosa dating from 1510 situated in the Reconciliation chapel.
Return to Soultz-Haut-Rhin and follow D 5 towards Cernay.

Cave vinicole du Vieil-Armand – This cooperative, situated on the outskirts of Soultz, groups 130 wine-growers looking after 150ha/371 acres of vineyards.
Two great wines are produced: Rangen, the most southern of Alsatian wines and Ollwiller, grown just beneath Vieil Armand. The cooperative organises tastings of regional wines. In the basement, the wine-grower's museum contains equipment used in the old days in vineyards and cellars.
Continue along D 5 then turn right onto D 35.

*Thann – *See THANN.*

VITRY-LE-FRANÇOIS

Population 17 032
Michelin map 61 fold 8 or 241 fold 30

Vitry-le-François is the capital of the **Perthois** area, a fertile plain extending from the River Marne to the Trois-Fontaines Forest. The town occupies a strategic position on the east bank of the Marne, at the foot of the Champagne limestone cliff and at the intersection of the Marne-Rhine and Marne-Saône canals.

Vitry was built by King François I who gave it his name. He commissioned an engineer from Bologna who designed the grid plan, the fortifications reinforced by bastions and a citadel destroyed in the 17C.

In 1940, the city was bombed and pounded by artillery fire to the point that 90% of it was destroyed. After the war, it was rebuilt along the lines of the original plan.

THE DINNER BELL

La Cloche – *34 r. A.-Briand* – ☎ *03 26 74 03 84 – closed 31 Jul-13 Aug, 18-31 Dec and Sun evening Oct-May – 130/280F.* Generous helpings of mouth-watering cooking based on good fresh produce make this a place definitely worth visiting. Two lovely old-fashioned buildings are separated by an inner courtyard, which serves as a terrace in summer. The rooms are plain and well-lit.

SIGHTS

Église Notre-Dame – The 17C-18C church overlooking place d'Armes is an interesting example of the Classical style with a harmonious and well-proportioned west front flanked by twinned towers adorned with scrolls and surmounted by flame vases. Inside, note the imposing nave and transept prolonged by a late-19C apse. The furniture includes a baldaquined altar, an organ case originally in the Abbaye de Trois-Fontaines and an 18C pulpit and churchwardens' pew in carved wood. The Crucifixion, painted in 1737 by Jean Restout is worth seeing in the last chapel along the north aisle.

Hôtel de ville – The town hall is housed in the 17C buildings of a former convent.

Porte du Pont – Fine triumphal arch (1748) erected in honour of Louis XIV. Taken down in 1938, it was only re-erected in 1984.

Ph. Gajic/MICHELIN

Church in St-Amand-sur-Fion

EXCURSIONS

★St-Amand-sur-Fion – *10km/6mi N along the Route de Châlons (N 44) then D 260.*
Lying on the banks of the River Fion, the village has retained timber-framed houses, six mills and a wash-house. The **church★** is a successful mixture of Romanesque (central doorway, part of the nave) and Gothic (chancel and nave) styles. The grace of the lofty interior is enhanced by the pink colour of the stone. The apse is pierced by windows on three storeys, the middle storey being a triforium which continues along the transept showing characteristics of the Flamboyant style. The beautiful arcaded porch dates from the 15C. Note the carved capitals and the 17C rood beam.

Vitry-en-Perthois – *4km/2.5mi along D 982.*
This village was rebuilt on the site of a medieval city destroyed by fire in 1544. From the bridge spanning the River Saulx, there is a pastoral view of the river with a mill.

Ponthion – *10km/6mi NE along D 982 then D 995.*
Situated between the Marne-Rhine canal and the River Saulx, Ponthion has a church dating from the 11C and 15C, preceded by a lovely 12C porch. In 754, a meeting between Pope Stephen II and Pepin the Short, the first Carolingian king, led to the creation of the Papal States.

VITREL‡‡

Population 6 296
Michelin map 62 fold 14 or 242 fold 29

This sought-after spa resort owes its fame to the therapeutic qualities of its water and its situation at the heart of a picturesque wooded area. The spa establishment lies outside the town; Vittel water is used mainly for the treatment of arthritis, gout, migraine and allergies, as well as kidney and liver disorders.
Outdoor activities including golfing and hiking are also part of the town's assets.

IN TOWN

★★Parc – This landscaped park, covering an area of 25ha/62 acres, is adorned with a bandstand where numerous concerts take place during the season. It is adjacent to vast sports grounds (horse racing, polo, golf, tennis etc). The new Palais des Congrès (Congress Hall) was inaugurated in 1970.

Institut de l'eau Perrier Vittel ☉ – The exhibition "Water and Life" is housed in the former baths built by Charles Garnier in 1884; it illustrates the scientific, technical and industrial aspects of water.

Usine d'embouteillage de Vittel SA ☉ – Situated on the western edge of town, this is the

Vittel park

most important bottling factory in Europe. Visitors can watch the production of plastic and glass bottles and the bottling and packaging process. The factory's turnover averages 5.4 million bottles of different sizes per day.

HEAD FOR THE HILLS

🟥 *3hr on foot there and back. Leave Vittel northwards along avenue A.-Bouloumié. With the riding centre on your right, follow a surfaced path on the left which runs across pastures then rises through woods. The itinerary crosses D 18 before reaching the Croix de mission de Norroy after a steep climb.*

Croix de mission de Norroy – The view extends north-west to the Vair and Mouzon valleys, south to a ridge known as the Crête des Faucilles and south-east to the Vosges summits.
Turn left and walk through a small wood.

Chapelle Ste-Anne – The chapel stands on the edge of the Châtillon Forest, beside a fine oak tree. The unassuming building contains a 16C altarpiece of the 12 Apostles (the heads are broken). Fine view north-west of the Vair Valley.
Continue straight on.

Walk through the Châtillon Forest. As you come out of the woods, there is another view of Vittel. *Return to the town.*

Eating out

MODERATE

Le Rétro – *158 r. Jeanne-d'Arc –* ☏ *03 29 08 05 28 – closed 19-30 Jun, 23 Dec-12 Jan, Sat lunchtime and Mon – 90/180F.* A good, simple place to eat, run by a keen young couple right in the middle of Vittel. Regional specialities and grills; nice atmosphere. The first dining room is the best, with its open fireplace and rustic decor.

On the town

Casino de Vittel – *near the baths –* ☏ *03 29 08 12 35 – daily from 11am – traditional games room from 9pm except Tue.* This is one of the main attractions of the spa resort, frequented by both tourists and spa patrons, and providing a little excitement for those restricted to drinking only water! Chance your luck with fruit machines, boule, roulette and black jack. Non-gamblers can enjoy lively evenings or Sunday afternoon tea-dances in the Cotton Club bar.

Shopping

Au Péché Mignon – *36 pl. du Gén.-de-Gaulle –* ☏ *03 29 08 01 07 – Tue-Sat 7.30am-12.30pm, 2-7.30pm, Sun 4.30am-12.30pm, 3-7pm – closed end Jun.* Apart from a few classic local dishes (pâté from Lorraine or Vittel) this home-made food shop sells wonderful varieties of chocolate: the "chocolate spa route" (four different chocolates, like the four Vosges spa towns), and *creuchotte* (a little chocolate cream frog).

Délices Lorraines – *184 r. de Verdun –* ☏ *03 29 08 03 30 – Mon-Sat 9am-12.30pm, 2.15-7.15pm, Sun 9am-12.30pm.* This shop sells a wide variety of regional specialities: honey, Lorraine wines (Côte de Toul), aperitifs and liqueurs from the Vosges (made from mirabelle plums or blueberries), sweets (Vittel sweets, *grès-rose des Vosges*), macaroons, madeleines, unusual wild fruit brandies etc.

EXCURSIONS

Domjulien – *8km/5mi NE along D 68.* The 15C-16C church, although considerably remodelled, contains some remarkable sculptures mainly situated in the north aisle: an altarpiece (1541) representing the Crucifixion and the 12 Apostles; an early-16C Entombment with angels carrying the instruments of Christ's Passion; statues of St George (16C) and St Julian (16C).
A fine 15C statue of the Virgin and Child playing with an angel stands on the right-hand side altar.

‡‡ **Contrexéville** – *4km/2.5mi SW (see Introduction: Architecture and art).* Known since the 18C, this popular spa town lying in wooded surroundings has five mineral springs used in the treatment of kidney and liver diseases, excess of cholesterol and obesity. In addition, the thermal establishment, built in 1912 in neo-Byzantine style, proposes slimming and fitness formulae.

Usine d'embouteillage ⊙ (bottling factory) – The manufactory offers an interesting insight into the bottling process and the conditioning of mineral-water bottles. The resort is also the ideal starting point of excursions through the region. The **Lac de la Folie** (1.5km/0.9mi north-west) is a large expanse of water (12ha/30 acres) surrounded by woods, with fishing facilities *(see Practical information).*

Thuillières – *9.5km/6mi SE.* The **castle** ⊙ was built by the architect Germain Boffrand (1667-1754) for his own use when he was working in the area.
Just beyond Thuillières on the left, the chapel of a former hermitage can be seen nestling inside the picturesque vale of Chèvre-Roche.
Continue along D 18 beyond the hermitage to Darney

Darney – *18.5km/11.5mi SE.* It was here that, in June 1918, President Poincaré of France, speaking in the name of the Allies, declared the independence of Czechoslovakia. A small **Czechoslovak museum** ⊙ is housed in the former town hall, known as the castle.
The church was consecrated in 1789; it contains some fine woodwork, particularly in the chancel.

Parc naturel régional des
VOSGES DU NORD★★

Michelin map 87 folds 2, 3 and 14 or 242 folds 11, 12, 15, 16 and 19

The northern Vosges are relatively low yet often steep mountains which differ considerably from the rest of the massif. Their sandstone cover has been torn open by deep valleys and shaped into horizontal plateaux or rolling hills generally less than 500m/1 640ft high.

Erosion has carved the sandstone crust forming isolated jagged rocks with strange shapes reminiscent of towers, giant mushrooms or huge arches. Apart from these rocks, real fortresses still stand on the densely forested heights.

The nature park – Created in 1975, the nature park aims to safeguard the natural heritage, preserve the quality of life and enable the public to enjoy it. Located in the northern part of the Vosges massif and covering an area of more than 120 000ha/296 532 acres, it extends from the north of the Lorraine plateau to the Plaine d'Alsace and from the German border in the north to the A 4 Metz-Strasbourg motorway in the south.

Forests covering more than 60% of the whole area consist of beeches, oaks, pines and spruces. Valleys are dotted with lakes and meadows.

Various activities (hikes, riding tours, bike tours, courses in nature discovery, themed excursions, lying in wait for game...) enable visitors to discover local flora and fauna in their natural environment and to get an insight into the lifestyle and economic activities of the region which offers a wealth of charming Alsatian villages and their picturesque traditions, as well as crystalworks, technical and folk museums

> **SIMPLE FARE**
>
> **Auberge des Mésanges** – 2 r. du Tiseur – 57960 Meisenthal – ☎ 03 87 96 92 28 – closed Feb – **P** – 20 rooms 240/290F – ☲ 40F – restaurant 78/120F. A good place to stay or eat after visiting the glass and crystal museum. The rooms are well equipped and impeccably kept. Simple, inexpensive meals, with tartes flambées and pizzas in addition to the usual fare at weekends.

and, of course, old castles full of mystery.

The Maison du Parc (park information centre) is in La Petite Pierre (see La PETITE-PIERRE).

The Parc naturel régional des Vosges du Nord has been designated by UNESCO as one of the biosphere's world reserves.

THE HANAU REGION

① Round tour from Saverne

125km/78mi – allow 4hr 30min

★**Saverne** – See SAVERNE.

Soon after leaving Saverne via Ottersthal, D 115 crosses the green Muhlbach Vale then passes beneath the motorway.

St-Jean-Saverne – See ST-JEAN-SAVERNE.

Just beyond St-Jean-Saverne, the ruins of **Haut-Barr Castle**★ (see Château du HAUT-BARR) can be seen overlooking Saverne from a wooded height; more to the right are the equally impressive ruins of Griffon Castle.

Bear left towards Dossenheim-sur-Zinsel.

★**Neuwiller-lès-Saverne** – See NEUWILLER-LÈS-SAVERNE.

Bouxwiller – This small town was, until 1791, the capital of the county of Hanau-Lichtenberg, extending across the Rhine. The princes' castle did not survive the Revolution, but the picturesque streets are lined with houses of the German Renaissance. Part of the ramparts have also been restored.

The **church** ⊘, dating from the 17C, contains a fine **pulpit**★ (c 1600) carved in stone and painted, an organ by Silbermann with an ornate organ case, a seigneurial box decorated with stuccowork and woodwork.

The **Musée du pays de Hanau** ⊘ houses collections of painted furniture, glassware from Bouxwiller, reconstructions of interiors...

The former synagogue (1842) houses the **Musée judéo-alsacien** ⊘ which illustrates the history and culture of the Alsatian Jewish community.

⚑ A 6km/3.7mi long **geological trail** *(information available from the town hall, the tourist office or the Maison de Pays)*, extremely rich in fossils, leads to the summit of Bastberg offering views of the town *(viewing tables)*. The summit is also accessible by car from Imbsheim *(from Bouxwiller, follow D 6 then turn right just before Imbsheim)*.

From Bouxwiller, drive to Ingwiller via Niedersoultzbach.

Ingwiller – This village offers a free guided tour of the **Sentier botanique et poétique du Seelberg** ⊙ (Seelberg botanic trail, *2hr*).

Drive out of Ingwiller along D 28, through Rothbach to Offwiller.

Offwiller – Stop by the **Musée des Arts et Traditions populaires** ⊙ which illustrates the region's rural and cultural appeal.

Follow D 28 to Zinswiller and turn left onto D 141 running along the north bank of the Zinsel du Nord between Offwiller Forest and Niederbronn Forest.

As you drive through the forest, you will see the ruins of Arnsbourg Castle on your right, near the GR 53 footpath.

Baerenthal – This charming village is situated on the north bank of the River Zinsel. It is possible to go round the Baerenthal Lake, a nature reserve with an exceptionally rich flora. An observation tower makes it possible to look at bird life, particularly in spring and autumn (migrating birds).

Between Baerenthal and Mouterhouse, the road follows the charming valley once dotted with numerous metalworks belonging to the De Dietrich family, now almost all gone. The Zinsel often widens, forming pools covered with water-lilies.

Continue along D 36 to Lemberg.

The shaded road is narrow and winding. On the right are the heights of Mouterhouse Forest. The road runs along the Breitenbach stream which widens in places and forms lakes lined with sawmills.

St-Louis-lès-Bitche – The former **cristalleries de St-Louis**, ⊙ founded in 1767, produce a variety of ornaments and objects used at the table.

Rejoin D 37 and turn right.

Goetzenbruck – The glass industry is the main activity of this community; important factory producing glasses for spectacles.

Meisenthal – In the centre of the village, the former glassworks (closed in 1970) house the **Maison du verre et du cristal** ⊙, a glass and crystal museum presenting a reconstruction of the manufacturing process (ovens, documentary film) and glassware produced by the works since the 18C.

Soucht – *2km/1.2mi beyond Meisenthal.* A former workshop houses the **Musée du Sabotier** ⊙ (clog-makers' museum).

Return to D 57.

From the **Colonne de Wingen**, there is a very fine view of the Meisenthal Valley with Rohrbach in the distance.

Pierre des 12 apôtres – This standing stone is very old but it was only carved in the 18C following a vow. Under the cross, one can see the 12 Apostles in groups of three.

It is in the area of **Wingen-sur-Moder** that the Lalique crystal and glassworks are situated.

Turn left in Wimmenau and follow D 157.

Reipertswiller – The old **Église St-Jacques** overlooking the village has a 12C square belfry and a Gothic chancel built c 1480 by the last member of the Lichtenberg family.

Château de Lichtenberg ⊙ – *Follow the Lichtenberg high street prolonged by D 257 to the path leading to the castle and leave the car.*
The castle, which has retained its 13C keep, was restored following damage caused by shelling during the 1870 Franco-Prussian War.

Follow D 113 SW via Sparsbach.

★**La Petite-Pierre** – *See La PETITE-PIERRE.*

Étang d'Imsthal – *The path leading to the lake branches off D 178 2.5km/1.5mi from la Petite-Pierre.*
The lake, lying at the bottom of a basin in the middle of pastureland surrounded by forests, offers a charming outing *(parking reserved for hotel clients)*.

Graufthal – In this hamlet of the Zinsel Valley, you can see troglodyte houses dug into the red-sandstone cliffs (70m/230ft high). They were inhabited until 1958.

Return to Saverne.

Dwellings built into the cliffs in Graufthal

CASTLE COUNTRY

Situated on the borders of the German palatinate, of Lorraine and of Alsace, this area is dotted with ruined castles built during the 12C and early 13C by the powerful dukes of Alsace, the Hohenstaufens, or by noble landowners who contested their authority. The castles were destroyed or abandoned even before the 18C. Today, their scattered ruins are full of romantic atmosphere.

② Round tour from Niederbronn-les-Bains

54km/34mi – allow 2hr 30min

‡‡ **Niederbronn-les-Bains** – *See NIEDERBRONN-LES-BAINS.*

Leave Niederbronn along the pleasant Flakensteinbach Valley. Opposite the ruins of Wasenbourg Castle, turn right onto a road branching off N 62 then left onto a forest road.

Le Wintersberg – Alt 580m/1903ft. This is the highest summit of the Vosges du Nord. From the tower there is a fine panorama of the lower Vosges region and of the plain.

The 6.5km/4mi forest road rejoins N 62; turn right then right again onto D 87 just beyond Philippsbourg. Drive on for 1km/0.6mi then turn left to Falkenstein Castle.

★**Château de Falkenstein** – *From Philippsbourg, follow D 87 and D 87^A which lead to a crossroads (3km/1.9mi); leave the car and continue on foot (45min there and back).*
🚶 *Follow the second path on the left (marked with blue triangles) for 15min then go up a few steps and turn left then right. Go through a doorway, turn left and walk round the peak on which the castle stands.*

The castle, built in 1128 on a sandstone peak overlooking the forest, was struck by lightning and damaged by fire in 1564. On your left you will see a vast cave carved out of the rock, known as the Salle des Gardes (guard-room). *Between the entrance doorway and the cave, there is another small doorway giving access to a flight of steps (with a handrail).* You will notice several natural caves, where the rockface has been carved by streaming water, as well as several man-made caves.

According to legend, the ghost of a cooper occasionally haunts the cellars at midnight and with a mallet, strikes a number of times corresponding to the number of casks of wine which will be produced during the year.

Further on, beyond a footbridge and some steps, you will see the top of the castle; walk to the viewpoint. It offers a fine **panorama**★.

Rejoin N 62 and turn right 3km/1.9mi beyond Philippsbourg; leave a small lake on the left and continue to Hanau Lake.

★**Étang de Hanau** – The lake is situated at the heart of a bog area, in pleasant wooded surroundings crisscrossed by marked footpaths.
🚶 Nature lovers have a choice between two hikes:
– the **Sentier botanique de la tourbière** *(access: 300m/328yd left of the restaurant parking area along D 162; start from the picnic area situated beyond the tennis courts, allow 45min)* and
– the **Promenade de l'arche naturelle de Erbsenfelsen** *(access: from the restaurant parking area, follow the no 3 blue markings, going via the back of the tennis courts, allow 1hr 30min).*
Follow the forest road running between the lake and Waldeck Castle to join D 35 which leads to Obersteinbach past the ruins of Lutzelhardt Castle on the left.

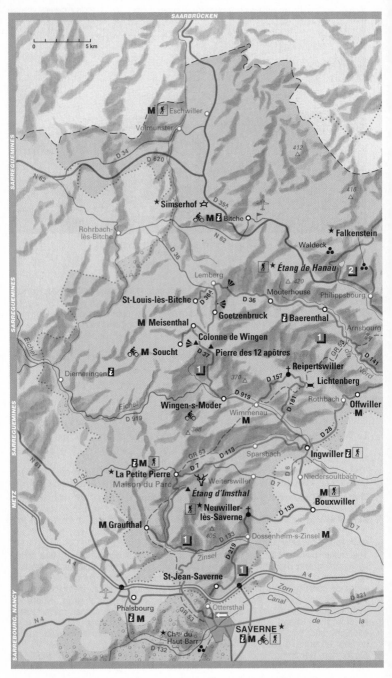

Obersteinbach – Picturesque village with timber-framed houses on red-sandstone bases.

The **Maison des Châteaux forts** is an information centre about castles, their history, their sites, their access and their owners.

On the way out, D 53 follows the winding route of one of the main medieval roads. It is overlooked by several ruins which probably formed part of a line of defence guarding Haguenau's imperial castle at the end of the 12C *(see HAGUENAU)*.

Schœneck Castle, standing on a rocky ridge, belonged to a member of the Lichtenberg family who also owned **Wineck** Castle facing it.

Turn left in Wineckerthal.

Châteaux de Windstein – *Parking area at the end of the left-hand branch of the road, in front of the restaurant-hotel Aux Châteaux.*

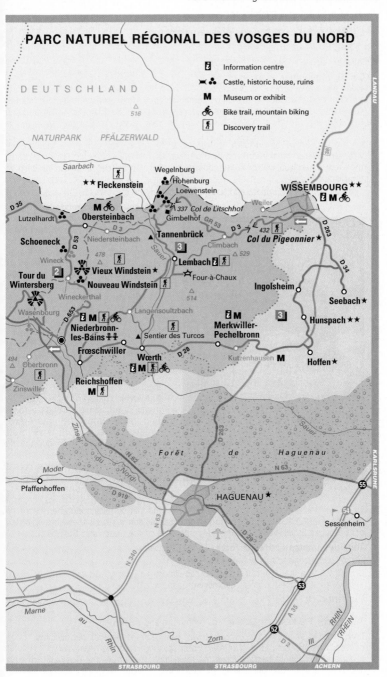

PARC NATUREL RÉGIONAL DES VOSGES DU NORD

The two Windstein castles, standing 500m/547yd apart, are believed to date from the end of the 12C (Old Windstein) and from 1340 (New Windstein). They were both destroyed in 1676 by French troops under the Baron of Montclar's command.

★**Vieux Windstein** (Old Windstein) – *45min on foot there and back.*

🚶 The dilapidated ruins stand at the top of a wooded knoll (alt 340m/1 115ft). The troglodyte part of the castle (stairs, bedrooms, cells, well 41m/135ft deep), is in a better condition. Admire the fine **panorama**★ of the surrounding summits and the Nagelsthal below.

Nouveau Windstein (New Windstein) – *30min on foot there and back.*

🚶 Standing on its own mound, the new castle is less picturesque but its ruins are nevertheless elegant: note the lovely pointed windows.

Return to Niederbronn along D 653.

A WELL-GUARDED BORDER
③ Round tour from Wissembourg
42km/26mi – allow half a day

★★Wissembourg – *See WISSEMBOURG.*

★Col du Pigeonnier – *Access on the left of the road coming from Climbach; 30min walk there and back.* Follow the Sentier de la Scherhol (marked with red circles) through the forest above the Club Vosgien refuge. After walking for about 15min, you will see a viewpoint offering a superb **view★** of the Plaine d'Alsace and the Black Forest. *Return along the same path or walk round the Scherhol through the forest and back to the pass (allow another 15min).*

On the way down, as the path comes out of the forest, there is a fine view of the village of Weiler on the left and of the green Lauter Valley. Beyond the crossroads, the view extends towards Wissembourg; the German border area can be seen in the distance.

Drive along D 3 to Climbach and turn right in the village towards the Col de Litschhof.

Fleckenstein

★★Château de Fleckenstein ○ – The castle was built in the 12C as part of the defence system of the northern border of the duchy of Alsace. In the 13C, it probably became an imperial possession and was one of the most powerful Alsatian baronies at the end of the 15C, including 35 villages. The castle was destroyed in 1680 and the Fleckenstein family became extinct shortly afterwards.

The ruins occupy a remarkable position near the German border, on a rock spur standing more than 20m/66ft high in wooded surroundings.

The lower courtyard surrounded by a wall is accessible through a fortified gate. Note the impressive square tower which was built against the main rock during the Gothic period.

Inside, stairs lead to several rooms hewn out of the rock, including the amazing Salle des chevaliers (Knights' Hall) with its central monolithic pillar, and then onto the platform (8m/26ft wide) where the seigneurial residence stood; there is a fine **view** of the upper Sauer Valley and of the confluence of the Sauer and Steinbach.

Tour des Quatre Châteaux forts – *See HIKE below.*
Go to Gimbelhof and follow the forest road.

On the way up you will see a disused red-sandstone quarry and then, on the right, a very densely forested area. **Hohenbourg** Castle stands opposite.

Tannenbrück – The Moselle army commanded by Hoche distinguished itself here in 1793.
The nearby Fleckenstein Lake offers swimming and relaxation.

Lembach – This charming small town has retained several **old buildings**: large houses, wash-houses, inns *(1hr round tour starting from the town hall)*.
A panoramic tour *(departure from the town hall; 1hr)* offers the possibility of fully appreciating the surroundings from viewpoints situated all round the village. On each site, explanations are centred on specific themes such as urban development, relief and vegetation, geology and biological environments such as orchards and hedges.

Along the road to Woerth on the left, 1km/0.6mi from the village, you will see the entrance of the **Ouvrage du Four à Chaux** *(see Ligne MAGINOT)*.

In Lembach, turn right onto the minor road which follows the River Sauer and leads to Reichshoffen.

The road goes through villages which were caught up in the 1870 Franco-Prussian War. Numerous monuments erected on the roadside commemorate the sacrifice of soldiers killed in the fighting.

Reichshoffen – The village witnessed the heroic cavalry charge which ended in a massacre in Morsbronn-les-Bains nearby. The **Musée du Fer** ○ illustrates the history of local mines and ironworks since the 14C.

Froeschwiller – Charming, typically Alsatian village.

Woerth – The castle houses the **Musée de la Bataille du 6 août 1870** ⊘: uniforms, weapons, equipment, documents and pictures concerning the two armies facing each other. Note the large diorama of the battle.

The **Sentier des Turcos** *(starting a few yards beyond the Alko France factory, on the left, on the way out of Woerth towards Lembach)* is a historic trail *(2km/1.2mi)* illustrating the main stages of the battle with the help of explanatory panels.

Merkwiller-Pechelbronn – This was the main centre of the oil fields of northern Alsace. All extracting operations stopped in 1970 but a small museum, the **Musée du Pétrole** ⊘, illustrates the main aspects of this former activity. Merkwiller-Pechelbronn is now a spa resort with a hot spring (Source des Hélions, 65°C/149°F) used for the treatment of rheumatism. *The spa establishment is closed for renovation.*

★**Hoffen** – This traditional village nestles round its church and its strange town hall supported by three wooden pillars. A lime tree planted during the Revolution stands next to the old public well.

★★**Hunspach** – White timber-framed houses with canopied façades line the streets of this typical Alsatian village, ranking among the most beautiful French villages, with a long-standing rural tradition (farmyards, orchards, fountains).

Ingolsheim – This large agricultural village is surrounded by orchards and dotted with gardens and farmyards.

★**Seebach** – This flower-decked village is typically Alsatian with its canopied timber-framed houses surrounded by gardens. The area has also retained its traditional costumes quite different from those of nearby villages.

Seebach typifies the beauty of an Alsatian village

HIKE

Tour des quatre châteaux forts (Tour of the four castles) – *4km/2.5mi. Allow 2hr.*

⬛ *Start from the parking area at the foot of Fleckenstein Castle (see above).* Walk along the path marked by a red rectangle then, a few yards further on, follow the picturesque Sentier des Rochers (red triangle) leading to the Maiden's fountain, which, according to legend, witnessed an unhappy love affair. Turn left (blue rectangle).

Across the German border stands **Wegelnburg**, another Imperial fortress taken over by brigands and largely destroyed at the end of the 13C. It offers a remarkable view of the border area. Retrace your steps to the Maiden's fountain and continue straight ahead (red rectangle) towards **Hohenburg**, another Fleckenstein possession destroyed in 1680; the lower Renaissance part has retained a powerful artillery bastion and the seigneurial residence. Continue southwards to **Loewenstein Castle**, destroyed in 1386 after serving as the headquarters of a group of robber-barons, including the cunning Lindenschmidt. The same path marked with a red rectangle runs past a typical red-sandstone crag (Krappenfels) on its way to the Gimbel farmhouse *(a farm-inn serving meals during the season).* Superb **view** of Fleckenstein Castle.

The path on the right (red-white-red rectangle) leads back to the Fleckenstein parking area.

VOUZIERS

Population 4 807
Michelin map 56 fold 8 or 241 fold 18

From a simple medieval village, Vouziers became an important trading centre following the creation in 1516 by King François I of one of the fairs which brought fame and prosperity to the Champagne region. The town was seriously damaged during the two world wars.

Roland Garros, the pilot who flew across the Mediterranean in 1913, was shot down nearby in October 1918 and was buried in the cemetery.

Église St-Maurille – The west front is adorned with an interesting triple **doorway★** in Renaissance style. Dating from the 16C, the richly decorated portals were the first part of a new church whose construction was interrupted by the Wars of Religion. For more than 200 years, the doorway stood isolated in front of the church. In 1769, it was joined to the existing edifice by means of two additional bays. The statues of the four evangelists are placed in recesses separating the three portals. The tympanum of the left-hand one represents a skeleton, whereas the right-hand one shows the risen Christ. A series of pendants representing the Good Shepherd and six Apostles hang from the first of the recessed arches of the central doorway. The tympanum depicts the Annunciation.

The church contains a lovely Renaissance Virgin.

St-Maurille church

EXCURSION

Le Mont Dieu 26km/16mi NE

This excursion to a remote Carthusian monastery takes in the Canal des Ardennes and the Lac de Bairon on the way.

Drive NE out of Vouziers along D 977, turn left after 1km/0.6mi onto D 14 to Semuy then right onto D 25 which follows the Canal des Ardennes as far as Le Chesne.

Canal des Ardennes – The canal which was dug during the reign of Louis-Philippe (1830-48), links the River Meuse to the River Aisne and to the waterways of the Seine Basin. There are 27 locks between Semuy and Le Chesne, over a distance of just 9km/5.6mi; the most interesting is in Montgon. Northeast of Le Chesne, the canal follows the green valley of the River Bar.

Leave Le Chesne N along D 991 and turn immediately right onto a narrow road leading to the Lac de Bairon.

Lac de Bairon – This lake (4km/2.5mi wide), set in hilly surroundings, is used as a reservoir of the Canal des Ardennes. It is divided into two by a causeway. There is a fine view of it from D 991. A section has been set aside as a bird sanctuary. The lake offers various activities including fishing, canoeing, walking...

From the lake, drive to D 12 which leads to D 977 and turn left.

The road runs through the Forêt du Mont Dieu. The former Carthusian monastery is signalled on the right.

★**Ancienne chartreuse du Mont Dieu** – Founded in 1132 by Odon, an abbot of St Remi in Reims, the monastery covered more than 12ha/30 acres surrounded by a triple wall. Damaged in the 16C, during the Wars of Religion, it was used as a prison at the time of the Revolution and was subsequently partly demolished. Little remains of the former monastery *(private property)* except some 17C buildings, built of pink brick with stone surrounds, set in a remote vale framed by dark woods.

WANGENBOURG

Population 1 176
Michelin map 62 fold 8 or 87 fold 14 or 242 folds 19 and 23

Lying some 40km/25mi west of Strasbourg, this charming summer resort forms an attractive **landscape**★ with its surroundings of meadows dotted with chalets and forests overlooked by the Schneeberg summit. A tree-felling competition takes place on the Sunday following the 14 July celebrations.

The ancient and powerful House of Dabo (Dabo is situated 15km/9.3mi north-west of Wangenbourg), also known as Dagsbourg, descended from the Duke of Alsace Étichon who was the father of St Odile. The most illustrious member of this dynasty was Bruno de Dabo, believed to have been born in 1002 in Dagsbourg Castle, who became Pope under the name of **Leo IX** and was later canonised.

Castle ruins – The ruins are accessible on foot *(15min there and back; leave the car in the parking area, 200m/220yd beyond the church; walk past a huge lime tree and follow a path which prolongs the main street)*. The castle, dating from the 13C and 14C, belonged to Andlau Abbey. The pentagonal keep and important sections of walls are still visible. The 24m/79ft high keep gives access to the platform offering a good overall view of the area. A path, which partly runs along the castle moat, takes you round the huge sandstone outcrop crowned by the ruins. A bridge leads to the old courtyard.

EXCURSIONS

The picturesque **Dabo-Wangenbourg region**★★ lies on the border of Alsace and Lorraine. Its austere sandstone massifs are separated by green valleys and calm rivers flowing on beds of fine sand.

Forêt de Saverne

78km/48.5mi round tour N of Wangenbourg – allow 3hr 30min

Obersteigen – This is a pleasant summer resort situated at medium altitude (alt 500m/1 640ft). Built of sandstone, the church is the former chapel of an Augustinian convent founded at the beginning of the 13C. It marks the transition between the Romanesque and Gothic styles: rounded arches, crocket capitals; note the ringed columns of the doorway.

Follow D 45 to Dabo.

The pleasant winding road enters a splendid forest and offers fine glimpses of the Rocher de Dabo and the surrounding area, of the fertile Kochersberg plateau and of the Plaine d'Alsace.

★**Rocher de Dabo** ⊙ – *Signposted Rocher St-Léon.* This sandstone rock is crowned by two viewing tables and a chapel dedicated to St Léon (Leo IX) whose statue is located in the chapel tower. Beneath the tower, to the left of the doorway giving access to the chapel, a small door opens onto a staircase *(92 steps)*. The **panorama**★ from the top of the tower includes the main summits of the sandstone Vosges mountains (Schneeberg, Grossmann, Donon etc). There is an interesting view of the village of Dabo which appears shaped like an X.

Dabo – This popular summer resort lies in a very pleasant **setting**★, at the heart of a beautiful forested area.

Slightly further on, the road runs down into the picturesque **Vallée du Kleinthal**.

On approaching Schaeferhof, one can see *(ahead to the right)* the hilltop village of Haselbourg.

Beyond Schaeferhof, bear left along D 45 and turn left again onto D 96 5km/3mi further on.

Cristallerie de Vallerysthal ⊙ – In 1838, Baron Klinglin transferred the old Plaine-de-Walsch glassworks to the present location; the new works prospered during the second half of the 19C, employing up to 1 300 workers in 1914. Nearly 40 000 pieces, displayed on the premises, illustrate the production from the 18C to today.

Return to D 98^C.

★**Rocher du Nutzkopf** – *Accessible by D 98^D from Sparsbrod then a forest track on the left and finally a footpath signposted on the left (45min on foot there and back).*

From the top (alt 515m/1 690ft) of this strange tabular rock, the **view**★ extends to the Rocher de Dabo, the village of La Hoube and the green valley of the River Grossthal.

Return to D 98^C then turn right onto D 98 which follows the Zorn Valley.

★**Plan incliné de St-Louis-Arzviller** ⊙ – *It is best seen from D 98^C.* Inaugurated in 1969, this boat elevator is equipped with an inclined plane 108.65m/356.46ft long in order to clear the 44.55m/146ft drop. It replaced 17 locks previously spread over a distance of 4km/2.5mi alongside the railway, which took a whole day to negotiate. Instead, a 43m/141ft long ferry truck going up sideways on rails along a concrete ramp by a system of counterbalance, transfers barges weighing 350t from one level to the other in 20min.

★**Vallée de la Zorn** – This pleasant valley, with its slopes covered with beeches and firs, is traditionally the busiest route through the northern Vosges mountains. Nowadays, the Marne-Rhine canal and the Paris-Strasbourg railway line run alongside the clear river which flows on a bed of sand and stones.
The ruins of the medieval Château de **Lutzelbourg** stand on a promontory; overlooking D 38-D 132.

★**Château du Haut-Barr** – See Château du HAUT-BARR.

★**Saverne** – See SAVERNE.

★★**Marmoutier** – See MARMOUTIER.

Forêt de Haslach

44km/27mi round tour S of Wangenbourg – allow 2hr 30min

Beyond Wolfsthal, D 218 climbs up to the beautiful **Haslach Forest**. A pleasant drive leads to the forest lodge then past a stela on the left, which commemorates the building of the road.
Further on *(500m/547yd)*, the road starts winding down towards Oberhaslach. Ahead and to the left stands the ruined tower of Nideck Castle.

The falls at Nideck

★★**Château and Cascade du Nideck** – *Leave the car in the parking area located below the forest lodge and follow the signposted footpath (1hr 15min on foot there and back).*
🚶 A 13C tower and 14C keep, standing in a romantic **setting★★**, are all that remains of two castles destroyed by fire in 1636. The German-speaking poet Chamisso de Boncourt, known as Adalbert von Chamisso, celebrated this site in his poems. From the top of the tower and the keep, there are fine views of the forest, Bruche Valley, Guirbaden Castle and the heights of Champ du Feu.
Walk to the right of the keep and follow a path on the left which leads to the waterfall. Bear right beyond a wooden shelter and a small bridge to the viewpoint (very dangerous in spite of the railing).
From the belvedere, there is a splendid **view★★** of the glacial valley and the wooded chasm into which the waterfall drops from the top of a porphyry wall. In order to see the waterfall, you must continue past the viewpoint along a marked path *(30min there and back).*
Return to D 218 and stop 1.2km/0.7mi further on.

Belvédère – The viewpoint is situated 20m/66ft off the road, near a stone marker. It offers a fine **view★** of the Château du Nideck and the valley below. Further on, to the left one can see the steep wooded slopes lining the River Hasel and its tributaries and, in the background, the Bruche Valley and the heights overlooking it to the south. The road winds down into the narrow, green valley of the Hasel towards Oberhaslach, Niederhaslach and the River Bruche.

Oberhaslach – This village is a place of pilgrimage, particularly lively on the Sunday following 7 November, when pilgrims come to pray to St Florent who, in the 7C, was believed to have the power to tame wild animals. Today, he still protects domestic animals but he also intervenes on behalf of pilgrims whatever their complaints. Numerous grateful acknowledgements testify to his efficiency.

The Baroque chapel, built in 1750 and restored in 1987, stands on the spot where the saint lived as a hermit before he became the seventh bishop of Strasbourg.

Église de Niederhaslach ⊘ – The village once had an abbey which, according to legend, was founded by St Florent in rather comic circumstances: for having cured his daughter, King Dagobert granted St Florent as much land as his donkey could delimit during the time the king spent washing and dressing; on the day in question, the king spent more time than he usually did and the donkey went galloping off, so that St Florent was given a considerable amount of land.

The church, begun in the mid-13C, was almost entirely destroyed by fire in 1287 but the son of Erwin von Steinbach (who designed Strasbourg Cathedral), Gerlac, partly rebuilt it in a plain yet elegant Gothic style. The doorway is framed by small statues and decorated with a tympanum illustrating the legend of St Florent curing King Dagobert's daughter.

Note the beautiful 14C-15C stained-glass **windows**★ in the aisles and in the apse. Bishop Rachio's funeral monument can be seen in the chancel, to the left of the main altar; a stone crucifix dating from 1740, flanked with John the Baptist and John the Evangelist, stands on the right. Gerlac's funeral monument and a 14C Holy Sepulchre are housed inside a chapel to the right of the chancel, which contains fine 17C stalls. A pilgrimage in honour of St Florent takes place in November.

Follow D 75.

Wasselonne – An old tower is the only part left of the castle overlooking this former stronghold whose houses are scattered on the slopes of the last foothill of the Kochersberg. The fortifications have completely disappeared except for a town gate and former keep. The **protestant church** ⊘ dates from the 18C (organ by Silbermann); in the cemetery *(along the Westhoffen road)*, there is an unusual domed pulpit. The Wasselonne fair *(last Sunday and Monday in August)* is a regional event, with an impressive procession of floral floats.

Drive W along D 224.

Vallée de la Mossig – Strange projecting sandstone rocks overlook the River Mossig. Strasbourg Cathedral is built of sandstone from this area.

WASSY

Population 3 291
Michelin map 61 fold 9 or 241 fold 34

This quiet little town, lying along the River Blaise at the heart of "humid Champagne", has retained the traditional ironworks which brought prosperity at a time when, before the First World War, Wassy was one of the main centres of iron-ore mining and metalwork in France. Try the local speciality, delicious small almond-flavoured meringues known as *caisses*.

The Wassy massacre

In 1562, François de Guise returned to Wassy one Sunday when the Protestant community was assembled in a vast barn. The duke's men began quarrelling with some of the Protestants and, having entered the barn, they massacred all those they could lay their hands on. The duke later disavowed the massacre although he had done nothing to stop it. This event deeply stirred the growing Protestant population of France and was one of the causes of the Wars of Religion which tore the country apart until 1598 when the Edict of Nantes was signed, granting religious freedom to all French subjects.

SIGHTS

Église Notre-Dame – Dating from the late 12C, the church has both Romanesque (belfry, capitals) and Gothic (doorway, vaulting) features.

Hôtel de ville ⊘ – Built in 1775, the town hall contains an interesting astronomical clock (early 19C) by François Pernot.

From place Notre-Dame, walk to rue du Temple.

Temple ⊘ – The Protestant church was built on the site of the barn where the massacre took place. It houses a **Protestant museum** illustrating the history of the reformed church of Wassy in the 16C and 17C.

Paul and Camille Claudel lived opposite with their parents. Paul later became a poet and playwright and his sister Camille a talented sculptor and close friend of Rodin.

Gare de Wassy – The imposing railway station was inaugurated in 1892. The **Train touristique de la Blaise et du Der** (tourist train) runs towards Éclaron and Doulevant-le-Château but it is possible to stop at Dommartin-le-Franc.

Lac-réservoir des Leschères – *1km/0.6mi S; signposted La Digue from Wassy.* This reservoir supplies the Canal de la Blaise, where swimming and fishing are possible.

EXCURSIONS

Osne-le-Val – *23km/14.3mi E.* This was the birthplace of ornamental cast-iron in France in the 19C. A building of the **Usine du Val d'Osne** ⊙, which closed down in 1986 houses an annual exhibition about ornamental cast iron (prints, photos, bronze-casting demonstration).

Vallée de la Blaise

Between Juzennecourt and St-Dizier, the Blaise Valley is a nature lovers' paradise. The river, abounding in trout, meanders through pastures between forested slopes. Hillside villages such as Lamothe-en-Blaisy or riverside ones like Daillancourt, are most attractive with their white-stone houses.

Metalwork is a long-standing tradition in the valley: as early as 1157, monks from Clairvaux founded the first industrial forge in Wassy and smelting works and workshops gradually settled along the river, burning wood from the nearby forests, using water power and iron ore mined locally.

Château of Cirey-sur-Blaise

In 1840, Osne-le-Val was the birthplace of ornamental cast iron. In 1900, Hector Guimard chose St-Dizier for his Art Nouveau creations. Today, the area produces urban furniture for many towns throughout the world: statues, fountains, benches...

In addition, some 100 highly specialised metalworks supply the aeronautical industry, the car industry, the chemical industry....

An unmarked road, known as the **Route du Fer** ⊙, links the main sites which testify to this ancient metalworking tradition.

34km/21mi itinerary from Wassy to Cirey-sur-Blaise

Drive S along D 2 to Dommartin-le-Franc.

Dommartin-le-Franc – The former **smelting works** ⊙ built in 1834 have been restored and are now used for exhibitions about metalwork in the past and ornamental cast iron.

Continue S along D 60 and turn right 2km/1.2mi further on.

Sommevoire – This village, nestling in a vale where the River Voire takes its source, became a centre of the metalwork industry during the 19C, specialising in the production of ornamental cast iron (fountains, lamps, vases, religious statues) initiated by Antoine Durenne. The **Paradis** Ⓥ houses a collection of his models, monumental plaster casts, some of them by eminent artists such as Bartholdi. The **Église St-Pierre** Ⓥ, deconsecrated, is used as an exhibition hall for cast-iron creations.

From Sommevoire drive SE along D 229 and rejoin the River Blaise in Doulevant-le-Château.

Doulevant-le-Château – This village, surrounded by beautiful forests, is well known for its wrought-iron and cast-iron workshops. The 13C-16C church has a fine Renaissance doorway.

Continue S along the river.

Cirey-sur-Blaise – Between 1733 and 1749, Voltaire stayed for long periods in the **château** Ⓥ of his friend the Marquise du Châtelet, whom he called the "divine Émilie". He wrote several of his works here, including two tragedies: *Alzire* and *Mahomet*.

The castle consists of a pavilion in the Louis XIII style and an 18C wing built by Madame du Châtelet and Voltaire. Note the **doorway** in the Rocaille style designed by Voltaire. The tour takes in the library, the chapel, the kitchens, reception rooms adorned with tapestries and Voltaire's small theatre.

WISSEMBOURG★★

Population 7 443
Michelin map 87 fold 2 or 242 fold 12

A village developed beside a prosperous Benedictine abbey and, by the 12C Wissembourg was already mentioned under its own name; the city became a member of Decapolis *(see MULHOUSE)* in 1354. Today, it still retains a considerable part of its fortifications and most of its ancient urban features. The River Lauter which flows here, splits into several arms, giving character to the town and creating a peaceful atmosphere. The annual fair which takes place on Whit Monday offers visitors the opportunity to see many Alsatian costumes.

Royal engagement – Stanislas Leszczynski, the deposed king of Poland *(see NANCY)*, having lost his fortune, settled in Wissembourg with his daughter Maria and a few loyal friends and led a simple life until, in 1725, Duc d'Antin arrived from Paris and announced that King Louis XV had decided to marry his daughter. The royal couple was married by proxy in Strasbourg Cathedral; Louis XV was 15 years old, Maria 22.

★OLD TOWN *1hr 30min*

Start from place de la République, in the lively town centre.

Hôtel de ville – Built of pink sandstone with pediment, small tower and clock (1741-52), the town hall stands on the square.
Turn left onto rue du Marché-aux-Poissons leading to the river. Note the lovely **vista** of the east end of St-Pierre-et-St-Paul at the other extremity of the street.

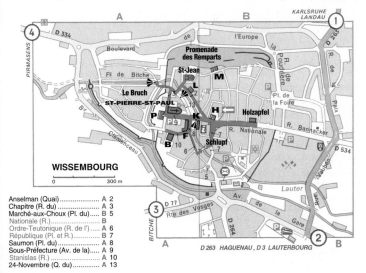

WISSEMBOURG

0   300 m

Eating out

MID-RANGE

Auberge du Pfaffenschlick – *Col de Pfaffenschlick – 67510 Climbach – 12km/7.5mi SW of Wissembourg on D 3, Lembach direction, and the mountain road on D 51 – ☎ 03 88 54 28 84 – closed 15 Jan-15 Feb, Mon and Tue – 110/160F.* A restaurant in the middle of the forest, just opposite a cabin used as a canteen during the construction of the Maginot Line. Formerly frequented by walkers, it still serves family style local meals, which are both solid and abundant. Attractive terrace and country decor.

Where to stay

MODERATE

Chambre d'hôte Klein – *59 r. Principale – 67160 Cleebourg – 7km/4.3mi SW of Wissembourg on D 7 – ☎ 03 88 94 50 95 – ⌷ – 3 rooms 170/230F – evening meal 70F.* Cleebourg is famous for its wine, and this 18C-19C Alsatian house in the village centre is a pleasant place to stay. Authentic decor with old furniture, and peaceful, friendly atmosphere. Regional cooking and good value for money.

On the town

Le Charles V – *31 r. Nationale – ☎ 03 88 94 09 39 – Sun-Wed, Fri 2pm-1am, Sat 10am-1am.* The only pub in Wissembourg, this barrel-shaped bar is the place to go at night to drink original beers and a selection of Alsace wines.

Shopping

Pâtisserie "Chez Éric" – *9 r. de la République – ☎ 03 88 94 01 58 – daily except Thu 8am-6.30pm – closed 2nd fortnight in Jan and Aug.* Situated in a charming, flower-decked little street that runs above the river, the terrace of this cake shop and tearoom is the ideal place to sample the town and the region's specialities: hazelnut tart, *kougelhopf* and Alsace wines.

Rebert – *7 pl. du Marché-aux-Choux – ☎ 03 88 94 01 66 – Tue-Sun 7am-6.30pm, tearoom Oct-Apr.* The speciality in this chocolate shop is the *pavés de Wissembourg*, little chocolate creams. Behind the shop, a lovely flower-decked courtyard serves as a tearoom in the summer.

Leisure

Espace Cycles – *8 r. de l'Ordre-Teutonique – ☎ 03 88 54 33 77 – Tue-Wed, Fri 8am-noon, 1.30-6.30pm, Thu 1.30-7.30pm, Sat 8am-noon, 1.30-4.30pm.* Bikes for hire.

Maison du Sel – This former hospital, slaughter house and salt warehouse dating from 1448 features balconied dormer windows protected by canopies.
Follow quai Anselman.

A l'Ancienne Couronne – This ancient aristocratic residence (1491) was used as an inn until 1603 before the Bartholdi family took possession in the late 18C.

Maison Vogelsberger – Dating from 1540, the house has a richly decorated Renaissance doorway and painted coat of arms.
Turn right onto rue du Presbytère.

Église St-Jean – The Protestant church dates from the 15C except for its belfry which is Romanesque. Inside, note the network vaulting of the north aisle. In the courtyard, on the north side of the church, there are ancient gravestones carved out of red sandstone. Martin Bucer *(see SÉLESTAT)* preached the reformed religion in this church before emigrating to England.
Return to the river and cross over.

Quartier du Bruch – From the bridge, there is a picturesque view of this old district. The canted corner of the first house, dating from 1550, is decorated with a small loggia or oriel. Note the 16C-17C mansion on the opposite bank.
Cross back and follow rue du Chapitre on the right.

★**Église St-Pierre-et-St-Paul** – The church, built of sandstone, is the former church of the Benedictine monastery, dating from the 13C.

The remarkable roof of the Maison du Sel, in the centre of town

The square belfry on the right side of the church is all that remains of the previous Romanesque edifice. The statues were beheaded during the Revolution and the paintings disappeared.

The ancient Head of Christ from Wissembourg, decorating the medallion of the 11C stained-glass window kept in Strasbourg, comes from the abbey church.

Inside, the Gothic style is predominant; note, in the south aisle, a red-sandstone Holy Sepulchre mutilated, which dates from the 15C; in the south transept there are traces of frescoes: the Apostles, Christ's Passion, the Resurrection, Whitsun, the Last Judgement. A 15C fresco, depicting St Christopher holding Jesus in his arms welcomes visitors who enter the church through the south door. It is the largest painted character known in France (11m/36ft).

The chancel is lit by 13C stained-glass windows, restored in the 19C. The oldest stained glass is the little rose on the gable of the north transept, which depicts the Virgin and Child (second half of the 12C).

On the north side of the church, a whole gallery and two bays are all that remain of a splendid **cloister** which was never completed, one of the finest cloisters in the whole Rhine Valley.

Sous-Préfecture – It is housed in an elegant late-18C pavilion situated at the end of avenue de la Sous-Préfecture.

Turn left onto avenue de la Sous-Préfecture to place du Saumon, then right onto rue Stanislas.

Tithe barn – The abbey's former tithe barn stands next to the house of the Teutonic Knights, dating from 1606. The order, founded in the 12C in the Holy Land, disappeared during the Revolution.

Ancien Hôpital – This was the residence of Stanislas Leszczinski from 1719 to 1725, when his daughter married Louis XV.

Walk back then turn right onto rue de l'Ordre-Teutonique.

Walk across the footbridge spanning the Lauter to reach the **Schlupf** district (Little Venice).

Turn left along rue de la République then right onto rue Nationale.

Holzapfel – The Gothic house flanked by corner turrets was a posting house from 1793 to 1854; Napoleon stayed there in 1806.

Walk back to return to place de la République.

PROMENADE DES REMPARTS

This picturesque itinerary which follows the bank of the former ramparts offers a good view of the old district and of the impressive towers of the Église St-Pierre-et-St-Paul, with, in the background, the undulating outline of the Vosges.

Part of the walls follow the river right through the town. Not far from the Maison Stanislas stands the Schartenturm, which is all that remains of the 11C wall surrounding the monastery.

Another section of wall extends from the end of faubourg de Bitche (fine 16C-17C mansion and Husgenossen tower) to the southern part of town.

ADDITIONAL SIGHT

Musée Westercamp ⊘ – Housed in a 16C building, the museum contains antique furniture (superb wardrobes), peasant costumes and mementoes from the 1870 battlefield as well as prehistoric and Roman exhibits.

EXCURSIONS

Vignoble de Cleebourg – The northern section of the Wine Road runs along the foothills of the northern Vosges, through vineyards specialising in two types of vines: Tokay Pinot Gris and Pinot Blanc Auxerrois.
There is wine-tasting in the Cleebourg cellars.

Altenstadt – *2km/1.2mi E.* The village has retained an interesting Romanesque **church** dating from the 11C and 12C. The nave and the aisles have ceilings. The chancel was raised in the 19C. As you enter, note the unusual porch (7m/23ft deep). The 11C belfry, decorated with Lombardy banding, was given a third storey in the 12C.

Ouvrage d'artillerie de Schoenenbourg – *12km7.5mi S along D 264 then D 65; signposting. See Ligne MAGINOT.*

THE AMAZING STORY OF JOAN OF ARC

No discussion of the history of Lorraine, the Vosges or Champagne would be complete without some mention of the history of *Jeanne d'Arc*, a simple country girl whose achievements were a decisive factor in awakening a national consciousness in France. The subject of a wide array of books, films and plays, Joan officially attained sainthood in 1920. However, her canonisation did not put an end to speculation on the divine or delusional nature of the voices that guided her. She remains a mystery and an amazement.

Born c 1412 in Dorémy, on the border of the duchies of Bar and Lorraine (and now in the Vosges *département*), Joan began life as the daughter of a tenant farmer of modest means and good reputation. According to the transcript of her trial, "at the age of 13, she received a voice from God, guiding her, and this voice came to her around noon, in the summer, in her father's garden". Joan believed that God spoke to her through the "voices" of Saint Michael, Saint Catherine and Saint Margaret.

The French crown was then in dispute between the Valois king (the "Dauphin" Charles) and the Lancastrian English king Henry VI (allied with the duke of Burgundy). The villagers of Dorémy were under constant threat from the Burgundians, and no champions of Henry. Charles needed to reach Reims to be crowned in the cathedral and reign legitimately, but Reims was deep in enemy territory.

Joan, possessed of remarkable courage and drive, made the dangerous journey to Chinon to speak to the Dauphin. Charles, 25 years old at the time, had known only war and intrigue, and was unable to reconquer his kingdom or make a peace agreement with the Burgundians. His father had been insane, his mother left Paris to ally herself with Burgundian duke John the Fearless, he was running out of money and his advisors were mostly untrustworthy. In a legendary confrontation, Charles, unsure and receiving contradictory counsel, made Joan wait several days before allowing her to enter the castle; then he disguised himself as an ordinary member of the court. Joan was not fooled an instant, kneeling before him without hesitation and saying that she wanted to go to battle with the English and accompany him to Reims for his coronation. While Charles vacillated, Joan pressed on. She bravely led attacks on Orleans, Beaugency and Patay, inspiring French troops and routing the English. Soon the mere sight of Joan's standard at the gates of a town was enough to make loyalties waver; thus Joan brought the Dauphin to Reims. She wrote the Duke of Burgundy, adjuring him to make peace with the legitimate monarch.

In 1430, when the Duke laid siege to Compiègne, Joan entered the town under cover of night and attempted a sortie, twice repelling the enemy. Protecting her rear guard to the last, Joan was unhorsed and captured. Charles, deep in his endless negotiations with the Burgundians, did nothing to seek her release. The Duke accepted an offer of 10,000 francs from the University of Paris, controlled by English partisans, to turn the young prisoner over to be tried – not for offences against the Lancastrian monarchy, but for heresy. Indeed, Joan's manner of direct discourse with her God threatened the powerful church hierarchy; proving her a heretic, or at least a witch, could also bring discredit on Charles. For five months, she was imprisoned in the harshest conditions while her health deteriorated, persecuted by her accusers, and her faith constantly called into question. Finally, her tormentors turned Joan over to the secular arm of justice, in order that she be condemned to death. On May 30, 1431, she was burned at the stake; witnesses to her death agreed that she died a faithful Christian.

Ruling as Charles VII, the new sovereign obtained a posthumous reversal of her sentence, perhaps more out of a perceived need to justify his coronation than a sense of justice. Despite his rather apathetic, indolent character, Charles VII made significant financial and military reforms which strengthened the French monarchy, and began to reunify the kingdom. He was helped in this by another remarkable woman, Agnès Sorel, his acknowledged mistress.

On 24 June, 1920, the French parliament declared a national festival in honour of Joan, held the second Sunday in May. Her greatest contribution to history may be her unfailing courage. Many factors complicate the analysis of her life and her impact on her times: she was victimised by both a foreign power and by France's internal struggles; the nature of her mission has been hotly debated by historians, theologians and psychologists; her recantation and whether or not she returned to wearing men's clothing of her own free will is still a subject of dispute. While the nature of her "voices" may be in doubt, none can question her heroic fortitude and profound conviction of the justice of her cause, nor the strength of her faith. She became, and remains, a symbol of the French spirit.

Ardennais horses

Practical information

Planning your trip

Climate and seasons

In Alsace, Lorraine and Champagne, weather patterns vary appreciably with the landscapes. The Ardenne uplands are known for heavy precipitation, low clouds, fog and frost; a bleak climate which may partially explain why this area has one of the lowest population densities in Europe. The lower plains of Champagne form part of the Paris Basin and share its milder climate; temperatures occasionally drop below freezing between November and March; the hottest days are in July and August.

In Alsace, comparable variations can be observed between the plain and the Vosges mountains. The average annual temperature in Colmar, for example, is 10.3°C/50.5°F, while the Grand Ballon (the highest summit) averages just 3°C/37.4°F. Prevailing winds arrive from the west or south-west, carrying rain and snow. When these weather systems run up against the Vosges, they result in precipitation, leaving the eastern plain fairly dry. Colmar holds the record for the lowest annual rainfall in France.

While the uplands are generally wetter and cooler throughout the area, visitors travelling on mountain roads may experience a curious phenomenon of temperature inversion, which occurs when atmospheric pressure is high. At such times, while a thick mist swathes the plain, the mountains bask in bright sunlight; temperatures may be 10°C/50°F higher than in the valley below. The luminosity and extensive view are uniquely magnificent.

Visitors will enjoy the summer months for holidays, but other seasons have their own charms. In the autumn, the vineyards and forests are rich with colour and harvest time livens up the villages, as the cool evening air brings red to your cheeks. Hunting season in the Ardenne Forest opens in November. Winter resorts in the Vosges are especially attractive to cross-country skiers and snowshoe enthusiasts, who appreciate the largely unspoiled beauty of the forest, and the traditional mountain villages; many areas have satisfactory downhill runs as well, and are equipped with snow-makers. The main resorts are Le Bonhomme (700m/2 297ft), La Bresse-Hohneck (650m/2 133ft), Gérardmer (750m/2 461ft), Saint-Maurice-sur-Moselle (560m/1 837ft) and Ventron (630m/2 067ft).

Champagne vineyards, early in the morning

Formalities

Passport – Nationals of countries within the European Union entering France need only a national identity card. Nationals of other countries must be in possession of a valid national **passport**. In case of loss or theft, report to your embassy or consulate and the local police.

Visa – No **entry visa** is required for Canadian, US or Australian citizens travelling as tourists and staying less than 90 days, except for students planning to study in France. If you think you may need a visa, apply to your local French Consulate.
US citizens should obtain the booklet *Safe Trip Abroad* (US$1), which provides useful information on visa requirements, customs regulations, medical care etc for international travellers. Published by the Government Printing Office, it can be ordered by phone – ☎ (202) 512-1800 – or consulted on-line (www.access.gpo.gov). General

passport information is available by phone toll-free from the Federal Information Center (item 5 on the automated menu), ☎ 800-688-9889. US passport application forms can be downloaded from http://travel.state.gov.

Customs – Apply to the Customs Office (UK) for a leaflet on customs regulations and the full range of duty-free allowances; available from HM Customs and Excise, Dorset House, Stamford Street, London SE1 9PS, ☎ 0171 928 3344. The US Customs Service offers a publication *Know before you go* for US citizens: for the office nearest you, consult the phone book, Federal Government, US Treasury (www.customs.ustreas.gov). There are no customs formalities for holidaymakers bringing their caravans into France for a stay of less than six months. No customs document is necessary for pleasure boats and outboard motors for a stay of less than six months but the registration certificate should be kept on board.

Americans can bring home, tax-free, up to US$ 400 worth of goods; Canadians up to CND$ 300; Australians up to AUS$ 400 and New Zealanders up to NZ$ 700. Persons living in a member state of the European Union are not restricted with regard to purchasing goods for private use, but the recommended allowances for alcoholic beverages and tobacco are as follows:

Spirits (whisky, gin, vodka etc.)	10 litres	Cigarettes	800
Fortified wines (vermouth, ports etc.)	20 litres	Cigarillos	400
Wine (not more than 60 sparkling)	90 litres	Cigars	200
Beer	110 litres	Smoking tobacco	1 kg

Embassies and consulates in France

Australia	Embassy	4 rue Jean-Rey, 75015 Paris ☎ 01 40 59 33 00 – Fax: 01 40 59 33 10.
Canada	Embassy	35 avenue Montaigne, 75008 Paris ☎ 01 44 43 29 00 – Fax: 01 44 43 29 99.
Eire	Embassy	4 rue Rude, 75016 Paris ☎ 01 44 17 67 00 – Fax: 01 44 17 67 60.
New Zealand	Embassy	7 ter rue Léonard-de-Vinci, 75016 Paris ☎ 01 45 01 43 43 – Fax: 01 45 01 43 44.
South Africa	Embassy	59 quai d'Orsay, 75007 Paris ☎ 01 53 59 23 23 – Fax: 01 53 59 23 33
UK	Embassy	35 rue du Faubourg-St-Honoré, 75008 Paris ☎ 01 44 51 31 00 – Fax: 01 44 51 31 27.
	Consulate	16 rue d'Anjou, 75008 Paris ☎ 01 44 51 31 01 (visas).
USA	Embassy	2 avenue Gabriel, 75008 Paris ☎ 01 43 12 22 22 – Fax: 01 42 66 97 83.
	Consulate	2 rue St-Florentin, 75001 Paris ☎ 01 42 96 14 88.
	Consulate	15 avenue d'Alsace, 67082 Strasbourg ☎ 03 88 35 31 04 – Fax: 03 88 24 06 95.

French tourist offices abroad

For information, brochures, maps and assistance in planning a trip to France travellers should apply to the official French Government Tourist Office / Maison de la France in their own country:

Australia – New Zealand
Sydney – BNP Building, 12 Castlereagh Street,
Sydney, New South Wales 2000,
☎ (02) 9231 5244 – Fax: (02) 9221 8682.

Canada
Montreal – 1981 Avenue McGill College, Suite 490,
Montreal PQ H3A 2W9,
☎ (514) 288-4264 – Fax: (514) 845 4868.
Toronto – 30 St Patrick's Street, Suite 700, Toronto, Ontario
☎ (416) 979 7587.

Eire
Dublin – 10 Suffolk Street, Dublin 2,
☎ (01) 679 0813 – Fax: (01) 679 0814.

South Africa
P.O. Box 41022, Craig Hall 2024,
☎ (011) 880 8062.

United Kingdom

London – 178 Piccadilly, London WIV OAL,
☎ (0891) 244 123 – Fax: (0171) 493 6594.

United States

East Coast – New York – 444 Madison Avenue,
16th Floor, NY 10022-6903,
☎ (212) 838-7800 – Fax: (212) 838-7855.
Mid West – Chicago – 676 North Michigan Avenue,
Suite 3360, Chicago, IL 60611-2819,
☎ (312) 751-7800 – Fax: (312) 337-6339.
West Coast – Los Angeles – 9454 Wilshire Boulevard,
Suite 715, Beverly Hills, CA 90212-2967,
☎ (310) 271-6665 – Fax: (310) 276-2835.
Information can also be requested from **France on Call**,
☎ (202) 659-7779.

On-line information

www.ambafrance-us.org
The French Embassy in America has a web site providing basic information (geography, demographics, history), a news digest and business-related information. It offers special pages for children, and pages devoted to culture, language study and travel, and you can reach other selected French sites (regions, cities, ministries) with a hypertext link.

www.franceguide.com
The French Government Tourist Office / Maison de la France site is packed with practical information and tips for those travelling to France. The home page has a number of links to more specific guidance, for American or Canadian travellers for example, or to the FGTO's London pages.

www.FranceKeys.com
Another site with plenty of information on most regions of France.

www.fr-holidaystore.co.uk
The French Travel Centre in London has gone on-line with this service, providing information on all of the regions of France, including updated special travel offers and details on available accommodation.

www.visiteurope.com
The European Travel Commission provides useful information on travelling to and around 27 European countries, and includes links to some commercial booking services (ie vehicle hire), rail schedules, weather reports and more.

Local tourist offices

To find the addresses of local tourist offices throughout France, contact the **Fédération Nationale des Comités Départementaux du Tourisme**, 280 boulevard St-Germain, 75007 Paris, ☎ 01 44 11 10 20. Below, the addresses are given for each local tourist office by region and *département*. The index lists the *département* after each town and the *départements* are delimited on the Map of principal sights in the introduction.

For **regional** information, address enquiries to the *Comité régional du tourisme (CRT)*:

Alsace – 6 avenue de la Marseillaise, B.P. 219, 67005 Strasbourg Cedex,
☎ 03 88 25 01 66 – Fax: 03 88 52 17 06 – www.tourisme-alsace.com.

Lorraine – 1 place Gabriel-Hocquard, B.P. 81004, 57036 Metz Cedex 1,
☎ 03 87 37 02 16 – www.cr-lorraine.fr.

Champagne-Ardenne – 15 avenue du Maréchal-Leclerc, BP 319, 51013 Châlons-en-Champagne Cedex, ☎ 03 26 21 85 80 – Fax: 03 26 21 85 90 – www.tourisme-champagne-ard.com.

For information on each *département*, address enquiries to the relevant **Comité Départemental du Tourisme (CDT)**:

Ardennes – 24 place Ducale, BP 419, 08107 Charleville-Mézières,
☎ 03 24 56 06 08.
Aube – 34 rue Dampierre, 10000 Troyes Cedex,
☎ 03 25 42 50 00.
Bas-Rhin – Agence de Développement Touristique, 9 rue du Dôme, B.P. 53, 67061 Strasbourg Cedex,
☎ 03 88 15 45 80.

Marne – 13 bis rue Carnot, B.P. 74, 51000 Châlons-en-Champagne,
☎ 03 26 68 37 52.
Meurthe-et-Moselle – 48 rue du Sergent-Blandan, B.P. 65, 54062 Nancy Cedex,
☎ 03 83 94 51 90.
Meuse – Hôtel du Département, 55012 Bar-le-Duc Cedex,
☎ 03 29 45 78 40.

Haute-Marne – 40 bis avenue Foch, 52000 Chaumont, ☎ 03 25 30 39 09.

Haut-Rhin – Maison du Tourisme de Haute-Alsace, 1 rue Schlumberger, BP 337, 68006 Colmar Cedex, ☎ 03 89 20 10 68 – www.tourisme68.asso.fr.

Moselle – Hôtel du Département, 1 rue du Pont-Moreau, BP 11096, 57036 Metz Cedex 1, ☎ 03 87 37 57 80 - www.moselle-france.com.

Vosges – 7 rue Gilbert, B.P. 332, 88008 Épinal Cedex, ☎ 03 29 82 49 93. The guide *Bonjour les Vosges* is available on request.

Tourist offices – Further information can be obtained from the tourist offices, or *Syndicats d'Initiative* as they are often called in smaller towns. Their addresses and telephone numbers are listed after the symbol 🛈, in the *Admission times and charges* section.

Tourist Pass: 100 sights for 280F

This pass gives unrestricted access to more than 100 historic buildings managed by the *Centre des Monuments Nationaux*. It is valid for one year throughout France as of the date of purchase and is for sale at the entrance to major historic buildings, monuments and museums. With the pass, you can save time by skipping the wait at the ticket window. For a list of all the monuments, plus details on their history, information on travel, and other entertaining features to help you plan your trip, visit the lively web site: www.monuments-france.fr.

Discounts – Significant discounts are available for senior citizens, students and children under 18 for public transportation, museums and monuments and for some leisure activities such as movies (at certain times of day). Bring student or senior cards with you, and bring along some extra passport-size photos.

Getting there

By air

Various international and other independent airlines operate services to **Paris** (Roissy-Charles de Gaulle and Orly airports) and there are regular air links to **Strasbourg** International Airport, **Basel-Mulhouse** (EuroAirport) and **Metz-Nancy-Lorraine** Airport from Paris and a host of other, mainly European, cities. There is a shuttle bus service into Strasbourg every 30min from Monday to Friday, and as planes arrive on weekends (journey time of 30min). The shuttle service from EuroAirport to Mulhouse train station also takes 30min. Metz-Nancy-Lorraine airport is situated between Metz and Nancy. The Aérolor shuttle runs from the airport to Metz (30min) or Nancy (40min) train stations.

Contact airline companies and travel agents for details of package tour flights with a rail or coach link-up, as well as fly-drive schemes.

Arriving by sea from the UK or Ireland

There are numerous **cross-Channel services** (passenger and car ferries, hovercraft) from the United Kingdom and Ireland and also the rail Shuttle through the Channel Tunnel (**Le Shuttle-Eurotunnel**, ☎ 0990 353-535). To choose the most suitable route between your port of arrival and your destination use the Michelin Tourist and Motoring Atlas France, Michelin map 911 (which gives travel times and mileages) or Michelin maps from the 1:200,000 series (with the yellow cover). For details apply to travel agencies or to:

P&O Stena Line Ferries	Channel House, Channel View Road, Dover CT17 9JT, ☎ 0990 980 980 or 01304 863 000 (Switchboard).
Hoverspeed	International Hoverport, Marine Parade, Dover, Kent CT17 9TG, ☎ 0990 240 241 – Fax: 01304 240088, www.hoverspeed.co.uk
Brittany Ferries	Millbay Docks, Plymouth, Devon. PL1 3EW, ☎ 0990 360 360, www.brittanyferries.com
Portsmouth Commercial Port (and ferry information)	George Byng Way, Portsmouth, Hampshire PO2 8SP, ☎ 01705 297391 – Fax: 01705 861165
Irish Ferries	50 West Norland Street, Dublin 2, ☎ (353) 16-610-511, www.irishferries.com
Seafrance	Eastern Docks, Dover, Kent, CT16 1JA, ☎ 01304 212696 – Fax: 01304 240033.

By rail

Eurostar runs via the Channel Tunnel between **London** (Waterloo) and **Paris** (Gare du Nord) in 3hr (bookings and information ☎ 0990 186 186 in the UK; ☎ 1-888-EUROSTAR in the US). From Paris (Gare de l'Est), the **SNCF** (French national railways) operates an extensive service to the region, including Nancy and Metz (2hr 30min-3hr), Strasbourg and Colmar (4-5hr), Reims (1hr 30min-2hr), Châlons-en-Champagne (1hr 15min), Troyes (1hr 30min), Charleville-Mézières (2hr 30min).

Eurailpass, Flexipass and **Saverpass** are travel passes which may be purchased in the US. Contact your travel agent or **Rail Europe**, 2100 Central Avenue Boulder, CO 80301, ☎ 1-800-4-EURAIL, or **Europrail International**, ☎ 1-888-667-9731. They may also be purchased in person in the UK from 178 Piccadilly London W1V OBA, ☎ 08705 848 848. Information on schedules can be obtained on web sites for these agencies and the **SNCF**: www.raileurop.com.us, www.eurail.on.ca, and www.sncf.fr.

The SNCF **youth discount card** (for those between ages 12-25) provides a 25-50% reduction on rail tickets, and also 25% reduction on the Eurostar, Avis rental cars, and United Airlines, Lufthansa, SAS and Air Canada flights. The card costs 270F for one year; you can pick it up at the train station (photo and proof of age required) or from an authorised SNCF agent *(Carte 12-25)*. Similarly, the **Carte Senior** offers 25-50% reductions on rail travel in France and from France to other European countries for travellers over 60. It is valid one year, costs 290F and requires a photo.

Strasbourg tramway

For EU citizens, a number of rail passes offer unlimited travel for a specified time. **Eurodomino** tickets are valid for unlimited rail travel within one European country over 3 to 8 days within any given month, while the **Interail** passes allow a month's unlimited travel within a specified zone, covering several countries. Both are available in the UK from Rail Europe at 178 Piccadilly, London WIV OBA, ☎ 08705 848 848. Tickets bought in France must be validated *(composter)* by using the orange automatic date-stamping machines at the platform entrance (failure to do so may result in a fine). Baggage trolleys (10F refundable coin required) are available at mainline stations.

A good investment is the **Thomas Cook European Timetable**, which gives all the train schedules throughout France and Europe, as well as useful information on travelling by train (from the US, ☎ 1 800 367 7984).

The French railway company SNCF operates a telephone information, reservation and prepayment service in English from 7am to 10pm (French time). In France, call ☎ 08 36 35 35 39 (when calling from outside France, drop the initial 0). Ask about discount rates if you are over 60, a student or travelling with your family.

By coach

Regular coach services operate from London to Paris and to large provincial towns:
Eurolines (London), 4 Cardiff Road, Luton, Bedfordshire, L41 1PP, ☎ 0990 143219 – Fax: 01582 400694, welcome@eurolinesuk.com and www.eurolines.co.uk
Eurolines (Paris), 28 avenue du Général-de-Gaulle, 93541 Bagnolet, ☎ 08 36 69 52 52

Travellers with special needs

The sights described in this guide that are easily accessible to people of reduced mobility are indicated in the *Admission times and charges* section by the symbol &.

Useful information on transportation, holidaymaking and sports associations for the disabled is available from the **Comité National Français de Liaison pour la Réadaptation des Handicapés** (CNRH), 236 bis rue de Tolbiac, 75013 Paris. Call their international information number ☎ 01 53 80 66 66, or write to request a catalogue of publications. Web-surfers can find information for slow walkers, mature travellers and others with special needs at www.access-able.com. If you are a member of a sports club and would like to practice your sport in France, or meet others who do, ask the CNRH for information on clubs in the **Fédération Française du Sport Adapté** (FFSA) in Paris, ☎ 01 48 72 80 72. For information on museum access for the disabled, contact La Direction, **Les Musées de France, Service Accueil des Publics Spécifiques**, 6 rue des Pyramides, 75041 Paris Cedex 1, ☎ 01 40 15 35 88.

The **Michelin Red Guide France** and the **Michelin Camping Caravaning France** guide indicate hotels and camp sites with facilities suitable for physically handicapped people.

Motoring in France

Planning your route – The area covered in this guide is easily reached by main motorways and national routes. **Michelin map 911** indicates the main itineraries as well as alternate routes for avoiding heavy traffic during busy holiday periods, and gives estimated travel times. **Michelin map 914** is a detailed atlas of French motorways, indicating tolls, rest areas and services along the route; it includes a table for calculating distances and times. The latest Michelin route-planning service is available on the Internet, **www.ViaMichelin.com**. Travellers can calculate a precise route using such options as shortest route, route avoiding toll roads, Michelin-recommended route, and gain access to tourist information (hotels, restaurants, attractions).

The roads are very busy during the holiday period (particularly weekends in July and August) and, to avoid traffic congestion, it is advisable to follow the recommended secondary routes (signposted as *Bison Futé – itinéraires bis*). The motorway network includes rest areas *(aires)* and petrol stations, usually with restaurant and shopping complexes attached, about every 40km/25mi, so that long-distance drivers have no excuse not to stop for a rest every now and then.

Documents – Travellers from other European Union countries and North America can drive in France with a valid national or home-state **driving licence**. An **international driving licence** is useful because the information on it appears in nine languages (bear in mind that traffic officers are empowered to fine motorists). A permit is available from the National Automobile Club, 1151 East Hillsdale Blvd, Foster City, CA 94404, ☎ 650-294-7000 (www.nationalautoclub.com); or contact your local branch of the American Automobile Association. For the vehicle, it is necessary to have the registration papers (logbook), the current insurance certificate and a nationality plate of the approved size. If the vehicle is borrowed, you should also carry a letter of authorisation from the owner.

Insurance – Certain motoring organisations (AAA, AA, RAC) offer accident insurance and breakdown service schemes for members. Check with your insurance company with regard to coverage while abroad. If you plan to hire a car using your credit card, check with the company, which may provide liability insurance automatically (and thus save you having to pay the optional fee for optimum coverage).

Highway Code – The legal driving age in France is 18. Traffic drives on the right. All passengers must wear **seat belts**. Children under the age of 10 must travel on the back seat of the vehicle. Full or dipped headlights must be switched on in poor visibility and at night; use sidelights only when the vehicle is stationary.

In the case of a **breakdown**, a red warning triangle or hazard warning lights are obligatory. In the absence of stop signs at intersections, cars must **yield to the right**. Traffic on main roads outside built-up areas (priority indicated by a yellow diamond sign) and on round-abouts has right of way. Vehicles must stop when the lights turn red at road junctions and may filter to the right only when indicated by an amber arrow.

The regulations on **drinking and driving** and **speeding** are strictly enforced – usually by an on-the-spot fine and/or confiscation of the vehicle.

Speed limits – Although liable to modification, these are as follows:

– toll motorways *(autoroutes à péage)* – 130kph/80mph (110kph/68mph when raining);

– dual carriageways and motorways without tolls – 110kph/68mph (100kph/62mph when raining);

– other roads – 90kph/56mph (80kph/50mph when raining) and in towns – 50kph/31mph;

– outside lane on motorways during daylight, on level ground and with good visibility – minimum speed limit of 80kph/50mph.

Parking regulations – In town, there are zones where parking is either restricted or subject to a fee; tickets should be obtained from the ticket machines (*horodateurs* – small change necessary) and displayed inside the windscreen on the driver's side; failure to display may result in a fine, or towing and impoundment. In some towns, you may find blue parking zones *(zone bleue)* marked by a blue line on the pavement or road and a blue signpost with a P and a small square underneath. In this case you have to display a cardboard disc with various times indicated on it. This will enable you to stay for 1hr 30min (2hr 30min over lunch time) free. Discs are available in supermarkets or petrol stations (ask for a *disque de stationnement*); they are sometimes given away free.

Tolls – In France, most motorway sections are subject to a toll *(péage)*. You can pay in cash or with a credit card (Visa, MasterCard). Sample tariffs can be found on the motorways web site – www.autoroutes.fr.

Petrol (US: gas) – French service stations dispense *sans plomb 98* (super unleaded 98 octane rating), *sans plomb 95* (super unleaded 95), *diesel/gazole* (diesel) and, increasingly, *GPL* (LPG). Petrol is considerably more expensive in France than in the USA. Prices are listed on signboards on the motorways, but it is also more expensive on these roads than elsewhere. The large hypermarkets on the outskirts of town are often cheaper places to fill up.

Car rental

There are car rental agencies at airports, railway stations and in all large towns throughout France. European cars have manual transmission; automatic cars are available in larger cities only if an advance reservation is made. Drivers must be over 21. Between ages 21-25, drivers are required to pay an extra daily fee of 50-100F; some companies allow drivers under 23 only if the reservation has been made through a travel agent. It is relatively expensive to hire a car in France; Americans in particular will notice the difference and should make arrangements before leaving – take advantage of fly-drive offers, or seek advice from a travel agent, specifying requirements.

Central Reservation in France:

Avis: ☎ 0 802 05 05 05

Budget France: ☎ 0 800 10 00 01

SIXT-Eurorent: ☎ 01 44 38 55 55

Baron's Limousine and Driver: ☎ 01 45 30 21 21

Europcar: ☎ 0 803 352 352

Hertz France: ☎ 0 803 861 861

National-CITER: ☎ 01 44 38 61 61

Worldwide Motorhome Rentals offers fully equipped campervans for rent. You can view them on the company's web pages (mhrww.com) or call (US toll-free) US ☎ 888-519-8969; outside the US ☎ 530-389-8316 or Fax 530-389-8316.

Overseas Motorhome Tours Inc. organises escorted tours and individual rental of recreational vehicles: in the US ☎ 800-322-2127; outside the US ☎ 1-310-543-2590; Internet www.omtinc.com

Basic information

Medical treatment

First aid, medical advice and chemists' night service rotas are available from chemists (*pharmacie* – identified by a green cross). Prescription drugs should be clearly labelled and foreign visitors are advised to carry a copy of the prescription.

It is advisable to take out comprehensive insurance cover as medical treatment in French hospitals or clinics must be paid for by the recipient. Nationals of non-EU countries should check with their insurance companies about policy limitations. Reimbursement can then be negotiated with the insurance company according to the policy held.

Americans concerned about travel and health can contact the International Association for Medical Assistance to Travelers, which can also provide details of English-speaking doctors in different parts of France: ☎ (716) 754-4883.

British and Irish citizens should apply to the Department of Health and Social Security **before travelling** for **Form E 111**, which entitles the holder to urgent treatment for accident or unexpected illness in EU countries. A refund of part of the costs of treatment can be obtained on application in person or by post to the local Social Security Offices (*Caisse Primaire d'Assurance Maladie*).

The American Hospital of Paris is open 24hr for emergencies as well as consultations, with English-speaking staff, at 63 boulevard Victor-Hugo, 92200 Neuilly-sur-Seine, ☎ 01 46 41 25 25. Accredited by major insurance companies.

The British Hospital is just outside Paris in Levallois-Perret, 3 rue Barbès, ☎ 01 46 39 22 22.

Currency

There are no restrictions on the amount of currency visitors can take into France. However, the amount of cash you may take out of France is subject to a limit, so visitors carrying a lot of cash should complete a currency declaration form on arrival.

French francs are subdivided into 100 centimes. The European Union's new currency units, **euros**, are being printed, and the banking and finance industries have already begun making the changeover. Euro banknotes and coins will go into general circulation from 1 January 2002 and, after **17 February 2002**, euros will be the only currency accepted as a means of payment. However, until the end of June 2002, notes and coins in francs can be exchanged in banks. After that, they will only be accepted by the Banque de France (3 years for coins and 10 years for notes). In the meantime, both euro and franc values (1 euro is roughly equivalent to 6.50F) are given in more and more instances (store and restaurant receipts, bank documents etc).

Tipping – Since a service charge of 15% is usually included (*service compris*) in the prices of meals and accommodation in France, it is not necessary to tip in restaurants and hotels. However if the service in a restaurant is especially good or if you have enjoyed a fine meal, an extra tip (this is the *pourboire*, rather than the *service*) is a well-appreciated gesture. Usually 10 or 20F is enough, but if the bill is big (a large party or a luxury restaurant), it is not uncommon to leave 50F or more. Taxi drivers should be given 10-15% of the metered fare. Tip hairdressers 10%, assistant 5%.

Banks

Banks are usually open from 9am to noon and 2pm to 5pm and are closed on Mondays or Saturdays (except on market days); some branches open for limited transactions on Saturdays. Banks close early on the day before a bank holiday.

A passport is necessary as identification when cashing cheques in banks. Commission charges vary and hotels usually charge more than banks for cashing cheques for non-residents.

One of the most economical ways to obtain money in France is to use **cash dispensers** (ATM) that accept international credit or debit cards. The machines are available everywhere and they often offer the best exchange rates. Virtually all ATMs in France take Visa and MasterCard, and many are linked to the Cirrus and Plus systems. American Express cards can only be used in certain machines. The code pads are numeric. If you know your PIN number in letters only, use a telephone dial pad to translate the letters into numbers.

Credit Card purchases – Visa (Carte Bleue) is the most widely accepted, followed by MasterCard/Eurocard (shops, petrol stations, supermarkets, toll booths, restaurants etc). American Express is more widely accepted in premium establishments. Most places post signs indicating the cards they accept, otherwise, if you want to pay with a card, it is a good idea to ask before ordering or selecting your purchases. Be sure to remember your PIN number, as you will often be asked to punch it when paying. If your card is lost or stolen, call one of the following 24-hour numbers:

American Express	☎ 01 47 77 72 00	**Visa**	☎ 08 36 69 08 80
MasterCard/Eurocard	☎ 01 45 67 84 84	**Diners Club**	☎ 01 49 06 17 50

Such loss or theft must be reported to the local police, who will issue a certificate to show to the credit card company.

Shops

Most of the larger shops are open Monday to Saturday from 9am to 6.30 or 7.30pm. Smaller, individual shops may close during the lunch hour. Food shops – grocers, wine merchants and bakeries – are generally open from 7am to 6.30 or 7.30pm; some open on Sunday mornings. Many food shops close between noon and 2pm and on Mondays. Bakery and pastry shops sometimes close on Wednesdays. Hypermarkets usually open until 9pm or later.

People travelling to the USA cannot import plant products or fresh food, including fruit, cheeses and nuts. It is acceptable to carry tinned products or preserves.

VAT refunds – There is a Value Added Tax in France *(TVA)* of 19.6% on almost every purchase (some foods and books are subject to a lower rate). However, non-European visitors who spend more than 1200F (182.94€) in any one participating store can get the VAT amount refunded. Usually, you fill out a form at the store, showing your passport. Upon leaving the country, you submit all forms to customs for approval (they may want to see the goods, so if possible don't pack them in checked luggage). The refund is usually paid directly into your bank or credit card account, or it can be sent by mail. Big department stores that cater to tourists provide special services to help you; be sure to mention that you plan to seek a refund before you pay for goods (no refund is possible for tax on services). If you are visiting two or more countries within the European Union, you submit the forms only on departure from the last EU country. The refund is worth while for those visitors who would like to buy fashions, furniture or other fairly expensive items, but remember, the minimum amount must be spent in a single shop (though not necessarily on a single day). For further details, call the French embassy or visit the web site for your country (in the US, go to French Customs Office, then Information for Private Individuals and finally Tax Refund for Visitors).

Public holidays

Public services, museums and other monuments may be closed or may vary their hours of admission on the following public holidays:

1	January	New Year's Day *(Jour de l'An)*
Easter Sun-Mon		*(Pâques)*
1	May	May Day
8	May	VE Day
40 days after Easter		Ascension Day *(Ascension)*
7th Sun-Mon after Easter		Whitsun *(Pentecôte)*
14	July	France's National Day (Bastille Day)
15	August	Assumption *(Assomption)*
1	November	All Saints' Day *(Toussaint)*
11	November	Armistice Day
25	December	Christmas Day *(Noël)*

National museums and art galleries are closed on Tuesdays; municipal museums are generally closed on Mondays. In addition to the usual school holidays at Christmas and in the spring and summer, there are long mid-term breaks (10 days to a fortnight) in February and early November.

Post and telephone

Main post offices are open Monday to Friday from 8am to 6pm and Saturday from 8am to noon. Smaller branch post offices close at lunchtime between noon and 2pm and in the afternoon at 4pm. French post boxes are yellow in colour.

Postage via airmail to:
> UK letter (20g) 3F
> US letter (20g) 4.40F
> Australia and New Zealand letter (20g) 5.20F
> South Africa letter (20g) 3.90F

Stamps may also be available from newsagents and tobacconists.
Stamp collectors should ask for *timbres de collection* in any post office.
Poste Restante (General Delivery) mail should be addressed as follows: Name, Poste Restante, Poste Centrale, postal code of the *département* followed by town name, France. **The Red Guide France** gives local postal codes.

Public Telephones – Most public phones in France use prepaid phone cards *(télécartes)*, rather than coins. Some telephone booths accept credit cards (Visa, Mastercard/Eurocard: minimum monthly charge 20F). *Télécartes* (50 or 120 units) can be bought in post offices, branches of France Télécom, *bureaux de tabac* (cafés that sell cigarettes) and newsagents and can be used to make calls in France and abroad. Calls can be received in phone boxes where the blue bell sign is shown; the phone will not ring, so keep your eye on the little message screen.

National calls – French telephone numbers have 10 digits. Paris and Paris region numbers begin with 01; 02 in north-west France; 03 in north-east France; 04 in south-east France and Corsica; 05 in south-west France.

International calls – To call France from abroad, dial the country code (33) + the 9-digit number (omit the initial 0). When calling abroad from France dial 00, then dial the country code followed by the area code and the number of your correspondent.

International dialling codes (00 + code):

Australia	☎ 61		New Zealand	☎ 64
Canada	☎ 1		United Kingdom	☎ 44
Eire	☎ 353		United States	☎ 1

To use your **personal calling card** dial:

AT&T	☎ 0-800 99 00 11	Sprint .... ☎ 0-800 99 00 87
MCI	☎ 0-800 99 00 19	Canada Direct .... ☎ 0-800 99 00 16

International directory enquiries, all countries: 32 12
International operator: 32 12 or 31 23
Local directory assistance: 12
Toll-free numbers in France begin with 0 800.

Cellular phones in France have numbers beginning with 06. Two-watt (lighter, shorter reach) and eight-watt models are on the market, using the Itinéris (France Télécom) or SFR network. *Mobicartes* are pre-paid phone cards that fit into mobile units. Cell phone rentals (delivery or airport pickup provided):

Rent a Cell Express	☎ 01 53 93 78 00, Fax: 01 53 93 78 09
A.L.T. Rent A Phone	☎ 01 48 00 06 60, E-mail:
Cell'Force	☎ 01 44 40 02 80, Fax: 01 44 40 02 88

Emergency numbers (free of charge):			
Police:	17	**"SAMU"** (Paramedics):	15
Fire *(Pompiers)*:	18		

Electricity

The electric current is 220 volts. Circular two pin plugs are the rule – an electrical adaptor may be necessary. US appliances (hairdryers, shavers) will not work without one. Adapters are on sale in electronics stores and also at international airports.

Time

France is 1hr ahead of Greenwich Mean Time (GMT).

When it is **noon in France**, it is

3am	in Los Angeles
6am	in New York
11am	in Dublin
11am	in London
1pm	in Pretoria
7pm	in Perth
9pm	in Sydney
11pm	in Auckland

In France "am" and "pm" are not used but the 24-hour clock is widely applied.

Accommodation

The **Map of places to stay** indicates recommended places for overnight stops, spas, and winter resorts; it can be used in conjunction with the **The Red Guide France** which lists a selection of hotels and restaurants.
Loisirs-Accueil is a booking service that has offices in most French *départements* and can help with many types of accommodation, including bed and breakfast, self-catering and camping. For further information, contact the tourist offices listed above or the head office of Réservation Loisirs Accueil, 280 boulevard St-Germain, 75007 Paris, ☎ 01 44 11 10 44, .

Hotels

A guide to good-value, family run hotels, **Logis et Auberges de France**, is available from the French Tourist Office, as are lists of other kinds of accommodation such as hôtel-châteaux, bed and breakfasts etc. **Relais et châteaux** provides information on booking rooms in luxury hotels with character: 15 rue Galvani, 75017 Paris, ☎ 01 45 72 90 00.

Economy Chain Hotels – If you need a place to stop en route, these can be useful, as they are inexpensive (about 200F for a double room) and generally located near the main road. While breakfast is available, there may not be a restaurant; rooms are small, with a television and bathroom. Central reservation numbers:
– **Akena** ☎ 01 69 84 85 17
– **B&B** ☎ 0 803 00 29 29
– **Etap Hôtel** ☎ 08 36 68 89 00 (2.23F per minute, from France)
– **Mister Bed** ☎ 01 46 14 38 00
– **Villages Hôtel** ☎ 03 80 60 92 70
The hotels listed below are slightly more expensive (from 300F), and offer a few more amenities and services. Central reservation numbers:
– **Campanile** ☎ 01 64 62 46 46
– **Climat de France** ☎ 01 64 62 48 88
– **Ibis** ☎ 0 803 88 22 22

Rural accommodation

Self-catering – **The Maison des Gîtes de France** is an information service on self-catering accommodation. *Gîtes* usually take the form of a cottage or apartment decorated in the local style where visitors can make themselves at home.
Contact the Gîtes de France office in Paris, 59 rue St-Lazare, 75439 Paris Cedex 09, ☎ 01 49 70 75 75, or their representative, in the UK, **Brittany Ferries** *(see address above)*. The web site is quite complete and has an excellent English version – www.gites-de-france.com or, specifically for Alsace, www.alsace-gites-de-france.com.

Places to Stay

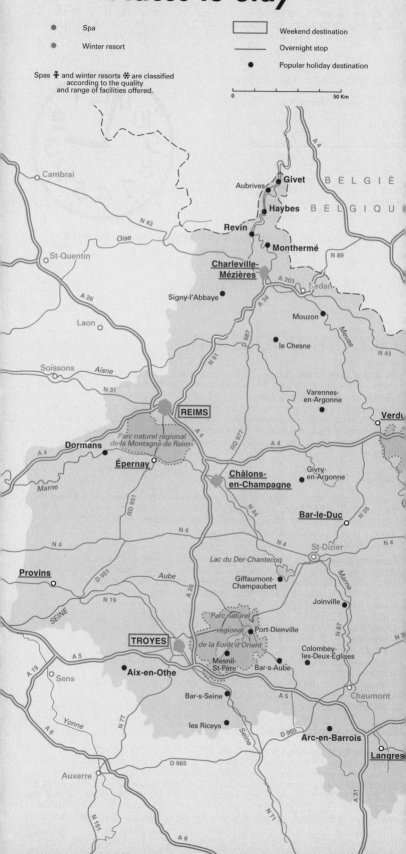

Legend:
- ● Spa
- ● Winter resort
- ▭ Weekend destination
- — Overnight stop
- ● Popular holiday destination

Spas ✠ and winter resorts ❄ are classified according to the quality and range of facilities offered.

0 — 50 Km

Cambrai

BELGIË
BELGIQUE

Aubrives · **Givet**
Haybes
Revin
Monthermé
Charleville-Mézières
Sedan
Signy-l'Abbaye ·
Mouzon ·
St-Quentin
le Chesne ·
Laon
Soissons
Aisne
Varennes-en-Argonne ·
REIMS
Verdu
Parc naturel régional de la Montagne de Reims
Dormans
Épernay
Givry-en-Argonne ·
Marne
Châlons-en-Champagne
Bar-le-Duc
N 4
N 4
St-Dizier
N 4
Provins
Lac du Der-Chantecoq
Giffaumont-Champaubert ·
Joinville
Aube
SEINE
Parc naturel régional de la Forêt d'Orient
Port-Dienville ·
Colombey-les-Deux-Églises ·
TROYES
Mesnil-St-Père ·
Bar-s-Aube ·
Aix-en-Othe
Sens
Bar-s-Seine ·
Chaumont
les Riceys ·
Arc-en-Barrois
Yonne
Seine
D 965
Langres
Auxerre
D 965

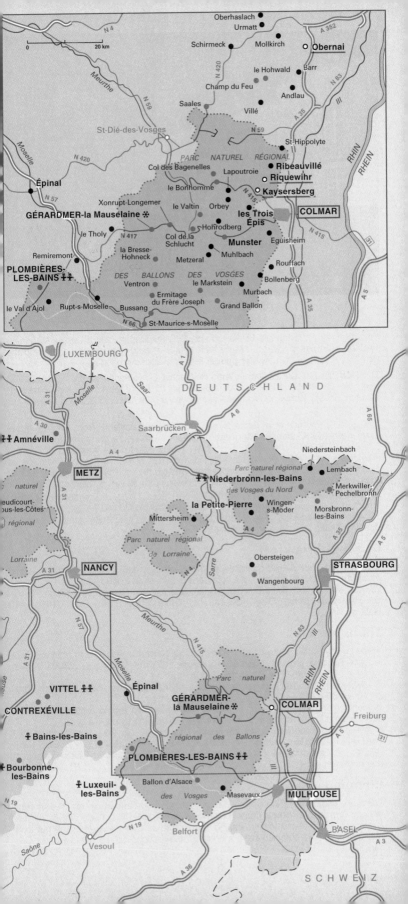

Bed and Breakfast at the Château de Châtel

Gîtes de France, Springfield Books Ltd and FHG Publications/World Leisure Marketing all publish listings of *gîtes* in France with details of how to book. Try contacting the local tourist offices, as they also publish lists of available properties.

The Fédération Française des Stations Vertes de Vacances, 6 rue Ranfer-de-Bretenière, 21000 Dijon, ☎ 03 80 54 10 50 – Fax: 03 80 54 10 55, is able to provide details of accommodation, leisure facilities and natural attractions in rural locations selected for their tranquillity.

The guide *Bienvenue à la ferme* is published by and available from the Assemblée Permanente des Chambres d'Agriculture, Service "Agriculture et Tourisme", 9 avenue Georges-V, 75008 Paris, ☎ 01 53 57 10 10. It includes the addresses of farmers providing guest facilities who have signed a charter drawn up by the Chambers of Agriculture. *Bienvenue à la ferme* farms, vetted for quality and meeting official standards, can be identified by the yellow flower which serves as their logo.

Ramblers can consult the guide entitled *Gîtes et refuges, France et Frontières* by A and S Mouraret (Editions La Cadole, 74 rue Albert-Perdreaux, 78140 Vélizy, ☎ 01 34 65 10 40). The guide has been written mainly for those who enjoy rambling, cycling, climbing, skiing and canoeing-kayaking holidays.

Bed and breakfast

Gîtes de France *(see above)* publishes a booklet on bed and breakfast accommodation *(chambres d'hôte)* which includes a room and breakfast at a reasonable price.

You can also contact **Bed & Breakfast (France)**, International reservations centre, PO Box 66, Henley-on-Thames, Oxon RG9 1XS, ☎ (01491) 578 803 – Fax: (01491) 410 806; e-mail: .

Youth hostels

There are two main youth hostel associations *(auberges de jeunesse)* in France:
- **Ligue Française pour les Auberges de Jeunesse**, 67 rue Vergniaud, 750013 Paris, ☎ 01 44 16 78 78 – Fax: 01 44 16 78 80, .
- **Fédération Unie des Auberges de Jeunesse (FUAJ)** 27 rue Pajol, 75018 Paris, ☎ 01 44 89 87 27 – Fax: 01 44 89 87 10 , .

Holders of an International Youth Hostel Federation card should contact the International Federation or the French Youth Hostels Association to book a bed.

Hostelling International/Youth Hostel Association () in the US (☎ 202 783-6161), the UK (☎ 01727 855215), Canada (☎ 613 273-7884) and Australia (☎ 2-9565-1669) sells a publication called *International Hostel Guide for Europe* – also available to non-members.

Camping

There are numerous officially graded sites with varying standards of facilities throughout the region; the **Michelin Camping Caravaning France** guide lists a selection of the best camp sites. An International Camping Carnet for caravans is useful but not compulsory; it can be obtained from motoring organisations or the Camping and Caravanning Club, Greenfield House, Westwood Way, Coventry CV4 8JH; ☎ (02476) 694-995.

Regional specialities and wines

The **Red Guide France** provides a very wide selection of restaurants, for all tastes and pocketbooks, serving the finest specialities in the regions of Alsace-Lorraine and Champagne-Ardenne as well as the rest of France.

When the word *repas* (meal) is printed in red, it refers to a high quality but reasonably priced meal. Pictograms indicate places with charming decor, a beautiful view, or a quiet setting.

Fermes-auberges (farm-inns) may or may not offer overnight accommodation, but they do serve farm produce and local speciality dishes.

The tradition of serving country fare to travellers is a century old in the Hautes-Vosges, where dairy farmers were known as *marcaires*. The *repas marcaire* proposed by many farms usually includes a *tourte de la vallée de Munster* (deep-dish pie with smoked pork, onions and garlic), followed by a blueberry tart. The *Guide des Fermes-auberges* in the Hautes-Vosges and Sundgau is available (40F) from the **Association des Fermes-auberges du Haut-Rhin et Départements Limitrophes**, BP 371, 68007 Colmar Cedex, ☎ 03 89 20 10 68. Write to the **Comité Régional du Tourisme de Lorraine** *(see address above)* for a catalogue of farms in the area entitled *Fermes-auberges, les Saveurs du Terroir Lorrain*.

Winstubs and brasseries are two very traditional types of eating house in Alsace. *Winstubs* were created by the Strasbourg wine producers to promote their wines and they provide a convivial setting in which to order a carafe of Alsatian wine to accompany a choice of different local dishes. For those who prefer beer, *brasseries* offer the chance to taste food from the region accompanied by a glass of beer brewed on site.

Gourmet guide – The Alsace-Lorraine region boasts a number of production sites, gastronomic itineraries, fairs and other events that particularly appeal to the gourmet traveller interested in discovering local specialities. Among those that have been awarded the special distinction of *site remarquable du goût* (tempting moments for the palate) are the Kronenbourg, Schutzenberger and Météor breweries for their beer, the sugar festival in the Erstein area (last weekend in August), the fried carp route in the Sundgau, the wine road in Alsace, the Kugelhopf festival in Ribeauvillé (first fortnight in June) and the cheeses of Cornimont (Munster, Géromé and Bargkass).

In Champagne-Ardenne, a number of chefs offering local recipes or products have formed a special group and display a sign with a chef's hat on a red background at the entrance to their establishments. In Ardenne, those who offer at least three or four specialities from the region display a blue and red sign.

Cookery courses – A number of restaurant owners in Alsace offer cookery courses with accommodation. They are usually held in winter:

Hôtellerie du Pape, 10 Grande Rue, 68420 Eguisheim, ☎ 03 89 41 41 21.
Hôtel-restaurant Alsace Villages, 49 rue Principale, 67510 Obersteinbach, ☎ 03 88 09 50 59.
Hôtel-restaurant Aux Deux Clefs, 50 Grand'Rue, 68600 Bisheim, ☎ 03 89 72 51 20.
Table d'hôte, Madame Fuchs, 22 rue de l'École, 67670 Waltenheim-sur-Zorn, ☎ 03 88 51 64 57.

Alsace-Lorraine

Choucroute is synonymous with Alsatian cuisine. The basic ingredient is white cabbage prepared in brine. The word is related phonetically to its German origin, *sauerkraut*. Typically, it is served with potatoes and a daunting portion of sausages, bacon, chops and other smoked or boiled pork. Modern tastes for lighter dishes have inspired many variations, in particular preparations using several varieties of fish or wildfowl; juniper berries add a burst of flavour. The choice of game is very wide, and partridge takes pride of place in seasonal *choucroute*. *Baeckeoffe* is a stew made of layers of different meats (usually mutton, pork and beef), potatoes and onions.

Yet pork remains the meat of choice, as evidenced by the many *charcuterie* shops selling salted and smoked hams, knuckles, trotters and bacon, Strasbourg sausages (pork and beef in a plump frankfurter), spicy *cervelas*, salamis, blood puddings and pork pies.

There is a long tradition of Jewish cuisine in Alsace too, and its influence is felt in the use of geese and goose fat in the place of pork, as well as the celebrated *carpe à la juive* (gefilte fish), a dish which is made ahead of time and served cold. Another popular freshwater fish dish is *matelote*, a stew made from a variety of species which may include pike, tench, perch, trout and eel. Frog soup has been a tradition in Alsace since at least the 13C.

The well-known quiche Lorraine joins other savoury pies, *tarte à l'oignon (ziewelküche)* and *tarte flambée (flammeküche)*, along with the delicious but unpronounceable *roï-gabragelti* (potato and onion hash) on menus in many popular establishments. Of course, while you are waiting, you may ask for a salty *bretzel* to go with your beer.

Munster is one of a variety of cheeses made in the region. This tasty, strong-flavoured cheese is named after a valley town in the Vosges mountains. Semi-soft, with a distinctive orange crust, a small portion of Munster is served at the end of a meal with a little dish of cumin or caraway seeds, and a glass of Gewürztraminer.

D.Hee/MICHELIN

Baked goods entice the visitor passing by the innumerable shops selling all sorts of breads, cakes and pastries. Among the specialities is the familiar *kugelhopf* (the name derives from the German *Kugel*, meaning ball), a light tube cake with raisins and almonds baked in a distinctive fluted and twisted mould. There are many seasonal treats, especially around Christmas time, starting early December with the St Nicholas *bonshommes*, in festive shapes, going on through New Year with *neujohrweke* brioche, and up until St Agatha's feast day (5 February), when the patron saint of bakers is celebrated. *Bredeles* are also associated with Christmas, although they can be bought all year round nowadays, and come in a variety of shapes; these buttery biscuits are flavoured with vanilla, lemon, aniseed or almonds. *Pain d'épice* (spice cake or gingerbread) also comes in every shape and size.

Mirabelles *(Prunus syriaca)* are found in orchards all over Lorraine. This golden-rose fruit weighs no more than 15g/0.5oz, stone included. It is used to make ice cream, tarts and jams, or served in syrup. *Mirabelle de Lorraine* is the official name of the distilled liqueur which is commonly served after a meal. Every year, the **Fête de la mirabelle** is held in Metz from the last weekend in August through to the first weekend in September.

Alsatian wines are predominantly white, and are identified by the grape types, rather than by the estate or village. The varieties are **Sylvaner**, **Muscat**, **Riesling**, **Pinot Gris**, **Gewürz-traminer**, **Pinot Blanc** and **Pinot Noir** *(see the Introduction for information on their distinctive qualities)*. There is also a wine called **Edelzwicker**, made from a blend, and this is often served by the carafe in restaurants. Wines labelled **Crémant d'Alsace** are sparkling (but without the finesse of Champagne). There is a single *Appellation Contrôlée* for the wines of Alsace (granted in 1962), and one superior *appellation*, **Alsace Grand Cru** (authorised in 1975). Yet restaurants distinguish wines by the names of the individual vineyards, and *by such designations as Réserve Particulière, Réserve Personnelle, Cuvée Spéciale or Cuvée Exceptionnelle* which, while they may help buyers keep track of vintages, are meaningless to the ordinary customer. The indication **Vendanges Tardives** signifies that the grapes were harvested late in the autumn, and this extra ripening time produces a subtler, sweeter, more complex wine, generally on the expensive side, and requiring a few years to develop fully in the bottle.

Champagne-Ardenne

Not surprisingly, cuisine in the region of Champagne production relies on sauces made from the sparkling wine, ladled generously over plump pullet hens, wild thrush, kidneys, stuffed trout, grilled pike, crayfish or snails. A delicious palate-freshener served between courses is a sorbet made from *marc de Champagne*.

Cabbage dishes are nearly as popular as in Alsace, served with smoked ham and sausage. Pigs' trotters are a speciality of Ste-Menehould, served in a white wine sauce flavoured with onions, mustard and pickles. Every French gourmet is familiar with *véritable andouillette de Troyes*, a traditional pure pork chitterling sausage seasoned with onions, although some may find it rather an acquired taste.

The once impenetrable Ardenne Forest is home to a great variety of game, and hunting is a popular pastime. Traditional recipes seem to have been handed down unchanged from the Dark Ages, robust restorative cookery for cold winter nights. *Sanglier* (wild boar) is emblematic of the region, and served in *pâtés* and *terrines*, or as a main course in a rich red wine sauce flavoured with spices and herbs, accompanied by potatoes and onions. *Marcassin* (young boar) is preferred for its subtler flavour and greater tenderness. A typical country inn menu may include: *Civet de lièvre* (jugged hare), *bécasse au champagne* (woodcock), *grives* (thrush), served up with sage leaves and juniper berries. *Jambon cru des Ardennes* is ham cured with green juniper or broom wood for a distinctive flavour; *boudin blanc* is a speciality sausage made from white pork, bacon, ham, fresh eggs and milk, especially in Rethel (a celebratory fair is held the last weekend of April) and Haybes-sur-Meuse (where the recipe includes onions).

Freshwater fish including *truite* (trout) and *brochet* (pike) are served stuffed, grilled, in sauce, in *matelote* (stew) or as *quenelles* (seasoned dumplings).

A few other local specialities are **Rocroi** cheese, apple and pear **cider**, sweet *galette au sucre* pastries and blue *ardoises*, nougat covered with white chocolate, shaped to resemble slate roof tiles.

Champagne is not only the name of a geographical region, but is, of course, the exclusive home of the world's best-loved sparkling wine. The *Introduction* to this guide gives an explanation of how it is made. Here is some information for travellers wishing to buy Champagne; there is no dearth of opportunities to do so.

Most Champagne is marketed by the *maison* (house) that blends and bottles it. Big companies with well-known brand names, *Grandes Marques*, open their cellars to visitors, and have a corner on the export market as well: **Moët et Chandon, Canard Duchêne, Heidsieck, Henriot, Krug, Lanson, Mercier, Mumm, Pommery et Greno, Roederer, Taittinger** and **Veuve Clicquot-Ponsardin**, to name a few.

Other companies act as a *Marque Acheteur* (buyer's own brand), and produce wines which are labelled for distribution under a specific trade name for supermarkets, department stores, restaurants etc. These companies may be subsidiaries of the *Grandes Marques*, but rarely sell Champagne under their own company name.

Finally, there are *Récoltant-manipulants*, small growers who produce unblended wines for sale to domestic markets, and *Négociant-manipulants*, small firms which blend local products, and may even provide some superior first-pressing juice to more prestigious houses. While the *Grandes Marques* generally offer better quality (at a higher price), some growers also produce exceptionally good sparkling wine.

Vintage Champagne is made with grapes harvested in a single year, although an admixture of 10% from another year is permitted, and the grapes do not all necessarily come from the same vineyard. To bear the vintage label, Champagne must be aged at least three years.

Vineyards in Champagne

Champagne is a fairly sweet wine, and while aficionados claim that it can accompany any part of a meal, whatever that meal's constituents, it is most often enjoyed as an aperitif before dinner, or with dessert. The sweetness of the wine comes from the final stage when sugar is added to stimulate the fermentation that creates its delightful, delicate bubbles. Truly dry Champagne is **Brut Zero** or **Brut Sauvage**, no sugar added, and rather astringent. With sugar percentages between 1 and over 6%, the order of sweetness is as follows: **Brut, Extra Sec** or **Extra Dry, Sec, Demi-Sec, Doux** or **Rich**.

Before the discovery of the *méthode champenoise*, a number of respectable still wines were made in the area, the most northerly wine-producing region in France. Red, white and rosé wines benefit from the *appellation contrôlée* **Coteaux Champenois**. **Bouzy Rouge** comes in an elegant bottle, like Champagne, and **Ratafia** is a popular fortified sweet wine served as an aperitif. A little-known wine which is hard to find outside the region is **Rosé des Riceys**, from a pretty village on the wine route – well worth a detour for those seeking something special!

415

Conversion tables

Weights and measures

1 kilogram (kg)	2.2 pounds (lb)	2.2 pounds
1 metric ton (tn)	1.1 tons	1.1 tons

to convert kilograms to pounds, multiply by 2.2

1 litre (l)	2.1 pints (pt)	1.8 pints
1 litre	0.3 gallon (gal)	0.2 gallon

to convert litres to gallons, multiply by 0.26 (US) or 0.22 (UK)

1 hectare (ha)	2.5 acres	2.5 acres
1 square kilometre (km²)	0.4 square miles (sq mi)	0.4 square miles

to convert hectares to acres, multiply by 2.4

1 centimetre (cm)	0.4 inches (in)	0.4 inches
1 metre (m)	3.3 feet (ft) - 39.4 inches - 1.1 yards (yd)	
1 kilometre (km)	0.6 miles (mi)	0.6 miles

to convert metres to feet, multiply by 3.28 . kilometres to miles, multiply by 0.6

Clothing

Women							Men
	35	4	2½	40	7½	7	
	36	5	3½	41	8½	8	
	37	6	4½	42	9½	9	
Shoes	38	7	5½	43	10½	10	Shoes
	39	8	6½	44	11½	11	
	40	9	7½	45	12½	12	
	41	10	8½	46	13½	13	
	36	4	8	46	36	36	
	38	6	10	48	38	38	
Dresses &	40	8	12	50	40	40	Suits
Suits	42	12	14	52	42	42	
	44	14	16	54	44	44	
	46	16	18	56	46	48	
	36	08	30	37	14½	14,5	
	38	10	32	38	15	15	
Blouses &	40	12	14	39	15½	15½	Shirts
sweaters	42	14	36	40	15¾	15¾	
	44	16	38	41	16	16	
	46	18	40	42	16½	16½	

Sizes often vary depending on the designer. These equivalents are given for guidance only.

Speed

kph	10	30	50	70	80	90	100	110	120	130
mph	6	19	31	43	50	56	62	68	75	81

Temperature

Celsius (°C)	0°	5°	10°	15°	20°	25°	30°	40°	60°	80°	100°
Fahrenheit (°F)	32°	41°	50°	59°	68°	77°	86°	104°	140°	176°	212°

To convert Celsius into Fahrenheit, multiply °C by 9, divide by 5, and add 32.
To convert Fahrenheit into Celsius, subtract 32 from °F, multiply by 5, and divide by 9.

Shopping

Christmas every day

The year-end holiday season is lively and popular in Alsace. There are about 50 different *Christkendelsmarkts* (Christmas markets) held during the month of December – all
week long in the larger towns, and weekends in smaller places. But even travellers
who visit at other times of the year will find the spirit of Christmas. The pretty towns
on the wine route are always festive with red geraniums, bright against the lush green
vineyards or the deeper green on the hillsides. **Kaysersberg**, for example, is known for
its Christmas market, but many of the shops are decked out year round with cookie
cutters, recipe and craft books, festive tableware, stockings to stuff, party linens, gift
boxes, sweets, candles, decorations for your tree...

Alsace has happily preserved the Germanic tradition of **toys** made of wood; they can be
found especially in Ingwiller and Éloyes in the northern Vosges.

A souvenir both typical and useful would be a **kugelhopf mould**; they are everywhere in
shop windows, some too lovely to think of putting in the oven! You will also find
glazed earthenware in the pottery villages of Betschdorf and Soufflenheim; the towns of
Longwy, Sarrguemines, St-Clément and Lunéville specialise in **faience**. Longwy is also
reputed for its **enamel work**.

Any friend at home would be pleased to receive a gift from **Baccarat**, the famous **crystal**
manufacturers who make useful and unique objects, including resolutely modern
jewellery, or from one of a number of other crystal works in Baccarat, Hartzviller,
St-Louis-lès-Bitche, Vallerysthal and Vannes-le-Châtel. Visitors to Mulhouse can enjoy
the fine shop in the **Musée de l'Impression sur Étoffes**; wonderful **fabrics** have been finely
made into ties, scarves and linens and there are some items that will go straight to
any designer's heart, including books and stationery.

Damask or jacquard tablecloths from Gérardmer would also make splendid gifts.

Christmas dreaming

Visitors to the Champagne-Ardenne region may like to purchase **crystal** from Bayel
(shop next to the crystal works), cane and **wickerwork** from Fayl-Billot (from the
school, craftsmen in the village or the coop in Bussières-les-Belmont) or perhaps
scissors and **knives** from Nogent. There is a wide choice of decorative **tableware** and **linen**,
particularly in Troyes, where there are many factory shops offering goods, **clothing**
included, at cut prices. Those in search of a gift for a child may like to visit the toy
shop Le Nain Jaune, 39 rue de la République in Charleville-Mézières, where there is a
selection of **marionnettes**.

Food and drink

There is certainly no shortage of ideas and suggestions for those who would like to
purchase wine, Champagne, cider from the Pays d'Othe or fruit brandies and liqueurs
from Lorraine. For those who are able, and brave enough, to travel with a cheese such
as Munster (short distances only recommended), the homeward journey may be
slightly less pungent if it is packed in an airtight container! Rather less aromatic
alternatives would be to take home some foie gras from Alsace, *biscuits roses* or
croquignoles from Reims, *madeleines* from Commercy or macaroons from Nancy, to
mention just a few of the delicious specialities available.

Active tours

Touring the region on foot

There is an extensive network of well-marked footpaths in France which make rambling *(la randonnée)* a breeze. Several **Grande Randonnée (GR)** trails, recognisable for the red and white horizontal marks on trees, rocks and in town on walls, signposts etc, go through the region. Along with the GR, there are also the **Petite Randonnée (PR)** paths, which are usually blazed with blue (2hr walk), yellow (2hr 15min-3hr 45min) or green (4-6hr) marks. Of course, with appropriate maps, you can combine walks to suit your desires.

Waymarked footpaths

To use these trails, obtain the *topoguide* for the area published by the **Fédération Française de Randonnée Pédestre**, 14 rue Riquet, 75019 Paris, ☎ 01 44 89 93 93, open Monday to Saturday from 10am to 6pm. Some English-language editions are available. Another source of maps and guides for excursions on foot is the **Institut National Géographique** (IGN), which has a boutique in Paris at 107 rue de la Boétie (off the Champs-Elysées); to order from abroad, contact IGN-Sologne, Administration des Ventes, 41200 Romorantin-Lanthenay, ☎ 02 54 96 54 42 – Fax: 02 54 88 14 66, or visit the web site (www.ign.fr) for addresses of wholesalers in your country. Among their publications, France 903 is a map showing all of the GR and PR in France (29F); the *Série Bleue* and *Top 25* maps, at a scale of 1:25 000 (1cm=250m), show all paths, whether waymarked or not, as well as refuges, camp sites, beaches etc (46-58F). In the region, you can find many of the publications cited above in bookstores, at sports centres or equipment shops, and in some of the country inns and hotels catering to the sporting crowd.

Le Club Vosgien – Founded in 1872, this is the oldest ramblers' association in France, and also the largest, with over 34 000 members. They have joined forces to protect natural and historic sites, and maintain the marks on 16 500km/over 10 000mi of trails. The club sponsors a quarterly publication, *Les Vosges*, and publishes detailed maps and guides to paths on the Lorraine plateau, in the Jura mountains of Alsace, the Vosges and the Alsatian plain. Check with local tourist offices for the dates of scheduled group rambles. The club's emblem is a holly leaf. As early as 1897, they began marking out a trail across the Vosges with a red rectangle, still seen on hiking trails in the region. Contact Le Club Vosgien, 16 rue Ste-Hélène, 67000 Strasbourg, ☎ 03 88 32 57 96.

The Grande Randonnée trails in the area are:

GR 2	Across the Pays d'Othe, through a hilly landscape and along the River Seine.
GR 5	From the border of Luxembourg to the Ballon d'Alsace, through the Lorraine Regional Nature Park.
GR 7	Across the Vosges from the Ballon d'Alsace to Bourbonne-les-Bains, and continuing into the region of Burgundy.
GR 12	A section of European footpath no 3 (Atlantic-Bohemia), cutting across the French and Belgian Ardennes.

GR 14	Follows the Montagne de Reims through vineyards and forest, then continues across the chalk hills of Champagne to Bar-le-Duc before turning towards the Ardennes.
GR 24	The loop starts at Bar-sur-Seine, goes through the Forêt d'Orient Regional Nature Park, vineyards and farmland.
GR 53	From Wissembourg to the Col du Donon, through the northern Vosges regional nature park.
GR 714	From Bar-le-Duc to Vittel, linking GR 14 and GR 7.
GR 533	Sarrebourg to the Ballon d'Alsace.

Stepping smart

Choosing the right equipment for a rambling expedition is essential: flexible hiking shoes with non-slip soles, a rain jacket or poncho, an extra sweater, sun protection (hat, glasses, lotion), drinking water (1-2l per person), high energy snacks (chocolate, cereal bars etc), and a first aid kit. Of course, you'll need a good map (and a compass if you plan to leave the main trails). Plan your itinerary well, keeping in mind that while the average walking speed for an adult is 4kph/2.5mph, you will need time to eat and rest, and children will not keep up the same pace. Leave your itinerary with someone before setting out (innkeeper or fellow camper).

Respect for nature is a cardinal rule and includes the following precautions: don't smoke or light fires in the forest, which are particularly susceptible in the dry summer months; always carry your rubbish out; leave wild flowers as they are; walk around, not through, farmers' fields; close gates behind you.

If you are caught in an electrical storm, avoid high ground, and do not move along a ridge top; do not seek shelter under overhanging rocks, isolated trees in otherwise open areas, at the entrance to caves or other openings in the rocks, or in the proximity of metal fences or gates. Do not use a metallic survival blanket. If possible, position yourself at least 15m/15yd from the highest point around you (rock or tree); crouch with your knees up and without touching the rock face with your hands or any exposed part of your body. An automobile is a good refuge, as its rubber tyres ground it and provide protection for those inside.

Touring the region by cycle

For general information concerning France, write or call the **Fédération Française de Cyclotourisme**, 8 rue Jean-Marie-Jégo, 75013 Paris, ☎ 01 44 16 88 88. Off-road and mountain bike (*VTT* in French) enthusiasts can contact the **Fédération Française de Cyclisme**, 5 rue de Rome, 93561 Rosny-sous-Bois Cedex, ☎ 01 49 35 69 00 and request the *Guide des centres VTT*. The IGN *(see address above, under Touring on foot)* offers Map 906, *Mountain bike and cycle touring in France* (29F).

Local tourist offices usually have a list of cycle hire firms. Regional associations and mountain bike centres include:

Association Vosges VTT,
Comité Départemental du Tourisme,
7 rue Gilbert,
88000 Épinal, ☎ 03 29 82 49 93.
Comité de Lorraine de la FFC,
Maison des Sports,
13 rue Jean-Moulin,
54510 Tomblaine, ☎ 03 83 21 35 12.

Centre VTT de la Forêt d'Argonne,
Argonne Passions, La-Grange-aux-Bois,
51800 Ste-Menehould, ☎ 03 26 60 81 16.

Lac du Der-Chantecoq,
Maison du Lac,
51290 Giffaumont-Champaubert,
☎ 03 26 72 62 80.
Office du Tourisme des Crêtes Préardennaises,
rue Roger-Ponsard,
08430 Launois-sur-Vence,
☎ 03 24 35 02 69.
Ligue d'Alsace de Cyclotourisme,
Maurice Arribet, 67540 Ostwald,
☎ 03 88 30 43 76.

Touring the region on horseback

The **Délégation Nationale au Tourisme Équestre**, 9 boulevard MacDonald, 75019 Paris, ☎ 01 53 26 15 50, publishes an annual review entitled *Tourisme et Loisirs Équestres en France*. It lists all the possibilities for riding by region and *département*. It is also possible to contact regional associations directly to obtain details of centres, activities, accommodation and itineraries of two to eight days:

Alsace

Comité Départemental du Tourisme Équestre du Haut-Rhin, Maison des Associations, 6 route d'Ingersheim, 68000 Colmar, ☎ 03 89 24 43 18.
Monday to Friday 2-6pm; brochure upon request.
Comité Départemental du Tourisme Équestre du Bas-Rhin, 4 rue des Violettes, 67201 Eckbolsheim, ☎ 03 88 77 39 64.

Lorraine	Association Régionale pour le Tourisme Équestre et l'Équitation de Loisirs (ARTEL), M.Yvon Hermann, 8 Grande-Rue, 54114 Jeandelaincourt, ☎ 03 83 31 40 58.
	Comité Départemental du Tourisme Équestre des Vosges, 13 rue Principale, 88240 Montmotier.
Champagne-Ardenne	Association de Champagne-Ardenne pour le Tourisme Équestre (ACATE), 51170 Arcis-le-Ponsart, ☎ 03 26 48 86 39.

The **Conseil Général des Ardennes** produces a topographical guide, *Les Ardennes à cheval*, showing 330km/205mi of bridle paths; it is available from the Hôtel du Département, 08011 Charleville-Mézières, ☎ 03 24 59 60 60.

The **Relais de la Largue**, 3 rue Ste-Barbe, 68210 Altenach, ☎ 03 89 25 12 92, organises seven-day trips in Sundgau and the Alsatian Jura by pioneer-style covered wagon, with overnight accommodation in good standard hotels or *gîtes*.

Touring the region on board a boat

There are numerous navigable waterways in the region, providing holidaymakers with an opportunity to enjoy a cruise or hire their own boat.
Voies Navigables de France, 175 rue Ludovic-Boutleux, 62400 Béthune, ☎ 03 21 63 24 24, can provide information on travelling the waterways, or you may like to contact the regional tourist office for information *(see Planning your trip, above)*.

Self-skippered holidays – The following hire fleet agencies and bases offer boats accommodating two to eight people:

Aquavac Plaisance	Port du Houillon, 57830 Languimberg, ☎ 03 87 25 94 22, .
	Base: Port du Houillon
Ardennes Nautisme	16 rue du Château, BP 78, 08203 Sedan, ☎ 03 24 27 05 15. Bases: Reims and Pont-à-Bar.
France Afloat	PO Box 249, Redhill, Surrey RHI 2FD, England, ☎/Fax: (0)8700 110 538, .
	Bases: Mittersheim, Meaux and Sillery.
Locaboat Plaisance	1 rue Thérèse, 75001 Paris, ☎ 01 42 61 59 39, .
	Bases: Reims and Lutzelbourg.
Nicols	Route du Puy-St-Bonnet,49300 Cholet, ☎ 02 41 56 46 56. Base: Saverne

Cruises – These can last a few hours to two weeks. In the region, you can travel on the Rhine, Moselle, Sarre, Neckar, Main, Danube, Meuse, Marne and Seine rivers.
The brochure *Lorraine au fil de l'eau* contains information on boat trips in the area and can be obtained from the **Comité Régional du Tourisme de Lorraine** *(see Local tourist offices above)*

River cruise

Alsace-CroisiEurope-Alsace Croisières, 12 rue de la Division-Leclerc, 67000 Strasbourg, ☎ 03 88 76 44 44, offers many trips out of Strasbourg. From March to December, you can tour the city while enjoying lunch or dinner on a boat leaving from quai Finkwiller, in the care of **Bateaux Touristiques Strasbourgeois**, 15 bis rue de Nantes, 67100 Strasbourg, ☎ 03 88 84 10 01. **Canaltour**, BP 8, 67026 Strasbourg Cedex, ☎ 03 88 62 54 98 offers a boat trip with a meal, leaving from Lutzelbourg and cruising via the inclined plain at Arzviller. Or you may like to contact **KD**, Croisirhin, 11 rue Richepance, 75008 Paris, ☎ 01 42 61 30 20 if you are tempted by a Rhine cruise lasting three to eight days between April and October, either departing or stopping at Strasbourg.

Croisi-Champagne, BP 22, 51480 Cumières, ☎ 03 26 54 49 51 offers trips on the River Marne. For the River Seine, the rendezvous is at Bray-sur-Seine; contact the **Association Loisirs Nautiques et Équestres**, 8 rue de la Ruelle-de-Mars, 77480 Montigny-le-Guesdier, ☎ 01 60 67 23 52. For a cruise on the River Meuse from Charleville, Monthermé and Revin, try **Loisirs Accueil en Ardenne**, 39-41 rue de la République, 08000 Charleville-Mézières, ☎ 03 24 56 00 63.

Touring the region from above

For a unique view and memorable experience, consider a **hot air balloon** ride:

Aérovision	4 rue de Hohrod, 68140 Munster, ☎ 03 89 77 22 81
Pilâtre de Rozier	6 place du Temple, 57530 Courcelles-Chaussy,
	☎ 03 87 64 08 08, www.pilatre-de-rozier.com
Champagne Air Show	15 bis place St-Nicaise, 51100 Reims,
	☎ 03 26 82 59 60

Flights in light aircraft – The **Aéroclub d'Alsace**, Terrain du Polygone, 67100 Strasbourg, ☎ 03 88 34 00 98 organises flights in the vicinity of Strasbourg, over the Château of Haut-Kœnigsbourg and the plain of the River Rhine, as well as weekends in Wissembourg with a flight, visits to châteaux and local wine and food tastings.

Flights in small planes are also arranged by the **Aéroclub du Sud Meusien**, BP 184, 55005 Bar-le-Duc, ☎ 03 29 77 12 14.

Helicopter flights on the outskirts of Strasbourg and Nancy are offered by **Proteus Hélicoptères**: Aéroport de Strasbourg-Entzheim, ☎ 03 88 64 69 30 or Aéroport de Nancy-Essey, ☎ 03 83 29 80 60.

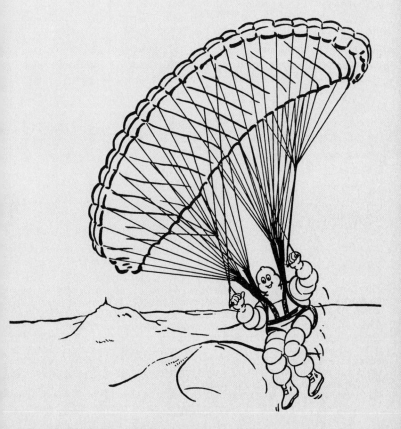

Sports and recreation

Water sports

The entire region covered by this guide is dotted with lakes, canals and rivers, providing many opportunities for recreational activities.

Fishing in France is regulated by the **Conseil Supérieur de la Pêche**, 134 avenue de Malakoff, 75116, Paris, ☎ 01 45 02 20 20, which publishes a map-brochure with commentary entitled *La Pêche en France*. The **Fédération de Pêche** (angling union) in each *département* is a good source of information for more localised fishing areas. When fishing in France, you will need to buy a permit, or *Carte de pêche*, and familiarise yourself with national and local regulations. Permits and information are available at tourist offices and in many cafés and bars located near popular fishing spots.

Lake/reservoir	Nearest town	Acreage	Swimming	Boating	Fishing
Alfeld	Kirchberg	25	–	–	⌇
Armance	Troyes	1 236	≈	–	⌇
Bairon	Le Chesne	297	≈	⌀	–
Blanc	Orbey	72	–	–	⌇
Blanchemer	La Bresse	14	–	–	⌇
Charmes	Langres	487	≈	–	⌇
Corbeaux	La Bresse	25	–	–	⌇
Der-Chantecoq	Vitry-le-François	11 861	≈	⌀	⌇
Folie	Contrexéville	25	≈	⌀	⌇
Gérardmer	Gérardmer	284	≈	⌀	⌇
Gondreange	Sarrebourg-	1 730	–	⌀	⌇
Hanau	Falkenstein-	44	≈	⌀	⌇
Lauch	Le Markstein	27	–	–	⌇
Liez	Langres	717	≈	⌀	⌇
Longemer	Gérardmer	188	≈	⌀	⌇
Madine	Hattonchâtel	2 718	≈	⌀	⌇
Mouche	Langres	232	–	–	⌇
Noir	Orbey	35	–	–	–
Orient	Troyes	5 683	≈	⌀	⌇
Pierre-Percée	Badonviller	692	–	⌀	⌇
Retournemer	Gérardmer	14	–	–	–
Temple	Troyes	4 522	–	–	⌇
Vielles-Forges	Revin	371	≈	⌀	–
Vert	Hohrodberg	556	–	–	–
Vingeanne	Langres	487	≈	⌀	–

Skiing

The Vosges mountains are perfect for easy going skiers. In the pine forests, gentle landscapes unfold between 600m/1 968ft-1 400m/4 600ft. Resorts offer downhill and cross-country trails, snowboarding, biathlon, ski jumping, snowshoeing, dogsledding, toboggan riding or simply peaceful walks through the wintry countryside.

Downhill skiers have 170 lifts to choose from and many stations are equipped with snow-making machines and lighting for night skiing, notably Gérardmer, La Bresse, Le Markstein and Lac Blanc. Schnepfenried is appreciated for the panoramic view of the crests forming the blue line of the Vosges. Cross-country skiers can enjoy more than 1 000km/621mi of marked and groomed trails.

For information and reservations, contact local tourist offices, or log in to www.skifrance.fr on the Internet, for the latest update on snow conditions; some sites also list available accommodation.

Cross-country at Champ de Feu

Hunting

The Ardenne Forest, thick and sparsely populated, is a good place to pursue deer and wild boar. For more information, contact the **Fédération Départementale des Chasseurs des Ardennes**, ☎ 03 24 56 07 35, the **Saint-Hubert Club de France**, 10 rue Lisbonne, 75008 Paris, ☎ 01 45 22 38 90 or the **Union Nationale des Fédérations Départementales des Chasseurs**, 48 rue d'Alésia, 75014 Paris, ☎ 01 43 27 85 76.

One-day and weekend hunting parties are organised on the estate of the **Maison Forestière de Germaine** in the hamlet of Vauremont, 5 rue de la Croix-Verte, 51160 Germaine, ☎ 03 26 51 08 27, including hunting from an observation tower, in a 400ha/988-acre park, or in a 1 200ha/2 970-acre wooded perimeter.

The **Pavillon du Territoire du Sanglier** at Mogues in the Ardennes *département* offers introductions to wild boar hunting. Contact the Office de Tourisme des 3 Cantons, ☎ 03 24 29 79 91.

And more ...

Golf is growing increasingly popular in France and the area covered in this guide is well equipped with courses, particularly Lorraine, where both regular players and novices are welcome. The Comité Régional du Tourisme *(see Planning your trip, Local tourist offices)* publishes a brochure-map with all of the addresses and services available, including nearby lodging. The **Golf Pass Lorraine** gives access to four different 18-hole courses in the region. For information, contact the **Ligue Lorraine de Golf de Champagne-Ardenne**, 2 chemin des Vignottes, 54690 Lay-St-Christophe, ☎ 03 83 22 91 15.

Canoeing-Kayaking can be practised on the majority of rivers in the Champagne and Ardenne regions. The more challenging courses are on the Blaise, Saulx, Rognon and Aire rivers. Gentler waters are the Meuse (at Sedan), the Aube and the Marne. In association with the **Fédération Française de Canoë-kayak**, 87 quai de la Marne, BP 58, 94344 Joinville-le-Pont, ☎ 01 45 11 08 50, the IGN *(address above, under Active tours, Touring on foot)* publishes map 905, *Water Sports in France*, with watercourses classified by level of difficulty.

In the Aube *département*, canoeing-kayaking can be practised on the Seine, Aube and Ource rivers or the lakes of the Forêt d'Orient. The brochure *Découverte des Rivières Auboises en Canoë-kayak* can be obtained from the **Comité Départemental du Tourisme de l'Aube** *(see Local tourist offices)*

Bases de Loisirs – These are recreational areas where travellers are likely to find various facilities for sports and recreation, such as beaches, camping and picnic areas, bike and hiking trails. When it is time to stretch your legs, keep an eye out for signs, or look for the green diamond on your Michelin map.

Spas and hydrotherapy

The Vosges mountains on the Lorraine side and the region of Lorraine itself are especially blessed with natural spring waters that have given rise to spa resorts. The Alsatian side of the range also has its share of resorts.

None of the waters are sulphurous, but all other types of spring water are found and used in treating various chronic affections.

Mineral springs and hot springs

Natural springs result when water filters through permeable layers of the earth's surface until it meets resistance in the form of an impermeable layer of rock. The water flows along this impenetrable layer until it breaks through to the open air, and the water surges forth.

A mineral spring can be water surging forth in the same way, or water rising from deep within the earth, collecting mineral substances and gases with therapeutic properties as it flows towards the surface. Hot springs produce water which hits the air at a temperature of at least 35°C/95°F.

Springs are found in zones where the earth's crust is fairly thin, where boulders have been thrown into place by eruptions or cracking. Hot springs are found along the Lorraine plateau fault line or near crystalline mountain ranges and outcrops.

Water, water everywhere – Water from mineral or hot springs is usually unstable, and contact with the air changes its properties. This is why its therapeutic virtues are best enjoyed at the source. Spa therapy is based on this principle.

The two geographic zones in the Vosges, the "plain" to the west and the "mountains" to the east and south-east, have different types of springs, each with its own specificity.

Cold springs – The plain is dominated by cold springs, water which has filtered through the earth's crust and re-emerges enriched with calcium and magnesium and, in some cases, lithium and sodium.

The best-known resort in the area is certainly **Vittel**; the waters were reputed in Roman times, then forgotten, only to be rediscovered in 1845. In 1854, the Bouloumié family began actively promoting and marketing the spring water.

Vittel and the neighbouring spa at **Contrexéville** treat kidney and liver ailments and Vittel also specialises in metabolic diseases. In conjunction with therapeutic activities at the spa, the water is bottled for sale, and many tourists visit the plants each year (with Évian, it is one of the world's largest bottling operations).

Hot springs – The springs found in the mountainous region are quite different. Of volcanic origin, their properties depend less on mineral content than on temperature and radioactivity.

Also known to the Romans, who appreciated warm springs, as did the Celts and the Gauls, these waters have a long-standing reputation. **Plombières**, with 27 hot springs, some of which reach 80°C/176°F, is reputed for the treatment of rheumatism and enteritis.

Bains-les-Bains is a spa specialising in the treatment of a number of heart and artery disorders, whereas **Luxeuil-les-Bains** treats gynaecological ailments.

The most recent arrival on the scene is **Amnéville**, where *curistes* come to relieve the symptoms of rheumatism and respiratory problems, using the therapeutic waters of the St-Éloy spring, which emerge at 41°C/106°F.

Bourbonne-les-Bains, located on the border of Lorraine and Champagne, boasts warm, radioactive water with a slight chlorine content. Louis XV created a military hospital on the site, for the treatment of soldiers with shot-wounds. Today, the spa is prescribed for the purposes of healing bones, arthritis, rheumatism and respiratory problems.

In Alsace, **Niederbronn-les-Bains** is recognised for the treatment of digestive and kidney afflictions and arteriosclerosis. **Morsbronn-les-Bains** is a small spa specialising in rheumatic disorders.

Hydrotherapy and tourism

The benefits of spa treatments were rediscovered in the 18C to 19C. At that time, "taking the waters" was reserved for wealthy clients with time to spare. Today, the French national health system recognises the therapeutic value of many spa treatments, and patients' stays are provided for, all or in part, by different social welfare organisations.

Treatment occupies only part of the day, so spas offer their guests many other activities to pass the time pleasantly – sports, recreation and various forms of entertainment. More often than not, the beautiful natural settings provide the opportunity for outdoor excursions.

Besides traditional courses of treatment, which usually last three weeks, many resorts offer shorter stays for clients with a specific goal in mind, such as stress relief and relaxation, fitness and shaping up, giving up smoking, losing weight etc.

The **Association des Stations Thermales Vosgiennes** publishes a brochure, *Vosges thermales*, with information on Bains-les-Bains, Contrexéville, Plombières and Vittel. To obtain a copy, write to BP 332, 88008 Épinal.

You can also get information by contacting the **Fédération Thermale et Climatique Française**, 16 rue de l'Estrapade, 75005 Paris, ☎ 01 43 25 11 85.

Via Internet, connect to www.thermes-de-france.com and choose a spa for precise information (in French in most cases) on accommodation, short-stay treatments, entertainment etc.

Or contact the spas directly:

Roman baths at Bain-les-Bains

Amnéville: rheumatic disorders, post-traumatic injury treatment and respiratory problems.
Open: February to December.
– Thermapolis, avenue d'Europe, 57360 Amnéville, ☎ 03 87 71 83 50.
– Centre thermal, rue des Thermes 57360 Amnéville, ☎ 03 87 70 19 09.
– Office de Tourisme, Centre Thermal et Touristique, 57360 Amnéville, ☎ 03 87 70 10 40.

Bains-les-Bains: cardiovascular ailments, rheumatic disorders, post-traumatic injury treatment.
Open: April to October.
– Thermes de Bains-les-Bains, 1 avenue du Docteur-Mathieu, 88240 Bains-les-Bains, ☎ 03 29 36 32 04.
– Office de Tourisme, 3 avenue André-Demazure, 88240 Bains-les-Bains, ☎ 03 29 36 31 75.

Bourbonne-les-Bains: rheumatic disorders, osteoarthritis, respiratory ailments, bone fractures.
Open: March to November.
– Établissement Thermal, BP 15, 52400 Bourbonne-les-Bains, ☎ 03 25 90 07 20.
– Centre Borvo, 52400 Bourbonne-les-Bains, ☎ 03 25 90 01 71.

Contrexéville: kidney and urinary problems, excess weight.
Open: April to October.
– Établissement Thermal, 88140 Contrexéville, ☎ 03 29 08 03 24.
– Office de Tourisme, 105 rue du Shah-de-Perse, BP 42, 88142 Contrexéville Cedex, ☎ 03 29 08 08 68.

Luxeuil-les-Bains: phlebology, gynaecology.
Open: March to November.
– Établissement Thermal, avenue des Thermes, BP 51, 70302 Luxeuil-les-Bains, ☎ 03 84 40 44 22.
– Office de Tourisme, 1 avenue des Thermes, BP 71, 70302 Luxeuil-les-Bains, ☎ 03 84 40 06 41.

Morsbronn-les-Bains: rheumatic disorders, post-traumatic injury treatment.
Open: year round.
– Établissement Thermal, 12 route Haguenau, 67360 Morsbronn-les-Bains, ☎ 03 88 09 83 00.
– Syndicat d'Initiative, rue Principale, 67360 Morsbronn-les-Bains, ☎ 03 88 09 30 18.

Niederbronn-les-Bains: rheumatic disorders, post-traumatic injury treatment, physical rehabilitation.
Open: April to December.
– Établissement Thermal, 16-18 rue du Maréchal-Leclerc, 67110 Niederbronn-les-Bains, ☎ 03 88 80 88 80 (year round).
– Établissement Thermal Saisonnier, place des Thermes, ☎ 03 88 80 30 70 (in season).
– Office de Tourisme, 2 place de l'Hôtel-de-Ville, 67110 Niederbronn-les-Bains, ☎ 03 88 80 89 70.

Plombières-les-Bains: Digestive ailments, nutritional problems, rheumatic disorders, post-traumatic osteo-articular therapy.
Open: April to October.
– Calodaé, 4 avenue des Etats-Unis, 88370 Plombières, ☎ 03 29 30 07 30.
– Société Thermale, 2 place Maurice-Janot, 88370 Plombières, ☎ 03 29 30 00 00.
– Office de Tourisme, "Sous les Arcades", 16 rue Stanislas, BP 15, 88370 Plombières, ☎ 03 29 66 01 30.

Vittel: Liver and kidney ailments, rheumatic disorders, post-traumatic injury treatment, nutritional problems.
Open: February to December.
– Thermes de Vittel, Parc Thermal, BP 43, 88805 Vittel Cedex, ☎ 03 29 08 76 54.
– Maison du Tourisme, 136 avenue Bouloumié, 88800 Vittel, ☎ 03 29 08 08 88.

Discovering the region

Excursion trains

Steam and diesel locomotives offer visitors to the region a charming ride through the countryside. Near Metz, a small steam train runs from Vigy to Hombourg along the **Vallée de la Canner**; at the southern end of the Route des Crêtes, you can enjoy a ride along the **Vallée de la Doller** from Cernay to Sentheim, or take the **forest train** from Abreschviller to Grand Soldat in the Massif du Donon. Just a short distance from Colmar, the Association CFTR offers combined boat and steam train trips along the **Rhine** between Neuf-Brisach and Baltzenheim *(see Admission times and charges)*.

Draisines – In the past, pedal cars, handcars and trolleys were propelled by railroad workers maintaining or inspecting the track. Today, this mode of locomotion can be used to explore the **Vallée de la Mortagne**. Energetic travellers can pedal along 20km/12mi of otherwise unused railways, starting from Magnières, near Baccarat. Rental is for 1hr or a half-day, 9am to 7pm. Information and reservations: ☎ 03 83 72 34 73.

Again in the **Vallée de la Canner**, instead of the train, you may prefer to take a *vélorail* and pedal the 11km/6.8mi from Vigy to Budange, ☎ 03 87 58 75 68.

Self-propulsion

Cl. Hinsinger

The **Chemin de Fer Touristique du Sud des Ardennes** steams down part of the Aisne Valley from Attigny to Challerange, passing through Vouziers (31km/19mi); or from Attigny to Amagne-Lucquy (9.5km/6mi). Another line follows the Meuse Valley from Mouzon to Stenay (24km/15mi). These trains run on Sundays from June to September. Information is available from the association **Les Amis de la Traction Vapeur en Ardenne**, cour de la Gare, 08130 Attigny, ☎ 03 24 42 26 14 or ☎ 03 26 04 86 06.

A steam locomotive travels along the **Chemin de Fer à Vapeur des 3 Vallées**; one of the three lines runs from Givet to Dinant in Belgium. *(See Admission times and charges for Givet)*. The **Train Touristique de la Blaise et du Der** departs from the 19C station of Wassy at 3pm on Sundays in July and August. For information, contact La Gare, 52130 Wassy, ☎ 06 07 50 55 72.

In the holiday season, **mini-trains** carry tourists around the historic districts of some towns, including Strasbourg, Colmar, Nancy, Riquewihr and Guebwiller in Alsace; Châlons-en-Champagne, Épernay, Langres, Reims, Troyes and around the Der-Chantecoq Lake in Champagne-Ardenne. Information at the local tourist office.

Thematic routes

Routes touristiques – In the areas covered by this guide, there are numerous tourist itineraries plotted out for motorists who wish to explore a particular aspect of the area. The best-known routes in Alsace are the **Route des Crêtes**, running along the ridge of the Vosges from the Col du Bonhomme to Thann, and the **Route des Vins**, or wine road, both described in this guide.

Motorists will notice many other itineraries signposted in the region: for example, the **Route du Rhin** from Lauterbourg to St-Louis along the River Rhine, the **Route de l'Amitié** from Paris to Munich, taking in the Lorraine region, both sides of the Vosges, Strasbourg, the Black Forest etc, the **Route du Cristal**, with visits to the principal crystal works in Lorraine and the **Route des Potiers**, featuring the pottery workshops of Soufflenheim and Betschdorf.

In Champagne-Ardenne, you may like to take the **Route Touristique du Champagne** through the Marne, Aisne and Aube *départements*, the **Route des Églises à Pans de Bois**, specialising in timber-framed churches, the **Route des Légendes de Meuse et Semoy**, **Route des Fortifications** or the **Route des Forêts, Lacs et Abbayes**, to name a few.

Routes historiques – These are heritage trails that guide motorists to towns, villages, châteaux, manors, abbeys, parks and gardens of architectural and historical interest. Among others, they include the **Route Historique Romane d'Alsace**, concentrating on Romanesque architecture, the **Route du Patrimoine Culturel Quebécois** in the Champagne region, retracing the history of the French who settled in Québec, including the founder of Montreal or the **Route du Vitrail en Haute-Marne**, taking in stained glass from Droyes to Joinville. Information from local tourist offices or the Fédération Nationale des Routes Historiques, Port Boulet, 37140 Bourgueil.

Routes gastronomiques – As you may expect, these itineraries are dedicated to unearthing regional culinary specialities, cheeses, beers, trout, *choucroute* etc.

These and other special itineraries are the subject of brochures which can be found in most local tourist offices.

Discovering animal life

Birdwatchers will find that the many lakes in Champagne-Ardenne attract a sizeable feathered population. A part of the **Lac de Bairon** has been set aside as a **bird refuge**, as has part of the **Lac d'Orient** in the Forêt d'Orient Nature Park. The **Lac du Der-Chantecoq** and nearby ponds have observatories and discovery trails. Here, the Ferme aux Grues is devoted to cranes, their migratory habits, how to observe them and conservation measures. The Maison de l'Oiseau et du Poisson is devoted to birds and fish and has exhibits and displays explaining the lake's ecosystem.

There are numerous communities of **storks** in Alsace, in particular in Eguisheim, Ensisheim, Kaysersberg, Molsheim, Rouffach, Soultz, Turckheim, Ungersheim and La Wantzenau.

There are many **animal parks** in the region, some offering entertainment in the form of shows and demonstrations, many keeping their animals in semi-captivity:
– Parc de Vision de Belval (tour in your car), ☎ 03 24 30 01 86.
– Parc Animalier de St-Laurent, near Charleville-Mézières (several tours available), ☎ 03 24 57 39 84.
– Parc Animalier de la Bannie, near Bourbonne-les-Bains, ☎ 03 25 90 14 77.
– Parc de Vision Animalier in the Forêt d'Orient Nature Park, ☎ 03 25 43 81 90.
– Parc Animalier de Ste-Croix, Lac de Madine, ☎ 03 87 03 92 05.
– Centre de Réintroduction des Cigognes (storks) and Centre de Reproduction de la Loutre (otter) in Hunawihr, ☎ 03 89 73 72 62.

– Serre à Papillons (butterfly conservatory) in Hunawihr, ☎ 03 89 73 69 58.
– Montagne des Singes (monkey mountain) in Kintzheim, near Sélestat, ☎ 03 88 92 11 09.
– Volerie des Aigles (eagle aviary) in Kintzheim, ☎ 03 88 92 84 33.
– Zoo and Botanical Gardens in Mulhouse, ☎ 03 89 31 85 10.
– La Pépinière (plant nursery), gardens and zoo in Nancy.
– Tropical Aquarium in Nancy, ☎ 03 83 32 99 97.
– Les Naïades Aquarium in Ottrott, ☎ 03 88 95 90 32.
– Zoo de l'Orangerie, opposite the Palais de l'Europe in Strasbourg.

Roaming the vineyards

In Alsace, the **Route des Vins** carries travellers from Marlenheim to Thann, linking up the charming little wine-growing villages of the region and incorporating the seven officially recognized *(Appellation d'Origine Contrôlée)* grape varieties in the area.

A number of small towns have waymarked tracks winding through the heart of the vineyards, punctuated by information boards explaining work in the vines and the different grape varieties. These *sentiers viticoles* can be

Cave Boeckel, Mittelbergheim

Alsatian wine pitcher

found in Soultzmatt, Westhalten, Pffaffenheim Eguisheim, Turckheim, Kientzheim, Bennwihr-Mittelwihr-Beblenheim-Zellenber-Riquewihr-Hunawihr (Grands Crus itinerary), Bergheim, Scherwiller, Dambach-la-Ville, Epfig, Mittelbergheim, Barr, Obernai, Dorlisheim, Molsheim, Traenheim, Dahlenheim and Marlenheim.

In the Champagne region, take the **Route du Champagne**, where many signposts indicate the way to vineyards, Champagne houses and cooperatives.

Visiting wine cellars

Many producers in both areas open their *caves* to visitors, and often offer tasting sessions. Here are just a few addresses among many, many others:

Wine cellars in Alsace:

Dambach-la Ville
39 rue de la Gare,
☏ 03 88 92 40 03
Eguisheim
Charles Baur, 6 Grand'Rue,
☏ 03 89 41 32 49

Kaysersberg
Caveau des Viticulteurs,
20 rue du Général-de-Gaulle,
☏ 03 89 47 17 87

Obernai
30 rue du Général-Leclerc,
☏ 03 88 95 61 18
Ribeauvillé
Domaine du Moulin de Dusenbach,
25, route de Ste-Marie-aux-Mines,
☏ 03 89 73 72 18
Rouffach
Domaine du Lycée Viticole,
8 Aux-Remparts,
☏ 03 89 49 60 17.

Other useful addresses:

CIVA, Conseil Interprofessionnel des Vins d'Alsace, Maison des Vins d'Alsace, 12 avenue de la Foire-aux-Vins, BP 1217, 68012 Colmar Cedex, ☏ 03 89 20 16 20. This organisation publishes a number of brochures on the wines of Alsace, including a guide-directory with details of wine cellars open to the public.

The **Espace Alsace Coopération** (☏ 03 89 47 91 33), in Beblenheim, on the wine route, has a good selection of regional wines produced by Alsace's 18 different cooperatives, along with other local products to taste.

The castle in Kientzheim houses the **Musée du Vignoble et des Vins d'Alsace**, with exhibits explaining various aspects relating to vines and wines. It also has a monumental winepress.

Wine festivals – Harvest festivals are held in October throughout Alsace, other celebrations take place from April to October:

April	**Ammerschwihr**
1 May	**Molsheim**
Ascension	**Guebwiller**
Mid-July	**Barr**
4th weekend in July	**Ribeauvillé**
1st half of August	**Colmar**
1st weekend of August	**Turckheim**
Last weekend of August	**Eguisheim**
September	**Riquewihr**

Sized to fit

Champagne comes in many sizes, one is sure to be right for your party! *See photo p 69.*

Magnum:	2 bottles		Methuselah:	8 bottles
Jeroboam:	4 bottles		Salmanazar:	12 bottles
Rehoboam:	6 bottles		Balthazar:	16 bottles
		Nebuchadnezzar: 20 bottles		

Wine cellars in Champagne

Ambonnay	Serge Pierlot, 10 rue St-Vincent, ☏ 03 26 57 01 11.
Ambonnay-Grand-Cru	Soutiran-Pelletier, ☏ 03 26 57 80 80.
Ay	Maison du Vin d'Ay, Pierre Laurain, 2 rue Roger-Sondag, ☏ 03 26 55 18 90.
Celles-sur-Ource	Marcel Vezien, ☏ 03 25 38 50 22.
Cogny	Breton Fils, 12 rue Courte-Pilate, ☏ 03 26 59 31 03.
Château-Thierry	Pannier, 23 rue Roger-Catillon, ☏ 03 23 69 13 10.
Fossoy	Déhu Père et Fils, 3 rue St-Georges, ☏ 03 23 71 90 47.
Gyé-sur-Seine	Cheurlin et Fils, 13 rue de la Gare, ☏ 03 25 38 20 27.
Hautvillers	J-M Gobillard et Fils, 38 rue de l'Église, ☏ 03 26 51 00 24.
Loches-sur-Ource	Jean-Paul Richardot, rue Renée-Guinton, ☏ 03 25 29 71 20.

Ludes	Forget-Chemin, 15 rue Victor-Hugo, ☎ 03 26 61 12 17.
Mardeuil	Beaumont de Crayères, 64 rue de la Liberté, ☎ 03 26 55 29 40.
Le Mesnil-sur-Oger	Launois Père et Fils, 3 avenue de la République, ☎ 03 26 57 50 15.
Oger	Jean Milan, 6 route d'Avize, ☎ 03 26 57 50 09.
Les Riceys	Morize Père et Fils, 122 rue du Général-de-Gaulle, ☎ 03 25 29 30 02.
Trélou-sur-Marne	Veuve Olivier et Fils, 10 route de Dormans, ☎ 03 23 70 24 01.
Verzy	Étienne Lefevre, 30 rue de Villers, ☎ 03 26 97 96 99.
Verzy	Fresnet-Juillet, 10 rue Beaumont, ☎ 03 26 97 93 40.
Vincelles	H Blin et Co, 5 rue de Verdun, ☎ 03 23 83 68 60.

Champagne and wine courses

For novices and enthusiasts who would like to learn more, there are a number of courses available:

In Alsace:

Centre de Formation, Lycée Viticole, 8 Aux-Remparts, 68250 Rouffach, ☎ 03 89 78 73 00.

In Champagne:

Institut Œnologique de Champagne, 10110 Bar-sur-Seine, ☎ 03 25 29 90 22.

La Maison du Millésime, Château de Pierry, 51201 Épernay, ☎ 03 26 54 05 11 for a tasting with commentary by appointment.

Les Celliers de Pierry, 1 rue Carnot, 51200 Pierry, ☎ 03 26 54 81 75.

La Palette de Bacchus, 51150 Ambonnay, ☎ 03 26 57 07 87.

Pretzels and beer, anyone?

Déhu Père et Fils, 3 rue St-Georges, 02650 Fossoy, ☎ 03 23 71 90 47.

Breweries

– **Heineken**, 4 rue St-Charles, 67300 Schiltigheim, ☎ 03 88 19 59 53.

– **Kronenbourg**, 2 rue Gabriel-Bour, 54250 Champigneulles, ☎ 03 83 39 50 50.

– **Kronenbourg**, 68 route d'Ober-hausbergen, 67000 Strasbourg, ☎ 03 88 27 41 59.

– **Météor**, rue du Général-Lebocq, 67270 Hochfelden, ☎ 03 88 02 22 22.

The tour is completed by a visit to the Stenay Beer Museum and the Musée Français de la Brasserie in St-Nicolas-de-Port.

– **Schutzenberger**, 8 rue de la Patrie, BP 182, 67304 Schiltigheim Cedex, ☎ 03 88 18 61 00.

Other local crafts and industries

Here are a few more suggestions for discovering the people and trades of the region:

– **Papeteries de Clairefontaine** (paper and stationery manufacturers), 19 rue de l'Abbaye, BP 1, 88480 Étival-Clairefontaine, ☎ 03 29 52 22 11.

– **Émaux St-Jean-l'Aigle** (enamels), château de la Faïencerie, 54400 Longwy, ☎ 03 82 24 58 20.

– **Manufacture de Niderviller** (ceramics), 2 rue de la Faïencerie, 57116 Niderviller, ☎ 03 87 23 80 04.

– **Seita** (cigar production), 7A rue de la Krutenau, 67070 Strasbourg cedex, ☎ 03 88 35 29 00.

– **Confiserie, Chocolaterie Roger Lalonde** (chocolates and confectionery), 2 avenue Milton, 54000 Nancy, ☎ 03 83 40 23 63.

– **Centre Européen de Recherche et de Formation aux Arts Verriers** (glass crafts), rue de la Liberté, 54112 Vannes-le-Châtel, ☎ 03 83 25 49 90.

– **Daum, Compagnie Française du Cristal** (crystal manufactory), 54112 Vannes-le-Châtel, ☎ 03 83 25 41 01.

– **Portieux** (crystal manufactory), 35 rue des Arts, 88330 Portieux, ☎ 03 87 23 80 04.

– **Fromagerie Jean Pire** (cheese makers), rue de la Grande-Chaudière, Tailette 08230 Rocroi, ☎ 03 24 54 10 84.

– **Bio-Plantes** (medicinal and savoury herbs), 10210 Pargues, ☎ 03 25 40 12 53.

– **Cristalleries Royales de Champagne** (crystal manufactory and *ecomuseum*), 13 rue Gustave-Marquot, 10310 Bayel, ☎ 03 25 92 37 60.

– **Automobiles Citroën**, BP 1, 08001 Charleville-Mézières, ☎ 03 24 56 65 65.

Excursions to neighbouring countries

The region is bordered by Germany to the north and east, Switzerland to the south-east, Belgium and Luxembourg to the north.

Visitors to Alsace will naturally be drawn to the other side of the River Rhine and such lovely towns as Freiberg, Belchen and Baden-Baden in the Black Forest. Consult **The Green Guide Germany** for tourist information, and **The Red Guide Deutschland** for hotels and restaurants.
Basel, in Switzerland, is also a popular tourist destination, especially at carnival time. The three days before the beginning of Lent mark the only Catholic ceremony to have survived the Reformation; a festival of parades and costumed revelry. **The Green Guide Switzerland** is useful for visiting Basel and the surrounding region. **The Red Guide Switzerland** makes it easy to choose where to spend the night and to find a special restaurant.
The Ardennes Forest covers most of the Belgian provinces of Luxembourg, Namur and Liège and part of the Grand Duchy as well as the French *département*. The valley of the River Meuse meanders to the North Sea by way of **Dinant**. This picturesque town is just 60km/37mi from Charleville-Mézières. Travellers can enjoy local honey cakes known as *couques*, baked in decorative wooden moulds, and may like to take advantage of a boat trip on the river (board in front of the town hall). Carry on to **Bouillon**, nestled in a bend of the River Semois and dominated by its medieval fortress. **Chimay** is known for its castle, but is also a familiar name to beer-lovers; the Trappist monks have their brewery at the abbey of Notre-Dame-de-Scourmount, just a few miles south of the town. Round off the excursion with a stop at **Orval Abbey**, in the Gaume Forest. Founded in 1070 by Benedictines from Calabria in southern Italy, it became one of Europe's wealthiest and well-known Cistercian abbeys. The tour includes a short film on monastery life, and a visit to the ruins dating from the Middle Ages to the 18C. From Dinant to Orval, the distance is 99km/61mi.
For further information, see **The Green Guide Belgium** and **The Red Guide Benelux**.

Monks on the Web! If you love Trappist beer and would like to know more about how it is made, take a virtual tour of the abbey where Chimay is brewed: www.chimay.be.

Suggested reading

Héloïse and Abélard

Latinists may regale themselves with the beautiful **Letters** written by these medieval lovers. Although their authenticity has sometimes been called into question (they may have been improved by scribes who came after), there is no denying the beauty and profound humanity of sentiment which rings true in all ages. If your Latin is rusty, there are various modern translations available.

Peter Abélard, by Helen Waddell, was first published in 1933 and has had over 30 reprints (London, Constable and Co Ltd, 1968). This slim volume is a novel but reads like a true account, moving in its simplicity.

Stealing Heaven: the Love Story of Héloïse and Abélard, by Marion Meade (NY, Soho Press, 1979), tells the story from a woman's perspective. This sensuous historical novel of epic proportions is an immersion in 12C France.

Poets for every purpose

The Complete Fables of La Fontaine, edited and with rhymed verse translation by Norman B Spector (Evanston, Ill., Northwestern University Press, 1988). No verse is unturned in this collection which presents the French text opposite its translation, keen wit intact.

Verlaine, a seminal Symbolist and critical author, left an extensive body of work. Readily available in translation (ie by Jacques LeClerque, Westport Conn., Greenwood Press, 1977) are such famous books as *Songs Without Words, Yesteryear and Yesterday, The Accursed Poets, Confessions of a Poet*.

Rimbaud got quite a few stanzas out before putting down his pen at age 20. His best-known works available in translation include *A Season in Hell* and *The Drunken Boat*. **Rimbaud and Jim Morrison: the Rebel as Poet**, by Wallace Fowlie (Durham NC, Duke University Press, 1994), was inspired by a letter written to the author by the Doors' founder and lead singer, thanking him for publishing his translations of Rimbaud. The illustrated volume is a twinned tale exploring the symmetry of two lives and the parallels between European literary tradition and American rock music.

The ravages of war

The Debacle, by Émile Zola (translated by LW Tancock, Penguin, 1972) takes place during the Franco-Prussian War of 1870, describes the tragic events of the defeat at Sedan as well as the uprising of the Paris Commune. The author carried out extensive research (arms, strategy, tactics) to produce this remarkably factual novel depicting the battle and its aftermath.

The Pity of War by Niall Ferguson (London, Allen Lane, 1998). This radical, readable reassessment of the powers driving nations and individuals into the terrible conflict of the First World War focuses on life in the trenches.

A Balcony in the Forest, by Julien Gracq (translated by Richard Howard, London, Harper Collins, 1992), is set in the Ardennes Forest in the winter of 1939-40, during the so-called Phoney War. Following a winter of solitude and contemplation of nature, a young officer on the Maginot Line must face attacking Panzer divisions.

A Time for Trumpets: The Untold Story of the Battle of the Bulge, Charles B MacDonald (NY, Morrow, 1984). The author was one of the 600 000 American soldiers who fought against Hitler's vanguard troops in the mists and snow of the Ardennes Forest on 16 December, 1944 – Germany's last desperate gamble and the turning point of the war.

Memoirs of Hope: Renewal and Endeavour, Charles de Gaulle (NY, Simon and Schuster, 1971). Written in Colombey-les-Deux-Églises, the General's memoirs also include descriptions of the landscape of the Champagne region beyond the windows of his study.

Words on wine

Among the many books on wines of the region: *The Wines of Alsace* (Tom Stevenson, London, Faber and Faber, 1993); *Alsace Wines* (Pamela V Price, London, Sotheby Publications, 1984); *The Wine Lover's Guide to Champagne and North East France* (Michael Busselle, NY, Viking, 1989); *The Glory of Champagne* (Don Hewitson, London, MacMillan, 1989).

A few films

La Grande Illusion (J Renoir, 1937), prisoners of war in the castle of Haut-Kœnigsbourg; *Tess* (R Polanski, 1978), filmed around Verdun; *Au Revoir les Enfants* (L Malle, 1987), filmed in Provins; *Camille Claudel* (B Nuytten, 1988), filmed in Villeneuve-sur-Fère; *Total Eclipse* (A Holland, 1995), the story of Verlaine and Rimbaud.

PELLERIN & Cᵉ, imp.-édit.   L'ILLUSTRE FAMILLE DES JEAN,   IMAGERIE D'ÉPINAL, Nᵒ 1337

Jeanfesse!   J'enseigne.   J'embrasse.   J'embrouille.   Jean pêche.

Jean jean.   Jean rage!!   Ô J'empeste!   Jean chante.   J'emmaillotte.

Imagerie d'Épinal

Calendar of events

Music

Joinville . . . . Les Claviers d'Hiver, keyboards (in the château).

March-May
Épinal . . . . Festival of classical music.

May
Vandœuvre-lès-Nancy . . . . . Musique Action, festival of contemporary music, ☎ 03 83 57 52 24.

Nancy . . . . Every other year – International festival of choir singing (5 000 choristers).

Sarrebourg . . . . International music festival.

Late May-mid June
Mulhouse . . . . Bach festival.

June
Strasbourg . . . . Music festival.

Fénétrange . . . . International festival of music and opera.

Vittel . . . . Guitar Festival.

Bar-le-Duc, Verdun, Bouchon-sur-Saulx . . . . Festival of organs in the Meuse *département*.

Mirecourt . . . . Festival of strings (classical).

July
Colmar . . . . International music festival, ☎ 03 89 20 68 94.

July and August
Reims . . . . Summer music festival.
Sound and light show on the cathedral façade.

July-September, Saturday
Reims . . . . Music and lights, St-Remi Basilica.

1st half of September
Cons-la-Grandville 57 2 *(1)* Rencontres Musicales, ☎ 03 82 44 97 66.

Late September-early October
Strasbourg . . . . Musica, international contemporary music festival, ☎ 03 88 21 02 02.

Mid-October
Nancy . . . . Nancy Jazz Pulsations, ☎ 03 83 37 83 79.

Mid-November
Metz and in Lorraine . . . . . Musiques Volantes, ☎ 03 87 32 43 98.

Culinary and wine festivals

Saturday or Sunday following 22 January
**In all wine-growing
towns** . . . . St Vincent festival, honouring the patron saint of winegrowers.

Thursday before Easter
Troyes . . . . Ham festival.

Late April
Rethel . . . . Boudin Blanc festival.

Around the feast of the Ascension
Ungersheim . . . . Pork festival.

Whitsun
Revin . . . . Bread festival.

June
Troyes . . . . Champagne Fair.

1st half of June
Ribeauvillé . . . . Kugelhopf festival.

Whitsun
Wissembourg . . . . Opening of the annual fun fair (until the following Sunday). Folk dancing, parade of traditional costumes, horse races.

1st half of June
Chaumont . . . . Graphic arts international forums.

2nd half of June
Châlons-en-Champagne . . . Furies street theatre and circus festival, ☏ 03 26 65 90 06.

2nd Sunday in June
Reims . . . . Fêtes Johanniques and folklore festival.

June
Monthermé, Nouzouville . . Three Valleys festival (story tellers, exhibits).

June-September
Riquewihr . . . . Sound and light show (Dolder).

2nd and 3rd weekend in June
Provins . . . . Sound and light.

3rd weekend in June
Provins . . . . Medieval festival.

3rd Sunday in June
Saverne . . . . Rose festival.

Saturday before 24 June (or after, if 24 June is a Thursday or Friday)
Vallée de St-Amarin . . . . . . Midsummer night festival: Bonfires light up the valley.

June-August
Provins . . . . Jousting tournament.

Late June-August
Braux-Ste-Cohière . . . . Summer festival.

End of June
Château-Thierry . . . . Jean de la Fontaine festival.

30 June
Thann . . . . Crémation des Trois Sapins: ceremonial fire, burning three pine trees in front of the church.

1st half of July
Épinal . . . . International festival of imagery.

July
Verdun . . . . Seasonal events and show.
Langres . . . . Theatre festival with the Compagnie Humbert.

Sunday after 14 July
Seebach . . . . Streisselhochzeit.

Late July-early August
Vendeuvre-sur-Barse
(weekends) . . . . Vindovera historical drama, ☏ 03 25 41 44 76.
Renwez . . . . Lumberjack competitions.
Chambley, near Metz . . . . . Biennale Mondiale de l'Aérostation, the world's second-largest international balloon festival. On odd-numbered years.

Mid July-end of August, weekend
Bussang . . . . Théâtre du Peuple: Dramatic arts interpreted by companies uniting professionals and amateurs.

July-August
Troyes . . . . Sound, light and heritage (St-Pantaléon and St-Nicolas).
Vendresse 56 8 *(1)* . . . . Sound and light show at the Cassine Château, ☏ 03 24 26 02 68.
Charleville-Mézières . . . . . . Marionnette show.

August
Langres . . . . La Ronde des Hallebardiers, historical drama.

2nd Sunday in August
Sélestat . . . . Flower-decorated floats on parade.

14 August

Gérardmer............... Light show and fireworks over the lake.

15 August

Marlenheim .... L'Ami Fritz marriage celebration. Regional costumes.

Last weekend in August

Haguenau .... Hops festival, world folklore festival.

Last Sunday in August

Provins.................. Harvest festival.

1st Sunday in September

Ribeauvillé.............. Fête des Ménétriers or Pfifferdaj (strolling fiddlers): Historical parade, wine flows freely.

1st half of September

Strasbourg .... European fair.

September, even-numbered years

Troyes .... 48-hour vintage car rally.

October

St-Dié-des-Vosges .... International geography festival.

December

Throughout Alsace and Lorraine................. St-Nicolas Feast.
Christmas markets.

Braux-Ste-Cohière .... Shepherd's Christmas.

(1) For places not described in the guide, the Michelin map number and fold are given.

St Nicholas

The legend of St Nicholas – St Nicholas, bishop of Myra in Asia Minor in the 4C, is known for offering a dowry to three impoverished girls. He is also said to have prevented the execution of three unjustly accused officers. Perhaps because of images relating to the number three, he has also been associated, since the 12C in France, with the miraculous resurrection of three young children who had been cut up and set to cure by a butcher.

These various legends have created a popular figure who, on the night of 5 December, distributed gifts to good children in the countries of northern Europe (Lorraine, Germany, Belgium, the Netherlands, Switzerland).

Fête de la St-Nicolas – The Feast is celebrated either on the eve of or on the 6 December, or sometimes the following Saturday or Sunday. Many towns in Lorraine have celebrations, especially St-Nicolas-de-Port (torchlit procession in the basilica), Nancy (parade and fireworks), Metz (musical parade), and Épinal (floats in a parade).

Useful French words and phrases

ARCHITECTURAL TERMS

See Introduction: Architecture and art

SIGHTS

abbaye	abbey	marché	market
beffroi	belfry	monastère	monastery
chapelle	chapel	moulin	windmill
château	castle	musée	museum
cimetière	cemetery	pan de bois	timber-
cloître	cloisters	(en)	framed
colombage	half-timbering	parc	park
cour	courtyard	place	square
couvent	convent	pont	bridge
écluse	lock (canal)	port	port/harbour
église	church	porte	gateway
fontaine	fountain	quai	quay
gothique	gothic	remparts	ramparts
halle	covered market	romain	Roman
jardin	garden	roman	Romanesque
mairie	town hall	rue	street
maison	house	statue	statue
		tour	tower

NATURAL SITES

abîme	chasm	grotte	cave
aven	swallow-hole	lac	lake
barrage	dam	plage	beach
belvédère	viewpoint	rivière	river
cascade	waterfall	ruisseau	stream
col	pass	signal	beacon
corniche	ledge	source	spring
côte	coast, hillside	vallée	valley
forêt	forest		

ON THE ROAD

car park	parking	petrol/	station essence
diesel	diesel/gazole	gas station	
driving licence	permis de conduire	right	droite
east	Est	south	Sud
garage	garage	toll	péage
(for repairs)		traffic lights	feu tricolore
left	gauche	tyre	pneu
LPG	GPL	unleaded	sans plomb
motorway/	autoroute	west	Ouest
highway		wheel clamp	sabot
north	Nord	zebra crossing	passage clouté
parking meter	horodateur		
petrol/gas	essence		

TIME

today	aujourd'hui	Monday	lundi
tomorrow	demain	Tuesday	mardi
yesterday	hier	Wednesday	mercredi
winter	hiver	Thursday	jeudi
spring	printemps	Friday	vendredi
summer	été	Saturday	samedi
autumn/fall	automne	Sunday	dimanche
week	semaine		

	zéro	15	quinze
	un	16	seize
	deux	17	dix-sept
	trois	18	dix-huit
4	quatre	19	dix-neuf
5	cinq	20	vingt
6	six	30	trente
7	sept	40	quarante
8	huit	50	cinquante
9	neuf	60	soixante
10	dix	70	soixante-dix
11	onze	80	quatre-vingt
12	douze	90	quatre-vingt-dix
13	treize	100	cent
14	quatorze	1000	mille

SHOPPING

antiseptic	antiseptique	grocer's	épicerie
bank	banque	newsagent	maison de la presse, marchand de journaux
baker's	boulangerie		
big	grand	open	ouvert
bookshop	librairie	pain killer	analgésique
butcher's	boucherie	plaster	
chemist's/		(adhesive)	pansement adhésif
drugstore	pharmacie	post office	poste
closed	fermé	pound (weight)	livre
cough mixture	sirop pour la toux	push	pousser
cough sweets	cachets pour la gorge	pull	tirer
entrance	entrée	shop	magasin
exit	sortie	small	petit
fishmonger's	poissonnerie	stamps	timbres

FOOD AND DRINK

beef	bœuf	lamb	agneau
beer	bière	lunch	déjeuner
butter	beurre	meat	viande
bread	pain	mineral water	eau minérale
breakfast	petit-déjeuner	mixed salad	salade composée
cheese	fromage	orange juice	jus d'orange
chicken	poulet	plate	assiette
dessert	dessert	pork	porc
dinner	dîner	red wine	vin rouge
duck	canard	salt	sel
fish	poisson	sparkling	
fork	fourchette	water	eau gazeuse
fruit	fruits	spoon	cuillère
glass	verre	still water	eau plate
grape	raisin	sugar	sucre
green salad	salade verte	tap water	eau du robinet
ham	jambon	turkey	dinde
ice cream	glace	vegetables	légumes
ice cubes	glaçons	water	de l'eau
jug of water	carafe d'eau	white wine	vin blanc
jug of wine	pichet de vin	yoghurt	yaourt
knife	couteau		

PERSONAL DOCUMENTS AND TRAVEL

airport	aéroport	railway station	gare
credit card	carte de crédit	shuttle	navette
customs	douane	suitcase	valise
passport	passeport	train/plane	billet de
platform	voie, quai	ticket	train/d'avion
		wallet	portefeuille

CLOTHING

coat	manteau	socks	chaussettes
jumper	pull	stockings	bas
raincoat	imperméable	suit	costume/tailleur
shirt	chemise	tights	collant
shoes	chaussures	trousers	pantalon

438

USEFUL PHRASES

goodbye	au revoir
hello/good morning	bonjour
how	comment
excuse me	excusez-moi
thank you	merci
yes/no	oui/non
I am sorry	pardon
why	pourquoi
when	quand
please	s'il vous plaît

Do you speak English?	Parlez-vous anglais?
I don't understand.	Je ne comprends pas.
Talk slowly.	Parlez lentement.
Where's...?	Où est...?
When does the ... leave?	À quelle heure part...?
When does the ... arrive?	À quelle heure arrive...?
When does the museum open?	À quelle heure ouvre le musée?
When is the show?	À quelle heure est la représentation?
When is breakfast served?	À quelle heure sert-on le petit-déjeuner?
What does it cost?	Combien cela coûte?
Where can I buy a newspaper in English?	Où puis-je acheter un journal en anglais?
Where is the nearest petrol/gas station?	Où se trouve la station essence la plus proche?
Where can I change traveller's cheques?	Où puis-je échanger des traveller's cheques?
Where are the toilets?	Où sont les toilettes?
Do you accept credit cards?	Acceptez-vous les cartes de crédit?
I need a receipt.	Je voudrais un reçu.

Admission times and charges

As times and charges for admission are liable to alteration, the information below is given for guidance only. Every sight for which there are times and charges is indicated by the symbol ⊙ in the main part of the guide.

Order: The information is listed in the same order as the entries in the alphabetical section of the guide.

Dates: Dates given are inclusive.

Last admission: Ticket offices usually shut 30min before closing time; exceptions only are mentioned below.

Charge: The charge is for an individual adult; where appropriate the charge for a child is given. Prices are given as they were reported to us, either in French francs (F) or in euros (€). Prices converted from francs to euros at the time of going to press appear between brackets {€}. In some cases, no price was indicated to our services, but the sight may not necessarily be free of charge.

Sights which have comprehensive facilities for disabled tourists are indicated by the symbol ⅙ below.

Guided tours: The departure time of the last tour of the morning or afternoon will be up to 1hr before the actual closing time. Most tours are conducted by French speaking guides but in some cases the term "guided tours" may cover group visiting with recorded commentaries; some of the larger and more frequented sights may offer guided tours in other languages. Enquire at the ticket office or bookstall. Other aids commonly available for the foreign tourist are notes, pamphlets or audio-guides.

Lecture tours: These are regularly organised during the tourist season in towns of special interest. The information is given under the appropriate heading. In towns labelled Villes d'Art et d'Histoire and Villes d'Art *, tours are conducted by lecturers/ guides approved by the Caisse Nationale des Monuments Historiques et des Sites.*

Churches: Admission times are indicated if the interior is of special interest. Churches are usually closed from noon to 2pm. Visitors should refrain from walking about during services. Visitors to chapels are accompanied by the person who keeps the keys. A donation is welcome.

Tourist offices 🛈 *: The addresses and telephone numbers are given for the local tourist offices, which provide information on local market days, early closing days etc.*

A

ALTKIRCH
🛈 Place Xavier-Jourdain – 68130 – ☎ 03 89 40 02 90

Musée sundgauvien – Sun and public holidays 2.30-5.30pm (Jul and Aug: daily except Mon). Closed Easter, 1 and 8 May, Whitsun, Christmas. 15F {2.29€}. ☎ 03 89 40 21 80.

Excursion

Luemschwiller: Church – Sun 10am-6pm. During the week, contact the town hall. ☎ 03 89 25 42 55.

AMNÉVILLE

Parc zoologique du bois de Coulange – ⅙ Apr to Sep: 9.30am-7.30pm, Sun and public holidays 9.30am-8pm; Oct to Mar: 10am to dusk. 12.20€ (children: 8.38€). ☎ 03 87 70 25 60.

Excursion

Walibi-Schtroumpf – Mid-Apr to end of Sep: 10am-6pm (Jul and Aug: 10am-9pm). Enquire about non-opening days. 129F {19.67€} (-1.40m: 62F {9.45€}; -1m: no charge). ☎ 03 87 51 90 52.

ARGONNE

Clermont-en-Argonne
🛈 5, place de la République – 55120 – ☎ 03 29 88 42 22

Église St-Didier – Tours by appointment. ☎ 03 29 87 41 20.

Chapelle Ste-Anne – Closed for renovation. Enquire at the tourist office.

Varennes-en-Argonne: Musée d'Argonne – Jul and Aug: 10.30am-noon, 2.30-6pm; May to Jun: 3-6pm; Apr and Sep to mid-Oct: Sat-Sun and public holidays 3-6pm. Closed Oct to Easter. 3.66€. ☎ 03 29 80 71 01.

Beaulieu-en-Argonne: Winepress – Mar to end of Nov: 9am-6pm.

Rarécourt: Musée de la Faïence – ⅙ Early Jul to early Sep: 10.30am-noon, 2-8.30pm. 25F {3.81€}.

B

BACCARAT

Musée du Cristal – ♿ Apr to Nov: 9.30am-12.30pm, 2-6.30pm (Jul and Aug: 9.30am-6.30pm); Nov to Mar: 10am-noon, 2-6pm. Closed 1 Jan and 25 Dec. 2.29€. ☏ 03 83 76 61 37.

BALLON D'ALSACE

Sentheim: Maison de la Géologie – Mar to end of Nov: tours by appointment; Jul to Sep: daily except Sat 9am-noon, 2-6pm (discovery paths, departure at 2.30pm). 10F {1.52€} (discovery paths 30F {4.57€}). ☏ 03 89 82 55 55.

Parc naturel régional des BALLONS DES VOSGES

Ste-Marie-aux-Mines   🚩 Place du Prensureux – 68160 – ☏ 03 89 58 80 50

Guided tours of the town – Contact the tourist office.

Maison de Pays – Jun to end of Sep: daily except Tue 10am-noon, 2-6pm (last admission 1hr before closing). 3.81€. ☏ 03 89 58 56 67.

Mine St-Barthélemy – Apr to Sep: guided tours (45min) by request; Jul and Aug: daily 10am-noon, 2-6pm. 30F {4.57€} (children: 23F {3.51€}). ☏ 03 89 58 72 28.

Mine d'argent St-Louis-Eisenthur – Guided tours (3hr) by appointment with the ASEPAM, Centre du Patrimoine Minier (mining heritage centre), 4, rue Weisgerber, 68160 Ste-Marie-aux-Mines. ☏ 03 89 58 62 11, Fax: 03 89 58 68 97 or at the tourist office. Wear sturdy shoes and warm clothes (boots, waterproof coats and helmets are provided).

Château-Lambert: **Musée de la Montagne** – Daily except Tue and Sun morning: 9am-noon, 2-5pm (Apr to Sep: 6pm). Closed 1 Jan, 1 Nov, 25 Dec. 20F {3.05€}. ☏ 03 84 20 43 09.

BAR-LE-DUC   🚩 5, rue Jeanne-d'Arc – 55805 – ☏ 03 29 79 11 13

Église St-Étienne – May to Sep: guided tours 10am-noon, 2-6pm; Oct to Apr: contact the tourist office. ☏ 03 29 79 11 13.

Musée Barrois – Wad-Sat 2-6pm, Sat-Sun and public holidays 3-6pm. Closed 1 Jan, 1 May, 14 Jul, 15 Aug, 1 Nov, 25 Dec. 1.83€. ☏ 03 29 76 14 67.

BAR-SUR-AUBE   🚩 33, rue d'Aube – 10200 – ☏ 03 25 27 24 25

Cellier aux moines – Daily except 9am-3pm, 6.30-10pm, Mon, Tue, Sun 9am-3pm. No charge. ☏ 03 25 27 08 01.

Église St-Pierre – Easter to All Saints: 9am-6pm; All Saints to Easter: daily except Sat-Sun. Evening guided tours available in high season, contact the tourist office.

Excursion

Nigloland – ♿ Apr to mid-Jul: 10am-6pm (last admission 2hr before closing time); mid-Jul to early Sep: 10am-7pm (Aug: 10am-8pm); beginning of Sep: Wed and Sat 10am-6pm, Sun 10am-7pm. 12.96€ (children: 11.43€). ☏ 03 25 27 94 52.

BAYEL   🚩 Rue Belle-Verrière – 10310 – ☏ 03 25 92 42 68

Crystalworks – ♿ Guided tours (1hr 30min) daily except Sun at 9.30am or 11am, Sat by request. Closed mid-Jul to mid-Aug, last week in Nov and public holidays. 25F {3.81€}. ☏ 03 25 92 42 68.

Écomusée du centre Mazzolay – 9am-1pm, 2-6pm, Sun and public holidays 2-6pm. Closed 1 Jan, 1 May, last week in Nov. 25F {3.81€}. ☏ 03 25 92 42 68.

Colombé-le-Sec: Ferme du Cellier – Guided tours (30min) May to Oct: Sat 2-6pm, by prior appointment with the Association Renaissance de l'abbaye de Clairvaux, 11, rue Nationale, 10200 Bar-sur-Aube. ☏ 03 25 27 88 17.

BITCHE   🚩 Hôtel de ville – Porte de Strasbourg – 57230 – ☏ 03 87 06 16 16

Citadel – Mar to mid-Nov: tour (with infrared listening device, 2hr) 10am-5pm (Jul and Aug: 6pm). 38F {5.79€} (children: 23F {3.51€}). ☏ 03 87 06 16 16.

BOURBONNE-LES-BAINS

Museum – ♿ Beginning of Apr to end of Oct: Tue, Thu, Fri 2-6pm, certain Sundays 3-6pm. Closed public holidays. 1.52€. ☏ 03 25 90 14 80.

Excursion

Parc animalier de la Bannie – Jun to Sep: daily except Fri 2-6pm, Sun 11.30am-6.30pm; Mar to May: daily except Fri 2-5pm, Sun 11.30am-6.30pm; Mid-Nov to end of Feb: Wed, Sat 2-5pm; Nov to end of Jan: closing time 4pm. Closed Sun and public holidays, 1 Oct to 15 Nov). No charge. ☏ 03 25 90 14 77.

BRIENNE-LE-CHÂTEAU

Musée Napoléon – Apr to end of Oct: daily except Tue 10am-12.30pm, 2-6pm. Closed public holidays. 20F (3.05€). ☎ 03 25 92 82 41.

Excursions

Brienne-la-Vieille: Écomusée de la Forêt d'Orient – May to Sep: 10am-6pm, Sat-Sun and public holidays 2-6pm; Oct to Apr: 2-5pm, Sat-Sun and public holidays by request. 25F (3.81€). ☎ 03 25 92 95 84.

Rosnay-l'Hôpital: Église Notre-Dame – Jul to end of Aug: Sun 3-5pm, Mon-Sat key available in exchange for an identity document. ☎ 03 25 92 40 67 or 03 25 92 45 20.

C

CHÂLONS-EN-CHAMPAGNE   🖪 3, quai des Arts – 51000 – ☎ 03 26 65 17 89

Guided tours of the town 🄰 – Contact the tourist office.

Bibliothèque – Closed temporarily.

Cathédrale St-Étienne – Jul to end of Aug: daily 10am-noon, 2.30-6pm. No charge.
Cathedral Treasury – As for the cathedral.

Église Notre-Dame-en-Vaux – Mon-Sat 10am-noon, 2-6pm.

Musée du cloître de Notre-Dame-en-Vaux – Daily except Tue 10am-noon, 2-5pm, Sat-Sun 10am-noon, 2-6pm (Apr to Sep: 6pm). Closed 1 Jan, 1 May, 1 and 11 Nov, 25 Dec. 3.96€. ☎ 03 26 64 03 87.

Musée municipal – Daily except Tue 2-6pm, Sun 2.30-6.30pm. Closed public holidays. 15F (2.29€). ☎ 03 26 69 38 53.

Église St-Alpin – Tue-Sat 10am-noon, 2.30-6pm.

Musée Garinet – Daily except Tue 2-6pm, Sun 2.30-6.30pm. Closed public holidays. 10F (1.52€). ☎ 03 26 69 38 53.

Église St-Loup – Tours by written request to the presbytery, 5, place Notre-Dame.

Musée Schiller-et-Goethe – Jul and Aug: 2-6pm, Sun 2.30-6.30pm; Sep to Jun: Sat 2-6pm, Sun 2.30-6.30pm. Closed public holidays. 10F (1.52€). ☎ 03 26 69 38 53.

Routes du CHAMPAGNE

Excursions

Oger: Musée des Traditions, de l'Amour et du Champagne – Mar-Nov: 9.30am-noon, 2-6pm, Sun 9.30am-noon, 3-6pm; Dec-Feb: by appointment. 5.34€. ☎ 03 26 57 50 89.

Le Mesnil-Sur-Oger: Musée la vigne and du vin – Guided tours (1hr 30min) Mon-Fri at 10am; Sat-Sun at 10.30am by appointment 1 day in advance. Closed 1 Jan, Easter and 20 Dec to early Jan. 5.34€. ☎ 03 26 57 50 15.

Fleury-la-Rivière: Coopérative vinicole – ♿ Guided tours (45min) daily except Tue 10am-noon, 2-6pm, Sun and public holidays 3-7pm. Closed 1 Jan and 25 Dec. 3.81€. ☎ 03 26 58 42 53.

Dormans: Mémorial des victoires la Marne – Apr to mid-Nov: Sat 2.30-6.30pm, Sun 10am-noon, 2.30-6.30pm; May to mid-Sep: daily except Tue 2.30-6.30pm, Sun 10am-noon, 2.30-6.30pm. ☎ 03 26 58 22 31.

Moulin d'en Haut – La Remise aux outils champenois – May to end of Oct: daily except Mon 2-6pm. Closed Nov to Apr. 3.81€. ☎ 03 26 58 85 16.

Church – Sun and holidays 10am-noon.

Œuilly: Écomusée – May-Nov: guided tours (1hr) daily except Tue 10am-noon, 2-6pm, Sat-Sun and public holidays 2-7pm; Dec to Apr: daily except Tue 2-6pm (last admission 1hr before closing). 5.33€ (children: 2.29€). ☎ 03 26 57 10 30.

Essômes-sur-Marne: Église St-Ferréol – Daily except Sat-Sun 9am-noon, 2-6pm. Contact Essômes town hall. ☎ 03 23 83 08 31.

Fossy: Le Varocien – Musée de la Vigne et du Vin – ♿ Guided tours (30min) daily by appointment. Contact Champagne DEHU, 3, rue St-Georges, 02650 Fossoy. Closed public holidays. 3.04€. ☎ 03 23 71 90 47.

CHARLEVILLE-MÉZIÈRES   🖪 4, place Ducale – 08109 – ☎ 03 24 33 00 17

Musée de l'Ardenne – ♿ Daily except Mon 10am-noon, 2-6pm. Closed 1 Jan, 1 May, 25 Dec. 25F (3.81€). No charge 1st Sun in the month. ☎ 03 24 32 44 60.

Musée Rimbaud – Daily except Mon 10am-noon, 2-6pm. Closed 1 Jan, 1 May, 25 Dec. 20F (3.05€). No charge 1st Sun in the month. ☎ 03 24 32 44 65.

CHARLEVILLE-MÉZIÈRES

Excursions

Mohon: Église St-Lié – 8am-noon. ☎ 03 24 57 13 15.

Warcq: church – Guided tours Mon-Fri 1.30-5.30pm. ☎ 03 24 59 48 20.

Parc animalier de St-Laurent – Apr to Sep: daily except Thu 2-6pm, Sat-Sun and public holidays 1.30-7pm; the rest of the year: daily except Thu 1.30-5.30pm. No charge. ☎ 03 24 32 44 80.

CHÂTEAU-THIERRY   🅱 12, place de l'Hôtel-de-Ville – 02400 – ☎ 03 23 83 10 14

Maison natale de La Fontaine – Apr to Sep: daily except Tue 9am-noon, 2-6pm; Oct to Mar: daily except Tue 10am-noon, 2-5pm. Closed 1 Jan, 1 May, 1 Nov, 25 Dec. 3.05€, no charge Wed. ☎ 03 23 69 05 60

Caves de champagne Pannier – ♿ Tours by appointment only 9am-12.30pm, 2-6.30pm (last admission 1hr before closing). Closed Sun and public holidays. 4.55€. ☎ 03 23 69 51 33.

Excursion

Condé-en-Brie: castle – Jun to Sep: guided tours (1hr) 2.30-4.45pm; May: Sun and public holidays 2.30-4.45pm. 6.40€. ☎ 03 23 82 42 25.

CHAUMONT   🅱 Place du Général-de-Gaulle – 52000 – ☎ 03 25 03 80 80

Donjon – Jun to end of Sep: daily except Tue 2.30-6.30pm, Sat-Sun 2.30-7pm. 1.53€. ☎ 03 15 03 80 80.

Musée – Daily except Tue 2-6pm (Jul to mid-Sep: 6.30pm) Closed 1 Jan, 1 May, 25 Dec. 1.52€. ☎ 03 25 03 01 99.

Les silos, Maison du livre et de l'affiche – ♿ Daily except Mon 2-7pm, Wed and Sat 10am-6pm, Sun 2-6pm (large exhibition hall only); summer: Tue-Fri 2-6.30pm, Sat 9am-1pm. No charge. ☎ 03 25 03 86 82.

Chapelle des Jésuites – Open during exhibitions. At other times, tours available by appointment with the tourist office. ☎ 03 25 03 80 80.

Excursion

Prez-sous-Lafauche: Zoo de bois – ♿ Jun to mid-Sep: daily except Mon 2.30-6pm. 2.29€ (children: 1.83€). ☎ 03 25 31 57 76.

Abbaye de CLAIRVAUX

Tour of the abbey – Apr to end of Oct: 2-6pm, guided tours (1hr 30min) Sat at 2pm, 3.30pm, 5pm (Jul and Aug: daily 4pm). 40F {6.10€}. ☎ 03 25 27 52 55.

COLMAR   🅱 4, rue Unterlinden – 68000 – ☎ 03 89 20 68 92

Guided tours of the town – Contact the tourist office.

Musée d'Unterlinden – Apr to Oct: 9am-6pm; Nov to Mar: daily except Tue 10am-5pm. Closed 1 Jan, 1 May, 1 Nov, 25 Dec. 5.34€ (children: 3.81€). ☎ 03 89 20 15 50.

Temple St-Matthieu – Mid-Jun to mid-Oct: 10am-noon, 3-5pm; end of Apr to beginning of May: call for information. ☎ 03 89 41 44 96.

Église des Dominicains – End of Mar to end of Nov: 10am-1pm, 3-6pm. 8F.

Boat trips – Jul and Aug: trips (30min) 10am-7.30pm; Apr to mid-Oct: 10am-7pm; Mar: Sat-Sun and public holidays 10am-6pm. 35F {5.34€} (children: no charge). ☎ 03 89 41 01 94.

Musée Bartholdi – Mar to end of Nov: daily except Tue 10am-noon, 2-6pm (last admission 20min before closing). Closed 1 May, 1 Nov, 25 Dec. 4€. ☎ 03 89 41 90 60.

Musée animé du Jouet et des Petits Trains – ♿ 10am-noon, 2-6pm (Jul and Aug: 10am-6pm. Closed 2 weeks in Jan, 1 Jan, 1 May, 1 Nov, 25 Dec. 25F {3.81€}. ☎ 03 89 41 93 10.

Muséum d'Histoire naturelle et d'Ethnographie – Daily except Tue 9am-noon, 2-5pm, Sun 2-6pm. Closed 1 Jan, 1 May, 1 Nov, 25 Dec. 4€. ☎ 03 89 23 84 15.

Excursion

Neuf-Brisach: Musée Vauban – ♿ Apr to Oct: daily except Tue 10am-noon, 2-5pm. 15F {2.29€}. ☎ 03 89 72 56 66.

COLOMBEY-LES-DEUX-ÉGLISES

La Boisserie – ♿ Daily except Tue 10am-noon, 2-5.30pm (May to Sep: 6pm). Closed Nov to Jan. 20F {3.05€}. ☎ 03 25 01 52 52.

Mémorial – Apr to Oct: daily except Tue 10am-7pm; Nov to Mar: 10am-noon, 2-4pm. Closed 1 Jan and 25 Dec. 12F {1.81€}. ☎ 03 25 01 50 50.

Route des CRÊTES

Haut-Chitelet: Jardin d'Altitude – Jul and Aug: 10am-6pm; Jun: 10am-noon, 2-6pm; Sep: 10am-noon, 2-5.30pm. 15F {2.29€}, no charge in Sep. ☎ 03 29 63 31 46.

Vieil-Armand: Monument national du Vieil-Armand – Apr to 11 Nov: 8am-noon, 2-6pm. 12F {1.81€}. ☎ 03 89 23 12 03.

Cernay:

Museum – May to end of Sep: daily except Tue 2-5pm. 20F {3.05€}. ☎ 03 89 75 88 85.

Tour of the Doller Valley – Steam trains: Jun to end of Sep: Sun and public holidays, departure from Cernay-St-André at 11am and 3.30pm, return trip at 3pm and 6.30pm. 55F {8.38€} return. Diesel trains: Jul and Aug: daily except Mon and Tue, departure from Cernay-St-André at 3pm, return trip at 5.30pm. 6.86€ return. ☎/Fax: 03 89 82 88 48.

D

Lac du DER-CHANTECOQ

Information available from the tourist office, Maison du Lac, 51290 Giffaumont-Champaubert. ☎ 03 26 72 62 80.

Giffaumont: Boat trips on the lake – May to Aug: daily except Mon 2-6pm (Jul and Aug: daily); Easter to Apr and first two weeks in Sep: Sat-Sun from 3pm (additional departure Sun at 11am). 33F {5.03€} (children: 21F {3.20€}).

Grange aux abeilles – Mar, Oct and Nov: Sat-Sun and public holidays in the afternoon; May to Sep: daily except Mon and Tue in the afternoon (Jul and Aug: mornings and afternoons). Closed Nov, Jan, Feb. No charge. ☎ 03 26 72 61 97.

Ferme de Berzillières (Agricultural museum) – May to end of Sep: Sat-Sun and public holidays in the afternoon; Jul and Aug: daily in the afternoon or by appointment. 20F {3.05€}. ☎ 03 25 04 22 52.

Maison de l'Oiseau et du Poisson – Beginning of Feb to end of Nov: 1.30-4.30pm, Sun 2-6.30pm (Jul and Aug: 10.30am-7pm); Nov to Jan: by appointment. 35F {5.34€}. ☎ 03 26 74 00 00.

Arrigny: Ferme aux Grues – Mid-Oct to Mar, Fri-Sun and public holidays 9am-5.30pm. No charge. ☎ 03 26 72 54 10.

Ste-Marie-du-Lac-Nuisement: Château d'eau panoramique – 10am-6pm. No charge. ☎ 03 26 72 62 80.

Massif du DONON

Abreschviller: Forest train – Jul and Aug: at 2.30pm and 4.15pm, Sun and public holidays at 11am, 2.15pm, 3.15pm, 4.15pm, 5.15pm; May and Jun: Sat at 3.15pm, Sun and public holidays at 11am, 2.15pm, 3.15pm, 4.15pm, 5.15pm; Sep and Oct: Sat at 3.15pm, Sun and public holidays at 2.30pm and 4.15pm. 7.62€ (children: 5.34€). ☎ 03 87 03 79 12.

Scierie de la Hallière – May to end of Oct: Sun and public holidays 2-6.30pm (Jul to Sep: daily except Mon). 2.29€. ☎ 03 83 74 49 71.

Lac de Pierre-Percée: Vedette "Cristal" – Apr to mid-Nov: Sun and public holidays departure at 2pm, 3pm, 4pm, 5pm (mid-Jun to beginning of Sep: daily). 40F {6.10€} (children: 20F {3.05€}). ☎ 03 83 73 15 25.

E

ÉCOMUSÉE D'ALSACE

Mid-Apr to Sep: 9.30am-7pm; Oct to mid-Apr: 10am-5pm. 12.96€ (children: 8.38€). ☎ 03 89 74 44 74.

EGUISHEIM
🛈 18, rue des Trois-Châteaux – 68420 – ☎ 03 89 23 40 33

Guided tours of the town – Contact the tourist office.

Excursion

Château de Hohlandsbourg – Easter to 11 Nov: guided tours (45min) Sat 2-6pm, Sun and public holidays 11am-6pm (Jul to early Sep: daily 10am-7pm). {3,81€}. ☎ 03 89 30 10 20.

ENSISHEIM

Musée de la Régence – Daily except Tue 2-5.30pm (Jan to Mar: daily except Tue 2-5.30pm, Thu 10am-12.30pm, 2-5.30pm). Closed public holidays and alternate weekends. 13F {1.98€}. ☎ 03 89 26 49 54.

ÉPERNAY

🖪 7, avenue Champagne – 51202 – ☎ 03 26 55 33 00

Moët et Chandon – Apr to mid-Nov: guided tours (1hr) 9.30-11.30am, 2-4.30pm (mid-Nov to end of Mar: daily except Sat-Sun and public holidays). 6.10€. ☎ 03 26 51 20 20.

Mercier – ⑤ Guided tours (45min) 9.30-11.30am, 2-4.30pm, Sat-Sun and public holidays 9.30-11.30am, 2-5pm (Nov to Feb: daily except Tue and Wed). Closed during Christmas school holidays. 30F {4.57€}. ☎ 03 26 51 22 22.

De Castellane – Beginning of Mar to end of Nov: guided tours (45min) 10am-noon, 2-6pm (last admission at 11.15am and 5.15pm). 5.34€ (children: 3.81€). ☎ 03 26 51 19 11.

Musée municipal – Closed for renovation.

Excursion

Parc du Sourdon – Apr to end of Sep: 9am-7pm. No charge. ☎ 03 26 59 95 00.

ÉPINAL

🖪 13, rue de la Comédie – 88000 – ☎ 03 29 82 53 32

Guided tours of the town – Contact the tourist office.

Imagerie d'Épinal (Exhibition gallery and Écomusée) – ⑤ Sep to Jun 9am-noon, 2-6.30pm, Sun and public holidays 2-6.30pm; Jul and Aug 9am-7pm, Sun and public holidays 2-7pm. Closed 1 Jan and 25 Dec. 4.57€ (children: 0.76€). ☎ 03 29 31 28 88.

Musée départemental d'Art ancien et contemporain – ⑤ Daily except Tue 10am-6pm. Closed 1 Jan, 1 May, 1 Nov, 25 Dec. 30F {4.57€} (children: no charge). ☎ 03 29 82 20 33.

Parc du Château – Apr to Sep: 7.30am-7pm (May to Aug: 7.30am-8pm); Nov to Feb: 8am-5pm (Mar and Oct: 7.30am-6pm). No charge. ☎ 03 29 68 50 61.

Église Notre-Dame – Closed Sun afternoons.

Excursion

Fort d'Uxegney – Mid-Jun to mid-Sep: guided tours (1hr 30min) Sat at 2pm and 4pm, unaccompanied visits Sun 1.30-5pm (Jul and Aug: daily). 20F {3.05€}. ☎ 03 29 31 03 01.

F

FISMES

Excursion

Courville: church – Contact Mrs Ronseaux, 5, rue de Bury. ☎ 03 26 48 44 31.

Parc naturel régional de la FORÊT D'ORIENT

Maison du Parc – 9am-noon, 2-6pm, Sat-Sun and public holidays 9.30am-12.30pm, 2.30-6.30pm (6pm from mid-Feb to end of Mar and 5.30pm Sun from Oct to mid-Feb). Closed 1 and 2 Jan, 24-26 and 31 Dec. No charge. ☎ 03 25 43 81 90.

Excursions

Lusigny-sur-Barse: Musée des Automates – Apr to mid-Sep: Sat, Sun and public holidays 3-6.30pm (last admission 1hr before closing). 7€ (children 3-12: 4.5€). ☎ 03 25 41 55 51.

Mesnil-St-Père:

Boat trips: Le Winger – Departures from Mesnil-St-Père harbour, mid-Mar to mid-Sep: daily. Time: 45min. 25F {3.81€} (children: 15F {2.29€}). ☎ 03 25 41 21 64.

Le Bateau Ivre – Mid-Mar to mid-Sep: trip (1hr) 9am-7pm; cruise including meal 11am-2pm and 6.30-8.30pm by appointment. Trip 4.57€ (children: 2.28€), meal 24.39€ (children: 13.72€). ☎ 03 25 41 20 72.

Parc de vision animalier – Apr to Sep: Sat-Sun and public holidays 5pm to dusk (Jul and Aug: daily except Thu and Fri); Oct to Apr: Sat-Sun and public holidays 2pm to dusk. Closed 1 Jan and 25 Dec. 20F {3.05€}. ☎ 03 25 43 81 90.

G

GÉRARDMER

Boat trips – Tour of the lake by launch (guided tour lasting 20min), 4€; by electric dinghy: 12.20€ for 30min, by pedal-boat: 5.34€ for 30min.

Excursion

Domaine de la Moineaudière – ⑤ 9.30am-noon, 2-6.30pm (Sep to Jun: Sat-Sun and public holidays 6pm). Closed 2 weeks in Jan, 2 weeks in Mar and from mid-Oct to end of Nov. 4.24€. ☎ 03 29 63 37 11.

GIVET

🗓 Place de la Tour – 08600 – ☎ 03 24 42 03 54

Tour Victoire – Jul and Aug: Mon, Tue, Fri and Sat-Sun 3-6pm, Wed and Thu 2-6pm; Jun: daily except Mon 3-6pm. 1.52€. ☎ 03 24 42 03 54

Centre européen des métiers d'art – 10am-noon, 2.30-6pm, Sun and Mon 2.30-6pm. No charge. ☎ 03 24 42 73 36.

Fort de Charlemont – Jul and Aug: 10am-noon, 2-6pm. 2.29€. ☎ 03 24 42 03 54.

Chemin de fer des Trois Vallées – May to mid-Sep: train ride (45min) with steam or diesel engines, Sat-Sun and public holidays, departure at 10.20am, return trip at 1.50pm and 4.50pm. Givet station. ☎ 03 24 41 36 04.

Excursions

Grottes de Nichet – Jun to Aug: guided tours (1hr) 10am-noon, 1.30-7pm; Apr to May and Sep: 2-6pm (last admission 1hr before closing). 4.57€ (children: 2.29€). ☎ 03 24 42 00 14.

Site nucléaire de Chooz – Guided tours (2hr 30min) by appointment (15 days in advance) Mon-Fri at 9am and 4pm. Children under 10 prohibited. Visitors must have identity papers with them. For foreign visitors (other than EEC members), send your request by mail enclosing a copy of your passport. ☎ 03 24 42 88 88.

Fumay: Musée de l'Ardoise – Apr to Sep: 10am-6pm (last admission 1hr before closing); Oct to Mar: 8am-noon, 1-5pm, Sat-Sun by appointment. 15F {2.29€}. ☎ 03 24 41 10 25.

GUEBWILLER

🗓 73, rue de la République – 68500 – ☎ 03 89 76 10 63

Guided tours of the town – Contact the tourist office.

Musée du Florival – ♿ Daily except Tue 2-6pm, Sat-Sun and public holidays 10am-noon, 2-6pm. Closed 1 Jan, 1 May, 25 Dec. 15F {2.29€}. ☎ 03 89 74 22 89.

Ancien couvent des Dominicains: centre polymusical (music centre) – Jul and Aug: 9am-noon, 2-6pm, Sat-Sun 10am-noon, 2-5pm; Sep to Jun: daily except Sat-Sun. ☎ 03 89 62 21 81.

H

HAGUENAU

🗓 Place de la Gare – 67500 – ☎ 03 88 93 70 00

Guided tours of the town – Contact the tourist office.

Musée historique – Jul to Sep: 10am-noon, 2-6pm, Tue, Sat-Sun and public holidays 2-6pm; Oct to Dec and Jan to Jun: 10am-noon, 2-6pm, Sat-Sun and public holidays 3-5.30pm. Closed 1 Jan, Easter, 1 May, 1 Nov, 25 Dec. 3.05€. ☎ 03 88 93 79 22.

Musée alsacien – 9am-noon, 1.30-5.30pm, Tue 1.30-5.30pm, Sat-Sun and public holidays 2-5pm. Closed 1 Jan, Easter, 1 May, 1 Nov, 25 Dec. 2.29€. ☎ 03 88 73 30 41.

Excursions

Soufflenheim: Ceramics workshops – Daily except Sat-Sun 9am-noon, 2-5pm. ☎ 03 88 86 26 97.

Betschdorf: Museum – Easter to All Saints: 10am-noon, 1-5pm. 20F {3.05€}. ☎ 03 88 54 48 07.

Morsbronn-les-Bains: Fantasialand (amusement park for children) – Apr to early Sep: 10am-6pm. ☎ 03 88 09 46 46.

Sessenheim: Auberge "Au bœuf" – Daily except Mon and Tue. Closed from beginning to mid-Feb and from end of Jul to mid-Aug. Postcard 0.76€.

Château du HAUT-BARR

Claude Chappe's telegraph tower – Jun to mid-Sep: guided tours (30min) daily except Mon noon-6pm. 10F {1.52€}. ☎ 03 88 52 98 99.

Château du HAUT-KŒNIGSBOURG

May to Sep: 9am-6pm (Jul and Aug: 6.30pm); Mar, Apr and Oct: 9am-noon, 1-5.30pm; Nov to Feb: 9.30am-noon, 1-4.30pm. Closed 1 Jan, 1 May and 25 Dec. 6.40€ (18-25s: 3.96€). ☎ 03 88 82 50 60.

Le HOHWALD

Ottrott: Les Naïades – ⏶ 9.30am-6.30pm; 25 Dec and 1 Jan: 9.30am-noon. 43F
{6.56€}. ☎ 03 88 95 90 32.

Le Struthof: Ancien Camp de Concentration – Jul and Aug: 10am-6pm (last admission 1hr
before closing); Mar to Jun: 10am-noon, 2-5.30pm (last admission 11.30am and
4.30pm); Sep to Christmas: 10am-noon, 2-5pm. Closed from Christmas to end of
Feb. 10F {1.52€}. ☎ 03 88 97 04 49.

J

JOINVILLE   🛈 Place Saunoise – 52300 – ☎ 03 25 94 17 90

Château du Grand Jardin – Apr to Oct: daily except Tue 10am-noon, 2-7pm (Jul and
Aug: daily 9am-8pm); Nov to end of Jan: daily except Tue 2-6pm (Nov to Jan: 5pm),
Sun and public holidays 10am-noon, 2-6pm. Closed between Christmas and New
Year's Day. 20F {3.05€}. ☎ 03 25 94 17 54.

Auditoire – Mid-May to end of Oct: guided tours (1hr 30min) Mon, Tue, Wed, Fri 9am-
2-6pm, Mon 2-6pm by appointment half day in advance with the tourist office (Jul
and Aug: Sat 4-7pm, Sun and public holidays 3-6.30pm; end of May to end of Jun: Sun
3-6pm; Sep and Oct: Sun 2.30-5.30pm) 20F {3.05€}. ☎ 03 25 94 17 90.

Église Notre-Dame – Guided tours available, contact the tourist office.

Chapelle Ste-Anne – In summer: daily except Mon and Sun. Contact the tourist
office.

K

KAYSERSBERG

Musée communal – Jul and Aug: 10am-noon, 2-6pm. 1.52€.

Musée Albert-Schweitzer – Easter to Nov: 9am-noon, 2-6pm. Closed Nov to Apr.
1.52€. ☎ 03 89 47 36 55.

L

LANGRES   🛈 Place Bel-Air – 52200 – ☎ 03 25 87 67 67

Guided tours of the town 🅰 – Contact the tourist office.

Cloître de la cathédrale – Tue and Thu 3-6pm, Wed and Sat 9.30-11.45am,
1.30-6pm, Fri 3-6.30pm and by appointment. ☎ 03 25 87 63 00.

Tours de Navarre et d'Orval – May to end of Sep: Sat-Sun and public holidays
2.30-5.30pm (Jul and Aug: daily 10am-12.30pm, 2.30-7pm). 15F {2.29€}.

Cathédrale St-Mammès:

Trésor – ⏶ Jul and Aug: daily except Tue 2.30-6pm. 15F {2.29€}
(ticket valid for visits to the Tour Sud). ☎ 03 25 87 67 67.

Tour sud – Jul to end of Aug: daily except Tue and during services 2.30-6pm. 15F
{2.29€} (tower and treasury).

Musée d'Art et d'Histoire – ⏶ Daily except Tue 10am-6pm (5pm in winter). Closed
1 Jan, 1 May, 1 Nov, 25 Dec. 3.20€. ☎ 03 25 87 08 05.

Excursions

Faverolles: Atelier archéologique – May to end of Sep: Sat-Sun and public holidays
3-6pm (Jul and Aug: daily except Tue 3-7pm). 15F {2.29€}. ☎ 03 25 87 67 67.

Château du Pailly – May to Sep: Sat-Sun and public holidays 2.30-5.30pm (Jul and
Aug: daily except Tue 3-7pm). 2.29€.

Fort du Cognelot – Jul to end of Aug: guided tours (1hr) Sun and public holidays at
3.30pm and 5pm. 20F {3.05€}. ☎ 03 25 87 67 67.

Fayl-Billot: Exhibition rooms of the national school of wickerwork – Daily except Tue 10am-
noon, 2-6pm. Closed 1 Jan and 25 Dec. 2.29€. ☎ 03 25 88 63 02.

Bussières-les-Belmont: Vannerie – Daily except Sat morning, Sun and public holidays
8am-noon, 2-6pm ☎ 03 25 88 62 75.

Parc Naturel Régional de LORRAINE

Hannonville-sous-les-Côtes: Maison des Arts and Tradition rurales – May-Jun: 9am-noon, 2-5.30pm, Sat, Sun and public holidays 2-6pm; Jul-Oct: daily except Mon and Tue 11am-noon, Sun 2-6pm; Nov-Apr: daily except Mon and Tue 2-6pm. 3.04€. ☎ 03 29 87 32 94.

Tarquimpol: Maison du Pays des Étangs: – ♿ School holidays: Wed-Sat 2-6pm, Sun 10am-noon, 2-6pm (Aug: 7pm); the rest of the year: Sat 2-6pm, Sun and holidays 10am-noon, 2-6pm. Closed 20 Dec to mid-Feb 3.05€. ☎ 03 87 86 88 10.

Rhodes: Parc animalier de Ste Croix – Jul-Aug: 10am-7pm, Sun and public holidays 10am-8pm; Sep to mid-Nov and Apr-Jun: 10am-6pm, Sun and public holidays 10am-7pm. Closed mid-Nov to Mar. 9.15€ (children 3-11: 6.10€). ☎ 03 87 03 92 05.

Hattonchâtel:

Musée Louise-Cottin – Apr to end of Sep: daily except Tue 10am-noon, 2.30-6.30pm, Sat-Sun and public holidays 2.30-6.30pm. 10F {1.52€}, 15F {2.29€} (ticket also valid for the guided tour of the village). ☎ 03 29 89 30 73.

Castle – Guided tours (30min) daily except Tue 9am-noon, 2-6pm, Sat-Sun and public holidays 9am-noon, 2-6pm. Closed in Oct. 3.05€. ☎ 03 29 89 57 44.

LUNÉVILLE

Château:

Chapel – Closed for restoration work.

Musée – Daily except Tue 10am-noon, 2-5pm (Apr to Sep: 6pm). Closed 1 Jan, Monday preceding Shrove Tuesday, 25 Dec. 2.29€. No charge 1st Sun in the month. ☎ 03 83 76 23 57.

Musée de la Moto et du Vélo – Daily except Mon 9am-noon, 2-6pm. 3.81€. ☎ 03 83 74 07 20.

LUXEUIL-LES-BAINS   1, avenue des Thermes – 70302 – ☎ 03 84 40 06 41

Guided tours of the town – Contact the tourist office.

Ancienne abbaye St-Colomban – Possibility of guided tours (2hr) at 3pm on the 3rd day of the month. tourist office. 25F {3.81€}.

Musée de la tour des Échevins – Summer: daily except Mon and Tue 10am-noon, 2-6pm, Sun 2-6pm; winter: daily except Mon and Tue 10am-noon, 2.30-5.30pm, Sun 2-5pm. Closed Nov, 1 Jan and 25 Dec. 12F {1.83€}. ☎ 03 84 40 00 07.

M

Ligne MAGINOT

Petit ouvrage de Villy-la-Ferté – Palm Sunday to All Saints: guided tours (1hr 30min) Sun and public holidays 2-5.30pm (Jul and Aug: daily except Mon). 3.05€. ☎ 03 24 22 06 72.

Gros ouvrage de Fermont – Jul and Aug: guided tours (2hr 30min) 2-4pm; Apr and May: Sat-Sun and public holidays at 2pm and 3.30pm; Jun: at 3pm, Sat-Sun and public holidays at 2pm and 3.30pm; Sep: 2pm and 3.30pm. Wear warm clothes and sturdy shoes. 4.57€. ☎ 03 82 39 35 34.

Fort de Guentrange – May to end of Sep: guided tours (1hr 30min) the 1st and 3rd Sun in the month at 3pm. 2.29€. ☎ 03 82 88 12 15.

Abri du Zeiterholz – May to end of Sep: guided tours (1hr 30min) the 1st and 3rd Sun in the month 2-4pm. 2.70€. ☎ 03 82 55 11 43.

Petit ouvrage de l'Immerhof – Apr to end of Sep: guided tours (1hr 30min) 2nd and 4th Sun in the month, public holidays 2-5pm. 20F {3.01€}. ☎ 03 82 53 09 61.

Gros ouvrage du Hackenberg – ♿ Apr to end of Oct: guided tours (2hr) Sat-Sun and public holidays 2-5.30pm. 25F {3.81€}. ☎ 03 82 82 30 08.

Gros ouvrage du Michelsberg – Apr to end of Oct: guided tours (1hr 30min) Sun and public holidays 2-6pm. 3.05€. ☎ 03 82 34 66 67.

Petit ouvrage du Bambesch – Apr to Sep: guided tours (1hr 30min) 2nd and 4th Sun in the month (Easter Monday, Whit Monday and 15 Aug 2-6pm). 3.05€. ☎ 03 87 90 31 95.

Rohrbach-lès-Bitche: Fort Casso – Apr to Oct: guided tours (1hr 30min) Mon-Fri at 9.30am, 10.30am, 2pm, 3pm and 4pm, Sat-Sun and public holidays at 3pm. 25F {3.81€}. ☎ 03 87 09 70 95.

Gros ouvrage du Simsershof – Closed for restoration until 2002.

Casemate de Dambach-Neunhoffen – May to end of Sep: Sun and public holidays 2-5.30pm. 1.52€. ☎ 03 88 09 21 46.

Lembach: Four à Chaux – Mid-Mar to mid-Nov: guided tours (1hr 30min) at 10am, 2pm, 3pm (Jul and Aug: at 10am, 11am, 2pm, 3pm, 4pm, 5pm; May to Sep: at 10am, 2pm, 3pm, 4pm). Closed mid-Nov to mid-Mar. 3.81€. ☎ 03 88 94 43 16.

Ouvrage d'artillerie de Schœnenbourg – May to Sep: 2-4pm, Sun and public holidays 9.30-11am, 2-4pm; Apr and Oct: Sun and public holidays 9.30-11am, 2-4pm. 5€. ☎ 03 88 80 59 39.

Hatten:

Musée de l'Abri – Mar to 11 Nov: Thu-Sat and public holidays 10am-noon, 2-6pm, Sun 10am-6pm (mid-Jun to mid-Sep: daily 10am-6pm). 25F {3.81€}. ☎ 03 88 80 14 90.

Casemate d'infanterie Esch – May to end of Sep: Sun 10am-noon, 1.30-6pm. 1.52€. ☎ 03 88 80 05 07.

Marckolsheim: Mémorial-musée de la Ligne Maginot du Rhin – & Mid-Mar to mid-Nov: Sun and public holidays 9am-noon, 2-6pm (mid-Jun to mid-Sep: daily). 1.22€. ☎ 03 88 92 74 99.

MARMOUTIER

Musée d'Arts et Traditions populaires – May to end of Oct: guided tours (1hr 30min) Sun and public holidays 10am-noon, 2-6pm. No charge. ☎ 03 88 71 46 84.

MARSAL

Maison du Sel – Mid-Jun to mid-Sep: Mon-Wed 2-6pm, Thu-Sun 10am-noon, 2-6pm; mid-Sep to mid-Jun: 2-6pm, Sun and public holidays 10am-noon, 2-6pm (Nov: Sat 2-6pm, Sun and public holidays 10am-noon, 2-6pm. Closed in Jan. Price information not provided. ☎ 03 87 01 16 75.

METZ   🚇 Place d'Armes – 57000 – ☎ 03 87 55 53 76

Guided tours of the town 🅰 – Contact the tourist office. In Jul and Aug, guided walking tours by night are also provided.

Cathédrale St-Étienne – Guided tours available. Contact the Association de l'Œuvre de la Cathédrale (Cathedral association), 2, place de Chambre or ask at the office inside the cathedral. ☎ 03 87 75 54 61.

Crypt and Treasury – Jan to Nov: daily except Sun morning 9am-6pm, public holidays noon-6pm. Closed 1 May and 15 Aug. 1.52€. ☎ 03 87 75 54 61.

Musée de la Cour d'Or – 10am-noon, 2-6pm. Closed 1 Jan, Good Friday, 1 and 8 May, 1 and 11 Nov, 25 Dec. 5.03€, no charge Wed and Sun mornings. ☎ 03 87 68 25 00.

Église St-Vincent – Closed for restoration.

Église St-Pierre-aux-Nonnains – & May to Sep: daily except Mon 2-6pm; Oct to Apr: Sat-Sun 2-6pm. Closed public holidays. No charge. ☎ 03 87 39 92 00.

Chapelle des Templiers – & Jun to Sep: daily except Mon 2-6pm. Closed public holidays. No charge. ☎ 03 87 39 92 00.

Excursions

Scy-Chazelles: Robert-Schuman's house – May to Sep: guided tours (1hr) daily except Tue 10am-noon, 2-6pm; Oct to Apr: daily except Tue 2-6pm. 3.05€. ☎ 03 87 60 19 90.

Vallée de la Canner – Train excursion – End of Apr to beginning of Oct: excursion on a train drawn by a steam or diesel engine Sun and public holidays, departure at 3pm and 5pm. 7.62€ return (children: 5.34€). Vigy train station (15km to the north-east of Metz by D 2 then D 52). ☎ 03 87 77 97 50.

Château de Pange – & Jun to end of Sep: 10am-4pm. No charge. ☎ 03 87 64 04 41.

Groupe fortifié de l'Aisne – & May to end of Oct: guided tours (2hr 15min) 1st Sun in the month at 2pm, 3pm and 4pm. Closed public holidays. 4€. ☎ 03 87 52 76 91.

Gorze: Maison de l'Histoire de la Terre de Gorze – Apr to end of Oct: Sat-Sun and public holidays 2-6pm (Jun to mid-Sep: daily except Mon). 10F {1.52€}. ☎ 03 87 52 04 57.

Méandres de la MEUSE

Levrézy: Musée de la Métallurgie – ♿ Jul and Aug: 10am-noon, 2-6pm; Jun and Sep: 2-6pm. 2.29€. Town hall, ☏ 03 24 53 94 20 or Tourist office, ☏ 03 24 32 11 99.

Château-Regnault: Centre d'exposition de minéraux – Mid-Jun to end of Aug: daily except Mon 2-6pm; Sep: Sat-Sun 2-6pm. 1.52€. ☏ 03 24 32 05 02.

Revin:

Maison espagnole – Beginning of May to end of Sep: 2-6.30pm, Sat-Sun and public holidays 2-6.30pm. 10F {1.52€}. ☏ 03 24 40 19 59.

Parc Maurice-Rocheteau – ♿ Beginning of May to mid-Oct: 10am-8pm. Closed public holidays. No charge. ☏ 03 24 41 55 65.

Galerie d'art contemporain – ♿ Wed, Sat-Sun and public holidays: 2-6pm. Closed Easter and 1 May. No charge. ☏ 03 24 56 20 53.

MOLSHEIM

Musée de la Chartreuse – May to mid-Oct: daily except Tue 2-5pm (mid-Jun to mid-Sep: daily except Tue 10am-noon, 2-6pm, Sat-Sun and public holidays 2-5pm) 16F {2.44€}. ☏ 03 88 38 25 10.

Parc naturel régional de la MONTAGNE DE REIMS

Olizy: Musée de l'Escargot de Champagne – ♿ Apr to mid-Nov: guided tours (1hr 15min) 1st Sat-Sun in the month 2-4.30pm, by appointment on other days. Closed first 3 weeks in Jul and public holidays. 3.05€. ☏ 03 26 58 10 77.

Mailly-Champagne: Carrière géologique – The geological specimens discovery path is open all year. Free admission. It would be advisable to purchase the "Carrière Pédagogique de Mailly-Champagne" guide (25F {3.81€}) from the reserve's offices in Pourcy if you intend visiting without a guide. Guided tours are organised by the Montagne de Reims regional nature reserve: contact the reserve's offices for the programme.

Faux de Verzy – Guided tours available May to Oct, once a month. 35F {5.34€}. Enquire at the Maison du parc naturel régional de la Montagne de Reims in Pourcy. Guide (45F {6.86€}) available at the Maison du Parc.

Germaine: Maison du bûcheron – Easter to All Saints: Wed, Sun and public holidays 2.30-6.30pm. 12F {1.83€}. ☏ 03 26 59 44 44.

Avenay-Val-d'Or: Église St-Trésain – Guided tours by appointment. Town hall. ☏ 03 26 52 31 33.

Pourcy: Maison du Parc – ♿ Information and documentation centre: Easter to All Saints 2.30-6.30pm. ☏ 03 26 59 44 44.

MONTHERMÉ   🛈 50, rue Étienne-Dolet – 08800 – ☏ 03 24 53 06 50

Église St-Léger – By request at the presbytery. ☏ 03 24 53 01 17.

MONTIER-EN-DER

Haras – 2.30-5.30pm, Sep to mid-Nov: presentation of stallions and harnesses every Thu. Closed 1 Jan and 25 Dec. No charge. ☏ 03 25 04 22 17.

MONTMÉDY

Citadelle – Jul and Aug: 9.30am-7pm; Apr to Jun and Sep to Oct: 10am-noon, 1.30-6.30pm; 16 Feb to 31 Mar, 1 to 15 Nov and Christmas holidays: 10am-noon, 1.30-5pm; 1 to 14 Feb and 15 to 30 Nov: 2-5pm. Closed Dec to Jan (except Christmas holidays). 25F {3.81€}. ☏ 03 29 80 15 90.

Musées de la Fortification et Jules-Bastien-Lepage – Feb to Nov: 10am-noon, 1.30-5pm (Sep to Oct: 10am-noon, 1-6pm, Jul and Aug: 10am-7pm). 25F {3.81€}. ☏ 03 29 80 15 90.

Excursions

Louppy-sur-Loison: Castle – Guided tours available (1hr), contact the "Office de tourisme du Pays de Montmédy", Citadelle, BP 28, 55600 Montmédy. ☏ 03 29 80 15 90, Fax: 03 29 80 05 79.

Marville: Cimetière de la chapelle St-Hilaire – Guided tours available by request at the town hall. ☏ 03 29 88 15 15.

MONTMIRAIL

Excursion

Verdelot: Church – Sat-Sun 8am-7pm.

MOUZON

Musée du Feutre – May to Sep: 2-6pm (Jun to Aug: 2-7pm, last admission 1hr before closing); Apr and Oct: Sat-Sun and public holidays 2-6pm. Closed Nov to Mar. 3.81€ (children: 0.76€). ☎ 03 24 26 50 76.

Musée de la Tour de la Porte de Bourgogne – Mid-May to mid-Sep: 3-6pm. 0.76€. ☎ 03 24 26 10 63.

Excursions

Parc de vision de Belval – &. May to beginning of Sep: daily except Tue and Wed 12.30-6pm. 4.57€ (children: 3.05€). ☎ 03 24 30 01 86.

Stenay:

Musée de la Bière – Mid-Apr to mid-Oct: 10am-noon, 2-6pm (mid-Jun to mid-Sep: 10am-6pm); Mar to mid-Apr and mid-Oct to end of Nov: 2-6pm. 4.57€ (children: 2.29€). ☎ 03 29 80 68 78.

Musée du pays de Stenay – Temporarily closed.

MULHOUSE   🗊 9, avenue du Maréchal-Foch – 68100 – ☎ 03 89 35 48 41

Guided tours of the town – Contact the tourist office.

Musée national de l'Automobile: collection Schlumpf – &. End of Mar to Aug: 9am-6.30pm; Sep to Easter: 10am-5pm. Closed 1 Jan and 25 Dec. 60F {9.15€} (children: 27F {4.12€}). ☎ 03 89 33 23 21.

Musée français du Chemin de fer – &. 9am-5pm (Apr to Sep: 9am-6pm). Closed 1 Jan, 25 and 26 Dec. 7.32€ (children: 3.81€). ☎ 03 89 42 83 33.

Électropolis: Musée de l'Énergie électrique – &. Daily except Mon (except Easter and Whit Mondays) 10am-6pm (Jul and Aug: daily). Closed 1 Jan, 25 and 26 Dec. 8€ (children: 4€). ☎ 03 89 32 48 50.

Musée de l'Impression sur étoffes – &. 10am-6pm. Closed 1 Jan, 1 May, 25 Dec. 5.49€. ☎ 03 89 46 83 00.

Rixheim: Musée du Papier peint – Jun to Sep: 9am-noon, 2-6pm; Oct to May: daily except Tue 10am-noon, 2-6pm. Closed 1 Jan, Good Friday, 1 May, 25 Dec. 5.34€. ☎ 03 89 64 24 56.

Temple St-Étienne – May to end of Sep: daily except Tue 10am-noon, 2-6pm, Sat 10am-noon, 2-5pm, Sun 2-6pm. No charge. ☎ 03 89 46 58 25.

Musée historique – Daily except Tue 10am-noon, 2-7pm (Sep to Jun: 6pm). Closed 1 Jan, Good Friday, Easter, Whitsun, 1 May, 14 Jul, 1 and 11 Nov, 25 and 26 Dec. Price information not provided. ☎ 03 89 45 43 20.

Musée des Beaux-Arts – Daily except Tue 10am-noon, 2-7pm (Sep to Jun: 6pm). Closed 1 Jan, Good Friday, Easter, Whitsun, 1 May, 14 Jul, 1 and 11 Nov, 25 and 26 Dec. No charge. ☎ 03 89 45 43 19.

Parc zoologique et botanique – &. May to Aug: 9am-7pm; Apr and Sep: 9am-6pm; Oct to Mar: 9am-5pm (Nov to Feb: 10am-4pm). 7.32€ (low season and children: 3.66€). ☎ 03 89 31 85 10.

MUNSTER   🗊 Place du Marché – 68140 – ☎ 03 89 77 31 80

Maison du parc naturel régional des Ballons des Vosges – May to Sep: daily except Mon 9am-noon, 2-6pm; Oct-Apr: daily except Sat-Sun 10am-noon, 2-6pm. No charge. ☎ 03 89 77 90 34, Internet: www.parc-ballons-vosges.fr.

Muhlbach-sur-Munster: Musée de la Schlitte – Jul to end of Aug: guided tours (45min) 10am-noon, 3-6pm. 10F {1.52€}. ☎ 03 89 77 61 08.

Gunsbach: Musée Albert-Schweitzer – &. Guided tours (1hr) daily except Mon 9-11.30am, 2-4.30pm. Closed Good Friday, Easter and from Christmas to beginning of Jan. ☎ 03 89 77 31 42.

Soultzbach-les-Bains: Church – To visit, contact the town hall or the presbytery.

N

NANCY   🗊 14, place Stanislas – 54000 – ☎ 03 83 35 22 41

Guided tours of the town 🅰 – Contact the tourist office.

Hôtel de ville – Jul to end of Aug: guided tours of the interior (30min) at 10.20pm (guides wear traditional costume on Fri and Sat). Closed 13 and 14 Jul. 15F {2.29€} (20F {3.05€} when guides are dressed in traditional costume).

Musée de l'École de Nancy – Daily except Tue 10.30am-6pm, Mon 2-6pm. Closed 1 Jan, 1 May, 14 Jul, 1 Nov, 25 Dec. 4.57€. ☎ 03 83 40 14 86.

Cathedral treasury – &. Visits by appointment: daily except Wed 8.30am-noon, 5-6.45pm, Sun 8.30am-noon, 6-8pm. Closed public holidays and alternating years Jul (even-numbered years) and Aug (odd-numbered years). No charge. ☎ 03 83 35 01 18.

Musée des Beaux-Arts – ♿ Daily except Tue 10am-6pm. Closed 1 Jan, 1 May, 14 Jul, 1 Nov, 25 Dec. 4.57€ (temporary exhibition: 5.34€), no charge 1st Sun in the month 10.30am-1.30pm. ☎ 03 83 85 30 72.

Palais ducal: Musée historique lorrain – Daily except Tue 10am-noon, 2-5pm, Sun and public holidays 10am-noon, 2-6pm (May to Sep: daily except Tue 10am-12.30pm, 1.30-6pm). Closed 1 Jan, Easter Sunday, 1 May, 14 Jul, 1 Nov, 25 Dec. 3.05€, 4.58€ including visit to the Couvent des Cordeliers. ☎ 03 83 32 18 74.

Église et couvent des Cordeliers: musée d'Arts et Traditions populaires – May to end of Sep: daily except Tue 10am-12.30pm, 1.30-6pm; Oct to end of Apr: daily except Tue 10am-noon, 2-5pm, Sun and public holidays 10am-noon, 2-6pm. Closed 1 Jan, Easter, 1 May, 14 Jul, 1 Nov, 25 Dec. 3.05€. ☎ 03 83 32 18 74.

Jardin botanique du Montet – ♿ Park: 10am-noon, 2-5pm, Sun and public holidays 2-6pm. Greenhouses: daily except 1st Tue in the month 2-5pm (Apr to end of Sep: 6pm). Closed 1 Jan and 25 Dec. Greenhouses 15F {2.29€}, park no charge. ☎ 03 83 41 47 47.

Maison de la Communication – Wed-Fri 10am-noon, 2-6pm. Closed public holidays. 15F {2.29€}. ☎ 03 83 34 85 89.

Musée-aquarium de Nancy – 10am-noon, 2-6pm. 30F {4.57€} (children: 20F {3.05€}). ☎ 03 83 32 99 97.

Excursions

Jarville-la-Malgrange: Musée de l'Histoire du Fer – Jul to Sep: daily except Tue 2-6pm; Oct to Jun: daily except Tue 2-5pm, Sat-Sun and public holidays 10am-noon, 2-6pm. Closed 1 Jan, Easter, 1 Nov, 25 Dec. 15F {2.29€}. ☎ 03 83 15 27 70.

Château de Fléville – Apr to mid-Nov: guided tours (45min) Sat-Sun and public holidays 2-7pm (Jul and Aug: daily). 6.10€. ☎ 03 83 25 64 71.

Parc de loisirs de la forêt de Haye: Musée de l'Automobile – ♿ Wed, Sat-Sun and public holidays 2-6pm (Jul and Aug: daily). Closed between Christmas and New Year's Day. 35F {5.34€}. ☎ 03 83 23 28 38.

NEUFCHÂTEAU
🛈 3, parking des Grandes-Écuries – 88300 – ☎ 03 29 94 10 95

Église St-Nicolas – Mid-Jun to mid-Sep: 2-6.30pm (Jul and Aug: 10am-6.30pm). Guided tours by request at the tourist office.

Église St-Christophe – Jul and Aug: guided tours 9am-noon, 2-6pm.

Excursions

St-Élophe: Museum – Apr to Sep: daily except Sat 9am-noon, 2-7pm; Oct to Mar: daily except Sat 2-5pm. Closed during Christmas school holidays. 1.52€. ☎ 03 29 06 97 94.

Grand:

Section of piping – Jul to end of Aug: guided tours (15min) Sun and public holidays 2-6pm. 10F {1.52€}. ☎ 03 29 06 77 37.

Amphithéatre – Apr to Sep: 9am-noon, 2-7pm; Oct to Mar: daily except Tue 10am-noon, 2-5pm. Closed mid-Nov to mid-Jan. 15F {2.29€}, mosaic and amphitheatre 20F {3.05€}. ☎ 03 29 06 77 37.

Mosaic – As for the amphitheatre.

NEUWILLER-LÈS-SAVERNE

Église St-Pierre-et-St-Paul – Unaccompanied visits of the church, guided tours of the tapestries by request to the church office, 5, cour du Chapitre. ☎ 03 88 70 00 51.

Église St-Adelphe – Apr to Oct: 8am-6pm; rest of the year by appointment. ☎ 03 88 70 00 19.

NIEDERBRONN-LES-BAINS

Maison de l'Archéologie – ♿ Mar to Oct: daily except Tue 2-6pm; Nov to Feb: Sun and public holidays 2-5pm. Closed between Christmas and New Year's Day. 2.29€. ☎ 03 88 80 36 37.

NOGENT-SUR-SEINE

Musée Paul-Dubois-Alfred-Boucher – Apr to end of Nov: Sat-Sun and public holidays 2-6pm (mid-Jun to mid-Sep: daily except Tue 2-6pm). Closed 1 May. No charge. ☎ 03 25 39 71 79.

Excursions

Centre nucléaire de production d'électricité – ♿ Guided tours (1hr 30min) daily except Sun 8.30am-12.30pm, 2-6pm by appointment (2 weeks in advance). Closed public holidays. No charge. ☎ 03 25 39 32 60.

Château de la Motte-Tilly – Park open to visitors, guided tours of the château (1hr), Mid-Mar to mid-Nov: daily except Mon and Tue 10am-noon, 2-6pm; mid-Nov to mid-Mar: Wed, Sat-Sun and public holidays 2-5pm. 5.49€. ☏ 03 25 39 99 67.

Ancienne abbaye du Paraclet – ♿ Mid-Jul to end of Aug: guided tours (15min) daily except Sun 10am-noon, 2-6pm. 10F {1.52€}. ☏ 01 42 27 88 24.

O

OBERNAI
🛈 Chapelle du Beffroi – 67210 – ☏ 03 88 95 64 13

Guided tours of the town – Contact the tourist office.

ORBAIS-L'ABBAYE

Church – Guided tours available. Information available at the presbytery. ☏ 03 26 59 20 35.

Excursions

Montmort-Lucy: Château – Mid-Jul to mid-Sep: guided tours (1hr) daily except Mon at 2.30pm and 4.30pm, Sun, 15 Aug and Whitsun at 2.30pm, 3.30pm, 5pm and 5.30pm. 5.34€. ☏ 03 26 59 10 04.

Étoges: Church – Easter to All Saints: 9am-6pm; All Saints to Easter: contact Mr. Scieur, 47 Grande-Rue, ☏ 03 26 59 20 28.

Val d'ORBEY

Lapoutroie: Musée des Eaux-de-vie – ♿ 9am-noon, 2-6pm. Closed 25 Dec. No charge. ☏ 03 89 47 50 26.

Fréland: Maison du Pays Welche – Jun to Sep: guided tours (1hr 30min) daily except Wed at 10am, 3pm, 4.30pm; mid-Mar to May, Oct and Nov: daily except Wed at 3pm; Dec to mid-Feb: Sun only at 3pm. Closed mid-Feb to mid-Mar. 15F {2.29€}. ☏ 03 89 71 90 52.

Musée de la Forge – Open year-round, visits by appointment. ☏ 03 89 47 58 30.

OTTMARSHEIM

Centrale hydro-électrique – Guided tours (2hr) daily except Sat-Sun 8am-noon, 2-4.30pm, Fri 8am-noon by written request 3 weeks in advance to EDF, Production Est, 54 av. Robert-Schuman, BP 1007, 68050 Mulhouse Cedex, ☏ 03 89 35 20 00.

P

La PETITE-PIERRE

Chapelle St-Louis: Musée du Sceau alsacien (Museum of Alsatian Heraldry) – ♿ Daily except Mon 10am-noon, 2-6pm. Closed in Jan. No charge. ☏ 03 88 70 48 65.

Maison du parc (Vosges du Nord regional nature reserve centre) – 10am-noon, 2-6pm. Closed in Jan, 24, 25 and 31 Dec. 25F {3.81€}. ☏ 03 88 01 49 59.

"Magazin" – ♿ Sat-Sun and public holidays: 10am-noon, 2-6pm (Jul to Sep: daily except Mon). Closed in Jan. No charge. ☏ 03 88 70 48 65.

PFAFFENHOFEN

Musée de l'Imagerie peinte et populaire alsacienne – ♿ May to Sep: daily except Mon 2-6pm; Oct to Apr: daily except Mon 2-5pm (Sat-Sun 2-6pm). Closed 1 Jan, 1 May, Good Friday, 1 Nov and from 24 Dec to 1 Jan. 3.80€. ☏ 03 88 07 70 55.

PLOMBIÈRES-LES-BAINS
🛈 16, rue Stanislas – 88370 – ☏ 03 29 66 01 30

Guided tours of the town – Contact the tourist office.

Étuve romaine, Bain romain and Thermes Napoléon – Apr to Oct: guided tours (2hr) Thu at 3pm (visitors must book in advance). Departure from the tourist office. 30F {4.57€}. ☏ 03 29 66 01 30.

Musée Louis-Français – Mid-May to mid-Oct: daily except Tue 2-6pm. 3.05€. ☏ 03 29 30 06 74.

Pavillon des Princes – Closed temporarily.

PONT-À-MOUSSON

🛈 52, place Duroc – 54700 – ☎ 03 83 81 06 90

Ancienne abbaye des Prémontrés – ♿ 10am-5.30pm. Closed 1 Jan and 25 Dec. 30F {4.57€}. ☎ 03 83 81 10 32.

Musée de Pont-à-Mousson – ♿ May to Sep: daily except Tue 2-6pm, Sun 10am-noon, 2-6pm; Oct-Apr: daily except Tue 2-5pm. 4.57€. ☎ 03 83 87 80 14.

Hôtel de ville – To visit the interior, contact the administration office 2 or 3 days in advance. ☎ 03 83 81 10 68.

PROVINS

🛈 Chemin de Villecran – BP 44 – 77160 – ☎ 01 64 60 26 26

Guided tours of the town 🅰 – Contact the tourist office.

Tour César – Apr to Oct: 10am-6pm; Nov to Mar: 2-5pm. Closed 25 Dec. 17F. ☎ 01 64 60 26 26.

Grange aux Dîmes – Apr to Aug: 10am-6pm; Sept to Nov: 2-6pm, Sat-Sun 10am-6pm; Nov to Mar: Sat-Sun, public and zone C school holidays 2-5pm. Closed 25 Dec. 22F. ☎ 01 64 60 26 26.

Musée du Provinois – Apr to Dec: 2-6pm (July and Aug: 2-7pm), last admission 30min before closing. Closed 25 Dec. 22F. ☎ 01 64 01 40 19.

Souterrains à graffiti – Apr to Nov: guided tours (45min) at 3pm and 4pm, Sat-Sun and public holidays 10.30am-6pm; Nov to Mar: Sat-Sun, public and zone C school holidays at 2pm, 3pm and 4pm. Closed 25 Dec. 22F. ☎ 01 64 60 26 26.

R

REIMS

🛈 2, rue Guillaume-de-Machault – 51100 – ☎ 03 26 77 45 25

Guided tours of the town 🅰 – Contact the tourist office.

Pommery – Easter to mid-Nov: guided tours (1hr) 10am-5pm, appointments preferred; mid-Nov to Easter: Mon-Fri by appointment. Closed end of Nov to beginning of Jan and 1 Nov. 40F {6.10€} (children: 20F {3.05€}). ☎ 03 26 61 62 56.

Parc Pommery – ♿ 9.30am-12.30pm, 2-6pm, Sat-Sun and public holidays 9am-7pm (Mid-Oct to end of Apr: ask for information at the park). 12F {1.83€}. ☎ 03 26 85 23 29.

Taittinger – Guided tours (1hr) 9.30am-noon, 2-4.30pm, Sat-Sun and public holidays 9-11am, 2-5pm (Nov to Feb: daily except Sat-Sun). Closed 1 Jan and 25 Dec. 35F {5.34€}. ☎ 03 26 85 84 33.

Veuve Clicquot-Ponsardin – Apr to Oct: guided tours (1hr 30min) by appointment 1 week in advance, daily except Sun 9am-12.30pm, 1.30-6pm (last admission 1hr 30min before closing); Nov to Mar: closed Sat-Sun and public holidays. No charge. ☎ 03 26 89 54 41.

Ruinart – Guided tours (1hr 30min) daily except Sat-Sun and public holidays, by appointment, contact the visits and receptions department, 4, rue des Crayères, 51100 Reims. No charge. ☎ 03 26 77 51 51.

Piper Heidsieck – Guided tours (30min) 9am-11.45am, 2-5.15pm (Jan and Feb: daily except Tue and Wed). Closed 1 Jan, 25 Dec. 6.90€. ☎ 03 26 84 43 44.

Mumm – Mar to Oct: guided tours (1hr) 9-11am, 2-5pm; Nov to Feb: Mon-Fri 9-11am, 2-5pm, Sat-Sun 2-5pm. Closed 1 Jan and 25 Dec. 25F {3.81€}. ☎ 03 26 49 59 70.

Église St-Jacques – Closed Sun.

Cryptoportique gallo-romain – Mid-Jun to mid-Sep: daily except Mon 2-5pm. Closed 14 Jul. No charge. ☎ 03 26 50 13 74.

Cathédrale Notre-Dame – 7.30am-7.30pm. Upper parts: mid-Jun to mid-Sep: 10-11.30am, 2-5.30pm, Sun 2-5.30pm. 3.81€. Contact the Palais du Tau.

Palais du Tau – Mid-Mar to mid-Nov: 9.30am-12.30pm, 2-6pm (Jul and Aug: 9.30am-6.30pm); mid-Nov to mid-Mar: 10am-noon, 2-5pm (Sat-Sun 6pm). Closed 1 Jan, 1 May, 1 and 11 Nov, 25 Dec. 32F {4.88€} (children under 12: no charge). ☎ 03 26 47 81 79.

Musée St-Remi – 2-6.30pm (Sat-Sun 7pm). Closed 1 Jan, 1 May, 14 Jul, 1 and 11 Nov, 25 Dec. 1.52€. ☎ 03 26 85 23 36.

Musée des Beaux-Arts – Daily except Tue 10am-noon, 2-6pm. Closed 1 Jan, 1 May, 14 Jul, 1 and 11 Nov, 25 Dec. 1.52€, no charge 1st Sat-Sun in the month. ☎ 03 26 47 28 44.

Musée-hôtel Le Vergeur – Guided tours (1hr) daily except Mon 2-6pm (Jun to Aug: 10am-noon, 2-6pm). Closed between Christmas and New Year's Day, 1 May, 14 Jul, 1 Nov. 3.81€. ☎ 03 26 47 20 75.

Ancien collège des Jésuites – Guided tours (45min) daily except Tue morning at 10am, 11am, 2.15pm, 3.30pm, 4.45pm, Sat-Sun at 2.15pm, 3.30pm and 4.45pm. Closed 1 Jan, 1 May, 14 Jul, 1 and 11 Nov, 25 Dec. 10F {1.52€}. ☎ 03 26 85 51 50.

Planétarium et horloge astronomique – ⑤ Sat-Sun and school holidays: shows at 2.45pm, 3.30pm and 4.45pm (be sure to arrive 15min in advance); Nov to Jan: "Étoile des rois mages" show presented at 2.15pm, 3.30pm and 4.45pm. Closed 1 Jan, 1 May, 14 Jul, 1 and 11 Nov, 25 Dec. 10F {1.52€}. ☎ 03 26 85 51 50.

Chapelle Foujita – May to end of Oct: daily except Wed 2-6pm. Closed 1 May and 14 Jul. 1.52€. ☎ 03 26 47 28 44.

Salle de Reddition – ⑤ Daily except Tue 10am-noon, 2-6pm. Closed 1 Jan, 1 May, 14 Jul, 1 and 11 Nov, 24, 25 and 31 Dec. 10F {1.52€}. ☎ 03 26 85 23 36.

Musée automobile de Reims-Champagne – ⑤ 10am-noon, 2-6pm (mid-Nov to mid-Mar: 5pm). 35F {5.34€} (children: 15F {2.29€}). ☎ 03 26 82 83 84.

Excursion

Fort de la Pompelle: Museum – ⑤ Daily except Tue 10am-5pm (Apr to Oct: 7pm). Closed 1 Jan, 1 Nov and from 24 Dec to beginning of Jan. 20F {3.05€}. ☎ 03 26 85 48 60.

REMIREMONT
🛈 2, rue Charles-de-Gaulle – 88204 – ☎ 03 29 62 23 70

Guided tours of the town – Contact the tourist office.

Musée municipal (Fondation Ch.-de-Bruyère) – Apr to Sep: daily except Tue 10am-noon, 2-6pm (Jul and Aug: Sun 7pm); Nov and Dec: daily except Tue 10am-noon, 2-5pm; Jan to Apr: daily except Sun and Tue 2-6pm. Closed in Oct, 1 Jan, 1 May, Ascension, 1 Nov, 25 Dec. 1.52€, no charge Sun. ☎ 03 29 62 42 17.

Musée municipal (Fondation Charles-Friry) – As for the municipal museum (Ch.-de-Bruyère foundation).

RETHEL

Église St-Nicolas – Jul and Aug: 2.30-5.30pm; Sep to Jun: Thu 8.45am-noon. Contact the presbytery. ☎ 03 24 38 41 50.

Vallée du RHIN

Fessenheim:

Bief – Information centre: daily except Sat-Sun 9am-noon, 2-6pm. Guided tours (3hr) by appointment (15 days' notice) daily except Sun 9am-noon, 2-5pm (minimum age 10 years if accompanied by parents, visitors must have identity papers with them). Contact EDF - Centre Nucléaire de production d'électricité, BP 15, 68740 Fessenheim, ☎ 03 89 83 51 23.

Maison de l'Hydraulique – ⑤ Jul and Aug: 2-6pm; Sep to Jun: guided tours by appointment (15 days' notice) with EDF – Énergie Est, 54, av. Robert-Schumann, 68050 Mulhouse Cedex.

RIBEAUVILLÉ
🛈 1, Grand'Rue – 68150 – ☎ 03 89 73 62 22

Guided tours of the town – Contact the tourist office.

Hôtel de ville: Museum – May to end of Sep: guided tours (1hr) daily except Mon and Sat 10-11am, 2-3pm. Closed Oct to Apr. No charge. ☎ 03 89 73 67 79.

RIQUEWIHR
🛈 2, rue de la 1ʳᵉ-Armée – 68340 – ☎ 03 89 49 80 80

Guided tours of the town – Contact the tourist office.

Musée d'histoire des P.T.T. d'Alsace – Beginning of Apr to beginning of Nov: daily except Tue 10am-noon, 2-6pm. 3.05€. ☎ 03 89 47 93 80.

Musée de la Diligence – ⑤ Beginning of Apr to beginning of Nov: daily except Tue 10am-noon, 2-6pm. 3.05€. ☎ 03 89 47 93 80.

Maison Hansi – Apr to Dec: daily except Mon 10am-6.30pm (Jul and Aug: daily); Feb and Mar: daily except Mon 2-6pm; Jan: Sat-Sun and public holidays 2-6pm. Closed 1 Jan and 25 Dec. 2€. ☎ 03 89 47 97 00.

Musée de la tour des Voleurs – Beginning of Apr to beginning of Nov: 10am-noon, 1.30-6.15pm. 1.52€. ☎ 03 89 49 08 40.

Musée du Dolder – Mid-Apr to end of Oct: Sat-Sun and public holidays 10am-noon, 1.30-6.15pm (Jul and Aug: daily). 1.52€. Tourist office. ☎ 03 89 49 08 40.

ROCROI
🛈 Place d'Armes – 08230 – ☎ 03 24 54 20 06

Musée – May to mid-Oct: 10am-noon, 2-6pm; Mid-Oct to end of Apr: 2-5pm. Closed 1 Jan and 25 Dec. 25F {3.81€}.

ROUFFACH
🛈 8, place de la République – 68250 – ☎ 03 89 78 53 15

Église des Récollets – Apply to the town hall for a guided tour. ☎ 03 89 78 03 00.

S

ST-DIÉ

🆉 31, rue Thiers – 88100 – ☎ 03 29 56 17 62

Cathédrale St-Dié – Jul to mid-Sep: 10am-12.15pm, 2-6.15pm, Sat 10am-12.15pm, Sun and public holidays 2-6.15pm. No charge. ☎ 03 29 56 12 88.

Église Notre-Dame-de-Galilée – As for the cathedral.

Musée Pierre-Noël – Musée de la vie dans les Hautes-Vosges – ♿ May to Sep: daily except Mon 10am-noon, 2-7pm, Sun 2-7pm; Oct to Apr: daily except Mon 2-6pm, Wed 10am-noon, 2-6pm. Closed public holidays. No charge. ☎ 03 29 51 60 35.

Bibliothèque – Daily except Sun and Mon 10am-7pm, Sat 10am-6pm (school holidays: daily except Sun and Mon 10am-noon, 2-6pm). Closed 1 Jan, 1 and 8 May, Ascension, 14 Jul, 15 Aug, 11 Nov and 25 Dec. No charge. ☎ 03 29 51 60 40.

Tour de la Liberté – 10am-6pm, Sat-Sun and public holidays 2-6pm (summer: 10am-8pm, Sat-Sun and public holidays 2-8pm). No charge. ☎ 03 29 42 22 22.

Jewelry Collection – Fri-Sun 2-6pm (Mid-Apr to mid-Oct: daily). Closed public holidays. 3.05€.

Excursions

Ban-de-Sapt: Jardins s Callunes – ♿ Late June to Sep: 10am-7pm; May to Jun: 10am-noon, 2-7pm; late Sep to 11 Nov and late Mar to Apr: 2-5.30pm. Closed 12 Nov to end of Mar. 4.57€. ☎ 03 29 58 94 94.

Étival-Clairefontaine: Church – Guided tour available by appointment. Contact the church office. ☎ 03 29 41 52 08.

Moyenmoutier: Church – Summer: guided tour by appointment. Contact the town hall. ☎ 03 29 42 09 09.

ST-MIHIEL

🆉 Palais abbatial – 55300 – ☎ 03 29 89 06 47

Bibliothèque – Apr to mid-Oct: Sat-Sun and public holidays 2-6pm (Jul and Aug: daily except Tue). 25F {3.81€}. ☎ 03 29 89 06 47.

Musée départemental d'Art sacré – ♿ Apr-Oct: Sat, Sun and public holidays 2-6pm (Jul and Aug: daily except Tue). 3,81€. ☎ 03 29 89 06 47.

Excursions

Sampigny: Musée Raymond-Poincaré – May to mid-Nov: daily except Sat 2-6pm, Fri 2-5pm (Jul and Aug: 2-6pm, Fri 2-5pm). 12F {1.83€}. ☎ 03 29 90 70 50.

Génicourt-sur-Meuse: Church – Guided tours by appointment. Contact the town hall. ☎ 03 29 87 75 01.

Commercy: Musée de la Céramique et de l'Ivoire – ♿ May to Sep: Sat, Sun and public holidays 2-6pm (Jul-Aug: daily except Tue). 3.05€. ☎ 03 29 92 04 77.

ST-NICOLAS-DE-PORT

Basilique St-Nicolas – Jul to mid-Sep: guided tours (1hr) Sun and public holidays 2-6pm. 20F {3.05€}, 10F {1.52€}the towers. Organ concerts every Sunday in August at 5pm, no charge. Visit with walkman daily except Sun and Mon 2-6pm. Collect walkman from 1, rue. des Trois-Pucelles, parvis de la Basilique. ☎ 03 83 46 81 50.

Musée français de la Brasserie – Mid-Jun to mid-Sep: 2.30-6.30pm; mid-Sep to mid-Jun: daily except Mon 2-6pm. Closed mid-Nov to beginning of Jan. 25F {3.81€}. ☎ 03 83 46 95 52.

Musée du Cinéma, de la Photographie and des Arts audiovisuels – ♿ Thu-Sat at 2pm, 3.30pm, 5pm, 6.30pm, Sun and public holidays at 2.30pm, 4pm, 5.30pm. Closed 1 Jan and 24 Dec to early Jan. 3,05€. ☎ 03 83 45 18 32.

STE-MENEHOULD

🆉 Place Leclerc – 51800 – ☎ 03 26 60 85 83

Musée – May to end of Oct: Sat-Sun and public holidays 3-6pm. No charge. ☎ 03 26 60 80 21.

Excursion

Château de Braux-Ste-Cohière – ♿ Mid-Jun to beginning of Sep: daily except Tue 10am-noon, 2-7pm. Price information not provided. ☎ 03 26 60 83 51.

SARREBOURG

🆉 Chapelle des Cordeliers – 57400 – ☎ 03 87 03 11 82

Chapelle des Cordeliers – May to Sep: 10am-noon, 1.30-6.30pm, Sun and public holidays 2.30-5.30pm; Oct to Apr: daily except Sun and Mon 2-6pm, Tue, Wed and Fri 8am-noon, 2-6pm, Thu 9am-noon, 2-6pm, Sat 9am-noon. Closed 1 Jan, 1 May, 11 Nov, 25 and 26 Dec. 3.05€. ☎ 03 87 03 11 82.

Musée du Pays de Sarrebourg – Daily except Sun and Tue 10am-noon, 2-6pm, Sat 10am-noon, 2-6pm (Apr to Nov: daily except Tue 10am-noon, 2-6pm, Sun 2-6pm). Closed public holidays, Good Friday, 26 Dec. 3.05€. ☎ 03 87 03 27 86.

Excursions

St-Ulrich: Villa gallo-romaine – Jul and Aug. No charge. Call for information, ☎ 03 87 03 27 86.

Hartzviller: Cristallerie – Daily except Sat-Sun 9-11am, 1-2pm. Factory shop 1.30-5.30pm. Closed between Christmas and New Year's Day and public holidays. No charge. ☎ 03 87 25 10 55.

SARREGUEMINES   🛈 Rue du Maire-Massing – 57322 – ☎ 03 87 98 80 81

Musée – 10am-noon, 2-6pm. Closed Tue from beginning of Oct to end of Jun, 1 Jan, Easter Sunday, 1 May, Whit Sunday, 1 Nov and 25 Dec. 2.29€. ☎ 03 87 98 93 50.

Musée des Techniques faïencières – ♿ 10am-noon, 2-6pm. Closed Tue from Oct to Jun, 1 Jan, 1 May, Easter, 1 Nov, 25 Dec. 3.81€. ☎ 03 87 98 93 50.

Circuit de la Faïence de Sarreguemines – Daily except Tue 10am-noon, 2-6pm. Closed public holidays. 30F {4.57€}. ☎ 03 87 98 80 81.

Excursion

Bliesbruck-Reinheim: Parc archéologique européen – Apr to Oct: daily except Mon 10am-6pm, Sun 10am-7pm; Nov to Mar: 10am-5pm. Closed from mid-Nov to mid-Jan (France) ☎ 03 87 02 25 79 or 03 87 02 22 32. For a visit to the museological reconstruction of the Celtic prince's tomb, (Germany) ☎ (00 49) 6843 9002 11.

SAVERNE   🛈 37, Grand'rue – 67700 – ☎ 03 88 91 80 47

Château: Musée – Mar to Nov: daily except Tue 2-5pm, Sun and public holidays 2-5.30pm (mid-Jun to mid-Sep: daily except Tue 10am-noon, 2-6pm); Nov to Feb: Sun and public holidays 2-5.30pm. Closed 1 Jan, Good Friday, 1 May, 1 Nov, 25 and 26 Dec. 2.44€. ☎ 03 88 91 06 28.

Roseraie – ♿ Jun to end of Sep: 9am-7pm. 15F {2.29€}. ☎ 03 88 71 83 33.

Excursions

Jardin botanique du col de Saverne – May to mid-Sep: daily except Sat 9am-5pm, Sun and public holidays 2-6pm (Jul and Aug: 9am-5pm, Sat-Sun and public holidays 2-7pm; Jun: daily except Sat 9am-5pm, Sun and public holidays 2-7pm). 15F {2.29€}. ☎ 03 88 91 80 47.

St-Jean-Saverne: Chapelle St-Michel – Open Sun. Closed Jan and Feb. Presbytery. ☎ 03 88 91 13 88.

SCHIRMECK

Waldersbach: Musée Oberlin – ♿ Daily except Tue 2-6pm. Closed 1 Jan, 1 May and 25 Dec. 2.29€. ☎ 03 88 97 30 27.

Mutzig: Musée régional des Armes – ♿ May to mid-Oct: daily except Mon and Tue 2-5.30pm, Sun and public holidays 2-6pm. 1.98€. ☎ 03 88 38 31 98.

SEDAN   🛈 Place du Château – BP 322 – 08202 Cedex – ☎ 03 24 27 73 73

Château fort (History Museum) – Mid-Mar to mid-Sep: guided tours (1hr 30min) 10am-noon, 1.30-5pm (Jul and Aug: 10am-6pm); mid-Sep to mid-Mar: daily except Mon 1.30-4.30pm, Sat-Sun, public holidays and school holidays 10am-noon, 1.30-5pm. Closed 1 Jan and 25 Dec. 6.86€ (children: 4.57€).

Dijonval – Tours by appointment. ☎ 03 24 27 73 73.

Manufacture du Point de Sedan – ♿ Daily except Sun 8am-noon, 2-6pm. Closed public holidays. No charge. ☎ 03 24 29 04 60.

Excursions

Aérodrome de Sedan-Douzy: Musée des débuts de l'aviation – ♿ Jun to Aug: daily except Mon 10am-noon, 2-6pm; May and Sep: daily except Mon 2-6pm; Apr and Oct: Sat-Sun and public holidays 2-6pm. Closed Nov to Mar. 2€. ☎ 03 24 26 38 70.

Bazeilles:

Maison de la dernière cartouche – Beginning of Jan to mid-Nov: daily except Mon 9am-noon, 1.30-5pm. 1.52€. ☎ 03 24 27 15 86.

Castle – Tours of the outside only. ☎ 03 24 27 09 68.

SÉLESTAT
🖈 Boulevard du Général-Leclerc – 67600 – ☎ 03 88 58 87 20

Guided tours of the town – Contact the tourist office.

Bibliothèque humaniste – Daily except Tue and Sun 9am-noon, 2-6pm, Sat 9am-noon (Jul and Aug: daily except Tue 9am-noon, 2-6pm, Sat-Sun and public holidays 9am-noon, 2-5pm). 3.05€. ☎ 03 88 58 07 20.

Excursions

Kintzheim:

Volerie des aigles – Jul and Aug: 2-5pm, demonstrations at 3pm, 4pm and 5pm (mid-Jul to mid-Aug: 10-11.15am, 2-5pm, demonstrations at 11.15am, 2.30pm 3.45pm and 5pm); Jun: 2-5pm, demonstrations at 2.30pm, 4pm and 5pm, Sat-Sun at 3pm, 4pm and 5pm; Apr, May, Sep and Oct: 2-4pm, demonstrations at 3pm (2.30pm in May) and 4pm, Sat-Sun and public holidays 3pm, 4pm and 5pm; beginning of Nov to 11 Nov: Wed and Sat-Sun 2-6pm, demonstrations Wed at 3pm and 4pm, Sat-Sun 3pm, 4pm and 5pm. 45F {6.10€} (children: 30F {4.57€}). ☎ 03 88 92 84 33.

Montagne des singes – & May to Sep: 10am-noon, 1-6pm (Jul and Aug: 10am-6pm); Apr, Oct: 10am-noon, 1-5pm; beginning of Nov to 11 Nov: Wed and Sat-Sun 10am-noon, 1-5pm. Closed from 12 Nov to end of Mar. 6.86€ (children: 4.57€). ☎ 03 88 92 11 09.

SIERCK-LES-BAINS

Château – Mar to Sep: 10am-7pm, Sun and public holidays 10am-8pm; Oct and Nov: 10am-noon, 2-4pm. Closed Nov to Feb. 23F {3.51€}. ☎03 82 83 67 97.

Excursion

Château de Malbrouck – Jul to Sep: daily except Mon 10am-6pm (Sat-Sun 7pm); mid-Apr to end of Apr and end of Sep to mid-Dec: daily except Mon 10am-5pm (Sat-Sun 6pm). 5.34€. ☎ 03 82 82 42 92.

Colline de SION-VAUDÉMONT

Museum – 3-5pm. ☎ 03 83 25 12 22.

Château de Haroué – Apr to 11 Nov: guided tours (1hr) daily except Mon and Tue 2-6pm (Jul and Aug: daily 10am-noon, 2-6pm). 38F {5.79€}. ☎ 03 83 52 40 14 or 03 83 52 55 57.

SOULTZ-HAUT-RHIN
🖈 14, place de la République – 68360 – ☎ 03 89 76 83 60

Guided tours of the town – Contact the tourist office.

La Nef des jouets – & Daily except Tue 2-6pm. Closed 1 Jan, 1 May and 25 Dec. 4.57€ (children: 1.52€). ☎ 03 89 74 30 92.

Musée du Bucheneck – May to Oct: daily except Tue 2-6pm. 2.29€. ☎ 03 89 76 02 22.

STRASBOURG
🖈 17, place de la Cathédrale – 67200 – ☎ 03 88 52 28 28

Guided tours of the town 🅰 – Contact the tourist office.

Cathédrale Notre-Dame

Tower – Apr to Jun and Sep: 9am-6.30pm (Jul and Aug: 8.30am-7pm); Nov to Feb: 9am-4.30pm (Mar and Oct: 5.30pm). 3.04€. ☎ 03 88 43 60 32.

Astronomical clock – & Clock chimes at 12.30pm. 0.76€. May be closed for exceptionally long services or concert rehearsals. ☎ 03 88 52 28 28.

Musée des Arts décoratifs – & Daily except Tue 10am-6pm. Closed 1 Jan, Good Friday, 1 May, 1 and 11 Nov and 25 Dec. 4.57€ (children: no charge), no charge 1st Sun in the month. ☎ 03 88 52 50 00.

Musée des Beaux-Arts – As for the Musée des Arts décoratifs.

Musée archéologique – & As for the Musée des Arts décoratifs.

Palais de l'Europe – & Pre-booked guided tours (1hr) daily except Sat-Sun, public holidays and during plenary sessions. ☎ 03 88 17 20 07.

Église St-Thomas – Closed Jan and Feb. ☎ 03 88 32 14 46.

Barrage Vauban – 9am-7pm (mid-Mar to mid-Oct: 8pm). No charge. ☎ 03 88 60 90 90.

Église St-Pierre-le-Jeune – Apr to end of Oct: daily except Mon 10am-noon, 1-6pm. ☎ 03 88 32 41 61.

Naviscope: Musée du Rhin et de la Navigation – Daily except Mon and Tue 2.15-6pm, Sat-Sun and public holidays 9.30am-noon, 2.15-6pm. Closed 1 Jan, 1 May, 1 Nov, 25 Dec. 25F {3.81€} (children: 15F {2.29€}). ☎ 03 88 60 22 23.

Musée alsacien – As for the Musée des Arts décoratifs.

Musée de l'Œuvre Notre-Dame – Daily except Mon 10am-6pm. Closed 1 Jan, Good Friday, 1 May, 1 and 11 Nov and 25 Dec. 4.57€ (children: no charge), no charge 1st Sun in the month.

Musée d'Art moderne et contemporain – ♿ Daily except Mon 11am-7pm, Thu noon-10pm. Closed 1 Jan, Good Friday, 1 May, 1 and 11 Nov and 25 Dec. 4.57€ (children: no charge), no charge 1st Sun in the month. ☎ 03 88 52 50 00.

Musée zoologique de l'université et de la ville – ♿ Daily except Tue 10am-6pm, Sun 10am-5pm. Closed 1 Jan, Good Friday, 1 May, 1 and 11 Nov and 25 Dec. 20F {3.05€} (children: no charge). ☎ 03 88 35 85 18.

Église St-Guillaume – Guided tours by appointment. ☎ 03 88 35 48 07.

Haras national – Daily except Sun 9-11.30am, 2-4.30pm. Closed Good Friday, Easter, Whitsun, 25 and 26 Dec. No charge. ☎ 03 88 36 10 13.

SUNDGAU

Oltingue: Maison du Sundgau – Mid-Jun to mid-Sep: Tue, Thu, Sat 3-6pm, Sun and public holidays 11am-noon, 3-6pm; Mar to mid-Jun and Oct to end of Nov: Sun and public holidays 2-5pm. Closed the 2 Sundays before Christmas and beginning of Jan to end of Feb. 12F {1.83€}. ☎ 03 89 40 79 24.

Hippoltskirch: Chapel – May to end of Sep: Sun 11am-6pm.

T

THANN   🛈 7, rue de la 1ʳᵉ-Armée – 68800 – ☎ 03 89 37 96 20

Collégiale St-Thiébaut – Daily 9am-noon, 2-6pm (Jul and Aug: 9am-7pm). Guided tours available, contact the tourist office. ☎ 03 89 37 96 20.

Musée des Amis de Thann – Mid-May to mid-Oct: daily except Mon 10am-noon, 2.30-6.30pm. 15F {2.29€}. ☎ 03 89 37 02 31.

THIONVILLE

Tour aux Puces: Musée municipal – Closed temporarily for restoration work.

Château de la Grange – Mid-Mar to mid-Nov: guided tours (45min) Sat-Sun and public holidays at 2.30pm, 3.30pm, 4.30pm and 5.30pm (Jul and Aug: daily). 4.60€. ☎ 03 82 53 85 03.

Excursions

Neufchef: Musée des Mines de fer – ♿ Guided tours (1hr 30min) daily except Mon 2-4.30pm. Closed 1 Jan, 24, 25 and 31 Dec. 5.34€. ☎ 03 82 85 76 55.

Aumetz: Musée des Mines de fer – May to Sep: guided tours (1hr 30min) daily except Mon 2-5pm. 5.34€. ☎ 03 82 85 76 55.

Vallée de la THUR

St-Amarin   🛈 60, rue Charles-de-Gaulle – 68550 – ☎ 03 89 82 60 01

Musée Serret et de la vallée de St-Amarin – May to end of Sep: daily except Tue 2-6pm. 20F {3.05€}. ☎ 03 89 38 24 66 or 03 89 38 24 24.

Husseren-Wesserling: Musée du Textile et des Costumes – ♿ 10am-noon, 2-5pm, Mon and Sat 2-5pm (Apr to Sep: 6pm). Closed 1 Jan, 1 May, 1 and 11 Nov, 25 and 26 Dec. 30F {4.57€}. ☎ 03 89 38 28 08.

TOUL   🛈 Parvis de la Cathédrale – 54203 – ☎ 03 83 64 11 69

Guided tours of the town – Contact the Tourist office.

Cathédrale St-Étienne – Daily except Sat-Sun 10am-noon, 2-5pm. ☎ 03 83 63 70 00.

Église St-Gengoult – Daily except Sat-Sun 10am-noon, 2-4pm. ☎ 03 83 64 11 69. For guided tours on weekdays, ask at the tourist office.

Musée municipal – Daily except Tue 2-6pm (Apr to Oct: daily except Tue 10am-noon, 2-6pm). Closed 1 Jan, Easter, 1 May, All Saints, 25 Dec. 2.59€. ☎ 03 83 64 13 38.

Excursions

Vannes-ﬂ-Châtel: Plate-forme verrière – ♿ Daily except Mon 8am-noon, 1-5pm, Sat, Sun and public holidays 2-6pm. Closed 1 May. No charge. ☎ 03 83 25 47 44.

Liverdun   🛈 Porte Haute – 54460 – ☎ 03 83 24 40 40

Guided tours of the town – Contact the tourist office.

Villey-le-Sec: Ensemble fortifié – May to end of Sep: guided tours (2hr) Sun and public holidays 2-4pm (mid-Jul to mid-Aug: daily except Mon at 3pm). 25F {3.81€}. ☎ 03 83 43 32 05.

TROYES

🚩 16, boulevard Carnot – 10014 – ☎ 03 25 82 62 70

Guided tours of the town – Contact the tourist office..

Cathedral Treasury – Jul to end of Sep: daily except Mon 10am-noon, 2-6pm, Sun and public holidays 2-6pm. No charge. ☎ 03 25 76 98 18.

Église St-Nicolas – Tue-Sat 4-6pm. Parish. ☎ 03 25 73 02 98.

Église St-Remy – Jul to end of Aug: 10.30am-12.30pm.

Église St-Nizier – Jul to end of Aug: 3.30-5.30pm.

Musée d'Art moderne – ♿ Daily except Tue 11am-6pm. Closed public holidays. 30F {4.57€}, no charge Wed. ☎ 03 25 76 26 80.

Maison de l'Outil et de la Pensée ouvrière – 9am-1pm, 2-6.30pm, Sat-Sun and public holidays 10am-1pm, 2-6pm. Closed 1 Jan and 25 Dec. 40F {6.10€}. ☎ 03 25 73 28 26.

Hôtel de Vauluisant (Troyes and Champagne history museum, Hosiery museum) – Daily except Mon and Tue 10am-noon, 2-6pm. Enquire for information on summer opening times. Closed public holidays. 30F {4.57€} (children: 5F {0.76€}), no charge Wed. ☎ 03 25 42 33 33.

Abbaye St-Loup – Daily except Tue 10am-noon, 2-6pm. Enquire for information on summer opening times. Closed public holidays. 30F {4.57€}, no charge Wed. ☎ 03 25 76 21 68.

Hôtel-Dieu-le-Comte: Pharmacy – ♿ Wed, Sat-Sun 2-6pm. Enquire for information on summer opening times. Closed public holidays. 20F {3.05€} (children: 5F {0.76€}), no charge Wed. ☎ 03 25 80 98 97.

Excursions

Isle-Aumont: Church – Apply to the town hall for a guided tour. ☎ 03 25 41 81 11 or Mr. Jacotin. ☎ 03 25 41 82 33.

Bouilly: Église St-Laurent – Contact Bouilly town hall. ☎ 03 25 40 20 09.

Maisons-lès-Chaource: Musée des Poupées d'antan et de la Tonnellerie – ♿ Daily except Tue 9am-noon, 2-6pm. Closed public holidays, Dec to Feb. 25F {3.81€} (children: 10F {1.52€}). ☎ 03 25 70 07 46.

Pont-Ste-Marie: Church – Contact the town hall, Mon-Fri 9am-12.30pm, 1.30-6pm (Fri 5pm). ☎ 03 25 81 20 54.

Ste-Maure: Church – Apply to the town hall to visit. Mon, Tue, Thu and Fri 9am-noon, 2-6pm, Wed and Sat 9am.noon. ☎ 03 25 76 90 93.

V

VAUCOULEURS

🚩 Place Achille-François – 55140 – ☎ 03 29 89 51 82

Chapelle castrale – Jul to Sep: guided tours 9am-6pm. ☎ 03 29 89 51 82.

Musée Jeanne d'Arc – Daily except Tue and Sat-Sun 8am-noon, 2-6pm (May to Sep: daily except Tue 10am-noon, 2-6pm, Sat-Sun 2-6pm) Closed between Christmas and New Year's Day, Easter, 1 and 11 Nov. 3.05€. ☎ 03 29 89 51 63.

Excursion

Domrémy-la-Pucelle: Maison natale de Jeanne-d'Arc – ♿ Apr to Sep: 9am-noon, 1.30-6.30pm; Oct to Mar: daily except Tue 9.30am-noon, 2-5pm. Closed 1 Jan, the last 3 weeks in Jan and 25 Dec. 20F {3.05€}. ☎ 03 29 06 95 86.

VERDUN

🚩 Place de la Nation – 55016 – ☎ 03 29 86 14 18

Musée de la Princerie – Apr to end of Oct: daily except Tue 9.30am-noon, 2-6pm. 1.52€. ☎ 03 29 86 10 62.

Citadelle souterraine – ♿ Apr to Sep: reconstitution (30min) 9am-6pm (Jul and Aug: 7pm); Oct and Nov: 9am-noon, 2-5.30pm; Jan: 2-5pm; Feb and Mar: 10am-noon, 2-5pm. Closed 1 Jan, 24, 25 and 31 Dec. 5.34€ (children: 2.29€). ☎ 03 29 86 14 18.

Centre mondial de la Paix (World Peace Centre) – ♿ Feb to mid-Nov: daily except Mon 10am-1pm, 2-6pm (Jun to mid-Sep: 9.30am-7pm). 35F {5.34€} (children: no charge). ☎ 03 29 86 55 00.

Monument de la Victoire – Easter to 11 Nov: 9am-noon, 2-6pm. No charge. ☎ 03 29 83 44 22 (town hall).

Excursions

Battlefields:

Fort de Vaux – ♿ Apr to Sep: 9am-6pm (Jul and Aug: 6.30pm); Feb to Mar and Oct to mid-Nov: 9.30am-noon, 1-5pm. Closed mid-Nov to end of Jan. 2.44€. ☎ 03 29 86 14 18.

Mémorial de Verdun – Feb to beginning of Apr: 9am-noon, 2-6pm (Apr to mid-Sep: 9am-6pm); beginning of Sep to end of Nov: 9am-noon, 2-5pm. 4.57€. ☎ 03 29 84 35 34.

Fort de Douaumont – Apr to Sep: 10am-6pm (Jul and Aug: 7pm); Oct, Nov, Feb and Mar: 10am-1pm, 2-5pm. Closed 1 Jan, 24, 25 and 31 Dec. 2.44€. ☎ 03 29 86 14 18.

Ossuaire de Douaumont – ♿ Mar to end of Nov: 9am-noon, 2-5pm (mid-Apr to beginning of Sep: 9am-6pm); cloister and chapel open all year. Ascent of the tower: 0.91€, films: 2.59€. ☎ 03 29 84 54 81.

Butte de Montfaucon: Monument – Daily except Mon and Tue 9am-5.30pm (Oct to mid-Apr: daily except Sat-Sun, closing time: 4.30pm). Closed public holidays. No charge. ☎ 03 29 85 14 18.

Senon: Church – Guided tours 2-6pm. Mr. Caillard. ☎ 03 29 85 98 07.

Route des VINS

Bœrsch: Marqueterie d'Art Spindler – ♿ Fri-Sat 9am-noon, 2-6pm and by appointment. ☎ 03 88 95 80 17.

Barr: La Folie Marco – Jul to Sep and Easter school holidays: guided tours (45min) daily except Tue, Sat-Sun 10am-noon, 2-6pm. 3.05€. ☎ 03 88 08 66 65.

Bergheim: Church – Jul and Aug: unaccompanied visits; Sep to Jun: contact the presbytery, 1, rue de l'Église.

Hunawihr:

Centre de réintroduction des cigognes – Apr to 11 Nov: 10am-noon, 2-5.30pm, Sat-Sun and public holidays 10am-5.30pm (Jul and Aug: 10am-6.30pm; Jun: 10am-6pm). 6.86€ (children: 4.57€). Ask for information by calling ☎ 03 89 73 72 62 or by visiting the web site www.cigogne-loutre.com

Jardin des papillons exotiques vivants – ♿ Jul and Aug: 10am-7pm. 30F {4,57€} (children: 20F {3.05€}). ☎ 03 89 73 33 33.

Kientzheim: Musée du Vignoble et des Vins d'Alsace – Jun to end of Oct: 10am-noon, 2-6pm; May: Sat-Sun and public holidays 10am-noon, 2-6pm. 2.29€. ☎ 03 89 78 21 36.

VITTEL

Institut de l'eau Perrier Vittel – ♿ Apr to end of Sep: daily except Tue 10am-12.30pm, 1.30-6pm. 3.05€ (children: no charge). ☎ 03 29 08 75 85.

Usine d'embouteillage de Vittel SA – ♿ Visits restricted according to work in progress. Jun to end of Sep 2000: 10.30am, 2pm, 3.30pm. No charge. ☎ 03 29 08 70 00.

Excursions

Contrexéville: Usine d'embouteillage – Apr-Sep: guided tours (1hr 30min) daily except Sat-Sun 9.30am, 2pm (except Mon morning); Sep: daily except Sat-Sun and Mon morning 9.30am and 2.30pm; Apr-May: daily except Sat-Sun 9.30am and 2.30pm; Oct to Mar by appointment. Closed public holidays. No charge. ☎ 03 29 08 80 20.

Thuillières: Castle – Jul to end of Aug: guided tours 2.30-5.30pm. 2.29€. ☎ 03 29 08 29 29.

Darney: Czechoslovak museum – Jul to end of Aug: daily except Sun and Tue 9am-noon, 2-6pm (end of Jul to mid-Aug: daily except Sun and Tue 10am-noon, 2-6pm). Closed public holidays. No charge. ☎ 03 29 09 33 45.

Parc naturel régional des VOSGES DU NORD

Bouxwiller:

Church – Jul to end of Aug: tours by appointment Fri 3-6pm, Sat 10am-noon, 3-6pm, Sun 11am-noon, 3-6pm. ☎ 03 88 70 72 06.

Musée du Pays de Hanau – May to Sep: daily except Mon 2-6pm; Oct to Apr: daily except Sat 2-6pm, Sun 2-5pm. Closed 1 Jan, Good Friday, 1 May, 24, 25 and 31 Dec. 15F {2.29€}. ☎ 03 88 70 70 16.

Musée judéo-alsacien – ♿ Mid-Apr to mid-Sep: daily except Mon and Sat 10am-noon, 2-5pm, Sun and public holidays 2-6pm. 6€. ☎ 03 88 70 97 17.

Ingwiller: Sentier botanique et poétique de Seelberg – From the village, a guided tour of the nature trail (2hr). By appointment. ☎ 03 88 89 23 45.

Offwiller: Musée des Arts and Traditions populaires – Jun to Sep: Sun 2-6pm. 1.83€. ☎ 03 88 89 31 31 or 03 88 89 36 56.

St-Louis-lès-Bitche: Cristalleries de St-Louis – Boutique open daily except Sun 9amnoon, 1-5pm, Sat 9am-noon, 1.30-5pm. ☎ 03 87 06 40 04.

Meisenthal: Maison du verre et du cristal – Easter to All Saints: daily except Tue 2-6pm. 5€ (children: 3€). ☎ 03 87 96 91 51.

Soucht: Musée du Sabotier – ♿ Easter to end of Oct: guided tours (45min) Sat-Sun and public holidays 2-6pm (Jul and Aug: daily). 1.52€. ☎ 03 87 96 86 97.

Château de Lichtenberg – Apr to end of Oct: 10am-noon, 1.30-6pm, Mon 1.30-6pm, Sun and public holidays 10am-7pm (Jun to Aug: daily except Sun 10am-6pm, Mon 1.30-6pm); Mar and Nov: 1-6pm. 2.29€.

Château de Fleckenstein – Jul and Aug: 9.30am-6.30pm; May to end of Jun, Sep and Oct: 10am-6pm; mid-Mar to end of Apr and from the 1st to mid-Nov: 10am-5pm. Closed mid-Nov to mid-Mar. 2.59€, 1.82€ in low season. ☎ 03 88 94 43 16.

Reichshoffen: Musée du Fer – Sun and public holidays 2-6pm (Jun to Sep: daily except Tue). Closed Good Friday, 25 and 26 Dec. 15F {2.29€}. ☎ 03 88 80 34 49.

Woerth: Musée de la Bataille du 6 août 1870 – Mid-Jun to mid-Sep: daily except Tue 10am-noon, 2-6pm; beginning to mid-Jun: daily except Tue 2-6pm; Apr, May and mid-Sep to end of Oct: daily except Tue 2-5pm; Nov to Mar: Sat-Sun 2-5pm. Closed in Jan. 20F {3.05€}. ☎ 03 88 09 30 21.

Merkwiller-Pechelbronn: Musée du Pétrole – ♿ Apr to end of Oct: Thu, Sun and public holidays 2.30-6pm. 3.05€. ☎ 03 88 80 91 08.

W

WANGENBOURG

Rocher de Dabo – Jun to mid-Sep: 9am-7pm; Mid-Mar to end of May: 9am-6pm, Sat 9am-6.30pm, Sun and public holidays 9am-7pm; mid-Sep to end of Oct: 9am-6pm. Closed Oct to mid-Mar. 1.52€. ☎ 03 87 07 40 12 or 03 87 07 47 51.

Cristallerie de Vallerysthal – ♿ 10am-noon, 1-6pm, Sat, Sun and public holidays 10am-noon, 2-6pm (Jan: 10am-noon, 2-5pm, Sat 10am-noon, 2-6pm, Sun and public holidays 2-6pm). Closed 1 Jan, 25 Dec. No charge. ☎ 03 87 25 62 04.

Plan incliné de St-Louis-Arzviller – Apr to end of Oct: guided tours including a descent in the boatlift in a launch (1hr 30min), times vary according to the season (Jul and Aug: at 10.15am, 11.30am, 1.35pm, 2.50pm, 4.05pm, 5.20pm). 6.10€. ☎ 03 87 25 30 69, Fax: 03 87 25 41 82.

Église de Niederhaslach – Guided tours by appointment. ☎ 03 88 50 90 29.

Wasselonne: Protestant church – Guided tours daily except Sat-Sun 10am-noon, 2-5pm. ☎ 03 88 59 12 00.

WASSY   🗓 Tour du Dôme – 52130 – ☎ 03 25 55 72 25

Hôtel de ville – By appointment (1 to 2 week's notice) with the tourist office. Closed Sat afternoon, Sun and public holidays. No charge. ☎ 03 25 04 08 70.

Temple and Protestant Museum – Mid-Jun to mid-Sep: daily except Mon 2-6pm. ☎ 03 25 04 08 70.

Excursions

Vallée de la Blaise: Route du Fer – Jul and Aug: Sun at 3pm leaving from Wassy railway station (to Éclaron on the 1st and last Sunday in the month; to Dommartin-Doulevant on the other Sundays). ☎ 06 07 50 55 72 (station).

Dommartin-le-Franc: Smelting works – Jul to end of Sep: Sat-Sun 2.30-6pm (Jul to end of Aug: daily except Tue 2.30-6pm). 3.05€. ☎ 03 25 05 00 41.

Sommevoire:
Paradis – Mid-Jul to mid-Sep: daily except Mon 2-6pm. By appointment in low season. 15F {2.29€}. ☎ 03 25 94 22 05.
Église St-Pierre – As for the Paradis.

Cirey-sur-Blaise: Castle – Jul to mid-Sep: guided tours (45min) 2.30-6.30pm; May to Jun: Sun and public holidays 2.30-6.30pm. 4.57€ (children under 10: no charge). ☎ 03 25 55 43 04.

WISSEMBOURG   🗓 9, place de la République – 67160 – ☎ 03 88 94 10 11

Guided tours of the town – Contact the tourist office.

Musée Westercamp – Apr to Oct: Mon, Wed, Thu 2-6pm, Fri and Sat 9am-noon, 2-6pm, Sun and public holidays 10am-noon, 2-6pm. Closed 25 Dec. 2.29€. ☎ 03 88 54 28 14.

Index

M

Madine (Lac) *Meuse*, 178
Maginot (Ligne), 182
Maginot Line, 52
Maginot (Monument) *Meuse*, 367
Mailly-Champagne *Marne*, 205
La Maix (Lac) *Vosges*, 131
Malbrouck (Château) *Moselle*, 316
Malgré Tout (Mont) *Ardennes*, 201
Mance, Jeanne, 170
Manises (Calvaire) *Ardennes*, 201
Manises (Monument) *Ardennes*, 201
Marckolsheim (Mémorial Musée de la Ligne Maginot du Rhin) *Bas-Rhin*, 188
Mareuil-sur-Ay *Marne*, 208
Marfaux *Marne*, 208
Marie-Antoinette, 95, 96
Le Markstein *Haut-Rhin*, 156
Marlborough, Duke, 316
Marlenheim *Bas-Rhin*, 372
Marmoutier *Bas-Rhin*, 188
La Marne (Source) *Haute-Marne* , 175
Marne (Vallée), 102
Marsal *Moselle*, 189
La Marseillaise, 320
Marville *Meuse*, 213
Masevaux *Haut-Rhin*, 339
Mathaux *Aube*, 146
Méhul, Étienne, 152
Meisenthal *Moselle*, 382
Mélaire (Lacets) *Haute-Marne*, 167
Merkwiller-Pechelbronn *Bas-Rhin*, 387
Merovingian dynasty, 32, 55
Mesnil-St-Père *Aube*, 146
Le Mesnil-sur-Oger *Marne*, 102
Métezeau, Clément, 105
Metz *Moselle*, 189
Meurthe (Upper valley) *Vosges*, 150
Meuse (Dames) *Ardennes*, 202
Meuse (Méandres), 198
Meuse (Vallée), 153
Mézy (Église) *Aisne*, 104
Michelsberg (Gros ouvrage) *Moselle*, 185
Mignard, Pierre, 352
Mirabelle, 414
Mittelbergheim *Bas-Rhin*, 163
Mittelwihr *Haut-Rhin*, 376
Mohon *Ardennes*, 108

Molhain (Ancienne collégiale) *Ardennes*, 153
Molsheim *Bas-Rhin*, 202
Moltke, Marshal, 38
Mondement *Marne*, 294
Mondorf-les-Bains *Luxemburg*, 317
Montagne de Reims (Parc naturel régional) *Marne*, 204
Mont-devant-Sassey *Meuse*, 216
Mont d'Haurs (Fort) *Ardennes*, 153
Mont Dieu (Ancienne chartreuse) *Ardennes*, 388
Montfaucon (Butte) *Meuse*, 370
Montier-en-Der *Haute-Marne*, 210
Montmédy *Meuse*, 213
Montmirail *Marne*, 214
Montmort-Lucy *Marne*, 247
Mont-St-Père *Aisne*, 104
Montsec (Butte) *Meuse*, 179
Moosch *Haut-Rhin*, 345
Morimond (Abbaye) *Haute-Marne*, 210
Morsbronn-les-Bains *Bas-Rhin*, 159
Le Mort-Homme *Meuse*, 370
Mossig (Vallée) *Bas-Rhin*, 391
La Motte-Tilly (Château) *Aube*, 244
La Mouche (Lac) *Haute-Marne*, 176
Mousson (Butte) *Meurthe-et-Moselle*, 258
Mouzon *Ardennes*, 215
Moyenmoutier *Vosges*, 292
Muhlbach-sur-Munster *Haut-Rhin*, 227
Mulhouse *Haut-Rhin*, 216
Munster *Haut-Rhin*, 225
Munster cheese, 65, 414
Murbach (Église) *Haut-Rhin*, 228
Musée du Pays du Der , 129
Mutigny *Marne*, 207
Mutzig *Bas-Rhin*, 307

N

Nancy *Meurthe-et-Moselle*, 230
Nancy, École, 56, 233
Nanteuil-la-Forêt *Marne*, 208
Napoleon, 214
Napoleon III, 94
Neuenberg (Sentier patrimoine) *Haut-Rhin*, 84

Neuf-Brisach *Haut-Rhin*, 122
Neufchâteau *Vosges*, 240
Neufchef (Musée des Mines de Fer) *Moselle*, 344
Neuntelstein (Rocher) *Bas-Rhin*, 164
Neuwiller-lès-Saverne *Bas-Rhin*, 242
Nichet (Grottes) *Ardennes*, 153
Nideck (Cascade) *Bas-Rhin*, 390
Nideck (Château) *Bas-Rhin*, 390
Niederbronn-les-Bains *Bas-Rhin*, 242
Niederbruck *Haut-Rhin*, 80
Niederhaslach *Bas-Rhin*, 391
Niedermorschwihr *Haut-Rhin*, 376
Nigloland *Aube*, 90
Nogent-l'Artaud *Aisne*, 104
Nogent-sur-Seine *Aube*, 243
Noir (Lac) *Haut-Rhin*, 249
Norroy (Croix de mission) *Vosges*, 379
Notre-Dame-de-Dusenbach (Chapelle) *Haut-Rhin*, 283
Nouzonville *Ardennes*, 199
Nutzkopf (Rocher) *Moselle*, 389

O

Oberhaslach *Bas-Rhin*, 391
Oberlin, Jean-Frédéric, 306
Obernai *Bas-Rhin*, 245
Obersteigen *Bas-Rhin*, 389
Obersteinbach *Bas-Rhin*, 384
Oderen *Haut-Rhin*, 346
Oeuilly *Marne*, 104
Offwiller *Bas-Rhin*, 382
Oger *Marne*, 101
Oiseau et du Poisson (Maison) *Marne*, 128
Olizy *Marne*, 205
Oltingue *Haut-Rhin*, 336
Orbais-l'Abbaye *Marne*, 247
Orbey *Haut-Rhin*, 250
Orbey (Val) *Haut-Rhin*, 248
Orient (Lac) *Aube*, 144
Orne (Valley) *Meurthe-et-Moselle, Moselle*, 344
Ortenbourg (Château) *Bas-Rhin*, 314
Osne-le-Val *Haute-Marne*, 392

469

Notes

Notes